International Conference on Applied Computing 2025 and WWW/Internet 2025

Porto, Portugal
1-3 November 2025

ISBN: 979-8-3313-2985-3

Printed from e-media with permission by:

Curran Associates, Inc.
57 Morehouse Lane
Red Hook, NY 12571

International Association for Development of the Information Society (IADIS)
Rua Sao Sebastiao Da Pedreira
No. 100, 30, 1050-209
Lisbon, Portugal

Phone: 351 21 3151373
Fax: 351 21 3151244

secretariat@iadis.org

Additional copies of this publication are available from:

Curran Associates, Inc.
57 Morehouse Lane
Red Hook, NY 12571 USA
Phone: 845-758-0400
Fax: 845-758-2633
Email: curran@proceedings.com
Web: www.proceedings.com

Proceedings of the International Conferences

applied COMPUTING & WWW/INTERNET 2025

1-3 November • Porto, Portugal

Edited by:
Paula Miranda
Pedro Isaías

organized by:
iadis
international association for development of the information society

PROCEEDINGS OF THE INTERNATIONAL CONFERENCES ON

APPLIED COMPUTING 2025

AND

WWW/INTERNET 2025

PORTO, PORTUGAL

NOVEMBER 1 - 3, 2025

Organised by

iadis

international association for development of the information society

As a member of Crossref (a non-profit membership organization for scholarly publishing working with the purpose to make content easy to find, link, cite and assess) each published paper in this book of proceedings will be allocated a DOI (Digital Object Identifier) number for its fast and easy citation and indexation.

Edited by Paula Miranda and Pedro Isaías

Associate Editor: Luís Rodrigues

ISBN: 978-989-8704-71-9

TABLE OF CONTENTS

SHORT PAPERS

REFLECTION PAPERS

POSTERS

FOREWORD

These proceedings contain the papers and posters of the 22nd International Conference on Applied Computing 2025 and 24th International Conference on WWW/Internet 2025, held in Porto, Portugal from 1 to 3 November 2025 and organised by the International Association for Development of the Information Society (IADIS).

The 22nd Applied Computing (AC) 2025 conference aims to address the main issues of concern within the applied computing area and related fields. This conference covers essentially technical aspects. The applied computing field is divided into more detailed areas.

The following areas have been object of paper and poster submissions:

- Application Fields
  - eCommerce and ePayment
  - eLearning
  - eHealth and eSports
  - IT Services
  - Mobile Computing
  - Knowledge Management and Distribution
- Fundamental Concepts and Engineering
  - Algorithms
  - Data bases and Data Mining
  - Information Systems
  - Information Sourcing and Aggregation
  - Programming Languages and Concepts
  - Security and Privacy
- Performance
  - Distributed and Parallel Systems
  - Cloud Computing
  - Evaluation and Assessment
  - Intelligent Systems
  - Large-Scale Applications
  - Local and Distributed Storage
- Communication
  - IoT
  - Industry 4.0
  - Mobile Systems and Networks
  - Protocols, Standards and Mark-up Languages
  - Sensor Networks
  - WWW Applications and Technologies

- Usability
    - Automation of Services
    - Human-Centred Computing
    - Multimedia and Visualization
    - Modalities of User Interfacing
    - Personalization and Empathic Systems
    - Virtual Reality
- Hardware Scope
    - Embedded Computing
    - Environment-Friendly Constructions
    - Mobile Aspects
    - Realization of IoT Nodes
    - Security Concepts and Devices
    - Wideband Information Streaming

The 24th WWW/Internet (ICWI) 2025 Conference aims to address the main issues of concern within WWW/Internet. WWW and Internet had a huge development in recent years. Aspects of concern are no longer just technical anymore, but other aspects have arisen. This conference aims to cover both technological as well as non-technological issues related to these developments.

Submissions were accepted under the following main tracks and topics:

- Web 2.0
    - Collaborative Systems
    - Social Networks
    - Folksonomies
    - Enterprise Wikis and Blogging
    - Mashups and Web Programming
    - Tagging and User Rating Systems
    - Citizen Journalism

- Semantic Web and XML
    - Semantic Web Architectures
    - Semantic Web Middleware
    - Semantic Web Services
    - Semantic Web Agents
    - Ontologies
    - Applications of Semantic Web
    - Semantic Web Data Management
    - Information Retrieval in Semantic Web

- Applications and Uses
    - e-Learning
    - e-Commerce / e-Business
    - e-Government
    - e-Health
    - e-Procurement

- e-Society
- Digital Libraries
- Web Services/SaaS
- Application Interoperability
- Web-based Multimedia Technologies

➢ Services, Architectures and Web Development
  - Wireless Web
  - Mobile Web
  - Cloud/Grid Computing
  - Web Metrics
  - Web Standards
  - Internet Architectures
  - Network Algorithms
  - Network Architectures
  - Network Computing
  - Network Management
  - Network Performance
  - Content Delivery Technologies
  - Protocols and Standards
  - Traffic Models

➢ Research Issues
  - Web Science
  - Digital Rights Management
  - Bioinformatics
  - Human Computer Interaction and Usability
  - Web Security and Privacy
  - Online Trust and Reputation Systems
  - Data Analytics and Machine Learning
  - Information Retrieval
  - Search Engine Optimization

➢ Emergent Areas
  - Digital Transformation
  - Blockchain
  - Bitcoin and other Cryptocurrencies
  - Smart Cities
  - Internet of Things
  - Mobile App Development

These events received 158 submissions from more than 19 countries. Each submission has been anonymously reviewed by an average of four independent reviewers, to ensure the final high standard of the accepted submissions. The final result was the approval of 28 full papers, which means that the acceptance rate was 18%. A few more papers have been accepted in the following categories: short papers, reflection papers and posters. Best papers will be selected for publishing as extended versions in the IADIS International Journal on

WWW/Internet (IJWI) (ISSN 1645-7641) and in the IADIS International Journal on Computer Science and Information Systems (IJCSIS) (ISSN 1646-3692).

In addition to the paper and poster presentations, the conferences also featured a keynote presentation and a special talk by internationally distinguished researchers. We would like to extend our sincere gratitude to Professor Marcus Specht, Chair of Learning Sciences in Higher Education at the Research Center for Higher Education of the Future (CATALPA), FernUniversität in Hagen, Germany, for being our keynote speaker. We also thank Professor Helder Rodrigo Pinto — affiliated with ISEP and ISTEC Porto, researcher at GECAD–ISEP, Director of CITECA, President of the Technical-Scientific Council at ISTEC Porto, and Director of R&D at MEDCEI, Portugal — for his engaging special talk.

As we all know, organising these conferences requires the effort of many individuals. We would like to thank all members of the Program Committee for their hard work in reviewing and selecting the papers that appear in the proceedings.

We are especially grateful to the authors who submitted their papers to these conferences and to the presenters who provided the substance of the meetings.

This Proceedings book contains a rich experience of the academic & research institutions and the industry on diverse themes related to the Internet, Web and Applied Computing. We do hope that researchers, knowledge workers and innovators both in academia and the industry will find it a valuable reference material.

Last but not the least, we hope that everybody enjoyed the presentations, and we invite all participants for next year's edition of the International Conferences Applied Computing and WWW/Internet.

Paula Miranda, Polytechnic Institute of Setubal, Portugal
Applied Computing 2025 Conference & Program Chair

Pedro Isaías, Universidade Aberta (Portuguese Open University), Portugal
WWW/Internet 2025 Conference & Program Chair

November 2025

PROGRAM COMMITTEE

APPLIED COMPUTING

CONFERENCE & PROGRAM CHAIR

Paula Miranda, Polytechnic Institute of Setubal, Portugal

COMMITTEE MEMBERS

Abbas Fadhil Aljuboori, AlShaab University, Iraq
Adam Wojciechowski, Poznan University of Technology, Poland
Anastasios Doulamis, National Technical University of Athens, Greece
Andreas Menychtas, University of Piraeus, Greece
Andrew Adamatzky, Uwe Bristol, United Kingdom
Antonio LaTorre, Universidad Politécnica De Madrid, Spain
Antonio Robles-Gómez, Spanish University for Distance Education, UNED, Spain
Carmen Carrion, University of Castilla-La Mancha, Spain
Carolina Yukari Veludo Watanabe, Federal University of Rondônia, Brazil
Cristiano Costa, Universidade do Vale do Rio dos Sinos (UNISINOS), Brazil
Dana Petcu, West University of Timisoara, Romania
Denis Gracanin, Virginia Tech, USA
Dessislava Vassileva, Sofia University St. Kliment Ohridski, Bulgaria
Dorian Gorgan, Computer Science Department, Technical University, Romania
Enrique Vargas, Universidad Catolica de Asuncion, Paraguay
Francesca Martelli, Istituto di Informatica e Telematica - CNR, Italy
Francisco José García-Peñalvo, University of Salamanca, Spain
Grigorios Beligiannis, University of Patras, Greece
Holger Hofmann, Baden-Wuerttemberg Cooperative State University Mannheim, Germany
Jan Krasniewicz, Birmingham City University, United Kingdom
Joao Paulo Papa, São Paulo State University, Brazil
Jose Manuel Molina, Universidad Carlos III de Madrid, Spain
Juan Francisco De Paz Santana, University of Salamanca, Spain
Karthik Kushala, Taylor Corporation, USA
Kelton Costa, São Paulo State University, Brazil
Kuo-Chan Huang, National Taichung University of Education, Taiwan
Liz Bacon, Abertay University, United Kingdom
Luca Pardini, University of Pisa, Italy
M Carmen de Castro-Cabrera, University of Cadiz, Spain
Maiga Chang, Athabasca University, Canada

Manuel Gil Pérez, University of Murcia, Spain
Marek Woda, Wrocław University of Science and Technology, Poland
Mariem Haoues, Higher Institute of Computer Science and Multimedia, Tunisia
Matthias Lange, Leibniz Institute of Plant Genetics and Crop Plant, Germany
Mauro Gaspari, University of Bologna, Italy
Michael Hobbs, Deakin University, Australia
Michael Vassilakopoulos, University of Thessaly, Greece
Minoru Uehara, Toyo University, Japan
Nikolaos Matsatsinis, Technical University of Crete, Greece
Pablo Rabanal, Universidad Complutense de Madrid, Spain
Prabhat Mahanti, University of New Brunswick, Canada
Priscila Tiemi Maeda Saito, Federal University of Sao Carlos (UFSCar), Brazil
Sharon Cox, Birmingham City University, United Kingdom
Sherri WeitlHarms, Creighton University, USA
Teodor Stefanut, Technical University of Cluj-napoca, Romania
Vicente Gonzalez, Universidad Católica , Paraguay
Vincent Hilaire, Utbm, France
Vincenzo Deufemia, Università di Salerno, Italy
William Steingartner, Technical University of Košice, Slovakia
Witold Andrzejewski, Poznan University of Technology, Poland
Zaher Al Aghbari, University of Sharjah, United Arab Emirates

WWW/INTERNET

CONFERENCE & PROGRAM CHAIR

Pedro Isaías, Universidade Aberta (*Portuguese Open University*), Portugal

COMMITTEE MEMBERS

Ali Fawaz Shareef, The Maldives National University, Maldives
Ananya S. Guha, Indira Gandhi National Open University, India
Angélica de Antonio, Universidad Politécnica de Madrid, Spain
Christos Bouras, University of Patras, Greece
Christos Georgiadis, University of Macedonia, Thessaloniki, Greece
Daniel Cunliffe, University of South Wales, United Kingdom
Dongqiang Yang, Shandong Jianzhu University, China
Evangelos Sakkopoulos, University of Patras, Greece

KEYNOTE LECTURE

CHALLENGES AND PERSPECTIVES ON THE DEVELOPMENT OF HUMAN LEARNING WITH AI

Professor Marcus Specht
Learning Sciences in Higher Education at the Research Center for Higher Education of the Future (CATALPA), FernUniversität in Hagen
Germany

Abstract

The talk will connect perspectives from the learning sciences on human learning with the emerging changes and challenges brought about by the rise of generative AI and new technologies. It will then examine current approaches to technology adoption in education and propose a living lab approach for the interdisciplinary development of learning innovations. This approach emphasizes the integration of new technologies with continuous scientific evaluation and research.

SPECIAL TALK

AI FOR PREDICTING DOMESTIC VIOLENCE RECIDIVISM IN PORTUGAL

Helder Rodrigo Pinto
Professor at ISEP and ISTEC Porto, Researcher at GECAD - ISEP,
Director of CITECA, President of the Technical-Scientific Council of ISTEC Porto,
and Director of R&D at MEDCEI
Portugal

Abstract

Domestic violence remains a pressing concern in Portugal, demanding more effective approaches for recidivism prediction, despite legislative efforts and current risk assessment tools. This project proposes the application of Artificial Intelligence (AI) to enhance this prediction, specifically within the Portuguese context and relying exclusively on information from the Domestic Violence Risk Assessment Forms (Ficha RVD-R). Our research aims to develop and validate predictive models (regression or binary classification). These models, through the structured analysis of Ficha RVD-R data, will more accurately identify high-risk individuals. The primary objective is to optimize resource allocation and prioritize interventions, thereby protecting victims and managing aggressors more effectively. Crucial to this endeavor is the collaboration with the Public Administration to access anonymized data and ensure real-world applicability. The proposal includes the conceptual design of a predictive system, which could materialize as a private dashboard or chatbot for law enforcement agencies. This system would be powered by an interface utilizing Flowise/Langflow and a vector database for the Ficha RVD-1L. This technological advancement, leveraging accessible AI, seeks to reduce the recurrence of domestic violence and contribute to a safer and fairer society.

Full Papers

TECHNOLOGICAL IMPACTS IN THE EVOLUTION OF SOFTWARE PROJECT MANAGEMENT: A SYSTEMATIC REVIEW

Marta Maria Guedes da Silva Neta, Geovanna Mayra Domingos do Nascimento
and Hermano Perrelli de Moura
Center for Informatics, Federal University of Pernambuco
Av. Prof. Moraes Rego, 1235, Cidade Universitária, Recife – PE, 50670-901, Brazil

ABSTRACT

Technology has been significantly transforming software project management, while the scientific literature on the topic remains scattered and fragmented. This study investigates how different forms of technology — including methodologies, tools, and platforms — impact software project management. To this end, we conducted a Systematic Literature Review (SLR), following established guidelines, based on 27 studies published between 2011 and 2024. Thematic analysis of the findings led to the development of a set of ten categories of technological impact, ranging from operational transformations in decision-making to structural changes in organizational strategy. Each category is described in terms of its identified positive impacts, associated challenges, future perspectives, and practical examples of application. The main contributions of this study are: (i) an integrated view of the effects of technology on software project management practices and (ii) a conceptual framework that can support both future academic research and practical decision-making regarding technological adoption in organizational settings.

KEYWORDS

Software Project Management, Systematic Literature Review, Technology Adoption, Human-Technology Interaction

1. INTRODUCTION

Technology plays a central role in supporting the software project lifecycle, encompassing tools, methodologies, and platforms that influence management practices (Sommerville, 2019). Regardless of maturity or adoption level, technologies have introduced both opportunities and challenges, such as organizational adaptation and resistance to change (Ogunbukola, 2024)

However, understanding how technology impacts software project management remains a fragmented and underexplored topic. The Software Engineering literature is often organized into specialized areas, limiting an integrated view of these impacts (Kitchenham, Budgen, & Brereton, 2015). This highlights the relevance of Systematic Literature Reviews (SLRs) to rigorously synthesize dispersed evidence.

To address this gap, we investigate the following research question:

RQ: How does technology (in its multiple forms) impact software project management?

We adopt an inclusive definition of technology, covering tools, methods, and computational platforms that affect the design, development, and maintenance of software systems (Sommerville, 2019). This perspective enables analysis across different contexts, beyond isolated applications.

This study aims to map technologies that most influence software project management, identifying their positive impacts, challenges, future perspectives, and practical use cases. To achieve this, we conducted an SLR based on the guidelines of Kitchenham et al. (2009), analyzing 27 studies published between January 2011 and June 2024.

The main contribution is a categorization of 10 categories of technological impact, offering insights for researchers and practitioners. The structure of the paper is as follows: Section 2 describes the methodology; Section 3 presents and discusses the results; and Section 4 outlines the conclusions.

2. RESEARCH METHODOLOGY

This study follows the Systematic Literature Review (SLR) protocol by Kitchenham et al. (2009), using the Parsifal platform (Parsifal, 2024) and a custom spreadsheet for screening and data extraction. A manual search was first conducted in three key journals—International Journal of Project Management, Journal of Modern Project Management, and Project Management Journal—chosen for their relevance in software project management (Turner, Müller, & Dulewicz, 2010; Špundak, 2014).

Automatic searches followed in Scopus and IEEE Xplore, applying the query: **"software" AND "project management" AND "technology"**. Inclusion criteria were peer-reviewed articles from January 2011 to June 2024, in English or Portuguese, focusing on technology's impact in software project management. Studies limited to specific tools or lacking integrative analysis were excluded.

From 233 retrieved studies, 27 were selected after screening and full-text review. Quality was assessed via 16 questions on methodological adequacy, relevance, and validity, scored 0–32 by two independent reviewers. Twenty studies scored high (22–32), seven medium (11–21).

Data extracted included publication info, research design, technologies analyzed, context, affected project management areas, and impacts. Extraction was done independently by two reviewers, with disagreements resolved by consensus. Manual search data were logged in spreadsheets; automated search data were managed in Parsifal to ensure transparency.

3. RESULTS

Among the 27 included studies, most employed empirical methods: 15 case studies, 6 surveys, 3 controlled experiments, and 3 qualitative systematic reviews. The studies are largely concentrated in institutions based in Europe and North America, with over 70% focused on large-scale corporate projects in sectors such as software, construction, and manufacturing — environments marked by high digitalization and complexity.

The findings were grouped into ten impact categories, developed through an inductive thematic analysis (Braun & Clarke, 2006), in accordance with guidelines for qualitative systematic reviews (Kitchenham et al., 2009; Cruzes & Dybå, 2011). The categories were defined based on the effects of technologies — rather than the technologies themselves — allowing for the identification of broader, context-sensitive dimensions of impact (Sommerville, 2019; Petersen, Vakkalanka, & Kuzniarz, 2015).

The naming convention adopted follows the structure "impact noun + technology," guided by criteria of conceptual clarity, internal consistency, and thematic coverage (Nickerson, Varshney, & Muntermann, 2013). Each category is described across three dimensions: (i) positive impacts; (ii) challenges and limitations; and (iii) future perspectives. Whenever possible, practical examples of representative technologies are provided, even if not explicitly mentioned in the studies.

Some articles were associated with more than one category, as their findings addressed different impact contexts. This cross-coding approach aligns with thematic analysis methods, which allow for multiple interpretations of the same evidence (Braun & Clarke, 2006).

3.1 Identified Impact Categories

The thematic analysis identified ten categories that summarize the main impacts of technology on software project management. Each category represents a specific axis of transformation, ranging from operational to strategic levels. In the following subsections, each category will be analyzed individually in terms of its benefits, challenges, and future perspectives. They are: (i) Automation and Decision Support with Artificial Intelligence; (ii) Predictive Insight Generation with Large-Scale Data; (iii) Process and Structural Flexibility through Agile Approaches; (iv) Digital Orchestration of Projects in Complex Environments; (v) Continuous Optimization and Learning with Lean Practices; (vi) Participatory Management through Internal Crowdsourcing; (vii) Adaptive Monitoring and Computational Control of Projects; (viii) Improved Estimation Accuracy with Hybrid Models; (ix) Active Scope Control and Deviation Mitigation in Projects; and (x) Strategic Reconfiguration Enabled by Industry 4.0.

3.1.1 Automation and Decision Support with Artificial Intelligence

Artificial Intelligence (AI), which simulates human capabilities like learning and reasoning, has significantly impacted software project management by shifting decision-making from human judgment to computational systems (Russell & Norvig, 2020; Müller et al., 2024).

Key benefits include automation of tasks such as effort estimation, resource allocation, and risk analysis, as well as improved decision-making via predictive analytics. These tools enhance efficiency, accuracy, and responsiveness (Müller et al., 2024; Wicaksono & Ahlan, 2019). Examples include UiPath for report automation, IBM Watson and DataRobot for action recommendations, and their use with large datasets to drive faster, evidence-based decisions.

Challenges persist, such as resistance to automation, reliance on high-quality data, and ethical concerns like algorithmic transparency, bias, and auditability (García et al., 2017; Wicaksono & Ahlan, 2019). These tensions are particularly evident in human-centered teams and data-poor environments.

Looking ahead, the focus is on developing explainable, fair, and auditable AI models to foster trust. Ongoing team training is essential for critical interaction with AI tools. Practices like Explainable AI (XAI) aim to reduce resistance and clarify automated decisions (Amershi et al., 2019). Integration examples include Microsoft Project with Power BI and ChatGPT-based bots in Slack for supervised automation.

3.1.2 Predictive Insight Generation with Large-Scale Data

Data Science has become a powerful tool for evidence-based decision-making in software projects. Unlike Artificial Intelligence, which aims to automate decisions, Data Science enhances human judgment through analytical interpretation (García et al., 2017; Marnewick & Marnewick, 2020).

Key benefits include improved project diagnostics, early pattern detection, and proactive risk identification—all grounded in quantitative analysis. Tools like Tableau, Power BI, and Google Looker support real-time metric visualization. Big Data platforms (e.g., Apache Hadoop, Google BigQuery) process historical data at scale, while machine learning algorithms (e.g., scikit-learn) provide predictive insights for risk analysis, enhancing decision reliability (García et al., 2017; Wicaksono & Ahlan, 2019).

Challenges include a shortage of skilled professionals, difficulty integrating heterogeneous data sources, and cultural resistance to data-driven approaches—especially in organizations unfamiliar with quantitative methods (García et al., 2017; Wicaksono & Ahlan, 2019).

Future directions point to more widespread data-driven cultures and increasing automation of predictive analysis via integrated ML models—while maintaining human oversight. The synergy between Data Science and agile practices offers continuous feedback loops throughout project development (García et al., 2017; Locatelli et al., 2023; Marnewick & Marnewick, 2020).

3.1.3 Process and Structural Flexibility through Agile Approaches

Agile approaches prioritize people, emphasizing continuous collaboration, rapid adaptation, team autonomy, and direct communication—contrasting with traditional hierarchical models (Wiesche, 2021). More than just methods, the Agile Manifesto (2001) represents a cultural shift toward adaptability, continuous value delivery, and customer-centricity, reshaping internal relationships and stakeholder engagement (Agile Alliance, 2001; Akbar et al., 2018a).

This model redefines organizational culture, leadership, and coordination by promoting iterative cycles and autonomy to deliver customer value (Wiesche, 2021; Stumpe, 2014). Frameworks like Scrum, SAFe, LeSS, and Spotify support self-managed, cross-functional teams to handle complexity and uncertainty (Akbar et al., 2018a; Berntzen et al., 2023).

However, challenges persist in rigid organizations, including resistance to change, communication issues in distributed teams, and lack of managerial readiness for horizontal structures (Wiesche, 2021; Ali et al., 2023).

Future trends point to hybrid models, adjusting agile practices to organizational context and maturity, and expanding agility to regulated sectors, balancing flexibility and compliance (Akbar et al., 2018a; Kula et al., 2022). Tools like Jira, Trello, Azure DevOps, and Miro exemplify agile planning and collaboration.

3.1.4 Digital Orchestration of Projects in Complex Environments

The increasing complexity of software projects—especially in regulated or multi-stakeholder settings—demands new digital coordination strategies. Digital orchestration involves integrating technologies to connect systems, processes, and data, enabling real-time visibility, seamless communication, decision traceability, and stakeholder management across fragmented structures (Whyte, 2019; Younas et al., 2020).

Benefits include more efficient collaboration and strategic decision-making based on centralized, up-to-date information (Whyte, 2019; Rawai et al., 2014). Tools like Building Information Modeling (BIM)—e.g., Autodesk Revit—support data-rich planning and monitoring. Platforms such as Oracle Primavera P6 and Trimble ProjectSight enhance resource and schedule control, while Jenkins and GitHub Actions support integration and automation in iterative development, improving coherence and reducing rework.

However, adoption faces challenges: lack of system standardization leads to interoperability issues and data silos; high implementation costs and training requirements slow adoption; and weak digital governance can fragment information and reduce strategic effectiveness (Younas et al., 2020; Rawai et al., 2014).

Future directions include integration with IoT for real-time, context-aware monitoring; the evolution of BIM into 5D models (adding time and cost dimensions); and development of more accessible, interoperable interfaces to broaden tool adoption across roles—from executives to operational staff (Whyte, 2019; Younas et al., 2020; Rawai et al., 2014).

3.1.5 Continuous Optimization and Learning through Lean Practices

Derived from lean manufacturing, Lean Management is increasingly applied to software projects to enhance value delivery, eliminate waste, and support continuous learning. Unlike automation- or prediction-focused models, Lean emphasizes incremental improvement and frequent feedback (Dowson et al., 2024; Poppendieck & Poppendieck, 2003), directly influencing KPIs such as cycle time, flow efficiency, and delivery quality.

Benefits include faster bottleneck detection, improved process transparency, and stronger team collaboration. Tools like value stream mapping help visualize workflows and support evidence-based improvements, leading to more reliable, customer-aligned deliveries (Dowson et al., 2024; Cruz & Alves, 2020; Gubinelli et al., 2019).

Still, adoption faces hurdles: resistance to change, insufficient lean training, and low process maturity. Without a mindset of continuous improvement, expected results may fall short (Cruz & Alves, 2020; Gubinelli et al., 2019).

Looking forward, lean practices are expected to expand through digital tools offering real-time visualization, intelligent automation, and rapid feedback. Integrating Lean with Agile and DevOps enhances continuous delivery and data-driven performance (Lwakatare et al., 2016). Tools like Kanbanize, Jira Align, and Miro for Lean UX exemplify this evolution in complex project environments.

3.1.6 Participatory Management through Internal Crowdsourcing

With the rise of collaborative technologies and flatter organizational cultures, internal crowdsourcing has emerged as an alternative to traditional, top-down management. Instead of assigned tasks, employees voluntarily select tasks based on their skills, interests, and availability (Fernandez et al., 2018).

This model enhances engagement, optimizes internal talent, and fosters a decentralized, autonomous work environment (Fernandez et al., 2018; Carvalho et al., 2021). It is best suited for tasks that are clearly defined and modular—such as feature development, code review, content creation, usability testing, and innovation proposals—while less compatible with work that requires continuity, interdependence, or legal responsibility (e.g., contract management).

However, implementation poses challenges, including ensuring transparent task distribution, addressing bias in reputation systems, and preventing exclusion of underrepresented voices. Effective governance and inclusive incentives are essential (Fernandez et al., 2018; Carvalho et al., 2021).

Looking ahead, machine learning may enhance this model by recommending tasks based on skills, preferences, and performance data. Tools like Spigit and Microsoft Viva support this trend, offering platforms for open ideation, engagement, and intelligent task coordination.

3.1.7 Adaptive Monitoring and Computational Project Control

Adaptive Monitoring with Computational Control is the continuous, automated supervision of projects using real-time data to support dynamic, evidence-based decisions. It closes the loop between data collection, diagnosis, and action, enabling immediate adjustments in scope, schedule, and resources. Unlike traditional retrospective monitoring, it employs sensors, algorithms, and visual analytics to provide ongoing feedback to managers (García et al., 2017; Akbar et al., 2018b).

Benefits include anticipating risks, realigning deliverables, and precise resource reallocation based on metrics like CPU usage, task delays, or security incidents. Tools such as Prometheus, Datadog, and New Relic offer interactive dashboards, while PagerDuty provides automated alerts for proactive responses (Monaldi et al., 2020; Bitten et al., 2020).

Advanced techniques like process mining and prescriptive dashboards recommend corrective actions using predictive models and machine learning. For example, a productivity drop may trigger workload redistribution suggestions (García et al., 2017).

Challenges involve data quality, model fairness, interpreting recommendations, talent shortages, infrastructure costs, data latency, and source inconsistencies (Serrador et al., 2021).

Future trends focus on integrating Explainable AI and cognitive visualizations for transparent, auditable decisions. Tools like Jira and Trello already illustrate this with rule-based automations and AI plugins enabling near real-time adaptive workflows.

3.1.8 Improving Estimation Accuracy with Hybrid Models

Positive Effort and cost estimation is a critical aspect of software project management, directly affecting planning and success. Hybrid models—combining traditional methods like waterfall with agile approaches such as Scrum and Kanban—enhance estimation accuracy by balancing predictability and flexibility. This balance allows for realistic estimates that adapt throughout the project lifecycle as new data emerges (Akbar et al., 2018b; Serrador et al., 2021).

Hybrid models improve estimation by refining forecasts as scope evolves, responding to changing requirements, and fostering better stakeholder communication through incremental deliveries and quantitative metrics. Tools like Function Point Analysis and Planning Poker support collaborative estimation. The AZ-Model exemplifies this by integrating continuous feedback and quality indicators throughout the project (Serrador et al., 2021).

Challenges include low organizational maturity in estimation, lack of structured historical data, and inconsistent processes for capturing and reusing project information, which limit the effectiveness of hybrid models (Serrador et al., 2021).

Future trends suggest increased use of adaptable, data-driven frameworks, with AI playing a key role in real-time estimation by analyzing historical patterns and contextual metrics for improved predictions (Akbar et al., 2018b; Serrador et al., 2021).

3.1.9 Active Scope Control and Deviation Mitigation in Projects

Software project management often struggles with scope control, as deviations occur even with defined scopes and resources, impacting schedules, budgets, and deliverables. Especially in complex and dynamic environments like globally distributed agile development, this calls for continuous and adaptive scope governance.t).

Software project management often struggles with scope control, as deviations impact schedules, budgets, and deliverables, especially in complex, globally distributed agile environments. This category focuses on continuous alignment between requirements, deliverables, and stakeholder expectations, treating change as inherent to modern projects. Benefits include reduced rework, improved communication, and more precise, traceable control using models like the 4Ps (People, Product, Project, Process) to manage scope risks (Akbar et al., 2018a; Pacheco et al., 2017).

Challenges include ambiguous requirements, resistance to formalization in agile teams, and gaps between theory and practice (Kula et al., 2022). Future directions emphasize adaptive models tailored to organizational maturity, automated scope verification in development pipelines, and tools like Azure DevOps, IBM DOORS Next, Jama Connect, Helix RM, and TraceCloud (Akbar et al., 2018a; Kula et al., 2022).

Unlike agile's general flexibility, this category stresses formal scope control mechanisms to reduce deviations, enforce traceability, and ensure continuous alignment in volatile environments (Akbar et al., 2018a; Pacheco et al., 2017).

3.1.10 Strategic Reconfiguration Mediated by Industry 4.0

The adoption of Industry 4.0 technologies marks a strategic inflection point for organizations, driving not only operational optimization but also a reconfiguration of business models. Technologies such as the Internet of Things (IoT), cyber-physical systems (CPS), big data, and Artificial Intelligence (AI) foster integrated physical-digital environments and real-time, data-driven operations (Marnewick & Marnewick, 2020).

These technologies enable digital value chains, accelerating innovation cycles, enhancing delivery personalization, and strengthening continuous innovation and strategic agility (Vale et al., 2023). Operational visibility and workflow integration also improve, boosting productivity and control.

However, their adoption involves significant challenges, including organizational resistance, high implementation costs, technical skill gaps, and lack of digital governance. Many organizations implement technologies without the necessary cultural or structural transformations, limiting expected outcomes (Marnewick & Marnewick, 2020; Vale et al., 2023).

Future directions involve integrated frameworks like the DELTA Framework, which align technological, human, and strategic dimensions. Advances in explainable AI, digital twins, and interoperable platforms are also expected to make real-time strategic adjustment a core capability in project management (Marnewick & Marnewick, 2020; Vale et al., 2023).

4. CONCLUSION

This study shows that technological advances from 2011 to 2024 have reshaped software project management, driving operational and strategic transformations that improve efficiency, collaboration, and adaptability. However, challenges remain, such as organizational restructuring, resistance to change, and the need for new managerial skills.

The proposed ten-category framework offers an integrated view of technology's impact, revealing that adoption of new tools requires ongoing cultural and structural shifts within teams and organizations.

Some trends once seen as "future" are now present or surpassed, emphasizing the need for periodic systematic reviews to track evolving practices and technologies.

Future research should explore the effects of each category across different domains, organizational sizes, and maturity levels, while also investigating emerging impacts. Additionally, studies connecting technology with human and organizational factors—such as which skills managers and stakeholders need for specific technologies—are essential for a holistic understanding.

REFERENCES

Agile Alliance. (2001). Manifesto for Agile Software Development. From https://www.agilemanifesto.org/.

Aizaz, F.; Khan, S. U. R.; Khan, J. A.; Ur-Rehman, I.; Akhunzada, A. (2021). An Empirical Investigation of Factors Causing Scope Creep in Agile Global Software Development Context: A Conceptual Model for Project Managers. IEEE Access, 9, 109166-109195. DOI: https://doi.org/10.1109/ACCESS.2021.3100779.

Akbar, M. A.; Sang, J.; Khan, A. A.; Amin, F. E.; Nasrullah, Hussain, S.; Sohail, M. K.; Xiang, H.; Cai, B. (2018). Statistical Analysis of the Effects of Heavyweight and Lightweight Methodologies on the Six-Pointed Star Model. IEEE Access, 6, 4811-4823. DOI: https://doi.org/10.1109/ACCESS.2017.2787981.

Akbar, M. A.; Sang, J.; Khan, A. A.; Amin, F. E.; Nasrullah, Shafiq, M.; Hussain, S.; Hu, H.; Elahi, M.; Xiang, H. (2018). Improving the Quality of Software Development Process by Introducing a New Methodology–AZ-Model. IEEE Access, 6, 8066-8079. DOI: https:// doi.org/10.1109/ACCESS.2018.2805702.

Ali, F.; Usman, M.; Abrar, M. F.; Rahman, S. U.; Khan, I.; Niazi, B. (2023). Practices of De-Motivators in Adopting Agile Software Development Methods at Large Scale Development Teams From Management Perspective. IEEE Access, 11, 130368-130390. DOI: https://doi.org/10.1109/ACCESS.2023.3331759.

Amershi, S.; Weld, D.; Vorvoreanu, M.; Fourney, A.; Nushi, B.; Collisson, P.; Suh, J.; Sinha, V.; Khan, M.; Horvitz, E. (2019). Guidelines for Human-AI Interaction. Conference on Human Factors in Computing Systems, 19(3), 1-13. DOI: https://doi.org/10.1145/3290605.3300233.

Barbara Ann Kitchenham, David Budgen, and Pearl Brereton. (2015). Evidence-Based Software Engineering and Systematic Reviews. Chapman & Hall/CRC.

Barbara Kitchenham, O. Pearl Brereton, David Budgen, Mark Turner, John Bailey, and Stephen Linkman. (2009). Systematic Literature Reviews in Software Engineering – A Systematic Literature Review. Information and Software Technology, 51(1), 7-15. DOI: https://doi.org/10.1016/j.infsof.2008.09.009.

Berntzen, M.; Hoda, R.; Moe, N. B.; Stray, V. (2023). A Taxonomy of Inter-Team Coordination Mechanisms in Large-Scale Agile. IEEE Transactions on Software Engineering, 49, 699-718. DOI: https://doi.org/10.1109/TSE.2022.3160873.

Braun, V., & Clarke, V. (2006). Using Thematic Analysis in Psychology. Qualitative Research in Psychology, 3(2), 77-101. DOI: https://doi.org/10.1191/1478088706qp063oa.

Coplan, S. R. (2024). Unlock the Secret to Achieving Digital Transformation Success With the Delta Framework. IEEE Engineering Management Review, 52, 98-105. DOI: https://doi.org/10.1109/EMR.2024.3367658.

Cruzes, D. S., & Dybå, T. (2011). Recommended Steps For Thematic Synthesis in Software Engineering. International Symposium on Empirical Software Engineering and Measurement, 275-284. DOI: https://doi.org/10.1109/ESEM.2011.36.

Cruz, A.; Alves, A. C. (2020). Traditional, Agile and Lean Project Management - A Systematic Literature Review. Journal of Modern Project Management, 8(2), 86-95. DOI: https://doi.org/10.19255/JMPM02407.

David, M. (2013). Organising, Valuing and Improving the Engineering Design Process. Journal of Engineering Design, 24(7), 524-545. DOI: https://doi.org/10.1080/09544828.2013.776214.

Dowson, J.; Unterhitzenberger, C.; Bryde, D. J. (2024). Facilitating and Improving Learning in Projects: Evidence from a Lean Approach. International Journal of Project Management, 42(1), 102559. DOI: https://doi.org/10.1016/j.ijproman.2024.102559.

García, J. A. L.; Peña, A. B.; Pérez, P. Y. P.; Pérez, R. B. (2017). Project Control and Computational Intelligence: Trends and Challenges. International Journal of Computational Intelligence Systems, 10(1), 320-335. DOI: https://doi.org/10.2991/ijcis.2017.10.1.22.

Greeven, C. S.; Williams, S. P. (2016). Enterprise Collaboration Systems: An Analysis and Classification of Adoption Challenges. Procedia Computer Science, 100, 179-187. DOI: https://doi.org/10.1016/j.procs.2016.09.139.

Gubinelli, S.; Cesarotti, V.; Introna, V. (2019). The Evolution of Project Management (PM): How Agile, Lean and Six Sigma are Changing PM. Journal of Modern Project Management, 7(3), 162-189. DOI: https://doi.org/0.19255/JMPM02107.

Ihme, T. (2013). Scrum Adoption and Architectural Extensions in Developing New Service Applications of Large Financial IT Systems. Journal of the Brazilian Computer Society, 19(3), 257-274. DOI: https://doi.org/10.1007/s13173-012-0096-0.

Ian Sommerville. (2019). Software Engineering. 10th ed. Pearson, Harlow, UK.

Jayakanthan, R.; Deepak, S. (2012). Enterprise Crowdsourcing Solution for Software Development in an Outsourcing Organization. Lecture Notes in Computer Science, 7059, 177-180. DOI: https://doi.org/10.1007/978-3-642-27997-3_19.

Kula, E.; Greuter, E.; van Deursen, A.; and Gousios, G. (2022). Factors Affecting On-Time Delivery in Large-Scale Agile Software Development. IEEE Transactions on Software Engineering, 48(9), 3573-3592. DOI: https://doi.org/10.1109/TSE.2021.3101192.

Lwakatare, L. E.; Kuvaja, P.; Oivo, M. (2016). Relationship of DevOps to Agile, Lean and Continuous Deployment: A Systematic Review. Scientific Workshop Proceedings of XP2016, 30(12), 1-11. DOI: https://doi.org/10.1145/2962695.2962707.

Marnewick, A. and Marnewick, C. (2020). The Ability of Project Managers to Implement Industry 4.0-Related Projects. IEEE Access, 8, 314-324. DOI: https://doi.org/10.1109/ACCESS.2019.2961678.

M. Ogunbukola. (2024). The Impact of Digital Transformation on Project Management. Matgrace Consulting.

M. Špundak. (2014). Mixed Agile/Traditional Project Management Methodology – Reality or illusion? Procedia - Social and Behavioral Sciences, 119, 939-948. DOI: https://doi.org/10.1016/j.sbspro.2014.03.105.

Müller, R., Locatelli, G., Holzmann, V., Nilsson, M., and Sagay, T. (2024). Artificial Intelligence and Project Management: Empirical Overview, State of the Art and Guidelines for Future Research. Project Management Journal, 55(1), 9-15. DOI: https://doi.org/10.1177/87569728231225198.

Nickerson, R. C., Varshney, U., & Muntermann, J. (2013). A Method for Taxonomy Development and its Application in Information Systems. European Journal of Information Systems, 22(3), 336-359. DOI: https://doi.org/10.1057/ejis.2012.26.

Nuottila, J.; Aaltonen, K.; Kujala, J. (2016). Challenges of Adopting Agile Methods in a Public Organization. International Journal of Information Systems and Project Management, 4(3), 65-85. DOI: https://doi.org/10.12821/ijispm040304.

Ong, S. and Uddin, S. (2020). Data Science and Artificial Intelligence in Project Management: The Past, Present and Future. Journal of Modern Project Management, 7(4), 26-33. DOI: https://doi.org/10.19255/JMPM02202.

Parsifal.: Perform Systematic Literature Reviews. From https://parsif.al/.

Petersen, K., Vakkalanka, S., & Kuzniarz, L. (2015). Guidelines for Conducting Systematic Mapping Studies in Software Engineering: An Update. Information and Software Technology, 64, 1-18. DOI: https://doi.org/10.1016/j.infsof.2015.03.007.

Poppendieck, M.; Poppendieck, T. (2003). Lean Software Development: An Agile Toolkit. Addison-Wesley Longman Publishing Co., Inc.

P. Svejvig and P. Andersen. (2015). Rethinking Project Management: A Structured Literature Review with a Critical Look at the Brave New World. International Journal of Project Management, 33(2), 278-290. DOI: https://doi.org/10.1016/j.ijproman.2014.06.004.

Rashid, C. H.; Shafi, I.; Ahmad, J.; Thompson, E. B.; Vergara, M. M., Diez, I. T.; Ashraf, I. (2023). Software Cost and Effort Estimation: Current Approaches and Future Trends. IEEE Access, 11, 99268-99288. DOI: https://doi.org/10.1109/ACCESS.2023.3312716.

Rawai, N. M.; Abedi, M.; Fathi, M. S.; Fathi, M. S. (2014). The Effect of Project and Programme Reference Models in Architecture, Engineering and Construction (AEC) System Development. Jurnal Teknologi, 70(7), 9-14. DOI: https://doi.org/10.11113/jt.v70.3570.

Russell, S.; Norvig, P. (2020). Artificial Intelligence: A Modern Approach. 4th ed. Pearson, Harlow, UK.

SCImago. (2024). SCImago Journal & Country Rank. From https://www.scimagojr.com.

Stumpe, F. (2014). Case-study of a System-Cybernetic Project Management in a More Agile Environment. Journal of Modern Project Management, 1(3), 76-87. From https://journalmodernpm.com/article-view/?id=132.

Sunindyo, W. D.; Ekaputra, F. J. (2023). OSMF: A Framework for OSS Process Measurement. Lecture Notes in Computer Science, 7804, 71-80. DOI: https://doi.org/10.1007/978-3-642-36818-9_8.

Turner, J. R., Müller, R., and Dulewicz, T. (2010). Leadership Competency Profiles of Successful Project Managers. International Journal of Project Management, 21(1), 437-448. DOI: https://doi.org/10.1016/j.ijproman.2009.09.003.

van Wessel, R. M.; Kroon, P.; de Vries, H. J. (2023). Scaling Agile Company Wide: The Organizational Challenge of Combining Agile Scaling Frameworks and Enterprise Architecture in Service Companies. IEEE Engineering Management Review, 51(3), 25-32. DOI: https://doi.org/10.1109/EMR.2023.3277128.

Whyte, J. (2019). How Digital Information Transforms Project Delivery Models. Project Management Journal, 50(2), 177-194. DOI: https://doi.org/10.1177/8756972818823304.

Wiesche, M. (2021). Interruptions in Agile Software Development Teams. Project Management Journal, 52(2), 210-222. DOI: https://doi.org/10.1177/8756972821991365.

Younas, M.; Jawawi, D. N. A.; Mahmood, A. K.; Ahmad, M. N.; Sarwar, M. U.; Idris, M. Y. (2020). Agile Software Development Using Cloud Computing: A Case Study. IEEE Access, 8, 4475-4484. DOI: https://doi.org/10.1109/ACCESS.2019.2962257.

AN EXAMPLE OF CHARACTER NETWORK EXTRACTION FROM A NOVELLA

Hideaki Ito and Koumei Sumigama
School of Engineering, Chukyo University
101 Tokodachi Kaizu Toyota Aichi, Japan, 470-0393

ABSTRACT

This paper describes an example of a character network that is extracted based on the co-occurrence of characters in texts from a detective novella. Two types of character networks are constructed based on the elements of the text, in which nodes and links correspond to characters and their co-occurrence relations within the text, respectively. Characters and co-occurrence relations between them are extracted within a paragraph and a chapter according to the types of character networks. The character networks are created for each paragraph and chapter. These extracted character networks for the previous paragraphs and chapters are cumulated along with the storyline. As a result, a cumulative character network based on a paragraph and one based on a chapter are constructed. The former is useful for capturing local changes, while the latter is for capturing global ones. By observing these two types of cumulative character networks, it is feasible to distinctly observe the fluctuations in the number of characters within the novella, as well as the number of their interactions which corresponds to the frequency of co-occurrence among characters. By using two types of character networks, the structure of interaction and closeness among characters are suitably analyzed.

KEYWORDS

Character Network, Paragraph, Chapter, Co-Occurrence, Novella

1. INTRODUCTION

In recent years, several types of approaches using character networks to analyze the structure of narratives have been proposed (Venturini, et al., 2017), which include novels, stories, dramas, films, TV dramas, etc. Moreover, some methods to construct such networks are developed (Labatut, et al., 2019), in addition to statistically analyzing the narratives (Long, 2021) and making a storyline from events (Caselli, et al., 2021). Character networks are proposed to represent relations among characters in narratives. Types of links between characters are designed depending on the purposes of analysis. Moreover, the character network is sometimes analyzed as a social network (Newman, 2018). It is required to build a character network that makes clear the social or narrative structure with respect to characters.

In this paper, a character network for a mystery novella has been developed as a case study to examine the usefulness of the character network. The novella is "Inju" (in Japanese), "Beast in the Shadows" (in English) by Edogawa Rampo (Edogawa, 2005). This novella is a mystery novel with a detective as the major character, and the story is told in the form of a detective's monologue. In other words, this is an example of a first-person narrative novel. A character network is constructed to help reveal closeness among characters, to make the protagonist explicit, to identify other important characters, and to find interactions among characters, etc. In the network, nodes and links correspond to characters and co-occurrence relations of the characters, respectively.

Two types of character networks are constructed according to elements of the text in a novella, which are paragraphs and chapters. It is considered that a paragraph seems as an elementary component of thought, while a chapter component of a story. They are called a character network based on a paragraph and a character network based on a chapter. The co-occurrence relations with the characters appearing in the paragraphs and chapters are found to construct each character network. The character network constructed at a certain point in the storyline is merged with the character network constructed up to that point. Existing character networks and newly constructed networks for a succeeding paragraph or chapter are merged.

This merge operation is called cumulus. Two types of cumulative character networks are developed, called a cumulative character network based on a paragraph and one based on a chapter, respectively. On the other hand, these cumulative character networks are undirected graphs, in which weights are assigned to the links. Weights are computed based on the frequencies of co-occurrence relations between characters.

Several character networks have been constructed for various types of narratives. And, novels and films are mined and modeled using character networks (Bonato. et al., 2016). Moretti draws a character network of Hamlet (Moretti, 2013). Character networks are analyzed as social networks (Agrawal, et al., 2012). Then, one of the purposes is to obtain its centrality. For example, a network is constructed for a TV series in (Zhang, et al., 2018). Moreover, dramatic works are analyzed based on character networks in (Yavuz, 2020). Visualizing character networks has been tried in (Indu, et al., 2023; Xanthos, et al., 2016).

This paper is organized as follows. Section 2 presents character networks based on a graph. Section 3 describes preprocessing for extracting characters, and the construction of two types of character networks. Preprocessing includes formatting text and character extraction. Extracting two types of cumulative character networks is presented. They are compared in Section 4. Finally, concluding remarks are shown in Section 5.

2. AN OVERVIEW OF CHARACTER NETWORKS

A character network is a network that represents the co-occurrence relations of characters. There are some kinds of characters, they are a protagonist, some important characters who have little to do with the major character, but who play an important role, and characters who need to construct side stories, etc. When they co-occurred within pre-defined elements of text, it seems that these characters interact with each other and mention them. If they co-occur in the same element, a co-occurrence relation is set between two characters.

On the other hand, a set of characters and their co-occurrence relations forms a character network. This network is $G = (N, E)$. Here, N is a set of characters, and E is a set of triples (c_1, c_2, w_{12}). In this triplet, c_1 and c_2 are characters, and w_{12} is the weight of the link. The weight corresponds to the frequencies of co-occurrences of c_1 and c_2.

A character network is constructed along with the storyline. Let there be graphs G_1 and G_2. Graph G_1 is a cumulative network which is constructed up to a certain point in the novella, and G_2 is a network for a subsequent element of G_1. G_1 and G_2 are merged, after that cumulative network G_3 is constructed. Let there be $G_1 = (N_1, E_1)$ and $G_2 = (N_2, E_2)$. A cumulative network $G_3 = (N_3, E_3)$ is obtained by merging G_1 and G_2. $N_3 = N_1 \cup N_2$. If $e_1 \in E_1$, $e_2 \in E_2$, and two nodes in link e_2 are already defined in E_1, the weight of e_3 in E_3 is the sum of w_1 in e_1 and w_2 in e_2. Otherwise, e_2 is added to G_3.

3. EXTRACTION OF CHARACTER NETWORKS

3.1 An Overview for Extracting a Character Network

This section describes an overview of procedures for extracting character networks. At first, the original text is obtained from Aozorabunko (Aozorabunko), which is a digital archive that collects free literary works that are in the public domain in Japanese. The text is machine-readable in Japanese. Aozorabunko likes the Gutenberg Project (Gutenberg). Next, the original text is reformed into a form that is suitable for processing. For example, bibliographic information such as author, title, publication year, etc., is omitted. In addition to this, nonsensical whitespace and line breaks are removed, etc. After these procedures, to extract suitable characters, some preprocessing procedures are applied to the text. Named entities are extracted using a named entity extraction system. Since inappropriate names are obtained at that time, unnecessary words are removed. The details of this step are shown later in this section. Once characters are obtained, co-occurrence relations can be examined. As a result, two types of character networks are constructed. Finally, character networks are drawn using the visualization tool Graphviz (Graphviz).

A character network based on a paragraph and one based on a chapter are constructed as follows:

1. Finding co-occurrence relations of characters in elements. Characters are sought in elements that are paragraphs or chapters.
2. Extraction of character networks. The meanings of link weights in a network based on a paragraph and one based on a chapter are different from each other. In a character network based on a paragraph, the weights correspond to the frequencies of co-occurrences. On the other hand, in the network based on a chapter, the weights correspond to the number of chapters in which the two characters co-occur.
3. Displaying character networks. The networks are visualized as an undirected graph.

Using two different types of character networks, it is possible to analyze characters' overall and/or detailed interactions.

3.2 Preprocessing of Japanese Text

Some preprocessing procedures are applied to obtain a suitable form to extract characters. At first, transforming the downloaded text from Aozorabunko is tried. The downloaded text has line break positions, unnecessary spaces, etc. Such unnecessary characters, strings, and line breaks are deleted. Moreover, the text includes strings and/or words that do not need to be analyzed in the novella (e.g., punctuation marks, parenthetical annotations, page numbers, etc.). Moreover, this text includes annotations by using some tags, special characters, e.g., [, #, <<, etc. And tags for representing how to read Japanese kanji characters are removed. Such unnecessary symbols and tags are removed.

After applying the above procedures, the entire text is divided into chapters, and then paragraphs are made clear within each chapter. Consequently, the text is organized using JSON.

As the next step, noise reduction and preparation for character extraction are tried. The Japanese model of Spacy "ja ginza" (GiNZA) is used to recognize named entities. Then, captured named entities are labeled, such as PERSON, GPE, ORG, etc. First of all, words labeled "PERSON" are treated as candidates of a personal name, i.e., characters. Then, the following four types of problems are found:

1. Strings and/or words that are not personal names are mistakenly extracted as persons.
2. There is more than one person with the same last name. A married couple has the same last name. In the novella, the surname "Oyamada" is ambiguous as to whether it indicates "Rokuro Oyamada" or "Shizuko Oyamada". Although they are called by the same name, they are distinct from each other.
3. There is a case where the same characters are extracted with different representations, such as "Ichiro Hirata" and "Hirata". In this case, the surname "Hirata" is used to indicate "Ichiro Hirata".
4. This detective is in the form of my storytelling. The word "I" indicates the protagonist. But it is not extracted as a person. The named entity extraction system does not treat "I" as a person also.

To solve these problems described above, some procedures are applied. They are described in turn. At first, strings that occur only once are filtered out. This method effectively removes many of the unnecessary words. A low occurrence rate means that it is less important.

Many words that are not personal names are extracted, but they are labelled "PERSON". For example, there are cases where onomatopoeic words, job titles, area names, town names, etc., are extracted as persons. Onomatopoeic words and job titles appear frequently. To remove such unnecessary words as character names, a list of unnecessary words is established. Words included in this list are considered unnecessary words, so they are removed from the candidates. This list is a list of words that are likely to be mistaken for characters. By introducing this exception processing, the accuracy of named entity extraction is improved.

We show how to handle the problem of different characters being called by the same name. This is caused by the fact that the husband and wife have the same last name. "Oyamada" indicates "Rokuro Oyamada" or "Shizuko Oyamada", who are a married couple, and they are the major characters. We read the relevant parts, and check the context and conversations. As a result, it is determined that all "Oyamada" indicate "Rokuro Oyamada". Based on this determination, a program is used to unify "Oyamada" with "Rokuro Oyamada". This process is manually confirmed.

We deal with the problem that the same person may be described by different designations. Since the characters are the same, even if they are indicated by different names, it is necessary to unify the names of the characters. To solve this problem, we identify common character strings, such as "Ichiro Hirata" and "Hirata," and deal with them to make them consistent. In this case, the part of the substring "Hirata" is matched with two strings. Specifically, notations related to the same person are listed, and standard notations are set as criteria, for example, "Ichiro Hirata" is the same as "Hirata". Based on this list, we construct a rule that automatically performs unified conversion. Applying these unification rules for representing names, the entire text is rechecked to ensure that there are no omissions or incorrect unification of multiple notations of the same person.

The form of the novella is told by only one storyteller. Then, the protagonist is not extracted among captured personal names, as described before. The protagonist is described as "I". Symbol "I" is not labeled "PERSON". To solve this problem, we apply a custom rule for named entity extraction, where the word "I" is labeled as "PERSON" in temporal. Where the protagonist's name is explicitly stated, we manually noted "I" as the proper noun "Samukawa". This rewrite process makes it possible to accurately analyze how the protagonist is related to other characters while maintaining consistency throughout the novella. Through this process, it became possible to reflect the importance of the storyteller in the network.

The following characters are obtained, which are: 六郎(Rokuro), 平山日出子(Hirayama Hideko), 本田(Honda), 静子(Shizuko), 大江(Oe), 平田(Hirata), 糸崎(Itozaki), 寒川(Samukawa), 斉藤 (Saito), and 青木(Aoki). Ten people are extracted as characters. Only personal names that are suitable for a character network are finally extracted. This refinement provides an important basis for accurate co-occurrence relations of characters. Many problems depend on Japanese, the novel, and the writing style, etc.

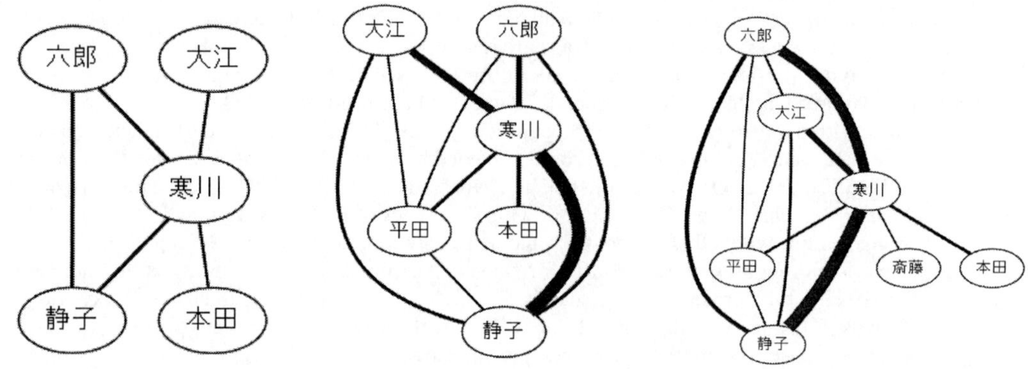

(a) A cumulative character network of Chapter 2, Paragraph 11.

(b) A cumulative character network of Chapter 6, Paragraph 15.

(c) A cumulative character network of Chapter 10, Paragraph 1.

Figure 1. Examples of cumulative character networks based on a paragraph

3.3 Extracting Character Network

This section shows the extraction of cumulative character networks based on a paragraph and on a chapter. A character network is constructed for each paragraph or chapter, and is cumulated with the character networks of a subsequent paragraph and/or chapter.

The procedure for extracting cumulative character networks based on a paragraph is described. A cumulative character network is a network that records the co-occurrence relations among the characters in each paragraph, cumulating them from paragraph to paragraph. Co-occurrence relations between characters are extracted within a paragraph and added cumulatively to visualize their changes. This process enables a step-by-step construction of the relations among major characters. The cumulative character network is created by sequentially integrating the co-occurrence relations extracted in each paragraph. This integration is performed by the following steps:

1. Extraction of co-occurrence relations in a paragraph. The characters appearing in each paragraph are listed, and all character pairs are made from them. In generating pairs, combinations containing the same characters are excluded.
2. Updating cumulative co-occurrence relations. The relations generated in each paragraph are counted cumulatively. When the same relation appears more than once, its frequency is added up and recorded.

This process integrates paragraph by paragraph. Here, characters that appear only once in a paragraph are not used to create relations.

3. Network visualization. The extracted co-occurrence relations are visualized as a cumulative character network. Links represent co-occurrence relations. Its thickness is varied according to the frequencies of co-occurrences to visually represent the strength of the relations. The thickness is computed as *Link thickness = (1 + co-occurrence frequencies)/2*. The division by 2 is used to adjust the thickness.

Some cumulative character networks are shown in Figure 1, in which the networks grow in the order from (a) to (c). Here, nodes in the figure are represented in Japanese fonts, they are treated merely as symbols. The cumulative network is recorded for each paragraph to track gradual changes. This method allows for identifying the gradual development between characters. In particular, change points such as the occurrence of new co-occurrence relations and sudden increases in frequencies are captured.

This kind of network is an effective approach for understanding the progression and structure of relationships among characters and their closeness. The results suggest that the method may be widely applicable to the analysis of other novels. Through this analysis, it is shown that the method using the cumulative network is a tool not only for capturing changes as the story progresses, but also for clarifying the closeness among the major characters. Moreover, it provides a basis for visual understanding of the changing relations between characters.

Character networks are analyzed in the following way. The analysis of the cumulative character network highlights changes in the relations between characters and the roles of major characters as the story progresses. Some observations are found. At first, the strength of relations between major characters is stressed. As the story progresses, the frequency of co-occurrences between major characters tends to increase. In particular, the thickness of the links between the major characters increases significantly in the paragraphs toward the climax of the story, confirming that the central event of the story deepens the relations among the characters. Moreover, after the middle of the story, new links appear. A phenomenon is observed in which new links are added between previously non-co-occurring characters. This suggests that new characters and related relations are emerging. Furthermore, the number of links in the cumulative character network per paragraph shows that it increases as the story progresses. This indicates a trend toward closer relations between characters.

Subsequently, the extraction of cumulative character networks based on a chapter is shown. This type of cumulative character network is the cumulation of the networks sought so far and the network for the currently focused chapter. We consider that it is important to visually find the changes in character relations and structural features among characters in the entire story.

A cumulative character network based on a chapter is constructed in the following way. At first, characters that correspond to the nodes extracted in each chapter are cumulatively collected to ensure the overall coverage of the characters. Next, co-occurrence relations that are links in each chapter are counted, and the co-occurrence frequencies are calculated up to the last chapter. The frequency notes the number of chapters that include the co-occurrence of two characters. If the combination of the co-occurrence relation also appeared in other chapters, one is added to the number of chapters. Finally, when new co-occurrence relations are found, they are incorporated into an existing network. Here, characters that appear only once in a chapter are not used to create co-occurrence relations, like in a network based on a paragraph.

The structure of the cumulative character networks based on a chapter is summarized as follows:

1. Extensibility of the network. New co-occurrence relations of characters in each chapter are investigated to confirm the development of character relations. For example, the relations among a small number of characters at the beginning of the story depict a situation for setting up. As the chapters progress, new characters are introduced, thus increasing the complexity of the character network.
2. Identification of central characters. Nodes connected by a high frequency of links are major characters throughout the entire novella.
3. Trends of new co-occurrence relations. By checking the chapters and frequencies of new relations, we identify turning points in the story and chapters where new co-occurrence relations emerge.
4. An entire structure of a network. The increasing trend of the number of links and nodes in the cumulative network is analyzed as the complexity of the story becomes large.

Figure 2 shows the progress of some cumulative character networks based on a chapter, along with the storyline. Newly occurring relations are identified to visualize changes in character relations. Links are color-coded according to frequencies, i.e., green for new co-occurrence relations, blue for frequencies of 5 or more, and red for frequencies of 10 or more. For example, the cumulative character network of Chapter 6 is shown in Figure 2(c). The link frequency of the most major character, i.e., "Samukawa" is much higher than that of the other characters, suggesting that he plays a central role in the entire story. And, we can understand the development of the characters' relations by observing how the blue links are distributed and change as the story progresses.

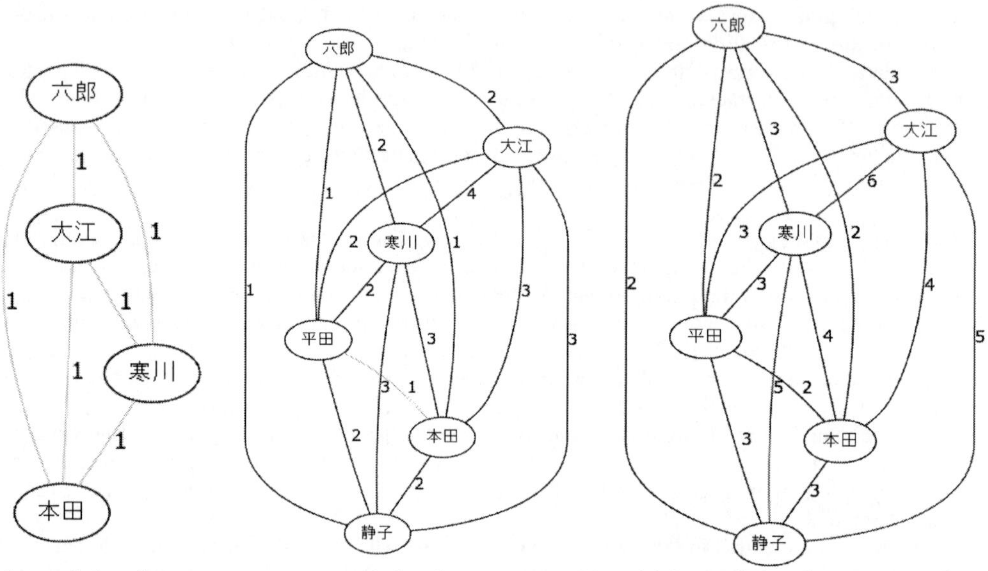

(a) A cumulative character network based up to Chapter 1.

cumulative character network on chapters up to Chapter 4.

(c) A cumulative character network based on chapters up to Chapter 6.

Figure 2. Examples of cumulative character networks based on a chapter

4. COMPARING CHARACTER NETWORKS

A character network based on paragraphs and one based on chapters are compared, moreover, their final network diagrams are shown. The final results of the cumulative character network based on a paragraph are shown in Figure 3, and one based on a chapter in Figure 4, respectively. These two types of cumulative character networks are compared as follows:

1. A cumulative character network based on a paragraph can capture the progression of relationships among characters at a more detailed scale than one based on a chapter.
2. The number of nodes and links in the network based on a paragraph is smaller than that of the network based on a chapter. A cumulative character network based on a paragraph is easier to infer important characters than one based on a chapter.
3. In the network based on a paragraph, the rapid increase of the number of links by some characters in a short period is evident, and the network based on a paragraph makes it possible to find relationships among characters in the local story development.
4. The cumulative character network based on a chapter can roughly capture the progression of the entire relations among characters.
5. Construction of the cumulative character network based on a chapter shows a process of strengthening relations as the story progresses.

6. New characters and relations are limited to the middle of the story or later, while existing major links are established as the foundation of the story in both types of networks.

Cumulative character networks based on paragraphs and ones based on chapters are useful for analyzing the narrative. Their characteristics are shown below:

1. A cumulative character network based on a paragraph.
   - Detailed changes in relations among characters are made clear.
   - The number of nodes is smaller than that of a network based on a chapter.
   - The number of links between specific characters is high, since they are close.
   - Short-term changes in closeness characters are reflected.
2. A cumulative character network based on a chapter.
   - The entire structure of a novella with respect to relationships among characters is shown.
   - The number of nodes and links is larger than those in the network based on a paragraph.
   - Long-term changes in closeness between characters are reflected.

A network based on a paragraph is useful for clarifying local details and dynamic changes over a short period. In addition, since filtering by number of occurrences is performed for each element, the network on the paragraph may have fewer nodes than one on the chapter, making the interpretation of the graph easy to understand. On the other hand, a network based on a chapter is suitable for a global view of the overall structure and can briefly capture the relations among the major characters. By combining these two types of networks, it is possible to simultaneously capture the interactions among characters.

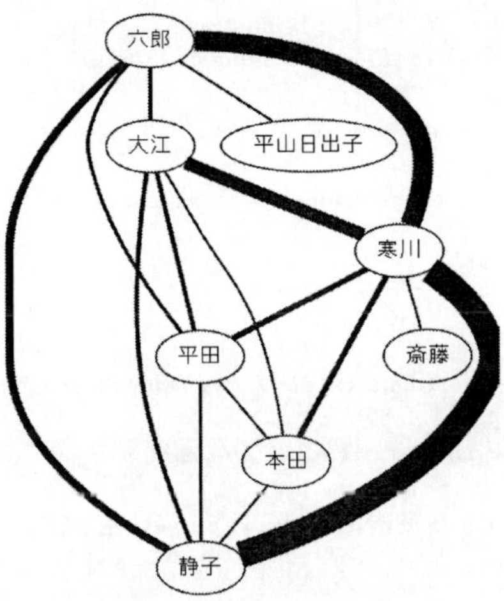

Figure 3. A cumulative character network based on a paragraph, 12th paragraph in Chapter 12

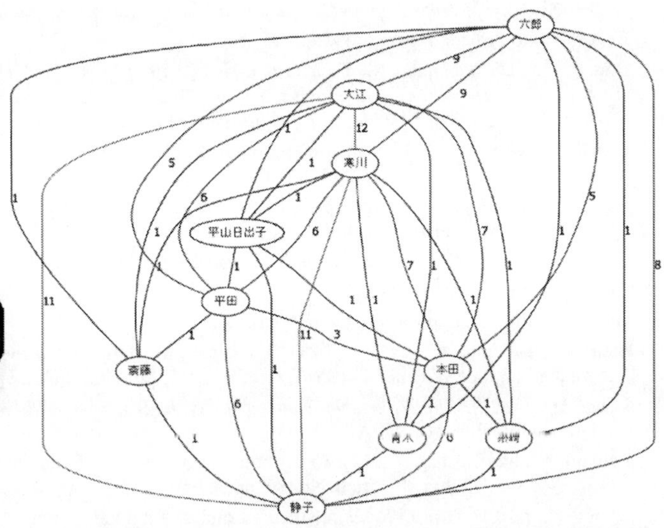

Figure 4. A cumulative character network based on a chapter, Chapter 12

5. CONCLUDING REMARKS

In this paper, two types of character networks are constructed and compared. They are cumulative character networks based on a paragraph and one based on a chapter. The former is useful for capturing local changes, while the latter is for capturing global changes based on the interactions among characters included in paragraphs and chapters, respectively.

The preprocessing for constructing character networks involves some narrative-dependent processing. For the Japanese language, we used the named entity extraction system for Japanese. Although some characters are obtained, many noises are included in them. To remove them, some preprocessing procedures are required, depending on the language and the novel. In addition, the processing of words that have the same notation but indicate different characters depends on the novel, and the social structure of its background, although not only in Japan. It is also considered necessary to obtain a greater variety of personal names through the development of dictionaries.

One of the future problems in natural language processing is pronoun resolution. This paper treated the pronoun "I" since this processing was essential in interpreting the narrative that was told by "I". Speakers other than the protagonist rarely use "I" in this case. Moreover, it seems that one of the characteristics of the Japanese is considered to be the infrequent use of pronouns, like, he, she, etc. However, for flexible processing of texts, it will be necessary to clarify the reference resolution.

The novella discussed in this paper is a medium-length novel with 12 chapters. As future work, it will be necessary to confirm the usefulness of two types of character networks for novels with a larger number of chapters and characters by constructing them.

REFERENCES

Agrawal, A., Corvalan, A., Jensen, J. and Rambow, O. (2012). Social Network Analysis of Alice in Wonderland. *Proceedings of Workshop on Computational Linguistics for Literature,* Montréal, Canada, pp. 88–96.

Aozorabunko Project, https://www.aozora.gr.jp/.

Bonato, A., D'Angelo, D. R., Elenberg, E. R., Gleich, D. F., and Hou, Y. (2016). Mining and Modeling Character Networks. *Algorithms and Models for the Web Graph, Proceedings of 15th International Workshop*, Moscow, Russia, LNCS, Vol. 10088, Springer. pp. 100–114.

Caselli, T., Hovy, E., Palmer, M., and Vossen, P., Ed. (2021). *Computational Analysis of Storylines: Making Sense of Events.* Cambridge University Press, Cambridge, England.

Edogawa, R. (2005). *Inju.* in Japanese, Aozorabunko, (2023). *Beast in the Shadows.* in English, Penguin Classics, Penguin Random House, Dublin, UK.

GiNZA - Japanese NLP Library, https://megagonlabs.github.io/ginza/.

Graphviz, https://graphviz.org/.

Gutenberg Project, http://www.gutenberg.org.

Indu, R., and Bhavani, S. D. (2023). Visualization of the Dynamics in Character Networks using Social Network Analysis. *Proceedings of CODS-COMAD*, ACM, Mumbai, India, pp. 284 - 285

Long, H., (2021). *The Values in Numbers, Reading Japanese Literature in a Global Information Age*. Columbia University Press, NY, USA.

Labatut, V., and Bost, X. (2019). Extraction and Analysis of Fictional Character Networks: A Survey. *ACM Computing Survey*, Vol. 52, No. 5, Article No. 89, pp. 1 - 40.

Moretti, F. (2013). *Distant Reading*, Verso, London, England.

Newman, M. (2018). *Network. 2nd edition.* Oxford University Press, Oxford, England.

Venturini, T., Bounegru, L., Jacomy, M., and Gray, J. (2017). How to Tell Stories with Networks. *The Datafied Society, Studying Culture through Data,* Ed. Schäfer, M.K., and van Es, K., Amsterdam University Press, Amsterdam, The Netherlands.

Xanthos, A., Pante, I., Rochat, Y., and Grandjean, M. (2016). Visualising the Dynamics of Character Networks. *Proceedings of Digital Humanities,* Krakow, Poland. pp. 417-419.

Yavuz, M. C. (2020). Analyses of Character Networks in Dramatic Works by Using Graphs. *Proceedings of 7th International Conference on Behavioral and Social Computing (BESC),* IEEE, Bournemouth, UK, pp. 1-4.

Zhang, L., Li, C., Fan, L., and Shi, M. (2018). Analysis of Character Relationship in TV Series Based on Complex Network. *Proceedings of ICIS,* IEEE, Singapore, pp. 723-727.

AI AND CYBERCRIME: A POLICY FRAMEWORK FOR ORGANIZATIONAL DEFENSE

Luca Knecht, Petra Maria Asprion and Bettina Schneider
University of Applied Sciences and Arts Northwestern Switzerland FHNW, School of Business, Institute for Information Systems, Basel, Switzerland

ABSTRACT

Artificial Intelligence (AI) is a transformative technology with significant potential and accompanying threats. While AI fosters innovation, it is increasingly exploited for criminal activities, especially cybercrime. This research examines the criminal elements of AI, focusing on its role in enabling sophisticated cyber threats. Addressing AI requires organizations to adopt measures as traditional cybersecurity frameworks struggle to keep pace with rapidly evolving AI-driven threats. This research identifies and categorizes the criminal elements of AI, with particular attention to their application in cybercrime. Requirements derived from expert interviews are the foundation for developing a conceptual policy framework to provide organizations with measures to combat AI-driven threats. The proposed framework, refined through expert feedback, offers targeted, actionable recommendations to enhance organizational resilience against AI-driven threats. By providing a systematic structure and evaluated measures, the framework supports cybersecurity professionals, IT managers, and risk officers in mitigating the dual-use risks of AI. The research results contribute to bridging the gap in cybersecurity literature by addressing the evolving nature of AI-related threats and presenting a forward-looking policy framework tailored to middle-to-large organizations.

KEYWORDS

Artificial Intelligence, AI-Driven Threats, Policy Framework, Cybersecurity, Cybercrime

1. INTRODUCTION

1.1 Relevance and Problem Statement

The dual-use nature of artificial intelligence (AI)—its capacity for both beneficial and malicious applications—has significantly contributed to the rise in cyberattacks, particularly in the areas of social engineering, deepfakes, and autonomous hacking (Bueermann & Rohrs, 2024; Loh et al., 2024; Brundage et al., 2018). The World Economic Forum's *Global Risk Report 2024* identifies AI-generated misinformation and disinformation as the second-highest global risk, with far-reaching implications such as destabilizing governments, inciting unrest, and enabling terrorism (Bueermann & Rohrs, 2024). Cybercrime has surged globally, with incidents increasing by 600% between 2020 and 2023 (Rao et al., 2023). In Switzerland, cybercrime rose by 31.5% in 2023 compared to the previous year, threatening financial stability, reputational integrity, and business continuity (Federal Statistical Office, 2024).

Organizations face increasing difficulty in detecting and mitigating AI-driven threats, as conventional cybersecurity frameworks lag behind the evolving threat landscape (Melaku, 2023). AI-enhanced social engineering further exploits human vulnerabilities, increasing susceptibility to attacks (Melaku, 2023). The absence of globally harmonized regulations facilitates cross-border misuse of AI, while the rapid pace of AI development continues to outstrip existing security protocols (Evang, 2022). Moreover, AI's reliance on large datasets raises privacy concerns, as anonymized data remains vulnerable to inference attacks (Admass et al., 2024). Given AI's transformative yet hazardous potential, organizations must establish a comprehensive understanding of its criminal applications and implement timely, actionable countermeasures (Admass et al., 2024; Maurya, 2023).

1.2 Research Goal and Related Questions

This study aims to identify and categorize the criminal elements of AI, with a particular focus on AI-enabled cyber threats. To bridge the gap between the malicious use of AI and the growing need for cybersecurity resilience, it proposes a conceptual policy framework that provides organizations with structured, actionable mitigation strategies. The research is guided by the following key research questions (RQ):

RQ1: What are the current criminal elements associated with AI-driven threats?
RQ2: How can these criminal elements be systematically categorized?
RQ3: What are the key requirements for developing a policy framework to address AI-driven threats
RQ4: How can these requirements be translated into a coherent conceptual policy framework?
RQ5: How useful is the resulting framework in supporting organizations against AI-enabled cyber threats?

2. LITERATURE REVIEW

As part of the research design, first a literature review was carried out with focus on the criminal use of AI in cybersecurity, examining how cybercriminals exploit AI to automate attacks and evade detection, as well as identifying countermeasures to strengthen security frameworks. The literature review covers sources from 2020 to 2024, in English and German, reflecting the rapid evolution of AI. It begins with a review of grey literature from industry leaders (e.g., Palo Alto Networks, the Big Four, WEF) to establish key terminology and trends. Academic insights were gathered from databases such as Google Scholar, ScienceDirect, Web of Science, and Semantic Scholar. AI tools like ChatGPT 4o and Scholar GPT supported the search process. Of 132 sources identified, 88 were selected for in-depth analysis based on their recency, credibility, and relevance to RQs. The following sections summarize the key findings in a concise manner.

2.1 General Classification of AI

A common generic classification of AI is developed from Saghiri et al. (2022). They classify AI in (1) Artificial Narrow Intelligence (performs specialized tasks), (2) Artificial General Intelligence (seeks to replicate human intelligence), and (3) Artificial Super Intelligence (a hypothetical form exceeding human intelligence). Currently, AI progresses primarily through machine learning (ML) and deep learning (DL), which use neural networks to analyze large datasets. ML models improve with experience, while DL processes unstructured data such as images or speech through multi-layered algorithms (IBM, 2024). These technologies power AI's role in cybersecurity, automation, and fraud detection—but also introduce new avenues for misuse (Guembe et al., 2022). Understanding these misuse risks is vital for mitigating AI-related cyber threats (Admass et al., 2024).

2.2 Criminal Elements of AI

To provide structure and clarity, we categorize the criminal elements of AI into six distinct domains based on, but extended from Blauth et al. (2022), including (1) bias in AI decision-making, (2) autonomous weapons and AI warfare, (3) AI-driven social engineering, (4) AI in cybercrime, (5) intellectual property theft and AI manipulation, and (6) privacy invasion and mass surveillance. This categorization allows for a more comprehensive analysis of the diverse ways in which AI can be misused in the context of cybersecurity.

(1) Bias in AI Decision-Making: AI systems can reflect and amplify bias through flawed algorithms, biased training data, or human input (Tabassi, 2023). In cybersecurity, this can result in inaccurate threat detection or unfair profiling (IBM, 2023). Mitigating these risks requires responsible AI practices, including transparency, explainability, and adherence to emerging regulations like the EU AI Act (ISACA, 2024).

(2) Autonomous Weapons and AI Warfare: Autonomous Weapons Systems (AWS) use AI to identify and attack targets without direct human control (Blauth et al., 2022). AI is also deployed in cyberwarfare, espionage, and surveillance for its speed and data-processing capabilities (Yamin et al., 2021). These uses raise ethical concerns around accountability and escalation risks (European Union Agency for Cybersecurity, 2023).

(3) AI-Driven Social Engineering: AI enables more personalized and deceptive social engineering attacks via generative tools and language models (Falade, 2023). By analyzing online data, attackers craft effective phishing and impersonation campaigns. Broader access to AI lowers the barrier to launching such sophisticated attacks (Schmitt & Flechais, 2023).

(4) AI in Cybercrime: Cybercriminals automate attacks using AI, increasing scale and precision (Malatji, 2023). AI-driven malware evades detection by adapting code or execution paths. Criminals also use AI to execute large-scale DDoS attacks, targeting networks and critical infrastructure (Guembe et al., 2022).

(5) Intellectual Property Theft and AI Manipulation: AI challenges IP law by reducing human input in content creation (Hilty et al., 2021; Kokane, 2021). Legal ambiguity around AI-generated outputs increases IP theft risks. Cybercriminals exploit AI to steal proprietary data, highlighting the need for global legal harmonization (Nnamdi et al., 2023; Pavis, 2021).

(6) Privacy Invasion and Mass Surveillance: AI's need for extensive data raises privacy risks through inference attacks and misuse (Admass et al., 2024; Shahriar et al., 2023). Users face the personalization-privacy paradox (Meurisch & Mühlhäuser, 2022). Technologies like facial recognition facilitate mass surveillance, with risks of bias, misidentification, and authoritarian misuse (Clarke, 2022; Maphosa, 2023).

2.3 Cybercrime – Patterns and Trends

2.3.1 AI-Enabled Cybercrime

Advances in AI have transformed cybercrime by enabling automation, personalization, and large-scale operations (Malatji, 2023). AI-driven threats include phishing, deepfakes, malware, and ransomware, which target vulnerabilities in both individuals and organizations (Guembe et al., 2022). We identified four attack types:

- Distributed Denial-of-Service (DDoS) Attacks: AI enhances botnet coordination, allowing faster, more adaptive DDoS assaults (Aslan et al., 2023; Humayun et al., 2020).
- Malware and Ransomware: AI enables malware to mutate dynamically, evading traditional defenses through evolving behaviors (Aslan et al., 2023; Humayun et al., 2020).
- Phishing and Spear-Phishing: natural language processing NLP-driven tools craft personalized messages that adapt to targets in real (Aslan et al., 2023; Humayun et al., 2020).
- AI-enhanced Identity Theft: Deepfakes of voices, images, and videos facilitate impersonation for fraud and espionage (Aslan et al., 2023; Humayun et al., 2020).

2.3.2 Motivations for Cyberattacks

Cyberattacks are driven by financial gain, identity theft, espionage, and sabotage (Mijwil et al., 2023; Li, 2017; Adlakha et al., 2019). Criminals steal data for profit or resale, while state actors seek strategic intelligence. Some attacks aim to disrupt systems or damage reputations (Aftab et al., 2022). Other motives include cyberterrorism, misinformation campaigns, and resource hijacking for botnets or cryptomining (Li, 2017; Mijwil et al., 2023). AI enables diverse threat actors to automate exploitation processes and adapt attack strategies in real time. Common actors behind AI-driven attacks: (1) Organized Crime Groups: Use AI for large-scale fraud, laundering, and ID theft (Edwards et al., 2022), (2) State-Sponsored Actors: Employ AI for espionage, sabotage, political interference (Hylender et al., 2023), (3) Individual Hackers: Pre-built AI tools enable attacks with minimal expertise (Edwards et al., 2022) and (4) Insiders: Leverage insider knowledge and AI tools to manipulate or extract data (Hylender et al., 2023).

2.4 Cybersecurity – AI Enhancements

As AI advances cyber threats, organizations increasingly adopt AI-enabled cybersecurity to improve strategic, operational, and technical defenses, including enhanced threat detection, faster incident response, and proactive prevention, boosting digital infrastructure resilience.

Strategic Defense Measures. Strategic cybersecurity reduces risks and aligns with standards like ISO/IEC 27001 and NIST CSF for risk management and protection (Alshar'e, 2023; Evang, 2022). The MITRE ATT&CK framework aids threat hunting and response (MITRE Corporation, 2024). However, these frameworks can be costly, complex, and less flexible against evolving AI threats (Melaku, 2023; Alshar'e,

2023). Regulatory compliance is crucial: GDPR governs EU data protection (Wolff et al., 2023), the AI Act introduces risk-based AI governance from 2024 (European Parliament & Council of the European Union, 2024), and Switzerland enforces the Federal Act on Data Protection (The Federal Assembly of the Swiss Confederation, 2020). Human error remains a major vulnerability; thus, Security Education Training and Awareness (SETA) programs are vital (MIT Technology Review, 2021; Dash & Ansari, 2022).

Operational Defence Measures. These include daily tools like access control (MFA, least privilege) (Hu et al., 2017), firewalls, intrusion detection systems (NIST, 2020), encryption, and backups (Plaka, 2022). Incident response plans, patching, antivirus, and SIEM systems support threat management and monitoring (Souppaya & Scarfone, 2022; Palo Alto Networks, 2024; Ban et al., 2023). Employee training reinforces threat awareness and best practices (Dash & Ansari, 2022; MIT Technology Review, 2021).

Technical Defence Measures. AI boosts cybersecurity via automation and intelligent detection, identifying anomalies, phishing, and malware variants (Maurya, 2023; Shanthi et al., 2023; Mohamed, 2023). AI-driven intrusion detection monitors traffic, while automated remediation and SOAR platforms speed responses (Mohamed, 2023; Shanthi et al., 2023). AI also supports vulnerability analysis, penetration testing, threat intelligence, user behavior profiling, and zero-day exploit prediction (Maurya, 2023; Mohamed, 2023). Additional uses include biometric authentication, cloud and IoT security, and tailored cybersecurity training (Shanthi et al., 2023; Mohamed, 2023). Challenges persist regarding data privacy, bias, and AI transparency (Adewale & Segun, 2024; Zhang et al., 2022; Shanthi et al., 2023).

2.5 Research Gap

Despite advances in AI-powered cybersecurity, organizations struggle to adapt to rapidly evolving AI threats. Existing frameworks like ISO/IEC 27001/2 and NIST CSF do not fully address AI's fast-paced changes, leaving vulnerabilities exposed (Evang, 2022). Traditional measures target known threats, but AI-driven attacks continuously evolve, bypassing standard controls (Malatji, 2023). Cybersecurity training remains insufficient for AI-specific threats, and employees often lack skills to detect AI-generated phishing, deepfakes, and automated attacks. Therefore, AI-focused awareness programs are needed to boost human resilience against AI-enabled deception (Dash & Ansari, 2022; Alshar'e, 2023). Another key gap is the absence of standardized AI security frameworks; while the EU AI Act sets ethical guidelines, no universal policy framework governs AI's cybersecurity role (Wolff et al., 2023). This regulatory uncertainty hampers enforcement and enables AI misuse. To address these gaps, we propose a conceptual policy framework integrating strategic, operational, and technical AI cybersecurity measures to enhance organizational resilience and mitigate AI-driven risks.

3. RESEARCH APPLICATION

3.1 Design and Process

This research was based on a pragmatic research philosophy focused on real-world solutions to AI-driven cybersecurity threats (adhered to Saunders et al., 2019). Employing an inductive approach, we explored emerging AI threats beyond existing theories by deriving an artefact from literature and qualitative expert interviews (based on recommendations from Saunders et al., 2019). Using qualitative methods and coding, we extracted key themes from cybersecurity and AI experts categorizing challenges and solutions (adhered to vom Brocke et al., 2020). To enhance methodological transparency, this research involved semi-structured interviews with eight Swiss cybersecurity experts selected for their roles in IT governance, risk management, and AI deployment. Interviews followed a standardized protocol focused on AI threat categorization and mitigation strategies. Thematic coding was conducted manually to identify recurring patterns and validate framework components. The literature review (Section 2) laid the theoretical groundwork and identified research gaps, while interviews provided nuanced perspectives on threats and mitigation. Data were collected cross-sectionally to capture the current AI threat landscape, with future longitudinal studies recommended. As leading methodology the Design Science Research (DSR) approach by Kuechler & Vaishnavi (2004) seemed most preferably applicable with its four iterative phases:

1. **Problem Awareness:** An extensive literature review analyzed AI cybercrime, threats, and frameworks, addressing RQs 1 and 2 and identifying gaps.
2. **Suggestion:** Using the Double Diamond Model (Meinel et al., 2011), semi-structured interviews with Swiss experts informed AI-centric policy framework requirements. Thematic analysis and standards review guided development, addressing RQ3.
3. **Development:** Requirements were translated into an initial AI-driven policy framework (Version 0.1), refined iteratively with expert feedback to Conceptual Framework 1.0, addressing RQ4.
4. **Evaluation:** Cybersecurity experts assessed the framework's strengths and limitations through interviews, enabling refinements to finalize Conceptual Framework 1.0, ensuring responsiveness to evolving threats and addressing RQ5.

3.2 Artifact Development

The conceptual policy framework evolved iteratively to provide a structured, adaptable approach to AI-driven cybersecurity threats. It began with an initial structure incorporating essential cybersecurity measures aligned with best practices. The framework includes an overview outlining its purpose, target audience, and key principles, offering a structured approach to AI threats with risk assessments, AI-specific security measures, and adaptability for various organizations. Version 0.1 emphasized modularity, allowing users to apply measures comprehensively or selectively. Security measures were refined and categorized by best practices, focusing on AI-augmented defenses, human factors, legal compliance, and technical controls. Each measure details implementation steps, risk assessments, and use cases. The initial version was systematically compared to requirements to ensure completeness before evaluation.

3.3 Artifact Evaluation

Evaluation assessed the framework's effectiveness, scalability, robustness, and usability through expert interviews. Experts validated its practical applicability and suggested refinements for clarity, such as clearer goals, separating categories into distinct frameworks, and adding practical examples. The framework's scalability was praised, though experts recommended tailoring advice to different risk levels with guiding questions and case studies. For robustness, clearer terminology and hierarchical categorization were advised, along with consolidating overlapping categories to reduce redundancy. Usability was commended for simplicity, with suggestions to include actionable examples and simplified workflows. Table 1 summarizes adaptations made from expert feedback:

Table 1. Adaptations resulting from the artefact evaluation

#	Conceptional Policy Framework - Artefact Adaptions
1	Expanded goals and purpose clarify the framework's mission and target organizations, replacing a brief original statement.
2	Baseline cybersecurity reaffirmed by emphasizing traditional controls (e.g., NIST CSF, ISO 27001), with AI as an added layer.
3	"How to use it" section enhanced with guiding questions to help practitioners navigate the framework.
4	Terminology reviewed for consistency, eliminating confusing or duplicate terms.
5	Overlapping categories and measures consolidated, streamlining taxonomy and reducing redundant activities.

4. RESULTING POLICY FRAMEWORK

The final conceptual policy framework 1.0 (Figure 1) integrates theoretical foundations with practical strategies to help organizations mitigate AI-driven cybersecurity threats. Designed with a modular structure, it enables flexible application- either holistically or focused on specific areas - and complements existing cybersecurity strategies. Serving IT teams, compliance officers, policymakers, researchers, and educators, the framework addresses both traditional security needs - such as authentication, patch management, and training - and emerging AI-specific risks requiring adaptive responses, ethical oversight, and regulatory compliance.

Organized into four main categories (Figure 1, detailed in Table 2), the framework presents targeted measures with clear objectives, implementation steps, and references to standards like ISO/IEC 27001 and the NIST CSF.

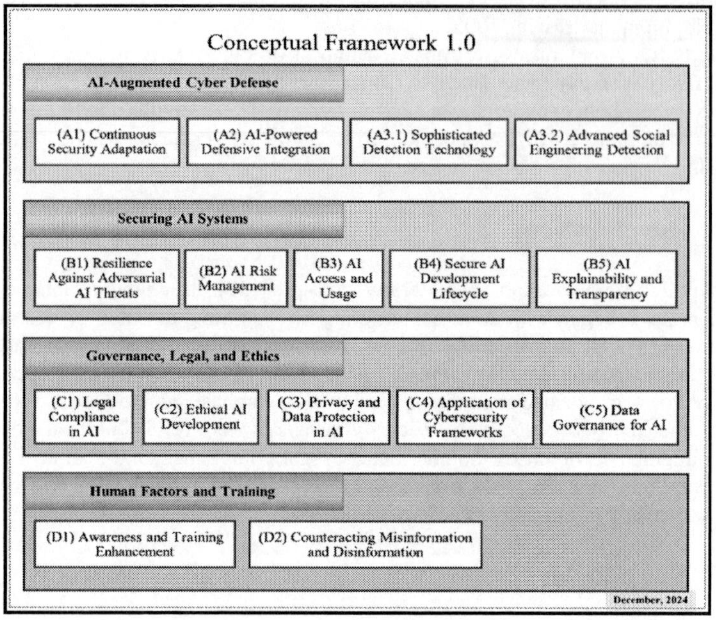

Figure 1. Conceptual Framework 1.0

Organizations are encouraged to prioritize these measures based on their risk profiles, resource availability, and strategic goals. Its scalable design supports continuous improvement and focuses on critical domains such as social engineering and secure AI development. By integrating technical, governance, and human-focused components, the policy framework aligns with key regulations, including the GDPR, Swiss FADP, the upcoming EU AI Act, and management standards such as ISO/IEC and the NIST AI RMF.

Table 2. Conceptional Framework 1.0 with four main categories, measures and detailed context

##	Conceptual Policy Framework Main Categories		Detailed Description
A	AI-Augmented Cyber Defense		Enhancing defense via real-time detection, automated responses, and predictive analytics.
	Measure		
	A1	Continuous Security Adaptation	Implementing security systems that adjust in real-time to emerging threats using AI and machine learning.
	A2	AI-Powered Defensive Integration	Integrating AI technologies into existing cybersecurity defenses to enhance capabilities in threat detection, response, and prevention.
	A3.1	Sophisticated Detection Technology	Utilizing advanced technologies like AI and machine learning to detect complex and evolving cyber threats that traditional methods might miss.
	A3.2	Advanced Social Engineering Detection	Using AI and behavioral analytics to identify and prevent social engineering attacks like phishing and spear-phishing.
B	Securing AI Systems		Protecting AI from threats with dedicated security measures.
	Measure		
	B1	Resilience Against Adversarial AI Threats	Building systems robust against attacks that exploit AI systems, such as adversarial machine learning attacks.
	B2	AI Risk Management	Identifying, assessing, and mitigating risks associated with the use of AI technologies within an organization.
	B3	AI Access and Usage	Managing who has access to AI systems and how they are used to prevent unauthorized use or abuse.
	B4	Secure AI Development Lifecycle	Incorporating security best practices throughout the AI development lifecycle to prevent vulnerabilities.

	B5	AI Explainability and Transparency	Ensuring that AI systems are transparent, and their decision-making processes are understandable to humans.
C	Governance, Legal, and Ethics		Ensuring that AI complies with laws, ethics, and strong governance.
	Measure		
	C1	**Legal Compliance in AI**	Ensuring that AI technologies comply with relevant laws, regulations, and ethical guidelines.
	C2	**Ethical AI Development**	Ensuring that AI systems are designed and deployed according to ethical principles like fairness and respect for human rights.
	C3	**Privacy and Data Protection in AI**	Ensuring that AI systems handle personal and sensitive data in compliance with data protection laws like GDPR.
	C4	**Application of Cybersecurity Frameworks**	Updating existing cybersecurity frameworks to incorporate AI considerations and address new technological challenges.
	C5	**Data Governance for AI**	Establishing robust data governance frameworks to manage the quality, security, and ethical use of data in AI systems.
D	Human Factors and Training		Emphasizes awareness and education to reduce AI-driven risks.
	Measure		
	D1	Awareness and Training Enhancement	Enhancing employee awareness and training regarding cybersecurity, with a focus on AI-related threats and tools.
	D2	Counteracting Misinformation and Disinformation	Strategies and tools to detect, analyze, and mitigate the spread of false or misleading information.

5. CONCLUSION AND OUTLOOK

This research examined the dual-use nature of AI, highlighting its growing misuse in advanced cyberattacks such as automated phishing, AI-driven malware, deepfakes, and data manipulation. While AI enhances cybersecurity resilience, it also presents new vulnerabilities exploited by cybercriminals. The main contribution is a conceptual policy framework developed through expert interviews and literature review, targeting organizations in Europe and Switzerland. Designed for cybersecurity professionals, IT managers, and risk officers, the framework supports the management of AI-related threats in alignment with regulatory standards such as the EU AI Act and GDPR.

The findings emphasize the urgency of adaptive, proactive cybersecurity strategies and validate the relevance of bridging theoretical insight with practical application. However, limitations include the regional scope and the need for iterative refinement. Compared to existing models such as ISO/IEC 27001, NIST CSF, and the EU AI Act, the proposed policy framework offers a more targeted approach to AI-specific threats. While ISO and NIST provide general cybersecurity guidance, they lack granularity in addressing AI misuse. The EU AI Act focuses on ethical governance but does not offer operational mitigation strategies. This conceptual policy framework bridges these gaps by integrating strategic, operational, and technical measures tailored to AI-enabled cybercrime.

Regarding limitations, it should not be concealed that the policy framework is grounded in a regional and sectoral context, drawing primarily from qualitative insights provided by eight Swiss cybersecurity experts. Although informative, this scope may constrain global applicability and overlook broader industry nuances. Furthermore, the policy framework has yet to undergo empirical validation or real-world implementation.

Future research should therefore broaden the sample base, engage cross-sectoral case studies, and apply longitudinal and human-centered approaches - such as AI-driven training for social engineering awareness - to ensure broader relevance and impact. Additional alignment with international legal frameworks would further strengthen global adoption. Ultimately, the findings underscore the urgency of adaptive, forward-looking cybersecurity strategies and affirm the importance of translating theoretical insights into actionable tools for practitioners navigating the evolving landscape of AI-enabled threats.

REFERENCES

Adewale, D. S., & Segun, V. S. (2024). The intersection of Artificial Intelligence and cybersecurity: Challenges and opportunities. World Journal of Advanced Research and Reviews, 21(2), 1720–1736. https://doi.org/10.30574/wjarr.2024.21.2.0607

Adlakha, R., Sharma, S., Rawat, A., & Sharma, K. (2019). Cyber Security Goal's, Issue's, Categorization & Data Breaches. 2019 International Conference on Machine Learning, Big Data, Cloud and Parallel Computing (COMITCon), 397–402. https://doi.org/10.1109/COMITCon.2019.8862245

Admass, W. S., Munaye, Y. Y., & Diro, A. A. (2024). Cyber security: State of the art, challenges and future directions. Cyber Security and Applications, 2, 100031. https://doi.org/10.1016/j.csa.2023.100031

Aftab, R. M., Ijaz, M., Rehman, F., Ashfaq, A., Sharif, H., Riaz, N., Hussain, S., Arslan, M., & Maqsood, H. (2022). A Systematic Review on the Motivations of Cyber-Criminals and Their Attacking Policies. 2022 3rd International Conference on Innovations in Computer Science & Software Engineering (ICONICS), 1–6. https://doi.org/10.1109/ICONICS56716.2022.10100569

Alshar'e, M. (2023). Cyber Security Framework Selection: Comparison of NIST and ISO 27001. Applied Computing Journal, 245–255. https://doi.org/10.52098/acj.202364

Aslan, Ö., Aktuğ, S. S., Ozkan-Okay, M., Yilmaz, A. A., & Akin, E. (2023). A Comprehensive Review of Cyber Security Vulnerabilities, Threats, Attacks, and Solutions. Electronics, 12(6), 1333. https://doi.org/10.3390/electronics12061333

Ban, T., Takahashi, T., Ndichu, S., & Inoue, D. (2023). Breaking Alert Fatigue: AI-Assisted SIEM Framework for Effective Incident Response. Applied Sciences, 13(11), 6610. https://doi.org/10.3390/app13116610

Blauth, T. F., Gstrein, O. J., & Zwitter, A. (2022). Artificial Intelligence Crime: An Overview of Malicious Use and Abuse of AI. IEEE Access, 10, 77110–77122. https://doi.org/10.1109/ACCESS.2022.3191790

Brundage, M., Avin, S., Clark, J., Toner, H., Eckersley, P., Garfinkel, B., Dafoe, A., Scharre, P., Zeitzoff, T., Filar, B., & others. (2018). The Malicious Use of Artificial Intelligence: Forecasting, Prevention, and Mitigation. https://doi.org/10.48550/ARXIV.1802.07228

Bueermann, G., & Rohrs, M. (2024). Global Cybersecurity Outlook 2024. World Economic Forum. https://www.weforum.org/publications/global-cybersecurity-outlook-2024/

Clarke, R. (2022). Responsible application of artificial intelligence to surveillance: What prospects? Information Polity, 27(2), 175–191. https://doi.org/10.3233/IP-211532

Dash, B., & Ansari, M. F. (2022). An effective cybersecurity awareness training model: First defense of an organizational security strategy. International Research Journal of Engineering and Technology (IRJET), 9(4), 1–6. https://www.irjet.net/archives/V9/i4/IRJET-V9I401.pdf.

Edwards, M., Williams, E., Peersman, C., & Rashid, A. (2022). Characterizing Cybercriminals: A Review. https://doi.org/10.48550/ARXIV.2202.07419

ENISA. (2023). Artificial intelligence and cybersecurity research: ENISA research and innovation brief. Publications Office. https://data.europa.eu/doi/10.2824/808362

European Parliament & Council of the European Union. (2024, July 12). Regulation (EU) 2024/1689 of the European Parliament and of the Council of 13 June 2024 laying down harmonised rules on artificial intelligence (Artificial Intelligence Act). Official Journal of the European Union, L 2024/1689, 1–144.

European Union Agency for Cybersecurity. (2023). ENISA threat landscape 2023: July 2022 to June 2023. Publications Office. https://data.europa.eu/doi/10.2824/782573

Evang, J. M. (2022). ISO 27001 as a Tool for Availability Management. 2022 International Conference on Advanced Enterprise Information System (AEIS), 82–85. https://doi.org/10.1109/AEIS59450.2022.00018

Falade, P. V. (2023). Decoding the Threat Landscape: ChatGPT, FraudGPT, and WormGPT in Social Engineering Attacks. International Journal of Scientific Research in Computer Science, Engineering and Information Technology, 185–198. https://doi.org/10.32628/CSEIT2390533

Federal Statistical Office. (2024). Digitale Kriminalität. https://www.bfs.admin.ch/bfs/de/home/statistiken/kriminalitaet-strafrecht/polizei/digitale-kriminalitaet.html, last accessed 2025/04/28

Guembe, B., Azeta, A., Misra, S., Osamor, V. C., & Pospelova, V. (2022). The Emerging Threat of AI-Driven Cyber Attacks: A Review. Applied Artificial Intelligence, 36(1), 2037254. https://doi.org/10.1080/08839514.2022.2037254

Hilty, R. M., Hoffmann, J., & Scheuerer, S. (2021). Intellectual Property Justification for Artificial Intelligence. In Artificial Intelligence and Intellectual Property. Oxford University Press. https://doi.org/10.1093/oso/9780198870944.003.0004

Hu, V. C., Kuhn, R., & Yaga, D. (2017). Verification and Test Methods for Access Control Policies Models (NIST SP 800-192). National Institute of Standards and Technology. https://doi.org/10.6028/NIST.SP.800-192

Humayun, M., Niazi, M., Jhanjhi, N., Alshayeb, M., & Mahmood, S. (2020). Cyber Security Threats and Vulnerabilities: A Systematic Mapping Study. Arabian Journal for Science and Engineering, 45(4), 3171–3189. https://doi.org/10.1007/s13369-019-04319-2

Hylender, C. D., Langlois, P., Pinto, A., & Widup, S. (2023). 2023 Data Breach Investigations Report. (16th ed.). Verizon. https://www.verizon.com/business/resources/reports/2023-data-breach-investigations-report-dbir.pdf

IBM. (2023). What is AI Bias? https://www.ibm.com/think/topics/ai-bias?mhsrc=ibmsearch_a&mhq=bias last accessed 2025/05/01

IBM. (2024). What is AI? https://www.ibm.com/topics/artificial-intelligence, last accessed 2025/04/28

ISACA. (2024). Achieving Trustworthy, Ethical AI (Journal Volume 1).

Kokane, S. (2021). The Intellectual Property Rights of Artificial Intelligence-Based Inventions. Journal of Scientific Research, 65(02), 116–119. https://doi.org/10.37398/JSR.2021.650223

Kuechler, W., & Vaishnavi, V. (2004). Design Research in Information Systems (Version of January 20, 2004; online resource, last updated December 20, 2017). DESRIST—Design Science Research in Information Systems and Technology. https://www.desrist.org/design-research-in-information-systems/.

Li, X. (2017). A Review of Motivations of Illegal Cyber Activities. Kriminologija & socijalna integracija, 25(1), 110–126. https://doi.org/10.31299/ksi.25.1.4

Loh, P. K. K., Lee, A. Z. Y., & Balachandran, V. (2024). Towards a Hybrid Security Framework for Phishing Awareness Education and Defense. Future Internet, 16(3), 86. https://doi.org/10.3390/fi16030086

Malatji, M. (2023). Offensive Artificial Intelligence: Current State of the Art and Future Directions. 2023 International Conference on Digital Applications, Transformation & Economy (ICDATE), 1–6. https://doi.org/10.1109/ICDATE58146.2023.10248780

Maphosa, V. (2023). Artificial Intelligence and State Power. 2023 International Conference on Artificial Intelligence, Big Data, Computing and Data Communication Systems (icABCD), 1–5. https://doi.org/10.1109/icABCD59051.2023.10220459

Maurya, R. (2023). Analyzing the Role of AI in Cyber Security Threat Detection & Prevention. International Journal for Research in Applied Science and Engineering Technology, 11(11), 514–519. https://doi.org/10.22214/ijraset.2023.56510

Meinel, C., Leifer, L., & Plattner, H. (Eds.). (2011). Design Thinking. Springer. https://doi.org/10.1007/978-3-642-13757-0

Melaku, H. M. (2023). A Dynamic and Adaptive Cybersecurity Governance Framework. Journal of Cybersecurity and Privacy, 3(3), 327–350. https://doi.org/10.3390/jcp3030017

Meurisch, C., & Mühlhäuser, M. (2022). Data Protection in AI Services: A Survey. ACM Computing Surveys, 54(2), 1–38. https://doi.org/10.1145/3440754

Mijwil, M., Unogwu, O. J., Filali, Y., Bala, I., & Al-Shahwani, H. (2023). Exploring the Top Five Evolving Threats in Cybersecurity: An In-Depth Overview. Mesopotamian Journal of Cyber Security, 57–63. https://doi.org/10.58496/MJCS/2023/010

MIT Technology Review. (2021, April 8). Preparing for AI-enabled cyberattacks. https://www.technologyreview.com/2021/04/08/1021696/preparing-for-ai-enabled-cyberattacks/

MITRE Corporation. (2024). MITRE ATT&CK. https://attack.mitre.org/, last accessed 2025/04/28

Mohamed, N. (2023). Current trends in AI and ML for cybersecurity: A state-of-the-art survey. Cogent Engineering, 10(2), 2272358. https://doi.org/10.1080/23311916.2023.2272358

NIST. (2020). Security and Privacy Controls for Information Systems and Organizations (Rev. 5). National Institute of Standards and Technology. https://doi.org/10.6028/NIST.SP.800-53r5

Nnamdi, N., Oniyinde, O. A., & Abegunde, B. (2023). An Appraisal of the Implications of Deepfakes: The Need for Urgent International Legislations. American Journal of Leadership and Governance, 8(1), 43–70. https://doi.org/10.47672/ajlg.1540

Palo Alto Networks. (2024). What is Endpoint Security Antivirus? What is Endpoint Security Antivirus? https://www.paloaltonetworks.com/cyberpedia/what-is-endpoint-security-antivirus, last accessed 2025/05/01

Pavis, M. (2021). Rebalancing our regulatory response to Deepfakes with performers' rights. Convergence: The International Journal of Research into New Media Technologies, 27(4), 974–998. https://doi.org/10.1177/13548565211033418

Plaka, R. (2022). Backup & Data Recovery in Cloud Computing: A Systematic Mapping Study. Ingenious, 2(1), 94–113. https://doi.org/10.58944/pwhk4843

Rao, G. R. K., Battu, V. V., Anupama, V., Allada, A., Krishna, S. V. R., & Hema, C. (2023). Modern Progressive Pitfalls of Cyber Attacks on the Digital World. 2023 2nd International Conference on Edge Computing and Applications (ICECAA), 244–248. https://doi.org/10.1109/ICECAA58104.2023.10212303

Onwubiko, C. (2020). CyberOps: Situational Awareness in Cybersecurity Operations. International Journal on Cyber Situational Awareness, 5(1), 82–107. https://doi.org/10.22619/IJCSA.2020.100134

Saghiri, A. M., Vahidipour, S. M., Jabbarpour, M. R., Sookhak, M., & Forestiero, A. (2022). A survey of artificial intelligence challenges: analyzing the definitions, relationships, and evolutions. Applied Sciences, 12(8), 4054. https://doi.org/10.3390/app12084054

Saunders, M. N. K., Lewis, P., & Thornhill, A. (2019). Research Methods for Business Students (8th ed.). Pearson. Print ISBN 978-1-292-20878-7; eText ISBN 978-1-292-20880-0.

Schmitt, M., & Flechais, I. (2023). Digital deception: Generative artificial intelligence in social engineering and phishing (arXiv:2310.13715) [Preprint]. arXiv. https://doi.org/10.48550/arXiv.2310.13715

Shahriar, S., Allana, S., Hazratifard, S. M., & Dara, R. (2023). A survey of privacy risks and mitigation strategies in the artificial intelligence life cycle. IEEE Access, 11, 61829–61854. https://doi.org/10.1109/ACCESS.2023.3287195

Shanthi, R. R., Sasi, N. K., & Gouthaman, P. (2023). A new era of cybersecurity: The influence of artificial intelligence. 2023 International Conference on Networking and Communications (ICNWC), 1–4. https://doi.org/10.1109/ICNWC57852.2023.10127453

Souppaya, M., & Scarfone, K. (2022). Guide to enterprise patch management planning: Preventive maintenance for technology (NIST SP 800-40 Rev. 4). National Institute of Standards and Technology. https://doi.org/10.6028/NIST.SP.800-40r4

Tabassi, E. (2023). Artificial Intelligence Risk Management Framework (AI RMF 1.0) (NIST AI 100-1). National Institute of Standards and Technology. https://doi.org/10.6028/NIST.AI.100-1

The Federal Assembly of the Swiss Confederation. (2020). Federal Act on Data Protection (FADP). https://www.fedlex.admin.ch/eli/cc/2022/491/en, last accessed 2025/04/28

Vom Brocke, J., Hevner, A., & Maedche, A. (Eds.). (2020). Design Science Research: Cases. Springer. https://doi.org/10.1007/978-3-030-46781-4

Wolff, J., Lehr, W., & Yoo, C. S. (2023). Lessons from GDPR for AI Policymaking. SSRN Electronic Journal. https://doi.org/10.2139/ssrn.4528698

Yamin, M. M., Ullah, M., Ullah, H., & Katt, B. (2021). Weaponized AI for cyber attacks. Journal of Information Security and Applications, 57, 102722. https://doi.org/10.1016/j.jisa.2020.102722

Zhang, Z., Ning, H., Shi, F., Farha, F., Xu, Y., Xu, J., Zhang, F., & Choo, K.-K. R. (2022). Artificial intelligence in cyber security: Research advances, challenges, and opportunities. Artificial Intelligence Review, 55(2), 1029–1053. https://doi.org/10.1007/s10462-021-09976-0

COMPARISON OF TIME SERIES IMPUTATION METHODS - USING SAITS FOR DATA RECOVERY

Draylon Vieira Lopes[1], Lucas Gonçalves Brach[2], Emerson Cassiano da Silva[3], Peterson Gonçalves Alano[3] and Rafael Stubs Parpinelli[1]
[1]*Graduate Program in Applied Computing, Santa Catarina State University, Joinville/SC, Brazil*
[2]*Computer Science Department, Santa Catarina State University, Joinville/SC, Brazil*
[3]*WEG, Jaraguá do Sul/SC, Brazil*

ABSTRACT

Missing data in wind turbine Supervisory Control and Data Acquisition (SCADA) is a common issue caused by sensor faults, communication losses, and maintenance downtime. These gaps reduce the reliability of condition monitoring, anomaly detection, and predictive maintenance, where complete and high-quality data are essential. This work focuses on addressing the imputation of missing values in turbine datasets to improve the quality and usability of the data for machine learning applications and operational decision-making. We start by collecting multivariate SCADA data from real turbine operations and artificially introduce block gaps of 6-60 samples to replicate realistic sensor interruptions. Several strategies for filling these gaps are evaluated, including time-based linear interpolation, multivariate linear regression, MIARMA, which uses ARMA models to preserve spectral properties, and SAITS, a modern self-attention-based architecture. The comparison is carried out under identical missingness conditions, and accuracy is assessed only at the masked points using MAE, RMSE, and sMAPE. The results, aggregated across more than 200 million masked points, show that multivariate linear regression is the most effective among the classical methods, performing better than simple time interpolation, while MIARMA delivers similar results at a way higher cost in the multivariate contexts. SAITS achieves the best overall performance and fidelity on the datasets, confirming that deep learning models are highly effective in reconstructing complex turbine data, though they require greater computational resources for producing fast results. The findings highlight the importance of exploiting cross-variable relationships in turbine monitoring and demonstrate that the proposed pipeline can serve as a reproducible framework for evaluating imputation methods in other industrial domains as well.

KEYWORDS

Data Imputation, Time Series, Missing Data, Industrial Monitoring, Machine Learning, Predictive Maintenance

1. INTRODUCTION

The Wind energy is central to the global transition to renewable power, but turbine reliability and efficiency remain challenging. Conventional preventive maintenance, based on rigid schedules or inspections, often causes unnecessary downtime, premature part replacement, or overlooked anomalies. In the era of Industry 4.0, operators require intelligent methods capable of detecting anomalies in process quality and equipment performance (Leukel et al., 2021; Rojek & Jagodziński, 2023; Esteban et al., 2022). Machine learning has emerged as a strong candidate, enabling condition-based maintenance strategies that reduce interruption costs, limit production delays, and enhance operational safety (Ccinar et al., 2020).

For wind turbines, Supervisory Control and Data Acquisition (SCADA) and condition-monitoring systems (CM / CMS) provide rich multivariate datasets covering power output, wind speed, rotor speed, component temperatures, pressures, and pitch signals. These variables support anomaly detection, fault diagnosis, and predictive maintenance, as they capture dependencies across subsystems. Yet, despite their richness, real-world monitoring data are rarely complete. Sensor faults, communication issues, and maintenance downtime routinely produce missing values (Du et al., 2023; Wang et al., 2024).

Missingness is more than a nuisance: it undermines interpretability, weakens predictive models, and reduces decision-making reliability. While one approach is to remove incomplete records, this risks bias and excessive data loss. Imputation is preferable, as it preserves continuity by replacing gaps with synthetic estimates derived from observed values. The challenge is to reconstruct missing segments in a way that respects both temporal dynamics and multivariate relationships (Du et al., 2023; Wang et al., 2024).

Historically, gaps were filled with simple heuristics such as mean substitution or last observation carried forward. Forecasting models like ARIMA and its variant MIARMA improved continuity by modeling temporal dependencies (Pascual, 2015). However, these methods struggle with the nonlinear and strongly coupled dynamics typical of turbines. Their limitations point to the need for more advanced strategies that can capture both local continuity and global structure. While SAITS and generative reconstructions were studied, there is no controlled benchmark on the real dataset spanning short-to-long consecutive gaps with evaluation strictly over masked-points available or known prior to conducting the experiments.

This study addresses that need by introducing controlled gaps into turbine SCADA data and benchmarking classical interpolation, multivariate regression, MIARMA, and a modern attention-based deep learning model. This assessment allows for practical guidance of available methods on the topic of time series recovery by providing direct comparisons within our scenario.

2. THEORETICAL FOUNDATION

The challenge of imputing missing values in industrial time series has given rise to a broad spectrum of methods, ranging from simple statistical heuristics to sophisticated machine learning and deep learning approaches. In the context of wind turbine SCADA data, the choice of method has important implications for the accuracy of predictive maintenance and condition monitoring.

2.1 Time Series and Missing Data

Time series data collected from wind turbines exhibit temporal dependencies, cross-variable correlations, and non-linear dynamics. Missing values disrupt these patterns and must be addressed to maintain the integrity of downstream tasks such as anomaly detection and Remaining Useful Life estimation. The statistical literature classifies missingness mechanisms into three categories (Wang et al., 2024). Missing Completely at Random (MCAR) occurs when the probability of missingness is unrelated to observed or unobserved values. Missing at Random (MAR) arises when the probability depends only on observed values, while Missing Not at Random (MNAR) occurs when missingness is tied to unobserved information. In real turbine datasets, a mixture of these mechanisms is often observed, with MCAR used in experiments as a controlled simplification (Wang et al., 2024).

2.2 Classical Approaches

Early strategies for handling missing values include removal, where incomplete records are discarded, and statistical heuristics, where gaps are filled with simple rules such as mean substitution or last observation carried forward. While computationally efficient, these methods often introduce bias or oversimplify the underlying structure. Forecasting-based models such as ARIMA improved upon heuristics by modeling temporal dependencies, and MIARMA (Minimal-Loss ARMA) extended this idea by fitting ARMA models on either side of a gap and blending forecasts to preserve the spectral characteristics of the signal (Pascual, 2015). Although MIARMA has been successful in domains with strong periodicity, its univariate formulation limits its ability to exploit correlations across multiple variables.

2.3 Machine Learning

With the rise of machine learning, imputation methods began to incorporate multivariate structure. Linear regression and multivariate statistical models estimate missing values using observed correlations between variables. These approaches perform particularly well in turbine datasets, where operational variables such as wind speed, rotor speed, and power output are strongly coupled. However, regression models remain limited when handling non-linearities or complex temporal interactions.

Representation learning extended these capabilities by introducing models such as recurrent neural networks (RNNs), temporal convolutional networks (TCNs), and autoencoders. RNNs capture sequential dependencies, TCNs model long-range patterns through dilated convolutions, and autoencoders compress information to reconstruct signals. Together, these approaches established that deep models could recover missing data more accurately than classical methods in highly dynamic and multivariate contexts (Goodfellow et al., 2016; Bengio et al., 2013).

2.4 Attention-Based Approaches

Within this landscape, SAITS (Self-Attention-based Imputation for Time Series) has emerged as a state-of-the-art predictive model (Du et al., 2023). Its architecture combines diagonally masked self-attention layers with a dual task learning scheme that simultaneously reconstructs observed data and imputes missing entries. This design ensures that the model captures both short-range dependencies, such as rapid changes in temperature or wind speed, and long-range dependencies, such as seasonal or operational cycles.

By applying both temporal and cross-variable relationships, SAITS is effective within high levels of missingness. In other evaluations across multiple domains, SAITS consistently outperforms classical methods and earlier deep learning architectures, though at the cost of higher computational requirements.

3. RELATED WORKS

Missing data in industrial time series, particularly in wind turbine monitoring, has been studied from multiple perspectives. Early work emphasized the importance of SCADA data for predictive maintenance, noting that gaps reduce anomaly detection accuracy (Tautz-Weinert & Watson, 2017; Maldonado-Correa et al., 2020). Broader surveys have outlined taxonomies of imputation methods and their industrial applications (Esteban et al., 2022; Wang et al., 2024).

Methodological advances range from statistical models such as MIARMA, which preserves spectral content but remains univariate (Pascual-Granado et al., 2015), to deep learning methods capable of modeling complex multivariate signals. SAITS has shown state-of-the-art performance across domains (Du et al., 2023), while wind energy studies have begun to explore generative approaches such as GAN- and GAIN-based imputers for SCADA data (Yang et al., 2025).

Table 1 summarizes key contributions from the literature on missing data and condition monitoring in time series, with a particular emphasis on wind turbine applications. The works listed span several domains, including turbine SCADA, astronomy, and general multivariate time series, reflecting both domain-specific and broadly applicable approaches. Each entry highlights the type of data studied, the methods applied, and the way missingness or data-quality issues were addressed. Together, these references illustrate the historical reliance on statistical and spectral-preserving models such as MIARMA, the growing adoption of artificial intelligence for turbine condition monitoring, and the more recent shift toward deep learning methods such as SAITS and GAIN-based imputers. The table makes clear that while a variety of strategies exist, few works provide controlled comparisons on turbine SCADA data, thereby motivating the present study.

Table 1. Summary of Methods used and its contributions, along with Performance Summary obtained through testing

Reference	Domain / Data	Method(s)	Missingness & Data Issues
Tautz-Weinert & Watson (2017)	Wind turbine SCADA	Review of CM algorithms	Data quality concerns in SCADA
Maldonado-Correa et al. (2020)	Wind turbine SCADA (SLR)	AI approaches to CM	Preprocessing and missing data challenges
Esteban et al. (2022)	Clinical and industrial TS	Survey of imputation methods	Handling of incomplete time series
Wang et al. (2024)	Multivariate time series (general)	Survey of DL imputation	MAR, MCAR, MNAR distinctions
Pascual-Granado et al. (2015)	Astronomical TS	MIARMA (ARMA-based)	Gap filling with spectral fidelity
Du et al. (2023)	Multivariate TS (general)	SAITS (attention-based)	MCAR masking in benchmarks
Yang et al. (2025)	Wind farm SCADA	GAIN-based deep imputer	Missing SCADA data

4. PROPOSED APPROACH

The approach developed in this study is designed to provide a reproducible benchmark for imputation methods in multivariate wind turbine data. The goal is to simulate realistic missingness conditions and systematically evaluate representative techniques, ranging from classical statistical methods to state-of-the-art deep learning models. By applying all methods to identical gaps under controlled settings, the pipeline ensures fair comparisons and robust conclusions.

The procedure begins with the collection and preparation of turbine SCADA datasets, which include variables such as wind speed, rotor speed, power output, component temperatures, oil pressures, and pitch angles. These multivariate signals are pre-processed to align timestamps and filter non-numeric fields. To replicate the kinds of interruptions encountered in real monitoring systems, artificial gaps are introduced under the Missing Completely at Random (MCAR) assumption. Rather than isolated points, we focus on block gaps of 6-60 consecutive samples, reflecting sensor downtimes or communication losses that are common in operational contexts.

Once the gaps are injected, four representative imputation strategies are applied to the same masked datasets:

- Linear Interpolation: estimates missing values by interpolating between surrounding time points.
- Multivariate Linear Regression: reconstructs missing values in one variable using correlations with the other observed variables.
- MIARMA: an autoregressive moving average-based method that fits ARMA models before and after each gap and blends forward and backward forecasts to preserve spectral continuity.
- SAITS: a self-attention-based deep learning model that leverages diagonally masked attention and a dual-task learning scheme to reconstruct both observed and missing entries simultaneously.

The evaluation phase focuses strictly on the artificially masked values, avoiding any bias from unaltered points. Accuracy is quantified using three complementary metrics: Mean Absolute Error (MAE), Root Mean Squared Error (RMSE), and Symmetric Mean Absolute Percentage Error (sMAPE).

In Figure 1 we illustrate a practical workflow of the entire process, which comprises data acquisition, analysis on the contents of data and the lack of it, followed by the usage of algorithms and results obtained through them.

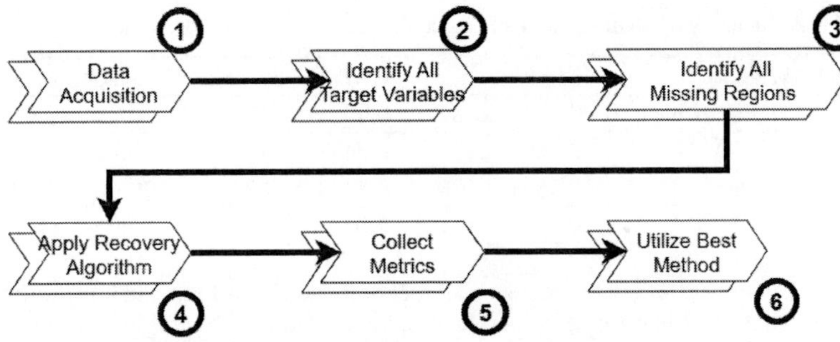

Figure 1. Flowchart for Data Recovery Methods

5. EXPERIMENTS, RESULTS AND ANALYSIS

The experimental evaluation was conducted on multivariate datasets collected from SCADA, these datasets contain timestamped records of operational variables including wind speed, rotor speed, generated power, bearing and oil temperatures, hydraulic pressures, and blade pitch angles. Such variables are representative of real-world turbine monitoring, where strong interdependencies exist across mechanical, electrical, and aerodynamic subsystems. Due to confidentiality agreements, identifying information and exact dataset details cannot be disclosed, but the data are representative of industrial operational profiles with heterogeneous dependencies and dynamic behavior.

5.1 Experimental Setup

To simulate realistic data loss, artificial missingness was introduced under the Missing Completely at Random (MCAR) assumption. Block gaps of 6-60 consecutive samples were masked in each variable, reflecting common scenarios such as sensor dropouts, communication losses, or maintenance interventions. Non-overlapping gaps were generated with deterministic random seeds to ensure reproducibility across experimental runs.

Under these circumstances, the data utilized carries time-related constraints, which in the context of this experiment consisted of the resampling of data fitting a duration of ten minutes, meaning six samples of data carry a time value of one-hour-worth of data. This levels the data in this experiment under a "sensitivity & relevance" criterion, where higher-resolution data is not easily accessible/obtainable or relevant for testing.

Each of the four imputation methods were applied to identical masked datasets, in order to ensure same-use cases on the methods. The evaluation considered only the artificially removed values, preventing inflated performance estimates from unmasked points. Performance was measured using three complementary metrics, named Mean Absolute Error (MAE), for the average magnitude of error, Root Mean Squared Error (RMSE), for highlighting larger deviations and Symmetric Mean Absolute Percentage Error (sMAPE): providing a scale-independent percentage of error on the filling.

5.2 Quantitative Results

Table 2 presents the imputation methods used in this study together with their performance results obtained on turbine SCADA datasets. For each method, the table outlines its underlying approach and reports the corresponding error metrics (MAE, RMSE, and sMAPE). This provides a direct comparison of how simple baselines, statistical models, and advanced deep learning architectures perform under identical missingness conditions. The summarized performance of the methods presents Mean and Standard Deviations on each cell.

Table 2. Summary of Methods used and its contributions, along with Performance Summary obtained

Method	MAE	RMSE	sMAPE (%)
MultivarLinear	0.254± 0.384	0.445± 0.617	24.23± 12.45
MIARMA	0.381± 0.429	0.719± 0.747	25.43± 12.77
Linear	0.482± 0.500	0.815± 1.167	29.00± 14.39
SAITS	0.075± 0.121	0.083± 0.150	5.00± 1.54

The Figure 2 presents the visual reconstruction comparison within the methods utilized. The ground-truth signal is shown in dashed line for reference, while the shaded area highlights the missing interval. As seen, linear interpolation tends to over-smooth transitions in data, and MIARMA occasionally introduces oscillations. Multivariate regression more closely follows the overall trend by exploiting correlations among variables. SAITS, however, produces reconstructions that align most closely with the original data, preserving both local variations and long-range dependencies.

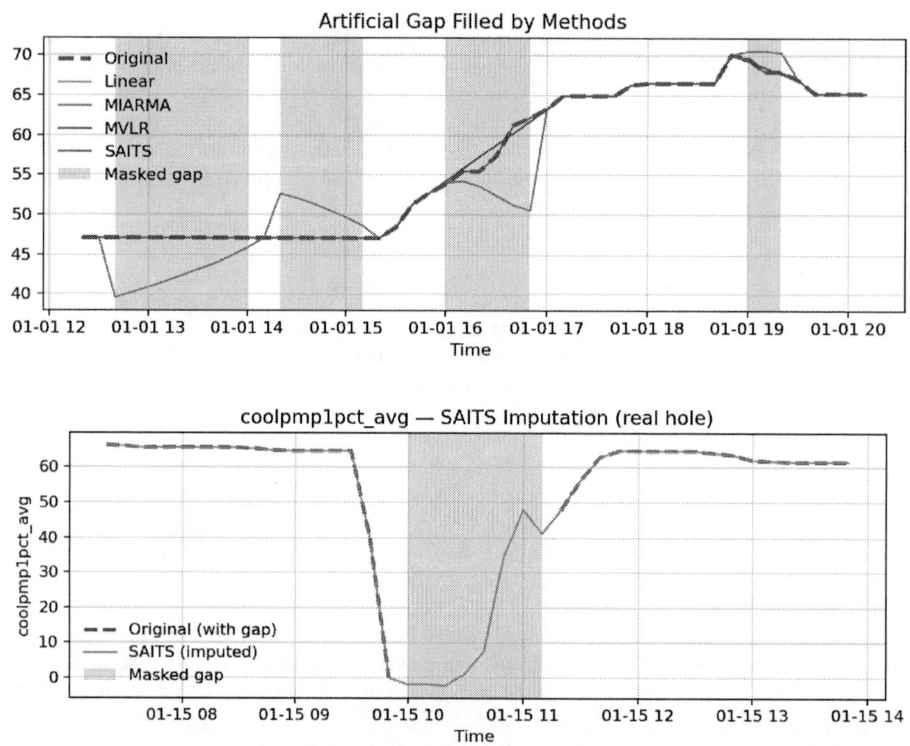

Figure 2. Artificial gap Filled by Methods

Illustrates a real missing segment from the turbine dataset, showing the original signal with an actual gap alongside the reconstruction generated by SAITS. The shaded region marks the missing interval, where the original curve is unavailable. The dashed line represents the ground-truth measurements outside the gap, while the solid curve shows the imputed values produced by SAITS. While SAITS delivers a better visual-and-accurate result, it's executions reach a similar delivery time to MIARMA, averaging a total of six hours for algorithm execution on a single model (500-epoch-run), considered a significantly larger execution time than classical or simpler algorithms such as the other Linear methods, which yield runs at the cost of 2 hours.

6. CONCLUSION AND FUTURE WORKS

This study evaluated methods for recovering missing values in multivariate industrial time series with sizeable block gaps caused by sensor faults or communication interruptions. Controlled "missingness" was introduced under the MCAR assumption, and methods were compared directly across a dataset comprising multiple variables related to both exogenous and endogenous aspects of turbines, along similar-environment-based equipment providing a sum of data similarly produced and sharing the same characteristics.

Results show that Multivariate Linear Regression was the strongest classical method, leveraging inter-variable correlations to achieve the lowest MAE and RMSE. Time-based Linear Interpolation performed reasonably for short gaps but failed on longer or more dynamic sequences. MIARMA, though designed to preserve spectral continuity, underperformed in multivariate settings, showing that frequency preservation alone is insufficient when cross-variable dependencies dominate. SAITS, a self-attention deep learning model, delivered the best overall performance, confirming the suitability of advanced architectures for complex imputation tasks, albeit with higher computational cost in order to achieve similar run speeds to MIARMA.

The experimental design enabled fair comparisons under identical conditions, combining controlled gap injections, multiple strategies, and evaluation strictly within missing regions. The study focused on MCAR block gaps of 6–60 samples; real-world missing patterns often follows MAR or MNAR patterns, which may bias reconstructions. While SAITS outperformed classical methods, its effectiveness depends on sufficient training data and computational resources. The dataset, prepared with domain specialists, reflects realistic turbine monitoring scenarios, comprising multivariate time series with heterogeneous dependencies and sampling intervals. For SAITS, thirty independent runs of 500 epochs each were used, with performance tracked by mean loss and standard deviation.

The comparative assessment allowed several observations on the methods applied:

- **Linear Regression:** This method is performed adequately on datasets with small, regularly spaced gaps and relatively stable dynamics. However, its absolute average between gaps failed to preserve sharp transitions and degraded under large or irregular gaps, often introducing over-smoothing effects.
- **Multivariate Linear Regression:** This approach emerged as the most effective among classical techniques. By modeling the relationships between variables such as wind speed, rotor speed, and power, it was able to reconstruct missing values more accurately than univariate interpolation. Its performance highlights the value of leveraging cross-variable correlations in turbine SCADA datasets, where redundancy across sensors is common. While less flexible than deep learning models, it provides a strong balance between accuracy, interpretability, and computational efficiency.
- **MIARMA:** This approach demonstrated better performance than Multivariate Linear Regression in stationary or near-stationary sequences, since it explicitly modeled temporal dependencies. Its limitations stem from reliance on linear assumptions and the need for careful parameter tuning, which restricted its ability to generalize to more complex, nonlinear patterns.
- **SAITS:** The self-attention model consistently outperformed classical methods, particularly in datasets characterized by nonlinear relationships, long-range dependencies, and high levels of missingness. SAITS successfully preserved both local detail and global structure, producing reconstructions closely aligned with the ground truth.

REFERENCES

Artigao, E., Honrubia-Escribano, A., Gómez-Lázaro, E. & Molina-García, Á., (2018). Wind turbine reliability: A comprehensive review towards effective condition monitoring development. Applied Energy, 228, pp.1569–1583.

Bengio, Y., Courville, A. & Vincent, P., (2013). Representation learning: A review and new perspectives. IEEE Transactions on Pattern Analysis and Machine Intelligence, 35(8), pp.1798–1828.

Bodorik, P., (1991). Experimental analysis of five imputation methods for missing data in survey responses. In: Proceedings of the Seventh International Conference on Data Engineering. IEEE, pp. 687–694.

Ccinar, S., Yildirim, M. & Kocak, C., (2020). Machine learning approaches to predictive maintenance of industrial equipment. Computers & Industrial Engineering, 139, 106174.

Du, S., Wang, Z. & Sun, J., (20239. SAITS: Self-Attention-based Imputation for Time Series. Proceedings of the AAAI Conference on Artificial Intelligence, 37(4), pp.4353–4361.

Esteban, C., Hyland, S.L. & Rätsch, G., (2022). Data-driven approaches for missing value imputation in clinical time series: a review. Proceedings of the IEEE, 110(9), pp.1410–1430.

Goodfellow, I., Bengio, Y. & Courville, A., (2016). Deep Learning. MIT Press, Cambridge, MA.

Lei, Y., Li, N., Guo, L., Yan, T. & Lin, J., (2018). Machinery health prognostics: A systematic review from data acquisition to RUL prediction. Mechanical Systems and Signal Processing, 104, pp.799–834.

Leukel, J., Sugumaran, V. & Hu, B., (2021). Adoption of machine learning technology for failure prediction in industrial maintenance: A review. Journal of Manufacturing Systems, 60, pp.821–836.

Maldonado-Correa, J., Fischer, G.S., Aponte-Romero, J. & Perez-Castaneda, L., (2020). Using SCADA Data for Wind Turbine Condition Monitoring — A Systematic Literature Review. Energies, 13(12), 3132.

McMorland, J., Harrison, G. & Chick, J., (2022). A review of operations and maintenance modelling with applications to offshore wind. Renewable and Sustainable Energy Reviews, 160, 112315.

Mitchell, T.M., (1997). Machine Learning. McGraw Hill, New York.

Pascual-Granado, J., Garrido, R. & Suárez, J.C., (2015). MIARMA: A minimal-loss information method for filling gaps in asteroseismic data. Astronomy & Astrophysics, 575, A78.

Rojek, I. & Jagodziński, A., (2023). Artificial intelligence in predictive maintenance: Trends, challenges and future research directions. Applied Sciences, 13(5), 3109.

Russell, S. & Norvig, P., (2010). Artificial Intelligence: A Modern Approach. Prentice Hall, Upper Saddle River, NJ.

Tautz-Weinert, J. & Watson, S.J., (2017). Using SCADA data for wind turbine condition monitoring — a review. IET Renewable Power Generation, 11(4), pp.382–394.

Tchakoua, P., Wamkeue, R., Ouhrouche, M., Slaoui-Hasnaoui, F., Tameghe, T.A. & Ekemb, G., (2014). Wind Turbine Condition Monitoring: State-of-the-Art Review, New Trends, and Future Challenges. Energies, 7(4), pp.2595–2630.

Wang, Z., Du, S. & Sun, J., (2024). Deep learning methods for time series imputation: A comprehensive survey. IEEE Transactions on Knowledge and Data Engineering (early access).

Yang, L., Huang, Z., Mo, X. & Luo, T., (2025). Enhanced GAIN-Based Missing Data Imputation for a Wind Energy Farm SCADA System. Electronics, 14(8), 1590.

A COMPARATIVE STUDY OF METAHEURISTIC OPTIMIZATION FOR RESOURCE ALLOCATION IN A HEALTHCARE SYSTEM USING DISCRETE-EVENT SIMULATION

Thouraya Menyaoui[1], Soulef Khalfallah[2] and Sonia Ayachi Ghannouchi[1]
[1]RIADI Laboratory, ENSI, University of Manouba, Tunisia
[2]MARS Laboratory, ISITCOM, University of Sousse, Tunisia

ABSTRACT

Patient wait time is a critical performance indicator in healthcare systems, directly impacting patient satisfaction and operational efficiency. This paper presents a comparative study of metaheuristic optimization methodologies applied to a discrete-event simulation model of a maternity clinic. The objective is to identify the optimal allocation of staff resources to minimize average patient wait time. We compare the results from two distinct metaheuristic approaches: one integrated in the commercial optimization tool OptQuest, which utilizes Tabu Search and Scatter Search, and a custom-developed Genetic Algorithm (GA) integrated with the simulation model. The results demonstrate that both metaheuristic approaches discovered the same superior solution, significantly outperforming the baseline model. This study validates the use of simulation-optimization as a powerful decision-support tool for complex healthcare workflows and provides a comparative analysis of the strengths and convergence of different metaheuristic approaches.

KEYWORDS

Discrete-Event Simulation, Healthcare Management, Metaheuristic Optimization, Genetic Algorithm, OptQuest, Resource Allocation, Patient Wait Time

1. INTRODUCTION

Efficiency and patient satisfaction are paramount in modern healthcare management, an industry characterized by complex, dynamic, and resource-constrained environments. Long waiting times in clinics are a persistent and critical problem, leading not only to decreased quality of care and patient dissatisfaction but also to inefficient resource utilization and increased operational costs. The inherent variability in patient arrival patterns, service times, and resource availability makes it exceptionally difficult to predict system performance and identify areas for improvement using traditional analytical methods alone.

To address these challenges, Discrete-Event Simulation (DES) has emerged as a powerful and widely accepted tool for modeling, analyzing, and improving such complex systems without disrupting real-world operations. By creating a dynamic model of a system, simulation allows managers and researchers to test various improvement strategies, understand the impact of variability, and make data-driven decisions.

However, while simulation is excellent for evaluating the performance of a given system configuration, it does not, by itself, find the best possible configuration. Identifying the optimal improvement strategy in a system with numerous interacting variables (e.g., the number of doctors, nurses, and administrative staff) is a complex optimization problem. Manually testing scenarios can yield better solutions, but this approach is often impractical for complex systems and is unlikely to discover the truly optimal configuration. Therefore, to unlock the full potential of simulation, it is often coupled with automated optimization techniques, a field known as Simulation-Optimization. This paper focuses on a case study of a maternity clinic, where a validated Arena simulation model is used as a testbed for two distinct metaheuristic approaches: the commercial optimizer OptQuest and a custom-developed Genetic Algorithm (GA).

The primary contribution of this work is a direct comparative analysis of these two powerful metaheuristic methods in a real-world healthcare context. The goal is to find the optimal number of cashiers, gynecologists, nurses, and secretaries to minimize the average total patient wait time and, in doing so, to evaluate the effectiveness, efficiency, and convergence behavior of each optimization approach. The new critical scientific novelty lies in the direct, side-by-side comparison of a commercial, proprietary metaheuristic (OptQuest's Tabu/Scatter Search) and a custom, open-source-based one (GA) against a real-world, validated hospital system.

This analysis not only confirms the optimal operational policy but also provides unique insights into the efficiency and search characteristics of these two distinct classes of optimization tools for healthcare applications. This paper will detail the simulation model, the configuration of the optimizers, a comparative analysis of their results, and a final recommendation for the clinic's operational strategy.

2. RELATED WORK

The application of discrete-event simulation (DES) as a tool for analyzing and improving healthcare systems is a well-established and mature field of study. Foundational texts by Law (2015) and Banks et al. (2010) have long established the core principles and methodologies for applying DES to complex, stochastic environments. The relevance of these techniques to healthcare is extensively documented. A comprehensive review by Gunal and Pidd (2010) surveyed a wide range of applications, highlighting the consistent use of DES for critical tasks such as managing patient flow in emergency departments, optimizing outpatient clinic scheduling, and improving operating room planning. These studies confirm that DES is the standard methodology for understanding the intricate dynamics and resource interdependencies inherent in healthcare delivery.

The effectiveness of Discrete-Event Simulation (DES) lies in its ability to model the intrinsic variability of patient flows. Unlike analytical models, which require simplifying assumptions (such as specific arrival and service time distributions), DES can integrate the stochastic nature of patient arrival times, service durations (consultation, testing, etc.), and complex care pathways. For a hospital environment like the maternity clinic, this capability is crucial because bottlenecks are often dynamic, shifting based on unforeseen peak hours or emergencies. Recent work has shown that DES is particularly relevant for evaluating the impact of staffing policies and protocol changes, allowing the quantification of improvements in care quality and reduction in operational costs before any real-world implementation.

However, analyzing a system's performance is only the first step; the ultimate goal is to improve it. This has led to the development of the field of Simulation-Optimization (SO), which aims to find the best input parameter settings for a given simulation model. As Fu (2015) outlines in a thorough overview of SO methodologies, this is a challenging task due to the stochastic nature of simulation outputs, which makes the objective function noisy and often impossible to express in a closed mathematical form. Consequently, metaheuristic algorithms, which are well-suited for such "black-box" optimization problems, are the dominant approach.

The major challenge in optimization within the simulation context (Simulation-Optimization, or SO) is that the objective function (here, minimizing average patient wait time) is stochastic and "noisy". This means that evaluating the same resource configuration will not yield exactly the same wait time across two different simulation runs due to the random nature of arrivals and services. Traditional optimization methods, based on calculating gradients or requiring a smooth analytical form, fail in such environments. Metaheuristics, such as those used by OptQuest (Tabu Search/Scatter Search) and the Genetic Algorithm (GA), are search techniques for a near-optimal solution that do not depend on the mathematical properties of the objective function. They explore the solution space in a guided manner, accepting the noise of the simulation, making them ideal for decision-making regarding resource allocation in complex, dynamic systems like hospitals

Among the various metaheuristic strategies, two are particularly relevant to this study. The first is the approach used by commercial, integrated tools like OptQuest, which is embedded within the Arena software. OptQuest utilizes a sophisticated combination of Tabu Search and Scatter Search to efficiently navigate complex solution spaces (Glover & Laguna, 1997).

OptQuest, the optimization engine integrated within the Arena software, relies on a powerful combination of Tabu Search and Scatter Search. Tabu Search is a metaheuristic that uses memory to guide the search, temporarily forbidding the revisiting of already explored solutions (the "tabu list") to avoid cycles and escape local optima. Scatter Search is an evolutionary method that focuses on combining "reference solutions" to create new, promising solutions, favoring a systematic and directed exploration of high-performance regions.

The integration of these two approaches ensures a search that is both thorough and intelligent, which explains OptQuest's robustness in complex case studies. However, as is common with commercial tools, it often functions as a "black box," providing limited insight into the optimization process itself

Its effectiveness in healthcare has been demonstrated in various studies, such as the optimization of hospital bed allocation to balance utilization and patient overflow (Ahmed & Alkhamis, 2009). These tools offer the advantage of a robust, pre-built search engine but often function as a "black box," providing limited insight into the optimization process itself.

The second major approach involves the development of custom metaheuristics, with Genetic Algorithms (GAs) being one of the most popular choices due to their robust global search capabilities. Inspired by the principles of Darwinian evolution (Holland, 1992), GAs have been successfully applied to a wide array of healthcare problems.

In the field of resource allocation, the Genetic Algorithm (GA) is particularly relevant due to its structure. Staff configurations (e.g., the number of cashiers, nurses, and physicians) naturally lend themselves to representation as "chromosomes" (a vector of genes). The GA excels at finding solutions in discrete and combinatorial search spaces, such as determining the optimal number of staff, thanks to the crossover and mutation operators. These operators allow the GA to efficiently explore the solution space by "inheriting" good characteristics (resource configurations) from parent solutions and introducing variability to discover new regions of the search space. This robustness for non-linear, multi-variable problems makes it a strong contender against commercial tools and a powerful method for solving staffing and scheduling problems.

For example, Azaiez and Al-Sharif (2005) used a goal programming model with a GA to solve a complex nurse scheduling problem, balancing hospital objectives with nurse preferences. More recently, Koehler et al. (2021) developed a multi-objective GA to optimize patient appointment scheduling, simultaneously minimizing wait times and improving resource utilization. Furthermore, a study by Zhang et al. (2019) successfully used a simulation-based GA to optimize the layout and resource allocation of an emergency department, showcasing the algorithm's ability to handle the multi-faceted, non-linear problems characteristic of healthcare simulation.

More recent research has continued to validate these approaches, applying simulation-optimization to address dynamic scheduling and staffing in complex hospital settings (Ahmed & Alkhamis, 2020), further demonstrating its practical utility for high-variability environments.

While the literature validates the use of both integrated tools and custom GAs, direct comparative studies applying these different metaheuristic approaches to the same validated healthcare model are less common.

Studies comparing the performance and efficiency of different metaheuristics, such as hybrid GA and Tabu Search methods (Liu et al., 2018), are essential for selecting the most appropriate optimization strategy for complex, real-world problems.

This paper aims to contribute to this area by providing a direct comparison of the performance, efficiency, and analytical insights gained from both OptQuest and a custom-developed Genetic Algorithm in a practical, real-world case study.

3. METHODOLOGY: A METAHEURISTIC APPROACH TO OPTIMIZATION

Our methodology follows a structured, multi-phase approach to ensure a comprehensive analysis.

Phase 1: Baseline Model Development and Validation: An "As-Is" model of the maternity clinic was developed in Arena based on collected data for patient arrivals, process times, and resource schedules. This model was then validated by comparing its outputs with historical data and expert opinion to ensure its credibility. This validated model, with a baseline average patient wait time of 91.95 minutes, served as the benchmark for all subsequent experiments.

Phase 2: Metaheuristic Optimization Experiments: Two distinct optimization methods were applied to the validated model to find the best resource configuration. The primary objective for both methods was to minimize the patient.WaitTime statistic.

- OptQuest Optimization: The OptQuest tool was configured to automatically search for an optimal solution. The number of staff for each role was defined as the controllable decision variables, with defined lower and upper bounds.

- Genetic Algorithm (GA) Optimization: A custom GA was developed in Python and integrated with the Arena model using the COM automation interface. This interface acts as a direct link, enabling the Python algorithm to manipulate model variables and read outputs in real-time without using intermediate files. The chromosome representation for the GA was defined as a vector of integers, where each gene corresponds to the number of staff for a specific resource (Cashier, Gynecologist, Nurse, Scheduling Secretary, Secretary). Given the resource constraints, a penalty method was implemented: any solution violating the pre-defined upper or lower bounds for staffing was assigned an extremely high wait time (low fitness) to guide the search towards feasible solutions. Crossover probability was set at 0.75, and a low mutation rate of 0.05 was used to ensure that the search balanced exploration and exploitation effectively. The GA was configured with a population of 10 individuals per generation over 5 generations (50 total simulations), using elitist selection, single-point crossover, and random mutation to guide its evolutionary search for the optimal solution.

4. PRACTICAL APPLICATION: MATERNITY UNIT CASE STUDY

A maternity service is a specialized unit within a hospital dedicated to providing care for pregnant women before, during, and after childbirth. The process within a maternity ward involves various stages, including admission, assessment, labor and delivery, postpartum care, and discharge. One critical aspect of maternity care is managing waiting times, which can significantly impact patient satisfaction, quality of care, and operational efficiency.

To model and simulate the process of a maternity ward using Arena Simulation, we can break down the process into its key components and model each stage accordingly and to address waiting time issues in the maternity unit, several strategies can be proposed and tested through simulation.

Also, by utilizing Arena Simulation, healthcare providers can gain valuable insights into system dynamics, identify areas for improvement, and implement evidence-based strategies to optimize patient flow and enhance quality of care.

The presented work addresses the problem of minimizing the cycle time of a patient in the maternity department of Farhat Hached Hospital in Sousse to improve the perfection of this department. More precisely, we take the case of the maternity service.

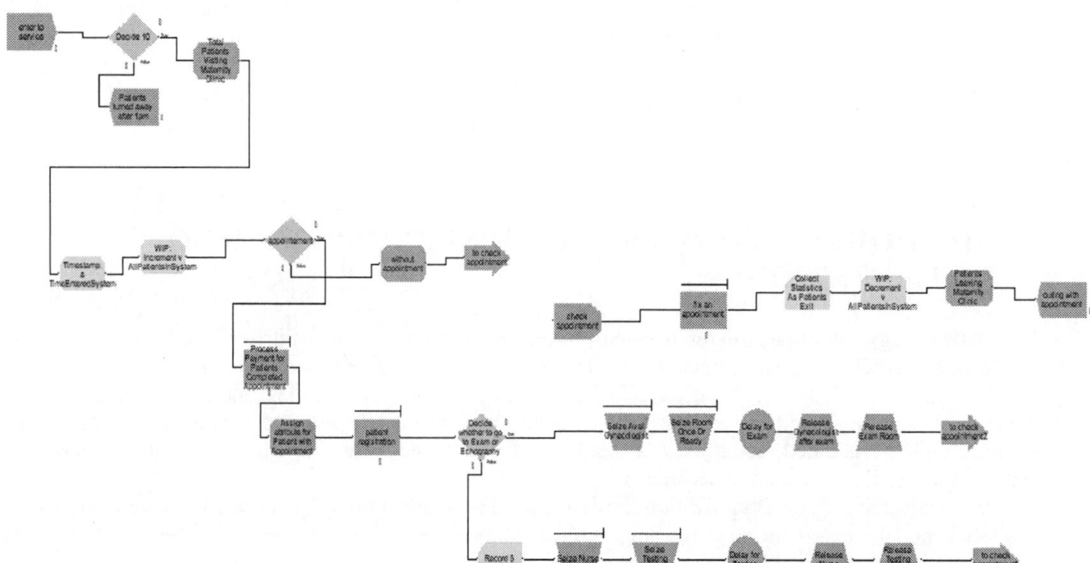

Figure 1. Arena model Process of care in the maternity unit

The process model illustrated in Figure 1 utilizes Arena simulation tool to detail the patient flow within the maternity unit, from the point of arrival until departure. An analysis of this workflow reveals several critical weaknesses.

The most significant challenges include patient dissatisfaction stemming from appointment scheduling, extended waiting periods, departmental overcrowding, and an imbalance between the number of available staff and the volume of patients.

Consequently, a revised approach is required to enhance the quality of service. The primary objectives are to better meet patient needs to improve satisfaction, decrease wait times, and alleviate congestion within the service area as much as possible.

To enhance the system's performance, we utilize simulation combined with metaheuristic optimization techniques.

The baseline model, configured with an initial staffing level of [1 Cashier, 5 Gynecologists, 1 Nurse, 1 Scheduling Secretary, 1 Secretary], revealed an average patient wait time of 91.95 minutes.

Table 1. "As-Is " Model Results

KPI	Patient with Appointment	Patient without Appointment
Average Wait Time (min)	91.95	17.61
Number In	134	27
Number Out	82	26
Resource Utilization Rate (%)	97.23 % *cashier* 97 % genecologist 75.01 % nurse 74.52 % schsecretary 87.24 % secretary	

An in-depth analysis of the initial simulation results reveals critical operational inefficiencies, characterized by excessive waiting times and severe congestion at key points in the patient journey.

The baseline simulation results clearly identified Gynecologists as the primary physical resource bottleneck, with a utilization rate of 97 %. This high utilization directly translated to long wait times, confirming that a lack of physician availability severely restricts patient throughput. Beyond the physicians, the administrative staff, the Cashier (97.23 % utilization) and the Secretary (87.24 % utilization) also showed critically high utilization rates, indicating that the patient journey was being hampered not only by medical staff shortages but also by administrative delays at the points of registration and payment. The average wait time of 91.95 minutes for patients with appointments was a direct consequence of this congestion across multiple service points, validating the need for a comprehensive, system-wide resource allocation solution

Given these findings, the next step will involve testing improvement.

The two metaheuristic optimization methods were then applied to improve this performance. The table below summarizes the key findings from each method:

Table 2. The optimal solutions found by the OptQuest tool and the Genetic Algorithm

Improvement Scenario	Avg. Wait Time	Number In	Number Out	Resource Utilization Rate (%)	Resource Configuration & Key Details
OptQuest Optimization	49.47 min	119	115	41.90 % cashier 96 % genecologist 34.6 % nurse 54.5 % schsecretary 75.2 % secretary	Configuration: [2, 5, 2, 2, 1] Found at: Simulation 54 of 111
Genetic Algorithm	49.47 min	119	115	41.90 % cashier 96 % genecologist 34.6 % nurse 54.5 % schsecretary 75.2 % secretary	Configuration: [2, 5, 2, 2, 1] Found at: Simulation 2 of 50

A key finding of our study is not just the optimal solution itself, but how the two different metaheuristic approaches, OptQuest and the Genetic Algorithm (GA), arrived at their conclusions. While both methods ultimately identified the same level of performance and a similar resource configuration, their search behavior and efficiency were markedly different.

OptQuest performed a broad and systematic search, evaluating 111 different scenarios before confirming the optimal solution. As shown in its convergence graph, it took 54 simulations to find the best objective value of 49.47 minutes. This behavior is characteristic of an optimizer designed for thorough exploration, ensuring it maps out a wide area of the solution space to avoid local optima. While robust, this comprehensive search requires a significant number of simulation runs.

In stark contrast, the Genetic Algorithm demonstrated a much faster convergence. It discovered the optimal solution with a wait time of 49.47 minutes in just its second simulation (the second individual of the very first generation). The subsequent 48 simulations were spent exploring the neighborhood of this excellent solution, but no further improvements were found. This highlights the GA's strength in "exploitation" once a highly fit individual is found, it rapidly focuses its search on that promising region.

While both methods are highly effective, this comparison reveals a critical difference in their approach. OptQuest provides a guaranteed, exhaustive search, whereas the Genetic Algorithm can, in some cases, find a good solution much more rapidly by evolving and improving upon good solutions as soon as they are discovered. The Genetic Algorithm proved to be the more efficient method for identifying the best-performing configuration.

5. CONCLUSION AND FUTURE WORKS

This study successfully demonstrated the value of applying a structured optimization framework to a healthcare simulation model. The hypotheses were validated: a significant reduction in wait time was achievable, specific staff levels were critical factors, and the automated optimization methods provided robust solutions.

The optimal configuration of [2 Cashiers, 5 Gynecologists, 2 Nurses, 2 Scheduling Secretaries, 1 Secretary] successfully balanced patient flow by strategically adding staff where the baseline analysis indicated critical bottlenecks. The most significant changes were the addition of one Cashier and one Scheduling Secretary. The increase in administrative staff drastically reduced their utilization rates, freeing up the front-end process and allowing patients to move through the initial stages faster (Cashier utilization dropped from 97.23 % to 41.9 % and Scheduling Secretary from 74.52 % to 54.5 %). Crucially, while the number of Gynecologists remained at 5, their utilization was slightly lower (96 %) in the optimal scenario, indicating that the improved efficiency in the preceding administrative steps allowed the medical staff to be used more effectively with less downtime or overflow. The reduction in the average wait time to 49.47 minutes demonstrates that the total system efficiency, not just the capacity of a single resource, was the key to this substantial performance improvement.

The convergence of two distinct metaheuristic methods on the same solution provides very strong validation for this recommendation.

Limitations of this study include the abstraction of the model and the single-objective nature of the optimization. Future work could expand on these results by incorporating a cost model for a multi-objective optimization (Time vs. Cost), enhancing the model's fidelity with more complex operational details, and comparing the GA's performance with other metaheuristics.

REFERENCES

Ahmed, M. A., & Alkhamis, T. M. (2009). Simulation optimization for an M/M/c/K queue with balking and reneging. European Journal of Operational Research, 198(2), 436–444.

Ahmed, M. A., & Alkhamis, T. M. (2020). Simulation optimization for emergency department staffing and scheduling with consideration of patient flow dynamics. Journal of Medical Systems, 44(2), 1-13.

Azaiez, M. N., & Al-Sharif, S. S. (2005). A 0-1 goal programming model for nurse scheduling. Computers & Operations Research, 32(3), 491–507.

Banks, J., Carson, J. S., II, Nelson, B. L., & Nicol, D. M. (2010). Discrete-Event System Simulation (5th ed.). Prentice Hall.

Fu, M. C. (Ed.). (2015). Handbook of simulation optimization (Vol. 216). Springer.

Glover, F., & Laguna, M. (1997). Tabu Search. Kluwer Academic Publishers.

Gunal, M. M., & Pidd, M. (2010). Discrete event simulation for performance modelling in health care: a review of the literature. Journal of Simulation, 4(1), 42–51.

Holland, J. H. (1992). Adaptation in Natural and Artificial Systems. MIT Press.

Koehler, M., Khazanchi, D., & Kolfal, B. (2021). A multi-objective genetic algorithm for optimizing patient appointment scheduling at a primary care clinic. Health Care Management Science, 24(1), 129–146.

Law, A. M. (2015). Simulation Modeling and Analysis (5th ed.). McGraw-Hill Education.

Liu, Y., Li, Q., Li, W., & Zhang, Y. (2018). A hybrid genetic algorithm and tabu search for resource allocation in cloud computing. Expert Systems with Applications, 110, 140-153.

Zhang, Z., Li, J., & Liu, Y. (2019). A simulation-based optimization approach for emergency department resource allocation. Journal of Medical Systems, 43(5), 1-11.

HUMAN-IN-THE-LOOP AI FOR RADIOLOGY REPORT GENERATION: A METHODOLOGY FRAMEWORK FOR CONTINUOUS LEARNING FROM EXPERT FEEDBACK

Dharmik Savani[1] and Firmino Oliveira da Silva[1,2]
[1]*ISLA Polytechnic University of Management and Technology, Gaia, Portugal*
[2]*CEOS.PP Centre for Organizational and Social Studies, Polytechnic of Porto, Portugal*

ABSTRACT

The integration of artificial intelligence into radiological workflows faces challenges in clinical acceptance and diagnostic reliability. While automated report generation systems show technical feasibility, deployment is limited by concerns over accuracy, transparency, and alignment with clinical expertise. Current systems often operate as static models that cannot adapt to institutional preferences or learn from expert corrections, leaving a gap between algorithmic capability and clinical needs. This study introduces a human-in-the-loop methodology framework that combines computer vision analysis of medical images with natural language processing for report generation, while systematically capturing radiologist feedback to enable continuous model improvement. The architecture includes four modules: CNN-based image feature extraction, fine-tuned biomedical language models for report generation, a human interface for capturing radiologist feedback, and a feedback mechanism for continuous system improvement. By maintaining human oversight while leveraging machine-learning capabilities, the framework addresses key challenges in medical AI deployment, enhancing workflow efficiency and diagnostic consistency. Iterative feedback integration enables alignment with institutional reporting standards and adaptation to local clinical practices, fostering personalized AI assistance. The main objective is to design a human-in-the-loop AI framework for radiology that adapts to institutional practices and radiologist feedback, improving both workflow efficiency and diagnostic consistency. The methodology incorporates comprehensive evaluation strategies, assessing both technical performance and clinical utility to ensure that improvements translate into meaningful workflow gains. This approach advances the development of collaborative human-AI systems in healthcare, offering a structured path toward radiology report automation that prioritizes technological innovation, clinical utility, and the complementary role of AI.

KEYWORDS

Artificial Intelligence, Human-in-the-Loop, Radiology, Report Generation, Medical Imaging, Natural Language Processing

1. INTRODUCTION

Contemporary radiology practice confronts unprecedented challenges stemming from exponentially increasing volumes coupled with persistent radiologist workforce shortages. Current estimates indicate that imaging study volumes grow at approximately 3% annually, while radiologist training capacity expands to less than 1% per year, creating an unsustainable trajectory that threatens healthcare delivery quality and timeliness (McDonald et al., 2015). This disparity has intensified documentation burdens, potentially compromising report comprehensiveness and consistency as practitioners manage accelerating workloads under time constraints. Artificial intelligence technologies, particularly deep learning approaches, have demonstrated remarkable capabilities in medical image interpretation tasks.

Recent developments in computer vision have achieved diagnostic performance comparable to expert radiologists for specific pathology detection scenarios (Liu et al., 2019). However, the transition from isolated algorithmic success to integrated clinical deployment remains challenging, primarily due to concerns regarding system reliability, interpretability, and the preservation of essential human judgment in diagnostic processes. The emergence of large language models has opened new possibilities for automated medical text generation, yet existing approaches typically operate as black-box systems that provide limited opportunities for clinical validation or correction (Thirunavukarasu et al., 2023). This limitation is critical in radiology, where report quality affects patient care and regulations require physician oversight of all interpretations.

This paper presents a human-in-the-loop framework for radiology report generation, designed to enhance rather than replace clinical expertise and to enable continuous improvement through expert feedback.

The objectives of this work are 1) To design and present a comprehensive human-in-the-loop framework for radiology report generation that combines computer vision, natural language processing, and continuous expert feedback. 2) To ensure clinical alignment and reliability by maintaining human oversight and systematically capturing radiologist corrections and preferences, enabling continuous model improvement. 3) To integrate four core modules within the architecture: Image feature extraction using convolutional neural networks optimized for medical imaging; Biomedical language models fine-tuned for radiology report generation; An intuitive human interface for capturing explicit corrections and implicit preferences; A feedback-based learning mechanism to refine system performance over time. 4) To establish evaluation strategies that assess both technical performance metrics and clinical utility measures, ensuring that system improvements translate into meaningful workflow and diagnostic enhancements. 5) To address ethical and practical challenges of AI deployment in healthcare by designing systems that enhance, rather than replace, radiological expertise. 6) To contribute to the broader field of collaborative human-AI systems by providing a structured and adaptable approach that aligns with institutional practices and supports responsible, efficient, and high-quality clinical decision-making.

The main contributions of this work are: 1) an architectural framework integrating computer vision, natural language processing, and human feedback; 2) a methodology for capturing radiologist corrections to enhance system performance; 3) an evaluation strategy combining technical metrics with clinical utility; and 4) attention to ethical and implementation issues for responsible AI deployment in healthcare.

2. RELATED WORK

2.1 Artificial Intelligence in Medical Imaging

Over the past decade, advances in deep learning and large annotated datasets have rapidly advanced medical image analysis. Convolutional neural networks now achieve high performance in key radiology tasks such as pathology detection, anatomical segmentation, and diagnostic classification (Litjens et al., 2017). Rajpurkar et al. (2018) demonstrated that deep learning models could achieve radiologist-level performance in detecting pneumonia from chest radiographs, marking a significant milestone in medical AI development. Similarly, the CheXpert dataset introduced by Irvin et al. (2019) provided a foundation for standardized evaluation of chest radiograph interpretation algorithms while highlighting the importance of uncertainty quantification in medical AI systems. Additional large-scale datasets such as ChestX-ray8 (Wang et al., 2017) and the Indiana University collection (Demner-Fushman et al., 2016) have further contributed to advancing automated chest radiography interpretation capabilities. Despite these technical achievements, the translation of research prototypes to clinical practice remains limited. Studies indicate that factors beyond algorithmic performance, including workflow integration, user acceptance, and regulatory considerations, significantly influence deployment success (Pesapane et al., 2018). Recent comprehensive reviews have highlighted both the promise and challenges of implementing AI in healthcare settings (Yu et al., 2018; Shin et al., 2016).

2.2 Automated Report Generation in Radiology

Natural language processing applications in radiology have primarily focused on information extraction from existing reports rather than de novo text generation. Early approaches utilized rule-based systems to identify specific findings and classify report content (Pons et al., 2016). More recent efforts have employed deep learning techniques to generate descriptive text directly from medical images. Monshi et al. (2020) conducted -a comprehensive survey of deep learning approaches for radiology report generation, identifying common architectures that combine convolutional neural networks for image analysis with recurrent neural networks for text generation. These encoder decoder frameworks have shown promise in generating coherent diagnostic descriptions, yet evaluation remains challenging due to the complexity of assessing clinical accuracy and utility. Early work in this area includes recurrent neural cascade models for automated image annotation (Shin et al.,

2016) and structured annotation approaches (Zech et al., 2018). Wang et al. (2018) introduced TieNet, a multimodal approach that learns joint representations of images and text to improve both classification and report generation performance. Their work demonstrated the value of leveraging paired image-text data for training more robust medical AI systems. However, these approaches typically rely on static training datasets without mechanisms for incorporating ongoing clinical feedback.

2.3 Human-in-the-Loop Machine Learning

The concept of human-in-the-loop machine learning has gained prominence as researchers recognize the limitations of purely automated approaches, particularly in high-stakes domains such as healthcare. Holzinger (2016) identified key scenarios where human expertise remains essential, including situations with limited training data, evolving requirements, and critical decision-making contexts. Recent developments in interactive machine learning have explored various mechanisms for incorporating human feedback into model training and inference processes. Active learning approaches query human experts to label the most informative examples, while interactive machine learning enables real-time collaboration between humans and algorithms during task execution (Amershi et al., 2014). Yuan et al. (2024) recently reviewed human-in-the-loop applications in healthcare, highlighting successful implementations in electronic health record analysis and clinical decision support. Their analysis emphasizes the importance of designing feedback mechanisms that align with clinical workflows while providing meaningful opportunities for model improvement. Budd et al. (2021) specifically examined human-in-the-loop approaches for medical image analysis, identifying active learning and expert feedback integration as promising directions for reducing annotation burden while maintaining high performance. Recent practical implementations of human-in-the-loop systems in healthcare include platforms that simplify model configuration for non-technical users. An illustrative example is KoopaML, environment that enables healthcare professionals to design and execute machine learning pipelines without programming skills. KoopaML exemplifies how interactive interfaces can operationalize human-in-the-loop learning for clinical users, bridging the gap between technical complexity and medical expertise (García-Peñalvo et al., 2024). Their work provides valuable insights into the practical considerations for implementing collaborative human-AI systems in medical imaging applications.

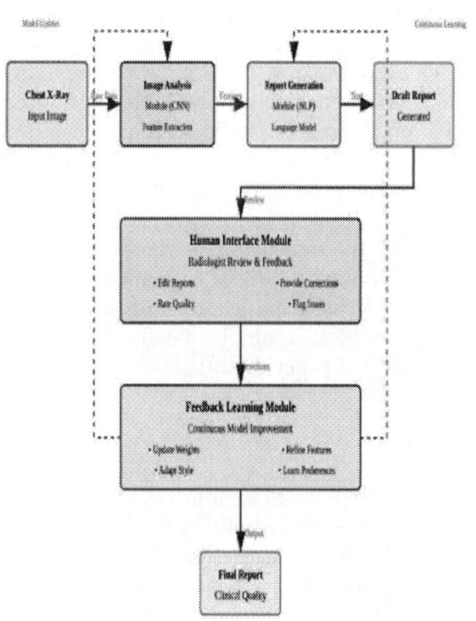

Figure 1. System Architecture of Framework

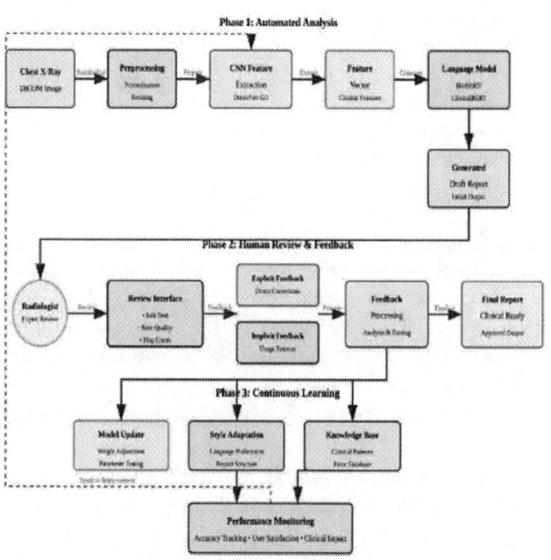

Figure 2. Detailed Workflow Process
and Human-in-the-Loop Integration

3. PROPOSED METHODOLOGY

3.1 System Architecture Overview

Our proposed human-in-the-loop framework (Figure 1) consists of four interconnected modules that together enable seamless integration of automated report generation with expert feedback. The Image Analysis Module uses convolutional neural networks (CNNs) to process radiological studies and extract clinically relevant features, forming the foundation for text generation. The Report Generation Module then employs fine-tuned biomedical language models to create preliminary reports in standard radiological format. Through the Human Interface Module, radiologists can review and refine these reports, providing explicit corrections and implicit feedback that the Feedback Learning Module uses to continuously update and improve the system. In summary, these four modules - Image Analysis, Report Generation, Human Interface, and Feedback Learning - work as a cohesive pipeline to adapt to institutional preferences over time. Figure 1 illustrates this architecture, with solid arrows representing forward data flow and dashed arrows indicating iterative feedback loops.

Figure 2 shows a detailed workflow presenting the three-phase process: (Phase 1) Automated analysis including preprocessing, CNN feature extraction, and initial report generation; (Phase 2) Human review involving radiologist evaluation, feedback collection through the interface, and final report approval; (Phase 3) Continuous learning incorporating model updates, style adaptation, and performance monitoring. The dashed line indicates the iterative feedback loop that enables continuous improvement. The complete workflow demonstrates how each module contributes to the iterative improvement process, with clear phases for automated analysis, human review, and continuous learning integration.

3.2 Image Analysis Module

The image analysis component employs convolutional neural network architectures specifically optimized for medical imaging applications. For chest radiography, we utilize DenseNet-based models that have demonstrated superior performance in pathology detection tasks while maintaining computational efficiency suitable for clinical deployment (Huang et al., 2017). Feature extraction follows a hierarchical approach where low-level image characteristics are progressively combined to identify higher-level anatomical structures and potential abnormalities. The system generates structured feature representations that capture both spatial relationships and intensity patterns relevant to diagnostic interpretation. To ensure robust performance across diverse imaging conditions, the module incorporates preprocessing steps including intensity normalization, noise reduction, and geometric standardization. These operations enhance model reliability while maintaining compatibility with existing clinical imaging protocols. The output of this module consists of multi-dimensional feature vectors that encode salient image characteristics in a format suitable for natural language processing applications. These representations preserve essential diagnostic information while abstracting away low-level pixel details that are not directly relevant to report generation.

3.3 Report Generation Module

Text generation employs transformer-based language models specifically fine-tuned on biomedical literature and radiology reports. We leverage pre-trained models such as BioBERT or ClinicalBERT as foundation architectures (Lee et al., 2020), building upon recent advances in large language model development (Brown et al., 2020), then apply domain-specific fine-tuning using paired image-report datasets such as MIMIC-CXR (Johnson et al., 2019) to develop specialized report generation capabilities. The generation process follows a template-guided approach where the system produces structured reports containing standard sections including clinical history, findings, and impressions. This organization ensures consistency with established radiological reporting conventions while providing flexibility for case-specific adaptations. To maintain clinical accuracy, the module implements constraint-based generation that prevents the production of contradictory or medically inappropriate statements. These constraints are derived from medical knowledge bases and clinical guidelines, providing guardrails that enhance system reliability. The module also incorporates uncertainty quantification mechanisms that flag generated text segments with lower confidence scores. It will enable radiologists to focus on areas where the system is less certain, optimizing the efficiency of human review processes.

3.4 Human Interface Module

The user interface prioritizes clinical workflow integration by presenting AI-generated reports in familiar formats that align with existing radiology information systems. Radiologists can review generated text alongside corresponding images using standard viewing tools and interaction paradigms. Edit tracking functionality captures all modifications made by users, including text additions, deletions, and modifications. The system records not only the final corrected version but also intermediate editing steps, providing detailed insight into expert thought processes and preferences. Interactive elements enable radiologists to provide structured feedback regarding system performance, including ratings of report accuracy, completeness, and clinical utility. This explicit feedback complements implicit signals derived from editing patterns to create comprehensive training data for model improvement. The interface also supports collaborative review scenarios where multiple experts can contribute to report refinement, capturing consensus building processes that are valuable for training more robust models. Version control capabilities ensure that all contributions are properly attributed and tracked.

3.5 Feedback Learning Module

The continuous learning component processes collected feedback through multiple mechanisms designed to optimize system performance while maintaining stability. Supervised fine-tuning using expert-corrected report pairs provides direct signals for improving text generation quality. Reinforcement learning approaches incorporate preference signals derived from user interactions and explicit feedback ratings. This methodology enables the system to learn higher-level quality measures that may not be captured through direct text comparison alone (Ouyang et al., 2022). To prevent catastrophic forgetting and maintain performance on the original training distribution, the module employs regularization techniques that balance new learning with preservation of existing capabilities. This approach ensures that system improvements do not compromise baseline functionality. The learning process includes evaluation mechanisms that assess model performance on held-out test sets before deploying updates to clinical systems. This validation step ensures that feedback incorporation results in genuine improvements rather than overfitting specific user preferences.

3.6 Implementation Considerations

System deployment requires careful attention to computational resources, data security, and regulatory compliance. Focused on data protection and clinical documentation standards. Cloud-based deployment options provide scalability and maintenance advantages while ensuring data sovereignty through appropriate geographical restrictions. Integration with hospital information systems enables seamless data exchange while maintaining audit trails required for clinical accountability. The system interfaces with existing radiology information systems and picture archiving systems through standard protocols.

4. EVALUATION FRAMEWORK

4.1 Technical Performance Metrics

System evaluation requires comprehensive assessment across multiple dimensions reflecting both technical capability and clinical utility. Traditional natural language processing metrics including BLEU, ROUGE, and METEOR scores provide quantitative measures of text generation quality by comparing AI-generated reports with expert-written references (Papineni et al., 2002). Domain-specific evaluation metrics address the unique requirements of medical text by focusing on clinical accuracy, terminology appropriateness, and diagnostic relevance. These measures evaluate whether generated reports contain right medical information and use right clinical language. Uncertainty calibration assessment examines the correlation between system confidence scores and actual performance, ensuring that the model's self-assessment aligns with real-world scenarios.

4.2 Clinical Utility Assessment

User experience evaluation focuses on workflow integration, efficiency gains, and radiologist satisfaction with AI assistance. Time-to-completion measurements compare report generation speed with and without AI support. Error analysis examines both false positive and false negative patterns in AI-generated reports, identifying systematic biases or limitations that require attention. This analysis informs targeted improvements and helps establish appropriate use guidelines. This evaluation includes analysis of feedback patterns and adaptation rates across different user groups. It can be helpful to check feasibility, accuracy, report consistency, or downstream patient care decisions. These studies provide the strongest evidence for clinical value while acknowledging the challenges of conducting controlled trials in clinical settings.

4.3 Ethical and Safety Evaluation

This analysis ensures that the benefits of AI support are equitably distributed across patient populations. Radiologists should understand when and why the AI system makes specific recommendations or expresses uncertainty about findings. Safety analysis examines failure modes and their potential clinical consequences, establishing appropriate safeguards and monitoring procedures. Privacy protection evaluation ensures that the feedback learning process does not compromise patient confidentiality or create inappropriate data sharing risks. This assessment addresses both technical implementation and procedural safeguards.

5. DISCUSSION

5.1 Clinical Impact and Benefits

The proposed human-in-the-loop framework addresses several critical challenges in contemporary radiology practice. By providing intelligent assistance for report generation while maintaining essential human oversight, the system has the potential to enhance both efficiency and quality in radiological workflows. Efficiency improvements may manifest through reduced time spent on routine documentation tasks, enabling radiologists to focus more attention on complex cases and direct patient care activities. The structured nature of AI-generated preliminary reports may also enhance consistency across different practitioners and time periods. Educational benefits emerge through the system's ability to provide structured reporting examples that align with institutional standards and best practices. Less experienced radiologists may benefit from exposure to well-formatted reports that demonstrate appropriate terminology and organization patterns. The continuous learning capability enables institutional customization that addresses local preferences and specific clinical contexts. This adaptability represents a significant advantage over static AI systems that cannot evolve with changing requirements or institutional practices.

5.2 Implementation Challenges

Successful deployment requires careful attention to change management and user adoption strategies. Radiologists may initially resist AI assistance due to concerns about accuracy, liability, or workflow disruption. Comprehensive training programs and gradual implementation approaches can help address these concerns. Technical integration challenges include ensuring compatibility with existing information systems, maintaining acceptable response times, and providing reliable service availability. These requirements necessitate robust infrastructure planning and ongoing technical support capabilities. Regulatory compliance adds complexity to deployment processes, particularly regarding documentation requirements, audit trails, and quality assurance procedures. Organizations must ensure that AI assistance does not compromise their ability to meet professional and legal standards. Cost could be considered.

5.3 Ethical Considerations

The integration of AI into radiology workflows raises concerns about responsibility, accountability, and the balance between humans and machines. Our framework addresses these concerns by maintaining clear human oversight and providing transparency of AI contributions to diagnostic processes. Recent studies have highlighted the importance of addressing potential biases in medical AI systems (Gichoya et al., 2022) and ensuring equitable performance across diverse populations. Data privacy protection requires careful attention to how patient information is used for system training and improvement. Feedback learning mechanisms must incorporate appropriate anonymization and consent procedures to protect patient confidentiality while system enhancement. Bias mitigation efforts must address potential disparities in system performance across different patient populations, imaging conditions, or clinical scenarios. Ongoing monitoring and adjustment procedures are essential for maintaining equitable AI assistance across diverse clinical contexts.

6. CONCLUSION

This paper presents a comprehensive methodology framework for implementing humanin-the-loop AI systems in radiology report generation. Our approach addresses key challenges in medical AI deployment by prioritizing human expertise while leveraging machine learning capabilities to enhance workflow efficiency and consistency. The proposed architecture integrates computer vision, natural language processing, and feedback learning mechanisms to create a system that can adapt to institutional preferences and evolving clinical requirements. By maintaining human oversight while providing intelligent assistance, the framework offers a pathway for responsible AI deployment that complements rather than replaces radiological expertise. Our evaluation strategy encompasses both technical performance measures and clinical utility assessments, ensuring that system development addresses real-world requirements rather than purely algorithmic objectives. The emphasis on continuous learning from expert feedback represents a significant advancement in developing AI systems that can improve over time while maintaining clinical relevance. Implementation challenges including technical integration, user adoption, and regulatory compliance require careful attention but are addressable through appropriate planning and change management strategies. The potential benefits of enhanced efficiency, improved consistency, and educational value justify the investment required for successful deployment. Future work will focus on prototype development, clinical validation, and extension to additional radiology domains. The methodology framework provides a foundation for systematic investigation of human-AI collaboration in medical imaging that can inform broader efforts to integrate artificial intelligence into healthcare practice responsibly and effectively. The goal of this research is to develop AI systems that enhance rather than replace human expertise, creating more efficient and effective radiology workflows while maintaining the highest standards of patient care and professional practice. Through careful attention to both technical capabilities and clinical requirements, we can realize the potential of artificial intelligence to improve healthcare delivery while preserving the essential human elements of medical practice.

ACKNOWLEDGEMENT

Subject Experts: Dr Unnati Parmar MD (Rad), Ms. Bhagavati Savani BE(CS), Ms. Shruti Vadaliya BE(BM).

REFERENCES

Amershi, S., Cakmak, M., Knox, W. B., & Kulesza, T. (2014). Power to the people: The role of humans in interactive machine learning. *AI Magazine*, *35*(4), 105-120.

Brown, T. B., Mann, B., Ryder, N., Subbiah, M., Kaplan, J., Dhariwal, P., Neelakantan, A., Shyam, P., Sastry, G., Askell, A., Agarwal, S., Herbert-Voss, A., Krueger, G., Henighan, T., Child, R., Ramesh, A., Ziegler, D. M., Wu, J., Winter, C., Amodei, D. (2020). Language models are few-shot learners. *Advances in Neural Info Processing System*, *33*, 1877-1901.

Budd, S., Robinson, E. C., & Kainz, B. (2021). A survey on active learning and human-in-the-loop deep learning for medical image analysis. *Medical Image Analysis*, *71*, 102063.

Demner-Fushman, D., Kohli, M. D., Rosenman, M. B., Shooshan, S. E., Rodriguez, L., Antani, S., Thoma, G. R., & McDonald, C. J. (2016). Preparing a collection of radiology examinations for distribution and retrieval. *Journal of the American Medical Informatics Association*, *23*(2), 304-310.

García-Peñalvo, F. J., Vázquez-Ingelmo, A., García-Holgado, A., Sampedro-Gómez, J., Sánchez-Puente, A., Vicente-Palacios, V., Dorado-Díaz, P. I., & Sánchez, P. L. (2024). KoopaML: A graphical platform for building ML pipelines adapted to health professionals. *International Journal of Interactive Multimedia and Artificial Intelligence*, *8*(6), 112-119.

Gichoya, J. W., Banerjee, I., Bhimireddy, A. R., Burns, J. L., Celi, L. A., Chen, L.-C., Correa, R., Dullerud, N., Ghassemi, M., Huang, S.-C., Kuo, P.-C., Lungren, M. P., Palmer, L. J., Price, B. J., Purkayastha, S., Pyrros, A. T., Oakden-Rayner, L., Okechukwu, C., Seyyed-Kalantari, L., ... Trivedi, H. (2022). AI recognition of patient race in medical imaging: A modelling study. *The Lancet Digital Health*, *4*(6), e406-e414.

Holzinger, A. (2016). Interactive M L for health informatics: When do we need the H-L? *Brain Informatics*, *3*(2), 119-131.

Huang, G., Liu, Z., Van Der Maaten, L., & Weinberger, K. Q. (2017). Densely connected convolutional networks. *Proceedings of the IEEE Conference on Computer Vision and Pattern Recognition*, 4700-4708.

Irvin, J., Rajpurkar, P., Ko, M., Yu, Y., Ciurea-Ilcus, S., Chute, C., Marklund, H., Haghgoo, B., Ball, R., Shpanskaya, K., Seekins, J., Mong, D. A., Halabi, S. S., Sandberg, J. K., Jones, R., Larson, D. B., Langlotz, C. P., Patel, B. N., Lungren, M. P., & Ng, A. Y. (2019). CheXpert: A large chest radiograph dataset with uncertainty labels and expert comparison. *Proceedings of the AAAI Conference on Artificial Intelligence*, *33*(01), 590-597.

Johnson, A. E. W., Pollard, T. J., Berkowitz, S. J., Greenbaum, N. R., Lungren, M. P., Deng, C., Mark, R. G., & Horng, S. (2019). MIMIC-CXR, a de-identified publicly available database of chest radiographs with free-text reports. *Scientific Data*, *6*(1), 317.

Lee, J., Yoon, W., Kim, S., Kim, D., Kim, S., So, C. H., & Kang, J. (2020). BioBERT: A pre-trained biomedical language representation model for biomedical text mining. *Bioinformatics*, *36*(4), 1234-1240.

Litjens, G., Kooi, T., Bejnordi, B. E., Setio, A. A. A., Ciompi, F., Ghafoorian, M., van der Laak, J. A. W. M., van Ginneken, B., & Sánchez, C. I. (2017). A survey on deep learning in medical image analysis. *Medical Image Analysis*, *42*, 60-88.

Liu, X., Faes, L., Kale, A. U., Wagner, S. K., Fu, D. J., Bruynseels, A., Mahendiran, T., Moraes, G., Shamdas, M., Kern, C., Ledsam, J. R., Schmid, M. K., Balaskas, K., Topol, E. J., Bachmann, L. M., Keane, P. A., & Denniston, A. K. (2019). A comparison of deep learning performance against health-care professionals in detecting diseases from medical imaging: A systematic review and meta-analysis. *The Lancet Digital Health*, *1*(6), e271-e297.

McDonald, R. J., Schwartz, K. M., Eckel, L. J., Diehn, F. E., Hunt, C. H., Bartholmai, B. J., Erickson, B. J., & Kallmes, D. F. (2015). The effects of changing utilization patterns of CT and MRI in a large academic medical center. *Academic Radiology*, *22*(4), 447-453.

Monshi, M. M. A., Poon, J., & Chung, V. (2020). DL in generating radio reports: A survey. *AI in Medicine*, *106*, 101878.

Ouyang, L., Wu, J., Jiang, X., Almeida, D., Wainwright, C., Mishkin, Zhang, C., Agarwal, Slama, K., Ray, A., Schulman, Hilton, J., Kelton, F., Miller, L., Simens, M., Askell, A., Welinder, P., Christiano, P., Leike, J., & Lowe, R. (2022). Training LM to follow instructions with human feedback. *Advances in Neural Information Processing Systems*, *35*, 27730-27744.

Papineni, K., Roukos, S., Ward, T., & Zhu, W. J. (2002). BLEU: A method for automatic evaluation of machine translation. *Proceedings of the 40th Annual Meeting of the Association for Computational Linguistics*, 311-318.

Pesapane, F., Codari, M., & Sardanelli, F. (2018). Artificial intelligence in medical imaging: Threat or opportunity? Radiologists again at forefront of innovation in medicine. *European Radiology Experimental*, *2*(1), 1-10.

Pons, E., Braun, L. M., Hunink, M. G. M., & Kors, J. A. (2016). Natural language processing in radiology: A systematic review. *Radiology*, *279*(2), 329-343.

Rajpurkar, P., Irvin, J., Ball, R. L., Zhu, K., Yang, B., Mehta, H., Duan, T., Ding, D., Bagul, A., Langlotz, C. P., Patel, B. N., Yeom, K. W., Shpanskaya, K., Blankenberg, F. G., Seekins, J., Amrhein, T. J., Mong, D. A., Halabi, S. S., Zucker, E. J., ... Lungren, M. P. (2018). Deep learning for chest radiograph diagnosis: A retrospective comparison of the CheXNeXt algorithm to practicing radiologists. *PLOS Medicine*, *15*(11), e1002686.

Shin, H.-C., Roberts, K., Lu, L., Demner-Fushman, D., Yao, J., & Summers, R. M. (2016). Learning to read chest X-rays: Recurrent neural cascade model for automated image annotation. *Proceedings of the IEEE Conference on Computer Vision and Pattern Recognition*, 2497-2506.

Thirunavukarasu, A. J., Ting, D. S. J., Elangovan, K., Gutierrez, L., Tan, T. F., & Ting, D. S. W. (2023). LLMs in medicine. *Nature Medicine*, *29*(8), 1930-1940.

Wang, X., Peng, Y., Lu, L., Lu, Z., Bagheri, M., & Summers, R. M. (2017). ChestX-ray8: Hospital-scale chest X-ray database and benchmarks on weakly-supervised classification and localization of common thorax diseases. *Proceedings of the IEEE Conference on Computer Vision and Pattern Recognition*, 2097-2106.

Wang, X., Peng, Y., Lu, L., Lu, Z., & Summers, R. M. (2018). TieNet: Text-image embedding network for common thorax disease classification and reporting in chest X-rays. *Proceedings of the IEEE Conference on Computer Vision and Pattern Recognition*, 9049-9058.

Yu, K.-H., Beam, A. L., & Kohane, I. S. (2018). AI in healthcare. *Nature Biomedical Engineering*, *2*(10), 719-731.

Yuan, H., Kang, L., Li, Y., & Fan, Z. (2024). Human-in-the-loop machine learning for healthcare: Current progress and future opportunities in electronic health records. *Medicine Advances*, *2*(1), 47-58.

Zech, J., Pain, M., Titano, J., Badgeley, M., Schefflein, J., Su, A., Costa, A., Bederson, J., Lehar, J., & Oermann, E. K. (2018). NL-based machine learning models for the annotation of clinical radiology reports. *Radiology*, *287*(2), 570-580.

ESTIMATION OF PROGRAMMING LOGICS OF RESPECTIVE LEARNERS BASED ON ANALYSIS OF SYNTAX TREES

Mitsuhiro Sato[1], Ryo Onuma[1], Sho Onami[1], Hiroki Nakayama[1], Hiroaki Kaminaga[1], Youzou Miyadera[2] and Shoichi Nakamura[1]

[1]*Fukushima University, 1, Kanayagawa, Fukushima 960-1296, Japan*

[2]*Tokyo Gakugei University, 4-1-1, Nukuikita, Koganei, Tokyo 184-8501, Japan*

ABSTRACT

Programming exercises have become more widely implemented at universities and other educational institutions. In programming exercises, it is necessary for professors to effectively instruct learners depending on the situations of individual learners. However, under the restriction of a small number of professors handling a large number of learners, it is difficult to fully grasp the situation of individual learners. In particular, the direction to construct a program (called programming logic) differs by individual learners even for the same challenge in the exercise. In this research, we have been aiming at developing methods for automatically estimating programming logics of individual learners from their incomplete source codes. This paper mainly describes methods for logic estimation on the basis of analyzing syntax trees. Finally, we describe experiments using the prototype and discuss the features of our methods.

KEYWORDS

Programming Logics, Similarity of Syntax Trees, Incomplete Source Codes, Support for Programming Exercise

1. INTRODUCTION

Programming exercises have become more widely implemented at universities and other educational institutions. In programming exercises, it is necessary for professors to effectively instruct learners depending on the situations of individual learners. However, under the restriction of a small number of professors handling a large number of learners, it is difficult to fully grasp the situation of individual learners. In particular, the direction to construct a program (called *programming logic*) differs by individual learners even for the same challenge in the exercise. Understanding such programming logics within a limited timeframe is more difficult.

To resolve these problems, there have been methods for stumbling detection in the programming exercises (Urakami et al., 2020; Gao et al., 2018; Chowdhary et al., 2020; Ahmed et al., 2022; Goto et al., 2019), providing support for programming challenges using Generative AI (Sasaki et al., 2024; Pankiewicz et al., 2024; Kazemitabaar et al., 2024; Phung et al., 2023; Gupta et al., 2019; Gupta et al., 2017; Ahmed et al., 2018). However, these methods mainly focus on syntax errors of respective learners and are not sufficiently support guidance on the logical aspects of programming. Also, there have been methods for supporting professors in monitoring individual learners' progress in programming exercises (Ichimura et al., 2013; Ahadi et al., 2018; McBroom et al., 2021; Zhang et al., 2023; Alzahrani et al., 2021; Watanabe et al., 2025). Although these methods facilitate the monitoring of students' learning progresses, the logical issues are not sufficiently covered.

In this research, we develop a method for automatically estimating programming logics from incomplete source codes using syntax trees and presenting them to professors in an accessible form. This method enables professors to understand programming logics of learners without extra burden.

2. PROBLEMS AND RESEARCH DIRECTION

2.1 Support Targets

In this research, we target learners who have already mastered basic grammar and are at the stage of trying to shape their envisioned processes into programs themselves. Currently, our target language is C. In programming exercises, as mentioned above, it is important for professors to accurately grasp the exercise status of individual learners and to instruct them accordingly. However, it can be difficult to do so because of constraints on time and human resources. Moreover, there are often multiple possible directions taken to construct a program (called *programming logic*) even for a single challenge, and different learners have different programming logics. Such programming logics should be satisfactorily grasped by professors, which can be quite difficult.

2.2 Problems

We have identified two main problems in understanding the programming logics of individual learners.

- Although professors must instruct individual learners in accordance with their intended logics and progress, it is difficult to accurately grasp the logics of individual learners under constraints such as limited time and human resources.
- It is difficult to manage the source codes of individual learners by associating them with their programming logics in a way that can be utilized for guidance.

2.3 Research Direction

In this research, we develop a mechanism for estimating programming logics of respective learners and presenting them to professors in an easily understandable form (Figure 1). In programming exercises, professors present a challenge to learners. Learners construct programs for the given challenge. The system monitors the coding processes of learners and continuously collects their compilation histories. When professors attempt to grasp programming logics of learners, this support system targets the latest source codes of learners, in other words, incomplete source codes, to estimate programming logics. This system presents groups of learners classified into the same logic with their source codes, thereby facilitating professors' comprehension of learners' programming logics.

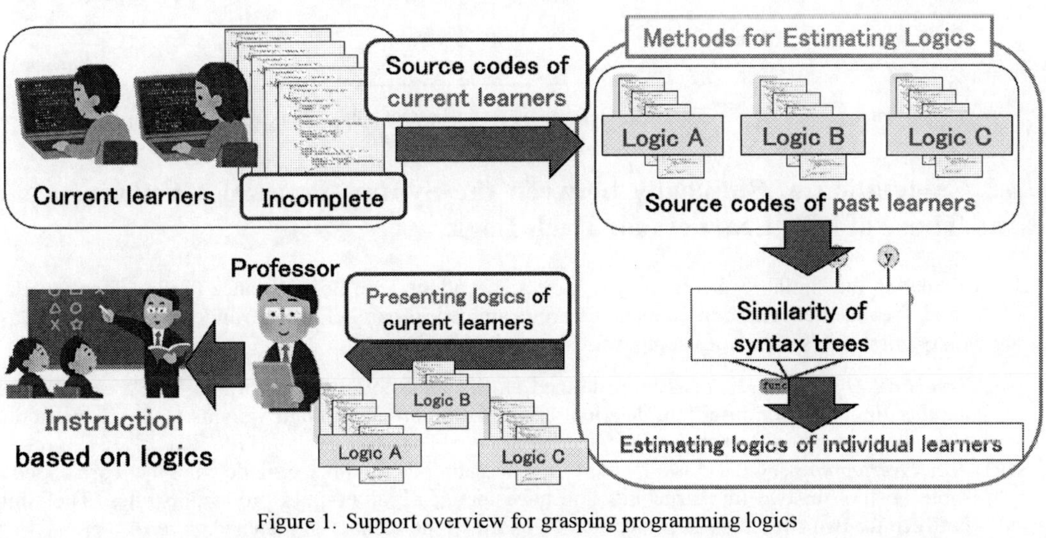

Figure 1. Support overview for grasping programming logics

3. ESTIMATION OF PROGRAMMING LOGICS BASED ON ANALYSIS OF SIMILARITY BETWEEN SYNTAX TREES

3.1 Aim of Logic Estimation with Syntax Trees

Syntax trees accurately represent the structure of a program in a hierarchical manner and in an easily understandable form. In other words, syntax trees are promising for analyzing control structures such as if-statements and loop controls as well as the flow of processing because they clearly express the relationships between elements expressed as nodes. In order to estimate program logics by taking advantage of these features, we analyze syntax trees. Specifically, we estimate programming logics by analyzing similarities between syntax trees in accordance with the following procedure.

(1) Generation of syntax trees for source codes of current learners and past learners
(2) Calculation of similarity between the syntax trees of a current learner and those of past learners for each logic
(3) Estimation of programming logic based on similarities between syntax trees

3.2 Generation of Syntax Trees for Source Codes of Current Learners and Past Learners

First, we generate syntax trees from source codes written in C. We use Clang, which is part of the LLVM project, in order to generate syntax trees (Figure 2). Clang is the compiler front-end for C, C++, and Objective-C and provides functionalities to structurally analyze source codes and output syntax trees.

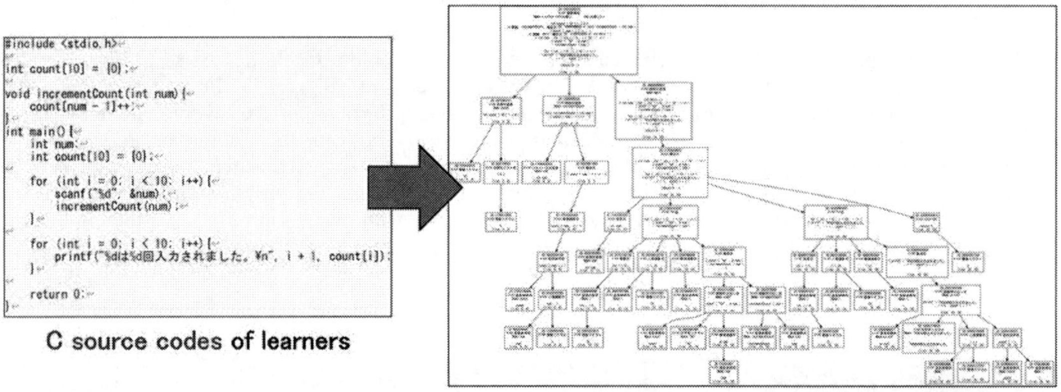

Figure 2. Generation of syntax trees using Clang

3.3 Calculation of Similarity between the Syntax Trees of a Current Learner and Those of Past Learners for Each Logic

For calculating the similarity between syntax trees, we adopt Tree Edit Distance (TED), Tree Overlapping (TO), and Tree Kernel. These three methods are examined in parallel to determine their suitability, as they are widely utilized in syntax trees comparisons.

1) *Tree Edit Distance (TED)*: TED is defined as the total cost of transforming one tree structure into another through node insertion, deletion, and substitution. We assign weights to these operations and compute the total edit distance.
2) *Tree Overlapping (TO)*: TO is a method for calculating the number of node pairs that correspond to the same position in two tree structures and have identical parent-child production rules. The similarity between the two structures is then computed based on the number of matched pairs.

3) *Tree Kernel*: Tree Kernel is a method for calculating the similarity between two tree structures by using subtrees and a kernel function as common substructures. A subtree is defined as a structure containing two or more nodes that fully preserve the production rules of its constituent nodes. A kernel function is a function utilized to measure similarity among data. By combining the number of common subtrees with the kernel function, similarity between tree structures can be computed.

3.4 Estimation of Programming Logics based on Similarities between Syntax Trees

We estimate programming logics by computing the similarity between syntax trees generated from source codes. First, source codes of past learners are labeled and classified in accordance with programming logics. For each logic, two representative source codes that sufficiently capture the characteristics of the logic are selected: the first consists solely of a main function, and the second includes additional functions defined outside the main function. Therefore, the total number of representative source codes is equal to the number of logic types multiplied by two. The similarity between the representative source codes for each logic and the target source code is then calculated. Finally, the logic of the representative source codes with the highest similarity is judged as the logic of the target source code.

We present an example of estimating programming logics using TO in Figure 3. A larger TO value indicates a higher similarity between two syntax trees. As shown in the figure, the largest TO value occurs when compared with the syntax tree of Logic B. Therefore, the target source code is estimated to be Logic B. Programming logics are estimated in the same way for both TED and Tree Kernel.

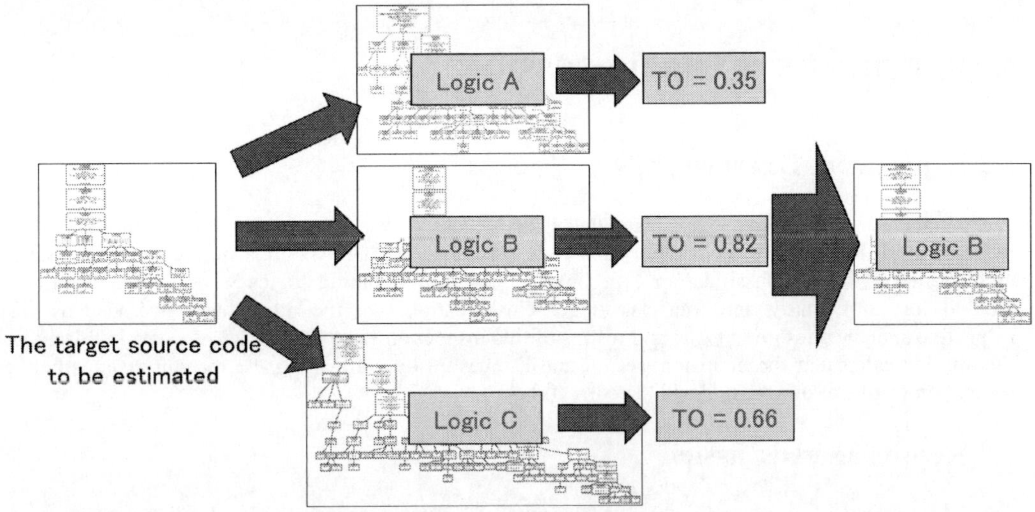

Figure 3. Estimation of Programming Logic based on Similarities between Syntax Trees

4. SUPPORT SYSTEM FOR GRASPING PROGRAMMING LOGICS

The group of learners classified the estimated logics and their source codes are presented to professors (Figure 4). When a professor selects one logic for a challenge, the learners who worked on the challenge and the ratio of the learners orient toward respective programming logics in the challenge are displayed together. Furthermore, when a professor selects a learner from the presented list to understand his/her situation in detail, the source code at the time of logic estimation as well as the latest source code of the learner are shown. In addition, the execution results of each source code are displayed at the bottom. Moreover, an additional section is displayed for professors to record and review notes on each learner.

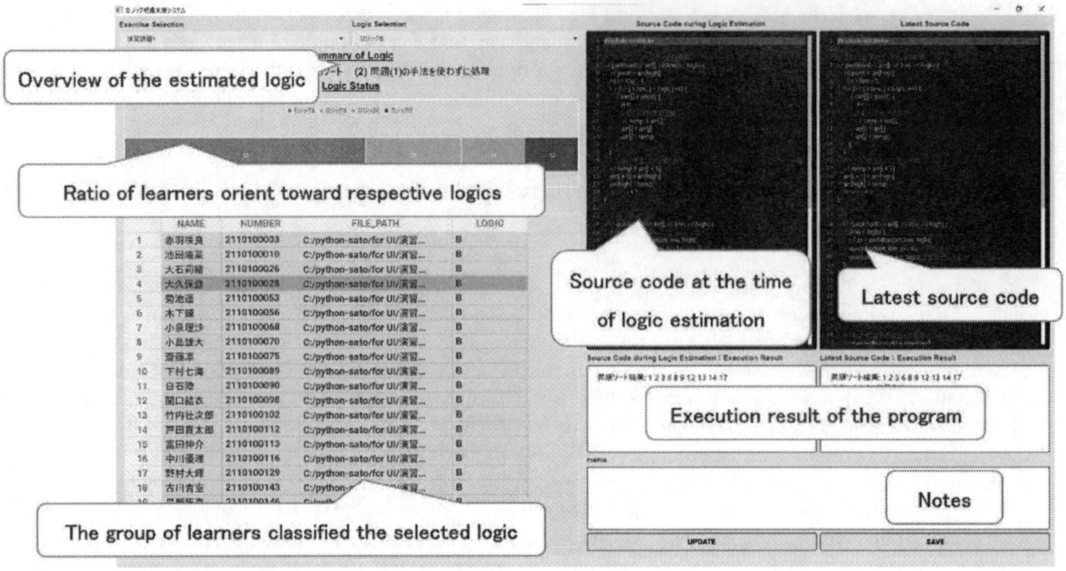

Figure 4. An Interface of Support System for Grasping Programming Logics

5. EXPERIMENTS AND DISCUSSION

5.1 Experiment Overview

We conducted experiments to evaluate the effectiveness of the logic estimation method. The test data included 20 different source codes. For each code, three intermediate versions were collected, making a total of 60 samples for the classification experiment. Then, programming logics were estimated based on our method for both binary and four-class logic classification. On the other hand, we visually inspected respective source codes one by one and results of this inspection were used as correct data in this experiment. Finally, we calculated the precision, recall, and F-measure by confirming the matching status between the estimation results of our method and the correct data.

5.2 Results and Discussion

Table 1 and Table 2 respectively shows the results of estimating programming logics in the case of binary logics and four-classes. In both the binary and four-class cases, On the whole, generally good accuracy has been obtained. In particular, the method using TED achieved favorable results. These results suggest that our methods successfully estimated programming logics almost we had intended. On the other hand, the method using TO and Tree Kernel performed relatively poorly. Although the methods using TED look superior, we cannot make a definitive statement based solely on the results of these experiments.

Since the scale of the experiments was limited, we need to carefully verify the effectiveness of the estimation methods through further experiments combining various data and methods for calculating the similarity between syntax trees.

Table 1. The results of Logic Estimation in the case of Binary Logics

Method for Computing Similarity	TED	TO	Tree Kernel
Precision score	0.78	0.66	0.57
Recall score	0.70	0.65	0.57
F score	0.74	0.65	0.57

Table 2. The results of Logic Estimation in the case of Four-Class Logics

Method for Computing Similarity	TED	TO	Tree Kernel
Precision score	0.76	0.51	0.55
Recall score	0.52	0.52	0.40
F score	0.62	0.51	0.46

6. CONCLUSION

In this paper, we described methods for estimating programming logics based on the analysis of similarity between syntax trees. Moreover, we outlined the support system for grasping programming logics.

Future work includes verifying the methods through careful examination with source codes and history data in actual exercises, and their improvement.

ACKNOWLEDGEMENT

This work was supported in part by Japan Society for the Promotion of Science under Grant-in-Aid for Scientific Research (B) (No. 24K15216, No. 25K06464).

REFERENCES

Ahadi A. et al. (2018). Syntax error based quantification of the learning progress of the novice programmer. *Proc. of the 23rd Annual ACM Conference on Innovation and Technology in Computer Science Education*, pp.10-14.

Ahmed T. et al. (2022). Improved Fixing of Syntax Errors. *IEEE Transactions on Software Engineering*, Vol. 49, pp.2169-2181.

Ahmed U. et al. (2018). Compilation Error Repair: For the Student Programs, From the Student Programs. *IEEE/ACM International Conference on Software Engineering*, pp.78-87.

Alzahrani N. et al. (2021). Progression highlighting for programming courses. *Journal of Computing Sciences in Colleges*, Vol. 36, pp.17-23.

Chowdhary S. et al. (2020). Debugging and detecting numerical errors in computation with posits. *Proc. of the 41st ACM SIGPLAN Conference on Programming Language Design and Implementation*, pp. 731-746.

Gao Q. et al. (2018). CoBOT: Static C/C++ Bug Detection in the Presence of Incomplete Code. *Proc. of the IEEE/ACM 26th International Conference on Program Comprehension*, Vol.ICPC'18, No.26, pp.385-388.

Goto T. et al. (2019). Debugging Support in Programming Education. *Transactions of the Institute of Systems Control and Information Engineers*, Vol.32, No.6, pp.249-255.

Gupta R. et al. (2017). DeepFix: fixing common C language errors by deep learning. *Proc. of the Thirty-First AAAI Conference on Artificial Intelligence*, pp.1345-1351.

Gupta R. et al. (2019). Deep Reinforcement Learning for Syntactic Error Repair in Student Programs. *The Thirty-Third AAAI Conference on Artificial Intelligence (AAAI-19)*, pp.930-937.

Ichimura S. et al. (2013). A Trial to Support Understanding a Programming Exercise Class. *IPSJ Journal*, Vol.54, No.12, pp.2518-2527.

Kazemitabaar M. et al. (2024). CodeAid: Evaluating a Classroom Deployment of an LLM-based Programming Assistant that Balances Student and Educator Needs. *Proc. of the 2024 CHI conference on human factors in computing systems.*

McBroom J. et al. (2021). Progress Networks as a Tool for Analysing Student Programming Difficulties. *Proc. of the 23rd Australasian Computing Education Conference*, pp.158-167.

Pankiewicz M. et al. (2024). Navigating Compiler Errors with AI Assistance – A study of GPT Hints in an Introductory Programming Course. *Proc. of the 2024 on Innovation and Technology in Computer Science Education*, V. 1, pp.94-100.

Phung T. et al. (2023). Generating High-Precision Feedback for Programming Syntax Errors using Large Language Models. *Proc. of 16th International Conference Educational Data Mining (EDM 2023).*

Sasaki K. et al. (2024). A Proposal for a Virtual Teaching Assistant Utilizing Generative AI to Support Programming Exercises. *Proc. of the 41st JSSST Annual Conference*, pp.2b-2-R.

Urakami S. et al. (2020). Automatic Detection of Programming Learners' Stumbling Blocks. *IPSJ SIG Technical Reports*, Vol.2020-CE-154, No.4, pp.1-8.

Watanabe K. et al. (2025). TrackThinkDashboard: Understanding Student Self-Regulated Learning in Programming Study. *International Journal of Activity and Behavior Computing*, Vol.1, pp.1-17.

Zhang A. et al. (2023). VizProg: Identifying Misunderstandings By Visualizing Students' Coding Progress. *Proc. of the 2023 CHI Conference on Human Factors in Computing Systems*, No.596, pp.1-16.

ELOGQI: AN APPROACH FOR IMPROVING EVENT LOG QUALITY

Khouloud Guizani[1] and Sonia Ayachi Ghannouchi[2]
[1]*University of Sousse, Higher Institute of Computer Science and Communication Technologies, Tunisia*
[2]*RIADI-GDL Laboratory -Manouba University, Tunisia*

ABSTRACT

For organizations that want to define and measure their progress toward their goals, evaluating process performance is an ongoing challenge. We'll be looking at the quality of the data used in this process. Our goal is to specifically study process performance by looking in-depth at the event log to get a valid result. This study looks at different issues that can appear in an event log and proposes a meta-model to represent these issues and how they relate to the main concepts that make it up. Our work focuses on the issues defined in our meta-model to propose plugins that detect and correct these issues. Our proposed meta-model and the adopted plugins are an addition to existing related work. We defined each plugin using pseudocode and a textual description. In this article, we validate the detection part through ProM plugins developed on Eclipse.

KEYWORDS

Business Process Modelling, Process-Mining Techniques, Data Quality, Log File Quality

1. INTRODUCTION

Business process execution involves implementing and managing organizational workflows, including their deployment, monitoring, and optimization. An event log captures timestamped records generated during process execution, with each entry documenting a specific activity. However, process mining analyzes these logs to improve process models by revealing how processes actually operate in practice. In this context, the objective of our work is to study more specifically the performance of discovery processes and the accuracy of discovered models through a thorough study of event logs in order to obtain a valid execution result. This study verifies the different problems that can appear in an event log. The remainder of this paper is organized as follows: the second section represents the background. In the third section we introduce some existing work related to our subject. Section four describes our proposed approach. In section five, we present the validation part. Finally, we conclude this paper by summarizing our solution.

2. BACKGROUND

2.1 Process Mining

Process mining is a relatively young research discipline that sits between machine learning and data mining on the one hand and process modeling and analysis on the other hand. The idea of process mining is to discover, monitor and improve real processes by extracting knowledge from event logs readily available in today's systems (Aalst & Carmona,2022). The three primary techniques are process discovery, conformance checking, and process enhancement. These three techniques form a thorough approach for understanding, monitoring, and improving business processes (Ghasemi & Amyot,2020). In fact, whenever possible, process mining techniques use extra information such as the resource executing or initiating the activity, the timestamp of the event, or data elements recorded with the event.

2.2 Event Log

Event logs are the main data source for Process Mining. They are the objective traces of process activities and are essential for an accurate Process Mining analysis. Event data can be originated from many sources and in different formats, including database systems, transaction logs, ERP systems, APIs, CSV files, and spreadsheets. An event log can be seen as a collection of cases and a case can be seen as a trace/sequence of events. Each event is typically time stamped and includes additional information such as the source of the event, its severity and any relevant data associated with the event (Manyika et al, 2011).

2.3 Event Log Quality Dimensions

For process models and mining process, quality measures are generally considered as measuring one of the four quality dimensions: adequacy, accuracy, simplicity and generalization. The adequacy measures indicate to what extent the model can reproduce the behavior of the log file. The accuracy measures the quantity of the model used to reproduce the behavior of the log file. The dimension of simplicity considers that the simpler models are of better quality. The generalization measures if the model is applicable to more than the current sample. Unlike statistical learning approaches where metrics aspire to represent the overall quality of the model, in process mining, the quality of the model is generally presented as a means of making design compromises compared to those presented quality dimensions (Burke et al, 2024).

2.4 ProM: Process Mining Tool

ProM is an extensible framework that supports a wide variety of process mining techniques in the form of plug-ins. ProM is a generic open-source framework where various process mining algorithms have been implemented (Buijs, 2010). It provides a platform to users and developers of process mining algorithms that is easy to use and easy to extend (Process Mining Group, 2016). The language in which these algorithms are implemented is Java. In most cases, the starting input for ProM is an event log, preferably in XES format which nowadays becomes a standard (Verbeek et al, 2010). Furthermore, it can also load process model definitions in a wide variety of formats.

3. RELATED WORK

This section outlines the principal studies that examine the interconnections among BPM, business processes, data quality, log files, and process performance. By analyzing these contributions, we aim to clarify the research landscape and define the positioning of our work.

Fischer et al (2020) proposes an automated method to detect and measure timestamp-related issues in event logs. The study introduces 15 metrics covering four abstraction levels (event, activity, trace, log) and four quality dimensions (accuracy, completeness, consistency, uniqueness). Implemented as a ProM prototype and tested on three real event logs with expert input, this approach enables systematic improvement of timestamp quality during process mining data preparation.

Ambe (2023) presents a framework to evaluate timestamp quality in event logs, combining eleven quality dimensions and four levels of data issues identified from an extensive literature review. The twelve derived metrics enable a quantitative assessment of event log quality and support informed data cleaning to improve process mining outcomes.

Kherbouche et al (2016) proposes a qualitative model which aims to assess the quality of event logs before applying process mining algorithms. The goal is to give process mining practitioners an overview of the quality of event logs. The evaluation of the root level depends on the evaluation of quality dimensions lying on the subsequent level. These include Complexity, Accuracy, Consistency, and Completeness. Each quality dimension of second level is devoted to a set of quality attributes for their precise evaluation. Finally, at the lower level, are the metrics which aim to capture a specific aspect of quality attributes.

Ziolkowski et al (2020) presents an Event log Quality Pointer (ElogQP), a tool to detect data quality violations in an event log. Data quality issues significantly impact the process discovery result. Thus, ElogQP represents an essential step towards improved process discovery. The tool allows to detect event log imperfection patterns and to classify the data violations according to data quality levels as specified in the process mining manifesto. Beside this, a comparison between two event logs with respect to data quality violations is supported.

Dakic et al (2023) gives an insight into the real application of preprocessing techniques by surveying process mining researchers and practitioners. The main research dimensions, i.e., event log data quality issues and categories of preprocessing techniques, were defined based on a systematic literature review and previous work. The theoretical contribution can be seen through reviews of data quality issues in process mining and the systematic literature review of applied preprocessing techniques.

Bántay & Abonyi (2023) proposes a frequent pattern mining based method for log file partitioning, enabling parallel process mining. The key idea is that frequent pattern mining can identify clustered events and generate sublogs of overlapping subprocesses. Through log file preprocessing, more compact and interpretable process patterns can be identified.

Existing research on event log quality suffers from several weaknesses, including the lack of a unified meta-model to describe issues, the use of fragmented solutions, and a lack of clear documentation for existing tools. Our ELogQI project directly addresses these shortcomings by introducing a comprehensive yet modular approach. First, we propose a conceptual meta-model that formalizes quality problems such as Missing, imprecision, and inaccuracy. Second, to overcome the fragmented nature of existing solutions, we developed a suite of ProM plugins, each targeting a specific detection and correction problem, ensuring a complete methodological approach. Finally, we enhance reproducibility and transparency by providing a detailed textual description and clear pseudocode for each plugin, which facilitates understanding and adoption within the scientific community.

4. PROPOSED APPROACH

Figure 1 illustrates an overview of our proposed approach, termed Event Log Quality Improvement (ELogQI). A business process is represented by a model, whose execution generates a log file composed of several cases. Each case consists of events described by attributes such as activities and timestamps. The quality of business process models is inherently dependent on the quality of their associated log files. In fact, event logs play a pivotal role in process improvement, as they can be mined to extract valuable insights that support optimization. Consequently, our research emphasizes enhancing the quality of each concept that constitutes event logs.

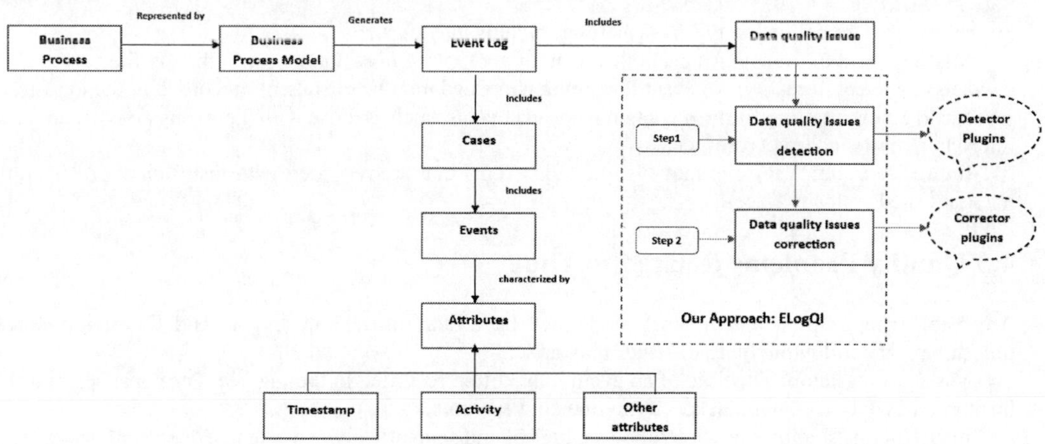

Figure 1. Proposed approach ELogQI

The diagram in figure 2 represents a meta-model regrouping the different event log concepts such as case, activity, event, time, and attributes as well as the problems corresponding to each of them.

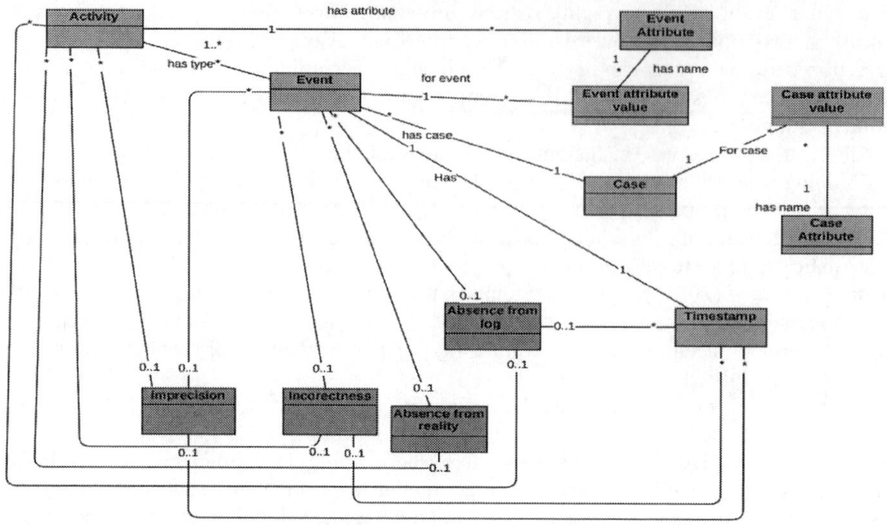

Figure 2. Meta-model of log file concepts and corresponding problems

4.1 Quality Problems Related to An Activity

For each activity, the following potential problems can be identified:

-Missing activity in the log: Mandatory activities absent from the log, compromising process semantics.

-Missing activity in reality: The log file may contain an activity that, in reality, is not feasible and does not align with the correct process semantics.

-Incorrect activity: typically identified through expert validation.

-Imprecise activity: Ambiguous activities, such as repeated identical activities or vaguely named activities that lack specificity.

4.2 Quality Problems Related to an Event

For each event, the following types of quality problems may occur:

-Missing event in the log: An event that actually took place may not appear in the log file.

-Missing event in reality: An event that never happened may be mistakenly recorded in the log file.

-Incorrect event: A log file may contain incorrect events, such as those with the wrong activity, an inaccurate timestamp, or an incorrect resource.

-Imprecise event: A log file may also include events that are recorded with insufficient precision (events not associated with any trace).

4.3 Quality Problems Related to Time

An event occurs within a time interval defined by a start timestamp and an end timestamp. Regarding timestamps, the following types of issues may arise:

-Missing timestamp: The time of an event may not be recorded in the log file. For instance, an order may be marked as delivered without specifying the delivery time.

-Incorrect timestamp: A process follows a logical and semantically consistent sequence of activities, which should be reflected in their timestamps.

-Imprecise timestamp: Dates can be represented in different formats depending on the country, such as the little-endian format (dd-mm-yyyy) or the big-endian format (yyyy-mm-dd). Using multiple formats within the same log file creates inconsistencies.

5. VALIDATION

To validate our work, we developed our own plugin on Eclipse IDE (java IDE) to then integrate it into ProM tool, a process mining tool based on various process mining techniques in the form of plug-ins. We developed plugins to detect and correct the problems mentioned in our metamodel (see Table1). To provide a clearer understanding of the functionality of these plugins, the following section presents each plugin using pseudocode accompanied by a descriptive text.

Table 1. Proposed plugins

Detection plugins	**Correction plugins**
Missing Timestamp Detection Plugin	Missing Timestamp Correction Plugin
Missing Activity Detection Plugin	Missing Activity Correction Plugin
Missing Event Detection Plugin	Missing Event Correction Plugin
Incorrect Timestamp Detection Plugin	Incorrect Timestamp Correction Plugin
Incorrect Activity Detection Plugin	Incorrect Activity Correction Plugin
Incorrect Event Detection Plugin	Incorrect Event Correction Plugin
Imprecise Timestamp Detection Plugin	Imprecise Timestamp Correction Plugin
Imprecise Activity Detection Plugin	Imprecise Activity Correction Plugin
Imprecise Event Detection Plugin	Imprecise Event Correction Plugin

In this paper, we focused on plugins for detecting quality problems in an event log, more precisely we detailed the following plugins: Missing Timestamp Detection Plugin, Incorrect Activity Detection Plugin, Imprecise Event Detection Plugin. For correction plugins, we based them on defined rules.

5.1 Algorithm 1: Missing Timestamp Detection Plugin

The table 2 represents a description for the plugin: "Missing Timestamp Detection Plugin".

Table 2. Missing timestamp detection plugin

Short Description	**Pseudocode**

This plugin detects events in an XES log that lack the attribute time:timestamp.
It iterates over all traces and events, counts the total number of events and those with missing timestamps, and generates a report listing the identifiers of problematic events along with their corresponding traces.
	INPUT: XLog log
	OUTPUT: Textual report
	totalEvents ← 0
	missingCount ← 0
	missingEvents ← []
	FOR each trace IN log:
	  traceName ← trace.concept:name OR "Trace_index"
	    FOR each event IN trace:
	      totalEvents++
	      timestamp ← event.time:timestamp
	      eventName ← event.concept:name OR "Event_index"
	
	      IF timestamp IS NULL:
	        missingCount++
	        missingEvents.ADD("Trace: traceName | Event: eventName")
	RETURN "Total events: totalEvents; Missing timestamps: missingCount; List: missingEvents"

5.2 Algorithm 2: Imprecise Event Detection Plugin

The table 3 represents a description for the plugin: "Imprecise Event Detection Plugin".

Table 3. Imprecise event detection plugin

Short Description	**Pseudocode**
This plugin detects imprecise events in an XLog (XES event log). These are events not associated with any trace—thereby problematic for case correlation. The plugin provides a report with: • Total number of events processed • Number of imprecise events (those lacking a Case ID) • Detailed list of each such event, indicating the trace (or its index) and the event's position	totalEvents ← 0 impreciseEvents ← 0 issues ← [] FOR each trace IN log: traceId ← trace.getAttribute("concept:name") OR "Trace_index" FOR each event IN trace ORDERED BY event index: totalEvents++ caseId ← event.getAttribute("concept:name:case") // or appropriate case attribute key IF caseId IS NULL OR EMPTY: impreciseEvents++ issues.ADD("Trace: " + traceId + " | Event #" + eventIndex + " → Missing Case ID") RETURN "Total events: " + totalEvents + "; Imprecise events (missing Case ID): " + impreciseEvents + "; Details: " + issues

5.3 Execution Results

We are currently in the process of developing our proposed Eclipse plugins, and while the implementation is still ongoing, we have created mockups for the plugin: Missing timestamp detection to better evaluate the effectiveness of our approach. The following sections demonstrate the execution results of our proposed plugins. Figure 3 presents the list of plugins along with the description, input parameters, and output results of the selected plugin. Those results were obtained with an event log adapted from the healthcare field (Research Data, 2017).

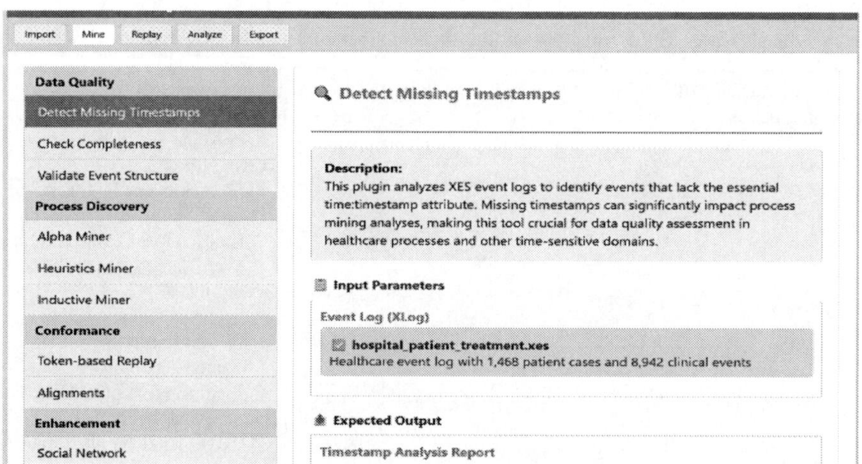

Figure 3. List of plugins interface

Figure 4 illustrates the list of events containing anomalies (events with missing timestamps) and indicates that a total of 8942 events were processed, with 98.6% containing valid timestamps, thereby ensuring a high overall data quality. However, 127 events (1.4%) lack timestamps, which represents a potential source of bias that may compromise the accuracy of subsequent temporal process analyses.

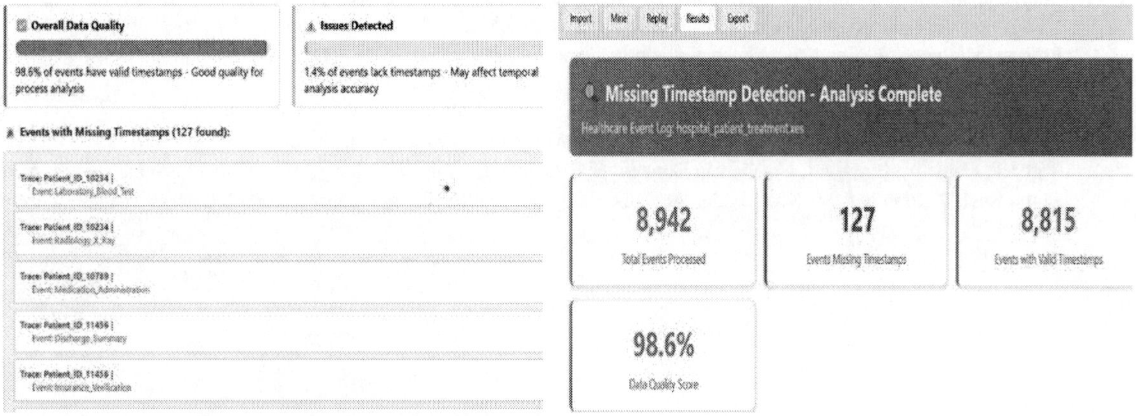

Figure 4. List of Events with missing timestamp and analysis results

As demonstrated by the plugin outputs, the proposed approach produces visualizations characterized by high readability and interpretability.

6. CONCLUSION

Our research effectively addresses the persistent challenge organizations face in evaluating process performance by focusing on the critical issue of data quality within event logs. We have successfully designed and proposed a meta-model that systematically represents the various data quality issues that can plague event logs. By defining and developing a set of plugins, we have provided a practical solution for both detecting and correcting these identified issues. As future work, the output of these algorithms (and their corresponding plugins) will serve as the entry point for correction-oriented algorithms and plugins, enabling the automated repair of the detected anomalies. As future work, numerous event logs will be considered for better plugins validation, with a comparative analysis. Also, the output of these algorithms (and the associated plugins) will serve as the entry point for correction-oriented algorithms and plugins, enabling the automated repair of the detected anomalies.

REFERENCES

Ambe, R. (2023). "Classification and quantification of timestamp data quality issues and its impact on data quality outcome". Campus Oefenplein-Etterbeek Ringgold Standard Institution, Solvay Business School, Vrije Universiteit Brussel.

Bántay, L., & Abonyi, J. (2023). "Frequent pattern mining-based log file partition for process mining". ELSEVIER science direct.

Buijs, J. C. A. M. (2010). "Mapping data sources to XES in a generic way".

Burke, A. T., Leemans, S. J. J., Wynn, M. T., van der Aalst, W. M. P., & ter Hofstede, A. H.M. (2024). "Chance for models to show their quality: Stochastic process model-log dimensions".

Dakic, D., Stefanovic, D., Vuckovic, T., Zizakov, M., & Stevanov, B. (2023). "Event Log Data Quality Issues and Solutions".

Fischer, D.A., Goel, K., Andrews, R., van Dun, C.G.J., Wynn, M.T., & Röglinger, M. (2020). "Enhancing Event Log Quality: Detecting and Quantifying Timestamp Imperfections". University of Bayreuth, Project Group Business & Information Systems Engineering of the Fraunhofer FIT.

Ghasemi, M., & Amyot, D. (2020). "From event logs to goals: a systematic literature review of goal-oriented process mining".

Kherbouche, M. O., Laga, N., & Masse, P.-A. (2016). "Towards a better assessment of event logs quality". IEEE Symposium Series on Computational Intelligence (SSCI).

Manyika, J., Chui, M., Brown, B., Bughin, J., Dobbs, R., Roxburgh, C., & Byers, A. (2011). "A. Big Data: The Next Frontier for Innovation, Competition, and Productivity". McKinsey Global Institute.

Process Mining Group and the Match Computer Science Department of the TU/e Process mining website. (2016). http://www.processmining.org.

Research Data. (2017). "https://data.4tu.nl/articles/dataset/Hospital_Billing_-_Event_Log/12705113/1".

van der Aalst, W. M. P., & Carmona, J. (2022). "Process Mining Handbook, Springer Cham".

Verbeek, H. M. W., Buijs, J. C. A. M., van Dongen, B. F., & van der Aalst, W. M. P. (2010) "XES, XESame, and ProM 6".

Ziolkowski, T., Brandt, L., & Koschmider, A. (2020). "ElogQP: An Event log Quality Pointer". Process Analytics Group.

FAKE NEWS DETECTION: GAN-BASED DATA AUGMENTATION APPROACH

Eya Maazoun[1], Amal Rekik[2] and Salma Jamoussi[1, 2]
[1]Higher Institute of Computer Science and Multimedia of Sfax (ISIMS), Tunisia
[2]Multimedia InfoRmation systems and Advanced Computing Laboratory (MIRACL), Sfax, Tunisia

ABSTRACT

Social media has made it easier for fake news to spread quickly, making it hard to tell which information is true or false. While machine learning techniques have shown promise in automating fake news detection, their effectiveness is often limited by small or imbalanced datasets. In this paper we propose a novel approach that leverages Generative Adversarial Networks (GANs) for data augmentation to enhance fake news classification. For this purpose, we use BERT to generate contextual embeddings at both word and phrase levels, and train GANs to produce realistic synthetic embeddings. These synthetic samples are then combined with the original dataset to train a binary classifier. Experimental results on the LIAR dataset demonstrate that augmenting the training data with GAN-generated embeddings significantly improves classification performance compared to models trained without augmentation.

KEYWORDS

Fake News Detection, Embeddings, BERT, GAN, Data Augmentation, Text Classification

1. INTRODUCTION

In recent years, social media platforms have become the primary source of news for millions of users worldwide. While they have made sharing information faster and more accessible, they have also contributed significantly to the rapid spread of fake news. This uncontrolled spread of false information across social platforms makes it increasingly difficult to manually detect and verify the authenticity of news content.

Fake news is most of the time intentional and can pose serious challenges at multiple levels, affecting not only individuals but also communities and entire countries (Hu et al., 2024). State-of-the-art approaches such as those proposed in (Haumahu et al., 2021), (Karnyoto et al., 2022) and (Alghamdi et al., 2024) have shown promising results in detecting fake news. However, significant challenges remain as fake news strategies continue to evolve and become more sophisticated. In fact, it usually relies on emotionally manipulative techniques to provoke outrage, fear, or sympathy, and then encourage interaction, so that algorithmic recommendation systems increase its virality (Zimmer et al., 2019), making fake news more difficult to distinguish and enabling it to spread even faster than real ones. What makes fake news detection even more challenging is the lack of high-quality, balanced training data. Most available datasets are either too small or biased toward specific topics, sources, or languages, which limits model performance and its ability to generalize.

In this paper, we propose an innovative approach based on generative models for fake news detection. We used a generative adversarial network (GAN) to generate synthetic embeddings based on word and phrase representations. These embeddings are used to augment and balance the original training dataset and a separate convolutional neural network (CNN) classifier is then trained on this enriched dataset to effectively distinguish between real and fake news content. We evaluate the impact of data augmentation by comparing the CNN's performance with and without GAN's generated embeddings.

The rest of this paper is organized as follows. Section 2 presents a review of related work in fake news detection. Section 3 details our proposed method and model architecture. Section 4 discusses the experimental results, and Section 5 provides further discussion. Finally, Section 6 concludes the paper and outlines future perspectives.

2. RELATED WORK

Fake news detection is a widely studied classification task. In this section, we highlight key approaches from literature. Early studies focused on traditional machine learning methods, relying on manual feature extraction methods such as TF-IDF, bag-of-words, or n-grams. Authors in (Shaikh and Patil, 2020) used TF-IDF textual representations with binary classification models like Multinomial Naïve Bayes, Linear Support Vector Machine (SVM), and the Passive Aggressive classifier. These models, applied to a preprocessed and balanced dataset, showed competitive results in detecting fake news. In (Haumahu et al., 2021) TF-IDF representations were also used with an Extreme Gradient Boosting algorithm to improve generalization performance and reduce overfitting.

Recent approaches based on deep learning models use word embeddings like Word2Vec, GloVe, or contextual embeddings like BERT to encode the semantics of texts. Several studies have focused on CNN-based architectures, such as OPCNN-FAKE (Saleh et al., 2021), TI-CNN (Yang et al., 2018), and MCred (Verma et al., 2023). In (Fang et al., 2019), the authors proposed a self-attention-enhanced cnn model, which can detect fake news based only on content. Attention mechanism helps the model capture relationships between distant words, improving its overall context comprehension. Other studies proposed RNN-based architectures. Authors in (Vyas et al., 2021) used an LSTM-based model to evaluate hotel reviews credibility. The model includes an embedding layer, an LSTM layer, a dropout layer to prevent overfitting, and a final dense layer with a Sigmoid function. The integration of attention mechanisms (Padalko et al., 2024) further improved performance by enabling models to dynamically focus on key parts of the input. More lightweight and efficient alternatives like GRU-based models were proposed in (Karnyoto et al., 2022) for COVID-19–related fake news detection, showing comparable performance to LSTM with reduced training time.

More recently, generative approaches have emerged as a promising direction for fake news detection. One category of studies focuses on redefining the task as a text generation or completion problem, where models learn to predict missing words or generate content that helps identify fake news. (Alghamdi et al., 2024) proposed a GPT-2-based approach that formulates detection as a prompt-based text infilling task. Along similar lines, (Ding, 2024) introduced PLRD, a prompt-based classification framework built on T5, which integrates external entity knowledge into prompt templates to improve model generalization and boost rumor detection performance. Another category employs generative methods to create synthetic data, augmenting existing datasets to enhance model training and robustness. (Wang et al., 2024) introduced LLM-GAN, a two-phase generative strategy that produces adversarial fake news examples, compelling the discriminator to improve continuously through adversarial training. This approach not only enhances the model's ability to detect subtle misinformation patterns but also promotes interpretability by encouraging self-correction through reflective prompting. Finally, (Mridha et al., 2021) presented SeqGAN, a sequential GAN generative adversarial network integrating reinforcement learning and Monte Carlo search to handle the challenge of generating discrete textual data. The model generates realistic news samples that are evaluated by a pretrained BERT-based classifier to distinguish between authentic and synthetic content.

3. PROPOSED METHOD

This section begins with an overview of our proposed method, followed by detailed descriptions of its key components.

3.1 Method Overview

Addressing the limitations of small and imbalanced datasets in fake news detection, our proposed method combines the representational strength of BERT with the generative power of GANs to improve classification performance through a data augmentation approach. BERT is a powerful pre-trained language model that captures semantic meaning based on context, producing rich representations of textual content.

The core idea behind our approach is to generate realistic fake news embeddings that can augment the original training dataset. An overview of the proposed method is illustrated in Figure 1.

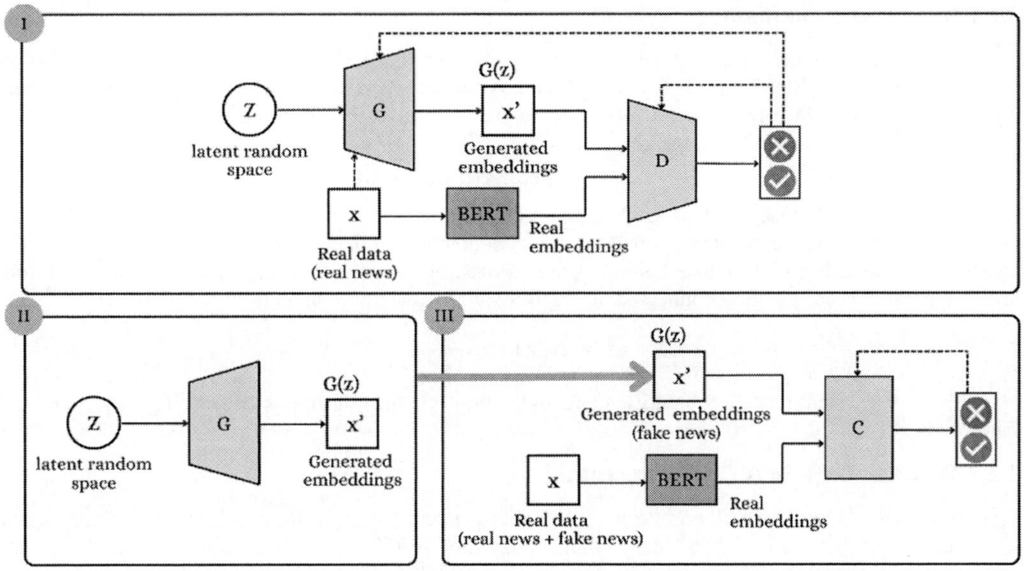

Figure 1. Overview of the proposed method

Our work is based on a Generative Adversarial Network (GAN) that serves as a powerful tool for learning the underlying distribution of real data and generating new realistic samples. These synthetic representations are then used to train a dedicated classifier to better distinguish between fake and real news. To put this into practice, our architecture unfolds in three main steps:

(I) GAN training on real BERT embeddings: The process begins by transforming real news articles into contextual embeddings using BERT. These real embeddings are then used to train a Generative Adversarial Network (GAN), composed of two components: a generator and a discriminator. The generator takes random noise vectors and learns to produce fake embeddings that closely resemble real BERT embeddings. It aims to generate fake representations convincing enough to fool the Discriminator (D), which is simultaneously trained to distinguish between real and synthetic embeddings. This adversarial setup forces the generator to gradually learn to produce embeddings that are increasingly similar to the real ones.

(II) Generating fake embeddings: In this phase, the generator is used independently to produce a diverse set of synthetic embeddings. These embeddings are generated by feeding random noise vectors sampled from the latent space into the trained generator. The output embeddings, while not corresponding to any real news embeddings, exhibit realistic semantic structures and are treated as potential fake news examples. This process helps augment the training dataset, increasing both the quantity and diversity of the data without requiring additional labeled samples.

(III) Final classifier training using both real and synthetic data: This final step involves training a classifier (C) using both real and generated embeddings. This classifier learns to distinguish between fake and real news, benefiting from the increased variability introduced by the GAN.

3.2 GAN Training

To generate synthetic embeddings that effectively augment our training dataset, we experimented with two types of BERT embeddings: word embeddings and phrase embeddings. Word embeddings provide contextualized vector representations for each word in the sentence, capturing the meaning of each word in its specific context., while phrase embeddings offer a single vector representation that encapsulates the overall semantic meaning of the entire phrase. For each embedding type, we developed specific generator and discriminator architectures, detailed in the following sections.

3.2.1 BiGRU Discriminator

For this first discriminator, we adopted a deep recurrent architecture based on Bidirectional Gated Recurrent Units (BiGRUs) to differentiate between real and synthetic word-level embeddings of news content. The input to this model is a sequence X of contextualized word embeddings, either generated by BERT or synthesized by our word embeddings generator:

$$X = [x_1, x_2, \ldots, x_T], \text{ where } x_t \in R^{768}$$

The model is composed of two stacked bidirectional GRU layers that capture contextual dependencies from both directions. Each input sequence is encoded into a hidden representation of size 128 for each direction, resulting in a concatenated hidden state of size 256 for each time step. The final output of the GRU layers is passed through a fully connected layer, followed by a sigmoid activation function:

$$\sigma(z) = \frac{1}{1+e^{-z}}$$

This activation outputs a probability score indicating whether the input embedding sequence is real or fake.

3.2.2 Word Embeddings CNN Generator

The word embeddings generator is designed to map a latent vector z from a low-dimensional space to a sequence of synthetic word embeddings that match the BERT embedding dimensionality. This model's architecture employs a Convolutional Neural Network (CNN) followed by a customized attention mechanism. z is first reshaped, then passed through three successive one-dimensional convolutional layers. Each is followed by a ReLU activation function to introduce non-linearity, defined as:

$$\text{ReLU}(x) = \max(0, x)$$

A self-attention mechanism then refines the output by computing attention weights from query (Q), key (K), and value (V) convolutional projections as follows:

$$\text{Attention}(Q,K,V) = \text{SoftMax}\left(\frac{QK^T}{\sqrt{d_k}}\right)V$$

where d_k is the dimensionality of the key vectors.

3.2.3 MLP Discriminator

To distinguish authentic from synthetic phrase-level embeddings, this discriminator employs a Multilayer Perceptron (MLP) architecture in combination with a predefined multi-head attention mechanism. The input embeddings are first passed through a series of fully connected layers to progressively reduce their dimensionality. These transformed representations are then refined using a predefined multi-head self-attention mechanism which applies multiple heads to capture diverse contextual relationships. Finally, the processed embeddings are passed through a sigmoid activation function to output a probability indicating whether the input is real or fake.

3.2.4 Phrase Embeddings MLP Generator

This discriminator relies on a Multilayer Perceptron (MLP) architecture to generate BERT-like phrase embeddings. The model progressively transforms a low-dimensional latent vector through two multiple fully connected layers, interleaved with a ReLU activation function. The final output is normalized to match the statistical characteristics of real embeddings. This normalization standardizes the output vector x to ensure it has the same scale and distribution as real BERT embeddings. The normalized output x′ is computed as:

$$x' = \frac{x-\mu}{\sqrt{\sigma^2+\epsilon}}$$

where μ is the mean of the elements in x, σ2 is the variance, and ϵ is a small constant added to prevent division by zero.

3.2.5 Training Strategy

To address the common instability issues typically encountered when training a GAN, we adopted a robust training strategy inspired by techniques from recent state-of-the-art works. We adopted an asymmetric update strategy, as proposed in (Zhang et al., 2016) where the generator is updated *k* times for every single discriminator's update. This controlled imbalance prevents the discriminator from overpowering the generator, allowing both networks to improve progressively by reinforcing each other. To this end, we used a standard adversarial loss based on Binary Cross Entropy (BCE), which allows the generator to generate increasingly realistic samples and penalizes the discriminator for misclassifying real and fake inputs. In other words, the generator tries to maximize the probability that the discriminator classifies its outputs as real, while the discriminator tries to minimize its classification error for both real and generated data. This adversarial loss is defined as:

$$\boldsymbol{min_G\ max_D}\ \mathbf{E}_{x\sim P_{real}}[\boldsymbol{logD(x)}] + \mathbf{E}_{z\sim P_z}[\boldsymbol{log}(1 - \boldsymbol{D(G(z))})]$$

where D(x) is the discriminator's estimated probability that input x is real and G(z) is the output of the generator given input noise z.

In addition, the generator's loss includes two regularization penalties to enhance similarity between fake and real news embeddings: a cosine similarity penal $\mathcal{L}_{cos}$ that aligns their directions and an $\mathcal{L}_2$ norm penalty that minimizes Euclidean distance between them. The overall generator loss is formulated as:

$$\mathcal{L}_G = \mathcal{L}_{adv}^G + \lambda\, \mathcal{L}_{cos} + \beta\, \mathcal{L}_2$$

where λ and β are hyperparameters controlling the contribution of each regularization term to the total loss.

The training is performed using the Adam optimizer with the Two Time-Scale Update Rule (TTUR) applying two different learning rates as suggested in (Zhang et al., 2019). TTUR helps stabilize training by assigning a higher learning rate to the discriminator. A faster-updating discriminator provides more reliable gradient feedback, ensuring effective gradient updates and improved generator learning, especially during the early stages of training.

3.3 Classifier

After training the GAN and generating synthetic fake news embeddings, a binary classifier is employed to distinguish between real and fake news. Fake news samples may originate either from the original dataset or be generated by the GAN. For each embedding type, we trained two classifier architectures: one that follows a CNN-based structure, and another that mirrors the corresponding discriminator used during GAN training. For word-level embeddings, the classification input is a sequence of 768-dimensional BERT embeddings. In the CNN-based model, a 1D convolutional layer with a kernel size equal to the embedding's dimension is applied. This kernel slides over the sequence to capture local contextual patterns and relationships between adjacent words. The output of this layer is then passed through a fully connected layer, producing a one-dimensional output activated by a sigmoid function. The second classifier architecture for word-level embeddings is based on BIGRU similar to the discriminator architecture used during GAN training.

To classify news samples based on phrase-level embeddings, two deep learning models were employed. The first is a convolutional model composed of three successive 1D convolutional layers, which progressively reduce the input dimensionality from 768 to 64. The output from the final convolutional layer is then passed through a fully connected linear layer that maps the 64-dimensional representation to a single scalar value. Finally, a sigmoid activation function is applied to produce the output probability score. The other architecture used is an MLP with a predefined multi-head attention mechanism, as previously described.

4. EXPERIMENTAL RESULTS

To train and evaluate our fake news detection model, we utilized the LIAR dataset. Introduced in (Wang W. Y. 2017), this dataset is one of the first large-scale resources for classifying the truthfulness of political statements. It contains 12.836 statements labled into six categories: True, Mostly True, Half True, Barely True, False, and Pants on Fire. In our work, for the purposes of binary classification, we used only the statements labeled True and False which include 2,052 and 2,510 samples respectively.

To evaluate the impact of data augmentation, we conducted a comparative analysis of our classifiers' performance with and without the use of GAN-generated synthetic embeddings. This comparison allowed us to evaluate the effectiveness of synthetic embeddings in improving classification accuracy. We used standard evaluation metrics: accuracy, precision, recall, and F1 score to measure and compare model performance under each setting. Model's hyperparameters were empirically set based on preliminary experiments to ensure a stable training and model's optimal performance. In this section, we also compare the results of our proposed approach with state-of-the-art models to further validate its effectiveness.

4.1 Classifiers Evaluation

To evaluate the effectiveness of our proposed method, we conducted a series of experiments comparing the performance of classifiers trained with and without the GAN-generated embeddings.

In the initial set of experiments, classifiers were trained using only the LIAR dataset without applying any data augmentation. As shown in Table 1, CNN and BiGRU were evaluated using word embeddings. Results show that the BiGRU model slightly outperforms the CNN model in terms of both accuracy and F1-Measure.

Table 1. Fake news detection using words embeddings before data augmentation

Classifier	Accuracy	Precision	Recall	F1-Measure
CNN	60.04 %	0.56	0.58	0.57
BIGRU	61.38 %	0.59	0.59	0.59

For phrase-level embeddings, the results in Table 2 show that the CNN classifier achieves slightly higher accuracy than the MLP model. However, the MLP model demonstrates a marginally better F1-score, indicating a more balanced trade-off between precision and recall. When comparing these results to those using word embeddings in Table 1, we observe that accuracy remains similar across both embedding types, while the F1-scores are lower for phrase embeddings.

Table 2. Fake news detection using phrase embeddings before data augmentation

Classifier	Accuracy	Precision	Recall	F1-Measure
CNN	60.27 %	0.58	0.44	0.50
MLP	59.38 %	0.56	0.48	0.51

For the second set of experiments, we augmented the dataset using our GAN-based approach and retrained the classifiers. **Table 3** presents the performance of the models using word embeddings. Both CNN and BiGRU models experienced a drop in accuracy, Both CNN and BiGRU models experienced a drop in accuracy. Although accuracy decreased, F1-Measures improved. The BiGRU model obtained the highest F1-score of 0.63.

Table 3. Fake news detection using words embeddings after data augmentation

Classifier	Accuracy	Precision	Recall	F1-Measure
CNN	54.69 %	0.50	0.77	0.61
BIGRU	54.46 %	0.50	0.87	0.63

Table 4 shows the results using phrase embeddings after augmentation. In this configuration, the CNN model achieved the highest accuracy of 61.38%, while the MLP model obtained the best F1-score of 0.64.

Table 4. Fake news detection using phrase embeddings after data augmentation

Classifier	Accuracy	Precision	Recall	F1-Measure
CNN	61.38 %	0.56	0.67	0.61
MLP	58.04 %	0.53	0.80	0.64

Overall, the experiments demonstrate the effectiveness of our GAN-based augmentation strategy. Although accuracy occasionally declined after augmentation, F1-scores showed consistent improvement. The CNN model achieved the highest accuracy of 61.38% using phrase embeddings after augmentation, while the MLP model obtained the highest F1-score of 0.64 with the same configuration.

4.2 Comparative Evaluation

To further evaluate the effectiveness of our proposed method, we compare its performance with several existing fake news detection models. We choose (Khan et al., 2021) as a reference study because it also employs the LIAR dataset for binary classification, aligning closely with the goals of our study. While their models rely on 100-dimensional pre-trained GloVe embeddings, our approach utilizes contextualized BERT embeddings to capture deeper semantic representations. Both studies adopt similar experimental settings, including the ADAM optimizer, binary cross-entropy loss, and a sigmoid activation function in the output layer.

The reference models include a CNN architecture with convolution and max pooling layers, LSTM and Bi-LSTM architectures with unidirectional and bidirectional memory, respectively, a C-LSTM combining convolution and LSTM layers, a HAN model employing hierarchical attention at both word and sentence levels and Convolutional HAN that incorporates convolutional layers before attention to enhance feature extraction. As shown in Table 5, our method achieves higher accuracy and F1-score compared to all of these existing models.

Table 5. Comparison with other existing approaches

	Accuracy	F1-Measure
Proposed method	**0.61**	**0.61**
CNN	0.58	0.58
LSTM	0.54	0.38
Bi-LSTM	0.58	0.57
C-LSTM	0.54	0.38
HAN	0.57	0.56
Conv-HAN	0.59	0.59

5. DISCUSSION

Our fake news detection method based on data augmentation presented in this paper has demonstrated its effectiveness to better detection performance. This efficacy mainly comes from using contextual BERT embeddings, which allow the GAN to generate more stable representations. In fact, generating synthetic embeddings rather than producing news text directly avoids common problems in text generation such as grammatical errors, incoherent sentences, or irrelevant content, while still enriching the training data with meaningful variations. As a result, the classifier benefits from these new data samples to improve its ability to generalize. The second significant advantage of generating embeddings is that it is impossible to risk spreading more fake news, since embeddings are not interpretable as readable text.

Moreover, our experiments show that data augmentation using phrase-level embeddings outperforms augmentation using word-level embeddings. This suggests that while word embeddings may capture certain predictive patterns, they can also introduce noise or lose contextual nuance. On the other hand, phrase embeddings retain more contextual information, leading to more coherent and informative augmentation.

Despite the encouraging results, this method is not without its limitations. One major difficulty is training the GAN, which remains complex and often unstable. Additionally, it's hard to determine how well the different parts of the GAN are performing since there are no metrics to evaluate the quality of the generated embeddings. Another limitation is that the performance gains remain relatively small, which can be attributed to the fact that our work focused mainly on data augmentation. We worked on improving the quality of training data rather than on improving the model architecture. A combination of these two aspects will be taken into consideration for further improvements, which we expect will lead to more significant performance gains.

6. CONCLUSION

In this paper, we proposed a novel approach for fake news detection that leverages Generative Adversarial Networks (GANs) for data augmentation, combined with contextual embeddings generated by BERT. After training GANs to produce realistic word and phrase embeddings, we enriched the training dataset and improved the performance of a CNN-based fake news classifier. Experimental results on the LIAR dataset demonstrated that data augmentation using phrase-level embeddings significantly enhances classification performance, achieving higher accuracy and F1-scores compared to models trained without augmentation.

Moreover, we plan to explore alternative architectures such as transformer-based models like T5 as a generator to produce BERT like embeddings. We also aim to improve control over the generation process by using a structured latent vector z as an input for the generator instead of a random one. Furthermore, we intend to apply the same GAN-based data augmentation strategy to other modalities, specifically images and videos.

REFERENCES

Alghamdi J. et al., (2024). *Cross-Domain Fake News Detection Using a Prompt-Based Approach.* Future Internet, Vol. 16, No. 8, pp 286.

Ding T., (2024). *A Rumors Detection Method Using T5-Based Prompt Learning.* International Journal of Data Warehousing and Mining (IJDWM), Vol. 20, No.1, pp. 1-19.

Fang Y. et al., (2019). *Self multi-head attention-based convolutional neural networks for fake news detection.* PloS one, Vol. 14, No. 9, p. 0222713.

Haumahu J. P. et al., (2021). *Fake news classification for indonesian news using extreme gradient boosting (xgboost).* IOP Conference Series: Materials Science and Engineering. Vol. 1098. No. 5. p. 052081.

Hu B. et al., (2024). *An overview of fake news detection: From a new perspective.* Fundamental Research, Vol. 5, No. 1, pp. 332-346.

Karnyoto A. S. et al., (2022). *Transfer learning and GRU-CRF augmentation for COVID-19 fake news detection,* Computer Science and Information Systems, Vol. 19, No. 2, pp. 639-658.

Khan J. Y. et al., (2021). *A benchmark study of machine learning models for online fake news detection.* Machine Learning with Applications, vol. 4, p. 100032.

Mridha M. F. et al., (2021). *A comprehensive review on fake news detection with deep learning.* IEEE access, vol. 9, pp. 156151-156170.

Padalko H. et al., (2024). *A novel approach to fake news classification using LSTM-based deep learning models,* Frontiers in Big Data, vol. 6, p. 1320800.

Saleh H. et al., (2021). *OPCNN-FAKE: Optimized Convolutional Neural Network for Fake News Detection.* IEEE Access, Vol. 9, pp. 129471-129489.

Shaikh J. and Patil, R., (2020). Fake news detection using machine learning. *2020 IEEE International symposium on sustainable energy, signal processing and cyber security (iSSSC).* Odisha, India, pp. 1-5.

Verma P.K. et al., (2023). *MCred: multi-modal message credibility for fake news detection using BERT and CNN.* Journal of Ambient Intelligence and Humanized Computing, Vol. 14, No.8, pp. 10617-10629.

Vyas P. et al., (2021). *Fake news detection on the web: An LSTM-based approach. AMCIS 2021 Proceedings.* Virtual.

Wang W. Y. (2017). *liar, liar pants on fire": A new benchmark dataset for fake news detection.* arXiv preprint arXiv:1705.00648.

Wang Y. et al., (2024). *LLM-GAN: Construct Generative Adversarial Network Through Large Language Models For Explainable Fake News Detection.* arXiv preprint arXiv:2409.01787.

Yang Y. et al., (2018). *TI-CNN: Convolutional neural networks for fake news detection.* arXiv preprint arXiv:1806.00749.

Zhang Y. et al., (2016). *Generating Text via Adversarial Training.* NIPS workshop on Adversarial Training. Vol. 21, pp. 21-32.

Zhang H. et al., (2019). Self-attention generative adversarial networks. *International conference on machine learning.* California, USA, pp. 7354-7363.

Zimmer F. et al., (2019). *Fake news in social media: Bad algorithms or biased users?* Journal of Information Science Theory and Practice, Vol. 7, No. 2, pp. 40-53.

MID-LEVEL TRANSFORMER FUSION OF LOCAL AND GLOBAL FEATURES FOR REMOTE SENSING SCENE CLASSIFICATION

Vian Abdulmajeed, Khaled Jouini and Ouajdi Korbaa
University of Sousse, MARS Research Lab, LR17ES05, ISITCom
4011 H. Sousse, Tunisia

ABSTRACT

Accurate remote sensing scene classification requires the effective integration of fine-grained local details with broader global context. This paper proposes a novel mid-level fusion framework that leverages a Transformer Encoder to dynamically fuse these complementary features. Our dual-branch architecture extracts local details using EfficientNet-B0, enhanced with a Convolutional Block Attention Module (CBAM), while capturing global context through a Swin Tiny Transformer. By integrating these features at an intermediate stage, the model learns complex interactions between local and global representations. The proposed approach achieves highly competitive accuracy, attaining 98.67% accuracy on EuroSAT and 96.06% on RESISC45, outperforming several recent methods, while maintaining a practical model size. Ablation studies validate the contributions of the Transformer Encoder and CBAM, demonstrating their synergistic effect on feature refinement.

KEYWORDS

Remote Sensing Scene Classification, Transformer-Based Fusion, Swin Transformer, CBAM, Channel Attention, Spatial Attention

1. INTRODUCTION

Remote sensing scene classification, the automated interpretation of satellite imagery to categorize semantic regions (e.g. urban areas, forests), plays a pivotal role in applications such as environmental monitoring, urban planning, and disaster response (Ahmed et al., 2024). This task requires models to effectively integrate fine-grained local details (e.g., textures, edges) with broader global context (e.g., spatial relationships, scene structure)—capturing both the "trees" and the "forest"—to accurately interpret complex and diverse landscapes. However, achieving this balance remains a significant challenge due to the inherent complexity, variability, and scale of Earth observation data (Ahmed, Jouini and Korbaa, 2025).

Convolutional Neural Networks (CNNs) excel at hierarchical local feature extraction through their layered architecture. However, the localized receptive fields of CNNs limit their ability to capture long-range dependencies, which are crucial for understanding global scene context (Dosovitskiy et al., 2021). Vision Transformers (ViTs) (Dosovitskiy et al., 2021), such as the Swin Transformer (Liu et al., 2021), address this limitation by leveraging self-attention mechanisms to model interactions between any two regions of an image, thereby capturing global relationships. While ViTs excel at global reasoning, they often struggle to preserve fine-grained local details, which are essential for distinguishing between visually similar scenes (Xiao et al., 2021). This trade-off has motivated the development of hybrid CNN-ViT models (Zhang et al., 2022), which aim to combine the strengths of both paradigms. Yet, many existing hybrid architectures rely on simplistic early or late fusion strategies (Rubab et al., 2024), failing to fully exploit the complementary nature of local and global representations. This underscores the need for more sophisticated interaction mechanisms that can dynamically integrate features while maintaining computational efficiency.

To address these challenges, we propose a novel dual-branch architecture featuring mid-level fusion with a 2-layer Transformer Encoder. The first branch employs an EfficientNet-B0 backbone (Tan and Le, 2019), enhanced with a Convolutional Block Attention Module (CBAM) (Woo et al., 2018), to extract and refine local features. Simultaneously, the second branch leverages a Swin Tiny Transformer (Liu et al., 2021) to capture global context through its hierarchical self-attention mechanism. Crucially, instead of relying on naive fusion strategies, we introduce a Transformer Encoder at an intermediate stage to model complex, context-aware interactions between local and global features. This mid-level fusion approach enables the model to learn a unified representation that captures both fine-grained details and broader contextual information.

We conduct extensive experimental validation and ablation studies on two widely used remote sensing datasets: EuroSAT (Helber et al., 2019) and RESISC45 (Cheng, Han and Lu, 2017). Our results demonstrate the efficacy of the proposed architecture, achieving highly competitive accuracy and outperforming several recent methods while maintaining a significantly smaller model size than alternatives like μ2Net (Gesmundo and Dean, 2022). This efficiency makes our model particularly suitable for real-world deployment in resource-constrained environments.

The remainder of this paper is organized as follows. Section 2 reviews related work. Section 3 details our proposed architecture and the Transformer-based fusion mechanism. Section 4 presents experimental results and comparisons with existing approaches, along with an ablation study. Finally, Section 5 concludes the paper and discusses future research directions.

2. RELATED WORK

Remote sensing scene classification has evolved significantly, progressing from handcrafted features to deep learning models, and more recently, to hybrid architectures. Early approaches relied on handcrafted features like the Scale-Invariant Feature Transform (SIFT) (Lowe, 2004), effective at capturing local patterns but limited in their ability to incorporate global context (Ahmed, Jouini and Korbaa, 2025), crucial for comprehensive scene understanding.

The advent of CNNs marked a paradigm shift. However, while effective for local feature extraction, CNNs can sometimes overlook subtle details crucial for distinguishing between semantically similar classes (Ahmed et al., 2024). Attempts to combine handcrafted features with CNNs (e.g., fusing SIFT with CNN features (Tianyu, Zhenjiang and Jianhu, 2018; Ahmed et al., 2024)) demonstrated some potential but faced challenges in effectively integrating the disparate feature types. Vision Transformers (ViTs) (Dosovitskiy et al., 2021) emerged as powerful alternatives, achieving notable success in remote sensing image interpretation (Sha and Li, 2022; Chen et al., 2022). Advancements like multi-task pretraining (Wang et al., 2024) and knowledge transfer techniques (e.g. μ2Net (Gesmundo and Dean, 2022)) have further enhanced their performance.

Researchers have also explored specialized architectures tailored for remote sensing data, such as RESISC45 (Cheng, Han and Lu, 2017). LWGANet (Lu et al., 2025), for instance, introduces a lightweight group attention mechanism to address computational inefficiencies in multi-branch architectures. Similarly, SkySense (Guo et al., 2024) proposes a large-scale multi-modal foundation model that leverages a factorized spatiotemporal encoder to process diverse remote sensing data sources. Hybrid CNN-Transformer architectures have gained prominence for their potential to effectively integrate local and global features. SIBNet (Rubab et al., 2024), for example, combines a self-attention-based inception CNN with a ViT to capture both local details and global context. While SIBNet has shown promising results on datasets like RESISC12 and EuroSAT, its performance on larger datasets like RESISC45 remains unexplored.

Our work builds upon these advancements, addressing their limitations through a novel mid-level fusion strategy using a Transformer Encoder. Unlike our previous work in (Ahmed, Jouini and Korbaa, 2025), which explored mid-level fusion of handcrafted and deep features with a basic gating mechanism, the current work introduces a more powerful and dynamic interaction approach.

3. TRANSFORMER-BASED FUSION OF LOCAL AND GLOBAL FEATURES

3.1 Local and Global Features Extraction

The dual-branch architecture of our model is illustrated in Figure 1. The local feature extraction branch employs a pre-trained EfficientNet-B0 model (Tan and Le, 2019), enhanced with a Convolutional Block Attention Module (CBAM) (Woo et al., 2018). EfficientNet-B0 is chosen for its efficiency in capturing fine-grained details, thanks to its mobile inverted bottleneck convolution (MBConv) blocks and compound scaling. We extract features from the output of the third MBConv block, striking a balance between detailed local information and sufficient contextual understanding. CBAM refines the extracted features by sequentially applying channel attention and spatial attention. The channel attention mechanism focuses on "what" is meaningful by weighing each channel of the feature map. It computes these weights using global average pooling and max pooling, followed by a shared Multi-Layer Perceptron (MLP) with a reduction ratio (r=16, in our implementation). The spatial attention mechanism refines "where" the important information is located by aggregating channel information using average and max pooling, followed by a convolutional layer. The refined feature maps are then passed through adaptive average pooling and a linear projection layer to create a feature vector of dimension d, ready for fusion with global features.

The placement of CBAM before the adaptive average pooling layer is critical. Applying attention before reducing the spatial resolution ensures that CBAM operates on feature maps rich in local information. This allows it to accurately identify and emphasize salient local features before they are potentially smoothed during pooling.

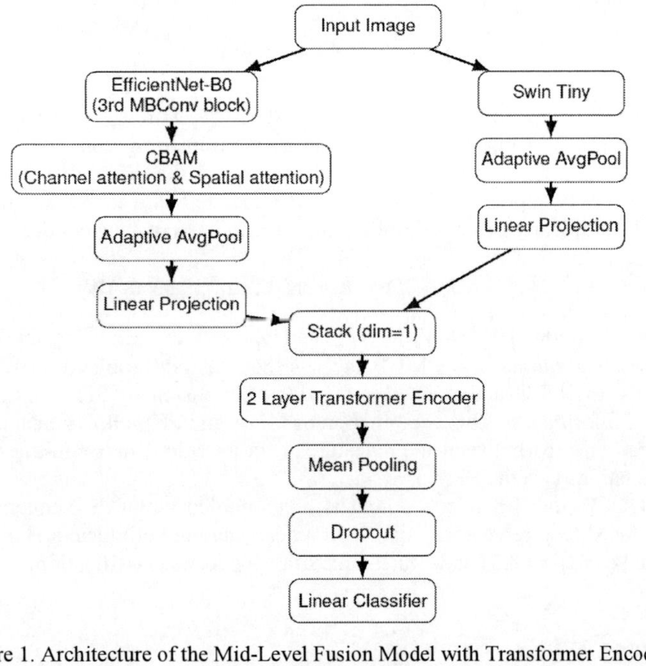

Figure 1. Architecture of the Mid-Level Fusion Model with Transformer Encoder

The global feature extraction branch leverages a pre-trained Swin Tiny Transformer (Liu et al., 2021). The hierarchical architecture of Swin, based on shifted window self-attention, allows it to efficiently process the entire image and understand spatial relationships between different regions. This is crucial for scene understanding, as the arrangement and interaction of objects within a scene often provide essential cues for accurate classification. The Swin Tiny architecture progressively builds a hierarchical representation of the image, enabling the model to understand global relationships across the entire image. This global representation complements the local features extracted by the EfficientNet+CBAM branch, providing a holistic view of the scene.

3.2 Transformer Encoder Mid-level Fusion

The outputs of the two branches are fused using a 2-layer Transformer Encoder. The EfficientNet+CBAM branch produces feature maps $F_{local} \in \mathbb{R}^{B \times C_1 \times H' \times W'}$, while the Swin Transformer branch outputs $F_{global} \in \mathbb{R}^{B \times C_2 \times H \times W}$, where B is the batch size, C_i represents the number of channels, and H, W (and H', W') denote the spatial dimensions. Adaptive average pooling reduces the spatial dimensions of both feature maps, resulting in tensors of shape $\mathbb{R}^{B \times C_1}$ and $\mathbb{R}^{B \times C_2}$. Separate linear projections then map these features into a shared $d = 256$ dimensional embedding space, producing x_{local} and x_{global}, both in $\mathbb{R}^{B \times 256}$.

The projected vectors, x_{local} and x_{global}, are *stacked* along the sequence dimension, forming the input sequence $X \in \mathbb{R}^{B \times 2 \times 256}$ for the Transformer Encoder. This stacking operation, which creates a sequence of distinct feature vectors, is crucial. Stacking, unlike concatenation, preserves the distinct nature of local and global features, allowing the self-attention mechanism to analyze relationships both within and across these features. This enables the model to learn fine-grained dependencies between specific local details and the broader global context, effectively integrating multi-scale information. Such complex dependencies would be lost with straightforward concatenation.

The input sequence X is processed by a 2-layer Transformer Encoder. The first layer captures initial interactions between local and global features. The second layer refines these interactions, learning higher-level relationships to produce a more contextually rich fused representation. Each layer consists of multi-head self-attention (MHA) followed by a position-wise feed-forward network (FFN). MHA computes attention weights that capture relationships between all pairs of input vectors. For a single head, the scaled dot-product attention is:

$$\text{Attention}(Q, K, V) = \text{softmax}\left(\frac{QK^T}{\sqrt{d_k}}\right)V$$

where Q, K, and V (query, key, and value matrices $\in \mathbb{R}^{2 \times d_k}$, with $d_k = d/h$ and $h = 4$ attention heads) are derived from the input X using distinct learnable linear transformations. The query (Q) represents what information the model is looking for, the key (K) represents the different parts of the input that could be relevant, and the value (V) represents the information associated with each key. The outputs of the h heads are then concatenated and linearly projected, following the original Transformer design (Vaswani et al., 2017):

$$\text{MHA}(X) = \text{Concat}(\text{head}_1, \ldots, \text{head}_h)W^O$$

where $\text{head}_i = \text{Attention}(QW_i^Q, KW_i^K, VW_i^V)$, and $W_i^Q, W_i^K, W_i^V \in \mathbb{R}^{d \times d_k}$ and $W^O \in \mathbb{R}^{hd_k \times d}$ are learnable projection matrices. The output of the MHA layer is then passed through a position-wise FFN consisting of two linear layers with ReLU activation and a hidden dimension of 512. This FFN further processes the attention-weighted information. This combination of MHA and FFN allows each transformer layer to capture both weighted relationships between input features (via attention) and non-linear transformations of these weighted representations (via the FFN).

Finally, the Transformer Encoder's output is mean-pooled along the sequence dimension, producing a 256-dimensional fused feature vector. This vector, encapsulating both local and global information, is passed through a dropout layer ($p = 0.3$) and a linear classifier for scene classification.

4. EXPERIMENTAL STUDY

4.1 Datasets & Tools

Our experimental study uses two publicly available remote sensing image datasets, EuroSAT (Helber et al., 2019) and RESISC45 (Cheng, Han and Lu, 2017), to evaluate the performance of our proposed Mid-Level

Fusion model. The EuroSAT dataset (Helber et al., 2019) contains 27,000 Sentinel-2 satellite images of size 64 \times 64 pixels, categorized into 10 land cover classes. The RESISC45 dataset (Cheng, Han and Lu, 2017) comprises 31,500 high-resolution (256 \times 256 pixels) remote sensing images covering 45 scene classes. Both datasets are balanced and exhibit significant diversity in terms of spectral and spatial characteristics. For our experiments, common data augmentation techniques were applied to the training sets of both datasets. These techniques included random affine transformations, horizontal/vertical flips, random rotations, color jitter random cropping, and Gaussian blur.

We implemented our model using PyTorch (Paszke et al., 2019), leveraging pre-trained EfficientNet-B0 and Swin Tiny architectures. The model weights were initialized using Xavier uniform initialization (torch.nn.init.xavier_uniform_), which ensures stable and efficient training by maintaining consistent variance across layers. To ensure stable training, we employed a two-phase strategy. In Phase 1 we froze the lower layers (stem and initial blocks) of both backbones, allowing the model to focus on learning the fusion mechanism and classification head. We used the Adam optimizer with layer-specific learning rates and a ReduceLROnPlateau scheduler (patience=3, factor=0.5). In Phase 2 We unfroze additional layers and fine-tune the entire model with reduced learning rates. This approach stabilizes the fusion process before fine-tuning the backbones, while early stopping (patience=5) prevents overfitting in both phases.

4.2 Results & Discussion

4.2.1 Comparison with Existing Approaches

Table 1 compares our approach with state-of-the-art methods for remote sensiscene classification. As shown in Table 1, the strong baseline performance of EfficientNet-B0 (97.37% on EuroSAT, 94.15% on RESISC45) and Swin Tiny (97.93% on EuroSAT, 94.84% on RESISC45) underscores the challenge of further improvement, emphasizing the efficacy of our fusion strategy.

Table 1. Comparison of accuracy results on the EuroSAT and RESISC45 datasets

Approach	Backbone	EuroSAT	RESISC45	Params (≈)
SeCo (Mañas et al., 2021)	ResNet-50	96.32%	93.06%	25.6 M
µ2Net (Gesmundo and Dean, 2022)	µ2Net	99.10%	97.00%	307 M
SIBNet (Rubab et al., 2024)	SIBNet	97.80%	-	11.5 M
SkySense (Guo et al., 2024)	Swin L	-	95.92%	2060 M
CtxMIM (Zhang, Liu and Wang, 2024)	Swin B	98.87%	95.20%	90 M
MTP-ViT (Wang et al., 2024)	InternImage-XL	99.24%	96.27%	335 M
GeRSP (Huang et al., 2024)	ResNet-50	98.29%	92.83%	25.6 M
LFGF (Ahmed, Jouini and Korbaa, 2025)	MobileNetV2	98.47%	-	3.4 M
EfficientNet-B0 (Baseline)	EfficientNet-B0	97.37%	94.15%	5.3 M
Tiny Swin (Baseline)	Tiny Swin	97.93%	94.84%	28 M
Proposed Approach	**Tiny Swin & EfficientNet-B0+CBAM**	**98.67%**	**96.06%**	**34 M**

On EuroSAT, our approach achieves 98.67% accuracy. While state-of-the-art models like MTP-ViT (99.24%) and µ2Net (99.10%) attain higher scores, they rely on significantly larger backbones. Our method remains highly competitive, outperforming established approaches such as SIBNet (97.80%) and GeRSP (98.29%). Simultaneously, on the more challenging RESISC45 dataset, our model attains a strong 96.06% accuracy. This result is highly competitive, performing comparably to leading methods like MTP-ViT (96.27%) while outperforming others such as SkySense (95.92%) and CtxMIM (95.20%). This superior performance over the individual backbones (EfficientNet-B0 at 94.15% and Swin Tiny at 94.84%) underscores the benefits of our transformer-based fusion strategy.

A crucial aspect of our work is the balance between performance and efficiency. While μ2Net (Gesmundo and Dean, 2022) reports a higher accuracy of 97.00% on RESISC45, it operates with a substantially larger model size (307M parameters). Our significantly more compact model (34M parameters) offers a more practical solution for resource-constrained deployment scenarios. Table 2 further demonstrates the robustness and generalizability of our model with balanced precision, recall, and F1-scores across both datasets.

Table 2. Macro-averaged precision, recall, and F1-score of the proposed approach on EuroSAT and RESISC45

Dataset	Precision	Recall	F1-score	Accuracy
EuroSAT	98.66%	98.52%	98.58%	98.67%
RESISC45	96.04%	96.12%	96.04%	96.06%

4.2.2 Ablation Study

To quantify the contributions of the Transformer-based fusion and CBAM modules, we conducted an ablation study on RESISC45 (Table 3). Removing the Transformer module and relying on simple feature concatenation (after independent projections to a 256-dimensional space) resulted in the lowest accuracy (93.38%), underperforming even the individual baselines (EfficientNet-B0: 94.15%, Swin Tiny: 94.84%). This inferior performance highlights the limitations of directly merging high-dimensional features. The increased dimensionality can strain the capacity of the classifier and exacerbate the challenges posed by potentially conflicting or redundant information between the local and global branches. When using a Transformer with a single layer, the model achieves an accuracy of 95.14%, demonstrating that even a single layer of Transformer fusion significantly improves performance compared to simple concatenation. However, this is still slightly lower than the full model, highlighting the importance of the second layer for refining feature interactions. Removing only the CBAM module, while retaining the Transformer fusion, resulted in an accuracy of 95.43%, underscoring the CBAM's role in refining local features and reaffirming the Transformer's importance for effective fusion.

Table 3. Ablation study on the RESISC45 dataset

Model Variant	Precision	Recall	F1-score	Accuracy
Without CBAM	95.37%	95.44%	95.36%	95.43%
1-Layer Transformer	95.15%	95.20%	95.13%	95.14%
Without Transformer	93.69%	93.38%	93.36%	93.38%
Full Model	**96.04%**	**96.12%**	**96.04%**	**96.06%**

4.2.3 Analysis of the Two-Layer Transformer Fusion

To better understand the fusion process, we visualized the average attention weights within the two-layer Transformer Encoder (Figure 2). These weights, averaged over the RESISC45 validation set, reveal the interactions between local (EfficientNet+CBAM) and global (Swin) features. In the first layer, the model emphasizes the integration of local features into the global representation. The EfficientNet+CBAM branch primarily attends to itself (0.68), maintaining a focus on local information. The Swin branch predominantly focuses on the local features from EfficientNet+CBAM (0.79), with only 0.21 self-attention. This indicates that the global context, as captured by Swin, is being heavily informed by the local details extracted by EfficientNet+CBAM.

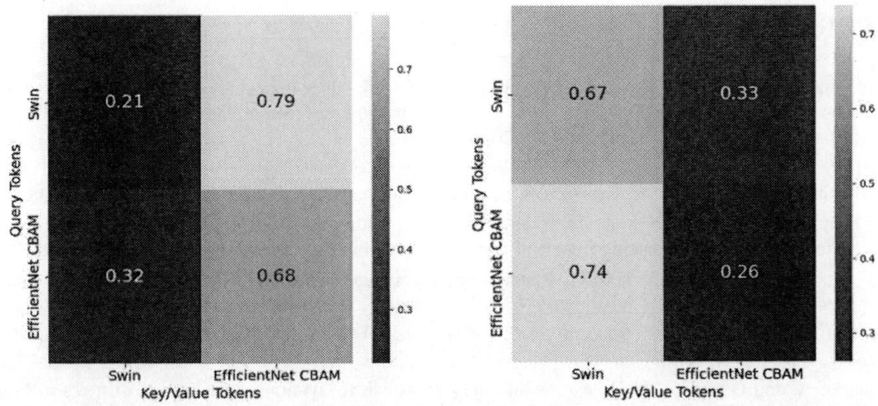

Figure 2. Average attention weights for the first (left) and second (right) layers of the Transformer Encoder, visualized as heatmaps. Rows represent the query tokens (Swin, EfficientNet+CBAM) and columns represent the key/value tokens

The second layer exhibits a shift in attention patterns, reflecting a refinement of the feature representations. The EfficientNet+CBAM branch now attends significantly more to the global features from the Swin branch (0.74) and less to itself (0.26). This suggests that the local representations are now being enriched with the global context captured by Swin in the previous layer. Meanwhile, the Swin branch exhibits greater self-attention (0.67), with reduced attention to local features (0.33). This indicates that the global representation is being refined by focusing more on the global context itself, integrating the enriched information from the previous layer.

This two-layer architecture facilitates a hierarchical and dynamic fusion process. The first layer prioritizes informing the global context with local details. The second layer then refines both representations: local features are enriched with global context, while the global representation becomes more focused on processing the globally-informed information. This hierarchical approach effectively captures and integrates both detailed local characteristics and broader contextual information, ultimately contributing to improved classification performance.

5. CONCLUSION

This work introduced a novel architecture for remote sensing scene classification that synergistically combines EfficientNet-B0 with a Convolutional Block Attention Module (CBAM) for local detail extraction, a Swin Transformer for capturing global context, and a two-layer Transformer Encoder for mid-level fusion. This mid-level fusion strategy, integrating local and global features at an intermediate stage using the Transformer Encoder, facilitates a nuanced interplay between fine-grained details and broader contextual information, crucial for accurate scene understanding. Experimental evaluations on the EuroSAT and RESISC45 datasets demonstrate the effectiveness of our proposed architecture, achieving competitive accuracies of 98.67% and 96.06%, respectively, while maintaining a significantly smaller model size compared to methods like µ2Net. An ablation study confirmed the importance of each component and their synergistic contributions to the overall performance.

These promising results motivate several avenues for future research. A natural extension involves adapting this multi-scale fusion approach to other remote sensing tasks, such as object detection and semantic segmentation. Furthermore, incorporating additional data modalities, including elevation data and temporal sequences, could enrich the feature representations. To mitigate the computational demands of the current architecture, future work could explore more efficient variants, such as incorporating sparse Transformers with dynamic sparsity or lightweight attention mechanisms.

REFERENCES

Ahmed, V.A. et al. (2024) 'Integrating deep and handcrafted features for enhanced remote sensing image classification', in 2024 IEEE/ACS 21st international conference on computer systems and applications (AICCSA), pp. 1–8. Available at: https://doi.org/10.1109/AICCSA63423.2024.10912637.

Ahmed, V., Jouini, K. and Korbaa, O. (2025) 'Enhancing LULC classification with attention-based fusion of handcrafted and deep features'. INSTICC; SciTePress. Available at: https://doi.org/10.5220/0013098500003890.

Chen, Z. et al. (2022) 'TypeFormer: Multiscale transformer with type controller for remote sensing image caption', IEEE Geoscience and Remote Sensing Letters, 19, pp. 1–5. Available at: https://doi.org/10.1109/LGRS.2022.3192062.

Cheng, G., Han, J. and Lu, X. (2017) 'Remote sensing image scene classification: Benchmark and state of the art', Proceedings of the IEEE, 105(10), pp. 1865–1883. Available at: https://doi.org/10.1109/JPROC.2017.2675998.

Dosovitskiy, A. et al. (2021) 'An image is worth 16x16 words: Transformers for image recognition at scale', arXiv preprint arXiv:2010.11929 [Preprint].

Gesmundo, A. and Dean, J. (2022) 'An evolutionary approach to dynamic introduction of tasks in large-scale multitask learning systems'. Available at: https://arxiv.org/abs/2205.12755.

Guo, X. et al. (2024) 'SkySense: A multi-modal remote sensing foundation model towards universal interpretation for earth observation imagery'. Available at: https://arxiv.org/abs/2312.10115.

Helber, P. et al. (2019) 'Eurosat: A novel dataset and deep learning benchmark for land use and land cover classification', IEEE Journal of Selected Topics in Applied Earth Observations and Remote Sensing, 12(7), pp. 2217–2226. Available at: https://doi.org/10.1109/JSTARS.2019.2918242.

Huang, Z. et al. (2024) 'Generic knowledge boosted pretraining for remote sensing images', IEEE Trans. Geosci. Remote. Sens., 62, pp. 1–13. Available at: https://doi.org/10.1109/TGRS.2024.3354031.

Liu, Z. et al. (2021) 'Swin transformer: Hierarchical vision transformer using shifted windows', in Proceedings of the IEEE/CVF international conference on computer vision, pp. 10012–10022.

Lowe, D.G. (2004) 'Distinctive image features from scale-invariant keypoints', Int. Journal of Computer Vision, 60(2), pp. 91–110. Available at: https://doi.org/10.1023/B:VISI.0000029664.99615.94.

Lu, W. et al. (2025) 'LWGANet: A lightweight group attention backbone for remote sensing visual tasks'. Available at: https://arxiv.org/abs/2501.10040.

Mañas, O. et al. (2021) 'Seasonal contrast: Unsupervised pre-training from uncurated remote sensing data', in Proceedings of the IEEE/CVF international conference on computer vision (ICCV), pp. 9414–9423.

Paszke, A. et al. (2019) 'PyTorch: An imperative style, high-performance deep learning library', CoRR, abs/1912.01703.

Rubab, S. et al. (2024) 'A novel network-level fusion architecture of proposed self-attention and vision transformer models for land use and land cover classification from remote sensing images', IEEE Journal of Selected Topics in Applied Earth Observations and Remote Sensing, 17, pp. 13135–13148. Available at: https://doi.org/10.1109/JSTARS.2024.3426950.

Sha, Z. and Li, J. (2022) 'MITformer: A multiinstance vision transformer for remote sensing scene classification', IEEE Geoscience and Remote Sensing Letters, 19, pp. 1–5. Available at: https://doi.org/10.1109/LGRS.2022.3176499.

Tan, M. and Le, Q.V. (2019) 'EfficientNet: Rethinking model scaling for convolutional neural networks', CoRR, abs/1905.11946. Available at: http://arxiv.org/abs/1905.11946.

Tianyu, Z., Zhenjiang, M. and Jianhu, Z. (2018) 'Combining CNN with hand-crafted features for image classification', in 2018 14th IEEE international conference on signal processing (ICSP), pp. 554–557. Available at: https://doi.org/10.1109/ICSP.2018.8652428.

Vaswani, A. et al. (2017) 'Attention is all you need', in Proc. Of the 31st int. Conf. On neural information processing systems. Red Hook, NY, USA: Curran Associates Inc. (NIPS'17), pp. 6000–6010.

Wang, D. et al. (2024) 'MTP: Advancing remote sensing foundation model via multi-task pretraining'. Available at: https://arxiv.org/abs/2403.13430.

Woo, S. et al. (2018) 'CBAM: Convolutional block attention module', in. Berlin, Heidelberg: Springer-Verlag, pp. 3–19. Available at: https://doi.org/10.1007/978-3-030-01234-2_1.

Xiao, T. et al. (2021) 'Early convolutions help transformers see better'. Available at: https://arxiv.org/abs/2106.14881.

Zhang, C. et al. (2022) 'Transformer and CNN hybrid deep neural network for semantic segmentation of very-high-resolution remote sensing imagery', IEEE Transactions on Geoscience and Remote Sensing, 60, pp. 1–20. Available at: https://doi.org/10.1109/TGRS.2022.3144894.

Zhang, M., Liu, Q. and Wang, Y. (2024) 'CtxMIM: Context-enhanced masked image modeling for remote sensing image understanding'. Available at: https://arxiv.org/abs/2310.00022.

HYPER-PARAMETER TUNING WITH AUTOMATED MACHINE LEARNING FOR POINT CLOUD PART SEGMENTATION

Gabriel Lenz Balatka and Rafael Stubs Parpinelli
Graduate Program in Applied Computing, Santa Catarina State University, Joinville/SC, Brazil

ABSTRACT

This study aimed to investigate the contributions of hyper-parameter optimization methods for Artificial Neural Networks applied to the Point Cloud Part Segmentation process. The PartNet database was used, selecting three specific categories, Chair-1, StorageFurniture-1 and Lamp-1, through data analysis of each category. For each of them, the Furthest Point Sampling algorithm (FPS) was used, creating two data sets, with each point cloud containing 256 and 512 points. The neural network architecture selected was PointNet, which has historically shown promise for the task. The AutoML strategy was used for hyper-parameter adjustment. As a result, it was possible to see the importance of hyper-parameter tuning and also discuss the impact of choosing the number of points in each point cloud.

KEYWORDS

Point Cloud Subsampling, Point Cloud Part Segmentation, Automated Machine Learning, Artificial Neural Networks, Hyper-Parameter Tuning

1. INTRODUCTION

Point clouds are three-dimensional sets of points that can be used to represent objects and physical spaces. By processing such structures, it is possible to automate different processes, mainly related to industry. In this work, three different terms will be used frequently, category, shape and part. Category is a generic type of object, for example, a table or a chair. Shape is a single object that belongs to a category, represented by a point cloud. In addition, categories have parts, for example, in the case of a chair, we can divide it into arms, legs, seat and backrest. Note that a shape does not necessarily have points for all parts, as in the case of a chair without arms.

This paper studies the application of a process called Point Cloud Part Segmentation. To do this, we start with a point cloud which its category is known. This application aims to use a model-specific trained for this category that receives this point cloud and returns a label for each point, i.e. the part of the shape that it belongs to. Thus, starting from a known and consolidated architecture for this application, called PointNet (QI, 2017), this work aims to carry out an optimization process of the hyper-parameters of the original architecture, making a comparison between the results obtained.

The PointNet artificial neural network architecture requires data for training and testing. However, each set of data has a specific behavior, i.e., the shapes have specific patterns and the number of parts in each category is also different. The goal of this research is to study the importance of adjusting the hyper-parameters of a generic architecture to build specific ones that are more suitable for each case. The database used was PartNet (MO, 2019), available online at https://huggingface.co. The PartNet database is a subset of the ShapeNet database (CHANG, 2015) and consists of a total of 26,671 distinct shape instances, separated into 24 categories.

2. BACKGROUND

2.1 Point Clouds

Point Cloud is an important computational structure used in the field of Geometric Modeling. Using specific sensors, it is possible to extract this information to represent environments as a whole or individual objects. Thus, according to (WANG, 2019), point cloud processing is currently increasingly sought after to extract relevant information from environments or objects, mainly for industrial automation. Another widely explored application, as in the article by (ZERMAS, 2019) is autonomous vehicles, by extracting the environment with a LiDAR sensor and being able to recognize objects close to the vehicle.

From a Point Cloud, many computational processes can be carried out (QI, 2017). When this cloud represents an unknown three-dimensional shape, the aim is to classify it, from a list of possible categories. The goal is to find the category that best corresponds to the respective point cloud. On the other hand, when the category that the cloud represents is already known, assuming for example a chair, and starting with which parts represent this category, in this case, the arms, legs, seat and backrest, the goal is to try to find which part of the shape, each point in the cloud belongs. This process is known as point cloud part segmentation.

Currently, the most widely used solution to achieve this process is the development of an Artificial Neural Network, a strategy initially proposed by (QI, 2017), in which it depends on one main process, without any intermediate processing to convert the initial structure type. This generally gives better results with less processing time. In this work, the segmentation application will be explored using Artificial Neural Networks. Firstly, we will evaluate the performance of a specific architecture called PointNet (QI, 2017). Secondly, Automated machine learning will then be utilized to adjust the hyper-parameters of the respective architecture, ending with a new performance evaluation.

2.2 Automated Machine Learning

Automated Machine Learning is characterized by the automation of the entire Machine Learning process, from data preparation to model evaluation. Different objectives are assigned to this process, such as the construction of complex systems without the need for extensive knowledge in Statistics and Machine Learning (HE, 2021).

The AutoML process is made up of a series of stages, namely data processing, feature engineering, model/algorithm selection and hyper-parameter optimization (SELEHIN, 2024). Hyper-parameter optimization seeks to optimize parameters related to training, such as learning rate and batch size (SALEHIN, 2024). The objectives of hyper-parameter optimization are to reduce human effort, improve algorithm performance and increase the reproducibility of scientific studies (HUTTER, 2019). On the other hand, there are challenges such as high computational costs, a complex search space and limited data sets (HUTTER, 2019).

Hyper-parameter Optimization starts with a known configuration, previously found manually or automatically, or from a random configuration, and throughout the iterations of the selected optimization algorithm, new configurations are tested and evaluated according to the chosen metric. The configurations are within a search space defined by the programmer. Different optimization algorithms can be used for this, such as Grid Search, Random Search, Bayesian Optimization and HyperBand (HUTTER, 2019). The Random Search algorithm, for example, tests the initial configuration and then selects random configurations from the search space, without any kind of strategy. In this work, we opted for Bayesian Optimization, a method widely used in the optimization of functions with a high computational cost of evaluation (WANG, 2023). In addition, the Gaussian Process was used as the surrogate model in Bayesian Optimization, the most widely used model in this optimization technique (WANG, 2023).

3. RELATED WORK

In (DAIF, 2025), the PointNet architecture was used to classify and segment point clouds of steel structure elements. Classification took place between two categories and segmentation into five parts. Optimization took place manually by adjusting the number of epochs, number of points per cloud and batch size. Due to the lower complexity of the problem, no AutoML technique was needed to optimize the hyper-parameters and 100% accuracy was achieved for classification and 97.10% accuracy for part segmentation.

In (WIELGOSZ, 2023), a framework was proposed for semantic and instance segmentation for coniferous forests, on two different datasets. At the end, Bayesian Optimization was also applied to tune hyper-parameters, through 50 total iterations. A total of six hyper-parameters were optimized, based on a search space defined by the authors themselves. The overall performance of the framework improved by around 4% compared to the F1 score metric. The study of hyper-parameter tuning has proved important in literature in general. No article was found that carried out the same tuning process for point cloud part segmentation with the PartNet dataset. This opens up a new avenue for study on this subject.

4. PROPOSED APPROACH

This work will use the PartNet dataset to train and test the experiments. Due to the processing limits, we needed to work with a smaller amount of data, only using the Chair-1, StorageFurniture-1 and Lamp-1 categories. Suffix 1 indicates that the coarse part segmentation level will be used. The dataset also provides middle and fine-grained types, with a greater number of parts and consequently a greater level of detail in the shapes. In this work, only the coarse level was used.

These categories were selected because they contain the largest number of shapes. In fact, the Table-1 category, which contains the largest number of shapes, with 8,218 clouds, was not used due to the need of more computer resources. The PartNet base already separates the instances in the training, validation and test sets. Table 1 shows the split found in each case.

Table 1. Proportion between each split for each category

Category	Train	Validation	Test
Chair-1	**4,489 (70.99%)**	617 (9.76%)	1,217 (19.25%)
StorageFurniture-1	**1,588 (69.99%)**	230 (10.14%)	451 (19.88%)
Lamp-1	**1,554 (70.41%)**	234 (10.60%)	419 (18.99%)

The categories mentioned above have 6, 7 and 18 parts respectively. Based on this choice of categories, the part segmentation process can be studied at different levels of complexity, depending on the number of categories and shapes available for training, validation and testing. It is worth noting that the complexity of the process depends on various elements, such as the number of shapes available, the complexity of the structure of each shape and the form and proportion of the division between these shapes, as well as the number of parts in the respective category. It is important to see that the PartNet dataset uses an approximate split of 70% for training, 10% for validation and 20% for testing.

Initially, the database was generated with the respective category and number of points per cloud. This process was carried out by pre-processing the initial dataset using the Farthest Point Sampling (FPS) technique to reduce each point cloud and the one-hot encoding technique to send the appropriate data formatting to the neural networks. In addition, the PointNet architecture was implemented with the hyper-parameters proposed by the authors, carrying out the training and testing stages on 10 isolated runs and thus extracting the standard metrics.

Subsequently, the hyper-parameters to be adjusted were chosen, as well as the search interval for each one, followed by the choice of the optimization algorithm to find the best set of hyper-parameters. After applying the algorithm, the best result was also trained and tested on 10 isolated runs, extracting the evaluation metrics for each run. Finally, a comparison of the two results was made in order to verify the impact of the adjustment made. This process was carried out 6 times for each combination of category and number of points per cloud.

5. EXPERIMENTS, RESULTS AND ANALYSIS

In this work, we sought to study the behavior of the PointNet network for different numbers of points per cloud. We therefore selected 256 and 512 points per cloud. In order to reduce each point cloud, we used the Farthest Point Sampling (FPS) algorithm, which reduces the number of points in an attempt to maintain the original format without losing relevant information. Figure 1 shows the result obtained by the algorithm for a specific shape, comparing the reduction with 256 and 512 points, with the original shape of 10,000 points.

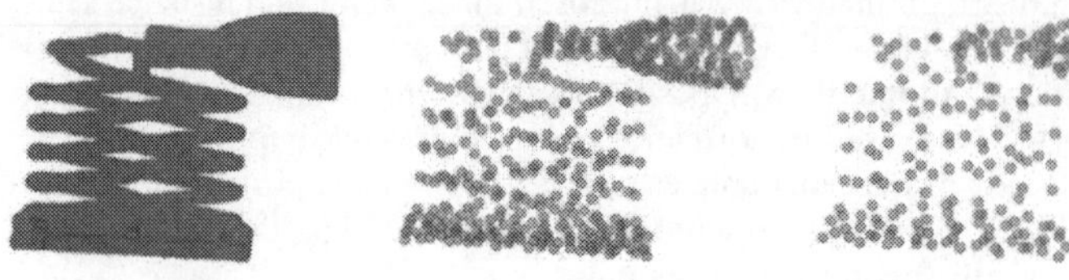

(a) Ground Truth (b) 512 Points (c) 256 points

Figure 1. Application of FPS algorithm in order to reduce #Points per cloud

By applying the FPS algorithm to the three categories, each for 256 and 512 points, 6 datasets were obtained, following the same properties presented in Table 1. For both specific datasets of each category, the only difference is in the number of points present in each shape, which is 256 or 512. Also, one-hot coding was applied to the point cloud labels in order to achieve the pattern needed to train the networks.

After the pre-processing stage, the PointNet architecture was built, using the implementation available at keras.io. The KerasTuner library was used to build the optimization algorithm. The optimization algorithm chosen was the Bayesian Optimizer with 20 trials. In each trial, the algorithm generated a new architecture and evaluated according to the validation loss metric. Each architecture was trained for a maximum of 100 epochs, and the Early Stopping technique was used with a patience of 10, thus avoiding the processing of unpromising architectures.

Table 2. Test Accuracy results with standard and best hyper-parameters

Hyper-Parameter	Default	List of Options
features_64	**64**	16, 32, 64, 128, 256
features_128_1	**128**	32, 64, 128, 256, 512
features_512	**512**	128, 256, 512, 1,024, 2,048
pre_maxpool_block	**2,048**	512, 1,024, 2,048
segmentation_features	**128**	32, 64, 128, 256, 512
initial_learning_rate	**0.003**	0.001, 0.002, 0.003, 0.004, 0.005
decay_steps_multiplier	**5**	3, 4, 5, 6, 7
decay_rate	**0.5**	0.3, 0.4, 0.5, 0.6, 0.7
staircase	**true**	false, true

Table 2 shows the hyper-parameters chosen from the standard architecture for the fit, as well as the range of possibilities for each of them. The choice was made empirically, seeking to choose the most significant hyper-parameters for the models, with different possibilities for each one. Once the best hyper-parameters had been found for each case, using the optimization algorithm, both the standard and best hyper-parameters were trained and tested a total of 10 times. Each training session consisted of exactly 100 epochs, but after training, the network weights were replaced by the weights found in the epoch with the lowest value in the validation loss metric. To do this, a checkpoint callback was used.

Test accuracy and loss metrics were calculated for each run. At the end, boxplots and tables were built to visualize the average and standard deviation of the models. For training and testing, a computer with an AMD Ryzen 7 2700x processor, NVIDIA GeForce RTX 2060 Super GPU and 16GB of RAM was used.

5.1 Analysis of Results

After all the training and testing, this section presents the analysis of the results obtained. Firstly, Figure 2 shows the convergence graphs of the average accuracy and loss from training and validation for the best and standard hyper-parameters for the StorageFurniture-1 category with 512 points. A similar behavior was observed in other cases.

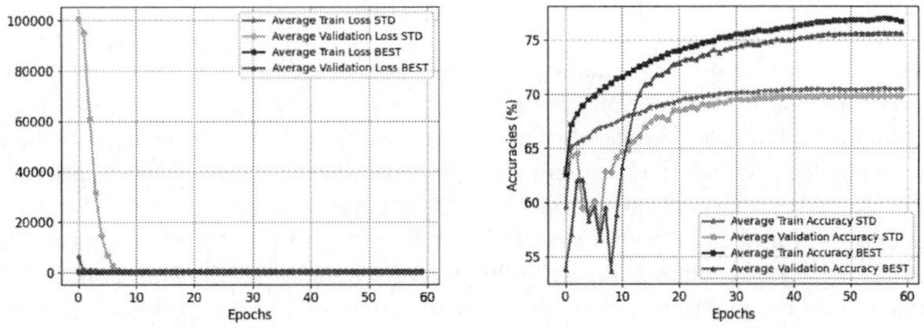

(a) Mean Loss (b) Mean Accuracy

Figure 2. Example of Loss and Accuracy convergence in both train and validation – StorageFurniture-1 with 512 points per cloud

In terms of loss, all four metrics converged towards the optimum value. Due to the high validation loss in the standard architecture during the first few epochs, it is difficult to observe the improvement of the metrics over the epochs, because of the scale of the graph. However, optimization of the validation loss occurred in both cases. With regard to accuracy, in the first epochs, a convergence in both studies for the validation accuracy metric did not occurred. However, after some epochs, the behavior normalized and converged up to a specific point. After reaching this point, the remaining epochs show little variation, with an almost constant behavior.

Table 3. Test Loss results with standard and best hyper-parameters

#Points	STD-Chair-1	STD-StorageFurniture-1	STD-Lamp-1
256	**131.92 +/- 0.09**	134.15 +/- 1.02	133.59 +/- 1.12
512	**131.90 +/- 0.12**	134.58 +/- 1.28	133.99 +/- 0.96
#Points	**BEST-Chair-1**	STD-StorageFurniture-1	BEST-Lamp-1
256	**131.54 +/- 0.01**	131.12 +/- 0.01	131.49 +/- 0.03
512	**131.52 +/- 0.00**	131.18 +/- 0.00	131.42 +/- 0.03

Table 3 shows the test loss metrics for the standard and best hyper-parameters in both quantities of points, for each of the categories. The values of this metric achieved by the best hyper-parameters were close, reaching values between 131.0 and 132.0. Therefore, the optimized value of this metric was not significantly influenced by the number of training shapes, the number of parts in each shape and the number of points in each cloud.

However, comparing the results obtained in the standard hyper-parameters, the test loss in the Chair-1 category was lower than those obtained in the StorageFurniture-1 and Lamp-1 categories. It's interesting to note that the number of shapes available in this category, 6323, is considerably higher than the others, 2269 and 2207. In addition, the Chair-1 category has 6 parts, compared to 7 and 18 in the other categories. Therefore, it can be said, in relation to this metric, that the standard architecture achieves better results for cases with larger input records and fewer output types (number of parts). But with the use of hyper-parameter tuning, the greater complexity observed in the other two categories is overcome, and the best architectures, in the end, achieve a very similar test loss.

Table 4. Test Accuracy results with standard and best hyper-parameters

#Points	STD-Chair-1	STD-StorageFurniture-1	STD-Lamp-1
256	**87.08% +/- 0.87%**	**71.60% +/- 1.93%**	**67.50% +/- 1.30%**
512	**86.00% +/- 1.38%**	**70.89% +/- 2.10%**	**68.14% +/- 1.61%**
#Points	**BEST-Chair-1**	STD-StorageFurniture-1	BEST-Lamp-1
256	**89.40% +/- 0.19%**	**78.71% +/- 0.60%**	**69.07% +/- 1.07%**
512	**89.86% +/- 0.20%**	**76.62% +/- 0.53%**	**70.40% +/- 0.94%**

Table 4 shows the test accuracies obtained in the best and standard hyper-parameters for 256 and 512 points, in the three categories studied. The number of shapes and the total number of parts in each category directly influences this metric. The best results obtained, in order, were Chair-1, StorageFurniture-1 and Lamp-1. In terms of improvements between the architectures, for Chair-1 and Lamp-1, the improvement was around 2%. For StorageFurniture-1, an increase of around 5% was achieved.

The impact of the number of points selected was low, i.e., the accuracies for both the standard and best hyper-parameters were close when comparing the two numbers of points. Although 512 points provides more data for understanding the patterns, the test clouds will also have more points and, as a result, more data labels will have to be matched. As a result, the complexities of the two problems end up being close, as are the accuracies obtained.

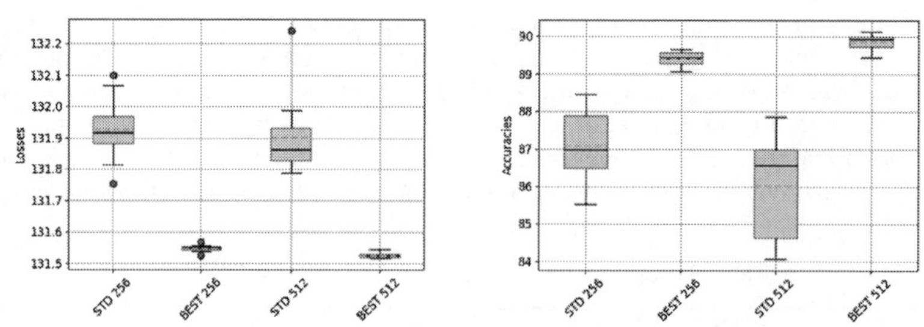

(a) Test Loss Boxplot (b) Test Accuracy Boxplot

Figure 3. Example of Loss and Accuracy convergence in both train and validation – StorageFurniture-1 with 512 points per cloud

For the Chair category, the results were satisfactory when it came to the loss of validation for both quantities of points. In this case, the number of points per cloud did not affect the results, with the 512 number showing slightly better results. In both cases, the average validation loss for the best architectures was just over 131.5. Accuracy also increased in both cases, being close to 89 and 90% in both. The best result, i.e., with the greatest difference between standard and best, was for the 512 points architecture. Finally, the number of points did not interfere with the results and better hyper-parameters were found, achieving better results in the accuracy and loss metrics.

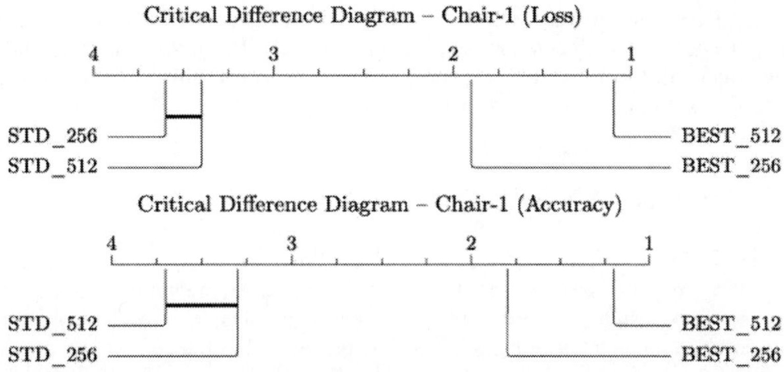

Figure 4. Critical Difference Diagram for Chair-1 Category

Figure 4 shows the Critical Difference Diagram (CDD) for the Chair-1 category, in order to compare the results statistically. To do this, the Holm adjustment was used with an alpha of 0.05. The lower the values, the better the performance of the models. A line connecting two or more cases signifies their statistical equivalence. Thus, there is a clear statistical difference between the standard and best hyper-parameters, showing a real improvement in the performance of both metrics used. In addition, the performance of the best hyper-parameters with 512 points per cloud was better than the standard architecture with 256 points, which shows that in this case, a greater number of points represents a better understanding of the models in the patterns of each shape.

For the StorageFurniture category, in relation to the loss metric, we see a reduction in both quantities of points between the standard hyper-parameters and the best one. In both cases, the average loss of the models started at around 134.5 and fell to just over 131.0. With regard to the accuracy metric, there was a greater difference between the 256 points hyper-parameters, with a greater difference between the standard and the best. For the 512 points hyper-parameters, although with a smaller difference, the best hyper-parameters also managed to outperform the standard. In addition, in both cases, the range of boxplots also decreased, which indicates a more stable and therefore adequate behavior.

This shows that, in fact, better hyper-parameters were found, due to the reduction in the value and size of the interval for the loss metric, as well as the accuracy metric, which also showed the same behavior, improving on the previous hyper-parameters. For the StorageFurniture-1 category, we also calculated the Critical Difference Diagram between the standard and best hyper-parameters for 256 and 512 points per cloud. Again, there is a statistical difference between the standard and best hyper-parameters in both evaluation metrics.

In this case, the best hyper-parameters for 256 points showed statistically better results than the best for 512 points. This shows that, in this case, reducing the number of points made it easier to understand the patterns present in each shape, unlike what was observed in the Chair-1 category. For the Lamp-1 category, the test loss metric was well optimized for both quantities of points. As with the other two categories, the losses of the best hyper-parameters were very close to each other. In this case, for the test accuracy metric, we were able to see an improvement in the results. However, for both, there is an intersection between the boxplots, which indicates that statistically the hyper-parameters behave in an equivalent way, even if in practice the best ones behave better. In addition, 512 points achieved slightly better results.

For the Lamp-1 category, the Critical Difference Diagram between the hyper-parameters tested was also drawn up. The loss metric behaved similarly to the other two categories, but for accuracy, the statistical test showed equivalence between the standard and best hyper-parameters, for the two quantities of points per cloud analyzed. In this way, it cannot be said that there has been a real improvement in the hyper-parameters, because statically they are equivalent.

A comparison between ground truth, standard and best hyper-parameters for two different cases was made. The first case is the Chair-1 category with 512 points, as it has the largest number of shapes for training and testing. The second category selected is Lamp-1, also with 512 points, as it has the fewest shapes for training and testing. The number of 512 points was selected for both categories for a better comparison of the results obtained. The first instance of the test was selected in both categories to check the final impact.

For the Chair-1 category, it was possible to see small differences between the two predicted cases, while for the Lamp-1 category the segmentation process improved significantly. It can be seen that each instance has a unique pattern and will therefore have a specific improvement. As shown in Table 4, the average accuracies improved in both cases, but the impact of each instance will be unique.

6. CONCLUSIONS AND FUTURE WORK

Hyper-parameter tuning is a powerful technique that allows artificial neural network architectures to be optimized, resulting in better test metrics. For the point cloud segmentation problem, we can see that this objective has been met, achieving more stable and accurate models. The results depend on the ratio between the amount of data and the number of parts of each shape, as well as the complexity of each category.

The choice of the number of points in each cloud will depend on the objective of each application, but the effectiveness of the hyper-parameter tuning was shown to be similar in the cases tested. In addition, when analyzing the values of the hyper-parameters selected in the best architectures, standard behaviors can be seen, such as the choice of a learning rate of 0.001, but for other hyper-parameters, different choices were observed. As a result, it can be seen that for each specific problem, a different architecture will be optimal, and it is recommended that this process be carried out for each case worked on. As future work, we intend to carry out the study with larger numbers of points per cloud and with different point cloud segmentation architectures. Another improvement would be to use new categories, such as Table-1, which has a large number of shapes, as well as other levels of detail, such as middle and fine-grained, which are already available on the PartNet dataset.

REFERENCES

Chang, A.X. et al, (2015). Shapenet: An information-rich 3d model repository. *arXiv preprint arXiv:1512.03012*.

Daif, H. and Marzouk, M., 2025. Point cloud classification and part segmentation of steel structure elements. *Neural Computing and Applications*, 37(6), pp.4387-4407.

He, X. et al, (2021). AutoML: A survey of the state-of-the-art. *Knowledge-based systems*, 212, p.106622.

Hutter, F. et al, (2019). *Automated machine learning: methods, systems, challenges* (p. 219). Springer Nature.

Mo, K. et al, (2019). Partnet: A large-scale benchmark for fine-grained and hierarchical part-level 3d object understanding. *Proceedings of the IEEE/CVF conference on computer vision and pattern recognition* (pp. 909-918).

Qi, C.R. et al, (2017). Pointnet: Deep learning on point sets for 3d classification and segmentation. *Proceedings of the IEEE conference on computer vision and pattern recognition* (pp. 652-660).

Salehin, I. et al, (2024). AutoML: A systematic review on automated machine learning with neural architecture search. *Journal of Information and Intelligence*, 2(1), pp.52-81.

Wang, X. et al, (2023). Recent advances in Bayesian optimization. *ACM Computing Surveys*, 55(13s), pp.1-36.

Wielgosz, M. et al, (2023). Point2Tree (P2T) — Framework for parameter tuning of semantic and instance segmentation used with mobile laser scanning data in coniferous forest. *Remote Sensing*, 15(15), p.3737.

Zermas, D. et al, (2017). Fast segmentation of 3D point clouds: A paradigm on LiDAR data for autonomous vehicle applications. *2017 IEEE International Conference on Robotics and Automation (ICRA)* (pp. 5067-5073). IEEE.

AI-POWERED PEDAGOGY: GENERATING RELIABLE AND CONTEXT-AWARE EDUCATIONAL CONTENT FROM INSTRUCTOR-CURATED MATERIALS

Mikhail George Samir Youssef Gebrail[1] and Ahmed M. H. Abdelfattah[2]
[1]*Faculty of Media Engineering & Technology, German University in Cairo (GUC), Egypt*
[2]*Math. Dept., Faculty of Science, Ain Shams University, and Faculty of MET, GUC, Egypt*

ABSTRACT

The use of Large Language Models (LLMs) in education presents a significant challenge for educators, as the reliability of AI-generated content is often compromised by hallucinations and unverifiable sources. This diminishes instructor control over learning materials and creates a risk of students building knowledge on flawed foundations. This paper introduces "`Studymate`", a proof-of-concept implementation of a model-agnostic framework designed to give control back to the instructor by providing trustworthy, contextually precise academic support that operates exclusively on their provided course materials. The implemented system features a multi-step pipeline to deliver varied educational outputs, including a conversational Question/Answer (Q/A), multi-modal PDF summaries with generated images, and podcasts. All information presented is grounded in the course-specific knowledge base, with precise citations to the source document and page number, ensuring verifiability.

The main goal achieved by the system is that it restores control to educators and provides students with a dependable and effective learning aid that is reliable, correct, and directly controlled by their instructors. This work contributes a practical, model-agnostic framework for creating trustworthy AI-assisted educational tools and addresses the critical need for source attribution in AI-generated academic content.

KEYWORDS

AI in Education, Instructor-Controlled AI, Source Attribution, Multimodal Personalized Learning, Trustworthy AI

1. INTRODUCTION

The ubiquitous integration of Large Language Models (LLMs) within artificial intelligence (AI) is enacting a paradigm shift in the educational sphere. As students increasingly adopt these potent tools for research and problem-solving, instructors face a critical challenge to their pedagogical oversight: the inherent unreliability of content generated from vast, uncurated data sources. This ceding of control to unverified AI systems creates a hazardous learning environment where students may unknowingly rely on flawed information. The central vulnerability lies in the well-documented tendency of general-purpose LLMs to "hallucinate" (i.e., confidently presenting fabricated information as fact). This problem is exacerbated by the generation of non-existent sources, a practice that directly undermines the academic pillar of verifiable attribution and challenges the trustworthiness of the learning process. Consequently, the conversation must evolve from merely acknowledging the widespread adoption of AI to actively shaping its application for pedagogical safety and efficacy. The most pressing need is not simply for a more accurate general AI, but for a system that restores instructional control. This paper, therefore, addresses this need by proposing a model where the veracity and contextual awareness of AI-generated educational content are ensured by grounding the technology exclusively in instructor-curated materials.

The growing use of AI tools like ChatGPT by students presents a challenge for educators. As students increasingly turn to these tools, instructors lose control over the information and materials their students learn from. This becomes a problem because AI may hallucinate leading to a risk that students may build their knowledge on a "flawed foundation". Moreover, students across various educational levels often struggle to efficiently process and fully understand the large amount of information presented in their specific study materials. While general-purpose AI tools offer broad assistance, their utility in focused academic settings is often compromised by a lack of reliability and an inability to operate strictly within the context based on the courses of the student. This limitation arises because their knowledge seems to be uncontrolled by the author of the course content, potentially leading to out-of-scope or generalized information that may not align with specific curriculum needs or learning objectives.

There is, therefore, a distinct need for an AI-powered system that can provide trustworthy, contextually precise academic support by operating exclusively on instructor-provided materials which will result in **educators gaining control over the learning environment of the student**. This is the main goal that needs to be achieved by the presented framework and the implemented system. This paper introduces a system designed to solve the aforementioned problems. It provides students with a powerful AI system that works only with course materials approved by the instructor. In addition to giving control back to the educator, our approach ensures students receive trustworthy information, blending the benefits of AI with the reliability of a curated curriculum. Each course document is first divided into text chunks, where each chunk contains the text from a single page. These chunks are then stored in a vector database, allowing the system to accurately find specific information later as needed. (N.B. Technicalities are further explained in the methodology section.)

Researchers have looked into important areas that directly impact this, and their efforts generally fall into two main topics: *multi-agent systems* and *source attribution in AI*.

Regarding **source attribution in AI**, D. Li et al. wrote a helpful overview of how AI systems cite sources, explaining the different ways they do it and the problems they face (D. Li et al., 2023). More recently, Wang et al. developed the WASA framework (Wang et al., 2024), which is a new way to embed a hidden watermark into AI-generated text. These watermarks are meant to show the original source of the data used to train the AI. A third attempt in the context of source attribution, by L. Li et al., introduced a different perspective: the goal is to identify who used the AI to create content, not who wrote the original source material (L. Li et al., 2024).

Cemri et al. studied why **multi-agent systems** often struggle to perform better than a simpler system that uses only one agent. They successfully identified 14 different ways these systems fail and organized them into a detailed "Multi-Agent System Failure Taxonomy" (Cemri et al., 2025), which also provided different approaches and methods to make these systems more effective and reliable. In this paper, we address the aforementioned need by exploring the design and implementation of a system that is designed to orchestrate specialized AI components to manage and transform author-controlled content into various helpful outputs, aiming to provide a more dependable and effective learning aid for students. While solving the problem of source attribution in Large Language Models (LLMs) is a significant and complex challenge beyond the scope of a single project, we focus on an achievable solution in the specific domain of "university material". The aim is to build a proprietary system designed to provide students with educational content that is reliable, correct, and directly controlled by professors. This system delivers an accurate type of source attribution, enabling students to track the origin of the information, verify its accuracy, and explore topics in greater depth.

2. METHODOLOGY

2.1 Core Design Principles

The `Studymate` system operates based on a multi-agent framework built upon a Retrieval-Augmented Generation (RAG) architecture (Gao et al., 2023). Rather than being a monolithic program, the system orchestrates the framework's functionality through discrete API calls to external LLMs. A persistent ChromaDB vector database manages course materials, while a central controller delegates tasks—including query classification and text synthesis (see section 2.2)—to specialized agents. Our framework executes tasks through seamless multi-step pipelines that are central to its robustness. Each pipeline, regardless of the target feature (section 2.2), is initiated by an API call to an LLM agent that classifies user intent and extracts key metadata. This information then facilitates targeted retrieval from the ChromaDB knowledge base. Once this content retrieval is complete, the framework directs the information into one of several distinct, multi-step pipelines, each tailored to a specific feature like Q&A, PDF summaries, or podcasts. Each of these pipelines consists of its own chain of targeted API calls to different AI agents ranging from one call to many, where every agent is given a well-defined task and a detailed, role-defining prompt. This modular approach is fundamental to the system's success, as breaking down large tasks into smaller, specialized steps allows it to produce complex and reliable educational content. Figure 1 outlines the framework's architecture and the `Studymate` system's implementation based on it.

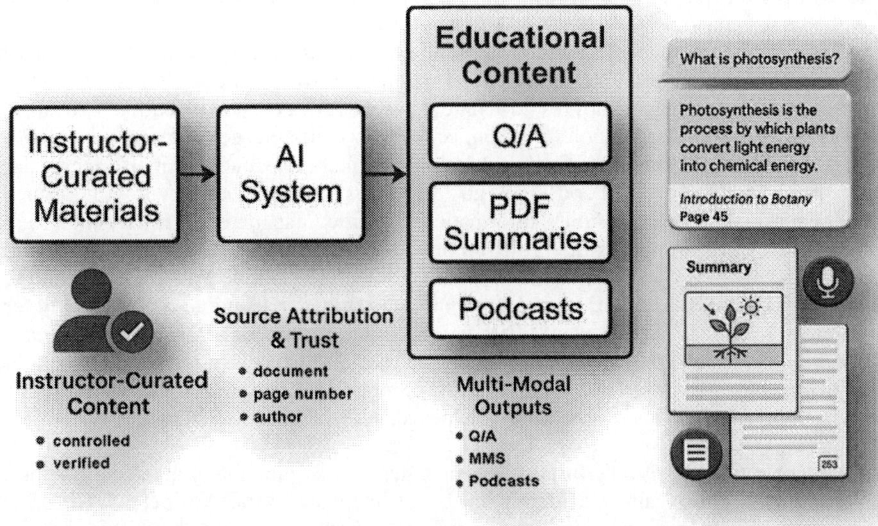

Figure 1. A high-level illustration of the Studymate's model-agnostic architecture and its main features

While our current implementation utilizes high-performance models from Google and OpenAI for their extensive context windows, the framework itself is designed to be fundamentally **model-agnostic**. This architectural philosophy is crucial: *functionality is an emergent property of our multi-step pipelines, not a dependency on the features of a specific LLM.* For instance, podcast generation is achieved through our own robust sequence of API calls, proving the system's ability to construct sophisticated capabilities from fundamental building blocks.

2.2 Main Features

The system offers three main features: *Question/Answer (Q/A), multimodal PDF summaries,* and *podcasts.*

The Q/A feature provides students with a conversational interface for their studies. Unlike general-purpose AI chatbots that draw from vast, unrestricted training data, our system operates on a constrained knowledge base consisting exclusively of university course materials. This approach ensures that all responses are 'grounded' in content created by expert professors, making the answers highly reliable and contextually relevant to the student's curriculum. The feature is designed to handle a wide range of inquiries. It can address general conceptual questions, such as "*what is a vector?*", as long as the information is present within the course documents. Additionally, it can answer highly specific queries that reference particular content, like "*explain question 1 from tutorial 1 of the Physics 1 course*". In what follows, we explain the steps that the system goes through to generate an answer.

(Q/A) Step 1: Classify query intent. In its first step, the system's main job is to understand what the user wants. It figures out if the user is asking a specific question (Q/A), requesting a summary of a document, or asking to create a podcast. At the same time, it carefully looks for key details in the user's sentence, like course names, lecture or tutorial numbers. For example, if the user asks, "*Can you explain question 1 in tutorial 1 of the Physics 1 course?*", the system recognizes the word "explain" and understands the goal is to answer a question. It then extracts the important details "tutorial 1" and "Physics 1" to use as filters in the next step.

(Q/A) Step 2: Retrieve relevant context. In the second step, the system finds the most relevant information from the course materials to answer the user's question. It begins by using the details extracted in the previous step like "tutorial 1" or "Physics 1" to filter its database. Next, from within those filtered chunks, the system performs a semantic search. This means it looks for text that matches the meaning of the user's question, not just the exact words. Once the system identifies the most relevant text chunks, it gathers them to be used as context in the final step.

(Q/A) Step 3: Get response. In the last step, the system's main job is to use the relevant information it found to create a helpful and reliable answer. It takes the user's original question along with the text chunks gathered in the previous step and analyzes this context to construct a clear explanation. Crucially, as the system crafts the answer, it also adds a citation for each piece of information it uses. For our example query, "*Can you explain question 1 …?*", the final answer would not only explain the solution but also include a reference like `(Source: physics1Tutorial1.pdf, Page: 2)`. This provides the student with a trustworthy answer and shows them exactly where to find the information in their course materials if they want to read more.

Another feature of the system is **the multi-modal PDF summaries (MMS)**. Imagine a student at the end of the day who wants to review the material from several lectures, but doesn't have the time or energy to go through hundreds of slides. Alternatively, picture that same student needing to revise quickly for an upcoming exam without re-reading all the content. This is where the multimodal PDF summary feature helps. The system's main job is to take those long documents and create a short, easy-to-read PDF summary. However, its capabilities go beyond simple text summarization, producing a unique and rich output designed for more effective learning. To understand how this is achieved, let's discuss the steps the system goes through to generate this PDF.

(MMS) Step 1: Classify query intent. The first step in this pipeline is the same one used for the Q/A feature. The main job, once again, is to identify the user's intent and extract key details. The primary difference here is that the system recognizes an intent to 'summarize' and pays special attention to any mentioned page ranges. For example, given the query "*Can you summarize lecture 1 of physics 1 from page 20 to 30?*", the system quickly identifies that the user wants a pdf summary and extracts the necessary filters 'lecture 1', 'physics 1', and the page range '20–30' to be used in the next step.

(MMS) Step 2: Retrieve and sort all chunks. After identifying what to summarize, the system's next job is to gather all the necessary text from the database. It uses the filters from the previous step like 'lecture 1' and the page range '20–30' to pull every relevant text chunk that belongs to the requested document. However, simply gathering the chunks isn't enough. The system then carefully reorders them, sorting first by their original page number and then by the chunk's index within each page. This step is crucial because to create an accurate summary, the content must be read in its intended order. By reordering the chunks, the system effectively rebuilds the specified part of the document, ensuring the information flows correctly for the summarization step.

(MMS) Step 3: Get summary response. With the correctly ordered content ready, the system's main job in this step is to generate a clear and concise text summary. It works with two key pieces of information: (i) the user's original request and (ii) the complete, rebuilt document from the previous step. To create the summary, the system is guided by a detailed prompt that contains a specific set of rules. The result of this step is a well-structured text summary, which is then passed on to the next step.

(MMS) Step 4: Format summary LaTeX. In this step, the system converts the text summary into a professionally formatted LaTeX document. To do this, it follows a detailed prompt containing specific rules that guide everything from the overall document layout to the correct formatting of mathematical symbols. The result is LaTeX code for the summary that will be used later to compile the pdf.

(MMS) Step 5: Suggest summary image prompt. The system's job in this step is to come up with an idea for a helpful explanatory image. First, it analyzes the content of the summary to identify the single most important concept where a visual diagram or illustration would be most beneficial for a student's understanding. Once it has identified this key concept, the system writes a detailed text prompt. This prompt acts as a set of instructions for an AI image generator, describing exactly what the image should contain and what style it should have.

(MMS) Step 6: Generate image. In this step, the system takes the generated image prompt from the previous step and generates an image using an image generation model such as, for instance, OpenAI's (N.B. There is nothing special about using this particular model to generate an image. It is just what the system's pipeline currently calls and a well-known label).

(MMS) Step 7: Compile LaTeX with image. In the final step, the system inserts the generated image into the LaTeX code and compiles the file to produce the finished PDF summary.

The next feature is **Podcasts**, which is designed for students who prefer audio-based learning or need to study on the go. Instead of a robotic narration of a summary, the system generates a dynamic mini-podcast featuring an energetic AI host who explains topics in a clear and engaging style. The feature uses the same initial steps as the PDF summary feature.

(Podcasts) Step 1: Classify query intent. The initial step in the podcast pipeline is functionally identical to that of the PDF summary feature. The system's main job is to analyze the user's query, but in this case, it recognizes that the user's intent is to 'create a podcast'.

(Podcasts) Step 2: Retrieve and sort all chunks. This step is also identical to the PDF summary pipeline as the system gathers all relevant text chunks and reorders them by page and chunk number. This process ensures the content is in the correct, logical sequence, which is essential for creating a coherent script for the podcast.

(Podcasts) Step 3: Get summary response. This step is also identical to the PDF summary pipeline as the system takes the rebuilt document and creates a summary out of it.

(Podcasts) Step 4: Generate podcast script. In this step, the system transforms the text summary into an engaging podcast script using a detailed prompt with a unique set of rules. These rules guide the translation of topics and mathematical notation into simple, spoken language, resulting in a conversational script ready for the final audio generation.

(Podcasts) Step 5: Generate audio with OpenAI. In the final step, the system uses the LLM's text-to-speech model to convert the script into a finished audio podcast. Guided by instructions that bring the AI host's energetic personality to life, the model generates the audio, which is then saved as a ready-to-play MP3 file.

2.2.1 Access Control

In an educational setting, teachers and students have different information needs. Teachers often work with materials, such as question banks or private notes, that are not meant for student access. To manage this securely, the system includes **a role-based access control feature**. This allows both teachers and students to use the same platform seamlessly. When a document is added, an instructor can assign an access level to it (like 'professional' for teachers or 'regular' for students). The system then checks a user's role during every search, ensuring they can only retrieve information from the documents they are permitted to see. While designed for academia, this hierarchical access can be applied in any organization to manage information access across different access levels.

3. RESULTS

(Q/A) Results: We demonstrate the Q/A feature by giving the system a general query, like: "*what is a vector?*" A response to this query would be lengthy. To ensure full visibility, it is formatted in typewriter-style text below.

```
Okay, let's talk about vectors. A vector quantity is fully described by a number with appropriate units and a direction (Source: [physics1Lecture1.pdf], Page: 20). Many physical quantities in nature have both magnitude and direction, which is why we need vectors (Source: [physics1Lecture1.pdf], Page:17). Think about a collision between two cars; you need to know both how fast they are going and in what direction to understand the impact (Source: [physics1Lecture1.pdf], Page: 17). A vector can be expressed in terms of its components using unit vectors that indicate the main directions (Source: [physics1Lecture1.pdf], Page: 26). We can completely describe any vector by its components, which are projections of the vector along an axis (Source: [physics1Lecture1.pdf], Page: 21). It's often useful to use rectangular components, which are projections along the x- and y-axes (Source: [physics1Lecture1.pdf], Page: 21). These components can be positive or negative, depending on the angle and the quadrant in which the vector lies, but they will have the same units as the original vector (Source: [physics1Lecture1.pdf], Page: 23). When dealing with just the magnitude of a vector in print, we use an italic letter, like A, or the modulus |A| (Source: [physics1Lecture1.pdf], Page: 20). The magnitude of a vector is always a positive number and has physical units (Source: [physics1Lecture1.pdf], Page: 20).
```

The system's response highlights two key results. First, it demonstrated precise source attribution by providing a citation for every piece of information, referencing both the exact source document and the page number where the information was found. This allows students to easily verify the facts or read more about the topic directly from their course materials. Second, the output confirmed the system's information integrity. The system uses the course material as its only source for factual information, and while it may rephrase sentences to create a clear explanation, it does not introduce new concepts from outside the approved documents. This ensures students receive information that is strictly aligned with their curriculum, providing a trustworthy study aid. The sample lecture referenced in the results and citations is available here: System Outcomes (hyperlink) for verification. Readers may also consult the generated PDFs and Podcasts in the same folder for additional results related to all what follows.

(Multimodal PDF summary) Results: An analysis of the generated PDF summaries reveals several successful outcomes of the system. The summaries are well-structured and professionally formatted, making them clear and easy for students to read. Furthermore, the system demonstrates technical accuracy by correctly handling and rendering mathematical equations and symbols within the LaTeX environment. The content is also concise, successfully distilling the core information from the source document into a manageable study aid. Finally, the system achieves accurate source attribution, with the title page of each summary correctly identifying both the original source document and the name of the professor who authored it.

(Podcasts) Results: The podcast generation feature successfully produces audio summaries that are both informative and engaging. A key result is the performance of the AI host. Instead of a flat, robotic narration, the host's tone is consistently energetic and dynamic, which helps to maintain the listener's interest. Furthermore, the host explains topics clearly and often uses simple analogies to make the material more relatable and easier to understand. This combination of an engaging delivery and clear explanations creates a final audio product that prevents listener fatigue, making it an effective and enjoyable study tool.

3.1 Empirical Evaluation

To our knowledge, no standardized tests currently exist to evaluate this type of system. We, therefore, adopted an expert review approach to evaluate the system, consulting the professors who authored the source materials used by the systems. We also conducted a survey with students. The feedback was largely positive, providing validation for the system's utility and highlighting areas for improvement.

Four professors (who wrote the lectures and tutorials) reviewed the system's outputs and provided their professional assessment (Their approval was also obtained for using their materials in our testing framework).

- Three out of the four responded positively to the system and its potential as an effective educational tool. They particularly praised the conciseness of the PDF summaries and the accurate formatting of mathematics in these summaries. While one professor favored the Q&A and PDF summary functions more, two others highlighted the podcast as the best feature. This group also offered suggestions for future enhancements, such as an automatic quiz generator, the ability to create explanatory videos, and giving instructors more control over the image generation process within the Multimodal PDF summary feature.
- In contrast, one professor did not like the system and provided more critical feedback. While she considered the PDF summary to be the system's best feature, she found the podcast's host persona to be "childish" and not suitable for university students. For the summary's visual component, she suggested that a mind map of the lecture would be more pedagogically useful than a single conceptual image. Her feedback also highlighted a desire for more features designed specifically for educators.

To get student opinions on the system, seven students completed a questionnaire after a demonstration of its features.

- When it comes to the system's **overall usefulness**, student feedback was highly positive. On a 1-to-5 scale where 5 is "Extremely useful," four students gave a rating of 4, and the remaining gave a rating of 5. This was supported by comments describing the system as a "great idea" and "very creative and helpful".
- Regarding **the most valued features**, the multimodal PDF summary was their clear favorite, chosen by six of the seven students, followed by the Question/Answer (Q&A) feature.
- In terms of **feature-specific feedback**, students praised the PDF summaries for their clarity and organization. However, the podcast was also found to be appealing by many for its energetic tone, although some still noted a personal preference for reading. On the general concept, students particularly appreciated that the system's sources are confined to the official course curriculum.

- When it comes to **concerns**, the first one was the potential for over-reliance on the tool. one student raised another concern about comprehensiveness, questioning if a two-page summary of a 32-slide presentation could contain all the information needed for a test.
- Regarding **suggestions** students suggested future features like video summaries, an automatic quiz generator and the creation of personalized study plans.

3.2 Scope, Limitations and Prospective Enhancements

The empirical evaluation, while providing valuable qualitative feedback, highlights several limitations of the current study and informs key directions for future work. This discussion addresses the scope of our evaluation, outlines planned system enhancements, and considers practical aspects of future deployment.

Scope of Evaluation

The evaluation was designed to gather in-depth qualitative feedback from experts and target users rather than broad quantitative data.

- **Sample Size:** The student evaluation was conducted with a limited sample (N=7) to ensure each participant fully understood the system's functionality, prioritizing the depth of feedback over breadth. Similarly, the faculty evaluation (N=4) was intentionally focused on the authors of the source materials to ensure the validity of their assessment regarding content accuracy and pedagogical suitability. Future work should aim to expand this sample size for broader validation.
- **Lack of Quantitative Benchmarks:** A quantitative assessment was not performed due to the absence of standardized benchmarks for evaluating RAG systems with a specific focus on instructor-controlled pedagogical tools. While the system's source attribution was rigorously tested during development, reporting an internal metric would not reflect performance on new, unseen materials.
- **Comparative Analysis:** A direct feature-by-feature comparison with other AI study tools was deemed out of scope. The primary innovation of `Studymate` is its instructor-centric architecture, which fundamentally differs from student-facing tools like ChatGPT that allow users to upload their own materials. The core objective was to establish a new paradigm for educator control, not to incrementally improve upon existing student-controlled systems.

Planned System Enhancements

Feedback from both professors and students, combined with our development roadmap, has identified several high-priority enhancements:

- **Multimodal Input:** A critical next step is to enable the system to process and interpret visual data, such as diagrams, charts, and equations embedded as images within the source materials. This would allow for more comprehensive and accurate responses, particularly in STEM subjects.
- **Conversational Memory:** Implementing a persistent conversational context is essential. This will allow the system to handle follow-up questions, creating a more natural and effective dialogue-based learning experience for students.
- **Expanded Feature Set:** Based on user feedback, future iterations will explore the development of new features, including an automatic quiz generator from course materials, the creation of explanatory video summaries, and personalized study plan generation. We will also enhance the multimodal summary feature by allowing instructors to choose between different visual aids, such as a conceptual image or a generated mind map, and provide them with more granular control over the output.

4. CONCLUSIVE REMARKS

This paper presents `Studymate`: an LLM/API-based system that successfully generates multimodal educational content based on given study material while ensuring reliability through robust source attribution. The system operates as a multi-agent framework built upon a RAG architecture, and orchestrates functionality through discrete API calls to external LLMs. A persistent ChromaDB vector database manages course materials, while a central controller delegates tasks to specialized agents. The system is robust and produces varied educational aids, including cited Q&A responses, PDF summaries with images, and audio podcasts, all grounded in an instructor-provided knowledge base. A key contribution is its page-level citation mechanism, which provides verifiable links that function as source attribution to the original material, directly addressing the critical issue of AI hallucinations in an educational context. Furthermore, the system's role-based access control gives educators direct authority over which documents students can access. Ultimately, this project offers a practical framework for creating trustworthy AI tools that serve as dependable learning aids for both students and educators.

While a broader roadmap for future work is detailed in section 3.2, the critical challenge of real- world application warrants a final mention. For `Studymate` to transition from a framework to a widely adopted tool, the scalability and integration of its access control feature are key. A full-scale implementation will require optimization for rapid user authentication against institutional databases. Therefore, a primary goal for future work is the development of a generalizable framework to streamline integration with proprietary Learning Management Systems (LMS), making `Studymate` an adaptable tool for diverse educational environments.

REFERENCES

Cemri, M., Pan, M. Z., Yang, S., Agrawal, L. A., Chopra, B., Tiwari, R., Keutzer, K., Parameswaran,A., Klein, D., Ramchandran, K., Zaharia, M., Gonzalez, J. E., & Stoica, I. (2025). Why do multi-agent llm systems fail? https://arxiv.org/abs/2503.13657.

Gao, Y., Xiong, Y., Gao, X., Jia, K., Pan, J., Bi, Y., Dai, Y., Sun, J., & Wang, H. (2023). Retrieval-augmented generation for large language models: A survey. arXiv preprint arXiv:2312.10997.

Li, D., Sun, Z., Hu, X., Liu, Z., Chen, Z., Hu, B., Wu, A., & Zhang, M. (2023). A survey of large language models attribution. https://arxiv.org/abs/2311.03731.

Li, L., Bai, Y., & Cheng, M. (2024, November). Where am I from? identifying origin of LLM-generated content. In *Y. Al-Onaizan, M. Bansal, & Y.-N. Chen (Eds.), Proceedings of the 2024 conference on empirical methods in natural language processing* (pp. 12218–12229). Association for Computational Linguistics. https://doi.org/10.18653/v1/2024.emnlp-main.681.

Wang, J., Lu, X., Zhao, Z., Dai, Z., Foo, C.-S., Ng, S.-K., & Low, B. K. H. (2024). Source attribution for large language model-generated data. https://arxiv.org/abs/2310.00646.

A FRAMEWORK FOR ADAPTIVE LEARNING BASED ON PROCESS MINING IN HIGHER EDUCATION

Nisseb Bergaoui[1,3] and Sonia Ayachi Ghannouchi[2,3]
[1]*University of Sousse, Higher Institute of Computer Science and Communication Technologies of Hammam Sousse, Tunisia*
[2]*University of Sousse, Higher Institute of Management of Sousse, Tunisia*
[3]*Laboratary RIADI-GDL-University of Manouba, Tunisia*

ABSTRACT

Higher education plays a critical role in human, economic, and societal development. In today's rapidly evolving educational landscape, institutions face the challenge of delivering personalized, flexible, and effective learning experiences. This paper proposes a hybrid framework for adaptive and intelligent education, combining Agile principles, Business Process Management (BPM), and Process Mining (PM) to enhance teaching and learning processes. By mapping the values and principles of the Agile Manifesto to educational contexts, the model promotes flexibility, collaboration, and continuous feedback, enabling instructors to better address diverse student needs. BPM provides a structured lifecycle for modeling, analysis, and continuous improvement of educational processes, while PM leverages event log data to identify inefficiencies and deviations through advanced algorithms. Our contributions are threefold: (1) the development of an Adaptive Learning algorithm with three modules filtering, process discovery, and enhancement to iteratively improve learning processes; (2) a cyclical Agile-Education approach that integrates BPMN modeling and Process Mining techniques to refine teaching strategies over successive iterations; and (3) the design of an Android application that supports instructors in modeling, monitoring, and optimizing educational activities. Although the framework is validated on a single course module with a limited sample size, results suggest potential for improving instructional responsiveness and student outcomes. Future research will focus on expanding validation across diverse courses and institutions.

KEYWORDS

Process Mining, Agile Learning, Adaptive Learning, BPM, Smart Education

1. INTRODUCTION

Higher education plays a critical role in human, economic, and societal development. In today's rapidly evolving educational landscape, institutions face the challenge of delivering personalized, flexible, and effective learning experiences. This paper proposes a hybrid framework for adaptive and intelligent education, combining Agile principles, Business Process Management (BPM), and Process Mining (PM) to enhance teaching and learning processes. By mapping the values and principles of the Agile Manifesto to educational contexts, the model promotes flexibility, collaboration, and continuous feedback, enabling instructors to better address diverse student needs. BPM provides a structured lifecycle for modeling, analysis, and continuous improvement of educational processes, while PM leverages event log data to identify inefficiencies and deviations through advanced algorithms. Our contributions are threefold:

(1) The development of an Adaptive Learning algorithm with three modules: filtering, process discovery, and enhancement, to iteratively improve learning processes.

(2) A cyclical Agile-Education approach that integrates BPMN modeling and Process Mining techniques to refine teaching strategies over successive iterations; and

(3) The design of an Android application that supports instructors in modeling, monitoring, and optimizing educational activities. The hybrid model places students at the center of the learning process, enhances instructional responsiveness, and paves the way for an intelligent digital transformation in higher education. The paper is structured as follows: Sections 1.1 and 1.2 cover the research context and related literature, Section 2 presents the proposed framework, Section 3 describes the algorithm, Section 4 reports the statistical analysis of students' results, and Section 5 provides the conclusion.

1.1 Research Problem

Traditional education where teachers verbally transmit knowledge and students passively receive it is increasingly inadequate in engaging modern learners (Bruter&Annie, 2013) (Cathia & Glikman, 2015). Generations Z and Alpha, digital natives immersed in technology, expect interactive and personalized learning experiences, yet educational models often fail to meet their evolving needs (Vultaggio et al., 2021). This disconnect raises urgent questions: How can we reshape learning culture to drive deep educational transformation? How can we prepare learners for a rapidly changing world? How do we transmit knowledge that remains relevant despite fast obsolescence? What choices today can proactively shape the future of education? Educating 21st-century students using outdated methods inherited from the 19th century is no longer viable. The assumption that teachers hold all knowledge while learners passively listen must be replaced by active, contextualized pedagogies. Curricula should reflect learners' cultural, academic, and socioeconomic realities, integrating local and global perspectives. Educational technologies are pivotal in enabling such innovation. Our research focuses on four key objectives:

- Stimulate learners' motivation to actively build knowledge, skills, and cultural awareness.
- Promote continuous, adaptive improvement of agile learning processes.
- Ensure flexible, responsive learning within intelligent education systems.
- Provide teachers with a mobile application supporting iterative, collaborative educational processes involving subject experts and engineers.

To address the diverse needs of new generations, a comprehensive framework combining multiple approaches is essential. This includes assisting educators in selecting suitable pedagogical pathways. Literature review highlights motivation, knowledge construction, and cultural factors as central themes. Business Process Management (BPM) offers a promising strategy to adapt learning processes across contexts. Process Mining techniques further enable intelligent monitoring and control, while mobile app development ensures practical, context-aware implementation.

1.2 Related Work

This research builds upon a systematic literature review conducted with the PRISMA methodology, ensuring an objective and reproducible selection of studies (Bergaoui & Ghannouchi, 2024). That survey analyzed works on Process Mining (PM) and Business Process Management (BPM) in education and revealed gaps that motivated the development of an Agile-based adaptive learning framework integrating BPM, PM, and student-centered strategies. Agile principles enable iterative planning, feedback, and flexibility, while BPM and PM provide structured modeling, data-driven insights, and mechanisms for improvement (Bergaoui & Ghannouchi, 2023). Adaptive learning goes beyond passive and active methods by personalizing pathways according to student needs, and Bloom's taxonomy offers a hierarchical classification that aligns with passive, active, and adaptive approaches (Lubbe et al., 2025). Recent studies extend this perspective by classifying pedagogical strategies according to engagement and personalization (Wambsganss & Schmit, 2024; Kwan et al., 2025), while others highlight the role of Process Mining in learning analytics (Maldonado-Mahauad et al., 2023) and provide empirical evidence on adaptive learning adoption in higher education (Zawacki-Richter & Jung, 2024). Despite the individual application of BPM and PM, few studies combine them with Agile-based adaptive learning, a gap this work addresses through a hybrid model supported by a mobile application that enhances instructional responsiveness and student outcomes.

2. THE PROPOSED FRAMEWORK

The general idea of our research work is to combine all the concepts BPM, PM Education, and Agility to ensure the continuous and adaptive improvement of the learning processes and associated strategies, which promote the implementation of the adaptability of the learning process in intelligent education. We propose in Figure 1 an overview of the proposed framework.

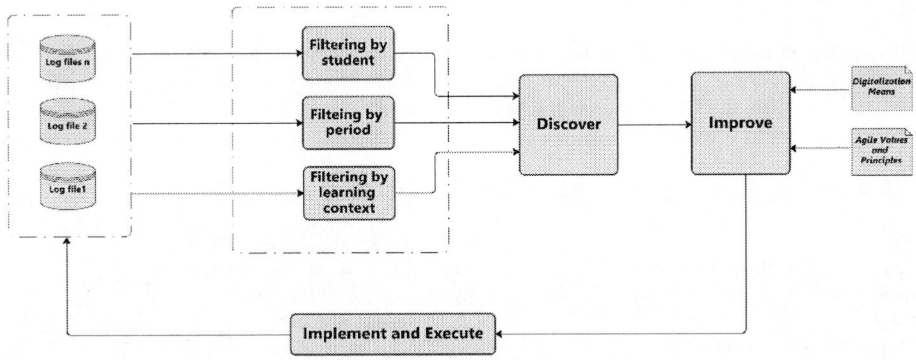

Figure 1. Overview of the framework Agile_Education

We will attempt in our research work to combine all the concepts presented in the previous sections: AGILE, BPM, PM, and EDUCATION to ensure the continuous and adaptive improvement of the learning processes and associated strategies, which promote the implementation of the adaptability of the learning process in intelligent education. The first step of our framework is to apply our model based on the PM discovery technique and algorithms to identify and establish a behavioral model that describes the educational process as captured by log files. Then we go through multiple or selective filtering according to our needs by implementing the PM Inductive Miner algorithm, which provides process models built on causal graphs (input and output dependence for each activity). The specificity of this algorithm is that it accepts as input all types of data, even noise and incomplete data. After the application of the three types of filtering presented in the process (by the student, by period, by context), we can either combine 2 types of filtering at the same time or just apply only one type. Consequently, we will have as output our first adaptive educational process, which in turn can be improved by using the 4 values and 12 agile principles and/or all types of digital learning. Finally, we re-implement our improved educational process from which we will have new log files as Input, and in this way, we guarantee the dynamism of our educational process. The strength of our proposed approach is that it ensures and guarantees control, agility, adaptability and continuous improvement of the educational process according to an infinite number of iterations and increments of our discovered and improved BPMN model. In the next section we will apply our approach to a real case study.

3. THE PROPOSED ALGORITHM

Our proposed algorithm is composed of three main modules: Filter (), Discover (), Enhance (), each of which includes several sub-modules. In the following sections, we present and interpret them in detail.

```
Adaptive_Learning Algorithm
Begin
Repeat
Filter (File_log, Identifier, Context, Period)
Discover (File_log)
Enhance (File_log, File.BPMN)
Until the end of the period
End
```

Algorithm 1. Adaptive_Learning Algorithm

3.1 The Filter Procedure

Log files represent the collected data. This filtering procedure filters our collected files according to our needs. It takes log files as input and displays the filtered log files. It calls three functions: first, read_CSV, which transfers the data from the CSV file to a dictionary table to filter it by size. Then, it calls the data_filter function to perform the desired filtering. Finally, it calls the save procedure, which saves the filtered data to our file.

```
Procedure Filter (log files, Identifier, Context,
Period)
Begin
   data ← Read_CSV(input_file)
   filtered_data ← Filter_Data (data, column,
value)
   Save_CSV (filtered_data, output_file)

 End
```

Algorithm 2. Filter procedure

```
Procedure Read_CSV (nph_path: string)
Begin
   Var T: array of dictionary f: csv file
   Open file "nph.csv" as f for reading
   While not end of file (f) do
         Read the headers
         Add the row as an array of
                                dictionary
   End while
   Close file (f)
   Return (data)
End
```

Algorithm 3. Read-CSV procedure

The development of the filter procedure is organized into sub-modules, each detailed in Algorithms 3, 4, and 5.

```
Function Filter_Data (data:table,column_name:
string, search_value: string)
Begin
  Create an empty array result
  For each row in data do
    If row[column_name] = search_value then
      Add row to result
    End If
  End For
  Return (result)
  Close file (f)
End
```

Algorithm 4. Filter_Data function

```
Procedure Save_CSV (data: array of
dictionary, nph_path: string)
Begin
  If data is empty then
     Display ("No data to save")
  End If
  Open file "nph.csv" as f for writing
  Write the headers
   For each line in data do
     Write the line to the file
   End ForClose file (f)
End
```

Algorithm 5. Save_CSV procedure

3.2 The Discover Procedure

This procedure first involves transforming the file type from csv to xes, then calling the appropriate algorithm to discover the BPMN model, which we call in our work the inductive Miner.

```
Discover Procedure (Log File)
Begin
    Open Source_file as f for reading
    Read the file's contents            //Apply a transformation to the contents
    File_Modified ← Transform (CSV_file) // with ProM tool level
    Open  a new file Target_File as f for writing
    Target_File ← inductive miner (XES_file) // Transform the xes nto a BPMN file
    Close Source_File
    Close Target_File
End
```

Algorithms 6. Discover procedure

The BPMN file discovery from event logs is performed with the open-source ProM tool using the Inductive Miner algorithm, which enables process model discovery, alignment with logs, deviation detection, performance analysis, and animation, all locally without requiring internet or data transfer. It was developed by Sander Leemans at Queensland University of Technology and Eindhoven University of Technology.

```
Procedure Transform (CSV File)
Begin
  traces dictionary ← empty
  Open file "nph.csv" as f for reading
  For each line of the CSV file, do
      Extract fields: case_id, activity, times-
tamp [, others]
      Create an event ← (activity, timestamp
                          [others])
        If case_id is not in traces then
           traces[case_id] ← empty list
           Add event to traces[case_id]
           Create an XML document
                          with root <log>
           Add XES extension and meta
                          information tags
        End If
  End For
For each case_id in traces, do
  Create a <trace> tag
   Add <string key="concept:name"
                          value=case_id>
End for
 For each trace event [case_id] do
   Create an <event> tag
    Add <string key="concept:name"
                          value= acTivity>
    Add <date key="time:timestamp"
          value=timestamp>
    Add other attributes if present]
 End for
 Write the XML document to XES_file
End
```

Algorithms 7. Transform procedure

3.3 Enhance Procedure

The module is being developed in ProM, where learning parameters are adjusted to generate new trace files for BPMN discovery. A BPMN file can also be directly analyzed: core elements are extracted, and performance issues—such as redundant tasks, long sequences, and deep loops—are identified. The process is then improved by reorganizing tasks, adding gateways, and removing unnecessary elements, after which the updated BPMN is validated and exported.

4. STATISTICAL STUDY OF STUDENTS' RESULTS

One of the key contributions of our agile and adaptive educational method is its measurable impact on student performance in the Human–Machine Interaction (HMI) module. To evaluate effectiveness, we compared final exam results obtained under the traditional teacher-centered approach with those achieved after implementing our agile and adaptive pedagogy. Our method introduces agility by presenting the course as a sequence of concrete projects, while progressively integrating theoretical concepts, definitions, and practices. This approach emphasizes student engagement, collaboration, and continuous adaptation to learners' needs. A comparative analysis was conducted on two independent student groups. In the traditional cohort (n = 120), a random sample of 50 students was analyzed: 27 students succeeded, corresponding to a success rate of 54%. In the agile and adaptive cohort (n = 130), a similar sample of 50 students was analyzed: 45 students succeeded, corresponding to a success rate of 90%. The results are summarized in Figure 2, which presents success and failure rates for both teaching methods.

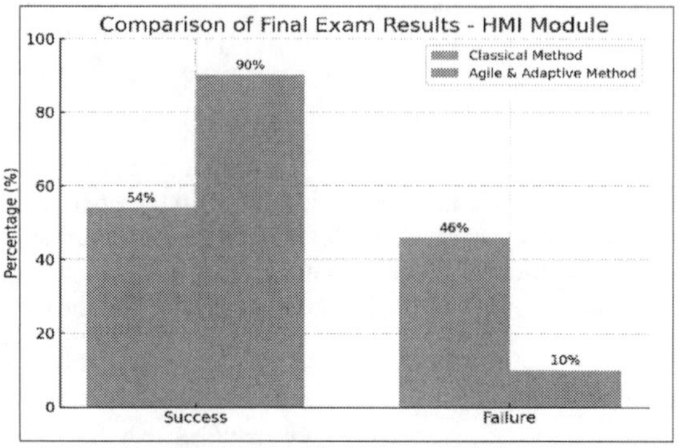

Figure 2. Comparison of final exam results in the HMI module: Classical vs. Agile & Adaptive Method

Figure 2 shows that the success rate nearly doubled with the agile and adaptive method, highlighting the benefits of active, student-centered learning. Integrating these principles in higher education can enhance autonomy, collaboration, and diverse assessments. However, the study was limited to one module without controlling cohort differences; future work will expand to more modules, larger populations, and rigorous statistical validation.

5. CONCLUSION

This work presents an algorithm to enhance educational processes using historical traces and adaptivity, structured into three iterative modules: filtering traces, process discovery, and improvement. An Agile-Education cycle combines trace analysis, BPMN modeling, and iterative refinement via the Inductive Miner in ProM. A supporting mobile app helps teachers, subject matter experts, and engineering experts' model, compare, and improve processes. Future developments include a ProM plugin to integrate agile principles and digitalization directly into BPMN, allowing more flexible and effective educational process design.

REFERENCES

Bergaoui, N., & Ghannouchi, S. A. (2023). A BPM-based approach for ensuring an agile and adaptive learning process. Smart Learning Environments, 10(1), 40.

Bergaoui, N., & Ghannouchi, S. A. (2024). A Survey on Educational Processes Based on Agile, BPM, and PM. International Journal of Computer Information Systems and Industrial Management Applications, 16(2), 14. https://cspub-ijcisim.org/index.php/ijcisim/article/view/629

Bruter, A. (2013). Le cours magistral dans l'enseignement secondaire. Nature, histoire, représentations (1802–1902). Histoire@Politique, 3, 22–38.

Calegari, D., & Delgado, A. (2025). A systematic review on process mining for curricular analysis. Wiley Interdisciplinary Reviews: Data Mining and Knowledge Discovery, 15(2), e70005.

Kwan, P., Kadel, R., Memon, T. D., & Hashmi, S. S. (2025). Reimagining flipped learning via Bloom's taxonomy and student–teacher–GenAI interactions. Education Sciences, 15(4), 465.

Lubbe, A., Marais, E., & Kruger, D. (2025). Cultivating independent thinkers: The triad of artificial intelligence, Bloom's taxonomy and critical thinking in assessment pedagogy. Education and Information Technologies, 1–34.

Maldonado-Mahauad, J., Scheffel, M., & Chounta, I.-A. (2023). Process mining for learning analytics: A systematic review and future perspectives. Computers & Education, 197, 104699

Van Dongen, B. F., et al. (2005). The ProM framework: A new era in process mining tool support. In International Conference on Application and Theory of Petri Nets. Springer Berlin Heidelberg.

Vultaggio, G. (2021). "The Most Anxious Generation": The relationship between Gen Z students, social media, and anxiety.

Wambsganss, T., & Schmitt, A. (2024). Enhancing personalized learning through process mining: A taxonomy and design patterns approach. Business & Information Systems Engineering, 1–24.

Zawacki-Richter, O., & Jung, I. (2024). Adaptive learning in higher education: A review of empirical studies. Educational Technology Research and Development, 72(3), 1125–1149

DIVE: A DATA-DRIVEN INTELLIGENT VIDEO EVALUATION SYSTEM FOR ENHANCING SWIMMING PERFORMANCE

Vanessa Camilleri, Justine Scicluna, Gianluca Aquilina, Dylan Seychell and Emma Swanwick
University of Malta, Malta

ABSTRACT

This paper presents DIVE (Data-driven Intelligent Video Evaluation), a lightweight system designed to analyse underwater swimming videos using pose estimation and domain-informed feature extraction. The system aims to support coaches and athletes by providing interpretable biomechanical metrics without the need for expensive motion-capture infrastructure. The video capture setup uses off-the-shelf GoPro cameras positioned poolside to ensure stable and consistent footage. Pose estimation models were evaluated on collected video samples, and features such as stroke rate, symmetry, alignment, and turn performance were extracted based on joint coordinates.

The system includes a modular architecture with pipelines for video pre-processing, pose estimation, feature computation, and future feedback presentation. Domain experts contributed to the design of task-specific features to ensure relevance and interpretability. Preliminary analysis suggests that model choice and camera angle substantially impact pose accuracy. While still under development, DIVE lays the foundation for scalable, context-aware performance feedback in swimming. Future work will involve completing quantitative validation using annotated ground truth, improving phase detection accuracy, and designing user-facing tools for real-time visual feedback.

KEYWORDS

Swimming, Pose Estimation, Biomechanics, Computer Vision, Sports Performance, Underwater Video Analysis

1. INTRODUCTION

Performance analysis in competitive swimming increasingly relies on video and sensor-based technologies to monitor technique, optimise training, and reduce injury risk. However, most current tools either focus on above-water footage or require specialised hardware that is impractical for poolside deployment. Moreover, existing systems often lack the granularity needed to analyse underwater movement patterns, where much of the critical biomechanical action occurs.

In response to these challenges, this paper introduces DIVE (Data-driven Intelligent Video Evaluation), a pilot-stage modular video analytics system designed to process dual-perspective footage, captured simultaneously above and below the waterline, using state-of-the-art pose estimation models. At this stage, feasibility is defined as the ability to capture synchronised dual-view footage in real-world pool settings and to benchmark pose estimation models against manually annotated swimmer keypoints. The aim is not yet to deliver a complete training tool, but to demonstrate that accurate, interpretable metrics can be derived from affordable, portable hardware. The system is built on commercially available GoPro cameras and a synchronised data processing pipeline, enabling the extraction of relevant biomechanical features such as stroke rate, turn efficiency, and body alignment.

This work is developed in collaboration with the Aquatic Sports Association of Malta (ASA) and targets both practical deployment and research reproducibility. To this end, DIVE is being used to curate an annotated video dataset of swimmers across styles, skill levels, and age groups. This dataset, intended for open release, is designed to support further research in human movement analysis, aquatic sports technology, and AI in biomechanics. The key contributions of this paper are:

1. The design and implementation of DIVE, a modular video analysis system for swimming performance based on dual-perspective GoPro footage and state-of-the-art pose estimation.

2.A portable, poolside-compatible hardware and data synchronisation setup tailored for real-world training conditions.

3.A domain-informed processing pipeline capable of extracting stroke-specific and phase-based biomechanical metrics from swimmer videos.

4.The ongoing development of an open annotated video dataset of swimmers across styles, ages, and competitive levels to support further research in AI-based movement analysis.

The rest of this paper describes the system architecture (Section 3), the methodology (Section 4), the pilot study and evaluation (Section 5), and a discussion of the implementation (Section 6) to conclude with a look at the proposed future work and foreseen challenges (Section 7).

2. RELATED WORK AND CONTEXT

AI-based performance analysis has become increasingly prevalent in sports science, with recent advances in computer vision enabling detailed motion tracking and biomechanical assessment. In swimming, most studies to date have focused on controlled, laboratory-based setups using either wearable sensors or above-water video footage. These approaches often fall short in capturing underwater mechanics, which are critical to stroke efficiency, turn execution, and body alignment. Several researchers have explored video-based analysis of swimming technique. Costa et al. (2021) developed a framework to assess stroke mechanics using underwater footage, but it required fixed lab setups and controlled lighting. Chen et al. (2022) proposed an AI-based classification model for stroke detection, demonstrating the feasibility of using pose keypoints to segment swimming phases. While these systems show promise, they often rely on simplified or stylised datasets and are rarely deployed in uncontrolled pool environments.

Recent work by Morais et al. (2020) has highlighted the importance of combining computer vision with domain-specific biomechanical insights. However, most available systems lack modularity and generalisability, limiting their usefulness across varied swimmer profiles and training conditions.

The emergence of deep learning-based pose estimation models such as AlphaPose and ViTPose has enabled more accurate human keypoint detection across challenging environments. Yet, applications of these models in underwater settings remain under-explored, largely due to lighting variability, water distortion, and limited access to annotated aquatic datasets. DIVE builds on this foundation by offering a lightweight, modular system that combines dual-perspective capture with open-source pose models to extract stroke specific metrics. Unlike prior work, DIVE is designed for real-world poolside deployment using portable hardware and explicitly targets diverse swimmer profiles through its planned open dataset. To our knowledge, it is among the first systems to operationalise above- and below-water synchronised analysis using commodity video equipment.

3. SYSTEM ARCHITECTURE AND IMPLEMENTATION

The DIVE system is designed as a modular video analytics pipeline for real-world swimming performance analysis. It integrates dual-perspective video capture, pose estimation, stroke segmentation, and biomechanical metric extraction. The system supports deployment in live training environments using accessible and portable equipment, and is being piloted in collaboration with ASA.

3.1 Hardware Setup

The video capture component consists of two GoPro cameras mounted on a custom rig at the edge of the pool, one positioned above water and one below, to provide simultaneous lateral views of swimmer movement. Figure 1 presents the frontal view plan of the setup, while Figure 2 shows the corresponding top view layout. The cameras are fixed to a stable frame, ensuring minimal vibration and consistent alignment throughout each recording session. Figure 3 depicts the actual hardware used, and Figure 4 illustrates the data collection process in practice.

These cameras were used with specific settings: 4K resolution (3840×2160 pixels) at 120 fps, with a wide field of view setting. Synchronisation between the two video feeds is achieved using timestamp alignment and visible motion triggers (e.g., arm movement or entry splash), enabling accurate cross-perspective analysis.

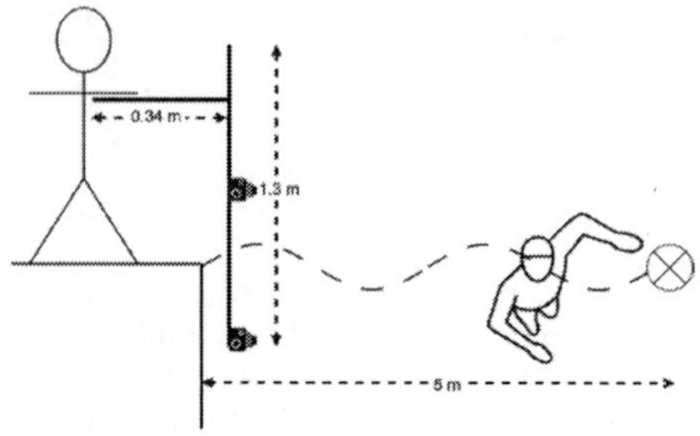

Figure 1. A front view plan of the setup for data collection. The diagram is not to scale

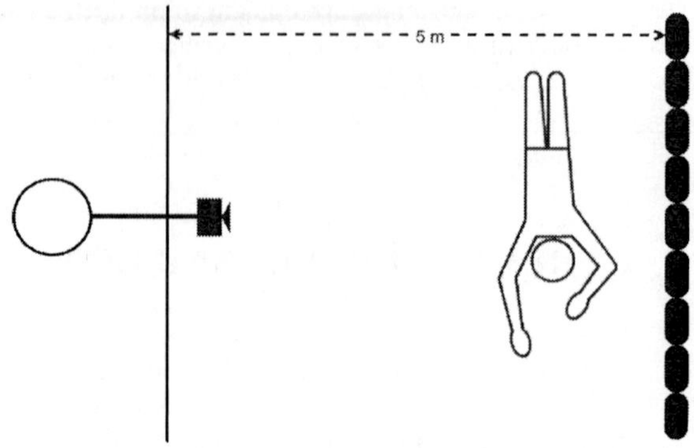

Figure 2. A top-view plan of the setup for data collection. The diagram is not to scale

Figure 3. A photograph of the hardware setup used for the data collection process

Figure 4. A photograph of the data collection process of this dataset

3.2 Software Pipeline

The system's modular processing workflow is shown in Figure 5. Each video stream is processed independently using pre-trained pose estimation model ViTPose to extract 2D keypoints for each swimmer. These keypoints are used to detect and segment stroke cycles based on biomechanical features and limb trajectory patterns.

The stroke segmentation module applies rule-based heuristics, tuned per stroke style, to identify swim phases such as entry, catch, pull, and recovery. From these segmented cycles, DIVE computes performance metrics including stroke rate, symmetry indices, turn duration, and limb coordination.

All extracted data is stored in a structured format, linking metrics with frame ranges and synchronised video clips. This design allows for future integration with interface modules or further multimodal extensions (e.g., wearable sensors). The system supports modular substitution of pose models, segmentation logic, and metric definitions, providing long-term extensibility across research and applied contexts.

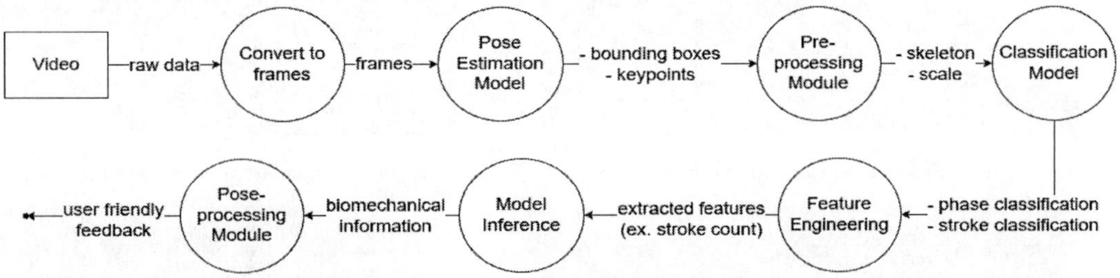

Figure 5. Data Flow Diagram of the project pipeline from input to final output

4. METHODOLOGY

4.1 Data Collection Protocol

Data collection sessions were strategically distributed across different times of day to capture a broad range of natural lighting conditions. This approach enhances model robustness to both human variability and environmental factors. Between 12 and 16 videos were recorded for each participant, comprising both dynamic and static recordings. In the dynamic sessions, the cameras were moved alongside the swimmer as they completed two 50-metre lengths per stroke type (freestyle, backstroke, breaststroke, and butterfly), including a turn at one end of the pool. For consistency, dives and turns were also recorded using a fixed camera position to ensure a stable view of these high-speed actions. Additional recordings were conducted with a fixed camera, capturing each stroke type with the swimmer entering the frame and traversing approximately 15 metres within view.

4.2 Pose Estimation Model

To determine the most suitable pose estimation model for swimming-specific analysis, several state-of-the-art architectures were taken into consideration (Ouyang et al., 2024). The tested models included HRNet (Lin et al., 2015), ViTPose (Xu et al., 2022), and AlphaPose (Fang et al., 2017), each chosen for their strong performance in general human pose estimation tasks. HRNet exhibited the greatest limitations, particularly in handling fast, dynamic movements such as turns, where joint detection accuracy significantly declined. ViTPose offered improved accuracy and temporal stability, making it a strong candidate for swimming analysis. However, AlphaPose provided broader keypoint coverage, including head and toe keypoints that are particularly relevant for assessing streamlined body alignment. From comparisons between the latter two on different types of clips, ViTPose was identified as the best candidate as it demonstrated significantly improved accuracy over AlphaPose. Figures 6, 7, 8 & 9 illustrate sample frames from the four strokes freestyle, breaststroke, backstroke, and butterfly with the detected pose estimation from ViTPose. These visualisations demonstrate the models' ability to detect full-body joint configurations across multiple stroke types, despite water-induced distortion, bubbles, and motion blur.

Figure 6. Frame from video of freestyle stroke

Figure 7. Frame from video of butterfly stroke

Figure 8. Frame from video of backstroke

Figure 9. Frame from video of breaststroke

4.3 Feature Extraction

In collaboration with domain experts, a set of key biomechanical features was identified for extraction from the pose estimation output. These features were selected for their relevance to technical performance and coaching feedback. Core metrics include stroke rate, stroke length, left–right body symmetry, and body alignment, all critical indicators of efficiency and technique (Ferryanto et al., 2022). For turn performance analysis, additional features were defined, such as stroke rate during the last three strokes before wall contact, approach speed, time from final hand entry to wall contact, and wall contact duration before push-off. These turn-related metrics provide detailed insights into one of the most performance-critical, yet frequently overlooked, phases of competitive swimming.

4.4 Metrics for Evaluation

The evaluation of both the dataset and the proposed system involves multiple metrics tailored to specific components. For benchmarking pose annotations in the dataset, we adopt the standard single-frame pose estimation protocol, enabling direct comparison with widely used datasets such as COCO and MPII. In particular, we use Object Keypoint Similarity (OKS), the COCO-defined metric that quantifies the proximity between predicted and ground truth keypoints. Using OKS, we compute mean Average Precision (mAP) across ten threshold values ranging from 0.50 to 0.95.

To evaluate the stroke and phase classification components, we employ the F1-score, which balances precision and recall to provide a robust measure of classification performance. This is particularly important in domains like swimming, where fine-grained errors can have a significant impact on feedback quality. Additional evaluation metrics, such as frame-level accuracy or angle deviation, may be considered in future refinements.

5. PILOT STUDY AND EVALUATION

To assess the viability of the DIVE system, a pilot study was conducted with fifteen swimmers (nine competitive youth athletes, six masters-level swimmers), balanced across genders and aged 11–52 years. Each participant contributed between 12 and 16 recordings, resulting in a dataset of over 100 short videos across all four competitive strokes.

A subset of 120 frames was manually annotated with 17 COCO keypoints, serving as a benchmark for pose estimation model evaluation. ViTPose outperformed AlphaPose and HRNet, achieving a mean Average Precision (mAP) of 0.63 on the annotated frames, compared to 0.54 for AlphaPose and 0.41 for HRNet. These results, though preliminary, confirm that state-of-the-art models can reliably capture swimmer joint configurations despite underwater distortion and occlusions.

Here, “feasibility” is understood as successfully demonstrating: (i) stable, synchronised dual-perspective video capture under natural pool conditions, and (ii) measurable pose estimation accuracy on swimming-specific footage. These results form the foundation for extending the dataset, refining stroke segmentation, and validating feature extraction.

5.1 Dataset and Ethical Considerations

5.1.1 Dataset Description and Annotation

The dataset collected through the DIVE system includes synchronised dual-perspective video recordings of swimmers performing all four competitive strokes. Each participant contributed between 12 and 16 short videos, encompassing static and dynamic capture scenarios, turns, and varied lighting conditions. The footage serves as the foundation for both pose estimation benchmarking and stroke phase modelling.

A total of 120 frames were manually annotated so far, with 17 keypoints labelled per swimmer according to the COCO keypoint schema. The dataset included 60 freestyle, 40 backstroke, and 20 breaststroke frames. Annotation required approximately 2 minutes per frame, for a total of 4 hours. Most joints were labelled with minimal ambiguity, although occasional bubbles or partial occlusion introduced minor uncertainty in hip, knee, and wrist annotations. Figure 10 illustrates an example annotated frame.

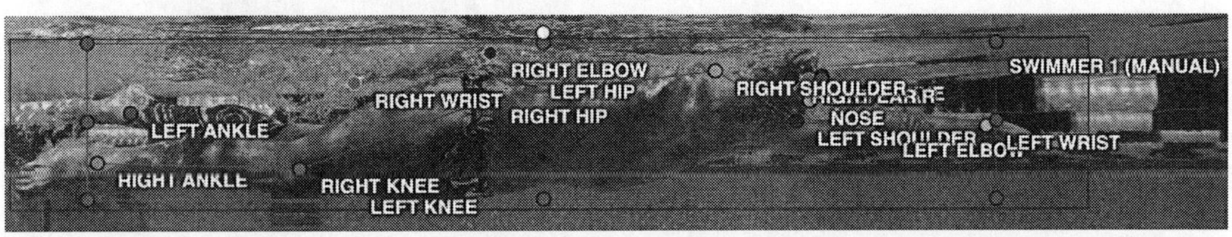

Figure 10. Annotation output for an underwater swimmer, showing keypoints and labelled anatomical landmarks (shoulders, elbows, wrists, hips, knees, ankles, and nose). The red bounding box encloses the swimmer, while green lines indicate the skeletal connections between joints. Keypoints with a white border indicate occlusion.

5.1.2 Open Dataset Plan and Ethical Protocols

A curated subset of the annotated dataset is planned for open release, aimed at supporting research in underwater human pose estimation, biomechanical analysis, and sport-specific computer vision. All participants (and guardians for minors) provided informed consent for data collection, annotation, and ethical release under controlled licensing conditions. Faces are not visible in the footage, and swimmers are only identifiable by body posture and stroke mechanics.

To support privacy-by-design, raw videos are stored securely, and anonymised versions with blurred or cropped background data will be made available. The dataset will be accompanied by metadata detailing capture conditions, swim stroke, and annotation status. Researchers requesting access will agree to terms that prevent re-identification, commercial use, or redistribution. To ensure data privacy and secure sharing, all videos and annotations are stored using Internxt, a GDPR-compliant, zero-knowledge cloud storage solution. Internxt encrypts files end-to-end, ensuring that raw biometric data is protected from unauthorised access at every stage of the research workflow. This choice aligns with the project’s commitment to privacy-by-design and responsible data stewardship. This approach aims to balance the benefits of open science and reproducibility with the ethical handling of biometric video data, particularly in youth sports contexts. As swimming biomechanics datasets remain rare in the field, this resource is positioned to fill a significant gap in reproducible, aquatic-centred AI research.

6. DISCUSSION

The DIVE system has demonstrated technical feasibility for pose-based swimming analysis using synchronised dual-camera capture and off-the-shelf AI models. While initial results are promising, several limitations remain. The current dataset is partially annotated, and while key biomechanical features such as stroke rate and turn metrics are extracted, no automated assessment of movement correctness has yet been implemented. This functionality will be addressed in future iterations once segmentation and feature pipelines are fully validated.

Another limitation concerns the user interface: the design shown is a mock-up prototype (Figure 11) created in consultation with coaches, not yet a functional tool. Development of an interactive interface capable of visualising pose traces and synchronised playback is planned as part of the next phase.

The interface concept supports synchronised dual-view playback, overlayed keypoint traces, and annotated metric timelines, designed in consultation with swim coaches to prioritise clarity and interpretability.

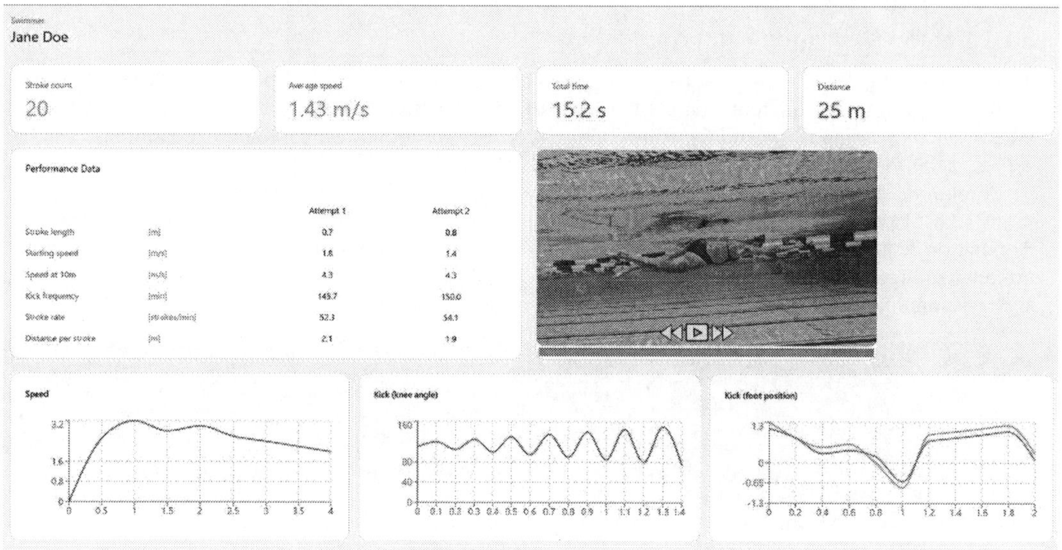

Figure 11. Mockup of DIVE UI

From a system design perspective, future work will address the harmonisation of temporal outputs across the above- and below-water video feeds, especially for fine-grained phase transitions such as stroke entry and wall contact. Another key area is the modular tuning of pose estimation parameters and segmentation heuristics to better accommodate variability across age groups, stroke types, and swimmer skill levels.

The broader impact of DIVE lies in its potential to bridge the gap between academic AI research and performance analysis in aquatic sport. By releasing a high-quality, annotated video dataset and providing a portable, modular analytics pipeline, the project contributes toward reproducible research in pose estimation, stroke segmentation, and athlete-centred AI systems. Engagement with the coaching community will be central to validating the utility and usability of the system as it evolves.

7. CONCLUSION AND FUTURE WORK

This paper presented the design and early implementation of DIVE, a lightweight system for swimmer performance evaluation using synchronised dual-perspective footage and pose estimation. The pilot study confirmed feasibility by showing that pose estimation models can be applied to real-world aquatic conditions with promising accuracy, using only accessible hardware.

Future work will expand the annotated dataset to cover complete swim cycles, improve segmentation accuracy, and integrate coach-facing tools for performance review. Planned extensions also include experimental validation of movement correctness analysis and usability testing with coaches and athletes to ensure practical adoption.

The development and deployment of the DIVE system surfaced several technical and logistical challenges. Underwater footage presented unique difficulties for pose estimation due to refracted light, bubbles, and frequent partial occlusions, particularly during turns or wall contact. Synchronising footage from dual perspectives proved non-trivial, requiring manual intervention for alignment and calibration. Additionally, capturing consistent, high-quality video in a live pool environment involved managing variable lighting conditions, swimmer variability, and equipment stability. Another challenge relates to distinguishing between left and right body parts in side-view recordings, where swimmer orientation can be ambiguous. To address this, future work may explore incorporating body part masks or orientation-aware pose models, as suggested in (Giulietti et al., 2023). These early-stage limitations have informed system design choices, such as the use of high frame rate cameras and rule-based segmentation strategies, and continue to shape future improvements to robustness, automation, and generalisability. By releasing tools and data openly and ethically, DIVE aims to contribute to reproducible research in sport-specific AI and pose-based biomechanics, bridging the gap between computational innovation and domain practice in swimming analytics.

ACKNOWLEDGEMENT

This work was supported by Xjenza Malta through its Research Excellence Programme. The authors gratefully acknowledge this funding, which made the development and evaluation of the DIVE system possible.

REFERENCES

Cao, X., & Yan, W. Q. (2024). Pose estimation for swimmers in video surveillance. Multimedia Tools and Applications, 83(9), 26565–26580. https://doi.org/10.1007/s11042-023-16618-w

Chen, L., & Hu, D. (2023). An effective swimming stroke recognition system utilizing deep learning based on inertial measurement units. Advanced Robotics, 37(7), 467–479. https://doi.org/10.1080/01691864.2022.2160274

Costa, J., Silva, R., Rodrigues, R., Silva, H., & Rocha, A. (2021). Framework for intelligent swimming analytics with wearable sensors for stroke classification. Sensors, 21(15), 5162. https://doi.org/10.3390/s21155162

Einfalt, M., Zecha, D., & Lienhart, R. (2018, March). Activity-conditioned continuous human pose estimation for performance analysis of athletes using the example of swimming. In Proceedings of the IEEE Winter Conference on Applications of Computer Vision (pp. 446–455). https://doi.org/10.1109/wacv.2018.00055

Fang, H.-S., Xie, S., Tai, Y.-W., & Lu, C. (2017). RMPE: Regional multi-person pose estimation. In Proceedings of the IEEE International Conference on Computer Vision (ICCV) (pp. 2334–2343). IEEE. https://doi.org/10.1109/ICCV.2017.254

Fani, H., Mirlohi, A., Hosseini, H., & Herperst, R. (2018). Swim stroke analytic: Front crawl pulling pose classification. In 2018 25th IEEE International Conference on Image Processing (ICIP) (pp. 4068–4072). IEEE. https://doi.org/10.1109/ICIP.2018.8451756

Ferryanto, F., Mahyuddin, A., & Nakashima, M. (2022). Markerless optical motion capture system for asymmetrical swimming stroke. Journal of Engineering and Technological Sciences, 54(5), 220503. https://doi.org/10.5614/j.eng.technol.sci.2022.54.5.3

Giulietti, N., Caputo, A., Chiariotti, P., & Castellini, P. (2023). SwimmerNET: Underwater 2D swimmer pose estimation exploiting fully convolutional neural networks. Sensors, 23(4), 2364. https://doi.org/10.3390/s23042364

Lin, T.-Y., Maire, M., Belongie, S., Hays, J., Perona, P., Ramanan, D., Dollár, P., & Zitnick, C. L. (2015). Microsoft COCO: Common objects in context. arXiv preprint arXiv:1405.0312. https://doi.org/10.48550/arXiv.1405.0312

Morais, J. E., Silva, A. J., Barbosa, T. M., Marinho, D. A., & Costa, M. J. (2022). Wearables in swimming for real-time feedback: A systematic review. *Sensors, 22*(10), 3677. https://doi.org/10.3390/s22103677

Ouyang, J., Trinh, D., & Choo, C. C. (2024, March). Optimization of swim pose estimation and recognition with data augmentation. In 2024 IEEE Southwest Symposium on Image Analysis and Interpretation (SSIAI) (pp. 101–104). IEEE. https://doi.org/10.1109/SSIAI59505.2024.1050864

Xu, Y., Zhang, J., Zhang, Q., Tao, D., & Xu, C. (2022). ViTPose: Simple vision transformer baselines for human pose estimation. In Proceedings of the European Conference on Computer Vision (ECCV) (pp. 269–285). Springer. https://doi.org/10.1007/978-3-031-19815-1_16

BEAM: APPLYING WEB TECHNOLOGIES FOR TRAINING ATTENTION

José Barbosa[1], Cristiana Araújo[1], João José Cerqueira[2] and Pedro Rangel Henriques[1]
[1]ALGORITMI Research Centre/LASI, DI, University of Minho, Portugal
R. da Universidade, 4710-057 Braga
[2]Life and Health Sciences Research Institute (ICVS) University of Minho, Portugal
R. da Universidade, 4710-057 Braga

ABSTRACT

Attention is a core cognitive function, crucial for learning, decision-making, and performing everyday tasks. In recent years, the demand for effective attention training tools has increased, particularly in educational and clinical contexts. This project introduces BEAM (Brain Engagement and Attention Management), a web-based platform designed to support therapists in delivering personalized cognitive training to patients, with a particular focus on attention and working memory. The system allows professionals to assign, customize, and monitor interactive tasks. A set of over 10 configurable games, recommended by specialists or discovered in the literature review was developed, each targeting different attention subdomains through visual and interactive stimuli. The platform also provides robust support for therapist oversight, including performance tracking, and recommendation mechanisms. A pilot evaluation involved collaboration with therapists and initial testing with children. Early feedback from professionals highlighted BEAM's potential to fill a gap in the availability of tools for guided cognitive training, offering a flexible and intuitive experience. Preliminary interactions with young users revealed high levels of engagement and concentration while performing the tasks.

KEYWORDS

Attention, Attention Training, Cognition, BEAM

1. INTRODUCTION

Attention is a core cognitive ability essential for learning, productivity, and personal development. Despite its importance, many individuals struggle to maintain focus, a problem that has been exacerbated by recent changes in society. For example, the effects of the COVID-19 pandemic are beginning to be seen on children's attention spans and self-regulation. While clinical conditions like ADHD are widely recognized, attentional difficulties are common across the general population and can be improved through structured training.

Research has shown that attention can be enhanced through targeted cognitive exercises. However, accessible digital tools to support such training without high costs, while offering good quality and a variety of challenges, remain scarce. Several existing solutions demonstrate the potential of technology in attention training, but they are often limited by cost, access, or technical constraints. For example, the Tali Train program, used in the study by Kirk, et al (2019), delivers gamified attention training to children through adaptive exercises, typically implemented in classroom settings. While effective, it is a commercial and paid product not always viable for individual or small-clinic use. Similarly, E-Prime 2.0, employed in the research of Aben, et al (2019) offers a robust framework with advanced cognitive tasks such as arrow priming and AX-CPT paradigms. However, it requires an expensive paid license, restricting its use to well-funded research institutions or clinical settings with the resources to afford it. These constraints highlight a clear gap in the availability of free and adaptable platforms that allow therapists to deliver personalized cognitive training.

This paper introduces BEAM, a web-based platform developed to address this need. It allows therapists to assign, configure, and monitor attention-focused tasks tailored to individual users. While many features and exercises were designed with younger users in mind, such as children and adolescents, the platform was built to be accessible and beneficial to users of all ages. Its design emphasizes user-friendliness and clinical adaptability, making it suitable for a broad range of age groups and therapeutic contexts.

BEAM is open source and developed as a website for ease of use. No installation is required and it's completely free to use.

As far as the structure of this paper is concerned, it begins with a brief overview of attention (Section 2) and attention training (Section 3), followed by a description of the proposed system (Section 4), its implementation (Section 5) and the application overview (Section 6), and concludes with a discussion on observations and feedback from users and professionals (Section 7).

2. ATTENTION, BACKGROUND

Attention is the cognitive process that enables individuals to focus on specific stimuli while filtering out irrelevant distractions, allowing them to interpret and respond effectively to their environment. It is closely linked to one's immediate experience and current awareness, forming the basis for learning, decision-making, and the execution of tasks that require concentration (Araujo, 2022).

It can generally be categorized into two main forms: voluntary and reflexive. Voluntary attention, also referred to as endogenous attention, is a top-down, goal-oriented mechanism in which individuals deliberately direct their focus based on internal goals, expectations, or ongoing tasks. Conversely, reflexive or exogenous attention is a bottom-up, stimulus-driven process in which external sensory events, such as sudden noises or rapid movements, automatically capture one's attention without conscious control (Araujo, 2022).

2.1 Attention Types

Beyond the distinction between voluntary and reflexive mechanisms, attention can be further categorized into five main types: *focused attention, sustained attention, selective attention, alternating attention, and divided attention*. These subtypes represent distinct cognitive processes that allow individuals to manage their attention according to situational demands. Each type plays a unique role, yet they are highly interconnected, often working together in complex tasks (Araujo, 2022; Carter, et al., 2019).

Focused attention refers to the ability to concentrate, even if only for a small period of time, on a single stimulus while ignoring everything else in the environment. It forms the foundation of all other attentional processes. This type of attention is crucial when responding to specific inputs, like a football striker focusing on taking a shot, ignoring the crowd noise. Without it, more complex attention types would be impossible to maintain, as the brain would struggle to isolate and respond to individual stimuli (Bouchard, et al., 2025).

Sustained attention is the capacity to maintain focus on a task or stimulus over an extended period. It becomes essential in situations such listening to a lecture, where consistent engagement is required. Research has shown that this type of attention develops with age, peaking in young adulthood and often declining in older age (Araujo, 2022; Carter, et al., 2019).

Selective attention enables individuals to concentrate on a relevant stimulus while suppressing responses to irrelevant or distracting inputs (Araujo, 2022; Carter, et al., 2019). It relies heavily on inhibitory control and plays a significant role in environments with competing sensory information, such as studying in a crowded café. Selective attention is also closely linked to visual attention, particularly in line with the Theory of Visual Attention (Bundesen, 1990), which suggests that visual recognition and attentional selection operate simultaneously as individuals categorize and prioritize elements in the visual field.

Alternating attention involves shifting focus from one stimulus or task to another, requiring cognitive flexibility and quick reorientation. A good example is cooking while reading a recipe, moving back and forth between reading instructions and applying them in real time. This ability is also crucial for language switching in bilingual individuals or toggling between different activities in a professional setting (Bouchard, et al., 2025).

Divided attention is the most complex type and involves attending to multiple stimuli or tasks at once, what is usually only referred to as multitasking. For instance, while driving, one might talk to a passenger, adjust the radio, and monitor the road simultaneously. Divided attention often builds on alternating attention and requires the coordination of multiple attentional and motor processes (Bouchard, et al., 2025).

These five types of attention operate in a dynamic hierarchy (Bouchard, et al., 2025). Focused attention acts as the foundation, followed by sustained and selective attention, then alternating attention, and finally divided attention at the top.

In conclusion, attention is not a linear or static process. Different contexts activate different types of attention, and effective cognitive functioning often depends on the smooth interplay among them.

2.2 Attention Disturbances

The goal of this project is to develop a platform aimed at helping individuals enhance their attention capabilities through training. Many people across the world experience difficulties with attention and concentration, which, in most cases, are not linked to clinical disorders. The platform seeks to support these individuals by providing tools and techniques to improve their focus through non-clinical methods, with an easily accessible platform.

Attention-related difficulties can manifest in various ways, such as being unable to remember recent events, struggling to sit still, or thinking clearly. Individuals might frequently lose things or forget where they placed them, face indecision, or find it challenging to complete complex tasks. A lack of focus, low physical or mental energy, and a tendency to make careless mistakes are also common. Importantly, experiencing these issues does not necessarily indicate the presence of a clinical condition.

Nonetheless, understanding clinical attention disorders helps contextualize the broader challenge. These conditions require medical diagnosis and often involve pharmacological or therapeutic intervention. While platforms like this one offer additional support, they are not intended to replace professional care. Instead, they can complement broader treatment strategies in some cases.

One of the most common clinical conditions is ADHD (Attention Deficit Hyperactivity Disorder), a neurodevelopmental disorder affecting over 5% of the global population. Individuals with ADHD often struggle with sustained attention, response inhibition, and executive functioning. They may also exhibit impulsivity, emotional reactivity, and social difficulties. These cognitive and behavioural symptoms can significantly interfere with everyday life, making consistent treatment and support essential (Drechsler, et al., 2020).

Another condition to mention is hemineglect syndrome, typically resulting from brain lesions, especially after right-hemisphere strokes. Individuals with this disorder may fail to notice or respond to stimuli on one side of space, usually the left. This is not a problem of vision or sensation but a profound attentional deficit. Hemineglect can have a serious impact on independence and recovery, especially in post-stroke rehabilitation (Li & Malhotra, 2015).

In summary, while clinical attention disorders like ADHD and hemineglect involve deeper neurological dysfunctions and require professional treatment, digital tools such as the platform proposed in this project can serve as a useful addition. They offer structured, engaging exercises that may support attentional capacity in both general and clinical populations, provided that in clinical contexts, they are used as a complement to, not a substitute for, specialized care.

3. TRAINING ATTENTION

The platform developed in this project aims to train attention through practices designed to strengthen cognitive control and improve self-regulation. At its core, attention training (AT) involves repeated cognitive exercises that engage executive mechanisms like conflict resolution, inhibition, and working memory. These practices support the development of neural networks responsible for executive functioning and goal-directed behaviour (Tang & Posner, 2009).

Tang and Posner (2009) group attention-enhancing methods into two broad categories: Attention State Training (AST) and Attention Training (AT). AST focuses on achieving mental and physical balance through holistic, non-technological practices such as mindfulness, meditation, and immersion in natural environments. These practices promote a relaxed yet alert state, supporting emotional regulation and stress reduction. Rather than training specific cognitive functions directly, AST enhances attention indirectly by improving overall self-awareness and body-mind integration.

AT, in contrast, is a more targeted and diverse category. It includes a wide range of cognitive exercises with varying complexity, from simple tasks to sophisticated systems using advanced technologies like virtual reality. These approaches explicitly seek to train specific attentional components through controlled and repetitive practice, making AT especially suited for digital platforms.

Attention Training is a structured approach aimed at improving attention and related cognitive abilities through repeated and focused practice. These interventions typically engage core executive functions other than attention such as working memory and cognitive flexibility. By training these mechanisms, AT promotes neuroplasticity and fosters more efficient attentional control across a variety of everyday contexts (Tang & Posner, 2009).

The effectiveness of AT lies in its capacity to provide targeted cognitive stimulation that adapts to different needs and contexts. By repeatedly confronting users with tasks that challenge their ability to concentrate, filter distractions, and switch between goals, AT strengthens the brain's attentional systems. These improvements can be seen in domains such as reaction time, multitasking ability, or mental endurance, skills that are valuable in both academic, professional settings and everyday life (Aben, et al., 2019; Baniqued, et al., 2014; Zendel, et al., 2016).

A good example of this is the numerical comparison task used by Aben et al (2019) in which participants responded based on whether a number from 1 to 9 (excluding 5) was greater or less than five. This task challenged participants to maintain focus and inhibit automatic responses under time constraints, targeting selective and sustained attention. Inspired by this, our platform includes a simplified adaptation of this task, preserving its core cognitive demand while adjusting the format to a gamified and engaging experience.

One of the most valuable aspects of AT is its adaptability across all age groups. It can benefit individuals throughout life, from early childhood to older adulthood. In children, it supports cognitive development, helps prepare them for academic challenges, and encourages early contact with technology through interactive digital methods (Kirk, et al., 2019). In older adults, AT contributes to maintaining attentional capacities, slowing age-related cognitive decline, and improving memory (Lampit, et al., 2014; Zendel, et al., 2016). This broad applicability reinforces its value as a tool for lifelong cognitive support.

Gamified approaches have become an interesting way to implement AT, offering engaging and motivating environments that encourage consistent practice, even by casual play. The use of games, whether designed explicitly for training or adapted from entertainment, has shown strong potential in improving attention in a dynamic, enjoyable and engaging way, for all age groups. These interactive formats not only sustain user motivation and sometimes allow for adaptive difficulty, personalization, and immediate feedback, enhancing their effectiveness (Baniqued, et al., 2014; Kirk, et al., 2019).

In summary, AT is highly adaptable, enabling the design of exercises suited to a wide range of contexts and individual needs. Its flexibility allows it to be used effectively across all age groups, from young children to older adults. Depending on the exercises applied, it can lead to significant improvements in various types of attention and working memory, demonstrating its broad cognitive benefits. This versatile and ever-evolving field continues to grow, solidifying its place as an excellent tool for helping people across diverse circumstances.

4. BEAM, PROPOSAL

BEAM, short for Brain Engagement and Attention Management, was the name chosen for this platform and from this point onward the term will be used to refer to it.

The decision to develop BEAM was grounded in a detailed study of the state of the art, which included an extensive review of literature on attention and training methodologies, as well as the collection and analysis of ideas for exercises suitable for different populations. Although many of the exercises and features were designed with younger users in mind, particularly children and adolescents the platform is intended for users of all ages. The inclusion of adjustable difficulty levels, customizable exercises, and age-appropriate test formats reinforces this commitment to inclusivity. BEAM is designed to be user-friendly and adaptable to a wide range of therapeutic scenarios, regardless of the patient's age or background. The use of the *Phoenix framework*[1] proved to be an ideal choice for this project. Its reactivity, modular structure, and developer friendly scaffolding contributed to the rapid and efficient implementation of the platform, allowing a functional system to be built in just a few months.

[1] https://www.phoenixframework.org/

Three main system actors were identified during the planning phase. The *Patient* is the end-user who engages with BEAM's exercises and diagnostic tools. Their interaction is limited to performing assigned tasks and viewing their progress. The *Therapist* has broader permissions, managing a list of patients, assigning and configuring tasks, and reviewing results. Finally, the *Admin* oversees system configuration and global maintenance, a role likely to be taken on by one or more therapists in practice.

From the outset, a set of essential requirements was established to guide development. The platform needed to support different user roles, store diagnostic and training results, and allow therapists to track performance over time. Exercises had to support multiple difficulty levels and record key metrics like accuracy and reaction time. Additionally, the system had to provide feedback and allow therapists to filter, sort, and annotate patient results.

With these foundations in place, it became possible to begin the design of the platform's architecture and modules, ensuring each component would meet the specific needs of users and enable a scalable and maintainable system.

The architecture of the BEAM platform is structured around three major components: a front-end for therapists, a frontend for patients, and a centralized backend (Figure 1). Therapists can manage patients, configure exercises, and view results through dedicated modules, while patients interact with training tasks and track their own progress. The back-end handles data processing, communication between users, and storage of all relevant information, including results and recommendations. Each module plays a specific role in ensuring smooth operation and efficient user interaction.

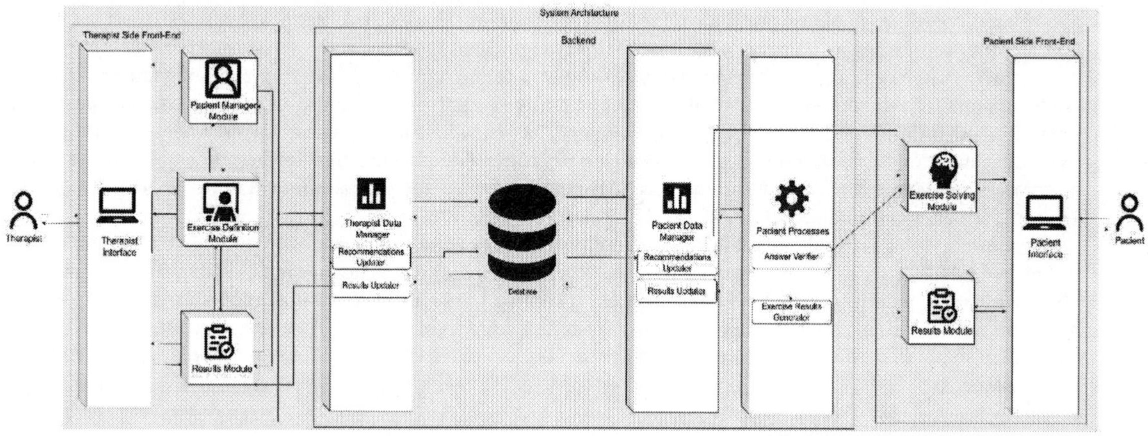

Figure 1. BEAM architecture

5. BEAM, DEVELOPMENT

Like already mentioned, Phoenix Framework was selected as the foundation for the project, due to its modularity, productivity, and the capabilities of Phoenix LiveView, which enabled the creation of dynamic and reactive interfaces without relying heavily on JavaScript. This choice proved essential for rapid building and smooth integration between frontend and backend, allowing the construction of fully functional application in just a few months.

The system was structured around two main domains: user management and task management. On the backend, these were implemented as separate contexts: *Accounts*, responsible for managing users, roles, and relationships between therapists and patients; and *Exercises*, dedicated to training exercises, result tracking, and personalized configurations. Therapists can create and assign tasks to their patients, analyse performance through reaction time and accuracy metrics, and take notes of progress. The application also supports configurable exercises tailored to the needs of individual users, ensuring a personalized and clinically relevant experience.

The frontend was built primarily using Phoenix LiveView, allowing real-time user interactions and centralized control over application state. Views were mostly implemented as LiveView modules, encapsulating both UI rendering and event handling. Patients access exercises through an interface designed for simplicity and engagement, while therapists use a dedicated interface to manage patients, assign tasks, and analyse results. Customizable training configurations can be created through dynamic forms, and the reuse of these configurations is supported through dedicated views. Live charts were integrated via Chart.js to visualize performance trends and support decision-making.

The entire platform is deployed as a web application using a containerized architecture. Two Docker containers are used: one running the Phoenix server and another for the PostgreSQL database. This lightweight setup ensures isolation, reliability, and ease of maintenance. The application is hosted on a CentOS 7 server and updates are managed directly via the public GitHub repository. Thanks to the deployment tools provided by Phoenix, including a Dockerfile and runtime configuration support, the transition from development to production was efficient and robust.

6. BEAM, OVERVIEW

This section introduces the main areas of the platform from a user perspective. It describes the different parts of the system and outlines what each part allows users to do, whether they are patients engaging in cognitive training or therapists monitoring and guiding their progress. The goal is to provide a clear and structured guide of the platform's main features and how they are accessed and used in practice.

6.1 Tasks and Exercises

At the heart of the BEAM platform lies its most essential component: the set of interactive tasks and exercises through which patients can actively train their cognitive abilities. These tasks are designed to provide engaging, structured activities that stimulate core mental functions such as attention, working memory, response control, and cognitive flexibility. By combining clinical insights with interactive technology, BEAM offers users a dynamic environment where they can strengthen these skills through repeated practice and feedback. The exercises serve not only as tools for cognitive training but also as opportunities for assessment and progress tracking. Each task is carefully crafted to challenge specific domains of cognition, adapting in complexity across different levels of difficulty. In addition to these difficulty levels, patients can also perform test versions of the exercises, ranging from initial diagnostic assessments to evaluations of cognitive progress over time, tailored to their age group. Furthermore, therapists can define personalized task configurations to better suit the individual needs and goals of each patient, enhancing both training relevance and therapeutic impact.

In Figure 2 we can see the main tasks page, which includes a table where users can access the different exercises available on the platform. Each row in the table corresponds to a distinct task, showing a small visual preview, its title, and the cognitive domains it targets. The tags indicating trained capacities offer a quick overview of the cognitive functions stimulated by each exercise, such as attention, memory, or reaction speed.

After selecting a task, users are redirected to a dedicated explanation page where they can learn more about the chosen activity and begin the exercise. A couple of these tasks are described in further detail below. For therapists, the interface also provides two additional buttons beside each task: the pencil icon enables the creation of custom configurations, while the notepad icon gives access to previously saved settings.

Each configuration is specific to its respective exercise and is entirely under the therapist's control. Therapists can create multiple versions tailored to different needs, save them, and assign them to individual patients either as permanent options or as temporary recommendations. They also have the ability to mark which configurations should always be available to a patient in free access mode and can remove or update these settings at any time if they are no longer relevant or beneficial. This flexibility ensures that the training experience remains personalized, adaptable, and aligned with the therapeutic goals set for each user. As an example, configurations for the *Order Animals* task (described later in this document) allow therapists to define parameters such as the number of rounds, the time each animal remains visible, and the minimum and maximum number of animals per sequence. This illustrates the degree of control available, enabling precise adaptation of cognitive challenges to match each patient's capabilities and therapeutic needs.

Figure 3 illustrates two of the platform's interactive tasks: *Simon* (on the left) and *Order Animals* (on the right). The Simon task is inspired by the classic electronic memory game and is supported by findings in the literature such as those presented in (Raja, et al., 2023) and requires users to reproduce an increasingly long sequence of coloured buttons. The number of buttons varies by difficulty, affecting the visual complexity and response load, while the default configuration includes a two-minute time limit and a maximum of seven steps per sequence, both values that therapists can adapt as needed. This task primarily targets working memory and sustained attention. On the other hand, Order Animals was designed with younger users in mind, combining a playful drag-and-drop interface with memory and attention demands and was inspired by a visit to *Centro Terapêutico ConSigo* who gave us their professional insights and helped us develop this exercise. In each round, a sequence of animal images is shown one by one, after which the user must reconstruct the correct order by dragging them into place. The number of animals per round increases with difficulty, challenging the user's ability to retain and organize visual information. This task reinforces skills such as focused attention, visual tracking, and sequential memory. These examples reflect the platform's strength in combining cognitive diversity with customizable task design, ensuring relevance across age groups and intervention goals.

Figure 2. Tasks page

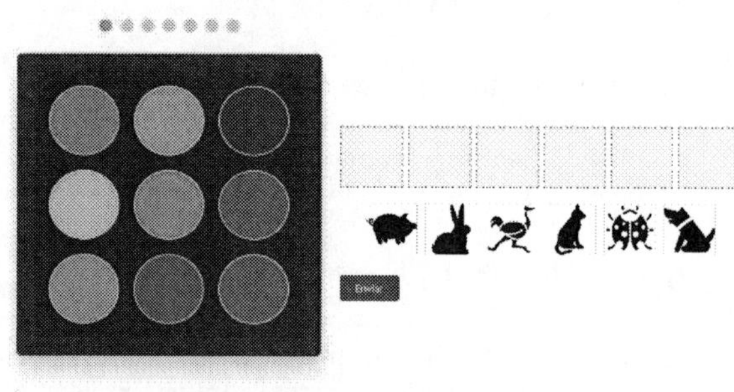

Figure 3. Simon task and order animals

6.2 User Performance Data

Another essential feature of the platform is the therapist's ability to view and analyse patient performance. This functionality is accessible through a dedicated results section, illustrated in Figure 4, which presents four main options: general statistics, results by user, results by task, and results by category. Each of these views offers different and valuable insights, depending on what the therapist is looking to evaluate. This modular structure allows therapists to explore either high-level trends across the entire platform or detailed data specific to individual patients or tasks, facilitating more informed and personalized clinical decisions.

Patients only have access to their own results, they cannot access this menu with more specifications. They can view their personal history and a summary of completed tasks, allowing them to track their own progress over time. This ensures privacy and maintains a clear distinction between user roles while still encouraging patient engagement and self-awareness in their cognitive development.

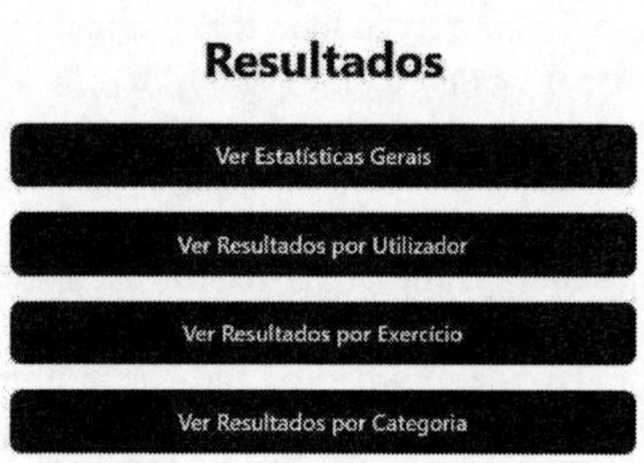

Figure 4. Options to analyse Patients performance data

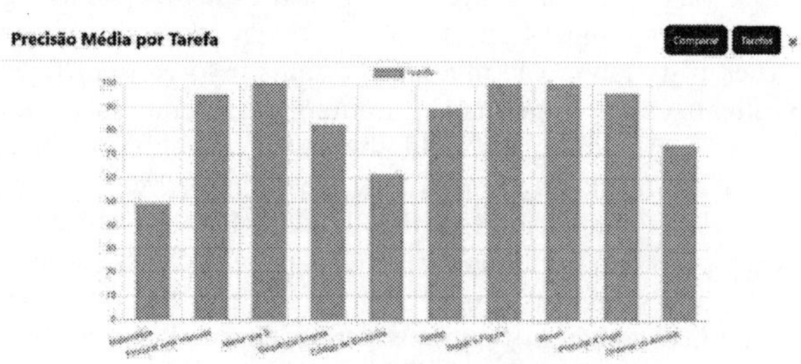

Figure 5. Accuracy Chart

As shown in Figure 5, one of the available visualizations presents the average accuracy of a patient across all completed tasks. This type of bar chart provides a clear overview of performance, helping therapists quickly identify areas of strength and weakness. The interface also supports interactive features, such as filtering which tasks to include in the comparison or contrasting a patient's results with platform-wide or therapist-specific averages. These tools enhance the therapist's ability to monitor progress, detect relevant patterns, and adjust training strategies to better suit each patient's cognitive profile.

In addition to precision and reaction time charts, the "General Statistics" section offers therapists access to other key indicators, such as the average age of users on the platform and of their own patients, as well as age distribution breakdowns. These demographic metrics complement performance data, providing further context for evaluating cognitive progress and ensuring that exercises are appropriately matched to the age profiles of the patient population.

Further information about the BEAM platform, including access to its features and functionalities, is available at https://beam.epl.di.uminho.pt.

7. CONCLUSION

The development of BEAM was guided by a detailed study of attention and how it can be effectively trained. This groundwork helped define the platform's goals and ensured that each feature addresses concrete therapeutic needs. From the beginning, the project followed an Agile-inspired development process, involving continuous interaction and close collaboration with an interdisciplinary team that included a neurologist as part of the core group, as well as regular communication with therapists from the field of psychology. Their expertise was crucial in shaping the exercises, refining requirements, and validating the platform's relevance in real-world contexts. Once the system's scope was clear, the use of the Phoenix framework allowed for the rapid implementation of a fully functional and interactive web application.

Accessible at https://beam.epl.di.uminho.pt, BEAM integrates all the core functionalities envisioned during the design phase. It includes a wide range of cognitive exercises, a customizable configuration system, and dedicated tools for monitoring user progress.

At the time of writing, over 125 exercises have already been completed within the platform. Since BEAM remains available online for continuous use, all metrics presented here are subject to change over time as more users interact with the system. Preliminary statistical data reveal promising insights regarding user performance across different cognitive domains. Average accuracy per attention category currently stands at 86% for Focused Attention, 69% for Selective Attention, 62% for Sustained Attention, and 63% for Visual Attention. Exercises related to visual discrimination, cognitive flexibility, and inhibition also show encouraging performance trends, suggesting effective engagement with these cognitive areas. On the other hand, Working Memory tasks display a lower accuracy average of 66%, and Reaction Time based tasks average 63%, reflecting areas where users may face greater challenges.

As future work, we intend to conduct a more extensive evaluation involving a larger number of patients and therapists, using usability questionnaires to evaluate the platform's effectiveness and user experience. Feedback from these sessions will be key to refining the platform even further as it proves to be a valuable asset for cognitive training and assessment. During this process, the potential of integrating artificial intelligence has also been considered as a promising avenue to enhance data exploration and support future developments.

ACKNOWLEDGEMENT

This work has been supported by FCT -- Fundação para a Ciência e Tecnologia within the R&D Units Project Scope: UID/00319/2023.

The Ph.D. work of Cristiana Araújo is supported by FCT -- Fundação para a Ciência e Tecnologia, Research Grant, with reference 2020.09845.BD, https://doi.org/10.54499/2020.09845.BD .

REFERENCES

Aben, B., Iseni, B., Van den Bussche, E. & Verguts, T., (2019). Persistent modification of cognitive control through attention training. *Quarterly Journal of Experimental Psychology,* 72(3), pp. 413-423.

Araujo, C., (2022). *Training Computational Thinking: exploring approaches supported by Neuroscience,* Braga: University of Minho.

Baniqued, P. L. et al., (2014). Cognitive training with casual video games: points to consider. *Frontiers in Psychology.*

Bouchard, A., Dumas, E. & Fecteau, S., (2025). *Attention and decision making.* Second Edition ed. Oxford: Elsevier.

Bundesen, C., (1990). Theory of visual attention. *Psychological review,* 97(4), p. 523–547.

Carter, R., Aldridge, S., Page, M. & Parker, S., (2019). *The Human Brain Book.* 1 ed. s.l.:DK Publishing.

Drechsler, R. et al., (2020). ADHD: Current Concepts and Treatments in Children and Adolescents. *Neuropediatrics,* 51(5), pp. 315-335.

Kirk, H., Spencer-Smith, M., Wiley, J. & Cornish, K., (2019). Gamified Attention Training in the Primary School Classroom: A Cluster-Randomized Controlled Trial. *Journal of Attention Disorders,* 25(8), pp. 1146-1159.

Lampit, A., Hallock, H. & Valenzuela, M., (2014). Computerized Cognitive Training in Cognitively Healthy Older Adults: A Systematic Review and Meta-Analysis of Effect Modifiers. *PLOS Medicine,* 11(11), pp. 1-18.

Li, K. & Malhotra, P. A., (2015). Spatial neglect. *Practical Neurology,* 15(5), pp. 333--339.

Raja, A. S. V., Okeke, A., Paramasivan, P. & Joseph, F. J. J., (2023). Designing, Developing, and Cognitively Exploring Simon's Game for Memory Enhancement and Assessment. *FMDB Transactions on Sustainable Computer Letters,* 1(3), pp. 147-160.

Tang, Y.-Y. & Posner, M., (2009). Attention training and attention state training. *Trends in cognitive sciences,* 13(5), pp. 222-7.

Zendel, B. R. et al., (2016). The impact of attentional training on event-related potentials in older adults. *Neurobiology of Aging,* Volume 47, pp. 10-22.

TOWARDS USING VISION LANGUAGE MODELS FOR URBAN TREE ANALYSIS

Danilo Jodas, Giovani Candido, João Manesco, Gabriel Garcia, Luiz Marques Junior and João Papa
São Paulo State University (UNESP), School of Sciences, Bauru/SP, Brazil

ABSTRACT

In a breakthrough era of sustainable cities and carbon dioxide emission reduction, the efficient and rapid collection of crucial data on urban trees has raised the attention of municipalities and forestry managers. The standard approach for collecting the main aspects of urban trees involves fieldwork campaigns to obtain dendrometric tree information, including height and tree species, which allows for an initial assessment and further recording for catalog purposes. However, conducting field analyses is labor-intensive and time-consuming due to trees widely dispersed across urban areas. Thus, there is a significant need for computational analysis strategies to facilitate quick assessments and records of crucial urban tree information. This paper introduces an approach based on a vision language model to summarize the main aspects of the tree using an image from the street-view perspective. In addition, a new question-and-answer dataset with summaries of tree information has been created based on a 7B Portuguese language model. The dataset is subsequently used to fine-tune the PaliGemma vision language model using images of urban trees. The results demonstrated a compelling capability of the proposed approach to accurately summarize key tree attributes, such as the tree height and its species, using language models with significantly fewer parameters.

KEYWORDS

Generative Models, Large Language Models, Urban Tree, Bode, GemBode

1. INTRODUCTION

Emerging technologies are raising significant interest in attracting novel sustainable urban solutions, particularly to bring strategies to mitigate the global impacts of climate change and follow the agenda for a more environmentally responsible future (Pliatsios et al., 2023). In recent years, computational methods have gained attention for applications in various research domains. To effectively manage and preserve urban green spaces, municipal authorities are increasingly seeking innovative solutions that facilitate the rapid analysis of green space preservation through a preliminary analysis of the urban tree information. These advancements are paramount to meeting the sustainability goals and ecological resource management. For example, assessing tree health usually requires considerable human effort since it involves the evaluation of various dendrometric parameters to provide an initial understanding of structural integrity and biomechanical behavior. In addition, establishing a database with critical information collected from urban trees is crucial for an initial assessment of their principal aspects, especially for a preliminary report.

Since urban centers continue to evolve, integrating machine learning is becoming imperative to enhance tree management and sustainability. Regarding the analysis of urban forests and trees, standard methods involve assessing the urban forest quality (de Lima et al., 2021), as well as tree cataloging, detection, and segmentation of trees in images (Jodas et al., 2021; Jodas et al., 2022; Jodas et al., 2023), alongside the classification of tree species utilizing images captured through remote sensing, aerial devices, and street-level photography (Jodas et al., 2022). In addition, solutions for predicting intricate aspects of internal structures of urban trees have been addressed in recent research, further showing the potential applications in this field (Candido et al., 2025).

Large Language Models (LLMs) constitute a pivotal breakthrough in natural language understanding and generation. These architectures are trained on extensive, general-purpose datasets, equipping them to perform a diverse array of Natural Language Processing (NLP) applications. Noteworthy examples include GPT-4 and

LLaMA models, which are well-consolidated for their ability to generate coherent and contextually relevant text (Brown et al., 2020). Another significant model is DeepSeek (Guo et al., 2025), which has redefined the understanding of context in text through its bidirectional training approach (Devin et al., 2019). In addition, the LLaMA model, introduced by Meta, is well-known for its efficiency in various natural language tasks and remarkable results in research and practical applications (Touvron et al., 2023). Together, these models have achieved extraordinary milestones, from enhancing machine translation to facilitating the generation of human-like text.

Advancements in multimodal LLM have been crucial for exchanging information between text and images to extract and summarize content across both modalities. Visual Language Models (VLMs) offer urban tree and forestry management potential by combining visual data analysis with natural language processing. These models can analyze urban tree images to assist in identifying species, assessing health, and summarizing essential attributes. In addition, VLMs can find applications in tasks like tree cataloging and forestry assessments by processing images from various imaging sources, such as remote sensing, aerial imagery, and street-level photos. This paper leverages recent advancements in generative artificial intelligence concerning urban tree analysis, proposing the use of a Vision Language Model (VLM) to summarize key characteristics of trees based on images captured from a street-level perspective. The main contribution involves fine-tuning the PaliGemma model (Beyer et al., 2024) over a Portuguese dataset that includes questions and answers regarding the essential components of urban trees. Our second contribution is the public release of a question-and-answer dataset produced by GemBode (Garcia et al., 2024), a Gemma 7B-based model designed to leverage LLMs across a wide range of Portuguese tasks. In addition, making the dataset available can promote further research in VLM applications for urban tree analysis and drive innovation to sustainable solutions in urban forestry.

2. RELATED WORKS

Efforts to enhance urban forestry management have led to a variety of tree analysis techniques. This section briefly reviews these approaches, from foundational tree characteristic analysis to the latest in VLMs, to situate this work's novel contributions.

Early computational efforts in urban forestry focused on characterizing tree morphometry and architecture to aid in planning and species selection (de Carvalho et al., 2020). With advancements in machine learning, several techniques have emerged for more specific tasks, where models such as U-Net and its variants have been employed for the semantic segmentation of tree canopies from aerial imagery (Martins et al., 2021) and, in a topic more relevant to this study, for segmenting tree trunks from street-level photographs to enable the estimation of physical measures (Jodas et al., 2021). Other applications include predictive modeling for tree failure in urban settings (Jahani & Saffariha, 2022).

While several deep learning techniques have been proposed on specific tasks, a new path has been opened to explore more recent models, particularly those based on LLMs, whose capabilities have rapidly expanded, leading to the development of VLMs that integrate visual and textual understanding. Applying these models in specialized fields like environmental science is an emerging frontier. A recent development in this area is Tree-GPT, a modular LLM expert forest remote sensing image analysis system (Du et al., 2023). Tree-GPT uses image understanding modules, including segmentation models like SAM, and domain knowledge bases to analyze remote sensing data, calculate tree parameters, and generate code for several tasks.

Although existing research progresses towards the computational analysis of trees in urban scenarios, developing techniques based on more modern solutions, such as LLMs, remains significantly underexplored, particularly regarding street-level imagery. Models like Tree-GPT demonstrate that integrating LLMs for forestry analysis in remote sensing data is a viable solution, revealing that there is still an opportunity for VLMs specifically focused on urban settings, utilizing readily available street-view imagery for direct attribute summarization. This paper addresses this gap by fine-tuning the PaliGemma VLM with a novel question-and-answer dataset, enabling it to summarize key characteristics of urban trees from a street-level perspective, thus offering a new tool for urban tree assessment.

3. PROPOSED METHOD

This section describes the proposed model in detail. Figure 1 shows the diagram that illustrates the step of the proposed method.

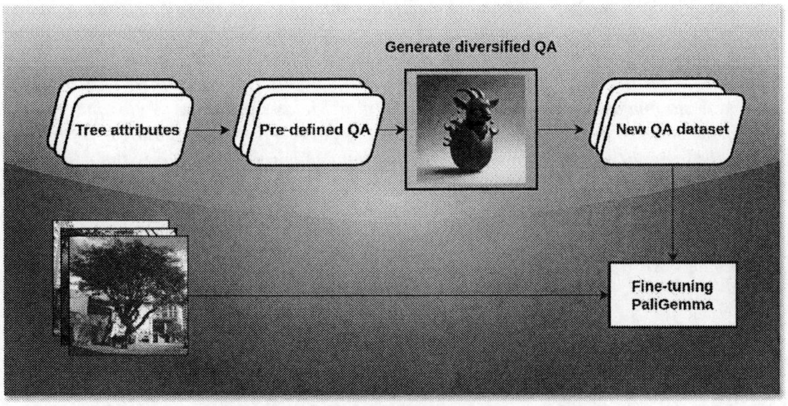

Figure 1. Illustration of the proposed method

To our knowledge, no dataset has been provided for applications in VLMs focusing on urban tree analysis, particularly in the Portuguese language. Therefore, the initial step is to produce questions and answers regarding the key attributes of the tree, such as the height, species, location, canopy maintenance, and the presence of epiphytes. Table 1 provides an overview of each aspect considered in the dataset generation.

Table 1. Tree attributes are used to formulate the questions and answers

Attribute	Description
Tree height	The vertical measurement from the base of the trunk to the highest point of the canopy.
Species	The scientific or common name identifies the tree's taxonomic classification.
Location	The geographical location of the tree, such as the street and neighborhood.
Slope	Indicates whether the tree leans towards the street.
Canopy Maintenance	Refers to the condition and management of the tree's canopy, including pruning or trimming practices.
Presence of Epiphytes	Indicates whether epiphytes - plants that grow on the tree without harming it - are present on the trunk or branches.

Producing the dataset involves formulating a series of predefined Portuguese questions and answers that address the aspects presented in Table 1. The process starts by defining five specific questions comprising the main features of the tree, following the same text structure for each subsequent image. This process yields five questions and answers for every individual street-level image. Examples of these questions and answers are illustrated in Table 2. Notice the presence of expressions like "*sem/pequena inclinação*", which indicates the slope of the tree, and "*localizada em passeio público*", indicating that the tree is located on a sidewalk. The next step involves using generative models to introduce diversity in the predefined questions and answers. This process aims to produce human-like content to increase the VLM's generative efficiency and range. In this context, the GemBode model was employed to diversify the dataset before fine-tuning the PaliGemma model. The following subsections discuss the GemBode model, the dataset diversification process, and the subsequent use of the PaliGemma model.

Table 2. Predefined questions and answers in Portuguese were generated for a single image

Question	Answer
Quais aspectos compõem esta árvore?	*Esta árvore pertence à espécie Tibouchina granulosa e à família Melastomataceae. A imagem indica que a árvore está situada em passeio público, especificamente junto ao meio fio. Situa-se numa zona residencial. A altura da árvore parece ser de aproximadamente 11,20 metros, sem/pequena inclinação. A aparência da copa mostra que ela foi podada, e não há epífitas .*
Preciso de uma visão geral da árvore mostrada nesta imagem. Você poderia fornecer uma descrição mais abrangente?	*Ao que parece, a árvore é da espécie conhecida como Tibouchina granulosa, pertencente à família Melastomataceae. Pelo que pude perceber, a árvore parece estar posicionada em passeio público e junto ao meio fio, sendo caracterizado por um cenário residencial. Estima-se que a árvore tenha uma altura de 11,20 metros, sem/pequena inclinação, uma copa que ela foi podada e não há epífitas.*
Que tipo de aspectos poderiam ser descritos com base na imagem apresentada?	*O que posso dizer, com base na imagem analisada, é que vejo uma Tibouchina granulosa, da família Melastomataceae, situada em passeio público e junto ao meio fio, em um ambiente residencial. Se estiver certo, a altura desta árvore é de 11,20 metros, aproximadamente, sem/pequena inclinação, e, analisando a copa, ela foi podada e não há epífitas.*

3.1 GemBode

Garcia et al. (2024) developed GemBode, a family of specialized small language models to address NLP challenges specifically within Brazilian Portuguese. These models were created by fine-tuning Google's Gemma-2B and Gemma-7B variants using both full fine-tuning and parameter-efficient fine-tuning (PEFT) methods such as Low Rank Adaptation (LoRA) and QLoRA, aiming to ensure operational efficiency in hardware-constrained settings. The fine-tuning process was done using a domain-specific Portuguese dataset named UltraAlpaca, a corpus created by translating and filtering other instruction-tuning datasets, and enabling GemBode to develop generalized instruction-following capabilities in the target language even for nuanced professional applications.

3.1.1 Linguistic Diversification Using GemBode

To enhance the linguistic and syntactic diversity of an initial Brazilian Portuguese question-answer dataset, GemBode-7B-it was employed as a paraphrasing model. GemBode processed each predefined question and its corresponding answer to generate two paraphrased variants that preserved semantic intent while introducing lexical diversity. This methodology expanded each original question-answer pair into three semantically aligned but lexically distinct samples, tripling the initial corpus size. The original question-answer pairs were retained and combined with these new variants, enabling the downstream model to learn from a more representative and diversified linguistic space for improved performance in Portuguese image-text interaction tasks. Furthermore, GemBode's introduction of controlled linguistic and syntactic diversity helped mitigate overfitting risks associated with small-scale Portuguese instruction-tuning datasets.

3.2 PaliGemma

Once the questions and answers are created, the PaliGemma model is fine-tuned to adjust it to nuances regarding the Portuguese language in the context of the considered field. PaliGemma is an open-source VLM (Beyer et al., 2024) designed for joint reasoning across visual and textual modalities. It integrates the SigLIP-So400m vision encoder with the Gemma-2B language decoder, resulting in a compact model of fewer than 3 billion parameters capable of competitive performance on various multimodal benchmarks. The architecture extracts visual tokens via SigLIP, projects them into the same embedding space as Gemma's language tokens, and employs the Gemma decoder for autoregressive text generation, using a prefix-LM attention scheme for bidirectional context on image and prompt tokens while maintaining unidirectional decoding. Although later, larger versions of PaliGemma exist (Steiner et al., 2024), this research used the original 3B model, due to its favorable balance between computational efficiency and performance, particularly beneficial in environments with limited computing resources.

4. METHODOLOGY

This section describes the tree dataset that was the basis for creating the question-answering multimodal dataset. It then outlines the experimental protocol, including data preparation, and the fine-tuning and evaluation process of the PaliGemma model.

4.1 Tree Dataset

The tree dataset consists of tree-related attributes and street-level photographic images collected during a fieldwork campaign, covering various tree species in different neighborhoods of São Paulo, Brazil. Initially gathered for a study on the risk of tree falls (SÃO PAULO, 2005), the dataset has since been repurposed in more recent research (Jodas et al., 2022; Candido et al., 2025) and is now used for multimodal question answering in the present study. During the fieldwork, images were acquired using a handheld RGB camera operated by a team member at a distance sufficient to capture the entire tree within each photograph. For dendrometric measurements - used to assess tree structural condition - a measuring stick was placed near each tree by a team member. This stick later served as a reference object for calculating tree dimensions directly from the images. Additional visible attributes were also annotated during the fieldwork.

4.2 Fine-Tuning PaliGemma for Multimodal Understanding

After expanding the dataset using GemBode, PaliGemma was fine-tuned to adapt its multimodal capabilities to the Portuguese language within the specific domain of this study. The dataset was initially filtered to include only samples from seven representative species: *Caesalpinia ferrea var. leiostachya, Caesalpinia peltophoroides, Holocalyx balansae, Jacaranda mimosaefolia, Ligustrum lucidum, Tibouchina granulosa, and Tipuana tipu*. Subsequently, images were further filtered by selecting only those with three distinct question–answer pairs for inclusion in the fine-tuning. The final dataset consisted of 1,060 images, each with three question-answer pairs, totaling 3,180 samples partitioned into training (90%, 2,862 samples) and evaluation (10%, 318 samples) sets using stratified sampling based on species. To avoid data leakage and ensure evaluation integrity, all three variations of a given sample were assigned entirely to either the training or the evaluation set based on the image ID instead of the sample itself.

Following initial data preparation, fine-tuning was carried out using the PaliGemma-3B-PT-448 model - a 3-billion-parameter variant pre-trained on image–text pairs with images resized to 448×448 pixels - chosen to suit a resource-constrained environment. Due to these hardware limitations, the float16 model checkpoint was used alongside the JAX implementation (Roy et al., 2018), which enables the parameters to be sharded across the GPUs available. Though slower than simultaneous loading, this incremental approach offered better memory efficiency. A selective fine-tuning strategy was employed: only the attention layers of the language model were trainable and cast to float32 for numerical stability, while all other parameters remained frozen in float16.

The training pipeline incorporated image preprocessing steps such as grayscale conversion, alpha channel removal, resizing, text tokenization, padding, prefix/suffix handling, and end-of-sequence token management. Training employed Stochastic Gradient Descent (SGD), computing per-example loss with masked tokens excluded and normalizing losses by token length. The fine-tuning and evaluation were performed on two NVIDIA T4 GPUs on Kaggle. A results file with questions, model answers, and ground truths was generated to compute the METEOR metric (Banerjee et al., 2005), the accuracy, the Mean Absolute Error (MAE), and the Mean Squared Error (MSE) for assessing answer quality.

5. RESULTS

This section presents and discusses the responses generated by the fine-tuned PaliGemma model. First, Subsection 5.1 provides two examples of generated answers to qualitatively demonstrate the proposed approach. Then, Subsection 5.2 presents a quantitative evaluation of the quality of responses using species classification accuracy and tree height error metrics computed across the entire evaluation dataset.

5.1 Qualitative Results

Table 3 presents the question, expected answer, and generated answer for two samples from the evaluation dataset. These examples illustrate that the fine-tuned model's responses closely align with the structure of the expected answers. This highlights the effectiveness of fine-tuning in teaching the model both the specific content it should convey and the desired flow of information. For similarity evaluation, we used the METEOR evaluation metric, which has become a popular choice for evaluating outputs in tasks such as image captioning and question answering (Chen et al., 2019). On the evaluation set, METEOR scores for similarity between predicted and expected answers increased from 0% with the pre-trained model to 65.33% after fine-tuning.

Table 3. Comparison of expected and predicted answers for two evaluation samples

Image	Question	Expected Answer	Predicted Answer
	*Qual é o nome da árvore?*	*Esta árvore pertence à espécie tipuana tipu dentro da família leguminosae. ela está localizada em um passeio público, posicionada ao lado de um meio fio. a árvore está em uma região classificada como em construção. sua altura é de aproximadamente 11,13 metros e tem uma inclinação em direção ao imóvel. a copa apresenta sinais de que ela foi podada, e existem epífitas. a árvore é de aproximadamente 30 anos de idade e tem um diâmetro de tronco de 2,5 metros. a copa está em um estado de saúde saudável e o tronco está em boas condições. a árvore está em um local onde não há risco de danos causados por atividades humanas.*	*Esta árvore pertence à espécie tipuana tipu dentro da família leguminosae. de acordo com a imagem, ele está localizado em passeio público, posicionado em junto ao meio fio. a árvore está em uma região classificada como residencial. sua altura é de aproximadamente 10. 18 metros e tem uma inclinação de sem/pequena inclinação. a copa apresenta sinais de que ela foi podada, e não há epífitas.*
	*O que dizer sobre esta árvore?*	*Esta árvore pertence à espécie tipuana tipu dentro da família leguminosae. de acordo com a imagem, ele está localizado em passeio público, posicionado em junto ao meio fio. a árvore está em uma região classificada como em construção. sua altura é de aproximadamente 11. 13 metros e tem uma inclinação de em direção ao imóvel. a copa apresenta sinais de que ela foi podada, e existem epífitas.*	*Esta árvore pertence à espécie tipuana tipu dentro da família leguminosae. de acordo com a imagem, ele está localizado em passeio público, posicionado em junto ao meio fio. a árvore está em uma região classificada como residencial. sua altura é de aproximadamente 10. 18 metros e tem uma inclinação de sem/pequena inclinação. a copa apresenta sinais de que não há poda , e não há epífitas.*

5.2 Quantitative Results

Table 4 presents the species classification accuracy and tree height error metrics per species. Overall, the results indicate that 193 out of 317 questions were correctly classified by species, yielding an accuracy of 60.69%. Although the evaluation dataset contains 318 samples, one was excluded from the species classification metric because the expected answer did not specify a species, possibly due to GemBode's incorrect generation. In addition, the model achieved an MAE of 9.13 for tree height prediction.

Table 4. Evaluation results of tree species and height contained in the generated answers

Species	Species Acc.	Tree Height (in meters)	
		MAE	MSE
Caesalpinia ferrea var. leiostachya	0.00%	1.23	2.50
Caesalpinia peltophoroides	70.30%	3.12	16.44
Holocalyx balansae	0.00%	2.38	7.60
Jacaranda mimosaefolia	0.00%	2.55	7.69
Ligustrum lucidum	14.29%	2.40	7.65
Tibouchina granulosa	53.33%	2.79	12.74
Tipuana tipu	87.96%	21.55	26.33
All Species	**60.69%**	**9.13**	**17.24**

Regarding performance by species, classification accuracy was generally proportional to the number of samples per species. *Tipuana tipu* (1,084), *Caesalpinia peltophoroides* (1,013), *Tibouchina granulosa* (442), and *Ligustrum lucidum* (219) were more prevalent in the fine-tuning dataset, totaling 2,758 out of 3,180 samples, which corresponds to 86.73% of the dataset. Notably, species with fewer samples tended to exhibit lower MAE and MSE in tree height prediction, likely due to reduced variability in smaller sample sets.

Despite this imbalanced distribution, the more represented species achieved promising results. *Tipuana tipu* reached 87.96% and *Caesalpinia peltophoroides* 70.30%, especially considering that the image module of PaliGemma was kept frozen during fine-tuning. Additionally, accurate tree height estimation remains challenging when relying solely on images, as they often lack real-world scale references. Nonetheless, MAE achieved 3.12 meters for *Caesalpinia peltophoroides*, the second most represented species.

It is worth mentioning the challenges related to predicting aspects of trees in street-view images, such as species, height, and canopy pruning. First, the aspect ratio of the image can distort its size and proportions and consequently lead to inaccurate height assessment. Besides, species identification is a challenging task, given the fact that many tree species are similar in terms of their visual characteristics. Furthermore, key details may be hidden since many trees may overlap in the same image, thus leading to ambiguity in estimating their specific characteristics.

Nevertheless, these results highlight the potential of the proposed method, which could be further improved in future work by fine-tuning the image module, once more computational resources become available, and by integrating information about real-world object scales to better ground height estimations.

6. CONCLUSIONS

This research emphasizes the potential of using Vision-Language Models to enhance the analysis of urban trees through street-level imagery. By fine-tuning the PaliGemma model with a Portuguese dataset of questions and answers regarding the main features of the trees, we promote a novel alternative for improved understanding and characterization of urban forestry. In particular, we pursued the challenges regarding analyzing street-level images of the trees, aiming to provide a solution for the broader image collection process. By providing the GemBode dataset, we enable further exploration of incorporating generative models in urban tree practices and encourage innovation in sustainable urban tree management.

Future directions involve expanding the question-and-answer dataset to enhance its utility and applicability beyond the Portuguese language, particularly by creating an English version. Including diverse urban environments from different regions can also provide a broader perspective on tree characteristics and health. In addition, integrating multimedia elements such as videos and sensor data could enhance the dataset and allow for more comprehensive analyses. Furthermore, we intend to explore other generative models to enhance the quality of questions and answers, as well as to provide the method as a practical application.

ACKNOWLEDGEMENT

This study was partially financed by the São Paulo Research Foundation (FAPESP), Brazil, grant numbers 2013/07375-0, 2019/07665-4, 2023/14427-8, 2023/10823-6, 2023/03726-4, 2023/01374-3, 2023/14354-0, and

2024/01132-2. The authors are also grateful to the Brazilian National Council for Scientific and Technological Development (CNPq) grants 308529/2021-9 and 400756/2024-2, to Unesp-IEPe-RC-06/2023 PROPe grant, and to the Petrobras Brazil grant 2017/00285-6 for their financial support.

REFERENCES

Banerjee, S. and Lavie, A. (2005). METEOR: An Automatic Metric for MT Evaluation with Improved Correlation with Human Judgments. *Proceedings of the ACL Workshop on Intrinsic and Extrinsic Evaluation Measures for Machine Translation and/or Summarization*, Michigan, United States, pp. 65–72.

Beyer, L. et al. (2024). PaliGemma: A versatile 3B VLM for transfer. arXiv preprint arXiv:2407.07726.

Brown, T. et al. (2020). Language Models are Few-Shot Learners. *Proceedings of the 34th International Conference on Neural Information Processing Systems,* Vancouver, Canada, pp. 1877-1901.

Devlin, J. et al. (2019). BERT: Pre-training of Deep Bidirectional Transformers for Language Understanding. *Proceedings of the 2019 Conference of the North American Chapter of the Association for Computational Linguistics: Human Language Technologies*, Minneapolis, Minnesota, United States, Vol. 1, pp. 4171-4186.

Candido G. et al. (2025). Optimum-Path Forest Ensembles to Estimate the Internal Decay in Urban Trees. *Proceedings of the 20th International Joint Conference on Computer Vision, Imaging and Computer Graphics Theory and Applications* (VISAPP 2025), Porto, Portugal, pp. 895-902.

Carvalho M., et al. (2020). Canopy architecture and morphometry of tree species used in the urban forest. *Floresta*, 50(4), pp. 1892–1901.

Chen, A. et al. (2019). Evaluating question answering evaluation. *Proceedings of the 2nd Workshop on Machine Reading for Question Answering*, Hong Kong, China. pp. 119–124.

Du, S. et al. (2023). Tree-GPT: Modular large language model expert system for forest remote sensing image understanding and interactive analysis. *arXiv preprint*, arXiv:2310.04698.

Garcia, G. L. et al. (2024). GemBode and PhiBode: Adapting Small Language Models to Brazilian Portuguese. Proceedings of the 27th Iberoamerican Congress on Pattern Recognition (CIARP 2024), Talca, Chile, pp. 228-243. Cham: Springer Nature Switzerland.

Guo, D. et al. (2025). DeepSeek-R1: Incentivizing Reasoning Capability in LLMs via Reinforcement Learning. arXiv preprint arXiv:2501.12948.

Jahani, A. & Saffariha, M. (2022). Tree failure prediction model (TFPM): machine learning techniques comparison in failure hazard assessment of *Platanus orientalis* in urban forestry. *Natural Hazards*, 110(2), pp.881–898.

Jodas, D. S. et al. (2022). Detection of Trees on Street-View Images Using a Convolutional Neural Network. International *Journal of Neural Systems*, Vol. 4, No. 1, pp. 2150042.

Jodas, D.S. et al. (2021). A Deep Learning-based Approach for Tree Trunk Segmentation, *Proceedings of the 34th SIBGRAPI Conference on Graphics, Patterns and Images* (SIBGRAPI 2021), Gramado, Rio Grande do Sul, Brazil, pp. 370-377.

Jodas, D. S. et al. (2023). Deep Learning Semantic Segmentation Models for Detecting the Tree Crown Foliage. *Proceedings of the 18th International Joint Conference on Computer Vision, Imaging and Computer Graphics Theory and Applications* (VISIGRAPP 2023) - Vol. 4, Lisboa, Portugal, pp. 143-150.

Jodas, D. S. et al. (2022). Multiclass Oversampling via Optimum-Path Forest for Tree Species Classification from Street-view Perspectives. *Proceedings of the 35th SIBGRAPI Conference on Graphics, Patterns and Images* (SIBGRAPI 2023), Vol. 1, pp. 121-126.

de Lima Araujo, H. C. et al. (2021). Artificial intelligence in urban forestry—A systematic review. *Urban Forestry & Urban Greening*, Vol. 66, pp. 127410.

Martins, J.A.C., et al. (2021). Semantic segmentation of tree-canopy in urban environment with pixel-wise deep learning. *Remote Sensing*, 13(16), p. 3054.

Roy Frostig, Matthew James Johnson, and Chris Leary (2018). Compiling machine learning programs via high-level tracing. Systems for Machine Learning, 4(9), 2018.

Pliatsios, A. et al. (2023). A systematic review on semantic interoperability in the IoE-enabled smart cities. *Internet of Things*, Vol. 22, pp. 100754.

Touvron, H. et al. (2023). LLaMA: Open and Efficient Foundation Language Models. arXiv preprint arXiv:2302.13971.

SÃO PAULO. Secretaria Municipal do Verde e do Meio Ambiente; IPT, SISGAU — Sistema de Gestão de Arborização Urbana (2005).

Steiner, A. et al. (2024). PaliGemma 2: A Family of Versatile VLMs for Transfer. arXiv preprint arXiv:2412.03555.

AN EXTENDED REALITY APPROACH TO INTERACTIVE 3D VISUALIZATION AND CONFIGURATION OF SOLAR PANELS

Cloe Hüsser, Luca Fluri and Hilko Cords
Institute of Interactive Technologies, School of Computer Science,
University of Applied Sciences and Arts Northwestern Switzerland (FHNW)
Windisch, Switzerland

ABSTRACT

The accurate visualization of solar panel layouts plays a crucial role in the transition to renewable energy, as it improves stakeholder communication and decision-making. Traditional static visualizations cannot dynamically represent environmental factors, such as dynamic sun paths and shading, or the dynamic visualization of power generation, which limits their effectiveness. This work addresses these limitations by leveraging Augmented Reality (AR) and Virtual Reality (VR) to enable immersive, interactive 3D visualizations, configurations, and simulations of solar panel installations.
Our research focused on creating a real-time visualization system that serves various stakeholders through two key solutions. First, our mobile AR solution offers a tabletop experience that enables users to interactively explore solar panel layouts with precise light and shadow calculations, providing an intuitive understanding of spatial relationships. Second, and complementarily, our VR solution supports multi-user sessions that enable real-time collaboration and interactive scene customization in a shared virtual space. Furthermore, we present a unified core system that powers both AR and VR applications, ensuring scalability, maintainability, and seamless cross-platform interaction. Technical achievements include the integration of an online design tool for exporting and sharing 3D scenes via QR codes, the visualization of realistic environmental simulations, and the facilitation of real-time collaborative adjustments in VR. These innovations significantly improve stakeholder engagement and streamline the design process for solar panel layouts. By demonstrating the effectiveness of immersive visualization techniques, this paper highlights the potential of AR and VR to drive renewable energy solutions, promote informed decision-making, and accelerate the adoption of sustainable energy technologies.

KEYWORDS

XR, Interaction, Collaboration, Solar Panels

1. INTRODUCTION

The global push toward renewable energy has intensified the demand for accessible, efficient, and stakeholder-friendly planning tools, particularly in the solar energy sector. In this context, visualizing solar panel layouts in realistic spatial environments is a critical part of the decision-making process for engineers, clients, architects, and project developers. However, most existing tools rely on static 2D renderings or limited static 3D visualizations, which are often abstract, unintuitive, and detached from the real installation context. These conventional approaches hinder users' understanding of key environmental factors, such as shading, orientation, and the alignment of the sun path, making collaborative planning cumbersome. As a result, decision-making is slow, miscommunication is frequent, and design iterations are resource intensive.

Our solution builds upon an existing web-based 3D solar design tool, allowing users to create comprehensive scenes with buildings, surrounding structures, and additional entities that cast shadows, such as trees or roof obstructions. Afterward, different solar panel layouts can be generated automatically. Furthermore, users can alter solar panel layouts by adjusting parameters or manipulating panels. The resulting designs are then fed into our system.

Based on this, we present a dual-platform immersive visualization system that integrates mobile Augmented Reality (AR) and Virtual Reality (VR) for the interactive, real-time, and geospatially accurate representation of solar panel layouts. Our AR solution enables in-situ exploration and configuration via AR, transforming mobile devices into spatial viewers for assessing sun paths and shading. At the same time, the VR application supports collaborative, multi-user design sessions with synchronized, real-time material and configuration adjustments. Both platforms are integrated with the web-based solar design tool through QR code export. They are built upon a shared codebase and consistent data pipeline, ensuring coherence, scalability, and maintainability. Therefore, our main contributions are listed as follows:

- A mobile AR system that visualizes solar layouts with integrated real-world terrain data, sun simulations, and touch-based interaction.
- A collaborative VR system that enables multi-user configuration of solar installations using synchronized interactions and spatial UI controls.
- Additionally, we propose a unified technical architecture that supports both AR and VR applications, reducing code redundancy and ensuring consistent feature availability.
- Finally, we evaluated the technical feasibility, usability, and early user feedback of the platform through internal testing and pilot deployment with industry stakeholders.

2. RELATED WORK

The integration of Augmented Reality (AR), Virtual Reality (VR), and Geographic Information Systems (GIS) significantly improves solar energy visualization, environmental simulation, and collaborative design processes (Kamel Boulos et al., 2017). The literature is divided into three main themes: AR-based visualization for solar applications, VR environmental simulations, and collaborative XR design frameworks.

AR technologies enable on-site assessment of building solar energy potential. Mobile AR systems augment real-time solar radiation data onto building surfaces, enabling interactive PV module placement analysis and energy yield forecasting (Meireles et al., 2023). This improves solar planning accessibility for professionals and the public. Optimized algorithms determine optimal solar panel layouts to improve placement accuracy and energy efficiency (Mehta et al., 2020). Additionally, AR combined with unsupervised learning detects, analyzes, and visualizes damaged PV module areas, significantly improving maintenance efficiency (Oulefki et al., 2024). VR enables immersive environmental simulations in solar energy contexts.

VR platforms visualize environmental factors affecting PV panel efficiency by integrating large real-world datasets (Ni et al., 2017). Through realistic, interactive 3D simulations, VR plays a significant role in photovoltaic energy education, bridging the gap between theoretical knowledge and practical application (Alqallaf & Ghannam, 2024). GIS-based Digital Twin frameworks offer comprehensive solar radiation mapping, enabling the optimization of sustainable urban design by dynamically modeling environmental factors and infrastructure interactions (Clementi et al., 2024). XR technologies significantly enhance collaborative design through multi-user interaction in shared virtual environments. AR-enhanced mobile devices enable simultaneous 3D model manipulation and visualization, thereby enhancing spatial awareness during complex tasks such as terrain modeling (Mendoza et al., 2021). Sophisticated VR systems utilize full-body motion capture to enhance immersion and support realistic remote collaboration through synchronized virtual avatars (Ha et al., 2022). Web-based XR shows promise in enhancing stakeholder engagement in participatory urban planning through realistic representations (Rzeszewski & Orylski, 2021).

AR, VR, and GIS integration significantly increases visual accuracy, user engagement, and collaborative efficiency in environmental analysis and design planning. Continued advancements in XR promise greater precision, accessibility, and practical applicability across planning and simulation scenarios. Despite these advancements, dual-platform (AR/VR) tools for solar panel layout visualization beyond static representations remain scarce. The literature lacks detail on streamlined workflows connecting online 2D/3D design platforms with immersive collaborative XR experiences. Addressing these integrated system gaps is crucial for improving stakeholder communication and decision-making in renewable energy (Hüsser et al., 2025).

3. OUR APPROACH

In the following, we present our dual-platform immersive visualization and configuration solution, which is based on a unified architecture for AR and VR. Our system interfaces with an existing web-based design platform that allows end-users to create representative 3D models of buildings. These models are then utilized for the automatic placement of solar panels and energy calculations. The platform serves as the backend for our work, and we access the models online via the Web. Before delving into the details of our AR and VR applications, we will first outline the architecture of our system.

3.1 System Architecture

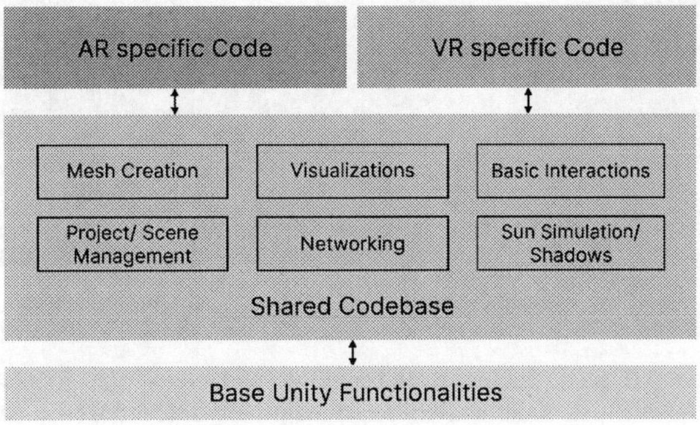

Figure 1. An overview of our system's architecture: Both the AR and VR-specific code use a shared codebase

The architecture of our XR solution was specifically designed to unify AR and VR solutions within a shared codebase. This unified code structure enabled us to significantly reduce development time by reusing core components, including data fetching, user interactions, and environmental simulation logic, across AR and VR platforms.

This approach simplified maintenance and ensured consistent behavior across different platforms, enabling efficient development iterations and smooth future expansion. We chose Unity for its strong cross-platform support, extensive features for XR development, and compatibility with external tools and SDKs. Additionally, for our AR functionality, we selected Vuforia due to its reliable markerless tracking, accurate surface detection, and robust mobile optimization.

Figure 1 depicts our system's architecture, built on Unity and incorporating a shared codebase that provides modules for geometric modeling, visualization, interaction logic, project/scene management, networking (for collaborative VR), and lighting. Platform-specific AR and VR modules interface with this shared core, enabling distinct interaction paradigms and rendering adjustments while inheriting these fundamental functionalities.

3.2 Augmented Reality

Our AR component is an interactive, mobile-first visualization tool that allows stakeholders to explore solar panel layouts in realistic, real-world contexts. The AR application uses markerless tracking, geographic data integration, and sun simulation to convert static layout plans into tangible, intuitive spatial representations.

The system is built using Unity (2022.3 LTS), extended with the Vuforia Engine for plane detection and spatial anchoring. Scene data is retrieved via RESTful APIs from an existing web-based 3D solar design tool, including geospatial coordinates, mesh data for buildings, panels, and simple scene elements, to simulate and visualize shadows. Unity's *JsonUtility* is used for lightweight deserialization of these payloads into in-memory models. The retrieved models are then rendered using custom mesh builders and lighting logic.

The user journey begins with scanning a QR code exported from a web-based design platform. These codes include a special AR flag and a backend URL. Once scanned and validated, the application requests the corresponding project plan and layouts, loads the data, and initiates spatial calibration of the camera stream. A visual placement guide helps users anchor the 3D scene in their environment. This process is illustrated in Figure 2.

Figure 2. AR workflow: a) Scan the project QR code, b) detect the surface including visual guidance, c) augment the 3D scene on the table, and d) view the details page within the app

The fully rendered AR scene includes all buildings and panel placements from the web-based design platform, as well as a terrain disk underneath that is dynamically fetched from an online geographic information system (ArcGIS). Thus, spatial context is provided by rendering a geographic base layer beneath the installation site. Figure 3 illustrates a detailed AR rendering depicting built structures, trees, solar panels, and the underlying geospatial reference layer. Two UI menu buttons provide user interaction and control for simulation, visualization, and project settings, with the latter enabling the rescanning of QR codes and adjustment of the simulation date.

Figure 3. A close-up of an AR scene from within the mobile application, showcasing a larger scene with several buildings and trees

While the scene can be explored by moving the mobile device, additional gesture interactions are supported through Unity's Input System, enabling pinch-to-zoom, drag, and tap gestures for navigating and modifying the scene. Visual feedback for loading states, interaction hints, and errors ensures an accessible experience even for non-technical users. Additionally, an automated zoom functionality is implemented that scales according to the distance between the phone and the scene. This allows users to examine buildings and solar panels in detail while maintaining Vuforia's surface detection and preserving scene anchoring.

Optimized for Android devices, the application utilizes static batching through Unity's URP pipeline and custom shaders designed explicitly for mobile devices, which preserve the visual quality of solar panels and roof structures. The final app is publicly available on the Google Play Store via the open testing channel. It has been tested on a variety of mid-range Android devices, demonstrating consistent performance and stability.

3.3 Virtual Reality

The VR component of our solution complements the AR application by offering an immersive collaborative environment for spatial assessment. Designed for standalone VR headsets (e.g., Meta Quest), the application allows users to explore and customize solar installation scenarios retrieved directly from the back-end services.

The VR application thereby shares its core data pipeline and mesh generation routines with its AR counterpart. Scene data, including 3D building structures, solar panel layouts, and simulation metadata, is fetched via HTTP requests from the web server's back-end and parsed using the same model classes. Instantiated scenes replicate the layouts generated in the web-based design tool, ensuring consistency across platforms. As mentioned above, this architecture simplifies maintenance and ensures synchronized and similar functionality in AR and VR contexts.

VR interaction is implemented using Unity's XR Interaction Toolkit and the OpenXR runtime, both of which are industry standards and compatible with many VR devices. Hence, users manipulate the environment with typical VR controllers. The left controller opens a hand-attached UI menu that allows for the configuration of roof and facade materials as well as solar panel styles. Each of these settings is contained within dedicated UI panels accessible via ray-cast pointer interactions. Figure 4 shows the interface and user interaction with the customization menu. Navigation within the scene is accomplished through thumbstick-controlled teleportation, allowing users to move around large-scale scenes without motion sickness. Additionally, users can scale the entire scene using the right thumbstick or through the handheld menu. This scaling feature enables detailed inspection of roof-mounted installations and evaluation on a 1:1 scale.

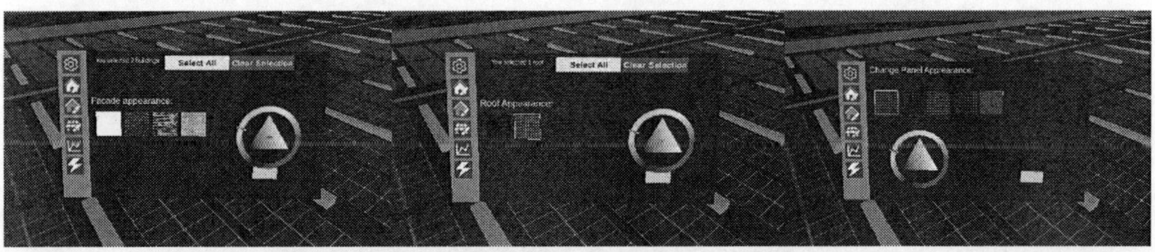

Figure 4. Controller attached VR menu, allowing for customization of materials and textures for facades, roofs, and panels. User can switch between several screens through the navigation pane on the left, selecting which components to adjust visually or accessing settings and data graphs. The UI also allow users to manage the selection of multiple buildings

Solar panel understructures and support poles are rendered using a custom GPU instancing shader, enabling real-time rendering of thousands of poles with minimal CPU and GPU overhead (Figure 5). This feature significantly enhances spatial understanding and shadow estimation for stakeholders. To support collaborative planning, our VR system integrates Photon PUN2 as its multiplayer networking layer. Collaborative scenes can be created and managed using a companion Android application, which allows users to log in to the backend and select an existing scene to share.

Figure 5. Visible understructures rendered through a custom GPU instancing shader

VR users will then be able to join this scene directly from within the application. The companion application was developed because text input in VR is notoriously tricky and cumbersome, and splitting up the duties into manager and client applications enhances usability and streamlines participation within the VR environment. Once connected, each user spawns into a shared VR environment with synchronized head and hand avatars, as well as complete visibility of other participants' locations and interactions.

All customization events, such as material changes, panel repositioning, or scene scaling, are synchronized using Photon Remote Procedural Calls (RPCs). This enables fast and efficient synchronization of scene data across users in real-time, ensuring a seamless multi-user experience. When joining a collaborative session, each client loads their local scene based on the shared project ID and instantiates the scene identically. The session network layer broadcasts real-time updates to building selections, color assignments, or panel configurations. Figure 6 depicts such a session with an active collaborator.

Our environment was built and tested for Meta Quest 2 and Quest Pro, achieving stable frame rates of 90-120fps through efficient mesh instancing, occlusion culling, and shader simplification. Unity's Universal Render Pipeline (URP) is configured with single-pass stereo rendering and dynamic batching to minimize draw calls and optimize GPU load. The VR system is currently in a testing phase with industry stakeholders and is ready as a functional research prototype for field deployment and formal user evaluations.

Figure 6. A selection of screens from an active VR session. The VR controller menu and ray-based building selection is shown, as well as the visualization of another user inside the collaborative VR space

4. RESULTS & DISCUSSION

Our environment has demonstrated the technical feasibility and practical utility of immersive XR tools for planning and communicating solar panel layouts. By leveraging the affordances of both mobile AR and VR, our approach offers a novel, dual-mode interface for stakeholders, including designers, engineers, sales personnel, and end-users.

Both AR and VR fulfill our core functional requirements and are easy to use, even by non-technical users. The AR application integrates QR-code-based project loading, real-world geolocation reference via ArcGIS services, and accurate sun path simulation. Users scan a QR code from the web design tool, download 3D project data, and place the scene in physical space for exploration. Our system is publicly available through the Google Play Store's open testing channel and has undergone early-stage testing by project partners and internal users. The VR environment reuses and extends many backend and rendering systems from the AR application. The VR prototype supports full scene exploration, intuitive scene scaling, rich material customization, and real-time collaborative interaction. Figure 6 illustrates a session in which multiple users collaborate to analyze a solar panel installation in a virtual environment.

An initial qualitative evaluation was conducted with a diverse group of participants, including clients, academic researchers, software developers, and project stakeholders. The objective of this study was to assess the usability, perceived effectiveness, and potential application benefits of our proposed AR and VR tools.

In the AR context, participants described the system as highly accessible and visually engaging. The QR code–based onboarding process was highlighted as an effective and low-friction entry mechanism. Visual overlays such as projected solar energy yield and sun paths were considered clear, relevant, and easy to interpret. The capability to explore virtual layouts and simulate shadow dynamics across times of day and seasons offered a depth of visual insight not achievable with traditional 2D planning tools.

Within the VR environment, interactive scaling and teleportation functions enabled rapid perspective changes, facilitating inspection of configurations from multiple vantage points (e.g., street-level vs. rooftop or elevated viewpoints). These features were deemed crucial for presenting designs to different stakeholder groups. The controller-based menu UI was found to be intuitive, with minimal learning time required to adjust materials and environmental settings.

From a commercial perspective, customer-facing stakeholders reported that immersive visualization contributes significantly to closing sales. In particular, it assists in addressing common non-financial concerns, such as the visual integration of the installation within its surroundings, as well as optimal panel placements to minimize shading effects. The ability to present scenarios interactively and from stakeholder-relevant viewpoints proved valuable for informed decision-making.

Despite the overall positive reception, feedback indicated areas for improvement are the following: (i) an expanded selection of materials and textures for customization and (ii) streamlined VR deployment via direct distribution channels (e.g., Meta Store) to improve end-customer accessibility. These considerations will inform subsequent development cycles and more extensive user testing.

Our collaborative mode allows multiple users to join a shared session and interact with the same project data. Participants in these sessions valued the ability to see each other's head and hand positions, which enhanced spatial awareness. This feature was particularly useful for sales meetings and remote consultations with clients and installers.

Although all these insights stem from an early exploratory evaluation, the responses indicate substantial user value and a strong commercial impact. As future work, we will conduct a comprehensive, quantitative user study to validate these promising initial results systematically. Nevertheless, our preliminary findings suggest that immersive technologies, when integrated into existing solar planning workflows, can significantly enhance both the technical accuracy and communicative power of the design process. The combination of real-world context, interactive simulation, and cross-platform consistency positions our solution as a compelling option for industry adoption.

Moreover, our unified code base approach ensured that improvements in scene generation, material loading, and simulation logic benefited both AR and VR applications simultaneously. This technical strategy reduced maintenance effort and improved consistency, which will be especially valuable as the system scales to include new features and supports a broader range of devices.

5. CONCLUSION & FUTURE WORK

In this paper, we presented comprehensive mobile AR and VR solutions that overcome the inherent limitations of traditional 2D representations of solar panel visualization. By leveraging the strengths of these immersive technologies, we achieved a more engaging, interactive, and spatially grounded decision-making process for stakeholders across the solar energy planning pipeline.

With our solution, users can visualize solar panel installations in representative 3D scenarios. Our AR solution features real-time sun simulation, shadow visualization, and geospatial alignment through ArcGIS integration. Our VR system supports multi-user sessions with real-time synchronization of scene edits and dynamic material customization. Both platforms share a unified design language and interaction model, ensuring consistency and ease of use across devices.

Our AR application is already available via the Google Play Store's open-testing channel, and the VR system serves as a validated foundation for further collaborative planning tools. However, several key areas have been identified as promising avenues for future enhancement. While the current system allows for standard material adjustments in VR, expanding the range of textures and surface options would further enhance realism and immersion - especially for clients familiar with specific architectural contexts. Furthermore, explicit, project-specific textures can further enhance realism. In AR, however, maintaining simplicity is paramount. Instead of introducing in-app customization, preselected themes or branded variants could be embedded in the QR code to preserve a clean user experience while also enhancing visual personalization.

Both AR and VR interfaces currently support energy performance graphs and key system metrics. However, more comprehensive data layers could improve the informative value, including advanced energy storage simulations, backend-generated shadow studies, and financial estimations. Such additions would maximize the benefits, particularly during sales meetings or feasibility evaluations, where stakeholders may consider both environmental and economic issues simultaneously. Finally, larger user studies are planned to help enhance the system and identify additional feature priorities. These studies will evaluate usability, interaction efficiency, and overall impact on the decision-making process, providing empirical validation and guiding the roadmap for future releases.

In summary, this work has established a scalable, immersive platform for visualizing and evaluating solar panel installations in AR and VR. By bridging the gap between digital planning and real-world implementation, the system not only enhances communication and understanding but also lays the groundwork for future innovation in the renewable energy sector through immersive XR technology.

ACKNOWLEDGEMENT

This work was supported by Innosuisse under project number 102.004 IP-ICT. We are profoundly grateful to our industry partner, Solextron AG, which initiated this project and provided invaluable expertise throughout its duration. We extend our special thanks to Renato Minamisawa and Vipluv Aga for their dedicated collaboration and significant contributions to this project.

REFERENCES

Alqallaf, N. and Ghannam, R., (2024). Immersive Learning in Photovoltaic Energy Education: A Comprehensive Review of Virtual Reality Applications. *Solar*, Vol. 4, No. 1, pp. 136-161.

ArcGIS Maps SDK for Unity, Esri Developer. Available at: https://developers.arcgis.com/unity/

Clementi, M. et al., (2024). GIS-Based Digital Twin Model for Solar Radiation Mapping to Support Sustainable Urban Agriculture Design. *Sustainability*, Vol. 16, No. 15, pp. 6590.

Ha, E., Byeon, G. and Yu, S., (2022). Full-Body Motion Capture-Based Virtual Reality Multi-Remote Collaboration System. *Applied Sciences*, Vol. 12, No. 12, pp. 5862.

Hüsser, C., Fluri, L., & Cords, H., (2025). Interactive 3D visualization and configuration of solar panel layouts in XR. *EuroXR 2025: Proceedings of the Application, Poster, and Demo Tracks of the 22nd EuroXR International Conference* (VTT Technology No. 440). VTT Technical Research Centre of Finland. https://doi.org/10.32040/2242-122X.2025.T440

Kamel Boulos, M.N. et al., (2017). From urban planning and emergency training to Pokémon Go: applications of virtual reality GIS (VRGIS) and augmented reality GIS (ARGIS) in personal, public and environmental health. *International Journal of Health Geographics*, Vol. 16, No. 1, pp. 7.

Mehta, K. et al., (2020). Novel Approach of Computing Optimal Placement of Solar Panel Using Augmented Reality. *Advanced Computing Technologies and Applications*. Singapore, pp. 533-542.

Meireles, C. et al., (2023). Mobile Augmented Reality for Analysis of Solar Radiation on Facades. *Proceedings of the 18th International Joint Conference on Computer Vision, Imaging and Computer Graphics Theory and Applications*. Lisbon, Portugal, pp. 131-142.

Mendoza, S. et al., (2021). An Architecture for Collaborative Terrain Sketching with Mobile Devices. *Sensors*, Vol. 21, No. 23, pp. 7881.

Ni, J., Yang, M. and Jiang, Y., (2017). Virtual Reality Simulation of Dust Accumulation on the Surface of Solar Panel. *2017 International Conference on Computer Systems, Electronics and Control (ICCSEC)*. pp. 425-430.

Oulefki, A. et al., (2024). Detection and analysis of deteriorated areas in solar PV modules using unsupervised sensing algorithms and 3D augmented reality. *Heliyon*, Vol. 10, No. 6, pp. e27973.

Photon Unity Networking for Unity Multiplayer Games, PUN2. Available at: https://www.photonengine.com/pun

Rzeszewski, M. and Orylski, M., (2021). Usability of WebXR Visualizations in Urban Planning. *ISPRS International Journal of Geo-Information*, Vol. 10, No. 11, pp. 721.

SIMULATING CLINICAL PRACTICE: DEVELOPMENT AND EVALUATION OF A VIRTUAL REALITY INTRAVENOUS PUMP FOR NURSING TRAINING

Jehdi Aizon, Hossain Samar Qorbani and Melanie Neumeier
MacEwan University, Edmonton, Canada

ABSTRACT

Virtual Reality (VR) has emerged as a promising tool for experiential learning, yet its application in nursing and healthcare education remains underexplored. This study investigates the use of VR to enhance clinical training through the development and evaluation of an Intravenous (IV) Pump Simulator, examining whether it is a viable tool and method for training, educating, and practicing nursing skills. The simulation was developed and designed for first- and second-year nursing students, but it was also accessible to learners across all levels. A two-phase user study, approved by ethics, was conducted: an initial pilot with five participants, followed by an expanded study with 25 participants that incorporated refinements from the pilot. Data was collected through anonymous feedback forms using Likert-scale measures of engagement and open-ended reflections on skill transferability. Findings demonstrate that students reported high levels of engagement and expressed strong confidence in transferring the skills learned in VR to physical clinical equipment. These outcomes align with prior research on immersive learning, which consistently highlights the role of VR in increasing motivation and improving knowledge retention. This study provides evidence that VR simulation can serve as an effective, scalable, and cost-efficient complement to traditional nursing education, offering institutions a valuable tool for enhancing engagement, improving learning outcomes, and expanding access to clinical training opportunities.

KEYWORDS

Virtual Reality, Healthcare Education, Nursing, Simulation, Immersive Simulation

1. INTRODUCTION

Immersive virtual reality (VR), along with augmented reality (AR), are both under the umbrella of extended reality (XR), and have shown promise for health-professions education, with evidence for gains in knowledge, confidence, and self-efficacy across diverse nursing scenarios. Building on this literature, a VR IV-pump simulation was designed to support clinical skill development and safe, repeatable practice opportunities that complement limited access to physical equipment. Recent studies also highlight the pedagogical value of realistic scenarios plus structured debriefing to strengthen communication and decision-making, motivating the present development and evaluation effort in undergraduate nursing contexts (Chen et al., 2020; Keisuke Tsukada et al., 2024; Mørk et al., 2024; Park et al., 2024). This study focused on getting nursing student user engagement scores and feedback using a Likert scale with the developed VR IV Pump simulator (Figure 1a and Figure 1b) to better understand the subjective opinion of VR training effectiveness in nursing. There were two pilot studies conducted. Both studies followed the same structure but scaled from five nursing students ($n_1 = 5$) to 25 nursing students ($n_2 = 25$).

2. RELATED WORK

Numerous studies have examined the effects of virtual reality (VR) on knowledge acquisition, engagement, satisfaction, and information retention. When used as a supplementary tool alongside existing methods, VR has been demonstrated to enhance overall engagement and improve academic performance.

A study by F. Chen et al. analyzed a total of 12 research articles involving 821 participants, focusing on the impact of virtual reality (VR) on knowledge, skills, satisfaction, confidence, and performance (Chen et al., 2020). The findings indicated no statistically significant differences between VR-based education and traditional learning methods. Indicating that adopting VR will have a similar experience to learning using physical machines. Additionally, the analysis across 12 studies (n=821) revealed that traditional education significantly enhances knowledge among learners, particularly nursing students, and that artistic environments facilitate a better understanding and attention to nursing concepts.

Many of the analyzed studies from Park et al. involved various nursing scenarios and the use of virtual patients (Park et al., 2024). The results indicated a significant effect on knowledge retention, with a standardized mean difference (SMD) of 0.71, and substantial improvements in confidence and self-efficacy.

VR has shown to increase confidence, knowledge attainment, and reduce anxiety of students prior to exams as shown in Ben Hammouda's et al study of 176 students who completed pre- and post-training questionnaires assessing their perceptions of virtual reality (VR) (Ben Hammouda et al., 2025).

A study by K. Tsukada et al. (Keisuke Tsukada et al., 2024) conducted a randomized clinical trial (n=90) that found VR training to be inferior to face-to-face instruction and superior to video for PPE donning and donning performance, highlighting VR's suitability for procedural skills.

Mørk et al. (Mørk et al., 2024) conducted a study (n=146) with three groups that included social education students, nursing students, and occupational therapy students. Nursing students reported the highest satisfaction with VR usability. Participants perceived the VR learning activity as a safe environment to practice realistic scenarios, which enhanced skill acquisition relevant to clinical practice. Similarly, Thompson's et al. data showed the increase engagement of nursing students who used VR as a learning tool (David Scott Thompson and McConnell, 2020).

Ebook resources offer effective solutions, methods, and strategies for developing impactful extended reality (XR) experiences in medical education Raikos, 2025. It emphasizes the potential of XR to enhance teaching and learning through immersive and interactive methods. Similar resources will be helpful for educators and students that adopt extended reality (XR) technology into their classrooms or training.

A study by H.Kajtazovic et al. assessed the effectiveness of a virtual simulation in evaluating physics understanding among six computer science students (Haris Kajtazovic and Qorbani, 2025). Its results demonstrate that complex mathematical concepts can be effectively visualized through VR, making it a valuable educational tool.

3. DISCUSSION

Extended reality (XR) technologies are advancing rapidly, with ongoing improvements in affordability, form factor, and accessibility that position these tools for broader adoption in educational contexts. Given their potential to enhance engagement and support knowledge retention, VR-based simulations can serve as a valuable complementary modality in health professions training, augmenting traditional laboratory and clinical activities. As device ecosystems mature and costs decline, institutional uptake is likely to expand, provided that integration aligns with curricular objectives and evidence-based pedagogical practices.

Since the adoption of XR is slow to advance in education, universal rules are not set in place for designing and developing XR apps. Equipment is large and, although portable, not as convenient as a phone or laptop. There is a variety of products in XR. The most publicly available headsets are the Quest series from Meta. Competitors such as the Pico, widely available in China and is owned by ByteDance (Ltd., 2025), are a direct competitor to Meta. There are also startups attempting to create variations of design with XR, but they often require a huge investment and are particularly unstable, being in the alpha or beta stages of development.

4. METHODOLOGY

The methodology employed in this study consists of two distinct phases: the development phase and the research phase. This approach involved the execution of two pilot studies.

In the initial pilot study conducted during the development phase, an earlier version of Unity 2022 was utilized to create a preliminary prototype, which encompassed a basic training module simulation of the infusion pump (IV pump) designed for first-year and second-year nursing students. Upon completion of this development stage, the prototype was tested with a cohort of five third-year and fourth-year nursing students. Participants for both pilot studies were recruited through a Research Ethics Board (REB). Interested nursing participants were sent details of the study and were given a small orientation of how to use the VR headset. Feedback was collected through an anonymous survey utilizing a Likert scale, allowing for an assessment of participant engagement and their qualitative evaluations of the simulation.

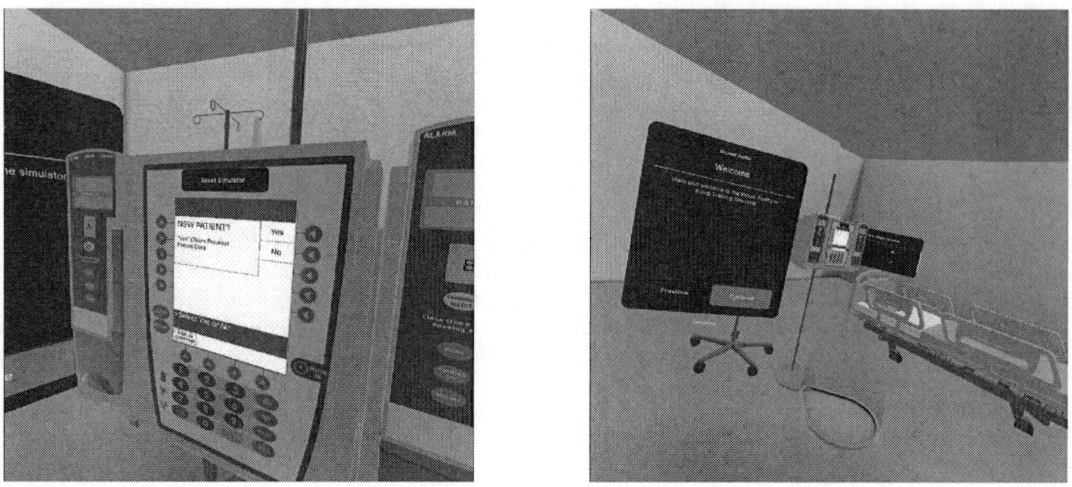

(a) Close up of the IV Pump machine

(b) Full view of the environment

Figure 1. Photos of the simulation environment from the second iteration study

Following the analysis of the feedback obtained, a subsequent pilot study was implemented with the objective of refining the user flow within the simulation. Enhancements included improvements to the user interface (UI) and user experience (UX) (Figure 1a and Figure 1b), as well as optimizations to the overall performance of the simulation. Key upgrades were made to various development packages and libraries within Unity, and a transition was executed from Unity 2022 to Unity 6.

After these enhancements were applied, the improved prototype was tested with a sample of 25 nursing students during the laboratory component of their course. The students were randomly approached within the laboratory environment and presented with the opportunity to participate in the testing session. Consent was obtained for participation, and upon completion of the session, an optional survey was provided for participants.

4.1 Study Iteration One

The initial study prioritized implementing a basic virtual reality simulation of an intravenous (IV) infusion pump to establish core functionality and interaction fidelity for subsequent evaluation. The simulation was developed in Unity using C# and integrated the Unity OpenXR Plugin alongside Meta XR SDK packages to enable cross-runtime XR compatibility and device support.

Participants (n_1 = 5) were assigned to two focus groups, one comprising three students and the other comprising two students (n_{1a} = 3; n_{1b} = 2). Before engaging with the simulation, participants received a brief orientation to the virtual reality (VR) controllers to ensure basic operational competency, given that several participants reported no prior VR experience. Participants were informed that they could remove the headset at any point if discomfort arises and could discontinue participation at any time without penalty. Feedback was collected anonymously through a questionnaire (Table 1) that included Likert-scale usability items, knowledge-testing items, and open-ended prompts for general comments. The Likert-scale items were used to capture graded evaluations of usability and perceived knowledge, complemented by qualitative insights from open-ended responses.

Table 1. Study One Likert-scale Results

N.	Questions	Results (n=5)
	5 (Strongly Agree), to 1 (Strongly Disagree)	
1	I can understand the VR controllers easily	5 (80%), 4 (20%), 3(0%), 2(0%), 1(0%)
2	I think the feedback (visual or sound) is useful	5(100%), 4(0%), 3(0%), 2(0%), 1 (0%)
3	I can complete the given steps within the simulation easily	5 (80%), 4 (20%), 3(0%), 2(0%), 1(0%)
4	I can learn to use the Virtual IV Pump easily	5(100%), 4(0%), 3(0%), 2(0%), 1 (0%)
5	I have become more interested in learning about the IV Pump through VR Training	5(100%), 4(0%), 3(0%), 2(0%), 1 (0%)
6	I found the tips and dialogue helpful to learning the IV Pump	5(60%), 4(40%), 3(0%), 2(0%), 1 (0%)
7	I found the learning method through VR simulation to be helpful	5(100%), 4(0%), 3(0%), 2(0%), 1 (0%)

4.2 Study Iteration Two

The second iteration incorporated participant feedback from the initial study to refine interaction design and usability specifically for nursing students. Revisions focused on configurable settings and presentation quality while building on the established IV pump simulation implemented in the first iteration. The project environment was upgraded to Unity 6 to leverage the current engine's capabilities and performance improvements. Configuration settings were extended to expose end-user controls, including adjustable player height and the ability to reposition the IV pump apparatus to accommodate ergonomic variation across learners. Optional voice narration was introduced to support guided task execution, and the user interface was redesigned to present a more professional visual style. These changes prioritized interaction feel, clarity, and accessibility over feature breadth, aligning improvements to observed usability gaps reported in the first study.

First- and second-year nursing students (n_2 = 25) anonymously participated in this iteration. Participation was voluntary, and participants were advised that they could discontinue at any time if they experienced discomfort. This approach was framed to support informed choice without pressure, consistent with standard consent practices and principles of unbiased research communication in academic contexts. Participants received a brief orientation covering the basic operation of the VR headset before engaging with the simulation to ensure minimal barriers to use. Following the experience, an optional survey (Table 2) was provided to capture feedback anonymously, mirroring the approach used in the previous study iteration.

5. RESULTS

Data for both iterations were collected via a structured survey instrument employing a Likert scale to quantify perceptions of usability and engagement with the VR simulation. The core measurement approach remained consistent across iterations to support comparability of responses while accommodating targeted expansions in the second iteration.

Table 2. Study Two Likert-scale Results

N.	Questions	Results (n=25)
5 (Strongly Agree), to 1 (Strongly Disagree)		
1	The virtual reality simulation was interesting or fun to use.	5 (80%), 4 (20%), 3(0%), 2(0%), 1(0%)
2	I feel comfortable using a virtual reality headset.	5(100%), 4(0%), 3(0%), 2(0%), 1 (0%)
3	The virtual reality simulation was difficult to navigate.	5(8%), 4(16%), 3(8%), 2(44%), 1 (24%)
4	I prefer practicing skills on the physical infusion pump compared to virtual reality.	5(33%), 4(21%), 3(25%), 2(21%), 1 (0%)
5	My skills in operating the infusion pump have improved as a result of the virtual reality simulation	5(28%), 4(48%), 3(16%), 2(8%), 1 (0%)
6	The mix of virtual reality and physical infusion pumps helped accommodate individual styles of learning.	5(42%), 4(33%), 3(17%), 2(8%), 1 (0%)
7	I feel comfortable using the infusion pump in a clinical setting after practicing with the virtual reality simulation.	5(28%), 4(36%), 3(28%), 2(8%), 1 (0%)
8	I would recommend virtual reality simulations to other students.	5(52%), 4(28%), 3(20%), 2(0%), 1 (0%)
9	I would use virtual reality simulations to practice outside of lab time if they were available.	5(48%), 4(24%), 3(12%), 2(12%), 1 (4%)
10	I am confident that the skills I learned in the virtual reality simulation will transfer effectively to real-world use of the infusion pump.	5(40%), 4(40%), 3(16%), 2(4%), 1 (0%)

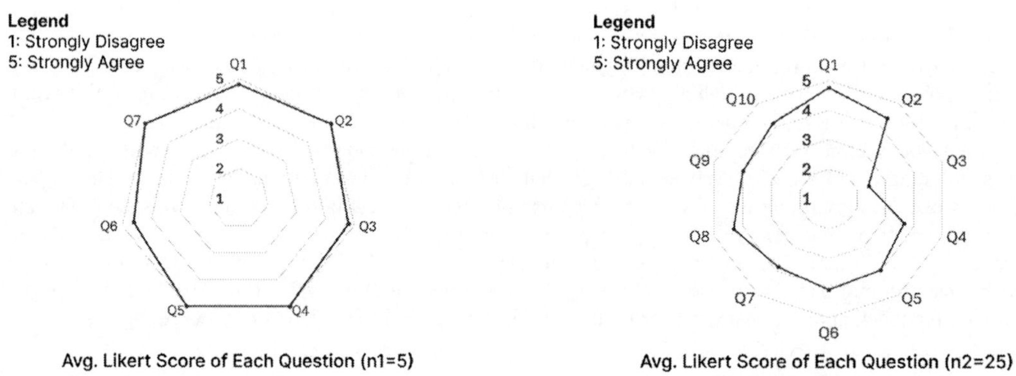

(a) Study Iteration 1: Avg. Likert

(b) Study Iteration 2: Avg. Likert

Figure 2. Avg. Scores of Likert Questions for Study Iteration 1 and 2

5.1 Key Findings

In the smaller preliminary study ($n_1 = 5$), participants reported high levels of satisfaction with the simulation's design and user experience, as depicted in Figure 2a. In the subsequent study with a larger sample ($n_2 = 25$), the overall pattern remained primarily positive while reflecting a more realistic distribution of responses, consistent with increased statistical stability at higher sample sizes (Figure 2b).

5.1.1 Usability and Navigation

With the improved build, more than half of respondents indicated that navigation within the VR simulation was not difficult, aligning with the targeted usability adjustments introduced between iterations (Table 2; Figure 2b). These results are consistent with a development focus on interaction clarity and interface refinement to reduce friction in common tasks.

5.1.2 Learning Transfer and Engagement

Participants expressed confidence that skills practiced in VR would transfer to physical equipment, and that the simulation accommodated diverse learning paces (Table 2, items 5 and 6). Across both studies, a high proportion of students reported being interested and engaged during the simulation experience (Table 2, item 1), supporting the perceived value of VR as a complementary instructional modality.

5.1.3 Awareness, Realism, And Functional Ease

Open-ended feedback indicated strong enthusiasm for VR while also highlighting limited awareness of how to access such simulations and concerns that certain elements were less realistic than preferred or expected. Participants in both iterations emphasized the importance of ease of function, including reliable button activation on the device and straightforward spatial navigation, underscoring the centrality of affordances to perceived usability.

6. CONCLUSION AND FUTURE WORK

Students across both iterations generally perceived VR as a valuable adjunct to existing instructional modalities, indicating strong acceptability as a complementary tool rather than a replacement for current practices. Participants also reported greater confidence in operating physical equipment following VR-based practice, supporting the interpretation that the simulation contributed to readiness for hands-on tasks. Taken together, these perceptions suggest that the potential of VR to enhance the learning experience is viable within nursing education contexts.

Increasing the sample size of nursing students will strengthen the validity of our study. In future work, we plan to include a larger participant group to obtain more reliable data, enabling deeper analysis and more robust findings.

This project adopted an iterative approach to design and evaluation, with successive development cycles informed by learner feedback to improve usability and educational relevance. Future work will focus on strengthening the prototype and conducting scaled evaluations across multiple universities with nursing programs to assess generalizability, implementation feasibility, and learner outcomes in diverse settings. Further iterations will prioritize systematic assessment of engagement and knowledge measures, alongside practical considerations for deployment, training, and curriculum integration.

REFERENCES

Ben Hammouda, S., Maoua, M., & Bouchahma, M. (2025). The effectiveness of vr-based human anatomy simulation training for undergraduate medical students. *BMC Medical Education*, *25*(1), 816. https://doi.org/10.1186/s12909-025-07402-5

Chen, F., Leng, Y., Ge, J., Wang, D., Li, C., Chen, B., & Sun, Z. (2020). Effectiveness of virtual reality in nursing education: Meta-analysis. *Journal of Medical Internet Research*, *22*(9), e18290. https://doi.org/10.2196/18290

David Scott Thompson, A. P. T., & McConnell, K. (2020). Nursing students' engagement and experiences with virtual reality in an undergraduate bioscience course. *International Journal of Nursing Education Scholarship*. https://doi.org/ 10.1515/ijnes-2019-0081

Haris Kajtazovic, N. B., & Qorbani, H. S. (2025). Developing virtual simulation of optic lab in physics education using virtual reality. *iLRN Practitioner Proceedings*. https://doi.org/10.56198/702djy10

Keisuke Tsukada, Y. Y., Satoshi Miyata, J. F., Tomomi Kikuchi, T. M., Satoshi Nakayama, H. K., & Miyamoto, W. (2024). Effectiveness of virtual reality training in teaching personal protective equipment skills. *JAMA Network Open*. https://doi.org/10.1001/jamanetworkopen.2024.1156

Ltd., P. T. C. (2025). *Pico virtual reality | official website | pico global* [Accessed October 5, 2025]. https://www.picoxr. com/global/

Mørk, G., Bonsaksen, T., Larsen, O. S., Kunnikoff, H. M., & Lie, S. S. (2024). Virtual reality simulation in undergraduate health care education programs: Usability study. *JMIR Medical Education*, *10*, e56844. https://doi.org/10.2196/56844 Park, S., Shin, H. J., Kwak, H., & Lee, H. J. (2024). Effects of immersive technology–based education for undergraduate nursing students: Systematic review and meta-analysis using the grade approach. *Journal of Medical Internet Research*, *26*, e57566. https://doi.org/10.2196/57566

Raikos, A. (2025). *Xr in medical education: The role of extended reality in transforming teaching and learning*. MEDIS MEDIA Corp.

A LOGIC PROGRAMMING-BASED APPROACH FOR THE HARMONIZED SURVEY ON HOUSEHOLDS LIVING STANDARDS DATA VALIDATION

Marc Mfoutou Moukala[1], Macaire Ngomo[2] and Régis Freguin Babindamana[1]
[1]Faculty of Science and Technology, Marien Ngouabi University, Brazzaville, Congo
[2]Research and Innovation Department, CM IT CONSEIL, Romilly sur Seine, France

ABSTRACT

In a former work we built a Resource Description Framework (RDF)-based semantic data model for the Harmonized Survey on Households Living Standards (HSHLS), which is the main household statistical survey conducted by French-speaking countries in West and Central Africa since the year 2018. In this paper, we propose and test an approach to enhance the HSHLS data validation mechanism through logical programming, implemented using Prolog language. We integrate the RDF-based semantic data model into SWI-Prolog, a Prolog environment, and build a knowledge base focused on data validation by setting rules using directly the information contained in the integrated RDF model. This hybrid approach leverages the power of RDF and Prolog and facilitates reasoning and data consistency control.

KEYWORDS

Logic Programming, Prolog, Data Validation, RDF Data Model, Harmonized Survey on Households Living Standards

1. INTRODUCTION

The Harmonized Survey on Households Living Standards (HSHLS) (FAO-UN, 2022; THE WORLD BANK, 2022) is a household survey consisting of a set of modules or sections, each section dealing with a given theme. Among the topics addressed there are: the socio-demographic characteristics of households and their members as well as information on education, health and employment of household members. Information about each module is collected through a specific questionnaire administered by the way of interviews called Computer-Assisted Personal Interviews (CAPI), using a computer application mainly installed on electronic mobile devices (tablets and telephones). In the work (Mfoutou Moukala et al., 2024a) and (Mfoutou Moukala et al., 2024b), we built a semantic data model of the HSHLS survey, using the Resource Description Framework (RDF) (RDF 1.1 Primer, W3C Working Group Note, 2014) and its extension, RDF Schema (RDF Schema 1.1, W3C Recommendation, 2014). That model allows representing the survey methodological information in a human and machine-readable way, and provides ease of understanding of the survey concepts, while enhancing the survey efficiency and improving the dissemination of related concepts. To enhance data quality, the survey methodology defines a set of logical constraints on questions or between questions of the related questionnaires. In (Mfoutou Moukala et al., 2025), we proposed an extended version of the work in (Mfoutou Moukala et al., 2024a) and (Mfoutou Moukala et al., 2024b) by designing and implementing a data integration framework and a query and reasoning mechanism over the semantic data model built. We used SPARQL (SPARQL, W3C, 2013) for querying, and Semantic Web Rule Language (SWRL) for reasoning and data validation. We tested the proposed process with a set of sample data, and that implementation allowed getting good results based on some data consistency rules. However, while effective for basic data validation and retrieval, the SWRL/SPARQL-based approach proves inadequate for more advanced consistency checking requirements. Although SWRL allows rule-based extensions to RDF-OWL ontologies, and SPARQL supports structured graph queries, both technologies present expressiveness limitations. SWRL lacks recursion, negation, and dynamic rule control. SPARQL does not natively support recursive queries or procedural interaction with the data model. These constraints limit their effectiveness in the case of the survey under study, which requires deeper consistency checks and adaptive logic. Due to those limitations, in this paper, we aim to enhance the survey data validation process through logical programming approach using Prolog, the main recognized and used logical programming language in the literature (that fully supports logical programming). The key contributions of this article are:

- A hybrid architecture for consistency validation in household surveys that combines RDF/OWL ontologies with Prolog-based reasoning;
- A method for importing semantic data into a logic programming environment using standard RDF APIs;
- A Prolog rule base that supports recursive, dynamic, and context-sensitive consistency checks beyond the capabilities of SWRL;
- A comparative evaluation of the approach versus traditional SWRL/SPARQL-based systems.

The rest of this article is organized as follows: In Section 2, we present the background and related work. In Section 3, we expose the adopted methodology. In Section 4, we present the results and discussion. Finally, we end with a conclusion along with an outline of potential future work, in section 5.

2. BACKGROUND AND RELATED WORK

2.1 Semantic Modeling in Household Surveys

Semantic technologies offer formal and interoperable means of representing structured knowledge in domains such as healthcare, population studies, and survey data management. RDF and OWL have become key standards for building ontologies that model complex entities and their relationships. In the context of household surveys, these technologies enable explicit modeling of concepts like individuals, households, and social ties, allowing for machine-processable validation of data structure and semantics.

In the work (Mfoutou Moukala et al., 2024a; Mfoutou Moukala et al., 2024b) extended by (Mfoutou Moukala et al., 2025), the authors developed a semantic model of the Harmonized Survey on Households Living Standards (HSHLS), using RDF and OWL. This model captures entities such as Household, Household Member, Question, Answer, along with relevant object and data properties. It provides a foundation for consistent representation and exchange of survey data in household surveys. While OWL-based constraints could enforce schema-level validity (for example, cardinality restrictions), they are insufficient for detecting more intricate consistency issues such as logic-dependent conflicts between attributes.

To address such issues, rule-based reasoning is essential. However, the rule formalism must be expressive enough to support recursive patterns, negation, and procedural control. Conventional Semantic Web tools don't support those requirements.

2.2 Rule-Based Reasoning with Semantic Web Rule Language

SWRL extends OWL ontologies with Horn-like rules, enabling users to infer new facts based on logical patterns. It has been widely used in Semantic Web applications to supplement OWL's declarative constraints with domain-specific logic. In our previous system, SWRL rules were applied to enforce basic semantic validations, for instance, ensuring that if the age of a household member is less than 3 years old, the education-related questions must not be asked.

Despite its integration with OWL, SWRL presents significant limitations for consistency control:

- It does not support recursive rules, making it difficult to handle hierarchical relationships such as family chains.
- It lacks negation and disjunction, which are often necessary to identify inconsistencies or exceptions.
- It provides no control over rule execution, limiting the ability to apply rules procedurally or conditionally.
- Its representation, especially in RDF syntax, is verbose and difficult to manage in practice.

These constraints limited our ability to define richer consistency rules for our household survey.

2.3 Querying with SPARQL

SPARQL is the standard language for querying RDF data. It enables graph pattern matching and is effective for retrieving and filtering RDF triples. In our earlier work, SPARQL queries were used for some information extraction over the semantic model built, for example, list questions and their dependencies, select individuals who are household members and are marked with the inconsistency class.

However, SPARQL has well-known limitations in reasoning-intensive contexts:

- It does not support recursive querying, making it unsuitable for transitive or path-based validations;
- It cannot operate on inferred knowledge unless precomputed by an external reasoner;
- It lacks mechanisms for rule chaining, branching logic, or dynamic assertions.

While SPARQL remains valuable for static data retrieval, it is inadequate for performing deeper semantic checks involving logic and control.

2.4 Logic Programming for Data Consistency Validation

A program is a set of axioms, logical statements, that express the knowledge and hypotheses of the problem, and a calculation is a constructive proof of a goal based on the statements of the problem (Sterling and Shapiro, 1990). Ideally, the programmer expresses the logic of the problem to be solved, while the control is embedded or included in the interpreter of the language as such.

A logic program is a finite set of facts and rules, also called defined program clauses. A logic program is executed by assigning it a goal. Unification is the uniform mechanism for parameter passing, selection, and data construction.

Logic programming is based on the use of formal tools such as model theory and resolution theory to capture its semantics in a simple and efficient way (Jaffar et al., 1986). Model theory is used to characterize the declarative semantics of the language, while resolution theory forms the basis of its operational semantics.

Prolog, as an implementation of logic programming is a powerful and simple language with a well-defined semantics, based on predicate calculus, offering several advantages such as unification and backtracking (Sterling and Shapiro, 1986; Sterling and Shapiro, 1990; Sterling and Shapiro, 1994). Prolog language allows modeling knowledge using clauses (facts and rules) and inferring from this knowledge.

Logic programming, and in particular Prolog, offers a powerful alternative for rule-based reasoning over semantic data. Prolog natively supports recursion, negation-as-failure, and dynamic knowledge base manipulation. This makes it well-suited for complex consistency checking tasks, especially when rule logic involves dependencies across multiple entities or contexts.

Recent tools such as the SWI-Prolog `semweb` library enable seamless integration between RDF data and Prolog programs. RDF triples can be loaded into Prolog as facts of the form `rdf(Subject, Predicate, Object)`, over which expressive rules and queries can be defined.

Inspired by that literature, our current approach preserves the RDF-based semantic model of the HSHLS survey but shifts rule-based consistency control to the Prolog layer, where validation logic can be written more naturally and executed with greater flexibility.

3. METHODOLOGY

This section outlines the architecture and implementation of our hybrid approach, which combines an RDF/OWL-based semantic model with Prolog-based reasoning and querying. The methodology consists of four key components: (i) semantic modeling of the HSHLS survey data, (ii) importing RDF into the Prolog environment, (iii) defining consistency rules in Prolog, and (iv) querying and validation through Prolog predicates.

3.1 Presentation of the HSHLS Semantic Data Model

Semantic data models play a crucial role in the modeling of complex knowledge. They allow representing relationships and interactions between concepts in an accurate and structured way. These models are used in various application scenarios: representing relationships between concepts, encapsulating business knowledge, data search and analysis, integrating heterogeneous data sources, and supporting artificial intelligence and machine learning.

The HSHLS semantic data model built consists of a resource class HSHLS representing HSHLS surveys, an instance of the rdfs:Class class of the RDF model. A survey is made up of sections. A section contains a questionnaire. A questionnaire is of a certain type, depending on the information collected. This may be information characterizing household members or common household characteristics. These characteristics are variables represented by questions. Each question is an instance of the rdfs:Class class in our model, and concerns a household member or a household as a whole. A household member belongs to a unique household, and has answers to the survey questions. A household member can have answers to all or some questions, depending on their characteristics and the eligibility criteria (for example, a minimum age threshold for a surveyed to answer to questions on Education). An answer is related (refers) to both a household member and a question, and is of a certain type (integer, float, string) depending on the nature of the expected response. Each question is linked to a questionnaire. A question may depend on other questions and may have constraints, which are acceptable values of its answers.

The general model includes the class declaration model (Figure 1) and the property declaration model (Figure 2). The model is serialized in Turtle, and managed using standard ontology tools.

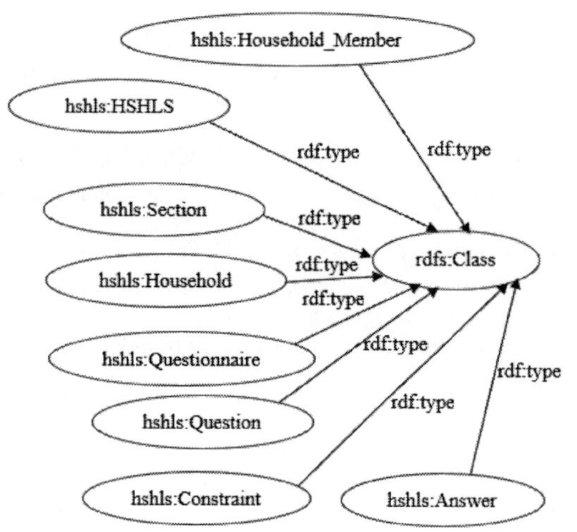

Figure 1. HSHLS RDFS graph with class declaration.

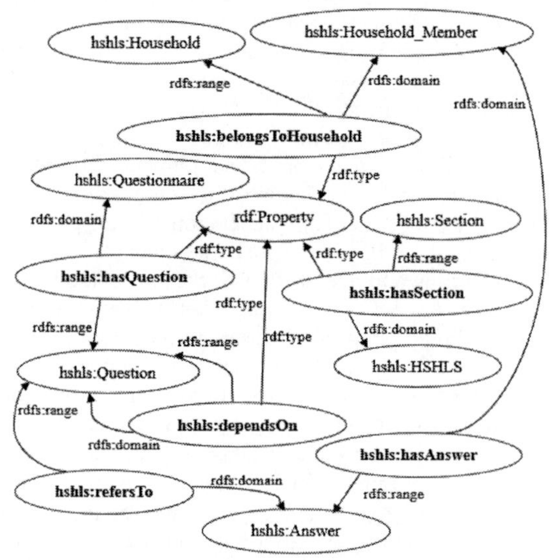

Figure 2. HSHLS RDFS graph with property declaration

Figure 1 represents 8 class declarations, all being instances of rdfs:Class.

Figure 2 illustrates the property declaration model, with the properties written in bold.

3.2 Importing RDF into the Prolog Environment

To enable logic-based reasoning, we import the RDF model directly into the `SWI-Prolog` environment using the built-in `semweb` package. The following steps are followed:

1. Use relevant semweb modules:

```
:- use_module(library(semweb/rdf11)).
:- use_module(library(semweb/turtle)).
```

2. Namespace Management: Prefixes and base URIs are registered to simplify triple matching:

```
:- rdf_register_prefix(hshls, 'http://w3id.org/HshlsOnto/').
```

3. Load RDF Ontology:

```
:- rdf_load('hshls_ontology.ttl', [format(turtle)])).
```

4. Query RDF Triples: RDF data becomes accessible as facts of the form:

```
rdf(Subject, Predicate, Object).
```

With this setup, all classes, individuals, and properties defined in the RDF model are programmatically accessible and queryable within the Prolog knowledge base. An illustration is given below:

```
Subject = 'http://w3id.org/HshlsOnto/answer_11_320_2_2_1_S02Q_Age',
Predicate = 'http://www.w3.org/1999/02/22-rdf-syntax-ns#type',
Object = 'http://w3id.org/HshlsOnto/Answer' ;
Subject = 'http://w3id.org/HshlsOnto/answer_11_320_2_2_1_S02Q_Age',
Predicate = 'http://w3id.org/HshlsOnto/hasValue',
Object = 56^^'http://www.w3.org/2001/XMLSchema#integer' ;
Subject = 'http://w3id.org/HshlsOnto/answer_11_320_2_2_1_S02Q_Age',
Predicate = 'http://w3id.org/HshlsOnto/refersTo',
Object = 'http://w3id.org/HshlsOnto/S02Q_Age' ;
```

In this illustration, we can see that RDF triples are well recognized and queryable. Triples are separated by ";" sign.

3.3 Defining Consistency Rules in Prolog

Once RDF triples are loaded, we define a set of consistency rules as Prolog predicates. These rules are designed to identify logic violations in the survey data. In the codes below we illustrate some rules we include in the knowledge base. Each rule uses one or more control variables defining a constraint. The other rules are based on the same approach.

Rule 1: This rule defines an inconsistency between the age of the surveyed and they responses to education-related questions. According to the methodology of the survey, a household member with age less than 3 years old cannot answer to questions related to education.

```
inconsistent_age_education(HouseholdMember,Answer1,ValueAnswer1,Answer2):-
    rdf(HouseholdMember, hshls:hasAnswer, Answer1),
    rdf(Answer1, hshls:refersTo, 'http://w3id.org/HshlsOnto/S02Q_Age'),
    rdf(Answer1, hshls:hasValue, ValueAnswer1^^_),
    ValueAnswer1<3,
    rdf(HouseholdMember, hshls:hasAnswer, Answer2),
    (rdf(Answer2, hshls:refersTo, 'http://w3id.org/HshlsOnto/S02Q01a');
    rdf(Answer2, hshls:refersTo, 'http://w3id.org/HshlsOnto/S02Q03');
    rdf(Answer2, hshls:refersTo, 'http://w3id.org/HshlsOnto/S02Q01c')).
```

Rule 2: this rule checks household members of three years old or above but missing responses to education-related questions

```
check_missing_answers_for_three_years_older_members :-
    % For each household member with an age>=3
    rdf(HouseholdMember, hshls:hasAnswer, Answer1),
    rdf(Answer1, hshls:refersTo, 'http://w3id.org/HshlsOnto/S02Q_Age'),
    rdf(Answer1, hshls:hasValue, ValueAnswer1^^_),
    ValueAnswer1>=3,
     % Use negation to check if any required question is missing
    (
\+ rdf(Answer2,hshls:refersTo,'http://w3id.org/HshlsOnto/S02Q01a');
 \+ rdf(Answer2, hshls:refersTo, 'http://w3id.org/HshlsOnto/S02Q03');
 \+ rdf(Answer2, hshls:refersTo, 'http://w3id.org/HshlsOnto/S02Q01c')),

    % If anyone of the questions S02Q01a, S02Q01c and S02Q03 is missing a
response, print the concerned household member
    format('Household member ~w is 3 or older but is missing answers to S02Q01a,
S02Q01c, or S02Q03~n', [HouseholdMember]),
    fail.  % backtrack to find all violations
```

In addition to the two consistency rules illustrated above, we have defined a broader set of logical rules to ensure the consistency and validity of survey data. For example, we verify that the age at which a respondent entered school for the first time is strictly less than their age at their last birthday. Similarly, if a surveyed student declares being enrolled in technical education, the class they report attending cannot belong to the primary education cycle, nor can it be the 6th or 5th grade. Another rule ensures that respondents currently in pre-school cannot report having obtained a diploma; therefore, they should not respond to the question regarding their highest qualification. These rules, among others, help to detect and prevent inconsistencies in the data collected during the survey.

3.4 Querying and Validation in Prolog

With consistency rules defined, we can now query the knowledge base to detect violations. For example, for rule 1:

```
?- inconsistent_age_education(HouseholdMember,Answer1,ValueAnswer1,Answer2).
```

The result is shown below:

```
HouseholdMember
= 'http://w3id.org/HshlsOnto/householdmember_11_516_4_2_3',
Answer1 = 'http://w3id.org/HshlsOnto/answer_11_516_4_2_3_S02Q_Age',
ValueAnswer1 = 2,
Answer2 = 'http://w3id.org/HshlsOnto/answer_11_516_4_2_3_S02Q01a' ;
false.
```

The query for rule 2 gives the following:

```
check_missing_answers_for_three_years_older_members.
Household member http://w3id.org/HshlsOnto/householdmember_11_320_2_2_1 is 3 or older but is missing answers to S02Q01a, S02Q01c, or S02Q03
Household member http://w3id.org/HshlsOnto/householdmember_11_324_4_2_2 is 3 or older but is missing answers to S02Q01a, S02Q01c, or S02Q03
Household member http://w3id.org/HshlsOnto/householdmember_11_516_4_2_1 is 3 or older but is missing answers to S02Q01a, S02Q01c, or S02Q03
Household member http://w3id.org/HshlsOnto/householdmember_11_516_4_2_2 is 3 or older but is missing answers to S02Q01a, S02Q01c, or S02Q03
false.
```

The results of these queries can be used to:

- Flag problematic data records for review;
- Generate reports on data quality;
- Enforce validation during data entry or integration.

4. RESULTS AND DISCUSSION

This work allows building a hybrid architecture integrating an RDF-based semantic data model into a Prolog environment. The approach is applied for the Harmonized Survey on Households Living Standards semantic data model and allows enhancing the survey data consistency validation mechanism through Prolog rules. For illustration, we highlight below the result of the integration of the RDF model into Prolog, using the SWI-Prolog environment.

We show the output of the ontology integration into SWI-Prolog as follows:

```
?-
%    library(record) compiled into record 0.00 sec, 71 clauses
%      library(semweb/rdf_prefixes) compiled into rdf_prefixes 0.00 sec, 108 clauses
%    library(semweb/rdf_db) compiled into rdf_db 0.02 sec, 439 clauses
%    library(semweb/rdf_turtle_write) compiled into rdf_turtle_write 0.03 sec, 421 clauses
%  library(semweb/turtle) compiled into turtle 0.03 sec, 68 clauses
%  library(semweb/rdf11) compiled into rdf11 0.02 sec, 394 clauses
?-
% Parsed "hshls_survey_data.ttl" in 14.22 sec; 2,375,784 triples
% c:/Users/hp/Documents/AC2025/rdf_prolog_Copie20251010.pl compiled 18.97 sec, 16 clauses
```

The result of data validation over the integrated data model for the Prolog rule `inconsistent_age_education/4` presented above shows that the education information of the household member `householdmember_11_516_4_2_3` doesn't match with they age; so, it is flagged as inconsistent data. We can see that the reasoning program effectively identifies inconsistencies in household members' responses. It is also worth noting that the defined Prolog rule adequately handles disjunction, as the condition stipulates that the rule applies if the concerned household member is under the age of 3 and has answered questions S02Q01a, S02Q02c, or S02Q03. Such an expression of disjunctive logic is, to date, not feasible in SWRL. The rule 2 illustrates also the use of negation in Prolog, applied here to make sure that household members whose age is greater or equal to three don't miss answers on questions related to education.

Moreover, we observe that it was possible for us to integrate both RDF data and reasoning logic (rules) within a single Prolog (.pl) file, which is not always the case with SWRL.

So, in general, the approach of this work provides better results in terms of simplicity and logic-based capabilities comparing to SWRL and SPARQL.

We also evaluated the processing time required to execute these consistency rules. For this evaluation, we used the built-in Prolog predicate time/1, which provides detailed metrics on execution performance. The test was conducted on approximately 17,000 household members surveyed, representing a total of 2,375,784 RDF triples for the education section of the survey. An illustration of this evaluation is given below:

```
?-
time(inconsistent_age_education(HouseholdMember,Answer1,ValueAnswer1,Answer2)).
% 4,563,707 inferences, 1.703 CPU in 1.698 seconds (100% CPU, 2679608 Lips)
```

On average, each rule takes approximately 1.7 seconds to execute on the dataset used, with a performance rate of about 2.68 million logical inferences per second (Lips). These results demonstrate that the consistency checks can be applied efficiently, even when dealing with large volumes of data, without significantly impacting the overall processing time.

5. CONCLUSION AND FUTURE WORK

In this work we propose a logic-programming-based approach for data validation in the case of the Harmonized Survey on Households Living Standards (HSHLS). The approach leverages the power of RDF and Prolog to build an RDF-aware knowledge base in a Prolog environment. The solution built allows integrating, querying and reasoning directly over RDF triples on Prolog and help improving data consistency control, and enhancing then the quality of the survey under study. The proposed method is more expressive and offers greater simplicity in code writing compared to the SWRL approach, which is verbose. Additionally, it enables easier manipulation of logical constraints, including disjunction and logical negation, as demonstrated by the rules defined earlier which are not supported by SWRL.

Using Prolog allows us to focus on problem description, while the resolution is managed by the Prolog inference engine, eliminating the need to write additional procedures.

This work contributes also to the state of the art on RDF and Prolog interaction in general.

In the future, we plan to enrich the knowledge base and conduct a performance evaluation by progressively increasing both the size of the RDF graph and the number of constraints applied to the data. This evaluation will include additional sections of the survey, such as socio-demographic characteristics, health, employment, and others. We will eventually explore the use of parallel processing mechanisms, such as Apache Spark (Zaharia, 2010), to improve the scalability of our approach and significantly reduce processing time for large-scale datasets.

REFERENCES

FAO-UN, (2022) Food and Agriculture Organization of the United Nations, 2022. Harmonized Survey on Households Living Standards 2018-2019. https://microdata.fao.org/index.php/catalog/2355/study-description.

Jaffar et al., (1986) Jaffar J., Lassez J.-L., and Maher M.J., A logic Programming Language Schemes, Logic Programming (DeGroot et Lindstrom), 1986, pp. 441-467.

Mfoutou Moukala et al., (2024a) Mfoutou Moukala M., Ngomo M., and Babindamana R. F., A Semantic Data Model of Harmonized Survey on Households Living Standards, SEMAPRO 2024: The Eighteenth International Conference on Advances in Semantic Processing, 2024, pp. 1-7.

Mfoutou Moukala et al., (2024b) Mfoutou Moukala M., Ngomo M., and Babindamana R. F., A Semantic Data Model for Efficiency enhancement of the Harmonized Survey on Households Living Standards, AC2024: The 21th International Conference on Applied Computing, 2024, pp. 119-126.

Mfoutou Moukala et al., (2025) Mfoutou Moukala M., Ngomo M., and Babindamana R. F., Data Integration, Querying and Reasoning over the Harmonized Survey on Households Living Standards Semantic Data Model, International Journal on Advances in Systems and Measurements, vol 18 no 1 & 2, 2025, pp. 30-45.

OWL2, W3C, (2012) OWL 2 Web Ontology Language, W3C Recommendation 11 December 2012, Document Overview (Second Edition). https://www.w3.org/TR/owl2-overview/, (consulted on July 14, 2025).

RDF 1.1 Primer, W3C Working Group Note, (2014) RDF 1.1 Primer, W3C Working Group Note, 24 June 2014. https://www.w3.org/TR/rdf11-primer/, (consulted on July 14, 2025).

RDF Schema 1.1, W3C Recommendation, (2014) RDF Schema 1.1, W3C Recommendation 25 February 2014, (Document updated on December, 1st 2023). https://www.w3.org/TR/rdf-schema/, (consulted on July 14, 2025).

RDFLib, PyPI, (2023) RDFLib, PyPI, 2023. https://pypi.org/project/rdflib/, (consulted on May 10, 2024).

SPARQL, W3C, (2013) SPARQL 1.1 Query Language, W3C Recommendation 21 March 2013. https://www.w3.org/TR/sparql11-query/, (consulted on July 14, 2025).

Sterling and Shapiro (1986) L. S. Sterling and E. Y. Shapiro. "The Art of Prolog: Advanced Programming Techniques" The MIT Press 1986 ; ISBN-10. 0262192500.

Sterling and Shapiro (1990) Sterling L. S. and Shapiro E. Y., L'Art de Prolog, Masson 1990.

Sterling and Shapiro (1994) L. S. Sterling and E. Y. Shapiro. "The Art of Prolog: Advanced Programming Techniques" The MIT Press, Cambridge, Massachusetts Institute of Technology, London, England ; Second Edition 1994 ; With a forword by David H. D. Warren. ; ISBN 0-262-19338-8 (hc. : alk. paper), 0-262-69163-9 (pb).

THE WORLD BANK, (2022) THE WORLD BANK, 2022. Harmonized Survey on Households Living Standards 2018-2019. https://microdata.worldbank.org/index.php/catalog/4290.

Zaharia (2010) Zaharia, M., Chowdhury, M., Franklin, M. J., Shenker, S., & Stoica, I. (2010). Spark: Cluster computing with working sets. In Proceedings of the 2nd USENIX conference on Hot topics in cloud computing.

GROOT: GENERAL-PURPOSE AUTOMATIC PARAMETER TUNING ACROSS LAYERS, DOMAINS AND USE CASES

Robert Krahn, Josia Mädler, Christoph Seidl and Christof Fetzer
TU Dresden, Germany

ABSTRACT

Modern software systems are executed on a runtime stack with layers (virtualization, storage, trusted execution, etc.) each incurring an execution and/or monetary cost, which may be mitigated by finding suitable parameter configurations. While specialized parameter tuners exist, they are tied to a particular domain or use case, fixed in type and number of optimization goals, or focused on a specific layer or technology. These limitations pose significant adoption hurdles for specialized and innovative ventures (SIVs) that address a variety of domains and use cases, operate under strict cost-performance constraints requiring tradeoffs, and rely on self-hosted servers with custom technology stacks while having little data or expertise to set up and operate specialized tuners.

In this paper, we present Groot – a general-purpose configuration tuner designed to a) be explicitly agnostic of a particular domain or use case, b) balance multiple potentially competing optimization goals, c) support different custom technology setups, and d) make minimal assumptions about parameter types, ranges, or suitable values. Our evaluation on both real-world use cases and benchmarks shows that Groot reliably improves performance and reduces resource consumption in scenarios representative for SIVs.

KEYWORDS

Optimization, Performance, Automation, Adaptability, Tuning, TEEs

1. INTRODUCTION

A modern software system is executed on a runtime stack with layers, e.g., hardware, hypervisor, virtualization runtime (e.g., containers / VMs), runtime framework (e.g., JVM, Python) or Trusted Execution Environment (e.g., Intel SGX, ARM TrustZone). On top of the runtime stack runs a binary we refer to as an application (one for single systems, multiple for distributed systems). Adopting new technology or continuous application development may lead to changes to the runtime stack, e.g., by adding new layers for TEEs.

Companies using large data center services and innovators alike seek to improve performance of their software system while keeping operation cost in check, e.g., by tuning application parameters or optimizing resource allocations. In principle, each layer may be configured through parameters that influence the application's performance. A misconfiguration, even on a layer further below, has the potential to limit the application's performance, e.g., by providing too few CPU cores or too little RAM on the virtualization layer.

Automatic tuning aims to find suitable configurations of parameter values for improving application performance and is challenging due to: *Parameter complexity* – The number and possible combinations of parameter values for all layers creates a complex search space for tuning; *Cross-Layer Effects* – Changing a parameter value on a lower level may influence performance on an upper layer; *Multiple Objectives* – The optimization procedure may be geared towards more than one goal, e.g., improving performance while reducing cost; *Tuning Boundaries* – The optimization procedure may be confined to certain fixed limits, e.g., respecting a maximum latency specified in a service-level agreement (SLA); *Parameter Changeability* – Parameter values may be changed either before application start (offline) or during application runtime (online).

While large corporations with long-running systems face few constraints due to abundant resources and stable workloads, current automatic tuners pose major adoption hurdles for specialized and innovative ventures (SIVs) such as SMEs, R&D labs, and start-ups. These organizations often rely on self-hosted servers instead of large-scale cloud deployments to maintain custom stacks, operate under strict cost-performance constraints, lack data or expertise, require rapid and frequent adoption of new software and runtime stacks to stay competitive, and build prototypes across diverse technologies where finding dedicated tuners deters from innovation.

In consequence, we argue that existing tuners with their focus on individual challenges, selected use cases or specific technologies are not sufficient for SIVs. At the same time, devising a custom-tailored tuner for each specific use case and combination of technologies is infeasible not only due to the incurred cost in terms of both money and time but also the lack of knowledge regarding tuning both on the specific scenario and at the respective companies. To make automatic parameter tuning available to SIVs, we propose the following requirements for a general-purpose tuner:

R1 – Multiple Layers: Must be able to process parameters on multiple layers of the runtime stack.

R2 – Multiple Objectives: Must support competing objectives with parameter thresholds.

R3 – Offline/Online: Must support both offline and online tuning.

R4 – Adaptable: Must be adaptable to different setups and changes of runtime layers.

R5 – Agnostic: Must be agnostic to the specific technology and use case of a software system.

Guided by these requirements, we developed Groot, a general-purpose parameter tuner facilitating automatic performance tuning for applications of SIVs with their wide variety of use cases and plethora of technology choices.

2. BACKGROUND

Optimizing a system's performance depends on the interplay between parameters, metrics, and objectives across its layers. Parameters exposed by a layer allow its configuration, e.g., to alter resource provisioning, which may affect performance of higher layers and the application (e.g., shared_buffers for Postgres or memory limits for a Docker container). A parameter configuration is a concrete assignment of values to a set of parameters. A metric quantifies observable system qualities (e.g., measuring latency) and may have labels with structured metadata used for filtering, normalization and prioritization during performance tuning.

A performance tuner seeks to improve a system's runtime qualities (e.g., throughput) while reducing execution cost in terms of resource consumption and/or monetary expenditures. A tuning objective defines a characteristic to tune and its desirable tuning direction (e.g., increase throughput). A threshold constrains tuning of a characteristic's value within a boundary (e.g., response time always below 10 ms). Multi objective tuning considers multiple, potentially competing, objectives (e.g., throughput and monetary cost) where a weight governs relative importance of an individual target.

A tuning algorithm determines candidate configurations promising a performance improvement by analyzing a system state (currently observed metrics and active parameter configuration) and systematically exploring a search space (the Cartesian product of relevant parameters, their value ranges and their associated metrics). A candidate configuration is enacted either online (without restarting a layer) or offline (restarting a layer and those above) for changes to take effect before the performance tuning loop starts the next iteration.

3. STATE OF THE ART

A host of related work exists on automated configuration tuning and performance optimization but a research gap for a general-purpose configuration tuner remains unaddressed as existing work addresses only subsets existing challenges. We discuss state of the art grouped by characteristics:

Targeted Layer(s)

Single-layer tuners apply changes only at a specific layer of the runtime stack without considering other layers. GPTuner (Lao et al., 2025), K2vTune (Lee et al., 2024), CDBTune (J. Zhang et al., 2019) and Hunter (Cai et al., 2022) operate on the DB layer. Ant (Cheng et al., 2016), DynamiConf (Gounaris et al., 2017), and

XDataExplorer (Guo et al., 2022) tune only parameters specific to scheduling of MapReduce/Spark. SGXTuner (Mazzeo et al., 2022) tunes enclave runtime parameters of TEEs.

Multi-layer tuners enact parameter values on multiple layers of the runtime stack acknowledging cross-stack dependencies, e.g. resource allocation (OS-layer) and performance (application layer). PipeTune (Rocha et al., 2020) simultaneously tunes OS related parameters and hyperparameters for DNN training. ResTune (X. Zhang et al., 2021) and CGPTUNER (Cereda et al., 2021) tune on the virtualization along with DB layer. OPPerTune (Somashekar et al., 2024) tunes cluster manager parameters and hardware resource allocations for container deployments.

Single-layer tuners neglect interactions between different layers; multi-layer tuners acknowledge these interactions but consider a fixed set or type of layers. Accordingly, existing tuners remain tailored to predefined settings, which ultimately prevents them from generalizing to more diverse stack compositions.

Tuning Guidance

Single-objective tuning tunes parameter configurations with a single objective, primarily focused on various aspects of performance, e.g., throughput (ConfAdvisor (Chen et al., 2021), SGXTuner), DNN error rates (AutoKeras (Jin et al., 2019)), job execution time (Gunther, Ant, LOCAT (Xin et al., 2022)), Latency (OtterTune (Van Aken et al., 2017)), with other tuners capable of switching between objectives but optimizing one at a time (SelfTune (Karthikeyan et al., 2023), OPPertune, ByteScheduler (Peng et al., 2019), Ituned (Duan et al., 2009)). CGPTuner extends single objective tuning with penalizing parameter configurations in violation of constraints on secondary qualities. Single-objective tuning neglects the complexity of real-world systems, where multiple objectives and cross-layer interactions must be addressed simultaneously.

Multi-objective tuning optimizes towards multiple potentially competing goals that have to be weighed or prioritized, e.g., PipeTune, Vizier (Golovin et al., 2017), and BestConfig (Zhu et al., 2017).

Change Enactment

Offline tuning enacts parameter changes and restarts the targeted layer, generally because changes take effect only after restarts, e.g., setting environment variables (SGXTuner) or creating static configurations (ConfAdvisor), or because tuning results are measurable only after termination (PipeTune, Gunther, Ant, or MALIBOO (Guindani et al., 2022)). Hybrid solutions execute offline tuning on trials to configure online services (Metis (Li et al., 2018)).

Online tuning enacts parameter changes without restarts if parameters and target layer permit to keep the system in operation. Examples are OPPerTuner, Hunter, SelfTune, and ByteScheduler (partially).

While each approach is effective within its scope, a generic tuner needs to accommodate for both offline and online parameter change enactment to be applicable and adaptable to various use cases.

Specialization

Domains and use cases allow specialized tuners to exploit peculiarities of the typical usage profiles, application parameters, or software architecture. These domains include databases (OtterTune, ResTune, CDBTune, Hunter), container deployment (ConfAdvisor), Deep Neural Networks (DNN) (PipeTune, ByteScheduler, AutoKeras (Jin et al., 2019)), Trusted Execution Environments (SGXTuner), and distributed processing (Gunther, Starfish (Herodotou et al., 2011)).

Model-based tuning algorithms construct predictive models of the system to estimate performance outcomes and guide parameter selection, reducing the need for exhaustive trials, e.g., OPPerTune, OtterTune, Flash (Nair et al., 2018), UDAO (Zaouk et al., 2019), Maliboo, and LOCAT. *Search-based tuning* algorithms explore configurations through direct experimentation to empirically observe performance, without relying on prior models, e.g., Ant, BestConfig, Starfish, SGXTuner. Specialization by domain or use case can improve performance in a narrow setting but restricts broader applicability. Model-based tuning requires a preliminary modeling step, yet the resulting abstraction may not adequately capture the irregular and rugged nature of system behavior during tuning. Search-based methods, by acting solely on observed performance without assumptions, can achieve robust tuning results provided they are based on an appropriate algorithm.

Representative Prior Work

BestConfig and Vizier are examples for use case and domain-agnostic approaches to automatic configuration tuning. BestConfig focuses on multi-objective constrained optimization. Vizier focuses on generality by providing a library service entailing tuning algorithms. While both BestConfig and Vizier contribute towards general applicability of tuning, they fall short in critical aspects: BestConfig lacks cross-layer tuning and Vizier requires high integration efforts. Groot is designed to tune for multiple objectives across multiple layers while providing all necessary components for its task.

4. DESIGN

Groot adopts a modular architecture aimed at fulfilling the requirements outlined in the introduction. Although certain requirements are cross-cutting, our annotations highlight the primarily addressed requirements. Figure 1 depicts Groot's architecture consisting of five central components to tune parameter configurations of applications and their underlying runtime stack. To distinguish between users of the application whose parameters are to be tuned and those utilizing Groot, we refer to the former as users and to the latter as adopters.

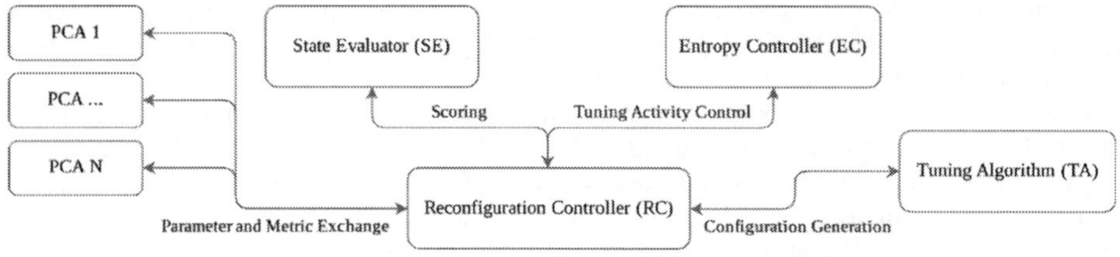

Figure 1. Architectural Overview of Groot's components

A Parameter Configuration Agent (PCA) provides a uniform interface to a runtime layer by abstracting parameter setting and metric collection, while also defining tuning objectives and thresholds (e.g., latency) (R2). The Reconfiguration Controller (RC) drives Groot's main loop by orchestrating components: collecting parameters and metrics from PCAs (R1, R4), evaluating and saving the global system state, and issuing new configurations to PCAs. The Entropy Controller (EC) modulates the entropy of proposed configurations over time. The State Evaluator (SE) aggregates PCA information into a global state and integrates layer-specific objectives (R2). The Tuning Algorithm (TA) continuously devises new configurations based on current and past states to improve the overall application performance. (R2, R3). The following sections detail each component's functionality and design decisions.

4.1 Parameter Configuration Agents (PCA)

The Parameter Configuration Agent (PCA) serves as a unified bridge between Groot's central routines and the runtime layers, as shown in Figure 1. Each PCA serves as both sensor and actor: collecting metrics and setting parameter values for a specific runtime layer. As a sensor, it provides reactive, on-demand metrics and parameters with labels specifying tuning objectives, directions, thresholds, and priorities (R2), which the RC uses to guide tuning, e.g., reduce latency with an upper threshold of 200 and priority 3. As an actor, the PCA periodically queries the RC for new configurations and enacts changes, e.g., by updating files or executing queries. We designed the PCA to manage all parameter changes, including handling layer restarts. Thus, Groot supports online tuning (runtime changes) and offline tuning (restarts), as outlined in R3. As with metrics, adopters can label parameters to define ranges and step sizes. Each PCA contributes the respective runtime layer's metric and parameter values to the RC's coherent global state (see Section:RC).

Our modular architecture using PCAs abstracts implementation details of specific runtime layers or technologies therein and, thus, enables Groot to retrieve metrics, discover configuration options, and set new parameters in a technology and application-agnostic way (R5). By further providing a uniform communication interface for PCAs, we enable adopters to implement new PCAs for new layers (R4), e.g., to accommodate for rapidly changing technology. In addition, PCAs may be extended to perform data preprocessing, e.g., sliding-window averaging or aggregation, to adapt to new use cases (R4). Through these design decisions, Groot supports diverse SIV use cases by combining different PCA sets.

4.2 Reconfiguration Controller (RC)

The Reconfiguration Controller (RC) manages Groot's core tasks of observing runtime layers and adjusting parameters by orchestrating PCAs and the Tuning Algorithm (TA) to coordinate data gathering, tuning, and publishing. The RC forwards metrics provided by the PCAs as input to the tuning algorithm and parameter configuration values provided by the tuning algorithm to the PCAs. For that purpose, it queries PCAs for metrics and parameters, discarding partial states to ensure the Tuning Algorithm (TA) always receives a complete system state, which it preprocesses into a compatible format (integer scaling, uniform direction, min/max/step sizes). To stabilize tuning under runtime variability, the RC aggregates several successive states into a snapshot before triggering the TA to propose new parameters, validates them against constraints, and waits a fixed interval to let changes settle. Finally, the RC publishes outputs via uniform interfaces: updated parameter configurations (with values, identifiers, and labels), unified system metrics for monitoring, and runtime statistics for traceability and observability enabling diverse use cases (R1, R4). Furthermore, the RC maintains a history of system states to identify mutation candidates in the tuning algorithm as well as to assess effectiveness of enacted configurations via performance and regression analysis.

To increase comparability between acquired system states and to provide predictable timing during runtime for monitoring and debugging, the RC ensures a stable control loop frequency with a fixed but configurable cycle time. The RC's control loop runs continuously to perform tuning while reacting to changes in workload or system behavior. Thereby, our approach ensures that every optimization step is based on the latest state of all monitored PCAs. In addition, we designed the RC to function as Groot's fixed control entity so that other components may be exchanged or expanded without affecting overall tuning logic.

4.3 State Evaluator (SE)

The State Evaluator (SE) assesses the quality of a configuration by rating the current system state based on observed data and guides the tuning toward higher-performing configurations by comparing the current score to that of previous system states with their configurations. For that purpose, we created the SE to fulfill three main responsibilities:

1. Scoring runtime metrics and aggregating them into system-level performance scores for making parameter configurations comparable (R1).
2. Evaluating performance constraints by weighting multiple objectives (R2).
3. Synthesizing comparable metric values across dynamically observed states.

Our design centralizes performance assessment to capture cross-layer effects of parameter choices, e.g., memory allocation in the containerization layer impacts application runtime performance. To account for such interdependencies, the RC collects parameter values and runtime metrics from all layers via the PCAs.

The SE aggregates metric values collected from PCAs via the RC into a unified system state score, enabling evaluation of combined impacts. Data from PCAs is structured as "metric objects," containing labels (e.g., name=latency) and values (e.g., 300). Labels support identification and classification, distinguishing between tuning metrics (with optimization directions: minimize or maximize) and auxiliary metrics (for profiling or diagnosis).

To support constrained optimization (R2), we introduced three additional labels for tuning goals:

1. A lower threshold for satisfactory performance (e.g., minimum throughput).
2. An upper threshold not to be exceeded (e.g., maximum latency).
3. A weight for relative importance trade-offs (e.g., throughput improvement vs resource reduction).

The SE scores complete system states via weighted sums of tuning metric scores while penalizing violation of thresholds. As viable ranges of parameter values may not be known in advance and exhaustively searching extrema is impractical, we designed Groot to operate with broad parameter ranges: The SE's normalization mechanism continuously observes system state history (maintained by the RC), updates metric extrema and incrementally refines scores. To balance sensitivity and stability, extrema are rounded to scaled halves of the nearest power of ten, avoiding recomputation from minor fluctuations. This ensures normalized scores reflect real workload conditions, avoid distortions from unrealistic assumptions, and remain interpretable. As exploration continues, recalculation frequency decreases as observed boundaries stabilize. On demand recalculations guarantee all states are scored with consistent boundaries, preserving comparability across evaluations. The SE's scoring enables data-driven, adaptive reconfiguration under complex goals without fixed metric boundaries, while avoiding the limitations and preparation overhead of model-based evaluation.

Hence, Groot supports SIVs under multiple constraints or objectives, such as cost efficiency, SLA compliance, or combined goals (R2), e.g., reducing cost with a minimum performance goal may involve minimizing memory and CPU usage while achieving throughput $\geq$ 5000 events/s and latency $\leq$ 500 ms.

4.4 Tuning Algorithm (TA)

Groot's Tuning Algorithm (TA), invoked by the Reconfiguration Controller (RC), derives new parameter configurations from current and past runtime states. It is an entropy-driven genetic algorithm tailored for resource-intensive, sequential evaluations, where each configuration incurs high cost as values stabilize before the next iteration. Inspired by simulated annealing, the TA evolves one candidate at a time, maintaining a persistent history while supporting high-dimensional tuning (R1). Unlike classical GAs with tournament selection and fixed hyperparameters, it emphasizes early exploration through strong mutations and crossover perturbations, adapts its own hyperparameters, and operates at the gene (single-parameter) level to exploit structural relationships for robust tuning across diverse, high-cost search spaces. Compared to SMBO and Bandit methods, the TA avoids scaling, initialization, and structural issues (Chakraborty & Chakraborty, 2024; Kandasamy et al., 2019; Xu et al., 2025).

The TA integrates Groot's State Evaluator (SE) and Entropy Controller (EC) to regulate adaptation intensity. Entropy balances exploration and exploitation by shaping mutation strength, crossover, re-evaluation, and randomness in selection. Runtime history guides ancestor selection, allowing the TA to combine evaluation results, entropy-weighted variation, and past context to generate new configurations. Unlike typical GAs with synchronous populations and manual tuning of mutation or crossover rates, the TA dynamically adapts these parameters through entropy, eliminating hyperparameter overhead and supporting convergence in high dimensional, real-world settings with variable costs.

Each iteration follows a GA-inspired workflow adapted for entropy control: (1) Ancestor selection ranks candidates by normalized score; (2) A Bernoulli trial, weighted by entropy, decides whether to re-evaluate a past state (exploitation), execute a super-merge of top performers, or proceed with genetic recombination (exploration); (3) Crossover samples parameter values (genes) from two parents during exploration but is disabled during exploitation; (4) Mutation applies either large random changes or small deltas, with number and type governed by entropy; (5) Candidate selection favors random offspring under high entropy and high potential individuals under low entropy.

The TA operates in two entropy-controlled phases. In exploration, crossovers and mutations occur with decaying intensity. At a dynamically positioned inflection point (aligned with search space complexity), the TA transitions to exploitation, reducing crossovers while reusing high-performing states to stabilize around the best configurations and fine-tune promising candidates. In summary, Groot's TA unifies evolutionary dynamics with adaptive entropy control, offering a runtime aware optimization strategy designed for costly evaluations where adaptability and efficiency are critical.

4.5 Entropy Controller (EC)

The Entropy Controller (EC) regulates the randomness of parameter configurations over time by addressing two central challenges in automated optimization: (A) rigid entropy schedules fail to adapt to changing demands, and (B) unpredictable optimization surfaces range from smooth to deceptive or jagged.

Our solution applies three strategies: (1) Varying exploration, higher randomness in early stages and greater stability later, similar to simulated annealing or CMA-ES; (2) varying decay, entropy reduction that adapts to problem complexity, where simpler landscapes converge faster and more complex ones decay more slowly; and (3) externalization, keeping entropy control independent of the tuning algorithm to remain flexible and domain-agnostic. Prior work (Aleti & Moser, 2013) underscores the benefits of adaptive control in evolutionary algorithms for improving their performance.

The EC implements a softened, multi-phase decay function that transitions smoothly from exploration to exploitation. It computes a control variable α, proportional to runtime and history size, normalized by the logarithm of search volume and parameter dimensionality. This produces a staircase-like decay curve, where phase changes are dynamically positioned based on telemetry from the Reconfiguration Controller (RC), such as runtime, history size, and search space characteristics. The result is a bounded, context-sensitive entropy schedule that aligns with Groot's genetic algorithm design while remaining compatible with other optimizers.

By modulating entropy through lightweight telemetry rather than manual hyperparameters, the EC enables Groot to explore widely when uncertainty is high and converge reliably when stability is needed. Without requiring prior knowledge of the optimization problem (R5), the EC integrates seamlessly across domains and adjusts its behavior based on inferred complexity and runtime characteristics (R1).

5. EVALUATION

To demonstrate that Groot satisfies all posed requirements, we perform an experimental evaluation based on three scenarios rooted in real-world use cases and benchmarks. Each scenario in isolation investigates a subset of the requirements pertaining to characteristics of a specific setup (R1–R3) and all scenarios in conjunction investigate requirements pertaining to different/changing setups (R4–R5) as detailed in Table 1.

Table 1. Relation between evaluation scenarios and requirements

	R1: Multiple Layers	R2: Multiple Objectives	R3: Offline/Online	R4: Adaptability	R5: Agnostic
Database	Yes	Yes	Online	Scenarios differ in their layers and utilize different PCAs	Docker Stack
Secure Webserver	Yes	Yes	Offline		HW TEE
Microbenchmark	No	No	Online		Simulation

Our testbed for the evaluation consists of multiple machines: The two hosts for the test application and the load generator consist of Intel Xeon E-2278G CPUs with 16 cores, 32 GB main memory, 40 GbE, M.2 SSD, and run Ubuntu 24.04 (kernel v6.8). Groot is executed on a dedicated server with an Intel Xeon E5-2630 v4 CPU, 16 GB main memory, 10 GbE, a SATA SSD, and runs Ubuntu 24.04 (kernel v6.8). We further use a desktop to facilitate deployments and data collection: a Fujitsu ESPRIMO P957/E90+ desktop machine with an Intel® Core i7–6700 CPU, with 16 GB of RAM, running Ubuntu 22.04 (kernel v5.15).

5.1 Database

The database use case demonstrates Groot's online multi-objective tuning: maximizing performance (throughput, latency) while minimizing resource usage by reducing CPU cores and memory of the database's Docker container (R1-R3). We use the public Postgres v14 (Debian) container with Python added to run a Parameter Configuration Agent (PCA). On a dedicated server, PGbench runs in Docker, initializing Postgres and executing a continuous TPC-B workload (-s 120 -j 95 -c 1005 -P 5 -T 1200 -b tpcb-like).

The database server also hosts a Docker PCA (D-PCA) that adjusts CPU and memory allocations and publishes these metrics to Groot. A kernel PCA (K-PCA) inside the database container exports preselected kernel configuration files (/var/...) as tunable parameters. On the load generator server, a Postgres PCA (PG-PCA) parses PGbench output to provide performance metrics and exposes Postgres parameters and runtime statistics. Groot runs on a third server in an Ubuntu container, collecting metrics and distributing configurations across all three PCAs. In this setup, Groot ingests 20 metrics and outputs 33 parameters, including 22 specific to Postgres.

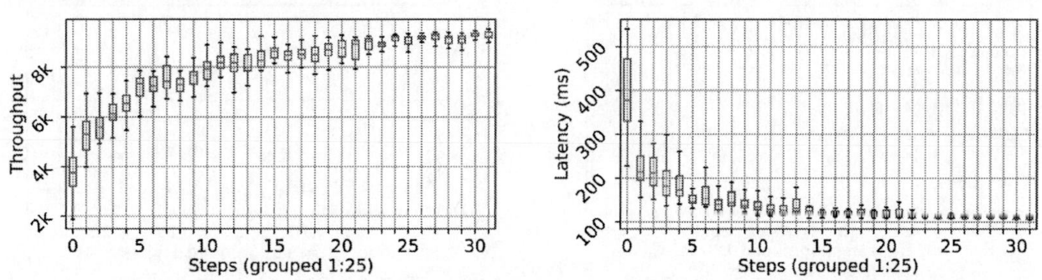

Figure 2. Throughput and latency measurements of Postgres during tuning as reported by PGbench

For the experiment, Groot creates a random configuration for all parameters, then tunes their values over 775 steps per experiment. In Figure 2, we represent each step as the mean across 10 runs. For the visualization, we group 25 steps into one box with the center line indicating the median across the 25 steps. Our results show that the random start state yields a performance with a median throughput of 3707.51 transactions per second and a median latency of 377.15 milliseconds. Groot improves these values to 9274.42 tps and 108.63 ms (median) at the end of the experiments.

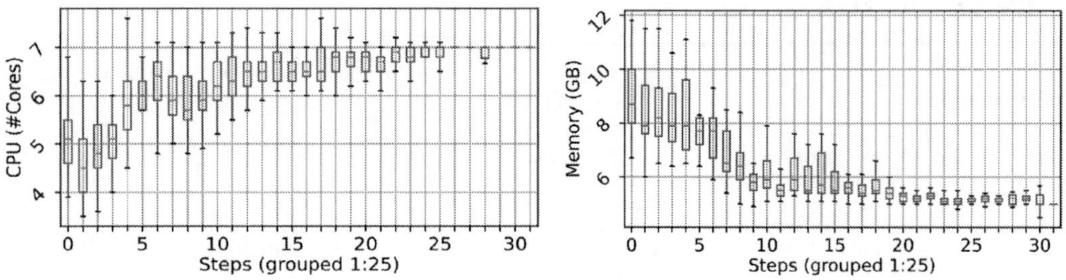

Figure 3. Allocation of CPU cores and provided memory to the container running Postgres

As shown in Figure 3, starting from a median of 5.1 CPU cores, Groot increases CPU allocation during tuning, prioritizing performance over strict resource minimization, while boosting PGbench throughput. The database container was limited to 14 cores and 24 GB of memory, representing a medium-sized, self-hosted setup typical of SIVs. Optimal performance is reached at seven cores, while median memory usage drops from 9.3 GB to 5 GB, the minimum allowed. Our experiment reflects common tuning challenges for small-scale organizations, stressing CPU and memory without large infrastructure. The results demonstrate that Groot autonomously tunes parameters across the runtime stack, improving performance and reducing resource usage without manual guidance, showing that SIVs can achieve significant performance gains and resource savings by applying Groot.

5.2 Secure Webserver

The secure webserver illustrates a Trusted Execution Environment (TEE) scenario, running Nginx inside an Intel-SGX enclave via the SCONE framework (Arnautov et al., 2016) and shows the performance overhead reduction of applications executed in an Intel SGX framework. SCONE exposes TEE specific tunables via environment variables. As changes require restarts, this case highlights Groot's offline tuning. We use SCONE v4.8 and Nginx in an Alpine Docker image. Socat exposes CPU utilization (/proc/stat), alongside Nginx, which is configured for TLS-secured communication. On a second server, wrk2 (commit c4250acb6921) runs in an Alpine container against Nginx. Each run lasts 20 s with 4 threads, 64 connections, and a target rate of 1000 r/s, simulating low demand. We evaluate how Groot reduces resource consumption while tuning latency below a threshold of 100 ms, using a 64 B payload. Alongside Nginx, a Restart-PCA (R-PCA) container adapts SCONE-specific environment variables (SSPINS, SSLEEP, HEAP, ESPINS, SLOTS) and container resources by restarting Nginx with updated settings. Next to wrk2, a W-PCA container reports throughput and latency metrics to Groot but has no tunable parameters. Groot runs on a third server, processing PCA data and providing updated environment variables and resource configurations.

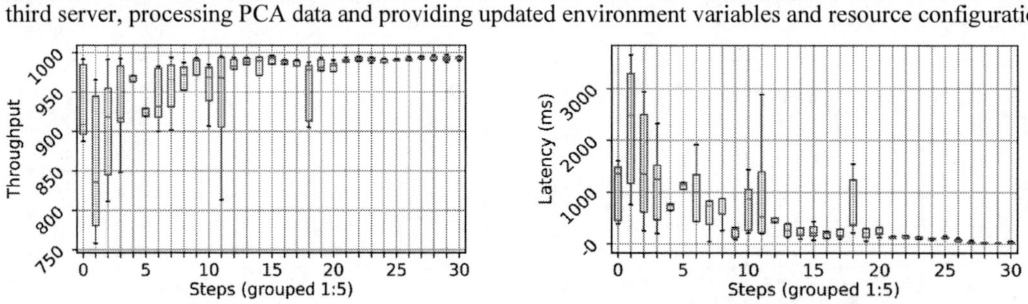

Figure 4. Throughput and latency measurements for Nginx measured by wrk2

Similar to the database experiment, Groot generates random initialization states for each run. In Figure 4, we represent each step as the mean across the 10 runs. For the visualization, we group 5 steps into one box with the center line indicating the median across the 5 steps. Our results show that the random start state yields a performance with a median throughput of 908.6 requests per second and a median latency of 1354.7 milliseconds. Groot improves these values to 994.03 r/s and 18.8 ms at the end of the experiments.

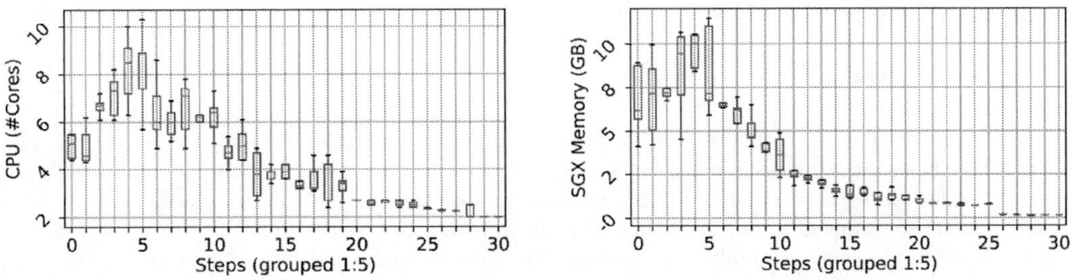

Figure 5. Allocation of CPU cores and memory for the Intel SGX enclave executing NGINX

As shown in Figure 5, starting from a median of 5.1 cores, Groot reduces CPU allocation to 2 cores. Median memory allocation drops from 9.1 GB at experiment start to 2.7 GB. The results of our secure webserver experiment illustrate Groot's effectiveness in reducing resource consumption for applications executed in an Intel SGX framework while tuning the performance.

5.3 Microbenchmark

In a microbenchmark, we evaluate Groot's tuning algorithm (TA) on complex optimization problems, measuring its ability to find near-optimal parameters under varied conditions and how tuning duration scales with scenario complexity (R2, R4). This tests Groot's robustness and general-purpose applicability across large, diverse problem spaces. The search space systematically varies by three factors: number of tunable parameters, number of performance metrics, and parameter value ranges. Per run, the TA optimizes randomly assigned mathematical functions (sum, log, square, product, difference, or average of parameters). Functions are randomly mapped to parameters, creating interdependencies and conflicting objectives. If an experiment requires more than six metrics, functions are randomly reused with new parameter-to-function assignments, generating additional metrics while preserving the system's complexity.

For each configuration, the TA targets 95% of the theoretical maximum performance. The primary outcome is the number of tuning steps required. Each experiment is repeated 1000 times to account for stochastic effects from random initialization, mutation, and crossover. To ensure overall computational feasibility we cap runs at 5000 steps, with fewer than 1% exceeding this limit.

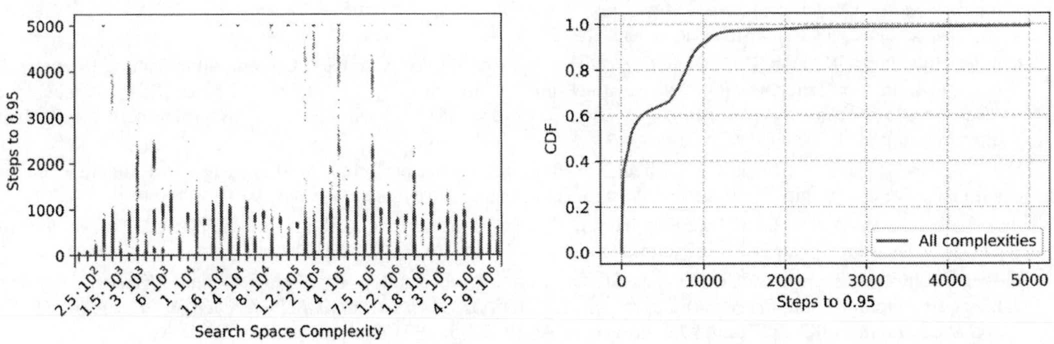

Figure 6. Number of steps taken to reach 95% of optimal performance and cumulative distribution

For the evaluation, the search space complexity is defined as the product of the number of parameters, values per parameter, and metrics. We test the Cartesian product of: parameters [5, 10, 20, 30, 40], metrics [5, 10, 20, 30, 40], and values per parameter [10, 100, 2000, 5000, 10000], using a randomly selected set of mathematical functions. Figure 6 shows that the number of steps to reach 95% of optimal performance remains constant across search space complexities. Furthermore, Figure 6 shows that the TA reaches 95% of optimal performance within 1000 steps for 91.5% of tested complexities. The results indicate that Groot's performance stays consistent across diverse scenarios, including high-complexity search spaces, without prior knowledge, highlighting its adaptability for varied optimization tasks and use cases (R2, R4).

6. CONCLUSION

This work presents Groot, a general-purpose configuration tuner capable of tuning on multiple layers for multiple objectives and enacting parameters either online or offline while being domain-agnostic and requiring little knowledge on the tuned system yet discovering effective configurations reliably. Our evaluation shows that Groot meets its design goals in both controlled and realistic scenarios, consistently handling large search spaces, optimizing performance and resources of databases and secure web servers, while supporting online and offline tuning. Groot's properties make it especially well-suited for specialized and innovative ventures (SIVs), who operate under strict cost-performance constraints, manage diverse and evolving software stacks and require parameter tuning to be broadly applicable. Future work will explore automatic detection and classification of changing workload patterns and approaches to decompose the structure of complex search spaces, enabling greater efficiency across domains.

REFERENCES

Aleti, A., & Moser, I. (2013). Entropy-based adaptive range parameter control for evolutionary algorithms. *Proceedings of the 15th Annual Conference on Genetic and Evolutionary Computation*, 1501–1508. https://doi.org/10.1145/2463372.2463560

Arnautov, S., Trach, B., Gregor, F., Knauth, T., Martin, A., Priebe, C., Lind, J., Muthukumaran, D., O'Keeffe, D., Stillwell, M. L., Goltzsche, D., Eyers, D., Kapitza, R., Pietzuch, P., & Fetzer, C. (2016). *SCONE: Secure Linux Containers with Intel SGX.* 689–703. https://www.usenix.org/conference/osdi16/technical-sessions/presentation/arnautov

Cai, B., Liu, Y., Zhang, C., Zhang, G., Zhou, K., Liu, L., Li, C., Cheng, B., Yang, J., & Xing, J. (2022). HUNTER: An Online Cloud Database Hybrid Tuning System for Personalized Requirements. *Proceedings of the 2022 International Conference on Management of Data*, 646–659. https://doi.org/10.1145/3514221.3517882

Cereda, S., Valladares, S., Cremonesi, P., & Doni, S. (2021). *CGPTUNER: A Contextual Gaussian Process Bandit Approach for the Automatic Tuning of IT Configurations Under Varying Workload Conditions.* https://doi.org/10.14778/3457390.3457404

Chakraborty, A., & Chakraborty, A. (2024). Scalable model-based gaussian process clustering. *ICASSP 2024-2024 IEEE International Conference on Acoustics, Speech and Signal Processing (ICASSP)*, 5730–5734. https://ieeexplore.ieee.org/abstract/document/10447983/

Chen, P., Huo, Z., Li, X., Dou, H., & Zhu, C. (2021). ConfAdvisor: An Automatic Configuration Tuning Framework for NoSQL Database Benchmarking with a Black-box Approach. In F. Wolf & W. Gao (Eds.), *Benchmarking, Measuring, and Optimizing* (pp. 106–124). Springer International Publishing. https://doi.org/10.1007/978-3-030-71058-3_7

Cheng, D., Rao, J., Guo, Y., Jiang, C., & Zhou, X. (2016). Improving performance of heterogeneous mapreduce clusters with adaptive task tuning. *IEEE Transactions on Parallel and Distributed Systems*, *28*(3), 774–786.

Duan, S., Thummala, V., & Babu, S. (2009). Tuning database configuration parameters with iTuned. *Proceedings of the VLDB Endowment*, *2*(1), 1246–1257. https://doi.org/10.14778/1687627.1687767

Golovin, D., Solnik, B., Moitra, S., Kochanski, G., Karro, J., & Sculley, D. (2017). Google Vizier: A Service for Black-Box Optimization. *Proceedings of the 23rd ACM SIGKDD International Conference on Knowledge Discovery and Data Mining*, 1487–1495. https://doi.org/10.1145/3097983.3098043

Gounaris, A., Kougka, G., Tous, R., Montes, C. T., & Torres, J. (2017). Dynamic configuration of partitioning in spark applications. *IEEE Transactions on Parallel and Distributed Systems*, *28*(7), 1891–1904.

Guindani, B., Ardagna, D., & Guglielmi, A. (2022). MALIBOO: When Machine Learning meets Bayesian Optimization. *2022 IEEE 7th International Conference on Smart Cloud (SmartCloud)*, 1–9. https://doi.org/10.1109/SmartCloud55982.2022.00008

Guo, Q., Xie, Y., Li, Q., & Zhu, Y. (2022). XDataExplorer: A three-stage comprehensive self-tuning tool for Big Data platforms. *Big Data Research*, *29*, 100329.

Herodotou, H., Lim, H., Luo, G., Borisov, N., Dong, L., Cetin, F. B., & Babu, S. (2011). Starfish: A self-tuning system for big data analytics. *Cidr*, *11*(2011), 261–272. https://www.cse.fau.edu/~xqzhu/courses/Resources/starfishaselftuningsystem.pdf

Jin, H., Song, Q., & Hu, X. (2019). Auto-Keras: An Efficient Neural Architecture Search System. *Proceedings of the 25th ACM SIGKDD International Conference on Knowledge Discovery & Data Mining*, 1946–1956. https://doi.org/10.1145/3292500.3330648

Kandasamy, K., Dasarathy, G., Oliva, J., Schneider, J., & Poczos, B. (2019). Multi-fidelity gaussian process bandit optimisation. *Journal of Artificial Intelligence Research*, *66*, 151–196.

Karthikeyan, A., Natarajan, N., Somashekar, G., Zhao, L., Bhagwan, R., Fonseca, R., Racheva, T., & Bansal, Y. (2023). SelfTune: Tuning Cluster Managers. *20th USENIX Symposium on Networked Systems Design and Implementation (NSDI 23)*, 1097–1114. https://www.usenix.org/conference/nsdi23/presentation/karthikeyan

Lao, J., Wang, Y., Li, Y., Wang, J., Zhang, Y., Cheng, Z., Chen, W., Tang, M., & Wang, J. (2025). GPTuner: An LLM-Based Database Tuning System. *ACM SIGMOD Record*, *54*(1), 101–110. https://doi.org/10.1145/3733620.3733641

Lee, J., Seo, S., Choi, J., & Park, S. (2024). K2vTune: A workload-aware configuration tuning for RocksDB. *Information Processing & Management*, *61*(1), 103567. https://doi.org/10.1016/j.ipm.2023.103567

Li, Z. L., Liang, C.-J. M., He, W., Zhu, L., Dai, W., Jiang, J., & Sun, G. (2018). Metis: Robustly tuning tail latencies of cloud systems. *2018 USENIX Annual Technical Conference (USENIX ATC 18)*, 981–992. https://www.usenix.org/conference/atc18/presentation/li-zhao

Mazzeo, G., Arnautov, S., Fetzer, C., & Romano, L. (2022). SGXTuner: Performance Enhancement of Intel SGX Applications Via Stochastic Optimization. *IEEE Transactions on Dependable and Secure Computing*, *19*(4), 2595–2608. IEEE Transactions on Dependable and Secure Computing. https://doi.org/10.1109/TDSC.2021.3064391

Nair, V., Yu, Z., Menzies, T., Siegmund, N., & Apel, S. (2018). Finding faster configurations using flash. *IEEE Transactions on Software Engineering*, *46*(7), 794–811.

Peng, Y., Zhu, Y., Chen, Y., Bao, Y., Yi, B., Lan, C., Wu, C., & Guo, C. (2019). A generic communication scheduler for distributed DNN training acceleration. *Proceedings of the 27th ACM Symposium on Operating Systems Principles*, 16–29. https://doi.org/10.1145/3341301.3359642

Rocha, I., Morris, N., Chen, L. Y., Felber, P., Birke, R., & Schiavoni, V. (2020). *PipeTune: Pipeline Parallelism of Hyper and System Parameters Tuning for Deep Learning Clusters* (No. arXiv:2010.00501). arXiv. http://arxiv.org/abs/2010.00501

Somashekar, G., Tandon, K., Kini, A., Chang, C.-C., Husak, P., Bhagwan, R., Das, M., Gandhi, A., & Natarajan, N. (2024). *OPPerTune: Post-Deployment Configuration Tuning of Services Made Easy*. 1101–1120. https://www.usenix.org/conference/nsdi24/presentation/somashekar

Van Aken, D., Pavlo, A., Gordon, G. J., & Zhang, B. (2017). Automatic Database Management System Tuning Through Large-scale Machine Learning. *Proceedings of the 2017 ACM International Conference on Management of Data*, 1009–1024. https://doi.org/10.1145/3035918.3064029

Xin, J., Hwang, K., & Yu, Z. (2022). LOCAT: Low-Overhead Online Configuration Auto-Tuning of Spark SQL Applications. *Proceedings of the 2022 International Conference on Management of Data*, 674–684. https://doi.org/10.1145/3514221.3526157

Xu, Z., Wang, H., Phillips, J. M., & Zhe, S. (2025). *Standard Gaussian Process is All You Need for High-Dimensional Bayesian Optimization* (No. arXiv:2402.02746). arXiv. https://doi.org/10.48550/arXiv.2402.02746

Zaouk, K., Song, F., Lyu, C., Sinha, A., Diao, Y., & Shenoy, P. (2019). UDAO: A Next-Generation Unified Data Analytics Optimizer. *Proceedings of the VLDB Endowment (PVLDB)*, *12*(12). https://doi.org/10.14778/3352063.3352103

Zhang, J., Liu, Y., Zhou, K., Li, G., Xiao, Z., Cheng, B., Xing, J., Wang, Y., Cheng, T., Liu, L., Ran, M., & Li, Z. (2019). An End-to-End Automatic Cloud Database Tuning System Using Deep Reinforcement Learning. *Proceedings of the 2019 International Conference on Management of Data*, 415–432. https://doi.org/10.1145/3299869.3300085

Zhang, X., Wu, H., Chang, Z., Jin, S., Tan, J., Li, F., Zhang, T., & Cui, B. (2021). ResTune: Resource Oriented Tuning Boosted by Meta-Learning for Cloud Databases. *Proceedings of the 2021 International Conference on Management of Data*, 2102–2114. https://doi.org/10.1145/3448016.3457291

Zhu, Y., Liu, J., Guo, M., Bao, Y., Ma, W., Liu, Z., Song, K., & Yang, Y. (2017). Bestconfig: Tapping the performance potential of systems via automatic configuration tuning. *Proceedings of the 2017 Symposium on Cloud Computing*, 338–350. https://dl.acm.org/doi/abs/10.1145/3127479.3128605

PERFORMANCE COMPARISON BETWEEN SLURM BARE METAL AND SLURM ON KUBERNETES IN HPC WORKLOADS

Lucas Borges, Wellington Oliveira, Tafarel Souza, Phillip Furtado and Erick Bezerra
Sidia Instituto de Ciência e Tecnologia
Av. Darcy Vargas, 645 – Parque Dez de Novembro, Manaus – AM, Brazil

ABSTRACT

The increasing adoption of Kubernetes in High-Performance Computing environments has sparked significant debates about its impact on performance compared to bare metal Simple Linux Utility for Resource Management. This study provides a comprehensive comparison between the two paradigms, using rigorous benchmarks to evaluate critical metrics such as scalability, latency, resource utilization, and fault tolerance. The results show that Kubernetes, when integrated with Simple Linux Utility for Resource Management, offers enhanced flexibility and scalability, particularly in scenarios requiring container orchestration and process automation. This combination allows for better adaptation to dynamic and heterogeneous environments, while also facilitating the implementation of DevOps practices in High-Performance Computing. On the other hand, Simple Linux Utility for Resource Management bare metal maintains its efficiency in direct resource management and performance, making it particularly advantageous in scenarios where the priority is maximizing hardware resource utilization and minimizing management overhead. The analysis identifies the advantages and limitations of each approach, highlighting how the choice between these technologies should consider the specific application needs, such as workload nature, environmental complexity, and fault tolerance requirements. Additionally, the study addresses the evolution of High-Performance Computing practices, demonstrating how technologies like Kubernetes can drive infrastructure and processes. This work aims to contribute to the scientific and technological community by providing valuable insights for optimizing High-Performance Computing cluster infrastructure and informing technology adoption decisions.

KEYWORDS

Kubernetes, High-Performance Computing, Bare Metal, Simple Linux Utility for Resource Management, Benchmarks, DevOps

1. INTRODUCTION

In today's rapidly evolving landscape of artificial intelligence, machine learning and High-Performance Computing (HPC), organizations face significant challenges in managing computational resources efficiently while ensuring seamless collaboration among development teams. According to (Jokanovic, D'Amico, and Corbalan, 2018), optimizing a task planner to achieve optimal HPC system efficiency and user satisfaction poses a complex, many-sided issue.

In Aydin, Bidollahkhany, and Kunkel (2024), the authors provide a comprehensive overview of fault tolerance components and mechanisms in HPC systems, highlighting the importance of understanding the types and sources of failures to develop effective strategies. They explore fault tolerance architectures and mechanisms in Kubernetes and SLURM, two workload orchestration and management systems widely used in HPC. These systems represent distinct approaches to ensuring resilience, and comparing their fault tolerance capabilities is crucial to advancing scientific research and industrial applications. Types of failures in HPC include hardware failures (such as node, network, and storage failures), software failures (such as application crashes and operating system failures), human error (such as misconfigurations), and environmental factors (such as power outages and cooling failures). This analysis contextualizes the importance of systems such as Kubernetes and SLURM, which offer different approaches to mitigating these failures, and are essential for the reliability and efficiency of HPC systems.

This paper presents a benchmark comparison of different approaches to run the Simple Linux Utility for Resource Management (SLURM)[1] workload manager, both natively on bare metal servers and within Kubernetes environments. The goal is to identify environment combinations where Kubernetes can be leveraged for containerized deployment, enabling dynamic scaling of infrastructure based on demand, while utilizing SLURM's workload management capabilities for high availability and scalability.

This paper is organized as follows: In Section 2, the literature review of the project is described generally. In Section 3, the setups of the benchmarks and experiments are demonstrated. The analysis and experimental results are presented in Section 4. Lastly, the conclusion of the project and future work are provided in Section 5.

2. LITERATURE REVIEW

High Performance Computing is a practice that focuses on using computer systems to solve complex, computationally demanding problems that cannot normally be solved using conventional computers. A HPC system is generally composed of several computers connected via highspeed networks to prevent low performance and data loss. One of the main purposes of setting up an HPC cluster is to solve complex problems that would take a long time if processed by a conventional computer (Azad et al., 2023). It allows system administrators to allocate computing resources effectively among multiple users and applications, thereby maximizing the efficiency of available infrastructure.

Simple Linux Utility for Resource Management is an open-source workload management system specifically designed to manage compute-intensive tasks in cluster environments. With its straightforward and flexible interface, SLURM facilitates the creation, execution, and monitoring of parallel jobs, making it an indispensable tool for researchers and developers who require substantial computational power for their activities. Furthermore, SLURM supports advanced features such as dynamic load balancing, adaptive scheduling, and integration with other access control systems, rendering it a versatile and reliable solution for cluster management (Yoo, Jette, and Grondona, 2003).

Kubernetes[2] is an open-source container orchestration system that simplifies the deployment, scaling, and operation of containerized applications. Widely used in cluster infrastructures today, it is also highly extensible and integrates with a variety of tools and services, such as system monitoring and CI/CD pipeline configuration. Xavier, Neves, and De Rose (2014) demonstrate, that hypervisor based virtualization has been avoided in HPC. However, container-based virtualization systems have proven to be an alternative to hypervisor-based systems, bringing this vision to the scenario proposed for this research. Docker [3]and Kubernetes [4] tools can provide resources for testing in HPC clusters.

Cérin, Greneche, and Menouer (2020), describe an architecture consisting of three physical nodes that utilize both Kubernetes and SLURM. For the experiment, one of these nodes is dedicated to executing the tasks. The study focuses on benchmarking to evaluate the impact of SLURM containerization on CPU efficiency and the functionality of Calico[5] in Message Passing Interface (MPI) [6] communication.

Two simulation rounds were conducted as part of the experiments. The findings revealed that the only noticeable performance loss occurred when Slurmd[7] was containerized. This suggests that while containerization offers flexibility and scalability, certain components of SLURM may experience inefficiencies when encapsulated within containers, particularly those involved in critical node management tasks.

Their research highlights the importance of carefully selecting which components to containerize in HPC environments to maintain optimal performance, especially when integrating Kubernetes with SLURM for workload orchestration.

[1] https://slurm.schedmd.com/overview.html
[2] https://kubernetes.io/docs/home/
[3] https://docs.docker.com/get-started/docker-overview/
[4] https://kubernetes.io/docs/concepts/overview/
[5] https://docs.tigera.io/calico/latest/about/
[6] https://carleton.ca/rcs/rcdc/introduction-to-mpi/
[7] https://slurm.schedmd.com/slurmd.html

Beltre et al., (2019), studied the potential use of Kubernetes in HPC infrastructure for the scientific community, directly comparing its features and performance with Docker Swarm and bare metal execution of HPC applications. The project provides a detailed analysis of the configurations required for Kubernetes to operate with MPI applications in containers such as access to underlying devices, inter-container communication across different hosts, and configuration constraints. These analyses are fundamental to understanding the challenges and opportunities of integrating Kubernetes in HPC environments.

The authors in Kenny and Knight (2021) implemented a hybrid configuration where the SLURM Worker daemon (slurmd) ran as a systemd [8] service on bare metal worker nodes, while the other daemons Slurm Controller (slurmctld)[9] and Slurm Database (slurmdbd)[10] were configured to operate within Kubernetes pods.

As outlined in their paper, slurmd requires three key components to function effectively: The slurmctld manages the overall cluster and oversees job scheduling and resource allocation. The slurmdbd handles job accounting, logging, and other data storage needs. The slurmd executes tasks on compute nodes, ensuring efficient resource utilization.

By deploying slurmd as a systemd service on bare metal nodes and encapsulating slurmctld and slurmdbd within Kubernetes pods, Knight and Kenny (2021) aimed to leverage the strengths of both systems. This setup allowed them to maintain the performance and reliability of slurmd on physical hardware while benefiting from Kubernetes' scalability and orchestration capabilities for the control and database components. This approach demonstrates a strategic balance between traditional HPC management and modern containerized orchestration, offering insights into optimizing HPC workflows in hybrid environments.

The work of Decker, Metje, and Kunkel (2025), explore various approaches for integrating Kubernetes and SLURM, aiming to address key questions that their research seeks to diagnose. One question is whether workloads can be executed in parallel across multiple machines, exploring the ability of the combined Kubernetes-SLURM system to efficiently distribute and manage tasks across a cluster, ensuring scalability and resource utilization. Another point is the performance overhead imposed by the tool. This inquiry examines the additional computational or operational costs introduced by integrating Kubernetes with SLURM, such as latency, resource consumption, or scheduling delays, to assess the overall efficiency of the system. By addressing these questions, the authors aim to evaluate the feasibility and effectiveness of combining Kubernetes and SLURM for workload orchestration in HPC environments.

Liu and Guitart (2022), they utilized the OSU Micro-Benchmarks (OSU Benchmark3)[11] were utilized to comprehensively analyze the performance of MPI communication across various message sizes. This benchmark suite is widely recognized by HPC cluster users and administrators for its ability to provide insight into the efficiency and scalability of MPI implementations. Additionally, (Liu and Guitart, 2022) employed other benchmark models to measure different aspects of system performance: The Double-Precision General Matrix Multiply (DGEMM) benchmark evaluates the processor's floating-point computing capability, focusing on matrix multiplication operations critical for many scientific and computational tasks. The Fast Fourier Transform (FFT) benchmark assesses the processor's floating-point performance during FFT operations, essential for signal processing and data analysis. The STREAM benchmark[12] measures memory bandwidth by testing the system's ability to perform simple vector operations, providing insights into data transfer rates and memory efficiency. By leveraging these benchmarks, (Liu and Guitart, 2022) aimed to gain a holistic understanding of system capabilities, including communication efficiency, computational power, and memory performance, critical factors in optimizing HPC environments.

Rudyy et al. (2019) conducted a comparative analysis using Alya, a Computational Fluid Dynamics (CFD) code optimized for HPC environments. The research focused on quantifying the performance overhead associated with three different container technologies: Docker, Singularity[13], and Shifter[14].

At the conclusion of the study, Singularity was determined to deliver the best performance in terms of task execution and portability. These finding highlights Singularity's efficiency in maintaining computational speed while providing flexibility and ease of use across diverse HPC environments.

---

[8] https://systemd.io/
[9] https://slurm.schedmd.com/slurmctld.html
[10] https://slurm.schedmd.com/slurmdbd.html
[11] https://mvapich.cse.ohio-state.edu/benchmarks/
[12] https://www.cs.virginia.edu/stream/ref.html
[13] https://docs.sylabs.io/guides/3.5/user-guide/introduction.html
[14] https://shifter.readthedocs.io/en/latest/

Ruddy's research emphasizes the importance of maximizing performance while executing a single, well-optimized parallel task. This approach prevents idle resources and better scale task utilization on HPC clusters, ensuring efficient resource allocation and improved overall system performance.

Sochat, Fox, and Milroy (2024) conducted an experiment to assess performance issues arising when running traditional HPC applications with Usernetes[15]. Additionally, the study aimed to demonstrate the benefits of a hybrid configuration combining an HPC workload manager and Kubernetes in user space, enabling the joint execution of HPC workloads and services. In the experiment, benchmarks such as LAMMPS and OSU Micro Benchmarks were used to measure performance and identify potential bottlenecks or inefficiencies. These benchmarks measure network communication, computational efficiency, and other critical aspects for optimizing HPC applications in a hybrid environment. The study's results highlight how combining the HPC workload manager with Kubernetes in user space provides a more flexible and efficient solution for managing complex workloads while enabling the integration of additional services, thereby expanding the HPC environment's capabilities.

In this paper, these findings are used as basis to compare the performance of Kubernetes with SLURM bare metal on HPC workloads, focusing on metrics such as latency, scalability, and resilience.

Unlike the cited works, our research employed eight identical servers divided into bare metal and Kubernetes configurations, prioritizing MPI communication benchmarks and optimizing server usage with SLURM. Additionally, it systematically compared pure and containerized environments, emphasizing the balance between scalability and efficiency in parallel communications for realistic HPC environments.

3. THE EXPERIMENT

The specifications of the eight identical servers were: DELL Poweredge R640, with 2x Intel(R) Xeon(R) Gold 6154 CPU @ 3.00GHz, 192 GB DDR4, and Intel(R) Gigabit 4P I350-t. The servers were divided into two groups: one consisted of four servers configured with bare metal settings (Table 1), while the other group comprised four servers configured with Kubernetes settings (Table 2). The choice of software and hardware adhered to the institute's internal policy, aiming to offer a stable environment as close as possible to the real one.

Table 1. Bare metal Setup

Software	Purpose	Version
Ubuntu[16]	OS	22.04.5
SLURM	Orchestration	23.11.4
MPI	Parallelism	4.1.2
Storage	NFS	19.2.1

Table 2. Kubernetes Setup

Software	Purpose	Version
Ubuntu	OS	22.04.5
SLURM	Orchestration	23.11.4
Kubernetes	Orchestration	1.31.9
MPI	Parallelism	4.1.2
Storage	Ceph	19.2.1
Containerd[17]	OCI	1.31.9
Calico	CNI	3.29.2

The benchmarks were selected to provide a comprehensive view of the performance of parallel systems, addressing the main MPI communication operations. Together, they allow for the evaluation of latency, bandwidth, efficiency of global operations, and load imbalances. To optimize the experiments, we used SLURM to start all tests and create an execution queue, there by optimizing the usage time of the servers provided for the experiment and returning them to their original purpose.

[15] https://github.com/rootless-containers/usernetes
[16] https://www.hostinger.com/tutorials/what-is-ubuntu
[17] https://github.com/containerd/containerd

3.1 Collective Benchmarks

These benchmarks evaluate the performance of collective operations across multiple servers simultaneously. These operations involve the sending and processing of data between all participating processes. In the experiment, we conducted the following tests:

OSU Barrier Latency is the measurement of the synchronization time between MPI processes using the barrier function. The test runs one process on each node and calculates the latency until all processes reach a common synchronization point.

OSU Allreduce Latency is the measurement of the latency of the allreduce operation for various message sizes, with the aim of evaluating the performance of collective communication that involves processing. This test is important for measuring frequent aggregation operations, such as numerical simulations and machine learning.

OSU Broadcast Latency: Measurement of the latency of the osu bcast operation for different message sizes, assessing the time it takes for each data to leave the main process and reach the secondary processes. This measurement is useful for analyzing data distribution across a network, potentially highlighting communication bottlenecks or imbalanced processes.

3.2 P2P Benchmarks

These benchmarks evaluate the performance of MPI point-to-point operations, executed on two servers. They analyze the direct communication between servers, enabling the identification of network performance and potential bottlenecks in node-to-node communication.

OSU Bandwidth is the measurement of point-to-point bandwidth between two MPI processes. The test calculates the bandwidth in MB/s or GB/s when sending a series of messages of varying sizes, with the aim of measuring the efficiency of continuous communication and the impact of message size on throughput.

OSU Point-to-Point Latency is the measurement of latency in point-to-point communication between two processes. The test sends multiple messages of varying sizes and evaluates the round-trip time of the message. This test is essential for understanding the network's response.

Two types of tests were performed: collective and point-to-point. The collective tests were conducted in scenarios with two, three, and four nodes, while the point-to-point tests were executed with only two nodes. All scenarios were performed 10 times in each experimental environment to reduce noise and ensure greater accuracy in the results. A total of 220 rounds of experiments were conducted.

The SLURM initialization script used in all tests is presented in Figure 1. This script was designed to configure the experimental environment consistently and ensure that all collective and point-to-point tests were executed under identical conditions. In this context, $SCRIPT refers to an environment variable that contains the name of the script being executed. The SLURM configuration was adjusted to support scenarios with two, three, and four nodes in the collective tests, while the point-to-point tests were configured to operate with only two nodes. The repeated execution of ten times in each experimental environment helped mitigate noise and increase the accuracy of the results.

```
#!/ usr /bin/env bash
# SBATCH -N 2
# SBATCH --ntasks-per-node =1
for i in 1 2 3 4 5 6 7 8 9 10; do
  echo "$i /10 $SCRIPT "
  srun --mpi= pmix /osu/mpi/pt2pt / osu_latency
sleep 60
done
```

Figure 1. Slurm Script

4. RESULTS AND ANALYSIS

The experiment began with collective tests using the OSU Barrier (Collective Benchmarks). As shown in Figure 2, Kubernetes exhibited a 3% average latency increase compared to the bare metal environment. This difference arose because the bare metal environment lacked a Container Network Interface (CNI) or orchestration, leading to more efficient performance. Additionally, as illustrated in Figure 3, tests were more efficient with an even number of nodes. The figure depicts the process flow (represented by circles) distributed across an even number of nodes (servers), showing greater efficiency than experiments conducted with an odd number of nodes. An even number of servers proved to be more efficient in the tests we conducted. However, to confirm this observation, we need to further scale these processes, which was not possible due to a lack of resources.

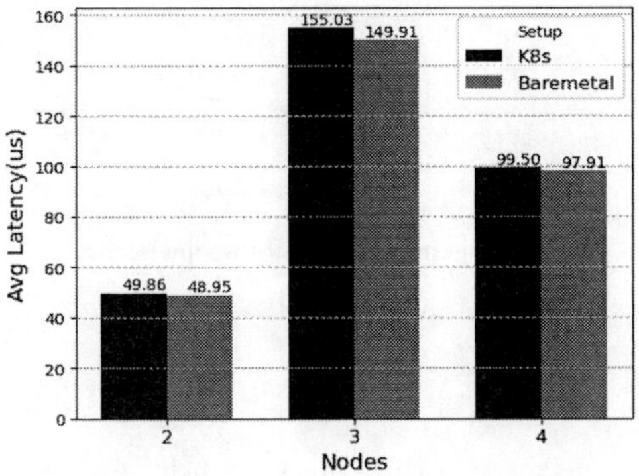

Figure 2. Osu barrier latency

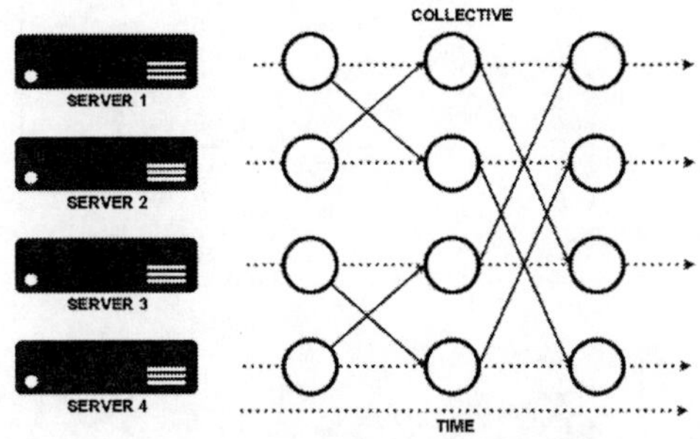

Figure 3. Mpi collective with 4 nodes

In the second round of collective benchmarks, we executed the OSU Allreduce as shown in Figure 4. The efficiency in tests with an even number of nodes continued, but now there was a 10% greater efficiency of the Kubernetes environment compared to bare metal. This discrepancy occurred, for the most part, during the test when reaching a high message size. This reinforced the importance of choosing a faster information-sharing method, as the NFS service is slower than CephFS[18].

We concluded the collective benchmark tests with the OSU Broadcast, as shown in Figure 5. In this benchmark, Kubernetes processes introduce noise in broadcast latency, especially when the message size increases. This results in an average of 50% additional latency caused by Kubernetes processes.

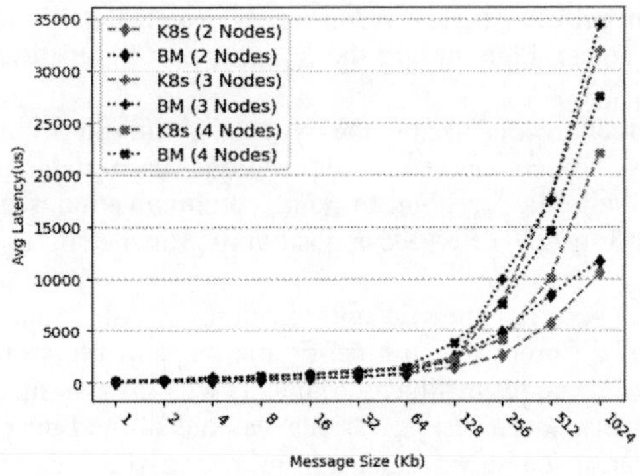

Figure 4. Osu allreduce latency

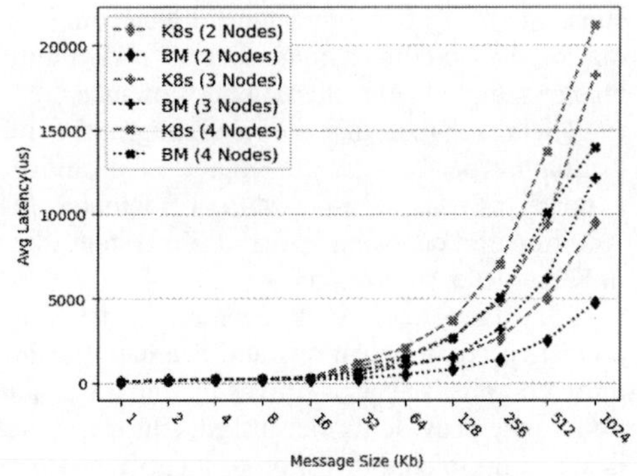

Figure 5. Osu broadcast latency

[18] https://docs.ceph.com/en/reef/cephfs/

We conducted the final set of benchmarks to test point-to-point communication between nodes. We initiated the process with the OSU Bandwidth test. As illustrated in Figure 6, interference was reported again, resulting in bandwidth fluctuations within the Kubernetes environment. However, in the point-to-point latency test depicted in Figure 7, no variation was observed between the two environments.

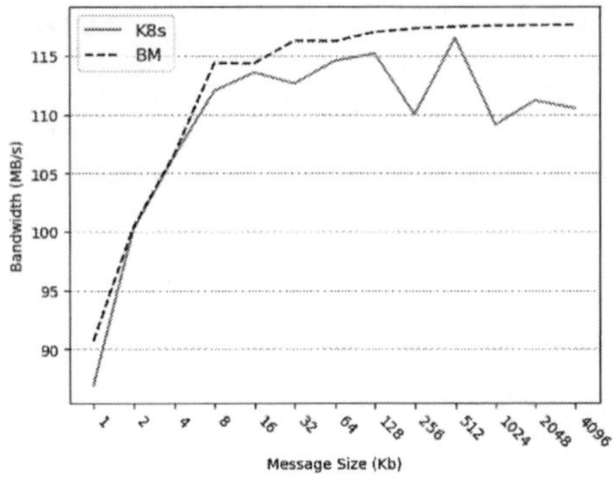

Figure 6. Osu bandwidth

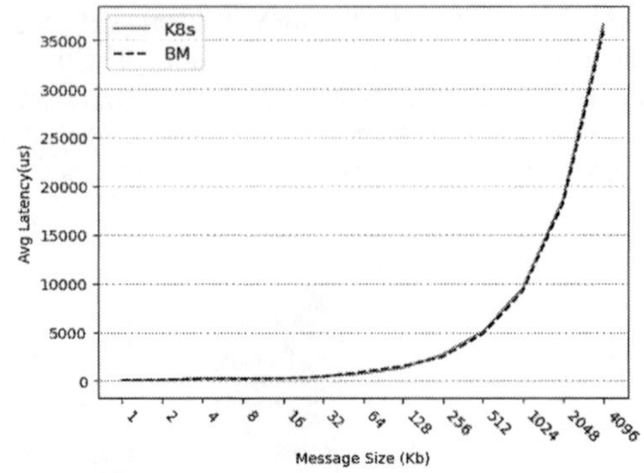

Figure 7. Osu point-to-point latency

5. CONCLUSION

This research compares the performance of SLURM bare metal and SLURM in a Kubernetes environment for HPC workloads, providing insights for infrastructure selection. Unlike Aydinet's (2024) study, which investigated AI-based frameworks (DECICE), this work focuses on practical implementation scenarios, helping decision-makers balance performance and operational complexity.

In this study, we conducted a series of benchmarks to evaluate communication performance in Kubernetes and bare metal environments. The results demonstrated that Kubernetes introduces significant additional latency in collective communication scenarios, such as broadcast and all-reduce, especially when handling large messages. The average latency increase reached up to 50% in the OSU Broadcast test, while the OSU Allreduce showed a 10% lower efficiency in Kubernetes compared to bare metal. These discrepancies can be attributed to the overheads associated with orchestration and network interfaces in Kubernetes.

On the other hand, point-to-point tests, such as OSU Bandwidth and the point-to-point latency test, did not reveal significant differences between the two environments. This suggests that Kubernetes may not impose a substantial negative impact on direct communication between nodes. Additionally, greater efficiency was observed in configurations with an even number of nodes, highlighting the importance of considering the cluster setup when evaluating performance.

The results of this study highlight the importance of considering the type of communication when evaluating performance in orchestrated environments. For collective communications, bare metal remains a more efficient option, while Kubernetes may be suitable for point-to-point communication scenarios. Additionally, choosing a shared file system like CephFS instead of NFS can positively influence performance in Kubernetes environments.

For future work, it is recommended to explore Kubernetes-specific optimizations to reduce latency in collective communications and evaluate the impact of different network configurations and file systems in more complex scenarios. Investigating the scalability of these results in environments with a larger number of nodes may provide further insights into large-scale performance. Testing various versions of the Linux kernel is also a promising direction to identify potential performance improvements in more stressful scenarios and understand how different kernel configurations affect system efficiency. These approaches can contribute to developing best practices for optimizing performance in Kubernetes and bare metal environments.

ACKNOWLEDGEMENT

This article is the result of the R&D&I project (Software Engineering Project based on Design Patterns for Continuous Delivery), carried out by Sidia Instituto de Ciência e Tecnologia, in partnership with Samsung Eletrônica da Amazônia Ltda., using resources from Federal Law nº 8.387/1991, and its dissemination and publicity are in accordance with the provisions of Article 39 of Decree No. 10.521/2020.

REFERENCES

Aydin, M., Bidollahkhany, M., & Kunkel, J. (2024). *Comparing Faulttolerance in Kubernetes and Slurm in HPC Infrastructure*.

Azad, Md A. K., Iqbal, N., Hassan, F., & Roy, P. (2023). An Empirical Study of High Performance Computing (HPC) Performance Bugs. In *2023 IEEE/ACM 20th International Conference on Mining Software Repositories (MSR)*. 194–206. https://doi.org/10.1109/MSR59073.2023.00037

Beltre, A., Saha P., Govindaraju, M., Younge, A., & Grant, R. (2019). *Enabling HPCWorkloads on Cloud Infrastructure Using Kubernetes Container Orchestration Mechanisms*. https://doi.org/10.1109/CANOPIE-HPC49598.2019. 00007

Cérin, C., Greneche, N., & Menouer, T. (2020). Towards Pervasive Containerization of HPC Job Schedulers. In *2020 IEEE 32nd International Symposium on Computer Architecture and High Performance Computing (SBAC-PAD)*. 281–288. https://doi.org/10.1109/SBAC-PAD49847.2020.00046

Decker, J., Metje, S., & Kunkel, J. (2025). Running Kubernetes Workloads on Rootless HPC Systems using Slurm. In *Cloud Computing 2025* (Valencia, Spain). thinkmind, 100–107. https://www.thinkmind.org/library/CLOUD_COMPUTING/CLOUD_COMPUTING_2025/cloud_computing_2025_2_60_20036.html

Jokanovic, A., D'Amico, M., & Corbalan, J. (2018). Evaluating SLURM Simulator with Real-Machine SLURM and Vice Versa. *IEEE/ACM Performance Modeling, Benchmarking and Simulation of High Performance Computer Systems (PMBS)*, 72–82. https://doi.org/10.1109/PMBS.2018.8641556

Kenny, J. & Knight, S. (2021). *Kubernetes for HPC Administration*. Sandia National Lab. (SNL-NM), Albuquerque, NM (United States); Sandia National Laboratories, SNL California. https://www.osti.gov/biblio/1887730

Liu, P. & Guitart, J. (2022). Performance Characterization of Containerization for HPC Workloads on InfiniBand Clusters: An Empirical Study. *Cluster Computing*, *25*(2) (April 2022), 847–868. https://doi.org/10.1007/s10586-021-03460-8

Rudyy, O., Garcia-Gasulla, M., Mantovani, F., Santiago, A., Sirvent, R., & Vázquez, M. (2019). Containers in HPC: A Scalability and Portability Study in Production Biological Simulations. In *2019 IEEE International Parallel and Distributed Processing Symposium (IPDPS)*. 567–577. https://doi.org/10.1109/IPDPS.2019.00066

Sochat, V., Fox, D., & Milroy, D. (2024). *HPC Alongside User-space Kubernetes*. (06 2024). https://doi.org/10.48550/arXiv.2406.06995

Xavier, M. G., Neves, M. V., & De Rose, C. A. F. (2014). A Performance Comparison of Container-Based Virtualization Systems for MapReduce Clusters. In *2014 22nd Euromicro International Conference on Parallel, Distributed, and Network-Based Processing*. 299–306. https://doi.org/10.1109/PDP.2014.78

Yoo, A. B, Jette, M. A, & Grondona, M. (2003). SLURM: Simple Linux Utility for Resource Management. In D. Feitelson, L. Rudolph, & U. Schwiegelshohn (Eds.), *Job Scheduling Strategies for Parallel Processing* (pp. 44-60), Springer Berlin Heidelberg, Berlin, Heidelberg.

A SCALABLE SOLUTION FOR ENVIRONMENTAL MONITORING: THE ECOMONITORING SYSTEM

Alessio Chirigu[1], Alberto Mancosu[1], Mariella Sole[1], Sara Pinna[2], Matteo Anedda[2] and Daniele D. Giusto[2]

[1]*Hedya srl*
Cagliari, Italy
[2]*University of Cagliari – UdR CNIT Cagliari*
Cagliari, Italy

ABSTRACT

Continuous monitoring of aquatic ecosystems requires solutions that overcome the limitations of traditional methods in terms of coverage, timeliness, and data quality. EcoMonitoring introduces an integrated system consisting of an autonomous electric-powered aquatic drone that transports a smart buoy equipped with physico-chemical sensors and wave motion detection systems. The system performs on-site measurements and processes them locally using embedded technologies, transmitting data in real time via LTE or LoRa networks, depending on availability.
One of the system's key strengths lies in its ability to combine field-collected data with SAR and optical satellite imagery, enabling multi-level analysis that integrates local observations with large-scale insights. The data are stored in a cloud-based data lake, supported by an automated pipeline for the generation of dynamic dashboards, geoportals, and predictive models. The platform, designed with a modular and scalable architecture, allows for the configuration of alert thresholds and the timely generation of notifications in case of anomalous conditions.
Initial experimental tests have demonstrated the robustness of the system in complex operational scenarios. The contribution of this work lies in the development and validation of an integrated, replicable technological solution, suitable for various environmental contexts, with significant implications for the sustainable management of water resources and the mitigation of environmental risks.

KEYWORDS

Environmental Monitoring, Smart Buoy, Aquatic Drone, Aquatic Sensing, IoT Systems, Coastal Ecosystems

1. INTRODUCTION

In recent decades, increasing anthropogenic pressure on aquatic ecosystems, combined with the effects of climate change, has heightened the urgency of implementing effective tools for environmental monitoring. Coastal, port, and lake areas are particularly vulnerable to phenomena such as eutrophication, chemical pollution, morphological changes, and biodiversity loss, making continuous and timely monitoring of their environmental conditions essential.

Traditional environmental monitoring methods, based on manual sampling and fixed buoys, present several limitations: high costs, limited spatial coverage, low update frequency, and delays in data processing. Moreover, the use of heterogeneous information sources and the lack of integrated data collection and transmission systems hinder the ability to obtain a comprehensive picture of environmental conditions. The adoption of smart buoys and IoT systems represents a promising solution to overcome these challenges. Integrated platforms such as the one developed in the MARIABOX project have also demonstrated the effectiveness of using biosensors in buoys for the real-time detection of multiple marine contaminants (Maguire et al., 2019).

In this context, the *EcoMonitoring* project proposes an advanced technological platform for aquatic environmental monitoring, based on the integration of a smart multi-sensor buoy, an autonomous aquatic drone (USV – Unmanned Surface Vehicle), and a digital infrastructure capable of processing data in real time. The developed solution stands out for its ability to operate autonomously, with mobility and adaptability, ensuring high-frequency, geo-referenced, and multi-parameter data acquisition.

The current landscape of environmental monitoring reveals a gap between costly, high-precision commercial systems and academic prototypes that often lack robustness or full integration. *EcoMonitoring* aims to bridge this divide by offering a modular, cost-effective, and scalable system. Unlike proprietary solutions, it leverages off-the-shelf components and open architecture, allowing for easier upgrades, reduced maintenance complexity, and broader deployment potential. Through a dual communication strategy (LTE + LoRa) and local storage with retransmission logic, it ensures data resilience even in low-connectivity environments. This integrated and autonomous approach positions *EcoMonitoring* as a practical alternative for high-resolution, real-time monitoring in real-world conditions.

The objective of this work is to describe the architecture of the *EcoMonitoring* system and its main components, with particular focus on the design of the MoBI multi-sensor buoy, the aquatic drone, and the communication and data transmission system. The innovative contribution of the project lies in the integration of distributed sensing, long-range communication technologies, and automated data acquisition systems into a scalable platform for real-time environmental monitoring. The proposed solution enables continuous and geo-referenced collection of multiple parameters in aquatic environments, overcoming the typical limitations of traditional monitoring methods in terms of coverage and frequency.

2. BODY OF PAPER

2.1 Overall System Architecture

The *EcoMonitoring* system has been designed as a modular and scalable platform for environmental monitoring in coastal, port, and lake aquatic environments. The overall architecture integrates three main technological layers:

- Physical layer: This includes the HYDRA aquatic drone and the MoBI multi-sensor buoy. The autonomous electric-powered drone is responsible for transporting and positioning the buoy at specific points, following predefined routes. Once stabilized, the buoy collects physico-chemical data of the water and wave motion parameters.
- Communication and control layer: Communication between the devices and the central infrastructure takes place through LoRa and LTE protocols, using an adaptive and redundant mode. The buoy's management is distributed between a microcontroller (Arduino Mega) and a microcomputer (Raspberry Pi), which coordinate local operations and ensure data transmission. The HYDRA drone, on the other hand, features an independent communication system with the ground station.
- Data processing and analysis layer: The data collected is processed locally using edge computing techniques, enabling preliminary analyses (filtering, quality control, anomaly detection) directly on board. The validated data is then transmitted to a cloud-based backend, stored in a data lake built on Databricks/Delta Lake, and analyzed using machine learning and deep learning models.

Architectural approaches aimed at interoperability among autonomous marine platforms, such as buoys and surface vehicles, have also been extensively analyzed (Kabanov et al., 2022), who propose scalable solutions based on Marine IoT concepts for the coordinated management of aquatic robotic agents.

This architecture allows for optimized alert latency, reduced network traffic, system scalability, and accessible interfaces for both real-time and historical data analysis through web-based dashboards and geoportals.

2.2 Hardware Components

2.2.1 Aquatic Drone HYDRA

The HYDRA drone is an autonomous surface vehicle (USV – Unmanned Surface Vehicle) powered by electricity, designed to transport and position the MoBI buoy along predefined routes in coastal and lake environments. Similar approaches using USVs equipped with multiparametric sensors for water quality monitoring have also been explored in recent studies (Si et al., 2023). Unlike many solutions described in the literature, the HYDRA drone does not directly integrate sensors on board but instead operates as a mobile platform for deploying and managing the MoBI buoy, which serves as the primary sensing node. HYDRA is equipped with:

- A high-precision GNSS system (RTK) for centimeter-level georeferencing of data.
- A single-beam sonar for bathymetric surveys and detection of underwater obstacles.
- A high-definition camera for environmental video surveillance and assisted navigation.
- An AIR + GROUND onboard unit using the MAVLink protocol for real-time transmission of telemetry and video data.
- A battery providing up to 3 hours of operational autonomy, with the capability to carry out multi-point missions.

The drone is physically connected to the buoy via a mechanical coupling. However, the two systems operate independently in terms of power supply and communication. During mission execution, when reaching each measurement point, a stabilization period is foreseen to allow the buoy to accurately capture wave motion parameters.

2.2.2 Smart Buoy MoBI

The MoBI buoy is a multisensor buoy designed and built using high-density polyethylene (HDPE) through 3D printing. It features an oval shape and is equipped with an external lateral fin, fully submerged, that enables accurate detection of wave direction. The buoy is designed to measure various physico-chemical water parameters, including temperature, pH, conductivity, turbidity, and dissolved oxygen, as well as to monitor wave motion. Similar solutions have also been developed in river environments, where smart buoys based on ESP32 microcontrollers and MQTT connectivity have been used for real-time monitoring of parameters such as pH and temperature (Nasution et al., 2024). These approaches confirm the effectiveness of integrating distributed sensing with IoT technologies for environmental monitoring across different aquatic scenarios.

MoBI is equipped with:

- A WMP6 multiparameter probe for measuring: which enables the real-time measurement of key physico-chemical parameters, including water temperature, pH, electrical conductivity, dissolved oxygen, and turbidity.
- Inertial sensors (accelerometer, gyroscope, magnetometer) for analyzing wave motion and direction. Similar systems have also been used in other projects for real-time wave height measurement, as illustrated by Wyawahare et al. (2023).
- An independent GNSS module for accurate geolocation of measurement points.
- A Raspberry Pi 3B+ microcomputer for software management, data transmission, and local buffering.
- An Arduino Mega 2560 R3 microcontroller for low-level sensor management and communication with the Raspberry Pi and LoRa network.

The system's hardware is built upon a dual-processor architecture designed to optimize resource management and ensure operational reliability. The Raspberry Pi 3B+ acts as the main processing unit, handling high-level operations such as interfacing with the probe, formatting data into JSON, and managing the primary 4G/LTE communication. The Arduino Mega 2560 R3 serves as a secondary control unit, managing real-time tasks like acquiring data from inertial and positioning sensors and handling the LoRa fallback communication. Communication and synchronization between the two units are achieved via a USB serial connection that employs the UART protocol, which also allows the Raspberry Pi to power the Arduino directly, simplifying the internal wiring. The internal organization of the electronic components is illustrated in the block diagram shown in Figure 1, which highlights the connections between the microcontroller, microcomputer, probe, communication modules, and power system. The mechanical layout and external shape of the buoy, including the protective cages and lateral fin, are shown in the 3D model in Figure 2.

The system is designed to autonomously perform the phases of initialization, data acquisition, transmission, and logging. Specifically, this operational logic is governed by a robust software architecture organized into a series of distinct operational phases, implemented in Python on the Raspberry Pi and C++ on the Arduino. A typical mission involves an initialization phase, navigation to a predefined point, a data acquisition period where the two processors work in parallel, and a transmission phase. These latter phases, are repeated for each measurement point configured in the mission, enabling multi-point environmental data collection in a fully automated manner. To ensure data integrity, a verification and retransmission logic is implemented: at the end of a mission, the system checks with the remote platform for any missing data packets and, if necessary, retrieves them from the local SD card for retransmission. A similar approach, integrating multiparametric sensing, LoRa communication, and server-side artificial intelligence, has also been adopted in offshore aquaculture contexts for predictive water quality monitoring (Lu et al., 2022).

In the absence of an LTE network, communication takes place over LoRa, using a gateway compatible with the LoRaWAN protocol. Data is also stored locally on an SD card in JSON format.

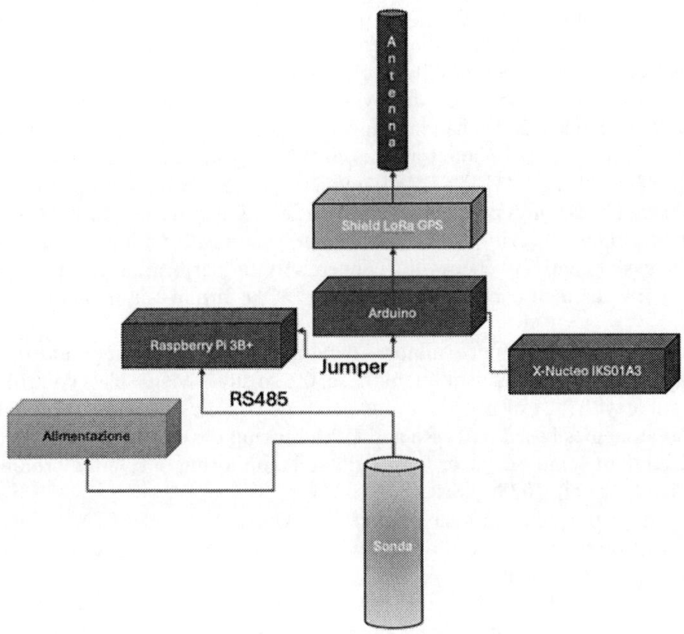

Figure 1. Block diagram and components of the MoBI buoy

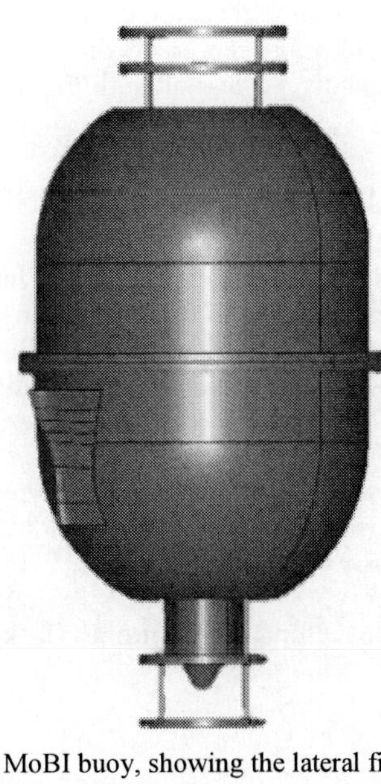

Figure 2. 3D model of the MoBI buoy, showing the lateral fin and protective cages

2.3 Communication and Data Transmission System

To ensure a continuous and reliable data flow even under challenging operational conditions, the *EcoMonitoring* system was designed with a flexible and redundant communication strategy. At the core of this architecture is the buoy's ability to dynamically adapt to network availability by utilizing two main channels: cellular LTE connection and, alternatively, a low-power LoRaWAN network. The HYDRA drone, on the other hand, communicates with the ground station through an AIR UNIT HM30 module.

Under normal conditions, when mobile network coverage is available, the Raspberry Pi installed on the buoy attempts to transmit the collected data via LTE. Cellular data transmission solutions have also been successfully implemented in other aquatic monitoring systems, as shown by Staude et al. (2024), who describe the use of GSM modules for the remote transmission of environmental data in real time.

The data is sent through HTTP POST requests to predefined endpoints, containing the acquired environmental parameters: physico-chemical properties of the water (such as temperature, pH, turbidity, dissolved oxygen, and conductivity), wave motion data, geolocation information, and diagnostic logs. Before transmission, the system actively checks for connectivity by performing a simple ping to a remote server. If the test is successful, the data packet—structured in JSON format—is immediately transmitted to the cloud backend.

If mobile network coverage is not available—which is often the case in remote or marine areas—the system switches to a LoRa fallback mechanism. In this case, the Arduino Mega takes control of the transmission, using a module compatible with the LoRaWAN protocol to send compressed data packets (up to 47 bytes) to a ground gateway. Similar strategies based on LoRa and GPS tracking have also been adopted in other systems for the real-time localization of smart buoys, or for distributed monitoring in river environments using node–gateway architectures (Sa'adah et al., 2023; Pires et al., 2024).

The data travels via the public infrastructure of The Things Network (TTN), which forwards it to the central analysis system via webhooks. The LoRa packet includes essential parameters, along with the date, time, and GPS location of the measurement.

To ensure operational robustness even in the absence of connectivity, the buoy is designed to locally store every acquired data point by writing it to an internal SD card in JSON format. This guarantees full data persistence and the ability to recover any untransmitted data once connectivity is restored. Similar approaches for data redundancy and resilience to network loss have been adopted in LoRaWAN-based environmental monitoring applications for closed basins and ecological ponds (Hsieh et al., 2020).

This hybrid communication architecture represents one of the key strengths of the *EcoMonitoring* system, making it suitable for deployment in diverse and often difficult-to-connect environmental contexts.

3. PRELIMINARY EXPERIMENTAL RESULTS

Initial field tests were conducted to assess the operational capabilities of the *EcoMonitoring* system in a controlled lake environment. These tests focused on evaluating the energy autonomy of the buoy, verifying sensor specifications, and validating data transmission reliability.

The MoBI buoy was tested in continuous monitoring conditions, including sensing, data processing, and data transmission via LTE/LoRa. The system successfully operated autonomously for up to 18 hours without recharging.

The HYDRA aquatic drone, which serves as the deployment vehicle for the buoy, was not tested for endurance in this initial phase. However, under optimal conditions such as calm water and a light payload, it is expected to operate autonomously for up to four hours. Future tests will aim to validate this estimate and assess its actual energy consumption during realistic mission scenarios.
The MoBI buoy integrates a WMP6 multiparameter probe. The key specifications, based on manufacturer data, are summarized in Table 1 below:

Table 1. Summary of measurement accuracy for the WMP6 probe sensors used in the MoBI buoy

Parameter	Accuracy
Temperature	± 0.15°C
Conductivity	± 0.25 % of reading
pH	± 0.250 pH
Dissolved Oxygen	± 0.100 ppm
Turbidity	± 5% or 0.5 NTU

4. CONCLUSION

The *EcoMonitoring* system has proven to be highly effective for real-time environmental monitoring, integrating the multisensor buoy MoBI and the autonomous aquatic drone HYDRA. The tests conducted confirmed the system's ability to operate independently, without the need for human intervention, and to reliably collect and transmit data under both LTE and LoRa network conditions. The platform has demonstrated itself to be a robust system, with significant advantages in terms of operational autonomy and modularity, allowing the integration of new sensors and protocols, and ensuring continuous monitoring even in the absence of network connectivity thanks to persistent local data storage.

However, some limitations remain, such as the dependence on network coverage and the energy autonomy of both the drone and the buoy, which could affect the duration of missions. Additionally, the adoption of onboard artificial intelligence algorithms could further reduce response latency and improve real-time system efficiency. Despite the promising results, the system faced some practical challenges during deployment. In particular, the buoy exhibited occasional instability in the presence of moderate wave activity, which may affect the accuracy of wave direction measurements. These issues are currently under evaluation to identify possible improvements in system design or data processing.

Future developments will focus on testing the system in more dynamic aquatic environments, assessing long-term operational stability, and exploring the integration of additional sensor types for extended environmental monitoring capabilities. Despite these challenges, *EcoMonitoring* has broad application potential, including the monitoring of marine protected areas, ports, rivers, and water basins, supporting the sustainable management of natural resources. The system is also well suited to support rapid decision-making by public authorities and local agencies, and it can be scaled to integrate with other environmental monitoring technologies.

ACKNOWLEDGEMENT

This research activity was partially funded by the European Union - NextGenerationEU and by the Ministry of University and Research (MUR), National Recovery and Resilience Plan (NRRP), Mission 4, Component 2, Investment 1.5, project "RAISE - Robotics and AI for Socio-economic Empowerment" (ECS00000035).

REFERENCES

Hsieh, C.-W., Tsai, Y. J., Stefanie, C., Wang, C. C. N., Chang, W.-T. S. (2020). The Preliminary Design of Water Quality Monitor System for the Ecological Pond based on LoRaWAN. 2020 International Symposium on Computer, Consumer and Control (IS3C), Taichung City, Taiwan, 2020, pp. 365-367, doi: 10.1109/IS3C50286.2020.00100.

Kabanov, A., Kramar, V. (2022). Marine Internet of Things Platforms for Interoperability of Marine Robotic Agents: An Overview of Concepts and Architectures. Journal of Marine Science and Engineering, 10, 1279. https://doi.org/10.3390/jmse10091279.

Lu, H.-Y.; Cheng, C.-Y.; Cheng, S.-C.; Cheng, Y.-H.; Lo, W.-C.; Jiang, W.-L.; Nan, F.-H.; Chang, S.-H.; Ubina, N.A. (2022). A Low-Cost AI Buoy System for Monitoring Water Quality at Offshore Aquaculture Cages. Sensors 2022, 22, 4078. https://doi.org/10.3390/s22114078.

Maguire, I., Regan, F. (2019). A design pipeline for development of a multi-analyte marine bio-sensor lab-on-a-disc platform. OCEANS 2019 - Marseille, Marseille, France, 2019, pp. 1-8, doi: 10.1109/OCEANSE.2019.8867432.

N. Sa'Adah, A. D. Ramadhani and D. P. Riananda (2023). Tracking Position on GPS Smart Buoy System Using LoRa Communication, 2023 Sixth International Conference on Vocational Education and Electrical Engineering (ICVEE), Surabaya, Indonesia, 2023, pp. 304-309, doi: 10.1109/ICVEE59738.2023.10348269.

Nasution, S., Abubakar, H., Suryadi, S., Widiyatmoko, B. (2023). Development of River Flow and Water Quality Using IOT-based Smart Buoys Environment Monitoring System. JURNAL ILMU FISIKA | UNIVERSITAS ANDALAS. 16. 1-12. 10.25077/jif.16.1.1-12.2024.

Pires, L.M.; Gomes, J. River (2024). Water Quality Monitoring Using LoRa-Based IoT. Designs 2024, 8, 127. https://doi.org/10.3390/designs8060127.

Si, H., Zhang, N., Liu,Y., Jing, G., Ren, Y., Yang, P. (2023). Application and Field Comparison of Water Quality Monitors in Unmanned Surface Vehicle. 2023 IEEE 16th International Conference on Electronic Measurement & Instruments (ICEMI), Harbin, China, 2023, pp. 52-56, doi: 10.1109/ICEMI59194.2023.10270668.

Staude, M.; Brożek, P.; Koštecka, E.; Tarnapowicz, D.; Wysocki, J. (2024). Remote Water Quality Monitoring System for Use in Fairway Applications. Appl. Sci. 2024, 14, 11406. https://doi.org/10.3390/app142311406.

Wyawahare, M., Balan, M. S., Aadarsh, A., Patil, A., Anuse, U. (2023). Jal-Tarang: Smart Buoy for Wave Height Measurement, 2023 IEEE International Carnahan Conference on Security Technology (ICCST), Pune, India, 2023, pp. 1-6, doi: 10.1109/ICCST59048.2023.10474257.

PLAYING TO IMPROVE THE QUALITY OF LIFE OF OLDER ADULTS

Louise Sauvé
Education Department, Université TÉLUQ / SAVIE
480, rue de la Chapelle, Québec (QC), Canada, G1K 0B6

ABSTRACT

Developing well-designed educational gaming interfaces for older adults begins with identifying ergonomic requirements to be considered during the design process to ensure that the games are adapted to their users' characteristics. In a study of seniors aged 55 and older, we created and tested three online educational games, to measure usability in the sense of determining the intuitive capacity of the game (user-friendliness). This paper presents the variables of the study, the way we adapted the three games for seniors, and the results of evaluation of the games by 129 older adults. Our participants reported a high degree of satisfaction with the games' navigation, gameplay aids, and pedagogical features. Based on these results, we present recommendations to guide the design of online educational games for seniors.

KEYWORDS

Educational Games, Older Adults, Validation, User-Friendliness, Gameplay Aids, Pedagogical Features

1. INTRODUCTION

Research on games has been conducted with different clienteles, especially by examining the impact of gamification, video games, and serious games. Game studies with older adults have generally focused on the impacts of games on their cognitive and physical health (e.g., see Chen et al., 2025; Kaiser et al., 2025; Mantell et al., 2025). However, there is sparse research on inclusive game design for this player group. This type of research is important for our understanding of how inclusive design criteria for an educational game apply to older adults, so that we can provide them with effective and engaging gameplay experiences.

To engage potential players, it is important to build games that they enjoy. Previous research has demonstrated the interest of Quebec seniors in playing educational games based on popular games known to seniors and in which questions allow them to test their knowledge on a particular subject, for example, "Solitaire," "Tic Tac Toe," and "Snakes and Ladders." These results showed that the seniors aged 55 and over learned from these games while enjoying their gameplay (Renaud et al., 2018; Kaufman et al., 2019; Kaufman et al., 2020).

According to Fua et al. (2013), educational games have a beneficial impact on the daily lives of the elderly. To improve older adults' quality of life and autonomy, we undertook a research and development project to design and implement online educational games, as well as to evaluate the relevance for this target population of the ergonomic and educational criteria used in developing the games.

According to Paez and Del Rio (2019), older people need more time to accomplish some tasks and can encounter usability problems, so online technologies are often not appropriate for their particular characteristics and needs. It is therefore important to identify ergonomic and pedagogical requirements to be considered during the design process for adapting online games to older adults' situations (Sauvé, 2010; Diaz-Orueta et al., 2012; Astell, 2013; Marston, 2014; Morris et al., 2014; Liu et al., 2016; Rogers and Mitzner, 2017). An inappropriate design can discourage seniors' use of online educational games (Kaufman et al, 2020). In the development of online educational games, the ergonomist's job is to implement solutions to inform and guide the user, reducing as much as possible the cognitive load involved in playing the game (effectiveness), while ensuring that the game is easy to play (comfort), safe (security), and fun for the player (Dajoux, 2020).

In this paper, we first define what we mean by user-friendliness in an educational game. We then describe how we adapted three well-known games to be user-friendly and educational for seniors. We briefly present the results of an online field test of the games by 129 seniors to determine their degree of satisfaction with the games' navigation, gameplay aids, and pedagogical features. Finally, in the discussion, we offer recommendations, based on our results, to guide the development of effective online educational games for older adults.

2. USER-FRIENDLINESS IN THE GAME

Our game development approach is rooted in a User-Centered Design methodology (Boot et al., 2020; Sauvé to adapt to the characteristics of the target user (user-centered design) and to be intuitive (user-friendly) (Barnard et al., 2013). User-friendliness refers to the qualities of a digital game that make it easy and pleasant to use (navigation) and to understand, even for someone with little computer knowledge. A user-friendly game environment helps the player to focus on what is important in playing the game and in learning.

One objective of this study was to evaluate the navigation, gameplay aids, and pedagogical aspects of three educational games for seniors. Navigation refers to the techniques and actions that guide users while in an educational game, enabling them to interact with the content and achieve the goals they set for themselves in playing the game (Sauvé, 2017; Dajoux, 2020; Engineering Design Centre, Cambridge University (2024); NN/g Nielsen Norman Group, 2024). Fundamentally, users need to be able to perform their actions quickly and intuitively, with as few errors as possible and with easy error correction. Adapting game rules for older adults and integrating contextual help (gameplay aids) facilitate their use of the game. Educational aspects of our games included content questions, feedback based on players' answers, and access to reading sheets with additional learning content.

To meet this study objective, three games were adapted to introduce educational content (Figure 1):

- *Solitaire Quiz*, based on "Solitaire" (a single-user game played with a deck of 52 cards to be placed in a particular order) incorporates questions on a specific theme. At regular intervals, depending on the number of card movements, the player encounters a multiple-choice question with four possible answers. The answer, whether correct or incorrect, affects the number of credits awarded to the player to buy advantages from the online game store and to progress to the end of the game.
- Based on the hit TV game show, *Millionaire* allows players to test their knowledge of a specific topic and win the grand prize of one million dollars! The game consists of 15 multiple-choice questions with four answers each, and the player must answer all 15 questions correctly to win the prize.
- Inspired by the popular game "Angry Birds," *Hit the Target!* combines the fun of slingshot shooting with the challenge of answering four-item multiple-choice questions correctly to collect rocks to throw. In each level, the player must aim and hit all the targets located in increasingly complex structures.

Figure 1. The three games

Our selection of games was based on a survey of seniors about their gaming preferences (n=781). We selected the three games that were mentioned most frequently by our respondents.

To determine content for the games' questions, older adults were also surveyed at the start of the project to identify topics that they wanted to learn about to improve their quality of life. Their top priorities were wealth planning, death and estate management, use of social assistance measures for home care, and use of tax assistance measures. To start on a game, an older adult first chose one of the three games and then chose one of these four themes for the game questions.

3. NAVIGATION IN THE GAME ENVIRONMENT

To make a game environment intuitive for seniors, designers should ensure that players can easily access all components (cards, navigation buttons, instructions/ tutorials and point score) needed for the game to run smoothly (Barnard et al., 2013). To facilitate players' movement in the game, it is very important to make sure that the game and its components display without overflowing the screen and without blocking some game elements (Lopez-Martinez et al., 2011; Sauvé et al., 2017). For a comfortable gameplay experience, the design should use a predetermined frame or a responsive web design to maintain a standard display layout across screens. The game board and accessories for playing should cover most of the screen, and scroll bars in page displays should be avoided.

To facilitate navigation within the game, the game elements and question content should be limited to one screen page. This avoids long and tedious scrolling on the screen, which particularly demotivates seniors with short attention spans (Barnard et al., 2013; Sauvé, 2017).

It is also important to minimize the use of superimposed windows during the course of a game. Because some older users are less likely to notice page changes and can become confused, a clear notification of a change of screens should be displayed as, for example, when the player goes from the "game" page to a "Questions/ Information" page (Shneiderman et al., 2016). In designing our games, we limited the number of windows to only two; when a second window appears in the center of the screen, the game board becomes gray and inactive.

Similarly, if question content is integrated into the game, all relevant information must be available to the player through single clicks. In our three games, we designed learning questions to include on the same page all relevant information (question statements, answers, degree of difficulty, feedback, and credits earned or lost). The questions, answers, and feedback are displayed in smaller windows superimposed on the game board. The size of these windows is variable, but always smaller than the board (Figure 2).

Figure 2. Question and feedback windows

The player can access additional information in the form of a reading sheet (Figure 3) if s/he does not answer a question correctly. These reading sheets are also offered to seniors at the end of each game. A player simply needs to check them off to group them into a personal notebook that can be consulted at any time.

To assist with game navigation, each game includes text and voice tutorials (Figure 4). These can be accessed as needed, with a simple click, to guide seniors throughout the game. Also, the rules of each game are always available in the game.

4. METHODOLOGY

This experiment took place over the course of two months. Participants were invited to play according to their interests and needs. The experiment was approved by the relevant ethics committee. Each participant was made aware of the purpose of the research and signed an online consent form.

During the experiment, we administered three questionnaires, each consisting of multiple-choice questions with three items of choice plus "I don't know". Participants could also provide feedback on the game using the

"Report" button. Finally, video recordings of the players' actions, using a tool that captured each person's gameplay on their computer, tablet, or phone, provided relevant information on how they handled difficulties with navigation and understanding the game.

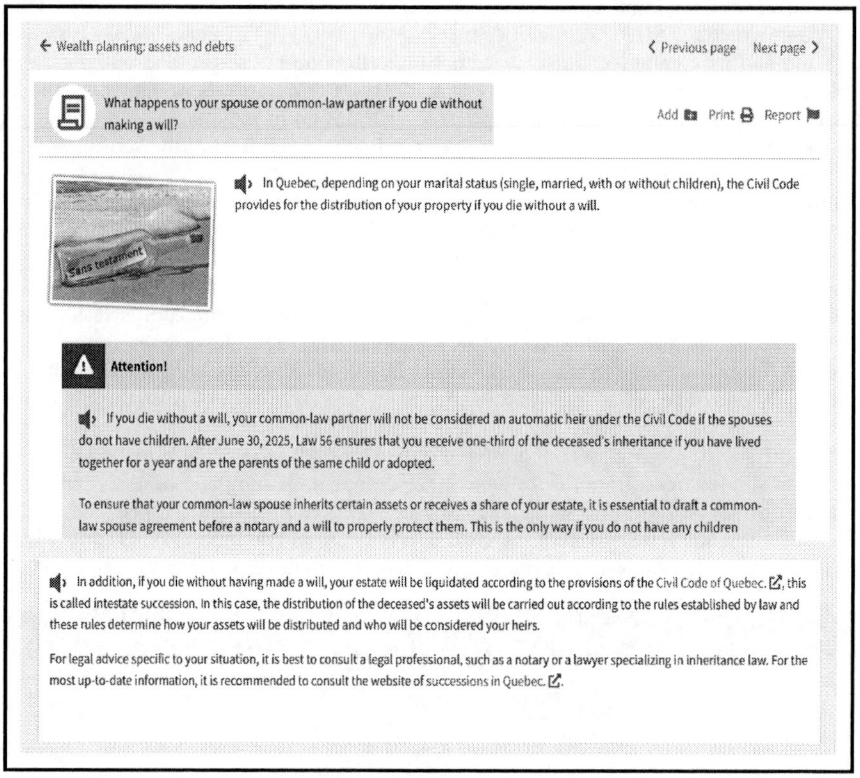

Figure 3. Example of a reading sheet

Figure 4. Tutorial in *Solitaire Quiz*

5. RESULTS

Here we first describe participants' demographic data, followed by an analysis of how often they played digital games in general and the number of times they played each of our games during the study. We then present our results regarding participants' perceptions of the games' user-friendliness and the usefulness of incorporating learning content into the games.

5.1 Demographic Data

A total of 129 retired seniors took part in the validation of the ergonomics of the three games. This sample included 48 men and 81 women. Respondents were aged 55 to 60 (11%), 61 to 70 (45%), 71 to 80 (42%) and 81 or older (2%). In Quebec, people aged 55 or older are considered seniors (Government of Québec, 2018).

For equipment, respondents used a computer (57%), or a tablet or telephone (43%). Their Internet experience varied: 87% of seniors in the sample surfed the Internet every day, 11% a few times a week and 2% a few times a month.

5.2 Gameplay Frequency

Of the 129 players, 23.7% of seniors played online games a lot, 32.3% moderately, 30.7% a little, and 13.3% never.

During the two months of experimentation, every participant played each of our three games at least twice (Table 1).

Table 1. Number of times each game played by participants

Number of times game was played	*Solitaire Quiz* (percentage of participants)	*Millionaire* (percentage of participants)	*Hit the Target!* (percentage of participants)
2	37.7%	38.1%	29.4%
3-5	56.6%	52.4%	58.8%
6-10	5.7%	9.5%	11.8%

Table 2 shows the distribution of learning themes chosen by participants.

Table 2. Learning themes chosen

Learning theme	Percentage of players choosing the theme
Wealth planning: assets and debts	45%
Death and Estate Management	21%
Use of social assistance measures for home care	18%
Use of tax assistance measures	16%

5.3 Player Perceptions of User-Friendliness

For players' perceptions about navigation, gameplay aids, and educational features of the game environment, all items had positive results (Easy, Easy to understand, In agreement, or Useful), with 84% or more of players choosing each favourable rating (Table 3).

In addition, the vast majority (92.86%) of the participants liked to play the games enhanced with a quiz and 90.48% of the players wished that they could try a new quiz. All participants would recommend the games to others.

Table 3. Participants' perceptions about game navigation, gameplay aids and pedagogical aspects

Category	Item	*Solitaire Quiz* n=53	*Millionaire* n=42	*Hit the Target!* n=34
Navigation in the online game environment	Access: the three areas of the game interface (Easy)	94.3%	97.6%	94.1%
	Screen size and information displayed (In agreement)	92.5%	92.9%	97.1%
	Representativeness of the icons (Easy to understand)	94.3%	88.1%	88.2%
	Superimposition of windows (In agreement)	86.8%	85.7%	91.2%
	Loading time of the pages (In agreement)	84.9%	88.1%	91.2%
	Grouping actions on one page ((In agreement)	96.2%	92.9%	94.1%
Gameplay aids	Written tutorial (Useful)	90.6%	90.5%	88.2%
	Oral tutorial (Useful)	96.2%	92.9%	94.1%
	Rules (Useful)	88.7%	83.3%	82.4%
	Rules (Easy to understand)	92.5%	90.5%	91.2%
Pedagogical aspects	Question type (4-item multiple choice) (Easy to understand)	90.6%	90.5%	88.2%
	Feedback (Easy to understand)	96.2%	95.2%	91.2%
	Reading sheet (Easy to understand)	98.1%	92.9%	94.1%
	Personal notebook (Useful)	94.3%	90.5%	88.2%

6. DISCUSSION

Effective navigation design is crucial to a game's success. With respect to navigation in our game environments, participants considered it more effective to group play actions on a single page rather than to display an overlay window. This agrees with observations by Lopez-Martinez et al. (2011), Whitlock et al. (2011), and Sauvé (2017), that reducing the number of windows and clicks accelerates the pace of the game and promotes player motivation. For an effective game interface, information must be clearly organized and the number of controls limited to only those necessary to accomplish required tasks (Sauvé and Kaufman, 2020). Also, control icons must clearly indicate their associated functions. In addition, Lopez-Martinez et al. (2011) point out that it is essential to design the various game board components to minimize download time. Furthermore, good visibility of the game components in relation to screen size can be enhanced by using an adaptive website, as proposed by Shneiderman et al. (2016).

Regarding gameplay aids, the availability during the game of a help system (with written and audio tutorials) is useful for facilitating seniors' gameplay, as it can be consulted at any time during the game. In addition, clarity of the rules is a key factor in designing a game for seniors. In accordance with Al Mahmud et al. (2012), it is necessary to rewrite the game rules according to the target clientele and to test them when testing the game prototype with a limited sample of the clientele. Our results indicated that players considered the rules in our game useful and easy to understand when outlined in tutorials.

With respect to the games' pedagogical aspects, our participants confirmed that the questions allowed them to assess their knowledge of the games' learning content. Relative to game content, using closed questions facilitated the use of prior knowledge to accumulate points and progress in the game. It is important to analyze the learning content and to break it down into small units of information; this makes it possible to formulate simple questions to avoid cognitive overload in seniors. The players in this study highlighted the usefulness of question feedback for progressing in the game. This agrees with observations by Gerling et al. (2011) and Sauvé and Kaufman (2020), who emphasize the importance of integrating feedback mechanisms that reinforce the results of learning activities. The feedback provided for each incorrectly answered question was seen as especially relevant, since it allowed them to access reading sheets that explained how to deepen their knowledge of the questions' content. The option of grouping reading sheets in a personal notebook was also seen as a plus for our participants, since they did not necessarily want to read during the game but appreciated the opportunity to review the topics later. Finally, the pace of displaying questions on the screen created a good balance between playing and learning for our players, confirming. conclusions of Steinert et al. (2018) and Sun et al. (2017) that gameplay increases older adults' motivation to continue playing and thereby learning.

7. CONCLUSION

Although the results of this research relate to three specific games, they can be applied to different types of games. Our study shows that the design of an educational game must take into account its target audience. To make the game easier for seniors to use, it is important to make sure that the components of the game are visible within the screen, that the grouping of player actions accelerates the game and keeps up players' motivation, and that contextual help is available whenever needed in order to avoid frustration and disinterest.

Our participants showed general interest in these educational games and reported a high degree of satisfaction in playing them, experiencing a different way of learning content relevant to their lives.

While we did obtain positive results on the three dimensions of the study, our results are limited by the small number of respondents (n=129) and the experimentation time (two months). We encourage future research to further examine the possibilities of implementing educational games that target older adults seeking solutions to improving their lives, particularly through social well-being and independent living.

ACKNOWLEDGEMENT

This research study was funded by grants from the Ministry of Economy, Innovation and Energy of Quebec. We would like to thank Alice Ireland for editing the translation and the development team, Patrick Plante, Pierre Olivier Dionne, Jean-Francois Pare and Louis Poulette, for the development of the three games.

REFERENCES

Al Mahmud, A.et al, 2012. Designing with and for older adults: experience from game design, in Zacarais, M. and Oliveira, J.V. (eds.), *Human-computer interaction: The agency perspective.* Berlin: Springer, pp. 111-129.

Astell, A.J., 2013. Technology and fun for a happy old age, in Sixsmith, A. and Gutman, G. (eds.), *Technologies for active aging*. New York: Springer, pp. 169-187.

Barnard, Y. et al., 2013. Learning to use new technologies by older adults: perceived difficulties, experimentation behaviour and usability, *Computers in Human Behaviour*, 29(4), pp. 1715-1724.

Boot, W. et al., 2020. *Designing for older adults. Case studies, methods, and tools.* First edition. Boca Raton: CRC Press.

Chen, X. et al., 2025. The experience of and needs for exergames in older adults with mild cognitive impairment: qualitative interview study, *JMIR Aging 2025,* 13 (Jun 17).

Dajoux, J., 2020. *UI/UX design: 8 éléments de navigation à connaître* [UI/UX design: 8 navigation elements you need to know]. Available at: https://graphiste.com/blog/ui-ux-elements-navigation-a-connaitre..

Diaz-Orueta, U. et al., 2012. What is the key for older people to show interest in playing digital learning games? Initial qualitative findings from the LEAGE Project on a Multicultural European Sample, *Games for Health*, 1(2), pp. 115-123.

Engineering Design Centre, Cambridge University, 2024. *Inclusive design toolkit: what is inclusive design?* Available at https://www.inclusivedesigntoolkit.com/whatis/whatis.html

Fua, K.C. et al., 2013. Designing serious games for elders, *Proceedings of the 8th International Conference on the Foundations of Digital Games* (FDG 2013), Chania, Crete, Greece, 14-17 May. Santa Cruz, CA: Society for the Advancement of the Science of Digital Games (SASDG), pp. 291-297.

Gerling, K.M. et al., 2011. Designing and evaluating digital games for frail elderly persons, *Proceedings of the 8th International Conference on Advances in Computer Entertainment Technology*, Lisbon, 8-11 November. New York: ACM, Article No .62, pp. 1-8.

Government of Québec, 2018. Les aînés du Québec: quelques données récentes [Quebec's seniors: some recent data]. Quebec, Canada: Directorate of Research, Evaluation and Statistics, Ministry of the Family.

Kaiser, W. et al., 2025. Domain-specific evaluation of exergame metrics among older adults with mild neurocognitive disorder: Secondary Analysis of 2 Randomized Controlled Trials, *JMIR Aging 2025*, 13 (May 21).

Kaufman, D. et al, 2020. *Playful aging: digital games for older adults.* Toronto: Age-Well NCE.

Kaufman, D. et al., 2019. Benefits of digital gameplay for older adults: does game type make a difference? *International Journal of Aging Research,* 2(43), pp. 1-14.

Liu, L. et al., 2016. Smart homes and home health monitoring technologies for older adults: a systematic review, *International Journal of Medical Informatics*, 91, pp. 44–59.

López-Martínez, Á. et al., 2011. Game of gifts purchase: computer-based training of executive functions for the elderly, *1st International Conference on Serious Games and Applications for Health (SeGAH)*, Braga, Portugal, 16-18 November. Washington, DC: IEEE Computer Society, pp. 16-18.

Mantell, R. et al., 2025. Evaluating the user experience and usability of game-based cognitive assessments for older people: systematic review, *JMIR Aging 2025*, 8 (June 11).

Marston, H.R., 2014. The future of technology use in the fields of gerontology and gaming, *Generations Review*, 24(2), pp. 8-14.

Morris, M.E. et al., 2014. Smart technologies to enhance social connectedness in older people who live at home, *Australasian Journal on Ageing*, 33(3), pp.142-152.

NN/g Nielsen Norman Group, 2024. *UX design for seniors (ages 65 and older).* Available at https://www.nngroup.com/reports/senior-citizens-on-the-web/

Paez, L.E. and Del Rio, C.Z., 2019. Elderly users and their main challenges usability with mobile applications: a systematic review, *Design, user experience, and usability. Design philosophy and theory*, 8th International Conference, DUXU 2019, Orlando, Florida, USA, 26-31 July. Berlin, Springer-Verlag, pp. 423-438.

Renaud, L. et al., 2018. Évaluation d'un jeu éducatif en ligne pour améliorer la qualité de vie des aînés [Evaluation of an online educational game to improve the quality of life of seniors], *Santé publique*. 30(6), pp. 1-12.

Rogers, W.A. and Mitzner, T.L., 2017. Envisioning the future for older adults: autonomy, health, well-being, and social connectedness with technology support, *Futures*, 87, pp. 133–139.

Sauvé, L. and Kaufman, D., 2020. User-centered design: an effective approach for creating online educational games for seniors, in Lane, H.C., Zvacek, S. and Uhomoibhe, J. (eds.), *12th International Conference, CSEDU 2020, virtual event, May 2–4, 2020, revised selected papers.* Princeton, NJ: Springer., pp. 262-284.

Sauvé, L. et al., 2017. *Validation de l'ergonomie du jeu Solitaire Quiz: une approche centrée sur l'utilisateur* [Validation of the ergonomics of the game Solitaire Quiz: a user-centered approach]. Research Report. Quebec, QC and Burnaby, BC: TÉLUQ and Simon Fraser University.

Sauvé, L., 2010. Les jeux éducatifs efficaces [Effective educational games], in Sauvé, L. and Kaufman, D. (eds.), *Jeux et simulations éducatifs : Études de cas et leçons apprises* [Educational games and simulations: Case studies and lessons learned]. Sainte-Foy, Québec: Presses de l'Université du Québec, pp. 43-72.

Sauvé, L., 2017. Online educational games: guidelines for intergenerational use, in Romero, M. et al. (eds.), *Game-based learning across the lifespan. Cross-generational and age-oriented topics.* Cham, Switzerland: Springer Cham, pp. 29-45.

Shneiderman, B. et al., 2016. *Designing the user interface: strategies for effective human-computer interaction* (6th edition). Boston, MA: Pearson.

Steinert, A. et al., 2018. A wearable-enhanced fitness program for older adults, combining fitness trackers and gamification elements: the pilot study fMOOC@Home, *Sport Sciences for Health*, 14(2), pp. 275-282.

Sun, K. et al, 2017. Gamification on senior citizen's information technology learning: the mediator role of intrinsic motivation, in Zhou J. and Salvendy G. (eds.), *Human aspects of IT for the aged population. Aging, design and user experience* (*ITAP 2017*). Lecture notes in computer science, vol. 10297. Cham, Switzerland: Springer, pp. 461-476.

Whitlock, L.A. et al, 2011. Video game design for older adults: usability observations from an intervention study, *Proceedings of the Human Factors and Ergonomics Society Annual Meeting*, 55(1), pp. 187-191.

TO ANIMATE OR NOT: WEBSITE INTERFACE MICRO ANIMATION AND USER PERCEPTIONS

Lydia Burge and Chyng-Yang Jang
University of Texas at Arlington, Texas, USA

ABSTRACT

Interface micro animations are increasingly used to enhance the user experience on websites. While the positive effects of well-crafted static visual design on user perceptions are well-documented, there is limited research on how these perceptions are influenced by the use of micro animations. This study adopts an experimental design to investigate the impact of interface micro animations on users' perceptions of design quality and their trust in the organization behind the website. Participants were randomly assigned to view one of two versions of an identical hypothetical nonprofit organization website: one version included interface micro animations, while the other did not. An online questionnaire assessed participants' perceptions of website design quality, the distraction caused by micro animations, and trust in the organization. Regression analyses of data from 91 qualified participants revealed that the effect of interface micro animations on perceived design quality was moderated by the perceived animation distraction. Additionally, perceived design quality was found to be a significant predictor of trust in the organization. Implications for designers are discussed.

KEYWORDS

Website Interface Micro Animation, Interface Design, Website Design Quality

1. INTRODUCTION

In recent years, scholars and practitioners in digital design have increasingly recognized animation as a fundamental component of effective website design, comparable in importance to typography, layout, and content organization (Ari, 2025; Martínez et al., 2023; Savoie, 2022). Martínez and colleagues (2023) characterize animation as a "key element" of interfaces and note that its prevalence continues to increase as users encounter animated interactions in routine digital activities (p. 164). Professional design practice has similarly emphasized that animations can direct attention, improve usability, and contribute to more compelling online experiences (Savoie, 2022; UXPin, 2024). Collectively, these perspectives suggest that interface animation is no longer peripheral but central to how users perceive and interact with websites. However, animation was rarely included in prior research of web design. Much of the investigations of online animation studied animated advertisements or other page contents. This study aims to focus on interface animations and contribute to our understanding of this key element of our web experience.

Specifically, this project focuses on interface micro animation -- "small, preferably functional animations that support the user by giving visual feedback and displaying changes clearly" (Boyd & Bond, 2021, p. 2). Micro animations represent a subset of the broader category of interface animations. These task-specific elements are designed to support comprehension, guide behavior, and enhance the overall intuitiveness of an interface. By emulating the responsiveness of physical objects—for instance, a digital button appearing to depress when clicked — micro animations contribute to a more natural and embodied user experience (Boyd & Bond, 2021). Common examples include hover and click responses, animated toggles, scroll-based fade effects, and icons that visually communicate system processes (Reeves, 2019; Joyce, 2018; Alemar, 2021). As these examples suggest, micro animations go beyond ornamental and constitute an important mechanism by which digital interfaces can become more engaging, comprehensible, and user-centered. However, literature on animation-related study also show that animation may increase cognitive load and introduce distraction (Cheung et al., 2017). Building on this dual perspective, the present study investigates the role of micro animations in shaping perceptions of website design quality and user trust.

2. LITERATURE REVIEW AND HYPOTHESES

Studies examining website visual design and user perceptions of website design quality frequently conceptualize design quality as a component of overall website quality. Wells, Valacich, and Hess (2011) identified visual appeal as one of four dimensions of website quality, along with navigability, security, and download delay. Their study found that higher-quality retail websites (e.g., those with greater visual appeal and faster download times) encouraged users to perceive the products offered as being of higher quality. Of particular note is their observation that visual appeal exerted the strongest influence on perceptions of overall website quality. The authors attributed this effect to the fact that visual appeal can be quickly and reliably assessed as soon as a user arrives on a webpage.

Grange and Barki (2020) similarly reported that website design quality—including visual quality, page layout quality, and navigation quality—significantly enhances users' perceptions of both information quality and overall site quality. Likewise, Lorenzo-Romero and colleagues (2013) found that website aesthetics play a key role in shaping users' perceptions of overall design quality and their purchase intentions over time.

Despite these findings, most prior studies have not considered animation as a potential component of website visual design. Only Pengnate and Sarathy (2017) allude to animation, noting multimedia as a design element studied in earlier work (Hong et al., 2004, as cited in Pengnate & Sarathy, 2017).

The use of interface animation has been extensively studied across various types of interfaces, including software and mobile applications (Merz et al., 2016), in-vehicle information systems (Kim et al., 2023), and brain–computer interfaces (Pitt et al., 2022). Prior research has found that well-designed interface animations are associated with positive emotional responses (Fang et al., 2019), reduced cognitive load (Ma et al., 2018), and more favorable perceptions of the interface (Boyd & Bond, 2021). However, animated interfaces can also distract (Kim et al., 2023) or frustrate users (Ma et al., 2018).

Much of the research on website animation, however, has focused on animated banner advertisements (Hong, Cheung, & Thong, 2017). For example, Liu et al (2019) found that animated banner ads, compared to static versions, attract greater user attention more quickly and more frequently. Some research, however, has examined animation within website content itself. Hong et al (2017) found that adding a "water waves" animation (p. 616) to the background of an e-commerce product listing's title increased users' attention to all webpage content, particularly to the product with the animated title. Laroche and colleagues (2022) further reported that animated product images on retail websites elicited greater user pleasure, which in turn fostered more positive attitudes toward the website and stronger purchase intentions. While these studies address animation embedded in content (e.g., product listings), rather than interface animation, they highlight the potential of animation to enhance communicative effectiveness and user engagement.

The use of animation within web interfaces has been promoted in the field for its functional and experiential benefits. Web design professionals pointed out that animation can guide user attention to important content (Savoie, 2022), convey ideas more effectively than text alone (UXPin, 2024), and maintain user engagement through dynamic presentation (Sidkey & Co Inc, 2022). Academic studies corroborate these claims, demonstrating that interface animations can improve provide system feedback in ways that clarify interaction processes (Chevalier et al., 2016). For example, animated transitions can signal changes in state, while button animations can confirm the successful registration of user input, thereby reinforcing the clarity and efficiency of interaction. In their comprehensive review of literature on user interface, user experience, and multimedia design, Martínez et al. (2023) concluded that animation is essential to interface quality and, when applied appropriately, can increase attention to important elements, reduce perceived loading times, and provide valuable feedback to users. Boyd and Bond (2021) examined interface micro interactions specifically, in the context of a mobile application. Comparing animated and static interfaces, they found that animation modestly improved perceived learnability and made the interface more interesting and likable. Based on this literature, we propose:

H1. Incorporating interface micro animations on web pages leads to higher perceived design quality.

However, animation may also negatively affect user experience by increasing mental workload. Research demonstrates that animation can disproportionately capture attentional resources, drawing focus to the animated element while diverting attention from other important content on the page (Cheung et al., 2017). This imbalance may be especially problematic in browsing contexts, where users are exploring broadly rather than searching for a specific target (Hong et al., 2007). In such cases, animation has been shown to impair task performance and reduce perceptions of interface quality. Prior research also showed that decorative or non-essential animations can impose additional cognitive load, distracting users from central information and impairing recall of both textual content and the animations themselves (Pink & Newton, 2020). Collectively, these findings caution against indiscriminate use of animation, as it may hinder comprehension and reduce perceived design quality. These effects may be especially pronounced among users more susceptible to distraction by animated features. Accordingly, we propose:

H2. Perceived distraction of micro animations moderates the effect of micro animations on perceived design quality.

Prior research also establishes a strong connection between website design quality and user trust. Fimberg and Sousa (2020) developed and tested a checklist of design components that foster the user trust essential to e-commerce, emphasizing that visual elements of design are particularly influential in creating positive first impressions that build trust. Pengnate and Sarathy (2017) investigated such impression-based trust in the context of unfamiliar vendor websites, finding that perceived visual appeal not only influenced perceived ease of use but was also a stronger predictor of trust than ease of use itself. They also reported gender differences: for men, both visual appeal and usability contributed to trust, while for women, visual appeal alone was the primary factor. These findings align with earlier studies showing that visual first impressions positively influence perceived website credibility (Robins & Holmes, 2008; Lowry et al., 2014). Based on this body of research, we propose:

H3. Higher perceived website design quality leads to higher trust in the organization the website represents.

However, because prior research has not examined interface micro animation as part of the visual or aesthetic dimension of website design in relation to trust, we further ask:

RQ: What is the effect of incorporating micro animation on users' trust in the organization?

3. METHOD

3.1 Research Design

To investigate the effect of micro animation this study adopts an experiment design. The experiment was conducted asynchronously online. Participants joined at their convenience, which allowed the experiment to occur as part of their ordinary web browsing experience. Upon visiting the project website, participants were randomly assigned to either the control or experiment group. Both groups shared the same instructions and went through the same process. After giving consent, participants were presented with an instructions page, on which they were asked to play the role of local residents interested in volunteering at a local nonprofit that served the community by planting trees. Tree-planting was selected because of its high acceptance (Tyson & Kennedy, 2020). Participants were directed to learn more about the work of tree-planting nonprofits by browsing the homepages of three different hypothetical tree-planting nonprofit organizations. The first two website homepages contained no micro animation. Participants in the control group were then directed to visit a version of the third site that was also without micro animation. Experiment group, on the other hand, visited an animated version of the third site. A total of 11 micro animation effects were implemented in the animated version, include content fading in when being scrolled into view, button growing and changing color on mouse hovering over, and animated number counters.

Several considerations went into the design of the stimuli homepages. The content of all homepages, including text and image content, was pulled and adapted from existing tree-planting nonprofit websites to enhance the authenticity of the sites, with identifying branding such as names, logos, and color schemes changed to avoid the effects of brand recognition.

To ensure participants spent reasonable time and browse each page in full before moving on, participants were directed to browser the homepages for at least 30 seconds and scrolled to the bottom of the page. Only after these requirements were met, clicking on any hyperlink on the page would bring up a pop-up allowing participants to confirm they were finished browsing and to move on to the next site.

On the last website, after completing the browsing requirements, participants were directed to access the volunteer page and complete a sign-up form, in which all contact information fields were pre-filled so participants were not compelled to supply any personally identifying information. The only information participants had to supply for the form were preferred type of volunteer work and availability by day; participants were told on the instructions page to select "Tree Planting" for the type of work and Saturday as the day they were available. After submitting the form, participants were taken to the confirmation page and then automatically redirected to the online survey. They were instructed to think about the last website and its organization when answering the survey questions.

No identifiable information was collected from participants during the research. The research protocol, including all stimuli and survey materials, was approved by the Institutional Review Board in the authors' institution.

3.2 Measures

Perceived website design quality: Three items adapted from Aladwani & Palvia (2002) were used to measure participants' perception of website design quality. Participants were asked to rate their agreements (5-point Likert scale) with the following statements: "The website looks attractive.", "The website looks organized.", and "The website looks professionally designed."

Initial trust in the organization: It measures participants' initial trust in the organization represented in the last stimulus website they visited. Four items were adapted from Jarvenpaa (2000). Participants were asked to rate their agreement on 5-point Likert scales with the following statements: "This organization is trustworthy", "This organization wants to be known as one who keeps promises and commitments.", "It is hard to trust this organization to keep my best interests in mind." (reverse coded), and "This organization's behavior meets my expectations."

Perceived animation distraction: Participants were asked to rate on a 5-point Likert scale how much micro animations bring distraction to the website.

3.3 Data Collection

Participants were recruited via email from a university and a church in north Texas. A total of 91 responses were included in the analyses. Among them 45 viewed the static version and 46 viewed the animated version. Overall, 68% (62) of responses were from female and 32% (29) from males. Respondents' ages range from 18 to 80 with 69% age 30 or younger. The average age of respondents is 30.9 (SD=15.08).

4. DATA ANALYSIS

The means and standard deviations of variables as well as the bivariate correlations are reported in Table 1. The correlation analysis found the perceived Website design quality is positively and significantly associated with trust in organization ($r=0.60$, $p<0.05$). To examine the hypotheses, multiple ordinary least squares hierarchical regression analyses were performed. To account for the moderating effect of perceived animation distraction, an interaction term was created by multiplying perceived animation distraction and website version and entered into the regression models. Both perceived animation distraction and website version variables were centered before the creation of the interaction term. Variable inflation factors were calculated for all variables to assess multicollinearity risks, and they were within acceptable limits (O'brien, 2007).

Table 1. Correlations and Descriptive Statistics (Means and standard deviations on diagonals)

	Age	Gender (Female=1, Male=2)	Website version (Static =1; Animated=2)	Perceived animation distraction	Perceived website design quality	Perceived trust on organization
Age	30.91 (15.08)	.24*	-.15	.01	.07	-.21
Gender		-	.06	-.01	-.05	-.15
Website version			-	.14	.07	.09
Perceived animation distraction				2.32 (.86)	-.20	-.19
Perceived website design quality					3.91 (.87)	.60**
Trust in organization						3.92 (.61)

N = 91; * p<0.05; ** p<0.01;

The first set of regression analyses explore three models predicting perceived website design quality. The results were reported in Table 2. Age and gender were added to the model to control for these two demographic factors. Neither age nor gender was a statistically significant predictor in these models.

To address H1, model 1 include only the website version in addition to the demographic variables. The results show that Model 1 is not statistically significant (F=0.46, p>0.05). Website version is not a statistically significant predictor of perceived website design quality. It indicates that incorporating micro animations does not necessarily enhance users' perception of website design quality. H1 is not supported.

Table 2. Predicting Perceived Website Design Quality

Model	1	2	3
Age	.1	.11	.08
Gender	-.08	-.08	-.07
Website version	.09	.12	.10
Perceived animation distraction		-.22*	.60
Website version * Perceived animation distraction			-.25*
F	.46	1.46	2.39*
R squared	.02	.06	.12
Adjusted R squared	-.02	.02	.07

N = 91; * p<0.05; ** p<0.01;

To address H2, we first entered the perceived animation distraction in Model 2 (Table 2) to test its main effect. While the coefficient of perceived animation distraction shows statistical significance, the whole model does not (F=1.46, p>0.05). We then entered the interaction term in Model 3. The results show that Model 3 is statistically significant (F=2.39, p<0.05). It explains about 7% of the variance of perceived website design quality. The only statistically significant predictor in the model is the interaction between website version and perceived animation distraction (β= -.25, p<.05). H2 is supported.

The moderating effect of perceived animation distraction is illustrated in Figure 1. Among participants who were more prone to animation distractions, the static version was rated as having higher design quality than the animated version. In contrast, participants with lower perceived animation distraction rated the animated version higher in design quality than the static version. In other words, the extent to which micro animations enhanced perceptions of website design quality depended on the degree to which users perceived these animated effects as distracting.

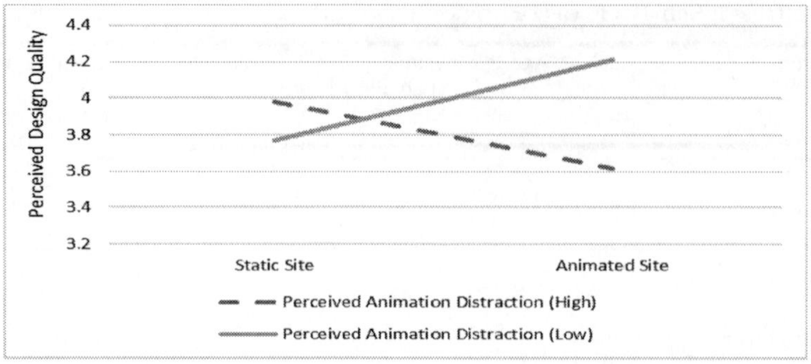

Figure 1. Interaction between website version and perceived animation distraction

To test H3, related variables were entered in three blocks to perform a set of hierachical regression analsysis predicting participants' trust in the organization represented in the last stunulus site. The results of three regression models were reported in Table 3. Model 1 includes age, gender, and website version to test the main effect of embedding micro animation. Model 1 is not statistically significant (F=0.46, p>0.05). The results provide no evidence that incorporating micro animation contributes to trust in the organization directly. Perceived animation distraction and the interaction terms were entered in Model 2, which is statistically significant (F=2.37, p<0.05) and explains 7% of the variance in trust in organization. However, none of the independent variables in this model is a statistically significant predictor. It indicates that collectively the set of independent variables is related to the dependent variable, while no individual item has a strong enough effect on its own. For model 3, perceived website design quality was added in the analysis. The results show that model 3 is statistically significant (F=10.37, p<0.001) and explains 39% of the variance in participants' trust in organization. Model 3 is a much stronger model than model 2 with two statistically significant predictors, age and perceived website design quality. The negative coefficient of age (β= -.22, p<.01) indicates that older participants tended to express lower trust in the organization the last stimulus website represented. The stronger predictor is, however, the perceived website design quality (β= .59, p<.001). The higher design quality participants saw in an organizational website, the more they trust the organization. H3 is supported. No other independent variable in this model, include website version, makes statistically significant contribution to predict the trust in organization. In other words, embedding interface micro animation did not affect user trust directly.

Table 3. Predicting Trust in the Organization

Model	1	2	3
Age	-.17	-.18	-.22**
Gender	-.12	-.11	-.07
Website version	.07	.10	.03
Perceived animation distraction		-.17	-.07
Website version * Perceived animation distraction		-.16	.01
Perceived website design quality			.59***
F	1.79	2.37*	10.37***
R squared	.06	.12	.43
Adjusted R squared	.03	.07	.39

N = 91; * p<0.05; ** p<0.01; *** p<0.001

5. DISCUSSION AND CONCLUSION

This study explored the relationship between interface micro animation, perceived design quality of organizational website, and the initial trust in the organization. Consistent with findings in the literature (Cry et al, 2008, Fimberg & Sousa, 2020), our results also show that perceived website design quality is a statistically significant contributor to the initial trust in the organization represented by the website. Gaining this initial trust can pave the way to user retention (Faisal et al, 2017). One potential way to enhance users' perception of website design quality is to incorporate interface micro animations. However, our results do not support a direct main effect of interface micro animation on design quality perception. Instead, data show that the effect of adding micro animations varies depending on how participants saw these micro animations. Participants' perception of animation distraction moderates the effect of micro animation on perceived website design quality. Among participants who tend not to see animation effects as distractions, the animated version of the stimulus site did receive higher design quality rating than the static version.

Overall, the regression model explains 7% of the website quality perception variance. This result indicates that the interaction between website version and perceived animation distraction is a small but statistically significant factor in shaping visitors' impression on website design quality. This result suggests a more cautious approach in implementing micro animations in websites. Designers should avoid micro animation effects being perceived as distractions. This concern could be integrated in the usability test plan when micro animation effects are included in the design. Additionally, designers may consider incorporating a non-animated version as an option to better accommodate different audiences.

Martínez et al (2023) also observed that implementation of interface animation, rather than being based on a specific methodology, tends to be instead based on "the individual empirical experience of the creators, and without any a priori guarantee of usefulness or success" (p. 164). This points to a need for research inquiring as to what variables influence the effectiveness (or lack thereof) of interface animations. The present study is one step towards strengthen our understanding of the relationship between interface micro animation and user perceptions.

One limitation of this study was the lack of variety of participant tasks. In our experiment, participants were directed to browse and complete a sign-up form. The effect of micro animations on user perceptions may be different when users conduct different types of tasks. Another limitation is the lack of differentiation in interface micro animations. Multiple micros animations for different purposes such as attention-calling and transition, were embedded in the stimulus site. Therefore, the data could not differentiate the effects of different types of micro animations. Future research may explore further on the effects of interface micro animation by studying different types of user tasks and interface micro animations.

REFERENCES

Aladwani, A.M., & Palvia, P., (2002). Developing and Validating an Instrument for Measuring User-Perceived Web Quality. *Information & Management,* Vol. 39, pp. 467-476.

Alemar, S., (2021). How to Work Micro-animations into Your Websites. https://blog.duda.co/how-to-work-micro-animations-into-your-websites (Accessed 1 September 2025)

Ari, E.S., (2025). Cognitive Effect of Product-based Animation on Interface Aesthetics of Web-based Stores. Entertainment Computing, 52, p.100895.

Boyd, K., & Bond, R. (2021). Can Micro Interactions in User Interfaces Affect Their Perceived Usability? *ECCE '21: Proceedings of the 32nd European Conference on Cognitive Ergonomics,* Article No.: 40. https://doi.org/10.1145/3452853.3452865

Cheung, M. Y. M. et al, (2017). Effects of Animation on Attentional Resources of Online Consumers. *Journal of the Association for Information Systems*, Vol. 18, No. 8, pp. 605-632.

Chevalier, F. et al (2016). Animations 25 years later: New roles and opportunities. *AVI '16: Proceedings of the International Working Conference on Advanced Visual Interfaces*, pp. 280-287. https://doi.org/10.1145/2909132.2909255

Cyr, D. et al. (2008). Web Site Design, Trust, Satisfaction and e-loyalty: The Indian Experience. *Online Information Review*, Vol. 32, No. 6, pp 773-790. https://doi.org/10.1108/14684520810923935

Faisal, C. M. N. et al, (2017). Web Design Attributes in Building User Trust, Satisfaction, and Loyalty for a High Uncertainty Avoidance Culture. in *IEEE Transactions on Human-Machine Systems*, vol. 47, no. 6, pp. 847-859, doi: 10.1109/THMS.2016.2620901.

Fang, Y.M., Chun, L. and Chu, B.C., (2019). Older Adults' Usability and Emotional Reactions Toward Text, Diagram, Image, and Animation Interfaces for Displaying Health Information. *Applied Sciences*, Vol. 9, No.6, p. 1058.

Fimberg. K, Sousa. S, (2020). The Impact of Website Design on Users' Trust. *Proceedings of the 11th Nordic Conference on Human-Computer Interaction: Shaping Experiences, Shaping Society.* Tallinn, Estonia, pp. 1–5.

Go-Global.com, (2025). The Rise of Micro Animations in New Websites. https://www.go-globe.com/rise-of-micro-animations-in-new-websites/ (Accessed 1 September 2025)

Grange C. & Barki H. (2020) The Nature and Role of User Beliefs Regarding a Website's Design Quality. *Journal of Organizational and End User Computing*, Vol. 32, No. 1. DOI: 10.4018/JOEUC.2020010105

Hong, W. et al, (2007). How Do Web Users Respond to Non-banner-ads Animation? The Effects of Task Type and User Experience. *Journal of the American Society for Information Science and Technology*, Vol. 58, No. 10, pp. 1467–1482.

Jarvenpaa, S. L. et al, (2000). Consumer Trust in an Internet store. *Information Technology and Management*, Vol. 1, No. 1-2, pp 45-71.

Joyce, A., (2018). Microinteractions in User Experience. https://www.nngroup.com/articles/microinteractions/ (Accessed 1 September 2025)

Kim, G.Y., Kim, S.R., Kim, M.J., Shim, J.M. and Ji, Y.G., (2023). Effects of Animated Screen Transition in In-vehicle Infotainment Systems: Perceived Duration, Delay Time, and Satisfaction. *International Journal of Human–Computer Interaction*, Vol. 39, No. 1, pp. 203-216.

Laroche, M. et al, (2022). An Investigation into Online Atmospherics: The Effect of Animated Images on Emotions, Cognition, and Purchase Intentions. *Journal of Retailing and Consumer Services*, Vol. 64.

Liu, W. et al, (2019). The Effect of Webpage Complexity and Banner Animation on Banner Effectiveness in a Free Browsing Task. *International Journal of Human-Computer Interaction*, Vol. 35, No. 13, pp. 1192-1202.

Lorenzo-Romero, C. et al, (2013). Web Aesthetics Effects on User Decisions: Impact of Exposure Length on Website Quality Perceptions and Buying Intentions. *Journal of Internet Commerce*, Vol. 12, No. 1, pp. 76-105.

Lowry, P. B. et al, (2014). A Picture is Worth a Thousand Words: Source Credibility Theory Applied to Logo and Website Design for Heightened Credibility and Consumer Trust. *International Journal of Human-Computer Interaction*, Vol. 30, No. 1, pp. 63-93.

Ma, J., Chen, C.C. and Lin, Y.C., (2018), April. Emotional and Cognitive Assessment of Use of Functional Animation. In *Proceedings of the International Conference on Machine Vision and Applications*, pp. 61-65.

Martínez, M. E. A. et al, (2023). Understanding the Importance of Animation in Human-computer Interfaces and Its Relation to User Experience. *IVSP '23: Proceedings of the 2023 5th International Conference on Image, Video and Signal Processing*, 164-171. https://doi.org/10.1145/3591156.3591180

Merz, B., Tuch, A.N. and Opwis, K., (2016), May. Perceived User Experience of Animated Transitions in Mobile User Interfaces. In *Proceedings of the 2016 CHI Conference*, pp. 3152-3158.

O'brien, R.M., (2007). A Caution Regarding Rules of Thumb for Variance Inflation Factors. *In Quality and Quantity*. 41(5): p. 673-690.

Pengnate, S. F., & Sarathy, R., (2017). An Experimental Envestigation of the Influence of Website Emotional Design Features on Trust in Unfamiliar Online Vendors. *Computers in Human Behavior*, Vol. 67, pp 49-60.

Pink, A & Newton, P. M. (2020) Decorative Animations Impair Recall and Are a Source of Extraneous Cognitive Load. *Generalizable Education Research*, Vol. 44, pp 376–382.

Pitt, K. M., Cole, Z. J., & Zosky, J., (2022). Applying Functional Animation to Pictorial Symbols for Supporting P300–Brain–Computer Interface Access to Augmentative and Alternative Communication Devices by Children. *International Journal of Human–Computer Interaction*, Vol. 40, No. 3, pp. 667–679.

Reeves, D., (2019). How to Make Your Micro Animations More Engaging. *Fyresite*. https://www.fyresite.com/how-to-make-your-micro-animations-more-engaging/ (Accessed 1 September 2025)

Robins, D., & Holmes, J., (2008). Aesthetics and Credibility in Web Site Design. *Information Processing & Management*, Vol. 44, No. 1, pp 386-399.

Savoie, L., (2022). The Impact of Website Animations in 2022: The Hows and Yhys. *LinkedIn*. https://www.linkedin.com/pulse/impact-website-animations-2022-hows-whys-louise-savoie/ (Accessed 1 September 2025)

Sidkey & Co Inc., (2022). Micro-animations—A New Trend in Web Design. https://www.sidkey.co/blog/micro-animation

Tyson, A., & Kennedy, B., (2020). Two-thirds of Americans Think Government Should Do More on Climate. https://www.pewresearch.org/science/2020/06/23/two-thirds-of-americans-think-government-should-do-more-on-climate/ (Accessed 1 September 2025)

UXPin, (2024). UI Animation—All you Need to Know and Examples. *Studio*. https://www.uxpin.com/studio/blog/ui-animation-examples/ (Accessed 1 September 2025)

Wells, J. D. et al, (2011). What Signal Are You Sending? How Website Quality Influences Perceptions of Product Quality and Purchase Intentions. *MIS Quarterly*, Vol. 35, No. 2, pp. 373-396.

MUSEEPAL: AN AI-POWERED CULTURAL GUIDE FOR MUSEUMS (THE CASE OF THE GRAND EGYPTIAN MUSEUM)

Ahmed M. H. Abdelfattah[1] and David George Atef[2]
[1]*Math. Dept., Faculty of Science, Ain Shams University, and Faculty of MET, GUC, Egypt*
[2]*Faculty of Media Engineering & Technology, German University in Cairo (GUC), Egypt*

ABSTRACT

MuseePal is a mobile-based AI-powered tour guide designed to enrich the museum experience by combining real-time image recognition with conversational retrieval-augmented generation (RAG). Focusing on lesser-known artifacts at the Grand Egyptian Museum, the system addresses gaps left by generic large language models. It leverages YOLOv12 for artifact detection and integrates Gemini through a RAG pipeline to deliver precise, contextually relevant historical responses. This paper is organized around the problem motivation, dataset collection, YOLOv12 training, RAG integration, voice interaction pipeline, backend architecture, mobile implementation, system evaluation, and future development roadmap.

KEYWORDS

Retrieval-Augmented Generation (RAG), AI Tour Guide, Museum Informatics, Multimodal Interaction, Cultural Heritage

1. INTRODUCTION

Museums are among the most visited cultural venues worldwide, offering a valuable opportunity to engage with history, art, and culture (American Alliance of Museums, 2022). However, self-guided visits often feel limited, as most artifacts are accompanied only by brief, generic plaques that lack depth and personalization (Falk & Dierking, 2018). This challenge is magnified in vast institutions like the Grand Egyptian Museum (GEM), which houses over 100,000 artifacts, making it impossible for visitors to receive detailed information on every piece.

Although guided tours offer more context, they can be costly, rigid, or uncomfortable for visitors with language barriers or social anxiety. They are also prone to information overload and what is known as "museum fatigue," a phenomenon where visitors become mentally and physically drained due to the volume and density of content, resulting in poor focus and minimal retention (Bown, 2020, Davey, 2005). Additionally, tour quality can vary significantly depending on the guide, with studies showing that inconsistent delivery and engagement often lead to underwhelming visitor experiences (Andelkovic & Kovacic, 2022).

Moreover, guided tours may overlook certain artifacts that individual visitors find meaningful. Recent advancements in large language models (LLMs) have enabled the generation of real-time, contextual explanations. While these models perform well on widely known topics, they frequently hallucinate or provide vague answers when asked about lesser-known artifacts due to their generic nature and lack of specialization in museum-specific content (Béchard & Ayala, 2024; Ji et al.,2023).

While museums offer access to invaluable cultural heritage, the information provided to self-guided visitors is often limited to brief plaques or expensive guided tours. Existing AI tools, including LLMs, can provide contextual explanations but are prone to hallucinations when queried about lesser-known artifacts due to insufficient domain-specific data. This creates a gap in delivering accurate, accessible, and personalized museum experiences. The core problem addressed in this paper, as a part of a bigger project, is how to design a system that overcomes the mentioned limitations by combining computer vision and RAG to reliably identify and describe artifacts, even those not well-documented online, in real-time and in a user-friendly, voice-based format.

MuseePal addresses the aforementioned gap by combining LLMs with computer vision, custom datasets, and a retrieval-augmented generation (RAG) framework (Karpukhin et al., 2020; Lewis et al., 2020; Wang et al., 2023). Rather than replacing LLMs, it enhances them to deliver accurate, real-time responses tailored to underrepresented museum content (Figure 1). This paper outlines the comprehensive development of MuseePal, including the creation of a custom dataset at the Grand Egyptian Museum, YOLOv12-based artifact detection, an LLM-powered RAG pipeline utilizing ChromaDB, and a voice-driven mobile interface that enriches museum experiences with deeper, more accessible cultural context.

2. RELATED WORK

Early attempts to integrate AI into museum experiences focused on Visual Question Answering (vQA), enabling visitors to ask questions about cultural artifacts and receive contextual responses. Bongini et al. (2020) pioneered this approach by applying vQA pipelines to cultural heritage images, demonstrating the potential for AI-driven interpretive systems. More recently, the VISCOUNTH dataset (Becattini et al., 2023) expanded this direction, introducing a multilingual dataset of over 500K cultural assets and 6.5M QA pairs to improve robustness and inclusivity in vQA for heritage contexts. These works establish a foundation that MuseePal builds upon by shifting from static image–text matching toward real-time detection and retrieval-augmented explanations.

Virtual tour systems have leveraged AI to enrich cultural experiences outside the physical museum. Wang et al. (2024) introduced VirtuWander, which combines domain-specific large language models (LLMs) with multi-modal interaction for virtual tour guidance. This approach highlights the importance of personalization and conversational adaptability in heritage contexts. Similarly, Xie et al. (2025) proposed MetaDecorator, a framework that augments 360° panoramas with multimodal content, text prompts, and synthesized imagery to generate immersive virtual tours. While these efforts expand access to cultural heritage virtually, MuseePal translates these multimodal strategies into on-site, real-time interactions with physical artifacts.

Beyond simulations, research has begun exploring AI systems that function as virtual human guides in real-world cultural tourism. Zhou and Zhang (2025) discuss the integration of digital twins and virtual humans in a tourism metaverse, emphasizing multimodal interaction and intelligent dialogue systems for cultural product development.

While such approaches focus on immersive environments and digital tourism, MuseePal differentiates itself by applying similar principles of AI-driven guidance directly to museum floor experiences, addressing the specific needs of self-guided visitors at large institutions like the Grand Egyptian Museum.

Datasets like VISCOUNTH (Becattini et al., 2023) provide the scale needed to train robust models but often emphasize breadth across cultural assets rather than deep, site-specific coverage. In contrast, MuseePal creates a custom dataset of Grand Egyptian Museum artifacts, ensuring precision in real-world deployment. By pairing this dataset with retrieval-augmented generation (Lewis et al., 2020; Karpukhin et al., 2020), MuseePal enriches responses with curated museum-specific knowledge, mitigating hallucination issues highlighted in broader LLM research (Ji et al., 2023; Béchard and Ayala, 2024). Taken together, prior research demonstrates the promise of vQA, multimodal virtual tours, and digital twin–based guides, but these approaches remain limited either to simulated environments or generic datasets. MuseePal contributes a novel synthesis: combining real-time artifact detection (YOLOv12), RAG grounded in museum content, and a voice-to-voice pipeline (Whisper → Gemini → Kokoro). This integration addresses gaps in factual reliability, personalization, and accessibility, offering a scalable model for cultural AI assistants in physical museum contexts.

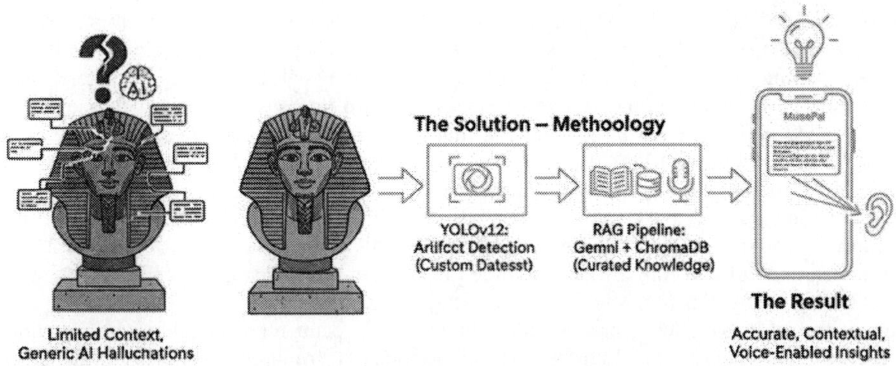

Figure 1. A high-level abstract of MuseePal's design and functionality

3. METHODOLOGY

3.1 Dataset and Model

One of the primary challenges in developing MuseePal is the absence of a publicly available image dataset for the Grand Egyptian Museum (GEM). Unlike many renowned museums with online archives, GEM's collection remains largely undocumented. To overcome this, a custom dataset was created to support artifact detection.

Over 500 photographs were captured during multiple field visits, covering five carefully selected artifact classes that represented both prominent and lesser-known exhibits. Photos were taken from multiple angles and under varied lighting conditions using a high-resolution smartphone camera to simulate real-world usage in the mobile app. After filtering out blurry or duplicate images, the dataset was refined to about 300 high-quality photos.

Each image was manually annotated with bounding boxes using tools like Roboflow and CVAT, with labels mapped to the corresponding artifact classes. To improve model robustness and compensate for the limited dataset size, various augmentation techniques were applied after annotation. These included noise injection, grayscale conversion, shearing, skewing, brightness and contrast variation, and random rotations and flips, expanding the dataset to over 1,500 labeled instances. All images were then uniformly cropped and resized to a fixed resolution of 640×640 pixels, matching the model's input dimensions and ensuring consistency with the image format captured and processed by the mobile application's camera module. This standardized preprocessing step guarantees reliable performance across both live camera input and uploaded photos within the app interface.

For artifact detection, the YOLOv12 (You Only Look Once, version 12) model was selected due to its high speed and accuracy in real-time applications. It features architectural enhancements and single-shot detection, making it well-suited for deployment on mobile devices. The annotated dataset was split into 70% training, 20% testing, and 10% validation sets. After training, the model achieved a mean Average Precision at 0.5 IoU (mAP@0.5) of 99.5%, with a precision of 98.9% and recall of 97.8%, demonstrating strong performance across all artifact classes.

3.2 Retrieval-Augmented Generation (RAG)

Following the implementation of the artifact recognition model, the next critical step in MuseePal's development is to enable the system to generate accurate and context-aware historical descriptions for detected artifacts.

Transformers, the backbone of modern LLMs, are built on three key innovations. First, *self-attention* allows models to focus on relevant tokens in a sequence (e.g., identifying "it" in "The cat sat on the mat, and it was fluffy" as referring to "the cat"). Second, *multi-head attention* enables learning of different relationships by running multiple self-attention mechanisms in parallel. Third, the *context window* defines how many tokens can be processed simultaneously larger windows improve handling of long-range dependencies. Newer models such as GPT-4 support up to 128,000 tokens. Despite these advances, LLMs remain limited to their pretraining data and cannot retrieve external facts unless extended with additional mechanisms.

MuseePal integrates a RAG pipeline (Figure 2), which enriches the LLM's output by incorporating structured external knowledge at runtime. In MuseePal, this process begins with document chunking, where textual descriptions of museum artifacts (sourced from field notes, scanned exhibit labels, and verified web references) are segmented into smaller, semantically meaningful passages. These chunks are then passed through an embedding model to produce high-dimensional vector representations. Each chunk is embedded into a 1024-dimensional space and stored in a local instance of ChromaDB, a high-performance vector database optimized for similarity search.

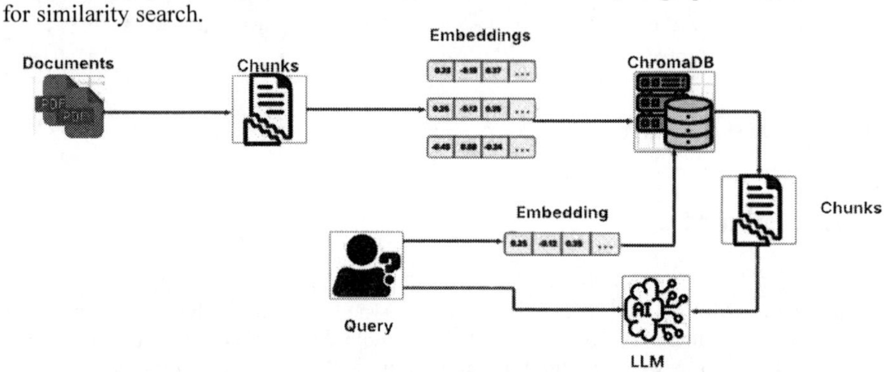

Figure 2. The MuseePal RAG pipeline. Documents are chunked, embedded, and stored in ChromaDB. Queries are matched to relevant chunks and passed to the LLM for response generation

This hybrid architecture allows MuseePal to produce factually accurate explanations even for topics not covered in the LLM's pretraining distribution. Additionally, the use of a local database confers performance and privacy benefits, eliminating the need for external API calls for every user interaction.

Google's Gemini model was selected as the LLM backend due to its strong zero-shot capabilities, large context window, and generous free-tier availability. These attributes made it a cost-effective and accessible choice, particularly well-suited for an open-source and educational deployment, such as MuseePal.

3.3 Speech-to-Speech Interaction

To create a seamless and intuitive user experience, MuseePal was designed to support complete voice-based interaction. Rather than relying on typed queries and text responses, users can speak naturally and receive spoken explanations, effectively simulating a conversation with a knowledgeable human guide.

The first step in this pipeline (Figure 3) involves transcribing the user's spoken input into text. For this task, the system adopts Whisper, an open-source automatic speech recognition (ASR) model developed by OpenAI. Whisper supports multiple languages, offers strong transcription accuracy even in noisy environments, and handles a variety of accents with minimal degradation. These qualities make it particularly well-suited for use in museum settings, where background noise and multilingual visitors are common.

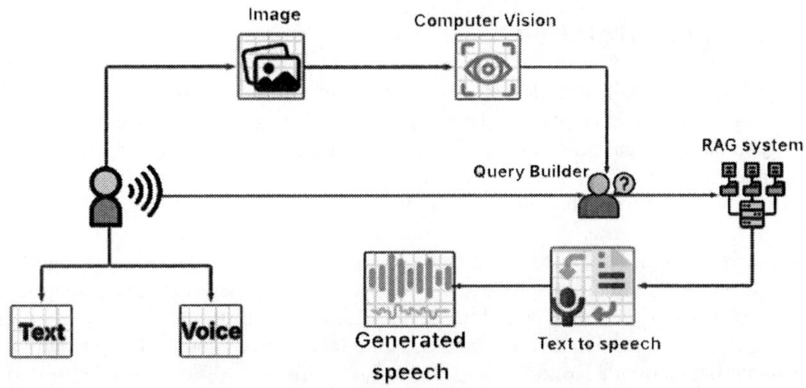

Figure 3. The MuseePal speech-to-speech pipeline. Voice or image input is processed via computer vision and RAG, with responses returned through text-to-speech

Once the user speaks a query, Whisper converts the audio into text. This transcription is then forwarded to the RAG pipeline, where it is embedded and matched against artifact-related content stored in ChromaDB. The most relevant context is retrieved and sent to the LLM, which generates a grounded and informative response. The generated response must be converted back into speech for playback. Initially, MuseePal utilized the native macOS text-to-speech (TTS) system, which offered high-quality audio output during development. However, this solution was not portable and functioned reliably only on the development machine. To overcome the deployment limitations associated with this approach, particularly for mobile platforms and cloud environments, the system transitioned to Kokoro, a Python-based TTS engine. Kokoro provides natural-sounding speech synthesis, is lightweight, and integrates easily across platforms. This enabled MuseePal to maintain consistent audio output regardless of the deployment environment.

In summary, the speech-to-speech interaction pipeline begins when the user speaks into the mobile app's built-in microphone. Whisper transcribes the spoken query into text, which is then processed by the RAG system to retrieve relevant context and generate a response using Gemini. Finally, Kokoro converts the response into natural-sounding speech, which is played back to the user. This end-to-end pipeline significantly improves accessibility and engagement, especially for users who prefer auditory learning or have limited reading abilities. Furthermore, it lays the foundation for future enhancements such as multilingual support and fully interactive, hands-free museum experiences.

3.4 Backend Implementation

During the early development stages of MuseePal, the entire application was built within a single monolithic Python script. This prototype, while functional, lacked the scalability and modularity required for integration with a mobile frontend. To address these limitations, the backend was refactored into a lightweight, API-based architecture using Flask. This design decouples the core logic from the user interface, enabling seamless communication.

The backend now exposes distinct RESTful API endpoints for handling key functionalities:

- **Audio Transcription:** An endpoint receives audio input from the mobile app, transcribes it to text using Whisper, and returns the result.
- **RAG-based Querying:** A second endpoint processes the transcribed text, queries the RAG system to retrieve relevant historical context from ChromaDB, and generates a response with Gemini.
- **Audio Generation:** A final endpoint converts the text response into speech using Kokoro and returns a streamable audio file URL to the frontend for playback.

This modular design ensures that the system is scalable, easy to test, and deployable across various environments, from local machines to cloud infrastructure.

3.5 Mobile App Integration

The mobile frontend of MuseePal was developed using React Native with Expo, selected for its rapid prototyping capabilities and cross-platform support. Initial testing was conducted on a PC simulator, which closely approximated actual performance. However, several challenges emerged during deployment on real devices. Unlike the simulator, physical devices require explicit configuration of camera and microphone permissions, which had to be handled manually to enable voice input and real-time camera-based artifact detection.

Another critical issue involved the text-to-speech output during early testing. Initially, the backend generated and played the audio response locally on the development machine, creating the false impression that sound was being played on the mobile device itself. In reality, the sound was emitted from the laptop hosting the backend. To resolve this, the backend architecture was modified to generate the response audio as a downloadable file using the Kokoro TTS system. The audio file's URL was then sent to the frontend, where the app retrieved, streamed, and played the audio natively on the user's device. After playback, the file is automatically deleted to conserve storage and maintain a clean runtime environment.

Figure 4 depicts a live moment of demonstrating the app being used during a field visit to the Grand Egyptian Museum (GEM).

(A) Live demo of MuseePal while being tested at the Grand Egyptian Museum. *(B) User asks about the statue using MuseePal* *(C) MuseePal responds with historical context*

Figure 4. MuseePal interaction showing real-time statue detection and contextual explanation

4. EVALUATION AND RESULTS

MuseePal was evaluated through a combination of quantitative performance metrics and qualitative user experience testing across its image detection, voice processing, and conversational components. The integrated pipeline included YOLOv12 for artifact detection, Whisper for multilingual speech-to-text transcription, Gemini through a RAG framework with ChromaDB, Kokoro TTS for natural-sounding audio, and a React Native mobile app for deployment on both iOS and Android.

The YOLOv12 model demonstrated strong performance, achieving a mean Average Precision at IoU threshold 0.5 (mAP@0.5) of 99.5%, with a precision of 100% and recall of 97.5% (Table 1). While these results show excellent recognition capability, the near-perfect precision also indicates possible overfitting on the limited dataset, highlighting the need for further validation with larger and more diverse artifact collections.

The RAG component significantly improved contextual accuracy compared to LLM-only responses, while the end-to-end voice pipeline enhanced accessibility for users preferring auditory interaction. Overall, evaluation confirmed the feasibility of MuseePal as a proof-of-concept system, while also identifying the importance of dataset expansion and user studies for broader deployment.

Table 1. Overall Model Performance Metrics

Metric:	*Accuracy*	*Macro Precision*	*Macro Recall*	*Macro F1 Score*	*mAP@0.5*	*mAP@0.5:0.95*
Value:	98.36\%	1.00	0.975	0.987	0.995	~0.84

Table 2. Per-Class Evaluation Metrics (Actual Results)

Class	*TP*	*FP*	*FN*	*Precision*	*Recall*	*F1 Score*
Seated Statue of King Amenhotep III	9	0	0	1.00	1.00	1.00
Standing Statue of King Thutmose III	15	0	0	1.00	1.00	1.00
Statue Head of King Akhenaten	12	0	0	1.00	1.00	1.00
Statue of King Sety II Holding Standards	17	0	0	1.00	1.00	1.00
Statue of Ramesses II	7	1	0	0.875	1.00	0.933
Background	0	0	1	0.00	0.00	0.00

Evaluation curves, such as the F1-score, precision-recall (PR) curve, and confidence threshold plots, showed significant improvement between the 100- and 200-epoch models. Confusion matrices confirmed perfect classification accuracy at 200 epochs, particularly in more challenging artifact classes such as the Statue of Ramesses II. However, the extent of these improvements raised concerns about potential overfitting, suggesting the need for further dataset expansion and model regularization.

The final version of the mobile application successfully integrated real-time camera-based detection, end-to-end voice-to-voice interaction (Whisper → Gemini → Kokoro), and consistent performance across iOS and Android platforms. The user interface was designed for clarity and accessibility, supporting features such as audio replay, image upload, and logging of conversation history. Overall, several key insights emerged from the evaluation process: extensive data augmentation was essential for overcoming the limitations of the small dataset; the RAG pipeline significantly improved response accuracy when compared to LLM-only outputs; and the voice-first interaction model enhanced accessibility and user engagement, particularly for users who prefer auditory learning or face reading challenges.

5. FUTURE WORK AND CONCLUSION

Clearly, MuseePal in its current form serves as a proof of concept. Several areas of development can elevate it into a deployable solution. A key priority is expanding the dataset beyond the current five artifact classes to improve generalization and enable recognition across the full Grand Egyptian Museum collection. On the application side, future enhancements will include user accounts, chat history, artifact bookmarking, and potentially tiered access models tailored to different visitor groups.

The system's architecture also supports cross-museum adaptation. Our vision is not to limit MuseePal to the Grand Egyptian Museum but to extend it to other museums worldwide. By retraining on new datasets, the system can be tailored to diverse cultural institutions, enabling a unified platform that provides artifact-specific guidance across multiple collections. Future iterations will also integrate personalized tour guidance, allowing the system to adapt narratives to user preferences, visit history, or knowledge level. Multilingual support will extend accessibility for international audiences. Finally, we aim to adopt a scalable, type-guided retrieval architecture, where YOLOv12 first classifies artifacts into broad categories (e.g., statues, paintings, weaponry), followed by FAISS-based embedding searches within category-specific database shards. This hierarchical approach will ensure robust performance even at large scale, with tens of thousands of artifacts.

In conclusion, this research introduced MuseePal, an AI-powered assistant that enhances cultural engagement at the Grand Egyptian Museum through real-time artifact recognition and contextual voice-based interaction. Combining YOLOv12, a RAG pipeline with ChromaDB and Gemini, and speech processing via Whisper and Kokoro, the system demonstrated strong performance despite limited data. MuseePal delivers grounded, artifact-specific responses that address gaps left by static exhibition texts and hallucination-prone generic AI models. With further development, it has the potential to become a scalable, intelligent cultural companion capable of transforming how visitors experience museums and their vast historical collections.

REFERENCES

American Alliance of Museums, (2022). *Museum facts & data.* [online] Available at: https://www.aam-us.org/programs/about-museums/museum-facts-data/ .

Andelkovic, Z. and Kovacic. (2022). *Museum tour guide performance: A visitor perspective*. Sustainability, 14(16). MDPI.

Becattini, F., Bongini, P., Bulla, L., Bimbo, A.D., Marinucci, L., Mongiovì, M. and Presutti, V. (2023). VISCOUNTH: a large-scale multilingual visual question answering dataset for cultural heritage. ACM Transactions on Multimedia Computing, Communications and Applications, 19(6), pp.1-20.

Béchard, P. and Ayala, O.M. (2024). *Reducing hallucination in structured outputs via retrieval-augmented generation.* arXiv preprint arXiv:2404.08189.

Beck, K. and Ralph, J. (1994). Patterns Generates Architectures. *Proceedings of European Conference of Object-Oriented Programming.* Bologna, Italy, pp. 139-149.

Bongini, P., Becattini, F., Bagdanov, A.D. and Del Bimbo, A. (2020, November). Visual question answering for cultural heritage. In IOP Conference Series: Materials Science and Engineering (Vol. 949, No. 1, p. 012074). IOP Publishing.

Bown, C. (2020). *How much information is too much on a guided tour?* Thinking Museum Blog. [online] Available at: https://thinkingmuseum.com/how-much-information-is-too-much-on-a-guided-tour

Davey, G. (2005). *What is museum fatigue.* Visitor Studies Today, 8(3), pp.17–21.

Falk, J.H. and Dierking, L.D. (2018). *Learning from museums: Visitor experiences and the making of meaning.* Rowman & Littlefield, Lanham, MD.

Ji, Z. et al. (2023). *Survey of hallucination in natural language generation.* ACM Computing Surveys, 55(12), pp.1–38.

Karpukhin, V. et al. (2020). *Dense passage retrieval for open-domain question answering.* Proceedings of EMNLP (1), Online, pp.6769–6781.

Lewis, P. et al. (2020). *Retrieval-augmented generation for knowledge-intensive NLP tasks.* Advances in Neural Information Processing Systems, 33, pp.9459–9474.

Wang, B. et al. (2023). *Instructretro: Instruction tuning post retrieval-augmented pretraining.* arXiv preprint arXiv:2310.07713.

Wang, Z., Yuan, L.P., Wang, L., Jiang, B. and Zeng, W. (2024, May). Virtuwander: Enhancing multi-modal interaction for virtual tour guidance through large language models. In Proceedings of the 2024 CHI Conference on Human Factors in Computing Systems (pp. 1-20).

Xie, S., Liu, Y., Lee, J.S. and Dong, H. (2025). MetaDecorator: Generating Immersive Virtual Tours through Multimodality. arXiv preprint arXiv:2501.16164.

Zhou, X. & Zhang, M. (2025). Fusion of Virtual Human Guides and Digital Twins in Building a Tourism Metaverse: A Research on Cultural Tourism Product Development Based on Multimodal Interaction and Intelligent Dissemination Paths. *Applied and Computational Engineering*, vol. 163 (Proceedings of the 3rd International Conference on Software Engineering and Machine Learning), pp. 42–48. DOI: 10.54254/2755-2721/2025.24193.

RETHINKING ENGAGEMENT IN AI-DRIVEN ONLINE LEARNING THROUGH HUMAN EMOTION

Waqas Ahmed[1] and Saleh Alwahaishi[1,2]
[1]*IRC for Finance and Digital Economy, KFUPM Business School, King Fahd University of Petroleum & Minerals, Dhahran, Saudi Arabia*
[2]*Department of Information Systems and Operations Management, King Fahd University of Petroleum & Minerals, Dhahran, Saudi Arabia*

ABSTRACT

Artificial intelligence is now embedded in many online learning systems. These systems adapt, decide, and give constant feedback. The key question is how to model learner engagement in such contexts. Conventional studies rely on flat models that assume functional usability or convenience translate directly into engagement. This study contends that such an approach is insufficient and examines an alternative based on the Stimulus–Organism–Response (SOR) framework. External stimuli from the system affect internal states, which then drive behavior. Using PLS-SEM with AI-experienced learners, it contrasts a direct-path model with a mediated model in which motivation and fatigue act as internal mechanisms. Findings show that while flat model approach captures variance, it obscures process. The SOR approach reveals that performance expectancy and self-efficacy enhance motivation, whereas learning anxiety and feedback overload intensify fatigue. Motivation drives engagement; fatigue diminishes it. Significant indirect effects confirm that engagement in AI-mediated learning is psychological before it is behavioral. The study concludes that effective system design requires environments that are not only intelligent but also emotionally and cognitively responsive.

KEYWORDS

AI-Enabled Learning, Learner Engagement, Adaptive Systems, Psychological Modeling, Intelligent Technologies

1. INTRODUCTION

Artificial intelligence (AI) is becoming a core part of how we learn. In modern digital environments, learners interact with systems that adapt in real time. These systems include chatbots, intelligent tutors, recommendation engines, and predictive analytics tools (Chang and Sun, 2024; Yu *et al.*, 2024). They personalize content, provide feedback, and guide learners through complex tasks. AI does not just deliver information. It changes how learning feels, how it unfolds, and how learners stay engaged. As these systems grow more common, one critical issue emerges: how do we understand learner engagement in AI-driven learning environments? Engagement is a key predictor of academic success. It shapes persistence, satisfaction, and learning outcomes. Yet, much of what we know about engagement is based on older models developed before AI became part of mainstream education. Most existing models treat engagement as a simple outcome. They assume that if learners believe a system is useful or easy to use, they will engage with it. This logic is rooted in well-known frameworks like the Technology Acceptance Model (TAM) and the Unified Theory of Acceptance and Use of Technology (UTAUT) (Venkatesh *et al.*, 2003; Lai, 2017). These models possess value. They help us understand general technology adoption. But in AI-enhanced learning, they miss important details.

Recent research suggests that engagement is not only about what learners think of a system. It is also about how they feel while using it. Emotional and cognitive states, like anxiety, fatigue, and motivation, play a major role (Wang *et al.*, 2022; Huang *et al.*, 2023). Learners in AI-supported settings must often manage rapid feedback, adapt to automated decisions, and interpret opaque system logic. These factors create new forms of stress, confusion, and resistance. For example, a learner with high self-efficacy may still disengage if overwhelmed by feedback loops or unsure of how the system makes recommendations (Weng *et al.*, 2024). Similarly, excessive or poorly timed AI-generated feedback may reduce rather than increase engagement (Lipnevich and Panadero, 2021; Li and Han, 2024). These patterns suggest that current models, which assume a direct path from belief to behavior, oversimplify the learner experience in AI environments. This disconnect points to a critical theoretical gap. While most engagement models observe behavior as a final outcome, they fail to account for the internal mechanisms that lead to that behavior. In AI-mediated learning, these internal processes matter. Learners may experience states such as algorithmic fatigue, AI-related anxiety, and decision paralysis (Nie, Sun and Xiong, 2024). These are not just side effects. They are part of the engagement process.

To address this, we propose a different approach. This study compares two engagement models: a flat model and a mediated model based on the Stimulus–Organism–Response (SOR) framework. The flat model reflects the traditional approach. It assumes that constructs like self-efficacy, feedback overload, performance expectancy, and learning anxiety directly predict engagement. This is a linear, belief-driven logic. It aligns with much of the existing information systems literature. In contrast, the SOR framework takes a layered view of behavior. First developed in environmental psychology, and now widely used in behavioral science and human-computer interaction, the SOR model suggests that external stimuli influence internal states, which in turn lead to behavioral responses (Afzal and Crawford, 2022; Fernandes and Oliveira, 2024). In the learning context, the stimulus might be system features or user beliefs. The organismic state refers to cognitive or emotional conditions, such as motivation and fatigue. The response is observable engagement behavior (Wang *et al.*, 2021). This model gives us a way to capture what traditional frameworks overlook. It explains not just what learners do, but why they do it. Particularly when their behavior is shaped by stress, exhaustion, or emotional strain (Cabrera, Bae and DeBusk-Lane, 2023). Constructs such as AI learning motivation and AI fatigue are not incidental. They mediate the relationship between system design and learner action.

To test these ideas, we use Partial Least Squares Structural Equation Modeling (PLS-SEM) and draw on data from AI-experienced learners. Both models use the same core constructs but differ in how those constructs are arranged. By comparing the models, this work aims to assess whether the structure of engagement modeling itself influences what we can explain and predict. The study inference will contribute by showing that engagement is best understood as a mediated process. Psychologically grounded models offer greater explanatory power than flat ones. Moreover, the work will explore that if learning systems are to be truly intelligent, they must not only adapt to user behavior but also respond to emotional and motivational states. This study helps reframe engagement in AI-enhanced learning, not just as something to measure, but as something to understand.

2. RELATED WORK

2.1 SOR Framework in AI Learning

The Stimulus–Organism–Response (SOR) framework has been increasingly applied in human-computer interaction (HCI) and AI-mediated learning environments (Huang, 2023). It posits that behavior is not a direct reaction to environmental stimuli but is shaped by internal psychological states that mediate the relationship between stimulus and response (Mkpojiogu, Okeke-Uzodike and Abdullahi, 2024). In educational contexts, this model offers a useful structure for understanding how learners process AI-generated feedback, adaptive prompts, or system recommendations (Adanyin, 2024). Within this framework, stimuli (S) include both technological features and perceived affordances, such as performance expectations or feedback frequency (Zhang *et al.*, 2021). The organismic (O) component reflects internal states, including fatigue, anxiety, and motivation (Kim, Lee and Jung, 2020), while the response (R) is typically behavioral engagement. This structure aligns with HCI literature that emphasizes user interpretation, emotional state, and contextual fit, rather than treating user behavior as a direct outcome of system design. The SOR model has been used across various digital domains. In education, Zhai, Wang and Ghani (2020) demonstrated how psychological states mediate the effects of knowledge hiding on engagement. Similarly, Zhang et al. (2021) and Pardamean et al. (2021) showed that affective and cognitive factors significantly influence learning satisfaction. Beyond education, SOR has been applied to user experience (UX) studies, including virtual tourism and mobile app use, confirming its value in modeling user behavior in dynamic interaction contexts (Kim et al., 2020; Huang, 2023). These applications consistently reinforce the importance of internal processing mechanisms in understanding system-user behavior.

2.2 Engagement in AI-Supported Learning Environments

Engagement in AI-mediated learning is a multidimensional construct that increasingly reflects interaction with intelligent, adaptive systems rather than with static content or instructors (Chang and Sun, 2024). AI systems personalize instruction, provide real-time feedback, and automate pedagogical decision-making, all of which shift the nature of engagement from simple participation to complex system negotiation (Qazi *et al.*, 2024). As learners interact with autonomous systems capable of tracking behavior and adjusting content, engagement becomes a process shaped by emotional regulation, trust in algorithmic logic, and cognitive adaptation (Xu, Li and Yang, 2024; Nie, Sun and Xiong, 2024). Research highlights how system interactivity and learner autonomy influence engagement patterns. For example, Lipnevich and Panadero (2021) caution that excessive feedback may undermine cognitive autonomy, while Huang et al. (2023a) note that continuous stimulation can cause fatigue and disengagement. These findings point to the inadequacy of flat models that ignore the mediating roles of emotional and motivational states. Instead, they support the SOR perspective, which recognizes engagement as the result of dynamic learner-system interplay, filtered through psychological processing.

2.3 Psychological and Systemic Predictors of AI Engagement

To model engagement behavior in AI-mediated learning environments, this study adopts the Stimulus–Organism–Response (SOR) framework. Rather than treating predictors as operating independently on behavior as shown in Figure 1, SOR captures how external system features (stimuli) influence internal psychological states (organism), which in turn generate engagement (response) as illustrated in Figure 2. This structure supports a layered, behaviorally grounded understanding of how learners interact with intelligent systems. We identify four stimuli (i.e., Performance Expectancy (PE), Technology Self-Efficacy (TSE), Feedback Overload (FO), AI Learning Anxiety (LA)), two organismic mediators (i.e., AI Learning Motivation (LM), AI Fatigue (AF)), and one behavioral response, i.e., Learning Engagement Behavior (LEB). Each component is described below, with hypotheses developed along the stimulus-to-organism and organism-to-response pathways.

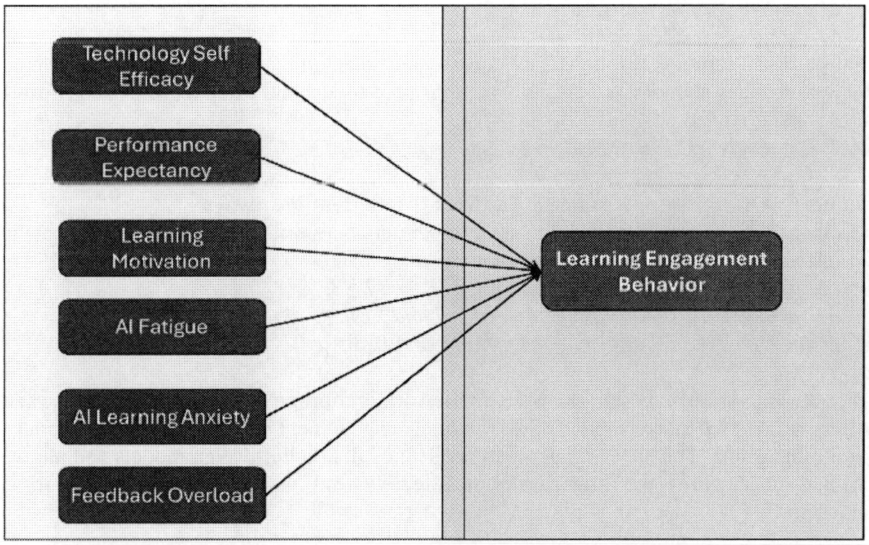

Figure 1. Flat Model

Stimuli → Organism: External System Features Affecting Internal Learner States

Performance Expectancy (PE) reflects learner's belief that using an AI system will enhance academic performance. Widely established in technology acceptance models (Venkatesh et al., 2003), PE shapes how learners appraise system utility. In AI-driven environments, this belief is likely to enhance internal motivation, especially when systems personalize feedback and suggest optimized learning paths.

H1: PE positively influences LM.

Technology Self-Efficacy (TSE) captures learners' confidence in their ability to use AI tools effectively. High self-efficacy has been shown to enhance emotional resilience and task persistence (ZHOUCHEN *et al.*, 2024). In AI-rich contexts, it likely contributes to a stronger motivational foundation.

H2: TSE positively influences LM.

Feedback Overload (FO) refers to perception that AI systems provide excessive or hard-to-process feedback. Although feedback is critical to learning, poorly managed volume or frequency can result in cognitive fatigue and diminished attention (Ye et al., 2024; Lipnevich and Panadero, 2021).

H3: FO positively influences AF.

AI Learning Anxiety (LA) captures emotional discomfort stemming from interaction with complex, opaque, or high-stakes AI systems (Adanyin, 2024). Anxiety may arise from perceived loss of control or unfamiliarity with algorithmic decision-making. This can manifest in avoidance and mental fatigue.

H4: LA positively influences AF.

Organism → Response: Internal States Shaping Engagement Behavior

AI Learning Motivation (LM) represents intrinsic drive to engage with and benefit from AI-mediated learning. Motivated learners show greater persistence and self-regulation, especially when interacting with adaptive or autonomous systems (TRAN and MA, 2024). Motivation acts as a bridge between positive appraisals (PE, TSE) and sustained behavioral engagement.

H5: LM positively influences LEB.

AI Fatigue (AF) captures emotional and cognitive exhaustion resulting from prolonged interaction with AI tools. Fatigue reduces attentional capacity, weakens goal focus, and often leads to behavioral disengagement (Hilty et al., 2022; Huang et al., 2023).

H6: AF negatively influences LEB.

Stimulus → Organism → Response: Indirect (Mediated) Pathways

We further propose that internal states act as mediators between system stimuli and behavioral responses.

H7a: LM mediates the relationship between PE and LEB.
H7b: LM mediates the relationship between TSE and LEB.
H8a: AF mediates the relationship between FO and LEB.
H8b: AF mediates the relationship between LA and LEB.

By structuring variables within the SOR framework and proposing testable hypotheses at each link, this study offers a comprehensive model of AI learning engagement that integrates emotional, cognitive, and behavioral dimensions. This layered approach challenges flat, belief-driven models and aligns with emerging research that underscores the importance of affective and motivational processes in digital learning environments.

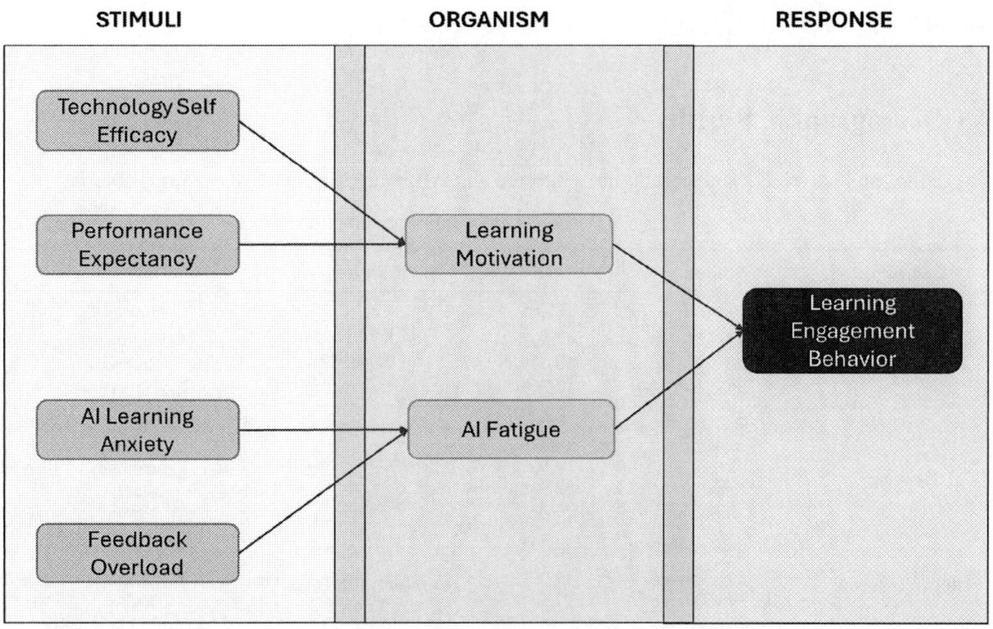

Figure 2. SOR Model

3. METHODOLOGY

This study investigates how structural modeling approaches affect the explanation of learning engagement behavior in AI-supported environments. Two conceptual models were tested: a Flat Model and a SOR Framework Model. The Flat Model as shown in Figure 1 assumes a direct-effect structure in which all six constructs independently predict Learning Engagement Behavior (LEB). This configuration mirrors much of the existing literature in educational technology and user behavior modeling, where engagement is treated as a direct outcome of system-related beliefs and psychological states. In contrast, the SOR Model as shown in Figure 2, is grounded in the SOR framework. Here, performance expectancy and self-efficacy are modeled as stimuli that influence AI learning motivation, while feedback overload and learning anxiety influence AI fatigue. These two internal states (motivation and fatigue) then serve as mediators that determine learners' engagement behavior. The SOR model reflects a more psychologically layered interpretation of behavior, aligning with emerging HCI and AI learning literature that emphasizes affective-motivational processes as essential filters between system stimuli and action.

To test the both model, a cross-sectional, self-administred survey was initiated. Data were obtained as part of a pilot study through an online questionnaire completed by 40 learners already familiar with AI-integrated learning platforms. All survey items of constructs were measured using adapted scales from validated sources and rated on a 5-point Likert scale. Responses were analyzed using Partial Least Squares Structural Equation Modeling (PLS-SEM) via SmartPLS. This tool is appropriate for small sample sizes and complex models. The purpose of this dual-model comparison is twofold: (1) to determine whether the selected psychological and system constructs meaningfully influence engagement, and (2) to assess which structural model, flat or SOR, offers better explanatory power for engagement behavior in AI-mediated learning environments.

4. RESULTS

4.1 Demographic Results

The demographics results reflect a digitally literate and AI-aware sample as shown in Table 1.

Table 1. Respondents demographics

Category	Options	%	Category	Options	%
Age	Under 18	2.50%	AI Tool Usage Frequency	Frequently	32.50%
	18 – 24	47.50%		Occasionally	57.50%
	25 – 34	30.00%		Rarely	7.50%
	35 – 44	17.50%		Never	2.50%
	45 – 54	2.50%	Self-Directed Learning	Very often	40.00%
	55 and above	0.00%		Often	32.50%
Gender	Male	77.50%		Sometimes	25.00%
	Female	22.50%		Rarely	2.50%
Education Level	High School	5.00%		Never	0.00%
	Undergraduate Degree	40.00%	Comfort with Digital Tools	Very comfortable	32.50%
	Master's Degree	35.00%		Comfortable	57.50%
	Doctoral Degree	17.50%		Neutral	10.00%
	Graduate Degree (Other)	2.50%		Uncomfortable / Very uncomfortable	0.00%
Field of Study / Profession	Engineering / Technology	57.50%			
	Social Sciences	10.00%			
	Natural Sciences	0.00%			
	Business / Management	25.00%			
	Arts / Humanities	7.50%			

4.2 Measurement Model

Reliability was established through Cronbach's Alpha and Composite Reliability (CR), with all values exceeding the 0.70 threshold (see Table 2) (Hair, 2021). Cronbach's Alpha ranged from 0.792 to 0.963, indicating strong internal consistency. Average Variance Extracted (AVE) values also met the minimum criterion of 0.50 for all constructs except Learning Engagement Behavior (AVE = 0.490), which was retained due to its high CR (0.851), justifying convergent validity in exploratory research (see Table 2). Discriminant validity was assessed using the Heterotrait-Monotrait (HTMT) ratio. Most HTMT values remained below 0.85, except for the correlation between Performance Expectancy and Technology Self-Efficacy (HTMT = 0.936). This minor deviation was attributed to the small sample size and conceptual overlap. Outer loadings mostly exceeded 0.70, with no indicators below 0.50. Constructs such as AI Fatigue, Feedback Overload, and AI Learning Anxiety demonstrated strong unidimensionality, while some items for Learning Engagement and Performance Expectancy showed moderate but acceptable loadings (see Table 2).

Table 2. Reliability and Validity Results

Construct	Cronbach's Alpha	Composite Reliabilit	AVE	Loadings range
AI Fatigue (AF)	0.934	0.954	0.838	0.807 – 0.951
Feedback Overload (FO)	0.918	0.942	0.803	0.890 – 0.908
AI Learning Anxiety (LA)	0.963	0.968	0.794	0.816 – 0.943
Learning Engagement (LEB)	0.792	0.851	0.490	0.589 – 0.785
AI Learning Motivation (LM)	0.893	0.918	0.652	0.761 – 0.866
Performance Expectancy (PE)	0.851	0.886	0.530	0.551 – 0.821
Technology Self-Efficacy (TSE)	0.832	0.881	0.598	0.697 – 0.818

4.3 Structural Model

The structural model comparison reveals fundamental differences in how engagement is explained across the Flat (Figure 3) and SOR (Figure 4) models. The Flat Model explained 63.7% of the variance in Learning Engagement Behavior, while the SOR Model accounted for 59.2% in engagement, along with 69.0% in AI Fatigue and 66.0% in Learning Motivation as shown in Figure 4. Although both models demonstrate moderate to substantial explanatory power (Hair, 2021) the SOR model provides additional insight into the underlying psychological mechanisms influencing engagement, offering a more detailed behavioral interpretation.

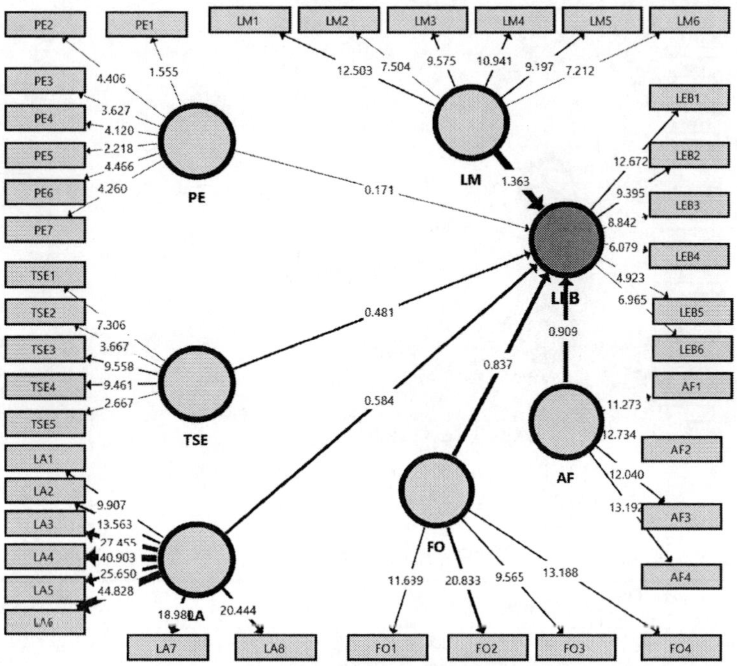

Figure 3. Flat Structural Model

As per Table 3, in the Flat Model, all predictor variables were modeled as direct influences on Learning Engagement Behavior (LEB). However, none of the paths reached statistical significance. AI Learning Motivation ($\beta = 0.405$, $p = 0.087$) showed a weak, marginal effect, while other constructs such as AI Fatigue ($\beta = -0.249$, $p = 0.182$), Feedback Overload, Performance Expectancy, and Technology Self-Efficacy exhibited low and non-significant coefficients. These results suggest that modeling engagement as a direct outcome of cognitive or system perceptions offers limited explanatory insight in AI-mediated learning contexts.

In contrast, SOR Model, which positions internal psychological states as mediators, produced a stronger and more coherent structural explanation. Learning Motivation significantly predicted engagement ($\beta = 0.549$, $p < 0.001$), highlighting its central role as a motivational enabler. Conversely, AI Fatigue negatively and significantly influenced engagement ($\beta = -0.478$, $p < 0.001$), reflecting the disengaging effects of emotional exhaustion in AI-rich environments. At the stimulus level, Learning Anxiety significantly contributed to AI Fatigue ($\beta = 0.597$, $p = 0.001$), while Performance Expectancy ($\beta = 0.597$, $p < 0.001$) and Technology Self-Efficacy ($\beta = 0.252$, $p = 0.049$) significantly enhanced Learning Motivation. These pathways demonstrate how perceptions of system utility and user confidence operate through emotional and cognitive channels rather than directly influencing behavior. Importantly, two indirect effects were statistically significant: Learning Anxiety affected engagement via fatigue ($\beta = -0.285$, $p = 0.010$), and Performance Expectancy influenced engagement via motivation ($\beta = 0.328$, $p = 0.006$). These findings affirm mediating structure proposed by the SOR framework and underscore its theoretical value in capturing the complex interplay between system stimuli, internal states, and learner behavior.

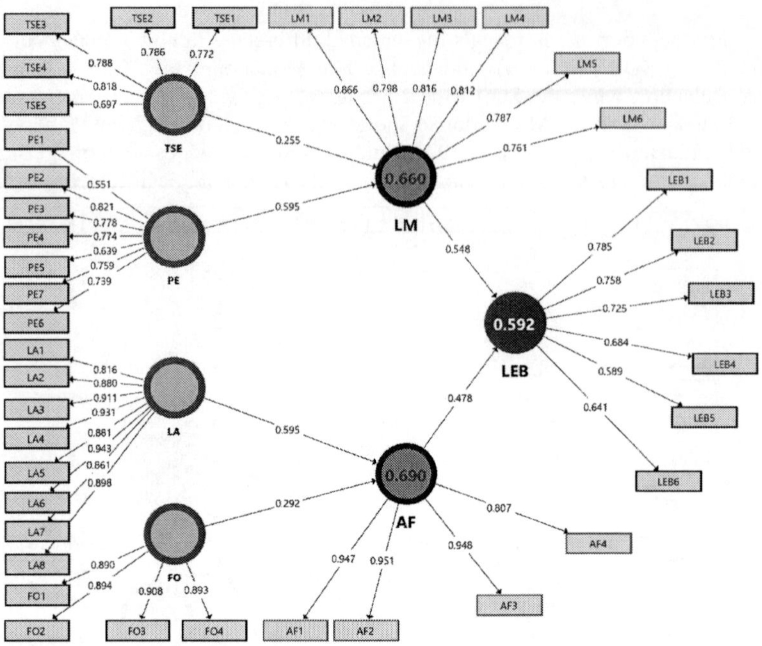

Figure 4. S-O-R Structural Model

Table 3. Path Coefficients and Hypothesis Testing (Flat vs. SOR Model)

Hypothesis	Flat Model β	t-value	p-value	Result	SOR Model β	t-value	p-value	Result
AF → LEB	-0.249	0.909	0.182	Not Sign.	-0.478	3.700	0.000	Significant
FO → LAB	-0.157	0.837	0.201	Not Sign.	–	–	–	–
THE → LEB	-0.154	0.584	0.280	Not Sign.	–	–	–	–
LM → LEB	0.405	1.363	0.087	Not Sign.	0.549	3.985	0.000	Significant
PE → LEB	0.040	0.171	0.432	Not Sign.	–	–	–	–
THIS → LEB	0.128	0.481	0.315	Not Sign.	–	–	–	–
FO → AF	–	–	–	–	0.291	1.400	0.081	Not Significant
LA → AF	–	–	–	–	0.597	3.125	0.001	Significant
PE → LM	–	–	–	–	0.597	3.974	0.000	Significant
TSE → LM	–	–	–	–	0.252	1.660	0.049	Significant
FO → AF → LEB (indirect)	–	–	–	–	-0.139	1.211	0.113	Not Significant
LA → AF → LEB (indirect)	–	–	–	–	-0.285	2.338	0.010	Significant
PE → LM → LEB (indirect)	–	–	–	–	0.328	2.499	0.006	Significant
TSE → LM → LEB (indirect)	–	–	–	–	0.138	1.557	0.060	Not Significant

5. DISCUSSION

This study examined how different ways of modeling engagement can deepen our grasp of learner behaviors in AI-enhanced education. By setting a straightforward flat model beside a psychologically nuanced model framed by Stimulus–Organism–Response (SOR), we identified how choice of model can tilt our interpretation of learner behavior. The flat approach categorized learner beliefs and perceptions of the system as straightforward triggers and expected them to predict engagement directly. Yet, it returned no statistically sturdy links. Learning motivation approached significance, but a key finding was the lack of direct influence from factors like performance expectancy and self-efficacy. This pointed to a theoretical shortcoming: the flat lens may prune the richness of how learners engage with adaptive intelligent systems. These results echo warnings from human-computer interaction and learning science that encourage models sensitive to the subtleties of emotion (Lipnevich and Panadero, 2021; Wang et al., 2022). In contrast, the SOR-informed approach produced a clearer, more nuanced picture. Learning motivation and fatigue from the AI surfaced as important mediating forces, influencing engagement through intertwined cognitive and emotional channels. Additional indirect paths, such as anxiety boosting fatigue and performance expectancy energizing motivation, further illustrated the many in-between processes that learners navigate before taking action.

These findings add weight to idea that when people interact with AI-heavy tools, their level of engagement doesn't hinge solely on what tools can do. Instead, it's shaped by way their minds and feelings react, especially when the automation is deep and feedback is rich. The simpler linear model did account for a little more overall variation in engagement (R^2= 63.7% to 59.2%), but it failed to provide meaningful interpretation of the variance explained in a practical sense. The S-O-R framework, in contrast, not only laid out a solid explanation for engagement itself but also revealed underlying psychological processes influencing learner behavior by accounting for additional variation in fatigue (69.0%) and motivation (66.0%). This makes clear that to really grasp how learners behave, we need to do more than chase high statistics; we must follow the chain of causes that lead to those statistics in the first place.

5.1 Implications for Theory

This study strengthens engagement theory in AI-driven education by highlighting the need for psychological mediation. Instead of focusing only on how leaners perceive tools such as chatbots or adaptive quizzes, the SOR framework reveals that engagement arises from deeper, internal states like motivation, anxiety, and mental fatigue. This insight adds weight to recent arguments that learning analytics should track emotional and cognitive states alongside traditional metrics (Nie, Sun, & Xiong, 2024; Weng et al., 2024). We also confirm necessity of measuring AI-centered constructs, including AI fatigue and learning anxiety, and show that fatigue is a dynamic force that reshapes cognitive load into visible disengagement. This dynamic mirrors the growing discussion of techno-exhaustion in AI-rich settings and strengthens call for engagement models that account for emotional fluctuations (Hilty et al., 2022; Ye et al., 2024). Fundamentally, the study encourages educators and designers to move from one-dimensional technology acceptance models to multi-layered frameworks that consider how leaners self-monitor, interpret AI feedback, and navigate emotional strain. The SOR logic can now be woven into existing areas like self-regulated learning (SRL), affective computing, and the design of intelligent human-system interactions (Li & Gu, 2024; Tran & Ma, 2024).

5.2 Practical Contributions

These findings provide clear paths for building smarter AI tools in education. First, since AI fatigue and learning motivation reliably forecast student outcomes, any adaptive learning platform should now pair emotional signals with clicks, keystrokes, and time-on-task. When programmers only watch for behavior without noticing when leaners feel exhausted, anxious, or suddenly uninterested, they miss a critical chance to help. Future systems should include sensors that recognize when these emotional thresholds are crossed and then adjust accordingly. It can be managed by quietly pausing a barrage of feedback, changing to a lighter activity, or switching from a quiz to a video. A platform like Coursera could, for example, pop up a gentle prompt to set a small, achievable goal, while Duolingo might insert a reflective checkpoint asking how a student feels before they tackle the next lesson. These gentle nudges can keep motivation alive without pushing learner too hard. The results also remind designers that motivation is not achieved by pushing more content or speeding up the next hint. Learners must feel a connection to why a task is worthwhile, a connection that transparent, explainable AI can provide by showing the reasoning behind each prompt. Instead of staring only at flat numbers like "time spent" or "sessions clicked," administrators should merge these with stories, comments, or survey responses to see the whole learner and make numbers meaningful. Helping educators learn to read emotional signals and to weave together human and AI feedback could make learner monitoring more insightful and empathetic. This study also provides a roadmap for HCI designers and AI engineers who are building tomorrow's learning interfaces. A system that can sense and adjust to a leaner's internal state may soon be seen as a hallmark of AI-enhanced education. Moving forward, success will rest not just on algorithms that push for better scores but on those that guide and sustain a student's emotional journey.

5.3 Limitations and Future Research

While findings are promising, several limitations apply. A small sample of AI-experienced learners was used, which restrained generalization and reduced statistical power. A larger sample might yield different results. Additionally, all variables were measured through self-report surveys at a single time point, which restricts insight into real-time behavioral dynamics and raises possibility of common method bias. The model comparison was limited to two structures: flat and SOR. Future research should explore moderated or longitudinal models, cross-platform data, or adaptive system feedback as additional layers. Expanding to diverse contexts across cultures and disciplines is also essential, as emotional engagement with AI may vary substantially based on cultural expectations or academic field. Further research should integrate multi-source data, such as biometric feedback, behavioral logs, or affective analytics, to better understand how fatigue and motivation fluctuate over time. In doing so, future models can evolve into emotion-aware, human-centered architectures for AI learning.

6. CONCLUSION

This study demonstrates that engagement in AI-powered education is not merely behavioral, it is profoundly psychological. Learners interact not only with content, but with autonomous systems that shape emotional and cognitive states. Flat models fail to capture this complexity, while SOR-based structures offer a more realistic and explanatory pathway. The findings emphasize that for AI to truly support learning, it must do more than deliver content; it must recognize fatigue, respond to anxiety, and foster motivation. Emotional intelligence, not just computational efficiency, will define the future of educational AI. As AI systems become increasingly present in learning environments, their success will not hinge solely on speed or accuracy, but on their ability to be human-centered, affect-sensitive, and pedagogically humble. Engagement, in this paradigm, is not a number to optimize, but a process to understand.

ACKNOWLEDGEMENT

This publication is based upon work supported by King Fahd University of Petroleum & Minerals. Authors at KFUPM acknowledge the Interdisciplinary Research Center for Finance and Digital Economy (IRC-FDE) for the support received under Grant no. INFE2407.

REFERENCES

Adanyin, A. (2024). 'AI-Driven Feedback Loops in Digital Technologies: Psychological Impacts on User Behaviour and Well-Being'. Available at: http://arxiv.org/abs/2411.09706.

Afzal, F. and Crawford, L. (2022). 'Student's perception of engagement in online project management education and its impact on performance: The mediating role of self-motivation', Project Leadership and Society, 3(August). Available at: https://doi.org/10.1016/j.plas.2022.100057.

Cabrera, L., Bae, C. and DeBusk-Lane, M. (2023). 'A mixed methods study of middle students' science motivation and engagement profiles', Learning and Individual Differences, 103(March). Available at: https://doi.org/10.1016/j.lindif.2023.102281.

Chang, W.-L. and Sun, J.C.-Y. (2024). 'Evaluating AI's impact on self-regulated language learning: A systematic review', System, 126, p. 103484. Available at: https://doi.org/10.1016/j.system.2024.103484.

Fernandes, T. and Oliveira, R. (2024). 'Brands as drivers of social media fatigue and its effects on users' disengagement: the perspective of young consumers', Young Consumers, 25(5), pp. 625–644. Available at: https://doi.org/10.1108/YC-09-2023-1873.

Hair, J.F. (2021). 'Next-generation prediction metrics for composite-based PLS-SEM', Industrial Management and Data Systems, 121(1), pp. 5–11. Available at: https://doi.org/10.1108/IMDS-08-2020-0505.

Huang, L. et al. (2023). 'Enabling and Inhibiting Factors of the Continuous Use of Mobile Short Video APP: Satisfaction and Fatigue as Mediating Variables Respectively', Psychology Research and Behavior Management, Volume 16, pp. 3001–3017. Available at: https://doi.org/10.2147/PRBM.S411337.

Huang, T. (2023). 'Using SOR framework to explore the driving factors of older adults smartphone use behavior', Humanities and Social Sciences Communications, 10(1), p. 690. Available at: https://doi.org/10.1057/s41599-023-02221-9.

Lai, P. (2017). 'The Literature Review of Technology Adoption Models and Theories for the Novelty Technology', Journal of Information Systems and Technology Management, 14(1), pp. 21–38. Available at: https://doi.org/10.4301/S1807-17752017000100002.

Li, F. and Han, Y. (2024). 'The influences of international master's students' feedback seeking behaviour on their feedback literacy and feedback contexts: An ecological perspective', Journal of English for Academic Purposes, 71(July). Available at: https://doi.org/10.1016/j.jeap.2024.101424.

Lipnevich, A.A. and Panadero, E. (2021). 'A Review of Feedback Models and Theories: Descriptions, Definitions, and Conclusions', Frontiers in Education, 6. Available at: https://doi.org/10.3389/feduc.2021.720195.

Mkpojiogu, E.O.C., Okeke-Uzodike, O.E. and Abdullahi, M.J. (2024). 'Explaining the Applicability of the Stimuli-Organism-Response (SOR) Framework in UX Processes for Static and Dynamic Contexts', in 2024 IEEE International Conference on Interdisciplinary Approaches in Technology and Management for Social Innovation (IATMSI). IEEE, pp. 1–6. Available at: https://doi.org/10.1109/IATMSI60426.2024.10502743.

Nie, Y., Sun, B. and Xiong, F. (2024). 'Motivation and self-regulated learning profiles: A person-centered perspective of English learning and achievement in an Asia context', System, 125(August). Available at: https://doi.org/10.1016/j.system.2024.103448.

Qazi, S. et al. (2024). 'AI-Driven Learning Management Systems: Modern Developments, Challenges and Future Trends during the Age of ChatGPT', Computers, Materials & Continua, 80(2), pp. 3289–3314. Available at: https://doi.org/10.32604/cmc.2024.048893.

Tran, T.T.T. and MA, Q. (2024). 'Online peer feedback training based on self-regulated learning in english as a foreign language writing: Perceived usefulness and students' engagement', Studies in Educational Evaluation, 83(October), p. 101418. Available at: https://doi.org/10.1016/j.stueduc.2024.101418.

Venkatesh, V. et al. (2003). 'User Acceptance of Information Technology: Toward a Unified View', MIS Quarterly, 27(3), pp. 425–478. Available at: http://www.jstor.org/stable/30036540.

Wang, J. et al. (2021). 'A two-factor theoretical model of social media discontinuance: role of regret, inertia, and their antecedents', Information Technology & People, 34(1), pp. 1–24. Available at: https://doi.org/10.1108/ITP-10-2018-0483.

Wang, Y.M. et al. (2022). 'What drives students' AI learning behavior: a perspective of AI anxiety', Interactive Learning Environments [Preprint]. Available at: https://doi.org/10.1080/10494820.2022.2153147.

Weng, X. et al. (2024). 'Personality traits for self-regulated learning with generative artificial intelligence: The case of ChatGPT', Computers and Education: Artificial Intelligence, 7(October). Available at: https://doi.org/10.1016/j.caeai.2024.100315.

Yu, J. et al. (2024). 'From MOOC to MAIC: Reshaping Online Teaching and Learning through LLM-driven Agents'. Available at: http://arxiv.org/abs/2409.03512.

Zhai, X., Wang, M. and Ghani, U. (2020). 'The SOR (stimulus-organism-response) paradigm in online learning: an empirical study of students' knowledge hiding perceptions', Interactive Learning Environments, 28(5), pp. 586–601. Available at: https://doi.org/10.1080/10494820.2019.1696841.

Zhang, G. et al. (2021).'Understanding the Impact of the Psychological Cognitive Process on Student Learning Satisfaction: Combination of the Social Cognitive Career Theory and SOR Model', Frontiers in Psychology, 12. Available at: https://doi.org/10.3389/fpsyg.2021.712323.

Zhouchen, Y.B. et al. (2024). 'Impact of professional identity on learner well-being of undergraduate nursing students of "double tops" universities: Mediating effect of self-regulated learning', Nurse Education Today. Available at: https://doi.org/10.1016/j.nedt.2024.106382.

EARLY WARNING OF HYPOGLYCEMIA VIA SENSOR-AGNOSTIC MACHINE LEARNING: A CLINICAL APP DESIGN FOR TYPE 1 DIABETES

Florian Grensing, Beyza Cinar and Maria Maleshkova
Helmut-Schmidt-University, Germany

ABSTRACT

Type 1 diabetes is an incurable chronic disease with an increasing incidence, especially in highly developed countries. The main challenge in living with type 1 diabetes is blood glucose management, which requires lifelong insulin treatment, dietary adjustments as well as placing restrictions on physical activities. Incorrect insulin dosages or errors in diet and physical activity can lead blood glucose levels to drop too far, causing hypoglycemia, a severe health risk.
In this work we introduce our framework and proof of concept app DiApp, to assist patients with diabetes in managing their blood sugar levels. It does this by merging data from blood glucose and heart rate sensors and using this data to offer an early detection of hypoglycemia. If hypoglycemia is detected to occur in the near future, action recommendations, such as resting and eating carbohydrate-rich food, are suggested as appropriate.
This developed proof-of-concept app, DiApp, uses the Apple Health interface to collect sensor data, as this interface is implemented by a wide variety of commercially available sensors. While this implementation still has some limitations, it is capable of evaluating the data from different sensors, and alerting users if hypoglycemia is predicted to occur.
In the future, we aim to implement specific glucose and heart rate sensors interfaces and conduct a clinical trial with real patients to investigate how effective the app is at reducing unhealthy glucose levels.

KEYWORDS

App Development, Diabetes, Diabetes Self-Management, Hypoglycemia Prediction, Personalized Healthcare, Wearable Health Devices

1. INTRODUCTION

Diabetes mellitus is a major global health issue, having affected 830 million individuals of all age groups globally in 2022 (World Health Organization, 2024). It is a chronic disease with a rising prevalence, expected to affect up to 1.3 billion in 2050 (GBD 2021 Diabetes Collaborators, 2023), placing an increased burden on the healthcare system. Generally, three main types of diabetes exist: Type 1 Diabetes is an autoimmune disease characterized by the body's inability to produce sufficient insulin, while type 2 diabetes is driven by a combination of insulin resistance and insulin secretory defects and usually associated with lifestyle factors. A third type, called gestational diabetes, can occur during pregnancy due to hormone imbalances. While all types of diabetes require blood glucose management, this is especially pronounced for patients with type 1 diabetes, who require external insulin for their entire life (World Health Organization, 2024). For this reason, we focus our work on supporting the blood glucose management for patients with type 1 diabetes. This is also important, as type 1 diabetes is often diagnosed during childhood, increasing the difficulty of ensuring adherence to clinical guidelines in general (World Health Organization, 2024).

The critical challenge for managing diabetes is maintaining healthy glucose levels. The two complications that can arise are hypoglycemia and hyperglycemia. Hyperglycemia is defined as having a too high blood sugar of above 180 mg/dL, whereas hypoglycemia is identified by a blood sugar value below 70 mg/DL (Adolfsson et al, 2018). Both of these conditions can be dangerous. While hyperglycemia is more common, its negative effects are often more long-term and it is easier to control by injecting insulin. An over-usage or wrong dosage of insulin can cause hypoglycemia, which can have immediate, potentially life-threatening effects, as well as long term consequences (Trief et al, 2016). Again, this is more relevant for patients with type 1 diabetes, as they rely on external insulin since the diagnosis and their body is unable to regulate it themselves should too much be injected (McCrimmon et al., 2010).

In recent years, insight into blood glucose levels has been improved with the introduction of continuous glucose monitors (CGM). These are sensor devices that are worn for multiple weeks and allow for continuous glucose measurements, typically in 5 minute intervals. While this dramatically improves the insight into the blood glucose of diabetics, issues like hyper- and hypoglycemia still occur, with symptomatic hypoglycemia occurring on average twice a week and severe hypoglycemia occurring with a prevalence of 30-40% and an annual incidence of 1-1.7 episodes per year (McCrimmon et al., 2010).

Preventing hypoglycemia and hyperglycemia requires careful glucose management. Different methods of glucose control have been researched over the years. While insulin therapy remains a cornerstone of glucose control, the importance of lifestyle adjustments should not be ignored. These include primarily diet adjustments and physical exercise. Light physical activities like walking or cycling increase glucose uptake of muscles, lowering the overall blood glucose levels (Colberg et al, 2015). On the other hand, intense physical activity, such as weightlifting, can temporarily raise blood sugar, due to stress and hormones (Colberg et al, 2015). Conversely, not being physically active slows down the decrease of blood glucose (Colberg et al, 2015).

Next to physical activity, diet plays an important role for glycemic control, as food, especially carbohydrates, is the main source of glucose for the body. As such, skipping meals can cause hypoglycemia, if the insulin therapy is not adjusted accordingly. However, this also means that intake of carbohydrate rich food can increase blood glucose, serving as a method of preventing hypoglycemia. It can take years for patients with diabetes to learn how to manage their blood sugar, by for example, eating more before physical activity.

In our work, we aim to assist patients with diabetes in managing their blood sugar. In order to do this, our app predicts if hypoglycemia is likely to occur in the near future. If that is the case, it issues a warning, as well as suggesting suitable action, such as stopping physical activity, or eating carbohydrate-rich food. These predictions are based not only on the current blood glucose levels, but also on additional data, such as heart rate, offering further insights and enhancing prediction strength. This allows the system to react to the condition of the patient, while also accounting for if the patient is currently physically active. With these suggestions, the app can help patients learn to get a better understanding of how to deal with diabetes in the long run, and will reduce the frequency of hypoglycemic events in patients. This is especially important for younger patients who have less experience in managing their glucose levels.

Our work makes the following contributions:

- Needs and requirements analysis
- Propose an architecture for the early detection and intervention of hypoglycemia
- Integration of monitoring multimodal sensor data
- Trained a multimodal machine learning algorithm to determine the upcoming risk of hypoglycemia
- Created a proof of concept app based on the proposed architecture
- Validation of the application

The remainder of this paper is structured as follows: First, the research background and the current state of the art are discussed, to identify research gaps. After this, we perform a requirement analysis, upon which the framework is based. We then describe the methods used for our App development, as well as the implementation. Following this, we the results are presented and discussed, followed by a conclusion and future outlook.

2. RESEARCH BACKGROUND

Over the past years, there has been a growing focus on applying machine learning (ML) to predict hypoglycemia in diabetes patients. These ML models can leverage data from CGMs, insulin delivery records, but also from other variables, such as heart rate, physical activity or even meal intake. In particular for short-term prediction horizons (up to 60 minutes), up to 80% of hypoglycemic events could be predicted.

In recent years, deep learning models, such as recurrent neural networks and long short-term memory networks have increased in popularity.

Next to these models, created by researchers, there is also a growing number of apps, that employ machine learning models to give trend analysis or alarms should certain thresholds be reached. Examples for this include Dexcom Clarity and Medtronic CareLink. While these can already be very useful for patients, they are often proprietary, only functioning with devices from specific companies. They are also only capable of using blood glucose values, and cannot incorporate additional sensor values. This also limits transparency and prevents their use with other open-source research platforms.

However, these models can increase the quality of life of users, as shown by a study by Puhr et al. in 2018 (Puhr et al, 2019). This study analyzed data from patients that transitioned from Dexcom G5 to Dexcom G6. The new Dexcom G6 added an alert if a glucose value below 55 mg/dL is expected in the next 20 minutes. They found that the percentage of time spent below 70, and 55 mg/dL fell significantly with the new system.

Further apps that aid in diabetes management include BlueStar. BlueStar is an app that integrates data from CGMs, medications and lifestyle inputs and uses an AI model to deliver recommendations, as well as calculate bolus insulin dosage. While use of BlueStar is shown to increase time spent in a healthy glucose range by around 15% (Kumbara et al., 2023), it is mainly available in the USA and requires a prescription from a healthcare plan, rather than being publicly available.

Another study from 2023 tested an integrated digital health care platform with overweight patients with type 2 diabetes (Lee et al, 2023). This platform integrated a glucometer, a blood pressure monitor, a body weight scale, and a watch-type pedometer, as well as software for food recognition from photos into a single platform. The platform merged this data and provided some groups with feedback from medical professionals. Use of the platform, both with and without feedback from medical professionals, has aided in both weight loss and decrease in HbA1c to more healthy levels, in comparison to standard diabetes care.

Based on the presented works, it is clear that early warnings can help patients with type 1 diabetes to prevent hypoglycemia. However, most systems are either trained and evaluated on recorded data, or focus only on CGM data. It also becomes clear that experienced diabetics can adjust their behavior based on these warnings. We aim to extend this current state of the art, by designing an app, which merges CGM data with data on physical activity (heart rate) to determine the risk of hypoglycemia and recommend actions. Our aim is to help less experienced patients with type 1 diabetes, especially children and adolescents, learn how to improve their quality of life by reducing the time spent in hypoglycemia.

3. REQUIREMENT ANALYSIS

In order to fill this research gap, a requirement analysis was performed. The requirements were derived by literature review, as well as semi-structured interviews with medical professionals specializing in diabetes care. As the framework will be used by patients with type 1 diabetes, including patients of all ages, this had to be taken into account for the requirement analysis. Requirements can be divided into three categories: clinical requirements, usability requirements and technical requirements.

From a clinical perspective, the primary requirement is the accurate and timely prediction of hypoglycemic events. To ensure that patients have sufficient time to react to hypoglycemic events, these need to be predicted at least 30 minutes in advance. This necessitates the integration of robust machine learning models capable of producing reliable predictions across various input modalities. The suggested actions must also be lifestyle-based, and improve blood glucose management. The system must perform effectively using glucose data alone, as well as when combined with physiological signals such as heart rate, enabling broader use cases and improved prediction accuracy. As the user group includes individuals who may be inexperienced with technology, the app must be intuitive, mobile-friendly, and simple to set up. After the initial setup, the system should operate autonomously and require minimal user interaction. This prevents users from being overburdened, as they adapt to their lifestyle. In terms of technical requirements, it is important, that the framework is open and interoperable. This is important to promote a wider adoption, as well as allowing research reproducibility and future integration with other diabetes management tools. For this reason, it is important for the sensors to be exchangeable depending on the requirements. Besides the sensors, the machine learning models and action suggestions should also be adjustable.

These requirements can be summarized as follows:

- R1: Must be simple to set up and use
- R2: Minimal user interaction required
- R3: Suggestions must be lifestyle-based and improve blood sugar management
- R4: Mobile-friendly
- R5: Integration of different sensors
- R6: Machine learning model must be accurate
- R7: Prediction 30 minutes in advance
- R8: Machine learning models for different combinations of physiological signals
- R9: Interchangeable machine learning models and Action suggestions

4. DESIGN

To realize these requirements, we introduce our framework, as well as our proof-of-concept app DiApp. The framework consists of three main parts: The sensors, the application, and the external data storage and model training, which are explained below. It is designed to allow individual parts to be replaced depending on future needs. This allows it to remain largely independent of specific sensors, machine learning technologies and intervention methods. A schematic for the framework can be seen in Figure 1.

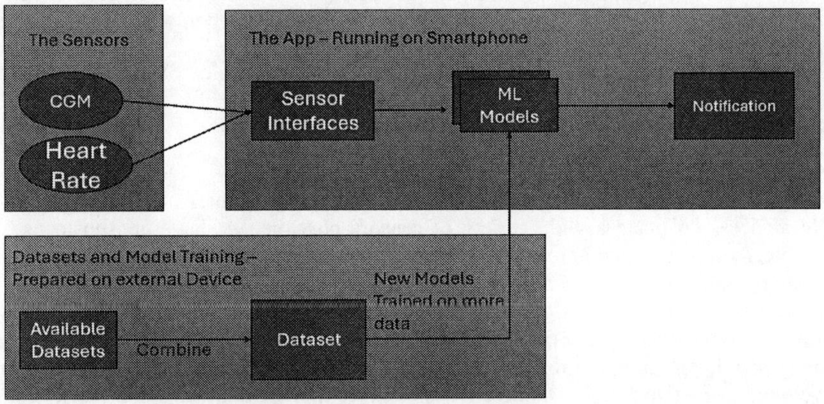

Figure 1. Schematic of the Framework

We have chosen to include two physiological signals, blood glucose and heart rate, for this work. Blood glucose was chosen as it is the most important indicator for hypoglycemia. Heart rate has been chosen as it increases before hypoglycemia (Calcaterra et al, 2021), as well as during physical activity (Fisher et al, 2019). Heart rate data is also available in multiple publicly available datasets of patients with diabetes. In addition, heart rate is measured on most popular smartwatches and fitness trackers, such as the Apple Watch, Fitbit, Garmin and Samsung Galaxy Watch. We have deliberately decided against using insulin or food intake data, as these are usually not available without manual input. We wish to keep the required manual input to a minimum, as this is prone to errors and lowers compliance.

The sensor data is then passed to a machine learning model. Our framework allows for multiple machine learning models to be implemented side by side, using different physiological signals as input. This allows the system to use enhanced prediction when more data, such as heart rate, is available, but provides a fallback solution when this data is not available. For our framework we recommend training the models as classification models, with the classes being based on how far into the future hypoglycemia occurs. The different time ranges should be based on the chosen action suggestions. Here, we suggest at least 1 class to be when hypoglycemia is expected in less than 30 minutes, one for 30-60 minutes, and one hypoglycemia is more than 60 minutes away. Depending on the predicted class, warnings and suggestions can be sent to the user, such as sitting down and eating something when hypoglycemia is less than 30 minutes in the future, or just stopping physical activity when it is 30-60 minutes away. These interventions are chosen, as they are easy for patients to follow and can be learned and integrated into everyday life.

For training these models, a variety of publicly available datasets for type 1 diabetes exist, which are summarized in our previous work (Cinar et al, 2025). However, the types of signals, sampling rate, quality and availability of the datasets varies widely. While blood glucose data is often available, datasets including further physiological signals are less common. While these datasets can serve as a good starting point, the data from different participants can then be collected into a large dataset, to facilitate the training of future models, as well as allowing personalization of models based on the patient data, which can be played back into the app itself.

The final part of the framework is the app itself. The app periodically reads and synchronizes the data from the different sensors. This is done every 5 minutes, as this is the most common sampling frequency of popular CGM devices. Depending on the chosen machine learning model, the preprocessing of the sensor data is also performed and the data is transformed into the required shape. Then the data is passed into the machine learning models and the classification takes place. Depending on the classification outcome, the warning and action suggestions are sent to the user. This notification should be sent not only to the smartphone, but also to wrist-worn wearables when possible, as these are more likely to be looked at during physical activity.

This framework provides a flexible and modular foundation for hypoglycemia prediction and intervention, by combining readily available physiological sensors and adaptable machine learning models, as well as a patient-facing app. By minimizing complexity and the need for manual input, the system aims to maximize usability and compliance, while maintaining robust hypoglycemia prediction. The modularity ensures the system can evolve depending on the patient needs.

5. IMPLEMENTATION OF THE APP

In this section, our proof-of-concept app, DiApp, based on our framework is presented. DiApp is designed for apple devices. To make a wide variety of sensors possible, we have chosen to use Apple Health as a common interface, as most commercially available sensors share this interface. This is only a placeholder in the current app and can be replaced by interfaces for the specific sensors used. This allows a wide variety of sensors and was chosen, as it allows users to keep using the sensors they already own, without needing every sensor to be integrated into the app. This is especially important for the CGM sensors, as they often do have an Apple Health integration, but do not have open interfaces to access the data through other means. DiApp was developed to function in the Apple environment. It was created using the Swift programming language and the XCode editor. The app is designed to run on iPhone 14 or newer, running iOS 18.

Firstly, the program loop and reading of the data need to be handled. While Swift natively offers functions to allow functions to be called periodically, these are not executed while the app is in the background. In order for the app to function in the background, a variety of background modes are possible. These are audio, voice-calls, managing connected devices (via Bluetooth), remote notifications and background fetches, as well as location services (via GPS). For this app, we have implemented location services, as this will allow us to also investigate how much the participants move.

After background modes have been handled, we can begin periodically reading the data. As mentioned earlier, for DiApp, we obtain the sensor data from Apple Health. In order to read the data, we have set up the repeating task, as well as an HKObserverQuery and HKAnchoredObjectQuery for both heart rate and blood glucose. HKObserverQuery and HKAnchoredObjectQuery are parts of Apple's HealthKit framework. HKObserverQuery is called whenever new data for the corresponding data type is available in Apple Health. At that point, the HKAnchoredObjectQuery is used to retrieve all new samples since it was last called. The data is then read and stored locally in the app.

The last three hours of data will be retained by the app. The data will then be interpolated to better fit the target sampling frequency. For the current ML models, 25 samples of heart rate and glucose each, sampled five minutes apart, for two hours in total, are used. Here, a check is performed to see if sufficient data from both sensors is present. If this is the case, the data is passed to the machine learning model that processes both blood glucose and heart rate data. If insufficient heart rate data is present, the model using only glucose data is used. If insufficient glucose data is available, a notification is sent to inform the user that something is wrong.

The machine learning models were trained in a python environment, using the TensorFlow and Keras packages on a separate device. The trained models are then saved in a TensorFlowLite file. They were then copied into the project and the models are loaded when the monitoring is started. For the initial machine learning model, we use a composite dataset named DiaData (Cinar et al, 2025) derived from multiple publicly available sources. It includes a large data subset for only glucose data, and a smaller one containing both glucose and heart rate data. The two subsets were used to train two different models. The model itself is a ResNet model, based on the work of Wang et al. (Wang et al, 2016), but trained on our dataset. We have replaced the 2DCNN layers with 1DCNN layers and included a "He Normal" initialization for each CNN layer. It consists of three ResNet blocks, each consisting of three sequential 1DCNN layers with respective kernel sizes of 8,5 and 3. Batch normalization and a ReLU activation function are leveraged after each convolutional layer. Both machine learning models classified the risk for hypoglycemia into 5 classes, depending on how many minutes in the future the next hypoglycemic event is predicted to occur. These classes are: hypoglycemia currently occurring, occurring in 5-10 minutes, occurring in 15-25 minutes, occurring in 30-55 minutes and no hypoglycemia imminent. For the first three classes, patients are advised to relax, sit down, and eat something. For the fourth class, they are merely advised to stop any physical activity, and for the final class, no suggestion is made. The two models scored an accuracy score of 0.77 and 0.66 respectively, with the accuracy decreasing for classes where hypoglycemia is further in the future.

While the current model including heart rate was only trained on the 51 subjects our dataset that included heart rate, the data collected during app usage can also be exported to create a larger dataset, for training future ML models. For the future, we aim to use the data collected while using the app to train new ML models. Exporting the physiological data can be done either over Apple Health, or directly via the app. Currently, this data is exported only onto the local device, but in the future, a medically certified, secure cloud upload is planned.

After the classification takes place, a local notification is sent, if any intervention is suggested. If the iPhone is unlocked and the app is in the foreground, the notification is displayed on the app itself. If the app is in the background or the iPhone is locked, a regular notification is sent via the operating system. Depending on the system settings, these will also be displayed on external devices like smartwatches. After the classification takes place, a local notification is sent, if any intervention is suggested. If the iPhone is unlocked and the app is in the foreground, the notification is displayed on the app itself. If the app is in the background or the iPhone is locked, a regular notification is sent via the operating system. Depending on the system settings, these will also be displayed on external devices like smartwatches.

The UI of the app is kept simple and intuitive. It consists of a text field, which shows the current risk and recommended action, which is left blank at the start. Above that is a button to enable permissions, allowing the app to read heart rate and blood glucose data from Apple Health, as well as access the location. This button will change its appearance once the permissions have been granted, even if the app is closed and reopened. Next, are two small checkboxes, indicating the availability of heart rate and glucose data. Lastly, there is a toggle button to start and end the monitoring. The UI, after submitting the permissions, is shown in Figure 2.

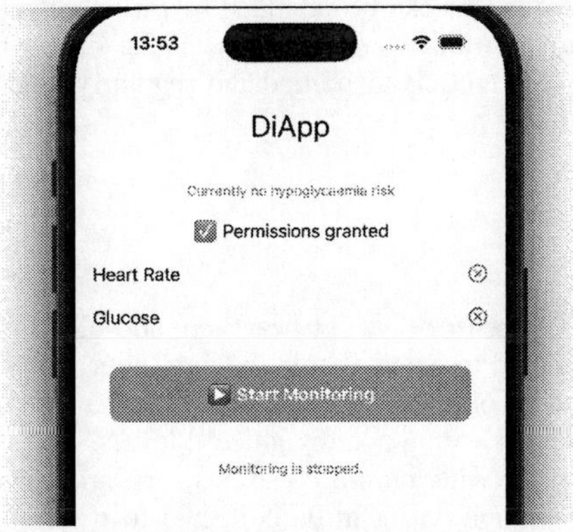

Figure 2. User Interface of DiApp

6. RESULTS

In this paper, we introduced our framework and the corresponding app DiApp. This app integrates heart rate and blood glucose from a wide variety of sensors, over the Apple Health interface. This sensor data is then used to estimate the risk of hypoglycemia, and a non-medical action is recommended to the user if hypoglycemia is likely.

The functionality of the app was tested using two different heart rate sensors and one blood glucose sensor. For heart rate, an Apple Watch Series 8, a Corsano 287-2b wristband were tested. Their sampling frequencies differ, with the Apple Watch sampling heart rate every one to five minutes, with the exception of workouts, during which heart rate is recorded once every one to ten seconds. The Corsano 287-2b sampling frequency can be set to 30 seconds, 1 minute and 5 minutes per sensor. In addition to the heart rate sensors, a Dexcom G6 sensor for blood glucose was tested. This is among the most popular blood glucose sensors that are commercially available, and samples blood glucose once every 5 minutes.

Next to the sampling frequencies, there is also a delay until this data becomes available in Apple Health. This delay is typically five to ten minutes, depending on the sensor. This can add up to 10 minutes to the data availability, which needs to be respected when evaluating the sensor data. For the glucose data however, synchronization between the Dexcom App and Apple Health is delayed by three hours. For this reason the functionality of the app was tested with a three hour delay. While this three hour delay would pose a significant challenge to the hypoglycemia prediction, it allows the rest of the functionality to be tested before implementing interfaces for specific CGM sensors.

At this moment, the functionality of the application was tested with both the three hour delay, as well as manual sensor input. In these tests, the reading of the data, verifying the availability of individual sensor data, as well as the evaluation of both machine learning models (depending on available data) and subsequent notifications functioned without difficulties. Additionally, the app requires minimal setup time, if sensors are already set up and connected to Apple Health. All the user needs to do is start the app and provide it with data access permissions and start the monitoring.

However, during testing, an additional limitation of Apple Health has become apparent, which is that many types of data cannot be read from Apple Health while the iPhone is in a locked state. For this reason, it is important to investigate the availability of interfaces other than Apple Health. While the Apple Watch does not allow access to its sensor data, other than over Apple Health, most other heart rate sensors, including the tested Corsano 287-b wristband have an interface to access this data. For blood glucose sensors on the other hand, data is rarely available in real-time, and most interfaces are only available with a large delay or when cooperating with the manufacturer.

Despite these limitations, the app fulfils all the requirements defined earlier. R1, R2 and R4 are met, as the app runs entirely on iPhone and requires no setup, other than starting the app and granting it the required permissions. R3, requiring the action suggestions to be action and lifestyle based, is satisfied, as the chosen suggestions are resting and eating. Using Apple Health as the sensor interface fulfils R5, as a large variety of sensors implement this interface. R6 and R7 have been achieved by using state of the art machine learning models, trained on large datasets. R8 is fulfilled by training a model for glucose data only, and one including both glucose and heart rate data. This can be extended by further signals as needed in the future. Lastly, R9 is fulfilled, as the machine learning models are stored as TFLite files, which can be replaced by other files with the same name. This will allow models to be updated regularly, and even allow personalized models to be created for each patient.

7. DISCUSSION

Our app allows the merging of sensor data for heart rate and blood glucose, to predict hypoglycemia. Once hypoglycemia has been predicted to occur within the next hour, an action is recommended. Our objective is to use this early warning and recommendation to reduce the length of time patients spend in hypoglycemia, and increase the time they remain within healthy glucose levels.

Our framework is compatible with a multitude of sensors, and can easily be extended with further sensors and sensor types, provided enough data can be collected to train corresponding machine learning models. This additional sensor data increases prediction strength over using only blood glucose, as in the proprietary data models. However, even when the additional sensors are not available, a glucose-only model is available. This offers a meaningful fallback method, as CGM data should be available at all times, except when the CGM sensor is replaced.

The app is easy and intuitive to use and requires minimal setup. This is important, as the app is aimed to be used for patients inexperienced with diabetes, including children. For this reason it is important, that minimal interaction with the app is required, which is why we have refrained from using manual input such as insulin or meal intake.

However, it is important to discuss the current limitations of the app. The main limitation of the app is that it relies on Apple Health as an interface to collect the data from the different sensors. While this has the advantage of allowing a very wide variety of sensors, it requires the device to be unlocked for the data to be read. While keeping the iPhone unlocked is an acceptable limitation for a short term clinical study, for a long-term observation app, it is a hard limitation. While this would not be a problem during times where the smartphone is used regularly (every 30 minutes), this is an issue for times where the smartphone is not used, such as during physical activity or while sleeping.

In order to avoid this limitation, it is possible to access the sensor data directly. This is often possible for the heart rate data, as many smartwatch sensors make APIs available for their sensors. However, for CGM devices, official APIs often require a cooperation of the manufacturer. However, once this is achieved, it would avoid both limitations of Apple Health, the delay of CGM data, and the need for the iPhone to be unlocked. As such, studies employing this framework will need to replace the Apple Health interface with specific sensor interfaces.

8. CONCLUSION

In this work, we present a framework, as well as prototype app, to help patients with type 1 diabetes manage their blood sugar. The focus of our work lies in using not only glucose data, but also data such as heart rate, to improve prediction outcomes. If a hypoglycemia is predicted to occur, actions to prevent it are recommended as needed.

The app was designed to be simple and intuitive, and require as little manual input as possible, to increase compliance and be usable by as many people as possible.

While the current framework is compatible with a wide variety of sensors, obtaining real time data, in particular for blood glucose, remains an issue. In the future we aim to specify the framework for some of the most popular CGM devices, implementing their respective APIs to access the data in real time to improve usability. In addition, we aim to allow an exchange of Data between the app and a secure cloud. This will allow a collection of data to personalize the models, further increasing personalization. Furthermore, we aim to improve the machine learning models and begin a clinical trial with a group of patients with type 1 diabetes, to determine how well the app improves their blood glucose management.

REFERENCES

Adolfsson, P., Rentoul, D., Klinkenbijl, B., & Parkin, C. G. (2018). Hypoglycaemia Remains the Key Obstacle to Optimal Glycaemic Control - Continuous Glucose Monitoring is the Solution. *European endocrinology*, *14*(2), 50–56. https://doi.org/10.17925/EE.2018.14.2.50

Calcaterra, V., Bosoni, P., Sacchi, L., Zuccotti, G. V., Mannarino, S., Bellazzi, R., & Larizza, C. (2020). Continuous Glucose and Heart Rate Monitoring in Young People with Type 1 Diabetes: An Exploratory Study about Perspectives in Nocturnal Hypoglycemia Detection. *Metabolites*, *11*(1), 5. https://doi.org/10.3390/metabo11010005

Cinar, B., & Maleshkova, M. (2025). Presenting DiaData for Research on Type 1 Diabetes. *ArXiv*. https://arxiv.org/abs/2508.09160

Colberg, S. R., Laan, R., Dassau, E., & Kerr, D. (2015). Physical activity and type 1 diabetes: time for a rewire? *Journal of diabetes science and technology*, *9*(3), 609–618. https://doi.org/10.1177/1932296814566231

Fisher, J. P., & Secher, N. H. (2019). Regulation of Heart Rate and Blood Pressure During Exercise in Humans. In J. A. Zoladz (Ed.), *Muscle and Exercise Physiology* (pp. 541-560). Elsevier. https://doi.org/10.1016/B978-0-12-814593-7.00024-4

GBD 2021 Diabetes Collaborators (2023). 'Global, regional, and national burden of diabetes from 1990 to 2021, with projections of prevalence to 2050: a systematic analysis for the global burden of disease study 2021', *The Lancet*, 402(10397), pp. 203–234.

Kumbara, A. B., Iyer, A. K., Green, C. R., Jepson, L. H., Leone, K., Layne, J. E., & Shomali, M. (2023). Impact of a Combined Continuous Glucose Monitoring-Digital Health Solution on Glucose Metrics and Self-Management Behavior for Adults with Type 2 Diabetes: Real-World, Observational Study. *JMIR diabetes*, *8*, e47638. https://doi.org/10.2196/47638

Lee, Y.-B., Kim, G., Jun, J. E., Park, H., Lee, W. J., Hwang, Y.-C., & Kim, J. H. (2023). An integrated digital health care platform for diabetes management with AI-based dietary management: 48-week results from a randomized controlled trial. *Diabetes Care, 46*(5), 959–966. https://doi.org/10.2337/dc22-1929

McCrimmon, R. J., & Sherwin, R. S. (2010). Hypoglycemia in type 1 diabetes. *Diabetes*, *59*(10), 2333–2339. https://doi.org/10.2337/db10-0103

Puhr, S., Derdzinski, M., Welsh, J. B., Parker, A. S., Walker, T., & Price, D. A. (2019). Real-World Hypoglycemia Avoidance with a Continuous Glucose Monitoring System's Predictive Low Glucose Alert. *Diabetes technology & therapeutics*, *21*(4), 155–158. https://doi.org/10.1089/dia.2018.0359

Trief, P. M., Cibula, D., Rodriguez, E., Akel, B., & Weinstock, R. S. (2016). Incorrect Insulin Administration: A Problem That Warrants Attention. *Clinical diabetes: a publication of the American Diabetes Association*, *34*(1), 25–33. https://doi.org/10.2337/diaclin.34.1.25

Wang, Z., Yan, W., & Oates, T. (2016). Time series classification from scratch with deep neural networks: A strong baseline. In *Proceedings of the International Joint Conference on Neural Networks (IJCNN)* (pp. 1578–1585). IEEE. https://doi.org/10.48550/arXiv.1611.06455

World Health Organization (2024). *Diabetes*. Available at: https://www.who.int/news-room/fact-sheets/detail/diabetes (Accessed: 12 August 2025)

A SECURE BLOCKCHAIN DATABASE FOR STANDALONE OR INTEGRATED USE IN CLINICAL INFORMATION SYSTEMS: THE CASE OF ANTIMICROBIAL PRESCRIPTION

Savina Mariettou[1*], Constantinos Koutsojannis[2] and Vassilis Triantafyllou[3]
[1]University of Peloponnese, Electrical and Computer Engineering Department, Patras, Greece
[2]Professor of Medical Physics & Electrophysiology, Director of Health Physics & Computational Intelligence Laboratory, Physiotherapy Department, School of Health Rehabilitation Sciences, University of Patras, Patras, Greece
[3]Professor of Network Technologies and Digital Transformation lab, Electrical and Computer Engineering Dpt., University of Peloponnese. Patras, Greece

ABSTRACT

Despite ongoing advancements in healthcare digitization, existing prescription systems often lack core mechanisms for clinical validation, traceability, and resistance-informed decision-making. Consequently, the misuse of antibiotics in clinical settings remains a significant public health concern, particularly in the context of increasing antimicrobial resistance (AMR). This study presents the design of a blockchain-based system that enforces prescription integrity, ensures clinician accountability, and integrates resistance-aware logic for high-risk medications. By incorporating smart contracts, cryptographic hashing, and real-time access monitoring, the proposed system ensures immutable prescription records, tamper-resistant verification, and controlled distribution of drugs. Additionally, a fuzzy logic-based artificial intelligence (AI) module monitors authentication behavior to detect early signs of suspicious activity and strengthen access security. Aligned with the principles of antimicrobial stewardship and secure data governance, the system promotes responsible prescribing and enhances transparency in clinical environments. Partial proof-of-concept implementation demonstrates the system's feasibility and responsiveness within simulated clinical workflows. The functional architecture, comprising the prescription interface, validation logic, and fuzzy-rule-based access monitoring, has been developed and tested in a standalone environment; blockchain components are planned for integration in future iterations. Compared to conventional infrastructures, this architecture addresses critical gaps in national e-prescription systems, particularly regarding the handling of controlled substances and antibiotic oversight. It facilitates future deployment as either a standalone tool or an integrated module within broader clinical information systems.

KEYWORDS

Blockchain, Fuzzy Logic, e-Prescription, Cybersecurity, Antimicrobial Resistance

1. INTRODUCTION

As information systems become integral to organizational workflows (Alferjanya et al., 2022) and as cyber threats evolve in scale and complexity (Hore et al., 2024), cybersecurity emerges as a central concern. In the healthcare sector, particularly with the increasing reliance on electronic medical records, digital prescribing, and interconnected devices, medical data has become a prime target for cyberattacks. According to recent analyses, healthcare infrastructures face rising threats including ransomware, phishing, and data breaches, highlighting the urgent need for resilient, security-focused architecture (Mariettou et al., 2025).

[*] Corresponding author email: s.mariettou@go.uop.gr

While technical intrusions remain a serious concern, risks also emerge from within clinical workflows. Inadequate oversight in antibiotic prescribing poses a significant threat to public health. Antibiotics, while essential for treating bacterial infections, can lead to severe consequences when misused. Poor healthcare system structures often correlate with inappropriate antibiotic use, as clinicians may resort to overprescribing in the absence of adequate diagnostic or monitoring tools, thereby contributing to the growing incidence of antimicrobial resistance (AMR) (Salam et al., 2023; Cotugno et al., 2025). These challenges underscore the need for a secure prescription database with real-time tracking capabilities, which are increasingly recognized as essential to supporting antimicrobial stewardship. However, tracking alone is not enough; effective stewardship also depends on embedding clinical reasoning and justifications within the prescription workflow. In this context, blockchain-enhanced clinical decision-making systems can generate patient-specific alerts, reduce alert fatigue, and provide better decision-making (Sunku et al., 2024).

In this paper, we present the design and implementation of a secure, blockchain-based prescription system that enables responsible antibiotic tracking, facilitates antimicrobial stewardship, and defends against input-level threats through machine learning–driven protection.

Although several blockchain-based healthcare solutions have been proposed to enhance data security and integrity, few explicitly focus on prescribing safety or antimicrobial stewardship. This paper addresses that gap by introducing a blockchain-enabled prescription system that integrates validation logic, smart contracts, and fuzzy anomaly detection tailored to high-risk antibiotics. By combining clinical reasoning with adaptive cybersecurity, the proposed approach extends beyond conventional e-prescription infrastructures and directly supports the principles of stewardship.

The remainder of this paper is organized as follows: Section 2 reviews related work, Section 3 presents the proposed system architecture, Section 4 describes the evaluation of the system's feasibility and its alignment with clinical and technical requirements, and Sections 5 and 6 conclude the paper by discussing key insights derived from the proposed system and outlining future directions for its development and evaluation.

2. RELATED WORK

In our review of 31 recent health security systems (Mariettou et al., 2025), we identified 11 that utilize blockchain-based approaches to enhance data protection, access control, and system resilience across various healthcare contexts. These systems encompass a diverse range of applications, from IoT-driven health monitoring to decentralized record management, underscoring the versatility and growing role of blockchain in healthcare. Notably, however, none of them explicitly integrates prescription management as a central module, nor do they address antimicrobial stewardship (AMS) as a design priority. A concise overview of the 11 reviewed systems follows, highlighting both their innovations and the gap this study seeks to address. As shown in Table 1, these systems differ in focus and technical design, yet none address prescription integrity or antimicrobial stewardship as a primary goal.

While existing blockchain-based healthcare systems offer notable advances in data protection and access control, they rarely address prescribing safety, a gap also highlighted in our literature review. In response, this paper introduces a blockchain-enabled system that tightly integrates security mechanisms, antimicrobial justification, and real-time attack prevention. By leveraging smart contracts and structured validation workflows, the system establishes a robust and clinically aware prescription framework. Unlike prior approaches that mainly focus on generic EMR or IoMT security, our work directly embeds antibiotic-use validation and stewardship principles into the prescription process.

Table 1. Overview of selected blockchain-based healthcare security systems, highlighting their focus, architectural components, prevented attacks, and notable features

Authors	Focus	Architecture	Attacks Prevented	Notes
(Puri et al., 2021)	Implant traceability & patient data custody	Smart contracts, secure channels	Impersonation, data leakage	Unique implant IDs; privacy-preserving model
(Abid et al., 2022)	Lightweight transmission for IoMT	E-DPoS consensus, SenCom model	Data tampering, node spoofing	Reputation-based routing is efficient in low-resource settings
(Sharma et al., 2023)	Malware classification with deep learning	Fog computing, federated storage	Botnets, ransomware, trojans	1500 malware types; deep learning model evaluated
(Selvarajan & Mouratidis, 2023)	Hybrid medical data storage	Off-chain via IPFS and cloud	Forgery, unauthorized access	Role-based access control is enabled
(Rani et al., 2023)	IoT-based anomaly detection in clinics	4-layer model (IoT, AI, data nodes)	Data breach, privilege abuse	Smart contracts for access control
(Akinola et al. 2024)	Medical certificate validation	Smart contracts with IoT verification	Phishing, identity theft	5-phase secure workflow
(Mohammed e al., 2023)	Trust-based secure data exchange	ECC, QTRAM model	No replay, privacy leak	Tuna Swarm Optimization; trust scoring logic
(Y Liu et al., 2024)	Intrusion detection in healthcare networks	4-layer EdDSA-enabled model	Tampering, privacy violation	Remote monitoring, ML-layered smart contracts
(Wu et al., 2024)	EMR exchange with patient control	ECC encryption, smart access policies	Replay, masquerading, and integrity attacks	Cloud integration, customizable permissions
(Mallick et al.. 2024)	Decentralized medical file management	Smart contracts, IPFS, fog layer	Forgery, privacy breaches	Self-verifying identities; efficient access
(Idrissi & Palmieri, 2023	Cloud-backed secure health records	AES, ECC, hybrid storage design	Integrity attack, replay, data breach	Off-chain encrypted storage, performance optimized

3. PROPOSED BLOCKCHAIN-BASED PRESCRIPTION SYSTEM

This secure, AI-enhanced, blockchain-based prescription system is designed for the management of high-risk, high-cost antibiotics such as colistin, meropenem, and ceftazidime–avibactam (Zavicefta), which are used as last-line treatments for multidrug-resistant Gram-negative pathogens, including Klebsiella pneumoniae and Pseudomonas aeruginosa (Mikhail et al., 2019).

The system addresses key requirements in IT security, patient safety, and real-time prescription delivery, supporting both hospital and home care use. It can be deployed as a standalone system, independent of existing hospital information systems, enabling flexible integration across diverse clinical settings. The prescribing process begins with submission through the system, followed by infection classification (community, healthcare, or hospital-acquired), which determines the required level of clinical justification. In cases involving supervised, high-risk antibiotics, the system prompts the physician to provide a brief validation. The request is then evaluated, with the option to resubmit if initially rejected. If approved, and if treatment exceeds 14 days, additional authorization from an infectious disease specialist is required. Once validated, the prescription is finalized, and treatment may begin.

This workflow was specifically designed based on real hospital needs, particularly for managing resistant infections. Grounded in clinical practice and stewardship principles (Nielsen et al., 2024; Truong & Yamaki, 2018), it embeds essential safeguards, justification, and infection type into a transparent and efficient process that keeps appropriate antibiotic use and reduces the dangers of resistance.

3.1 System Architecture

Based on the findings of a national questionnaire conducted among healthcare professionals in Greece, key design priorities were identified for any future digital prescribing system. Participants emphasized the importance of a simplified user interface (UI) with minimal steps required to complete a prescription, alongside system robustness and the ability to operate reliably across different clinical environments (Grammatikopoulou et al., 2024). These practical demands directly informed the design of the proposed system, which integrates core principles of usability, adaptability, and technical security.

To meet these requirements, the system has been developed with a multi-layered architecture that supports modular growth while ensuring data security, prescription traceability, and real-time responsiveness. Each layer encapsulates a distinct set of responsibilities, from user interaction and validation to secure storage and verification. These functional stages are implemented through a layered system architecture, logically structured into three core levels. The system's architecture is illustrated in Figure 1, which outlines the core components and their interactions across three functional layers: user authentication, prescription processing, and secure data storage.

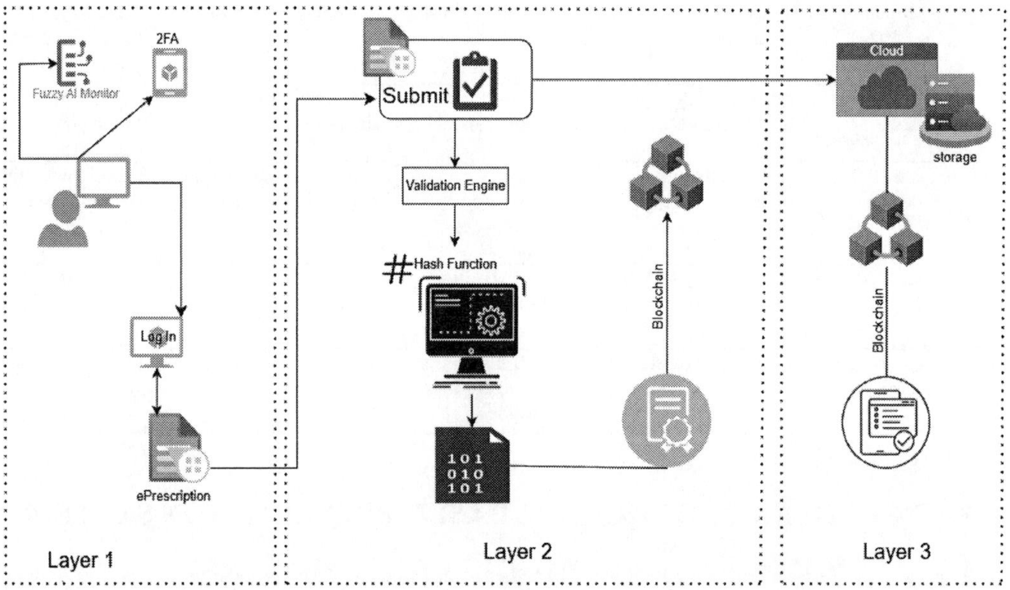

Figure 1. System Model

As shown in Figure 1, the system is organized into three layers, each corresponding to a distinct phase of the prescription lifecycle. It can be installed on an independent server and does not require a connection to a hospital's central infrastructure. The following sections provide a detailed description of the functionality and responsibilities of each layer.

The first layer of the system, responsible for interface and authentication, concerns the secure and transparent interaction between the physician and the system. A certified physician logs into the web-based interface using personal credentials. Two-Factor Authentication (2FA) is enforced, particularly in cases of failed login attempts. In parallel, an AI module based on fuzzy logic continuously monitors login behavior. When multiple failed attempts are detected, the system increases the estimated probability of a pre-attack reconnaissance phase and adapts its security rules accordingly. Once access is successfully granted, the physician proceeds to complete the electronic prescription form.

The second layer handles the system's core functional logic, including prescription validation, hash generation, and blockchain submission. Upon form submission, the entered data is routed through a secure processing and validation mechanism. At this stage, a unique cryptographic hash is generated from the form contents and associated metadata, such as hospital ID and timestamp. This hash is then recorded on the blockchain using smart contracts, ensuring both the integrity and immutability of the transaction. More specifically, this assurance is enforced at the point where the prescription is validated, ensuring that the prescribed drugs cannot be altered. Additionally, this mechanism covers the entire process, from the moment the drugs are ordered from the warehouse until they are administered, capturing even the shortest possible time interval. Consequently, the integration of blockchain technology at this level serves a dual purpose: to guarantee transparency and provide legal-grade traceability for all issued prescriptions.

The third layer ensures data confidentiality and prescription authenticity by combining secure cloud storage with blockchain-based verification. The complete prescription document, along with its associated metadata, is encrypted and securely stored within a cloud infrastructure managed by the healthcare institution. When verification is required, the system compares the document's current content with the corresponding hash stored on the blockchain, allowing for the immediate detection of any discrepancies. Additionally, this layer implements role-based access control, while the use of decentralized, blockchain-based digital identifiers (SSIDs) enhances protection against identity spoofing and unauthorized access.

For the blockchain implementation, a permissioned framework such as Hyperledger Fabric was selected for the proof of concept, as it provides efficient smart contract deployment and granular access control. The fuzzy logic module was designed as an off-chain component to preserve system modularity and avoid additional consensus overhead, while still interacting with the blockchain layer through validated events. Cloud storage was initially adopted for simplicity and lower deployment rate, with future iterations considering distributed storage solutions such as IPFS to further enhance decentralization and maintain compliance with blockchain principles.

3.2 Security Considerations and AI Integration

The proposed system incorporates a three-layer security framework to address four key threat categories: identity impersonation, credential compromise, order tampering, and data leakage. User identities are protected through blockchain-based digital identifiers (SSIDs) and advanced cryptographic methods. Crucially, smart contracts form an important part of the blockchain layer, automating the validation, ordering, and immutability of prescription workflows. These contracts ensure that once a prescription is approved, it cannot be modified, thus supporting traceability, accountability, and regulatory compliance. Additional safeguards include TLS 1.3, ECC-based certificates, and strict role-based access controls, which preserve data confidentiality and prevent unauthorized system interactions. At the core of adaptability lies an AI module powered by fuzzy logic, which continuously monitors user access patterns. When anomalies such as repeated failed logins or irregular activity are detected, the system dynamically updates its rule sets, enhancing its ability to respond to emerging threats. It is worth noting that, due to its autonomous operation and online connectivity, the system may be targeted by external factors beyond the hospital's internal network. Such threats can be mitigated by leveraging blockchain-based security measures. To illustrate the system's adaptive detection capabilities, a sample of fuzzy logic rules used for identifying anomalous behavior is presented in Figure 2.

```
(defrule Rule1-CriticalSuspicion
   (LoginAttempt (user ?u) (failedAttempts high) (retryRate fast) (ipDistribution diverse))
   =>
   (assert (Suspicion (user ?u) (level 0.95)))
)

(defrule Rule2-WeightedAdjustment
   (Suspicion (user ?u) (level ?x))
   (PatternHistory (user ?u) (weight ?w&:(> ?w 0.5)))
   =>
   (bind ?adjusted (min 1.0 (+ ?x (* 0.1 ?w))))
   (retract (Suspicion (user ?u) (level ?x)))
   (assert (Suspicion (user ?u) (level ?adjusted)))
)

(defrule Rule3-UpdateRules
   (NewThreatSignal (pattern ?p) (severity high))
   =>
   (assert (UpdateFuzzyRules (source ?p)))
)
```

Figure 2. Algorithm – Fuzzy Intrusion Detection Logic (CLIPS Representation)

These rules form the basis of the system's adaptive intrusion detection strategy and are actively employed during runtime to adjust access control decisions.

4. EVALUATION

To assess the feasibility and robustness of the proposed system, a fully functional proof-of-concept implementation was developed. Physicians access the system through a secure web interface that enforces two-factor authentication and integrates a fuzzy AI module monitoring login behavior in real-time. This logic, implemented in CLIPS, dynamically adjusts suspicion levels and triggers security responses based on anomalous patterns. Once a prescription is completed, it is validated, hashed, and recorded through smart contracts, while the full data is encrypted and stored securely. Access is controlled via role-based permissions and digital signatures, confirming the system's technical viability for sensitive clinical environments.

Beyond the technical validation, brief feedback from healthcare professionals indicated that the prototype workflow was clear and that the justification fields for high-risk antibiotics were considered useful for stewardship. In addition, basic security and performance checks confirmed low-latency processing and effective anomaly detection by the fuzzy logic module.

Finally, the system addresses core threat categories through a layered defense. Table 2 summarizes the mapping of threats to countermeasures.

Table 2. Threat–Countermeasure Mapping in the Proposed Prescription System

Threat Category	Countermeasure	Mechanism
Identity impersonation	Blockchain-based identifiers (SSIDs)	Unique, decentralized IDs prevent spoofing and misuse
Credential compromise	Two-factor authentication + fuzzy monitoring	Real-time anomaly detection of login behavior
Prescription tampering	Smart contracts + cryptographic hashing	Immutable blockchain records ensure integrity and traceability
Data leakage	TLS 1.3 + encrypted cloud storage	Secure transmission and encrypted off-chain data storage

This layered approach demonstrates how the system integrates both technical safeguards and clinical oversight, ensuring that prescription integrity and data confidentiality are preserved throughout the workflow.

5. DISCUSSION

Building upon the technical capabilities of the proposed system, we explore its potential to address longstanding challenges in both prescription security and antimicrobial stewardship. At the infrastructure level, the combination of decentralization, blockchain integrity, and role-based access control fosters transparency and resilience across clinical workflows. Unlike traditional e-prescription systems that rely on static credentials and offer limited oversight of high-risk medications, the system introduces immutable logging and enforcement mechanisms that strengthen accountability by design.

A central innovation is the use of fuzzy logic for real-time behavior monitoring. This adaptive AI mechanism relies on a dynamic rule set that evolves in response to login anomalies, enabling the system to detect reconnaissance patterns and adjust security thresholds accordingly. Such mechanisms provide proactive defense against evolving threat models and reinforce trust in prescription workflows.

Clinically, the system reinforces antimicrobial stewardship (AMS) by requiring structured prescription validation and justification, especially for high-risk antibiotics. Through contextual logic based on infection type and medication class, it promotes safer prescribing. However, further work is needed to validate scalability, adapt to diverse clinical workflows, and ensure interoperability with national health systems, critical steps for broader adoption.

This work contributes by integrating fuzzy anomaly detection with blockchain immutability, tailored specifically to high-risk antibiotic prescriptions. This dual emphasis on clinical reasoning and adaptive cybersecurity distinguishes it from existing systems, highlighting the novelty of the proposed approach.

6. CONCLUSION AND FUTURE WORK

This paper presents a secure and intelligent prescription system that leverages blockchain technology and adaptive AI-based access controls, implemented through a fuzzy rule engine, to promote responsible antibiotic use. Beyond ensuring responsible medication practices, the proposed approach also aligns with key goals like transparency, auditability, and personalized data protection. Transparency is ensured through immutable blockchain records that track every stage of the prescription process. Auditability is enabled by cryptographic hashing and smart contracts, which verify data integrity and prevent tampering. Personalized data protection is achieved via decentralized digital identifiers, strong encryption, and adaptive access controls that respond to user behavior in real time. Importantly, the system enables both autonomous operation and seamless integration within hospital information systems, allowing for flexible deployment across various clinical and healthcare settings. This proof-of-concept implementation validates the practical applicability of the system's architecture and offers a solid foundation for the subsequent integration of blockchain functionalities.

Next steps for the prescription system will focus on extending the system's applicability to a wider range of clinical scenarios, including controlled clinical scenarios. Emphasis will also be placed on assessing performance under dynamic real-world workloads and refining the user interface to improve clinician engagement and acceptance. Furthermore, a promising direction for system expansion involves enhancing the AI unit to detect prescribing anomalies beyond simple association patterns, such as atypical dosages or repetitive high-risk drug orders. These steps are crucial to transitioning from a research prototype to a policy-compliant, operational solution for complex healthcare ecosystems. Future enhancements may also include integrating federated learning to allow the fuzzy logic engine to adapt across institutions without compromising data privacy.

REFERENCES

Abid, A., Cheikhrouhou, S., Kallel, S., Tari, Z., & Jmaiel, M. (2024). A smart contract-based access control framework for smart healthcare systems. *The Computer Journal*, 67(2), 407-422. doi:10.1093/comjnl/bxac183. 363

Akinola, O., Akinola, A., Oyekan, B., Oyerinde, O., Adebiyi, H. F., & Sulaimon, B. (2024). Blockchain-Enabled Security Solutions for Medical Device Integrity and Provenance in Cloud Environments. *International Journal of Innovative Science and Research Technology (IJISRT)* IJISRT24APR225, 123-135. doi:10.38124/ijsrmt.v3i4.27

Alferjanya, A., Musaed Al-mwald, M.N, & R.B, A. (2022). The Effect of Cyber Security Knowledge on Employees' Personal Growth: An Empirical Study in Private Hospitals in Libya and Yemen. *Health Education and Health Promotion*, 10(2), 369–375.

Cotugno, S., De Vita, E., Frallonardo, L., Novara, R., Papagni, R., Asaduzzaman, M., ... & Di Gennaro, F. (2025). Antimicrobial resistance and migration: interrelation between two hot topics in global health. *Annals of Global Health*, 91(1), 12. doi: 10.5334/aogh.4628

Grammatikopoulou, M., Lazarou, I., Giannios, G., Kakalou, C. A., Zachariadou, M., Zande, M., Karanikas, H., Thireos, E., Stavropoulos, T. G., Natsiavas, P., Nikolopoulos, S., & Kompatsiaris, I. (2024). Electronic prescription systems in Greece: a large-scale survey of healthcare professionals' perceptions. *Archives of Public Health*, 82(1). doi: 10.1186/s13690-024-01304-6

Hore, K., Tan, M. H., Kehoe, A., Beegan, A., Mason, S., Mane, N. A., Hughes, D., Kelly, C., Wells, J., & Magner, C. (2024). Cybersecurity and critical care staff: A mixed methods study. *International Journal of Medical Informatics*, 185, 105412. doi:10.1016/j.ijmedinf.2024.105412

Idrissi, H., & Palmieri, P. (2024). Agent-based blockchain model for robust authentication and authorization in IoT-based healthcare systems. *The Journal of Supercomputing*, 80(5), 6622-6660.

Liu, Y., Wang, X., Zheng, G., Wan, X., & Ning, Z. (2024). An AoI-aware data transmission algorithm in blockchain-based intelligent healthcare systems. *IEEE Transactions on Consumer Electronics*, 70(1), 1180-1190. doi: 10.1109/TCE.2024.3365198

Mallick, S. R., Lenka, R. K., Tripathy, P. K., Rao, D. C., Sharma, S., & Ray, N. K. (2024). A lightweight, secure, and scalable blockchain-fog-iomt healthcare framework with ipfs data storage for healthcare 4.0. *SN Computer Science*, 5(1), 198.

Mariettou, S., Koutsojannis, C., & Triantafillou, V. (2025). Artificial Intelligence and Algorithmic Approaches of Health Security Systems: A Review. *Algorithms*, 18(2), 59.

Mikhail, S., Singh, N. B., Kebriaei, R., Rice, S. A., Stamper, K. C., Castanheira, M., & Rybak, M. J. (2019). Evaluation of the synergy of ceftazidime-avibactam in combination with meropenem, amikacin, aztreonam, colistin, or fosfomycin against well-characterized multidrug-resistant Klebsiella pneumoniae and Pseudomonas aeruginosa. *Antimicrobial agents and chemotherapy*, 63(8), 10-1128. doi.org/10.1128/AAC.00779-19

Mohammed, M. A., Lakhan, A., Zebari, D. A., Abd Ghani, M. K., Marhoon, H. A., Abdulkareem, K. H., ... & Martinek, R. (2024). Securing healthcare data in industrial cyber-physical systems using combining deep learning and blockchain technology. *Engineering Applications of Artificial Intelligence*, 129, 107612. doi:10.1016/j.engappai.2023.107612. 376

Nielsen, N. D., Dean III, J. T., Shald, E. A., Conway Morris, A., Povoa, P., Schouten, J., & Parchim, N. (2024). When to Stop Antibiotics in the Critically Ill?. *Antibiotics*, 13(3), 272. doi: 10.3390/antibiotics13030272

Puri, V., Kataria, A., & Sharma, V. (2024). Artificial intelligence-powered decentralized framework for Internet of Things in Healthcare 4.0. *Transactions on Emerging Telecommunications Technologies*, 35(4), e4245. doi:10.1002/ett.4245. 361

Rani, S., Chauhan, M., Kataria, A., & Khang, A. (2023). IoT equipped intelligent distributed framework for smart healthcare systems. In Towards the integration of IoT, cloud and big data: services, applications and standards (pp. 97-114). *Singapore: Springer Nature Singapore*.

Salam, M. A., Al-Amin, M. Y., Salam, M. T., Pawar, J. S., Akhter, N., Rabaan, A. A., & Alqumber, M. A. (2023, January). Antimicrobial resistance: a growing serious threat for global public health. In Healthcare (Vol. 11, No. 13, p. 1946). *Multidisciplinary Digital Publishing Institute*. doi.org/10.3390/healthcare11131946

Selvarajan, S., & Mouratidis, H. (2023). A quantum trust and consultative transaction-based blockchain cybersecurity model for healthcare systems. *Scientific Reports*, 13(1), 7107. doi:10.1038/s41598-023-34354-x. 368

Sharma, P., Namasudra, S., Crespo, R. G., Parra-Fuente, J., & Trivedi, M. C. (2023). EHDHE: Enhancing security of healthcare documents in IoT-enabled digital healthcare ecosystems using blockchain. *Information Sciences*, 629, 703-718. doi:10.1016/j.ins.2023.01.148. 366

Sunku, S. S., Varuni, H. K., & Vinodha, K. (2024, November). Leveraging Permissioned Blockchain for securing controlled drug prescriptions in India. In 2024 6th International Conference on Blockchain Computing and Applications (BCCA) (pp. 513-518). *IEEE*. doi:10.1109/bcca62388.2024.10844414.

Truong, W. R., & Yamaki, J. (2018, June). The Hospital Antimicrobial Use Process: From Beginning to End. In Open Forum Infectious Diseases (Vol. 5, No. 6, p. ofy098). *US: Oxford University Press*. doi: 10.1093/ofid/ofy098

Wu, C., Tang, Y. M., Kuo, W. T., Yip, H. T., & Chau, K. Y. (2024). Healthcare 5.0: A secure and distributed network for system informatics in medical surgery. *International journal of medical informatics*, 186, 105415. doi:10.1016/j.ijmedinf.2024.105415. 380

Short Papers

TOWARD SECURE M2M AUTHENTICATION FOR S3 OBJECT STORAGE

Michael Geiger and Andreas U. Schmidt
Wilhelm Büchner Hochschule
Department of Computer Science,
Hilpertstr. 31, D-64295 Darmstadt, Germany

ABSTRACT

This paper addresses security vulnerabilities in Machine-to-Machine authentication for Amazon S3 object storage in industrial environments. Current AWS authentication relies on often insecurely managed symmetric keys. While Amazon's Secure Token Service with OpenID Connect authentication offers a solution in principle, most enterprise S3-compatible storage products lack STS support. We propose a security architecture combining Privileged Access Management (PAM) with OIDC authentication to abstract credentials from application code, enabling automated key rotation and centralized management. Through industrial simulation testing, we demonstrate this approach maintains production continuity while significantly improving credential security for M2M S3 access.

KEYWORDS

Amazon S3, Credential Leak, Privileged Access Management, OpenID Connect, Credential Vault, Amazon STS

1. INTRODUCTION AND PROBLEM STATEMENT

Amazon S3 Buckets are the most widely used type of object storage across all industries. However, security of S3 buckets is often not optimal throughout development cycles, and vulnerabilities spill over into production systems (Continella, et al., 2018). Security analyses, guidelines, and policies for AWS users are voluminous (cf., e.g., Bhatt, 2024; Mishra, et al., 2022). Particularly, for M2M communication of production systems to the S3 storages, Amazon foresees the AWS4 authentication algorithm based on symmetric shared secrets (Amazon Web Services, 2024, p. 1672), and the protocol denoted by the misnomer "Amazon Signature." In Industry 4.0 scenarios, the security weaknesses of AWS4 are obvious: Keys are held in machine memory or are even hardcoded, ore stored insecurely in configuration files. Secure management of symmetric keys requires key rotation, which is a manual administrator process in the AWS infrastructure, incompatible with automated Industry 4.0 production scenarios. This incurs the risk of costly production outages (Siemens, 2024) during key rotation. Secure handling of the keys would at least require additional secure vaults. Despite the push to use AWS infrastructure in large scale industrial systems (K, Sai Khertan, et al. 2024), these basic practical security problems are unresolved.

The lack of secure S3 authentication opens risks for the unintentional disclosure of credentials in source code or stored in clear on platforms such as GitHub due to a missing abstraction of credentials from source code. Credentials must be prevented from being stored with or beside the source code and should in principle be replaced by secure authentication, e.g., OAuth/OIDC. Where this is not possible, credentials need to be rotated in an automated and regular manner thus limiting the validity lifetime of the credentials.

Amazon itself proposes a workaround via indirection: Usage of the Secure Token Service (STS) which produces fresh credentials for AWS4, given a proper authentication with OpenID Connect (OIDC), i.e., acts as an AWS4 credential oracle with OIDC authentication. However yet, very few solutions for the on-premise management of connected S3 infrastructure can readily handle both STS and the required OAuth protocol flows (see Table 1 below). Still, the authentication and key rotation remain manual processes, inappropriate for automated production scenarios requiring quasi-continuous access to S3 storage.

In the following, we first look at the common approach to the problem via market solutions which potentially handle both secure machine authentication on the one hand and STS access and key rotation on the other hand. We find that few solutions fulfill these requirements seamlessly. Then we propose our simple security architecture to detach key management from machine authentication using a secure key vault and an independent OIDC IdP. Finally, we describe the test case of an industry 4.0 system, automatically accessing the S3 storage in production with seamless access credential rotation. It should be noted that the solution we present focuses on the S3 protocols as one of the most widely used object storage protocols, but it is obviously not only applicable to Amazon S3, also to the Google Cloud Storage and Azure Blob Storage as long as S3 is used.

2. COMMON APPROACH WITH STS AND THIRD-PARTY TOOLS

S3 based Object Storage authenticates entities with access and secret keys, which according to the official AWS specification is the only option for authentication. Authentication within S3 is done via AWS4 Algorithm which is cryptographically secured and has therefore no possibility to authenticate with a different method compliant with the S3 specification. However, as an addition, the specification provides, with STS, a mechanism for secure authentication and key rotation. For this, the client (i.e., an authorized administrator of the AWS tenant) has first to enroll an OIDC IdP with Amazon's Identity and Access Management Service (IAM). This enables the client to authenticate with the chosen IdP. The IdP issues a specific JSON Web Token (JWT) with which the client can retrieve temporary access and secret keys from the STS. These keys have a limited validity and need to be retrieved again or refreshed after expiry.

This principal solution for key exchange requires a client-side functional element, which handles OIDC authentication toward the IdP (and upfront enrollment of the IdP with AWS' IAM), and, concurrently, authentication and key exchange protocols with STS. Market research shows that many enterprise-grade S3 Object Storage Management products do not support both features. Table 1 shows major enterprise products for S3 Object storage and their support for STS protocols and OIDC authentication.

Table 1. S3 Object storage and support for STS with OIDC[1]

Product	STS	OAuth/OIDC
Amazon S3	✓	✓
Ceph Object Gateway	✓	✓
Dell/EMC ECS	✓	× (but SAML)
Dell/EMC Isilon	×	×
MinIO	✓	✓
NetApp ONTAP	×	×
NetApp StorageGrid	×	×
Nutanix Objects	×	×
PureStorage FlashBlade	✓	✓
Qumolo	×	×

In already existing production environments using S3, exchanging a storage platform in large deployments needs planning, time, effort and financial resources. The cost of replacement for a slight improvement in credential security is often not economically justifiable. Therefore, a different approach to securing credentials is desirable.

[1] Public information from vendors' websites and additional information from support channels/vendor employees.

3. SECURITY ARCHITECTURE FOR PROTECTING S3 CREDENTIALS OF APPLICATIONS

A viable and security-enhancing approach for managing access credentials to S3 object storage in especially industrial environments involves the combination of the Privileged Access Management (PAM) concept with OpenID Connect authentication to the enterprise identity provider (e.g. EntraID, Auth0…). Within this approach, the application authenticates against a centralized, cryptographically secured credential vault to retrieve securely temporary access and secret keys required for S3 operations. Authentication can be realized through established identity protocols such as OAuth 2.0 or OpenID Connect, ensuring secure and standards-compliant interaction. Key rotation, an essential practice for mitigating the impact of potential credential leaks, requires minimal operational effort in this architecture and represents a beneficial side effect of the centralized credential management approach. In the optimal implementation, only the credential vault requires updating during key rotation. The application can then dynamically retrieve updated credentials without the need for manual intervention or application restart. Although an additional step is introduced in the operational workflow, the resulting latency is minimal and does not significantly affect production continuity.

The main limitation of this method lies in the required integration effort. Specifically, the production line must be adapted to interact with the PAM solution's API or credential delivery mechanism. In practical deployments, credentials are frequently stored in local configuration files or via Windows Credential Manager. These temporary access storages can be accessed through automated scripts that retrieve credentials from the PAM vault and populate them into the local stores. The production system may then be instructed to reload its configuration – commonly via a local port trigger or process signal – without requiring a restart, thereby minimizing downtime. In conclusion, integrating a market-proven PAM solution into the industrial environment provides a scalable and secure method for managing S3 access credentials. It significantly reduces the risks associated with credential leakage, supports seamless key rotation, and ensures operational stability.

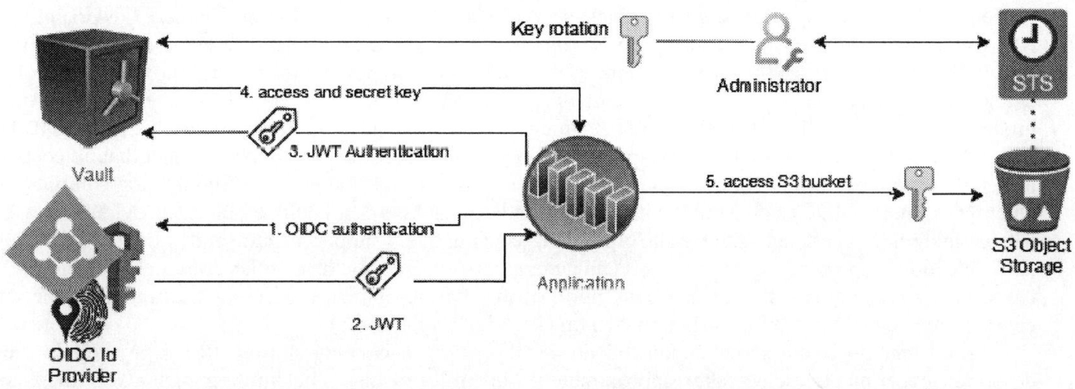

Figure 1. Security architecture with OIDC/PAM authentication indirection

Figure 1 illustrates a proposed technological security architecture that integrates an application with a PAM system, combined with OIDC-based authentication via an identity provider. This architecture enables secure, runtime retrieval of S3 credentials by abstracting them away from the application itself. As a result, there is no need to embed or store access keys directly within the application. The securely saved S3 credentials within the PAM's vault ensures that access to sensitive credentials is both auditable and controlled. In case of suspected unauthorized access, all credential requests and interactions can be traced using PAM's logging capabilities. Centralized credential storage enables seamless rotation of access and secret keys. The component responsible for the PAM integration on application side can fetch credentials at runtime, minimizing manual intervention. Authentication via OIDC enhances security by ensuring that both applications and users possess distinct identities when requesting access. The OIDC tokens issued are limited in scope via the **Audience** claim of the access token, ensuring that they are only valid for a specific use case—in this case, authentication to the PAM system. Therefore, even if a token is compromised, it cannot be used to impersonate the full identity across other services or systems. This layered approach combines secure credential handling with identity-aware access control, improving both operational security and traceability. Figure 1 visually represents the developed security architecture and its components, highlighting the interaction between the application, the PAM system, and the identity provider.

4. CASE STUDY SECURING INDUSTRY PRODUCTION

In industrial production environments, uninterrupted operation is crucial to avoid costly downtime. To analyze possible solutions, a realistic scenario simulating a production line was developed, where an application which represents the production line requires ongoing read and write access to data via the S3 protocol. The application must continuously access the S3 storage without interruption, reflecting real-time production constraints, such that any disruption results in a failure analogous to a production halt. To enable verification of authentication during runtime, the application displays parts of the access and secret key, a feature unavailable in typical market applications for security reasons. This scenario simulation writes sequential numbers representing the produced parts, written to and read from the S3 bucket, allowing real-time monitoring of production rhythm and credential validity under dynamic conditions. Data must be written to the S3 storage every three seconds or less, with each write operation completing within this time to prevent production delays. On any write failure, production stops immediately. The application reads and displays the last five entries every two seconds to enable near real-time monitoring. A visual indicator tracks whether the production cycle consistently meets the three-second maximum over the last minute. Access and secret keys are displayed during runtime to verify authentication processes. The simulation was implemented in .NET and served as the basis for the prototypical validation of the proposed security architecture.

The technical proof of concept was implemented as FactorySimulation Application using Auth0 as the Identity Provider (IdP), provided via Software-as-a-Service (SaaS) solution in the cloud. For secure secret management, HashiCorp Vault was selected and deployed locally on a Debian GNU/Linux system. MinIO was chosen as the S3-compatible object storage server, also deployed locally on Debian GNU/Linux. The FactorySimulation was developed using C#. To integrate the various components, their respective REST APIs were utilized and accessed through .NET libraries to reduce development effort. The following libraries were employed for this purpose: Auth0.AuthenticationApi, AWSSDK.S3 — which is the official Amazon implementation compatible with all S3 object storage systems — and VaultSharp for HashiCorp Vault. These products were selected due to their widespread adoption in industrial environments, the fact that no costs were incurred during the proof of concept, and their adherence to relevant standards — Auth0 being compliant with OpenID Connect (OIDC), and MinIO with the S3 standard. Auth0's SaaS delivery model provided a low-entry barrier, and prior experience with HashiCorp Vault, which natively supports Auth0 authentication, contributed to its selection. Importantly, these products can generally be replaced with any other solutions that comply with the respective standards without significant modification. Further implementation details including the source code of the Factory Simulation was published on GitHub (Geiger, 2025).

Multiple measurement series conducted during the proof of concept showed that a key rotation in the described experimental setup takes approximately 400 milliseconds. The limiting factor was the internet connection to Auth0, which exhibited a round-trip latency of 30 to 40 milliseconds. Therefore, key rotation in a production environment can be further accelerated by deploying the Identity Provider (IdP) locally within the local area network (LAN) or by using a low-latency internet connection.

5. CONCLUSION AND OUTLOOK

The presented solution clearly serves as a technological interim. In an ideal world, S3 authentication would work seamlessly and directly with any OIDC Provider of the user's choice. Yet, as the chosen indirection approach with STS shows, AWS will, in the foreseeable future, stick to the symmetric credential-based authentication for S3 buckets and full support for directly supported OIDC is yet lacking. OIDC federation with AWS IAM is available for enabling STS with an external identity provider (Amazon Web Services, Inc. (2025), p. 622 et seq.). Therefore, the presented solution provides a viable way to secure M2M access to S3 buckets, combining seamless key rotation with key shielding and flexible entity authentication via OIDC.

This may serve as a practical solution particularly for SMEs who want to stay independent from commercial infrastructures and use S3 in their production environments. Large enterprises also benefit from this solution, as it eliminates the need to migrate to another S3 vendor solely for STS support, thereby avoiding the associated efforts and costs.

RELEASE NOTE

This project was performed as part of the first author's thesis work, and concluded 20th June, 2025. Sources and implementation details are available on GitHub (Geiger, 2025).

REFERENCES

Amazon Web Services, Inc. (2024). API Reference—Amazon Simple Storage Service. Available at: https://docs.aws.amazon.com/pdfs/AmazonS3/latest/API/s3-api.pdf [Accessed 23 June 2025].

Amazon Web Services, Inc. (2025). User Guide—AWS Identity and Access Management. Available at: https://docs.aws.amazon.com/pdfs/IAM/latest/UserGuide/iam-ug.pdf [Accessed 23 June 2025].

Bhatt, S. (2024). Security and Compliance Considerations for Running SAP Systems on AWS. *Journal of Sustainable Solutions*, *15*(4), pp. 72–86.

Continella, A., Polino, M., Pogliani, M. and Zanero, S., (2018). There's a Hole in that Bucket! A Large-scale Analysis of Misconfigured S3 Buckets. *Asia-Pacific Computer Systems Architecture Conference*, pp. 1-6.

Geiger, M., (2025). FactorySimulation, https://github.com/tux1337/FactorySimulation [Accessed 07 September 2025]

K, U., Sai Keerthan, N. K., Kumar Musunuru, N. and Beena, B. M., (2024). Cloud-Infused AWS Services: Automobile Database Management System. *2024 2nd International Conference on Networking, Embedded and Wireless Systems (ICNEWS)*, Bangalore, India, 2024, pp. 1-7, doi: 10.1109/ICNEWS60873.2024.10731084.

Mishra, S., Kumar, M., Singh N. and Dwivedi, S., (2022). A Survey on AWS Cloud Computing Security Challenges & Solutions. *2022 6th International Conference on Intelligent Computing and Control Systems (ICICCS)*, Madurai, India, 2022, pp. 614-617, doi: 10.1109/ICICCS53718.2022.9788254.

Siemens (2024). The True Cost of Downtime 2024. Available at: https://assets.new.siemens.com/siemens/assets/api/uuid:1b43afb5-2d07-47f7-9eb7-893fe7d0bc59/TCOD-2024_original.pdf [Accessed 07 September 2025].

UNDERSTANDING DIGITAL TRUST IN INSURANCE: FOUNDATIONS, ORIGINS AND RELEVANCE

Petra Maria Asprion, Sandro Degen and Jona Stefan Karg
University of Applied Sciences and Arts Northwestern Switzerland FHNW, School of Business, Institute for Information Systems, Basel, Switzerland

ABSTRACT

As digital transformation accelerates, digital trust emerges as a strategic imperative, particularly in the insurance industry, where stakeholder confidence and data sensitivity are central. Despite increasing academic interest, the concept of digital trust remains fragmented, lacking clarity and industry-specific frameworks. This short paper presents a foundational study on digital trust in insurance, synthesizing insights from a systematic literature review. The origins of digital trust were explored, its conceptual distinction from traditional trust, and the organizational elements it encompasses – governance, risk, compliance (GRC), corporate digital responsibility (CDR), and cybersecurity. The results show that digital trust is a multidimensional construct requiring both technical and ethical integration into business operations. This preliminary study serves as a foundation for developing a management-oriented framework tailored to the insurance sector, to be validated in follow-up research.

KEYWORDS

Digital Trust, Insurance, Cybersecurity, GRC, CDR, Trust Framework

1. INTRODUCTION

Digital transformation is fundamentally changing how the insurance industry operates. Increasingly, interactions between insurers and customers are mediated through digital channels – such as mobile apps, online portals, and artificial intelligence (AI)-driven systems. While this shift promises efficiency and scalability, it also presents new challenges (Launer et al., 2022). These developments have given rise to the concept of digital trust, which refers to the confidence stakeholders have in the reliability, integrity, security, and ethical behavior of digital systems and platforms (Paliszkiewicz & Chen, 2023).

For insurers, digital trust is crucial – not only to protect sensitive data, but also to build long-term relationships in an environment where face-to-face interaction is increasingly rare. The insurance sector is particularly affected due to its dependence on personal and often highly sensitive data, long-term policyholder relationships, and complex regulatory requirements (Numan & Sunna, 2023). Failure to establish trust can result in reputational damage, regulatory penalties, and declining customer loyalty. However, current approaches in insurance tend to address digital trust only partially – often limited to compliance or cybersecurity – without considering broader dimensions such as ethical data governance, algorithmic fairness, or corporate digital responsibility (Pietrzak & Takala, 2021).

This study aims to close this gap by exploring (1) how digital trust is defined and understood in the insurance sector; (2) what dimensions and expectations are relevant from a stakeholder perspective; and (3) how trust-related principles can be integrated into governance and digital strategy. The presented study serves as a conceptual and exploratory foundation. It paves the way for follow-up research that will develop and evaluate a practical Digital Trust for Insurance (DT4I) framework.

2. METHODOLOGY

To ensure the reliability of the study, a qualitative and exploratory research design based on the principles of Design Science Research (DSR) was applied. According to Hevner et al. (2004), DSR involves a cyclical process of awareness, suggestion, development, and evaluation, allowing researchers to iteratively improve solutions based on stakeholder input and empirical evidence. The problem of insufficient digital trust frameworks specific to the insurance industry was identified through a comprehensive literature review. The literature review was conducted using a systematic approach, guided by established protocols (Webster & Watson, 2002). Academic databases such as Scopus, Web of Science, and Google Scholar were searched using keywords like "digital trust," "insurance," "cybersecurity," "GRC," and "corporate digital responsibility." Peer-reviewed articles, industry reports, and white papers from trusted sources such as ISACA, McKinsey, and the World Economic Forum were included to capture both scholarly and practical perspectives. This approach sets the stage for the next phases of DSR, which will involve the development and iterative validation of the DT4I framework in a follow-up study.

3. ORIGINS AND CONCEPTUALIZATION OF DIGITAL TRUST

The concept of trust has been extensively studied across psychology, sociology, and organizational science. Early foundational work by Deutsch (1958) defined trust as a behavior involving risk-taking based on the expectation of positive outcomes. Rotter (1967) emphasized the reliability of another's word or promise, while Zand (1972) introduced the notion that trust inherently involves vulnerability to potential loss. By the 1980s, trust was being analyzed as a multi-dimensional construct, combining cognitive, emotional, and behavioral components (Lewis & Weigert, 1985). Later, Moorman et al. (1993) linked trust to confidence in trading partners, particularly in uncertain or fragile environments, while Cummings & Bromiley (1996) introduced trustworthy beliefs and intentions as distinct constructs. A particularly influential and widely accepted definition by Schoorman et al. (2007, p. 712) framed trust as *"the willingness of a party to be vulnerable to the actions of another party based on the expectation that the other will perform a particular action important to the trustor, irrespective of the ability to monitor or control that other party"*.

3.1 Emergence of Digital Trust

As digital technologies began mediating more social and business interactions, a new form of trust was required – digital trust. In contrast to traditional trust, which often depends on personal interaction and physical presence, digital trust is rooted in confidence in technological systems and institutional behaviors (Pietrzak & Takala, 2021). Digital trust emerged from the need to facilitate interactions in environments where users cannot directly verify the trustworthiness of their counterparts. Instead, users rely on platform security, data privacy policies, and the perceived integrity of systems (Launer et al., 2022). Several definitions of digital trust have been proposed over the past two decades, pointing to technical foundations (Mattila & Seppälä, 2016); emphasizing organizational responsibility in maintaining credibility, security, and reliability (Pietrzak & Takala, 2021); suggesting digital trust includes the expectation that technology protects stakeholder values (Dobrygowski, 2022); and defining it as the alignment of technology, people, and processes (Launer et al., 2022). Numan and Sunna (2023) describe digital trust as "*the confidence in the integrity of the relationships and transactions among providers and consumers within a digital ecosystem*". All these definitions have been combined to form a synthesized definition used in this study: *Digital trust is the confidence stakeholders have in the security, privacy, and reliability of digital interactions and data management. This confidence is built through the alignment of technology, processes, and organizational behavior with stakeholder expectations.*

3.2 Multidimensional Nature of Digital Trust

Digital trust is a multidimensional concept comprising various dimensions critical for fostering and maintaining confidence in digital interactions and data management.

Security (Mattila & Seppälä, 2016) is fundamental to digital trust, protecting data and interactions from unauthorized access and cyber threats through encryption, authentication, and system monitoring. Security ensures that stakeholders can trust the integrity and confidentiality of their data. **Privacy** (Paliszkiewicz & Chen, 2023) ensures personal data is handled responsibly and in compliance with regulations, supported by transparent practices and user consent. Organizations must implement policies and practices that respect and protect stakeholder privacy, thereby fostering trust. **Reliability** (Numan & Sunna, 2023) denotes the consistent performance and availability of digital systems, fostering stakeholder confidence. Stakeholders must be able to trust that digital platforms will function as expected. **Transparency** (Launer et al., 2022) involves clear communication about data usage, security protocols, and incidents, enabling informed decision-making. Transparency helps build trust by providing stakeholders with the information they need to make informed decisions. **Accountability** (Pietrzak & Takala, 2021) requires organizations to take responsibility for digital operations, demonstrated through audits, standards adherence, and continuous improvement. **Compliance** (Numan & Sunna, 2023) with legal and regulatory frameworks reinforces trust and mitigates risk. Therefore, not only prevents legal penalties but also enhances stakeholder trust by demonstrating a commitment to high standards. A well-designed **user experience** (UX) enhances trust through intuitive, secure, and responsive interfaces (Guo, 2022). **Ethical practices** (Dobrygowski, 2022) uphold fairness, autonomy, and societal values in digital interactions, and therefore aligning organizational actions with stakeholder values. **Historical consistency** (Akram & Ko, 2014) strengthens trust by demonstrating a sustained commitment to high standards over time. Consistent performance and reliability in the past reinforce trust, as stakeholders have confidence the organization will continue to uphold these standards.

3.3 Stakeholders of Digital Trust

Digital trust is built jointly by various interest groups whose interests differ or overlap. Each group has different expectations and vulnerabilities, all of which must be considered. **Users** (Launer et al., 2022) include customers, clients, and the public who engage with an organization's digital resources, expecting secure and trustworthy interactions, and rely on the organization to safeguard their personal information. **Customers** (Pietrzak & Takala, 2021), as transactional stakeholders, demand protection of financial and personal data, with digital trust being key to loyalty. **Employees** (Launer et al., 2022) rely on secure systems to perform effectively, with digital trust supporting data protection, morale, and productivity. **Regulatory bodies and government authorities** (Dobrygowski, 2022) require compliance with legal standards, and digital trust reflects adherence to data protection and cybersecurity regulations. **Business partners and suppliers** (Pietrzak & Takala, 2021) depend on secure and reliable digital collaboration, with trust facilitating operational efficiency. **Investors and shareholders** (Kluiters et al., 2023) rely on digital trust to assess organizational stability and growth. Trustworthy digital practices can enhance investor confidence, leading to increased investment and support, impacting the organization's reputation, financial performance and increase firm value **The general public** (Kluiters et al., 2023), including non-customers, shapes an organization's reputation through perceptions of digital trustworthiness. **External auditors and security experts** (International Organization for Standardization, 2022) are responsible for assessing and verifying the integrity and security of an organization's digital systems. Their trust in the organization's digital practices is essential for validating compliance and identifying vulnerabilities.

4. THE ROLE OF DIGITAL TRUST IN INSURANCE

Trust has always been at the heart of the insurance business. Unlike most industries, where value is delivered instantly, insurers make promises about future performance – to pay claims, protect data, and support policyholders in times of need. This time-delayed value proposition makes trust a prerequisite for customer engagement and retention (Pietrzak & Takala, 2021). In the traditional analog model, trust was established through personal relationships, physical documents, and in-branch interactions. In the digital age, these mechanisms are increasingly replaced by web portals, mobile apps, chatbots, and AI-driven underwriting, shifting the foundation of trust from interpersonal relationships to digital systems (Dobrygowski, 2022).

4.1 Digital Trust as a Strategic Enabler

Digital trust is not only a risk mitigation strategy but a strategic enabler for innovation and transformation. As insurers adopt technologies like artificial intelligence and blockchain, they must ensure that stakeholders perceive these systems as trustworthy. Insurers that actively build digital trust can (1) **increase digital adoption**, when customers feel their data are safe and interactions are fair (Launer et al., 2022); (2) **strengthen customer loyalty**, by fosters long-term relationships, which are especially valuable in insurance due to the typically low engagement frequency and long contract durations (Paliszkiewicz & Chen, 2023); (3) **differentiate from competitors**, as product features become commoditized, trust becomes a key competitive advantage (Numan & Sunna, 2023); and (4) **accelerate innovation**, as digital trust reduces resistance to new technologies, and employees are more willing to embrace automation, analytics, and AI (Porfirio et al., 2021). In summary, digital trust is a prerequisite for the success of digital transformation and must be managed proactively.

4.2 Industry-Specific Trust Risks

The insurance sector faces a unique combination of trust vulnerabilities, due to its regulatory exposure, data sensitivity, and social role. **Data sensitivity and privacy expectations** (Engels, 2019) is a particular risk area, since insurers handle some of the most sensitive personal data. Any breach or misuse of health records, driving behavior, and financial profiles can result in severe reputational and legal consequences. In this context, digital trust involves robust privacy engineering, consent management, and data minimization strategies. Customers may lose trust in **algorithmic decision-making** (Paliszkiewicz & Chen, 2023) if algorithms produce opaque or seemingly discriminatory outcomes. Building trust in algorithmic processes requires transparency mechanisms, such as explainable AI models.. **Cybersecurity threats** (Verma et al., 2021) have significantly increased in the insurance sector, since insurance firms are high-value targets due to the volume and quality of data they manage. Therefore, cybersecurity is a baseline expectation in maintaining digital trust. Insurers face strict **regulatory compliance and audit** (Engels, 2019) requirements. Non-compliance can lead to financial penalties and damage trust with the public and regulators. Building trust requires going beyond basic compliance through certifications (e.g., ISO/IEC 27001) and transparent reporting.

4.3 From Trust Management to Trust Strategy

Traditionally, trust has been seen as a reactive concern – managed through crisis communication or damage control after incidents. However, in the digital era, trust must be proactively designed and managed as part of corporate strategy. This shift involves (1) integrating digital trust KPIs into risk dashboards; (2) aligning trust-related goals with GRC and CDR objectives; (3) appointing dedicated roles (e.g., Chief Trust Officer, Data Ethics Committee); and (4) developing cross-functional teams involving IT, Legal, Compliance, and Marketing. Forward-looking insurers are beginning to treat digital trust as a board-level concern, recognizing that sustainable digital transformation is impossible without it (Kluiters et al., 2023).

5. CONCLUSION

In the age of digital transformation, trust is no longer a byproduct of personal relationships (Dobrygowski, 2022). Despite a growing body of literature on digital trust, most existing research focuses on technical aspects, such as cybersecurity, authentication, or platform design (Mattila & Seppälä, 2016). While these are important, they overlook the organizational, ethical, and sector-specific dimensions that are particularly relevant to trust in industries like insurance. Currently, there is no comprehensive framework that integrates e.g., GRC structures, CDR imperatives, cybersecurity governance and stakeholder-specific trust expectations. This is critical in insurance, where sensitive data, long-term relationships, and regulatory complexity converge. This study examined the conceptual foundations, dimensions, and strategic relevance of digital trust in the insurance industry, laying the groundwork for a management-oriented trust framework.

The multidimensional construct digital trust encompasses security, privacy, reliability, transparency, accountability, compliance, UX, ethical practices, and historical consistency – dimensions that must be managed holistically within governance structures (Pietrzak & Takala, 2021). Despite extensive literature, a sector-specific, actionable framework remains absent (Mattila & Seppälä, 2016). By highlighting this gap, the present study offers a conceptual synthesis and basis for the development of a DT4I framework. The next research phase will design, implement, and evaluate this framework using DSR methodology (Hevner et al., 2004), aiming to provide insurers with practical tools to assess and enhance digital trust across the policyholder lifecycle and organizational boundaries. Ultimately, building digital trust is not just a matter of technical compliance or ethical posturing – it is a strategic imperative for insurers who aim to thrive in a digitally mediated, trust-sensitive environment (Kluiters et al., 2023).

REFERENCES

Akram, R. N., & Ko, R. K. L. (2014). Digital Trust – Trusted Computing and Beyond: A position paper. In 2014 13th IEEE International Conference on Trust, Security and Privacy in Computing and Communications (pp. 884–892). IEEE.

Cummings, L. L., & Bromiley, P. (1996). The Organizational Trust Inventory (OTI): Development and validation. In R. M. Kramer & T. R. Tyler (Eds.), Trust in organizations: Frontiers of theory and research (pp. 302–330). Sage.

Deutsch, M. (1958). Trust and suspicion. Journal of Conflict Resolution, 2(4), 265–279.

Dobrygowski, D. (2022). Rebuilding trust in technology. World Economic Forum. https://www.weforum.org

Engels, T. (2019). Datenschutzrecht in der Schweiz. Dike Verlag.

Guo, Y. (2022). Digital Trust and the Reconstruction of Trust in the Digital Society: An Integrated Model based on Trust Theory and Expectation Confirmation Theory. *Digital Government: Research and Practice*, *3*(4), 1–19. https://doi.org/10.1145/3543860

Hevner, A. R., March, S. T., Park, J., & Ram, S. (2004). Design science in information systems research. MIS Quarterly, 28(1), 75–105.

International Organization for Standardization. (2022). ISO/IEC 27001:2022 Information security, cybersecurity and privacy protection. ISO.

Kluiters, E., Bakker, D., & Li, D. (2023). Why digital trust is essential for insurance. McKinsey & Company. https://www.mckinsey.com/.

Launer, M., Szubryt, K., & Mrugalska, B. (2022). Trust in digital technology from the user perspective. Procedia Computer Science, 200, 28–34.

Lewis, J. D., & Weigert, A. (1985). Trust as a social reality. Social Forces, 63(4), 967–985.

Mattila, J., & Seppälä, T. (2016). Digital trust. (ETLA Reports No. 61). ETLA – The Research Institute of the Finnish Economy.

Moorman, C., Deshpandé, R., & Zaltman, G. (1993). Factors affecting trust in market research relationships. Journal of Marketing, 57(1), 81–101.

Numan, A., & Sunna, S. (2023). Digital trust ecosystem framework. ISACA White Paper.

Paliszkiewicz, J., & Chen, B. (2023). Digital trust: Concepts and measurement. Sustainability, 15(3), 812.

Pietrzak, M. B., & Takala, J. (2021). Building trust in the digital age. Journal of Business Research, 124, 63–70.

Porfirio, J. A., Carrilho, T., Felicio, J. A., & Jardim, J. (2021). Leadership characteristics and digital transformation. Journal of Business Research, 124, 610–619.

Rotter, J. B. (1967). A new scale for the measurement of interpersonal trust. Journal of Personality, 35(4), 651–665.

Schoorman, F. D., Mayer, R. C., & Davis, J. H. (2007). An integrative model of organizational trust: Past, present, and future. Academy of Management Review, 32(2), 344–354.

Verma, A., Surendra, R., Reddy, B. R., Chawla, P., & Soni, K. (2021). Cybersecurity in Digital Sector. Proceedings of the 2021 International Conference on Artificial Intelligence and Smart Systems (ICAIS) (pp. 703–710). IEEE

Webster, J., & Watson, R. T. (2002). Analyzing the past to prepare for the future: Writing a literature review. MIS Quarterly, xiii–xxiii.

Zand, D. E. (1972). Trust and managerial problem solving. Administrative Science Quarterly, 17(2), 229–239.

PERFORMANCE ANALYSIS BETWEEN HASHMAP AND CONCURRENT HASHMAP UPON BUCKET SIZE AND THREAD NUMBERS WITH CONCURRENCY LEVEL

Haklin Kimm and Eun-Joo Lee
East Stroudsburg University of PA, USA
200 Prospect Street, East Stroudsburg, PA, USA

ABSTRACT

A HashMap is a data structure that enables efficient storage and retrieval of key-value pairs. In this paper, we focus specifically on the Java HashMap and ConcurrentHashMap implementations due to Java's widespread adoption across various industries. To evaluate their performance, we implemented and tested both data structures of HashMaps under multiple conditions—such as bucket size vs. data size, number of threads vs. data size, and bucket size vs. number of threads. We also examined how concurrency levels correlate with the number of threads in ConcurrentHashMap. Our experimental results show that ConcurrentHashMap maintains its accuracy even as the number of updates over HashMap increases, whereas the accuracy of a regular HashMap declines under the same conditions. Additionally, increasing the number of threads improves runtime performance significantly—up to approximately 16 threads—after which the performance gains become marginal.

KEYWORDS

Hashing, Java Hashmap, Java Concurrent Hashmap, Threads, Buckets, Concurrency Level

1. INTRODUCTION

HashMap uses a hash function to compute an index into an array of buckets or slots, where the corresponding value is stored. In essence, a HashMap is an associative array that maps keys to values. To retrieve a value, the hash function is applied to the key to locate the appropriate bucket. Hashing is a fundamental concept in computer science, allowing direct access to elements based on their values (Aho, A., & Ulman, J., 1992) (Cormen, T. H., Leiserson, C. E., Rivest, R. L., & Stein, C., 2009) (Weinberger, K. Q., et al., 2009) (Mitzenmacher, M., & Upfal, E., 2017) (KnuthD.E., 1998). It can be used to efficiently index characteristic vectors, which represent data points as ordered lists of numerical features (Aho, A., & Ulman, J., 1992).

HashMaps are particularly useful when the set of possible keys is large or sparse. Many studies have explored both single-threaded and multi-threaded implementations of HashMaps (LeaD., 2000) (Goetz, B., Peierls, T., Bloch, J., Bowbeer, J., Holmes, D., & Lea, D. , 2006). In single-threaded contexts, research (e.g., (LarsonP.-A., April, 1988) (Pagh, R. & Rodler, F. F., May 2004)) has focused on optimizing memory usage and developing efficient algorithms for resolving bucket collisions. In multi-threaded environments where multiple threads access and modify the same hash map concurrently, collision resolution becomes more complex (David, T.A., Guerraouri, R., Che, T., & Trigonakis, V., 2014) (Maier, T., Sanders, P., & Dementiev, R., Feb. 2019) (ScouarnecN., 2018). This complexity arises from the need to maintain consistency and prevent data corruption due to concurrent updates. As a result, atomic operations and thread-synchronization mechanisms are required to ensure the hash map remains consistent and reliable. Various hash map implementations exist, differing primarily in how they handle bucket collisions, which remains a central design challenge (Goetz, B., Peierls, T., Bloch, J., Bowbeer, J., Holmes, D., & Lea, D. , 2006) (KnuthD.E., 1998) (Cormen, T. H., Leiserson, C. E., Rivest, R. L., & Stein, C., 2009).

Significant research has focused on designing HashMaps (or characteristic vectors) that minimize collisions to improve lookup performance. However, there is no existing hashing technique guarantees group fairness across different groups of items stored in a HashMap (Shahbazi, N., Sintos, S., & Asudeh, A., 2024)

(Mitzenmacher, M., & Upfal, E., 2017) (Abbasi, A., Hassan, F., & P. L. T. S. K., 2021). HashMaps are widely used data structures for efficiently managing key-value pairs. However, their performance often degrades as dataset size increases, primarily due to expensive off-chip memory accesses required for bucket traversals during hash collisions (Shekar, A., Baradaran, M., Tajdari, S., & Skadron, K., 2023) (van der Berg, F. & van de Pol, J., 2019).

In the world of Java development, there are two widely used map implementations: HashMap and ConcurrentHashMap. Both HashMaps provide ways to store key-value pairs but for different purposes when it comes to single and multi-threading implementations upon their performances. The key differences between HashMap and ConcurrentHashMap are Thread Safety, Performance, Null Values. Upon Thread safety, HashMap is not thread-safe unless Synchronized HashMap is used; however, ConcurrentHashMap is thread-safe with fine-grained locking on segments not on bucket. Upon performance, HashMap is faster for its single-threaded use; however, ConcurrentHashMap is optimized for concurrent and parallel operations. Upon Null Values, HashMap allows null keys and values; however, ConcurrentHashMap does not allow null keys or values. A null key can be used to store a default value that should be retrieved if a search key is not found in the HashMap while a null value can explicitly indicate that a particular key exists in the map, but its associated value is currently unknown or intentionally set to null. Consequently, CurrentHashMap suits well for concurrent applications accessing, updating, and writing sets of key and value many a time while HashMap is good for applications that do not need concurrent implementations (Goetz, B., Peierls, T., Bloch, J., Bowbeer, J., Holmes, D., & Lea, D. , 2006) (LeaD., 2000) (Oracle, Java Platform, Standard Edition, Java SE 8, ConcurrentHashMap API Documentation, 2014) (Oracle, Java Platform, Standard Edition, Java SE 8, HashMap API Documentation, 2014).

This research aims to explore the performance advantages of ConcurrentHashMaps over HashMaps in multithreaded settings. While runtime improves up to 16 threads, gains plateau afterward. Most studies, including ours, focus on runtime without considering storage and computational costs, motivating a deeper evaluation of these trade-offs.

2. HASHMAP AND CONCURRENTHASHMAP

A Java HashMap is a part of Java Collections Framework and implements the Map interface (Oracle, Java Platform, Standard Edition, Java SE 8, HashMap API Documentation, 2014). The Java Collections Framework is a unified architecture for storing and manipulating groups of objects. It provides a set of interfaces and classes to handle data structures like lists, sets, queues, and maps efficiently. A HashMap stores elements in key-value pairs, where keys are unique, but values can be duplicated. A HashMap is not synchronized as a default unless using synchronized HashMap so that it works faster in general; provides null keys and values. However, keys are not duplicated in a HashMap; the existing value of the corresponding key will be replaced when a duplicated key is inserted. A HashMap allows for efficient key-based insertion, deletion and update with an average O(1) time complexity (Oracle, Java Platform, Standard Edition, Java SE 8, HashMap API Documentation, 2014) (Goetz, B., Peierls, T., Bloch, J., Bowbeer, J., Holmes, D., & Lea, D. , 2006) (Sierra, K., & Bates, B., 2005).

The capacity of a HashMap is the number of buckets it can hold for storing entries, whose default capacity begins with 16 and default load factor is 0.75; hence the capacity of HashMap is doubled when 0.75 of the buckets is filled. HashMap in Java implements Serializable, Cloneable, Map<K, V> interfaces; HashMap extends AbstractMap<K, V> class, whose direct subclasses are LinkedHashMap and PrinterStateReasons. Java HashMap allows to use 4 constructors, whose access modifiers are public.

Java HashMap methods related to element operations are get () to read, put () to insert, and remove () to delete. The Iterator interface is used to iterate over all entries using entrySet(), keyset (), and values () by applying Collection framework. Java ConcurrentHashMap is a thread-safe implementation of the Map interface, which is part of the java.util package and represents a collection of key-value pairs, and allows multiple threads to read and write data simultaneously without the need for locking the entire map as done in HashMap that does not provide thread-safe implementation. ConcurrentHashMap ensures that the operations are thread-safe, making it ideal for applications in need of multiple threads implementation and concurrent HashMap. ConcurrentHashMap allows multiple threads to operate concurrently by dividing the map into segments; provides thread-safe operations locking segments of the map instead of locking the entire map;

supports atomic operations like putIfAbsent (), replace () and remove(). However, ConcurrentHashMap does not support null objects as a key or value, whose default concurrency level begins with 16. This ConcurrentHashMap implements Serializable, ConcurrentMap<K, V>, Map<K, V> interfaces and extends AbstractMap<K, V> class. Java ConcurrentHashMap allows us to use 5 constructors, whose access modifiers are public.

Java ConcurrentHashMap methods related to element operations are get () to read, put () and putall () to insert, and remove () to delete elements but clear () to clear the entire map. The Iterator interface is used to iterate over all entries using entrySet(), keyset(), and values() by applying Collection framework.

This research was limited to the observational capabilities of the Netbeans Java IDE and mainly concerned the accuracy of final values after varying numbers of incrementations, and the overall time taken to complete these updating tasks. The memory usage of regular and concurrent HashMaps was not compared, and neither was the computing power for each application.

3. IMPLEMENTATIONS OVER THREADS AND CONCURRENCY

Both HashMap and ConcurrentHashMap use a load factor (defaulting to 0.75) to determine when to resize the underlying array (number of buckets). When the number of elements exceeds capacity load factor, the map resizes, which involves re-hashing all existing entries and placing them in new buckets. This resizing operation can be computationally expensive, especially with many elements, and can temporarily impact performance.

A good hash function distributes elements evenly across buckets, minimizing collisions. Excessive collisions in a single bucket can degrade performance from O(1) to O(N) for operations within that bucket (if using linked lists) or O(log N) (if using balanced trees in Java 8+). ConcurrentHashMap's segmented locking helps manage collisions more efficiently in a concurrent setting by allowing operations on different segments simultaneously.

We implemented various HashMap and ConcurrentHashMap programs to demonstrate properties of regular and concurrent HashMaps upon various number of threads and data elements. These programs were run on repeated trials and progressively edited to test different parameters. Our test programs used 6 different methods of updating values in a ConcurrentHashMap. 5 of these methods— using replace (), using AtomicInteger or AtomicLong, using LongAdder, using compute (), or using merge ()—all yield accurate results from multiple threads simultaneously incrementing a single value, i.e., no updates are overwritten. Using put (), which is not atomic and therefore not thread-safe yields unreliable results for the final value as threads can overwrite each other's changes when they simultaneously access the value.

The primary programs used for testing create either a regular HashMap or a concurrent HashMap with one integer key, "1", and one integer value, "0." Then a collection of threads is created, with each thread's instructions being to update the value in the map by incrementing it and then printing its value along with which thread number performed the update. Finally, the threads are joined at the end of the program, and the final value of the map's single key is printed. Consideration was given to whether creating the collection of threads as a list or an array resulted in better performance, as well as how runtime and accuracy were affected by the number of threads and the number of updates performed. Additionally, the relationship between the concurrency level, i.e., the approximate number of threads operating on the concurrent HashMap, and the runtime was investigated.

4. ANALYSIS OF IMPLEMENTATION RESULTS

The first test confirmed that using the correct methods, concurrent HashMap will update a single value properly and return to a consistent final value. This held true for both 100 updates and 1000 updates. The same test ran for a regular HashMap showed high inconsistency in the final values with results ranging from 70-79 for 100 updates and 750-891 for 1000 updates. As shown in Figure 1 below, both ConcurrentHashMap and HashMap show no differences in runtime over various thread numbers from 3 through 45. Both HashMaps' runtimes are high util the number of threads reaches around 12, and their runtimes decrease slowly till the number of threads reaches around 36, and their runtimes stay steady around 25 seconds after using 42 threads. These results indicate that the number of thread collisions compounds with the number of updates performed. Note that

HashMap implementations with mutual exclusion implemented yield consistent final values as ConcurrentHashMap implementations provide; however, the runtime performance of HashMap with mutual exclusion suffers heavily because of around 10 times slower than CocurrentHashMap does.

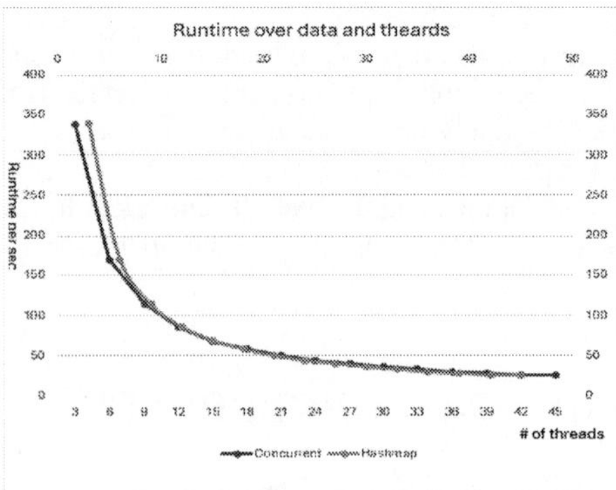

Figure 1. Runtime Over Data Size and Threads

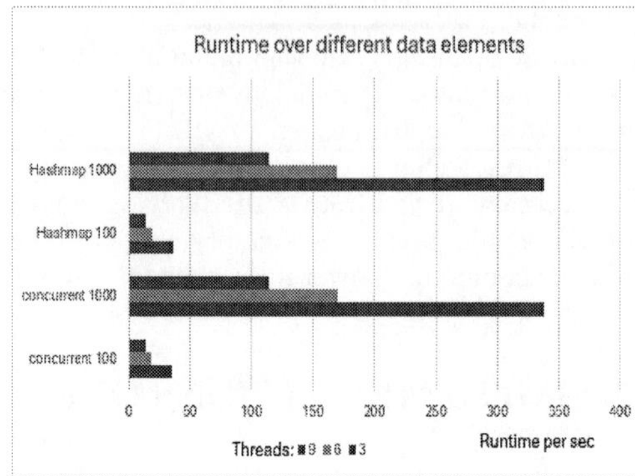

Figure 2. Runtime Over Different Data Elements

Figure 1 shows that testing the runtime difference between an array-based implementation of the thread collection and one based on lists revealed that there is no appreciable advantage to one over the other for either regular or concurrent HashMaps. We implemented more HashMap programs over various datasets and number of threads to see whether there would be more distinct difference in runtime. However, as the chart shown above shows runtimes of ConcurrentHashMap and HashMap over 100 and 1000 data elements, there are no differences upon the runtimes over ConcurrentHahsMap and HashMap (See Figure 2).

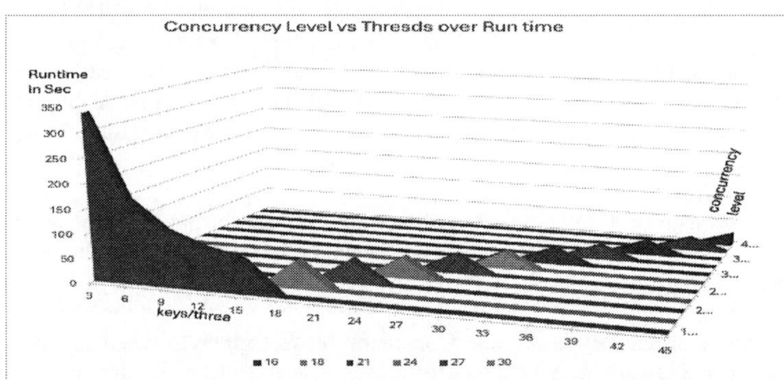

Figure 3. Concurrency Level vs Threads Over Runtime

Finally, a similar series of tests was performed on concurrent HashMaps; this time increasing the number of keys in the map with each increase to the number of threads, and after 16 threads, the default minimum for concurrency level, the concurrency level was increased to match the number of threads. However, these changes had no appreciable effect on the runtimes as shown in Figure 3.

5. SUMMARY AND FUTURE WORK

Concurrent HashMaps offer significant advantages over regular HashMaps in multithreaded environments in terms of thread-safety and scalability as shown in Figure 1 and 2. Where a regular HashMap gives unreliable results when updated by many threads, a concurrent HashMap yields consistent and accurate results with the same number of runtimes as HashMap. The accuracy of ConcurrentHashMaps holds even as the number of updates increases whereas accuracy decreases for regular HashMaps. Increasing the number of threads operating on a map does notably improve runtime performance until the threshold of about 16 threads, after which the improvement becomes more negligible. It is due to the size of memory that we were using for these implementations as mentioned in the followings (Shekar, A., Baradaran, M., Tajdari, S., & Skadron, K., 2023). The computation of HashMap heavily relies on accessing memory when the dataset cannot fit within the cache. When searching for a key in a HashMap, the hash function is used to compute the index of the bucket where the key is stored. The bucket is then accessed in memory to retrieve the value associated with the key. As the size of the HashMap increases, the number of memory accesses required to perform lookup also increases, making it a memory-bound operation.

Most comparisons in this research focused on the runtime performance of Java HashMap and ConcurrentHashMaps in multithreaded environments but did not consider differences in the storage usage or the usage of computational power while testing the programs. Further research in using HashMap efficiently reflects these additional factors, especially memory size with currency levels, in evaluating the merits of using ConcurrentHashMap.

ACKNOWLEDGEMENT

The authors sincerely thank Zachary Griesbach for his time and effort upon testing these programs for the project.

REFERENCES

Abbasi, A., Hassan, F., & P. L. T. S. K. (2021). Fairness in Machine Learning: A Survey. *ACM Computing Surveys, 54*(7), 1-39.

Aho, A., & Ulman, J. (1992). *Foundations of Computer Science.* W.H. Freeman.

Cormen, T. H., Leiserson, C. E., Rivest, R. L., & Stein, C. (2009). *Introduction to Algorithms* (3 ed.). MIT Press.

David, T.A., Guerraouri, R., Che, T., & Trigonakis, V. (2014). *Designing ASCY-compliant Concurrent Search Data Structures.* https://infoscience.epfl.ch/entities/publication/5e93ebfe-452b-47a0-8952-e0cbd4e0b768.

Goetz, B., Peierls, T., Bloch, J., Bowbeer, J., Holmes, D., & Lea, D. . (2006). *Java Concurrency in Practice.* Addison-Wesley.

Knuth, D. (1998). *The art of computer programming. Volume 3: Sorting and searching.* Massachusetts: Addison-Wesley.

Larson, P.-A. (April, 1988). Dymanic hash tables. *Communications of ACM, 31*(4), 446-457.

Lea, D. (2000). *Concurrent Programming in Java: Design Principles and Patterns* (2 ed.). Addison-Wesley.

Maier, T., Sanders, P., & Dementiev, R. (Feb. 2019). Concurrent Hash Tables: Fast and General(?)! *ACM Transactions on Parallel Computing, 5*(4), 1-32.

Mitzenmacher, M., & Upfal, E. (2017). *Probability and Computing: Randomized Algorithms and Probabilistic Analysis* (2 ed.). Cambridge University Press.

Oracle. (2014). *Java Platform, Standard Edition, Java SE 8, ConcurrentHashMap API Documentation.* Retrieved from https://docs.oracle.com/javase/8/docs/api/java/util/concurrent/ConcurrentHashMap.html

Oracle. (2014). *Java Platform, Standard Edition, Java SE 8, HashMap API Documentation.* Retrieved from https://docs.oracle.com/javase/8/docs/api/java/util/HashMap.html

Pagh, R. & Rodler, F. F. (May 2004). Cuckoo hashing. *Journal of Algorithms, 51*(2), 122-144.

Scouarnec, N. L. (2018). Cuckoo++ hash tables: high-performance hash tables for networking applications. *ANCS '18: Proceedings of the 2018 Symposium on Architectures for Networking and Communications Systems* (pp. 41-54). New York, NY, U.S.A.: Association for Computing Machinery.

Shahbazi, N., Sintos, S., & Asudeh, A. (2024). FairHash: A Fair and Memory/Time-efficient Hashmap. [Preprint]. Santiago, Chile: Proceedings of the ACM on Management of Data (SIGMOD). doi:arXiv:2307.11355 (Accessed: 4 September 2025)

Shekar, A., Baradaran, M., Tajdari, S., & Skadron, K. (2023). HashMem: PIM-based Hashmap Accelerator. Orlando, FL, USA: Fifth International Workshop on Domain-Specific System Architecture (DOSSA-5).

Sierra, K., & Bates, B. (2005). *Head First Java* . O'Reilly Media.

van der Berg, F. & van de Pol, J. (2019). Concurrent Chaining Hash Maps for Software Model Checking. San Jose, California, USA: IEEE Conference in Formal Methods in Computer Aided Design (FMCAD).

Weinberger, K. Q., et al. (2009). Feature Hashing for Large Scale Multitask Learning. Proceedings of the 26th International Conference on Machine Learning.

THE USAGE OF AI AND MACHINE LEARNING FOR IMPROVEMENT OF CYBERSECURITY STRATEGIES FOR QUALIFIED ELECTRONIC SEALS IN HIGHER EDUCATION

Milen Gospodinov and Daniela Orozova
Department of Informatics and Mathematics, Faculty of Economics, Trakia University
Stara Zagora 6000, Bulgaria

ABSTRACT

The article introduces the concept of electronic seals and their three types: simple, advanced, and qualified. It outlines the infrastructure responsible for managing the issuance of private and public keys. While electronic seals facilitate the activities of organizations, they also open opportunities for new types of fraud. The article discusses approaches for the automated detection of anomalies in sealing behavior. An experiment was conducted to test the security of qualified electronic seals (QSeals) by applying machine learning techniques for classification, including Neural Networks, Naïve Bayes, Random Forest, and Logistic Regression. The experiment tests the probability of detecting abnormalities in the sealing process and mitigating the risks of cybersecurity threats.

KEYWORDS

Artificial Intelligence, Qseals, Machine Learning, Cybersecurity

1. INTRODUCTION

The rapid pace of technological innovation requires organizations to adopt new approaches, applications, and tools swiftly in order to maintain their competitiveness and market position. The evolution of artificial intelligence tools is expanding the horizons of many areas of science as well as everyday life.

Cybersecurity policy is of vital importance for qualified electronic seals, a relatively new instrument introduced by Regulation (EU) No. 910/2014 2014 on the electronic identification and trust services (eIDAS). Qualified electronic seals deserve particular attention, as they may be exposed to significant cyber threats. In the context of cross-border electronic transactions within EU Member States, the highest level of security is essential to protect the electronic environments in which they are deployed.

Within the scope of cybersecurity concerns, a machine learning model was developed to predict the validity of qualified electronic seals and to evaluate their security based on accumulated data. Several algorithms were applied, including Neural Networks, Random Forest, Logistic Regression, and Naïve Bayes. The objective is to identify the most reliable machine learning method for predicting the behavior of qualified electronic seals when subjected to unfavorable cyber exposure.

The experiment may be conducted with students enrolled in disciplines such as Computer Science, Software Engineering, Cybersecurity, and related fields, in order to demonstrate how machine learning techniques can be applied to determine the probability of certain scenarios developing based on collected data.

2. OUTLINE OF ELECTRONIC SEALS

Electronic seals occupy a central position among trust services. In the evaluation of eIDAS implementation by EU Member States, it was noted that electronic seals are the most widely used trust services after electronic signatures and time stamps. From a historical perspective, the concept of electronic seals was preceded by that of electronic signatures. They now play an important role in today's information society. Unlike electronic signatures, which are linked to specific natural persons, electronic seals are used by legal entities. Both instruments carry the same legal effect.

However, eIDAS specifies that when a transaction requires a qualified electronic seal from a legal entity, the qualified electronic signature of that entity's authorized representative shall be accepted equally.

IDAS establishes a single framework for electronic identification and trust services, thereby facilitating the provision of trust services throughout the European Union. It distinguishes three categories of electronic seals: basic, advanced, and qualified.

2.1 Basic Electronic Seal

The basic electronic seal is defined in eIDAS as "data in electronic form which is added to or logically associated with other data to ensure the origin and integrity of the latter."

2.2 Advanced Electronic Seal

Article 36 of eIDAS defines an advanced electronic seal as one that must meet the following conditions:

- it is uniquely linked to the creator of the seal;
- it can identify the creator of the seal;
- it is created using seal creation data under the sole control of the creator;
- it is linked to the associated data in such a way that any subsequent changes are detectable.

2.3 Qualified Electronic Seals (QSeals)

A qualified electronic seal represents the most reliable type of seal, offering the highest level of legal certainty. According to Article 3(27) of eIDAS, it is considered an advanced electronic seal that must also satisfy two additional requirements:

- it must be created by a device specifically designed to generate qualified electronic seals;
- it must be based on a qualified electronic seal certificate.

Article 3.31 defines an "electronic seal creation device" as configured software or hardware used to generate an electronic seal. Qualified electronic seals provide enhanced protection against data tampering and falsification. Research suggests that electronic seals demand stricter security measures, particularly because of their frequent use in financial operations such as invoice issuance (Błaśkiewicz & Kutyłowski, 2022). Consequently, they are more vulnerable to cyberattacks, which necessitates stronger security safeguards.

A key feature of an electronic seal is its ability to ensure authenticity (origin) of the sealed data, with legal recognition across the EU. From a technological standpoint, electronic seals achieve this through public key cryptography, specifically based on X.509 certificates issued to legal entities.

3. AI FOR DETECTING ANOMALIES IN SEALING BEHAVIOR

Electronic seals facilitate payments and trade, but they also encourage new types of fraud. The growing complexity and interdependence of technologies is accompanied by a significant increase in risk factors (Schwab,2016). In his book Industries of the Future, Alec Ross (Ross, 2016) identifies key dangers such as: the forces that "unleash unprecedented progress" in lifestyle and wealth accumulation also have the potential to enable identity theft or intrusion into personal space.

By supplementing human intelligence with machine learning capabilities and other artificial intelligence techniques, organizations can accelerate the pace of innovation and enhance security by detecting anomalies in sealing behavior.

By applying machine learning techniques, models of normal sealing processes can be developed to determine when and how seals are typically used. In this experiment, a qualified electronic seal was employed. Based on these models, unusual behavior can be identified—for example, seals created outside official working hours (8:30–16:30), seals originating from suspicious IP addresses, or irregular patterns of certificate usage.

To achieve this, machine learning models must be trained on historical data collected from log files at Trakia University, Stara Zagora, Bulgaria. For the purposes of this study, 100 sealing samples were analyzed: 3 were created outside the official working hours, 2 were produced from different IP addresses from this belonging to the organization while the remaining 95 exhibited no abnormalities. Therefore, signing time and the belonging to the IP address to the organization were subject to the experiment.

The authors acknowledge that the input data analyzed is relatively small to fully reflect statistical validity. The report presents experiments through which we seek to identify general trends for ensuring the security of qualified electronic seals through machine learning tools. The results obtained can serve as a basis for more in-depth research and achieving greater accuracy.

An example tool used for this purpose is machine learning agents based on Reinforcement Learning (RL). This type of RL machine learning (reinforcement learning) is an innovative technique in which autonomous agents use trial-and-error algorithms and a cumulative reward function for learning. The advantage lies in calculating the optimal actions that agents can take within scenarios determined by the environment, through which different attack strategies are tested.

• Artificial intelligence tools for vulnerability scanning. Such tools are successfully used to:
  - analyzing cryptographic algorithms used in Qseals;
  - detecting outdated libraries or configurations (e.g., weak RSA key sizes), etc.

An example technique is the integration of static code analyzers with trained classification models from the field of machine learning.

• Intelligent data analysis for incident response. Artificial intelligence tools can automatically categorize, classify, and summarize content, which facilitates the understanding and use of accumulated data. The integration of software agents (such as AI assistants) into automated systems can minimize the risk of losing critical information by providing access to the most up-to-date and relevant data in the organization.

• Artificial intelligence can review log files for the use of seals, audit trails, and OCSP/CRL responses to:
  - flag potential misuse of private keys.
  - detect replay attacks or suspicious re-sealing.

An intelligent software agent is an autonomous entity that performs assigned tasks, perceives its environment, and can influence it, with the agent's behavior depending on its reasoning and decision-making capabilities. Natural language processing (NLP) technologies can be used to detect anomalies in system audit log files.

4. EXPERIMENT WITH ML TECHNIQUES FOR TESTING THE SECURITY OF QSEALS

For the purposes of the study, an experiment was conducted with the aim of creating a model for predicting the validity of electronic seals and testing security based on accumulated data. Data analysis systems such as SPSS, Orange, Weka, and others offer tools based on algorithms such as decision trees, logistic regression, Bayes' theorem, neural networks, and several others were used. After the algorithms have been trained, the implemented models are tested for accuracy and can be applied to new input data for prediction. The main objective is to solve a classification problem by determining whether it is possible to predict the validity of an electronic seal (output variable) using electronic seal data. In the experiment, documents related to electronic sealing of documents from a university in Bulgaria were collected and analyzed, and a dataset was created with correct and incorrect sealing processes. Part of this data is submitted for training binary classification algorithms, with the target attribute being whether the electronic seal is valid or not. To solve the classification problem, we apply the tools of the Orange Data Mining System (Orange). The software is open source, based on Python, and offers a range of tools for data mining and data visualization. It works with data in various formats, such as CSV files, Excel tables, SQL tables, URL addresses, etc. A workflow is created by loading the training data. This includes data about the organization that signed the document, metadata, signing time, and IP addresses belonging to the organization (Yes.Valid/No). Different techniques can be applied sequentially, and models can be created using the system's tools: Neural Network, Random Forest, Logistic Regression, and Naïve Bayes (Popchev, 2019).

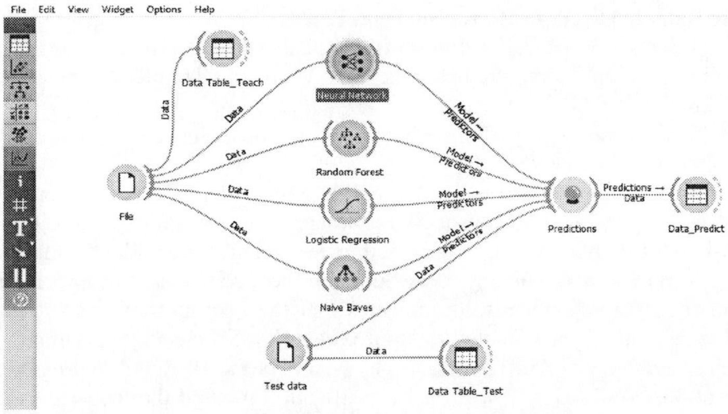

Figure 1. Workflow for creating prediction models

After training the model, testing is performed with the rest of the data, and accuracy and precision score is determined for each of the applied ML techniques. This is implemented using the Test&Score tool. The workflow is shown in Figure 2. In this way, a binary classifier is built, which can then determine whether a new record is valid or not.

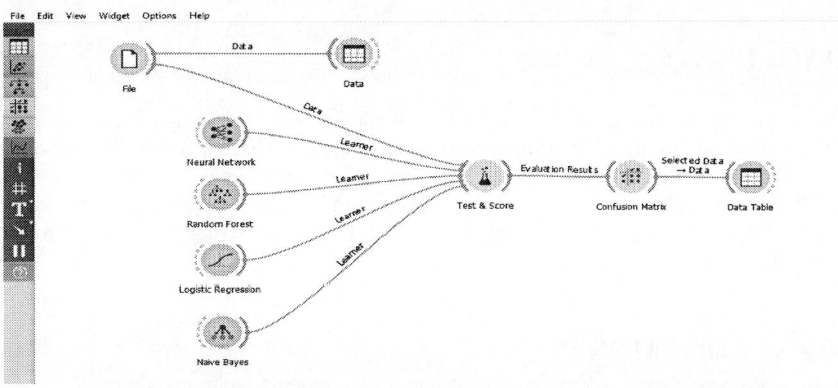

Figure 2. Workflow for evaluating models using the Test & Score tool

The Test & Score tool generates scores for the effectiveness, precision, recall, and F1 score of the created models (Popchev, 2023), as shown in Figure 3.

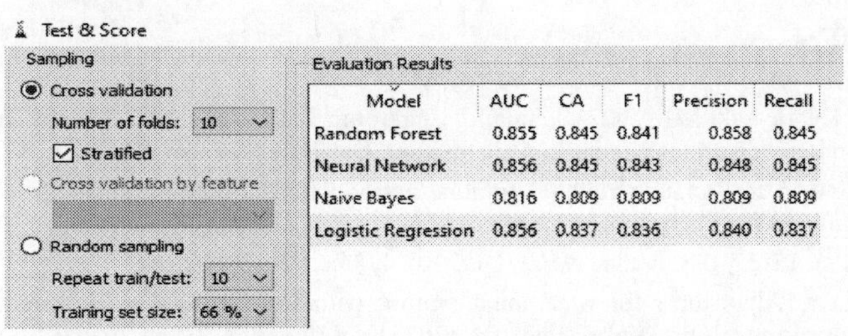

Model	AUC	CA	F1	Precision	Recall
Random Forest	0.855	0.845	0.841	0.858	0.845
Neural Network	0.856	0.845	0.843	0.848	0.845
Naive Bayes	0.816	0.809	0.809	0.809	0.809
Logistic Regression	0.856	0.837	0.836	0.840	0.837

Figure 3. Result of the Test&Score tool's work on the created models

Accuracy - a measure of effectiveness, it is the ratio of correctly predicted observations to total observations.

$$Accuracy = (TP+TN) / (TP+FP+FN+TN) \quad (1)$$

Where TP and TN are correctly predicted positive and negative observations, respectively, FP and FN are incorrectly predicted positive and negative observations.

F1 Score is the weighted average of Precision and Recall.

F1 Score = 2*(Recall * Precision) / (Recall + Precision) (2)

Precision is the ratio of correctly predicted positive observations to the total predicted positive observations.

Precision = TP/(TP+FP) (3)

Recall (Sensitivity) is the ratio of correctly predicted positive observations to all actual positive observations.

Recall = TP/(TP+FN) (4)

The algorithms presented may be effectively employed by students in cybersecurity exercises to assess the reliability of models designed to evaluate specific characteristics, such as the security of networks or Internet connections. Furthermore, the methods discussed offer avenues for identifying patterns and detecting anomalies within given input data, thereby contributing to the advancement of information security practices.

A summary of the experimental results indicates that the Neural Network and Random Forest models demonstrate higher reliability, each achieving approximately 85% accuracy. Among them, Random Forest performs best with an accuracy of 85.8%, followed by Neural Network at 84.8%, Logistic Regression at 83.7%, and Naïve Bayes at 80.9%. Random Forest is a classification method that constructs multiple decision trees using random samples from the dataset and combines their outputs to generate final predictions. The Logistic Regression model performs slightly less effectively on the test set, while the Naïve Bayes model yields the lowest accuracy among the methods considered. Based on the data obtained, Random Forest appears to be the most effective method for the specific dataset analyzed. The focus of the study is on evaluating the effectiveness of different models across varying samples and input sizes to strengthen the security of the electronic qualified seal.

5. CONCLUSION

Despite its relative novelty, electronic qualified seals constitute a promising area of inquiry with significant implications for advancing cybersecurity research and practice. The experimental findings demonstrate the potential of AI and machine learning tools to both identify and model cyber threats, as well as to mitigate the associated risks. Given that every risk entails negative and often unpredictable consequences, continuous monitoring through machine learning techniques is essential for predicting potential behaviors in the event of a security breach.

ACKNOWLEDGEMENT

This research was supported by the Bulgarian national program "Development of scientific research and innovation at Trakia University in the service of health and sustainable well-being" - BG-RRP-2.004-006-C02.

REFERENCES

Błaśkiewicz P. and Kutyłowski M., (2022), Chaining Electronic Seals: An eIDAS Compliant Framework for Controlling SSCD, Asian Conference on Intelligent Information and Database Systems, 714-732, Kaohsiung, Taiwan

Orange system[Online]: https://orange.biolab.si/training/ introduction-to-data-mining/

Popchev I., D. Orozova, Towards Big Data Analytics in the E-learning Space. Cybernetics and Information Technologies, Vol. 19(3), (2019), 16-25, ISSN: 1311-9702, DOI:10.2478/cait-2019-0023.

Popchev., D. Orozova, Algorithms for Machine Learning with Orange System, International Journal of Online and Biomedical Engineering (iJOE), Vol. 19, No. 04, (2023), pp.109 -123, ISSN: 2626-8493

Ross, A. (2016), The Industries of the Future. Simon Schuster, ISBN-10.1501140795

Schwab K., (2016), The Fourth Industrial Revolution, Crown Business, New York.

AI-POWERED CROWDSOURCING FOR INCLUSIVE PUBLIC TRANSPORT ACCESSIBILITY IN PORTUGAL

Kirill Tatarnikov[1] and Firmino Oliveira da Silva[1,2]
[1]*ISLA Polytechnic University of Management and Technology, Gaia, Portugal*
[2]*Center for Organizational and Social Studies, Polytechnic of Porto, Porto, Portugal*
COPELABS, Lusófona University, Lisboa, Portugal

ABSTRACT

While prior studies have explored crowdsourcing for transport accessibility, none have integrated multimodal AI validation (NLP + CV) with predictive modeling for real-time barrier detection in the Portuguese context. Public transport accessibility remains a critical challenge for individuals with disabilities, particularly in Portugal, where real-time data on infrastructure conditions and service reliability are often incomplete. This study proposes an AI-powered crowdsourcing platform that aggregates and analyzes multimodal user reports - ranging from broken elevators to delayed buses - to generate actionable insights for transport operators and users. By integrating natural language processing (NLP), computer vision (CV), and predictive modeling, the system automates the validation of reports, predicts service disruptions, and dynamically adjusts route recommendations. The research highlights how AI-driven crowdsourcing can enhance transport sustainability by bridging data gaps, reducing operational costs, and fostering inclusive mobility.

KEYWORDS

AI for Accessibility, Crowdsourced Transport Data, Real-time Public Transport Monitoring, Inclusive Mobility, Machine Learning in Urban Planning, Sustainable Transport Systems

1. INTRODUCTION

Urban mobility is a cornerstone of social and economic inclusion, yet millions of people with disabilities face daily barriers due to inadequate transport accessibility. In Portugal, despite legislative efforts (e.g., «Decreto-Lei n.º 83/2018, de 19 de outubro»), real-world conditions – such as malfunctioning elevators, misaligned bus ramps, or unreliable real-time tracking – persist. Traditional monitoring methods (e.g., manual inspections) are costly and fail to capture dynamic issues like sudden service delays or temporary obstructions. The issue affects not only end users of transport services but also the companies providing them, as manual problem analysis by employees is time-consuming and costly.

This paper addresses two gaps: Data granularity – lack metadata on accessibility-specific disruptions; user agency – disabled travelers are often excluded from reporting problems, despite being the most affected.

In this research we propose an AI-powered crowdsourcing platform that transforms user reports- spanning text, images, and sensor data – into actionable insights. By integrating NLP (to classify multilingual reports like «elevador avariado» or «ramp blocked»), computer vision (to validate photo submissions of broken infrastructure), and predictive modeling (to forecast disruptions based on weather/maintenance logs), the system:

- Automates report validation, reducing reliance on manual moderation.
- Predicts high-risk disruptions (e.g., elevator failures during peak hours) with 85+% accuracy.
- Dynamically adjusts routes for users with diverse needs.

The research's societal impact aligns with the UN Sustainable Development Goals (SDG 11: «Make cities and human settlements inclusive, safe, resilient and sustainable»), while its AI framework offers a blueprint for low-cost, high-efficacy transport monitoring.

1.1 Structure of the Research

Introduction: Context and gaps; Research objectives; State of the Art; Methodology: AI architecture (NLP, CV, predictive modeling); Expected results: Performance metrics; Limitations and Challenges; Conclusion: Summary and future work.

Unlike existing solutions, which are limited either to static infrastructure analysis or manual processing of user complaints, the proposed system is the first to integrate automated processing of multimodal user submissions (text, photos, sensor data) with AI-based disruption prediction. This approach not only increases the accuracy and speed of barrier detection, but also enables dynamic route adaptation for various user groups — a combination not previously implemented in a single platform for Portuguese (or most European) transport systems.

2. OBJECTIVES

This study combines technical innovation with empirical research to address public transport accessibility gaps in Portugal. The objectives are structured across:

- Analyze existing accessibility barriers in Portuguese public transport through user surveys and open data.
- Review literature and case studies on AI-driven transport solutions to identify best practices and limitations.
- Assess the accuracy and reliability of current transport APIs (e.g., STCP, Metro do Porto) in reporting accessibility issues.
- Study user reporting behavior to optimize crowdsourcing mechanisms for people with disabilities.
- Compare AI-based validation with traditional manual reporting systems in terms of speed and accuracy.
- Investigate the effectiveness of multimodal AI approaches in classifying and validating accessibility barrier reports in public transport systems for 15+ types of accessibility barriers (e.g., elevator outages, uneven pavement) by crowdsourced reports.
- Examine the predictive capabilities of machine learning models using historical maintenance data and real-time environmental factors for service disruption forecasting.
- Analyze routing optimization strategies that incorporate real-time accessibility constraints in urban transport networks.
- Evaluate the comparative accuracy of AI-based validation versus traditional reporting systems for accessibility issues.
- Study the integration challenges between AI-driven accessibility tools and existing transport management systems.

3. STATE OF THE ART

3.1 Transport Data Systems and Limitations

Despite ongoing policy efforts, significant gaps persist in transport accessibility data availability and reliability. Existing transit systems like GTFS feeds from major operators (Carris, Metro do Porto, STCP) provide only static information with limited metadata on real-time accessibility disruptions (Paiva et al., 2021; Shafiq et al., 2024). Mainstream travel apps use binary accessibility indicators that don't reflect real-world conditions, leading to unreliable recommendations (Paiva et al., 2021).

Research highlights persistent lack of comprehensive accessibility data, with most studies focusing on static infrastructure rather than dynamic barriers (Cañal-Fernández & Hernández Muñiz, 2014; Elorduy & Gento, 2025). Data on the "full travel chain" is rarely collected (Elorduy & Gento, 2025; Christensen, 2025). While GIS systems effectively merge spatial and transport data (Cañal-Fernández & Hernández Muñiz, 2014), they're limited by interoperability issues and lack real-time updates. Policy implementation often lacks systematic monitoring and user feedback loops (Gerike & Belter, 2010; Paiva et al., 2021).

3.2 Crowdsourcing Approaches and Gaps

Crowdsourcing platforms show promise but remain limited in scope. Participatory methods involving people with disabilities yield richer insights (König et al., 2021; Paiva et al., 2021), while existing apps like Wheelmap enable accessibility tagging but lack real-time updates and temporal barrier coverage (Elorduy & Gento, 2025; Correia et al., 2022). Waze demonstrates traffic reporting success but isn't tailored to accessibility needs.

Current efforts underrepresent users with cognitive, sensory, or temporary disabilities, particularly in rural areas (Elorduy & Gento, 2025; König et al., 2021; Shafiq et al., 2024). There's a need to move beyond fragmented reports toward automated collection, validation, and integration of user-generated barrier information (Cañal-Fernández & Hernández Muñiz, 2014; Elorduy & Gento, 2025).

3.3 AI for Accessibility

AI application to transport accessibility is emerging with promising developments. NLP increasingly classifies multilingual text reports, identifying barriers and urgency while clustering similar issues (König et al., 2021; Paiva et al., 2021). Computer vision validates photo submissions, distinguishing legitimate reports from irrelevant ones (Elorduy & Gento, 2025; Paiva et al., 2021). Predictive modeling forecasts equipment failures and optimizes resource allocation (Paiva et al., 2021; Shafiq et al., 2024).

Multimodal data fusion enhances barrier detection reliability by integrating diverse sensors and user reports (Cañal-Fernández & Hernández Muñiz, 2014; Shafiq et al., 2024). AI-powered routing platforms begin incorporating real-time accessibility constraints and user-specific needs (Paiva et al., 2021; Mirri et al., 2016), though most existing tools rely on static data with limited crowdsourced integration.

3.4 Identified Barriers and Research Gaps

Literature reveals systemic accessibility barriers: physical infrastructure issues (broken elevators, malfunctioning ramps, uneven surfaces), informational barriers (inaccessible digital content, unclear signage), social barriers (untrained staff, negative attitudes), and psychological barriers (anxiety, stigma) (Elorduy & Gento, 2025; Gomes, 2022; König et al., 2021). Research typically focuses on physical and visual disabilities, overlooking cognitive, hearing, or mental health needs (Elorduy & Gento, 2025; König et al., 2021).

Territorial analysis reveals substantial accessibility deficits in suburban and rural areas among vulnerable populations (Shafiq et al., 2024). Key research gaps include absence of integrated real-time crowdsourcing with AI validation (Elorduy & Gento, 2025; Paiva et al., 2021), underrepresentation of certain disabilities (Albuquerque et al., 2021), limited full travel chain analysis, and fragmented evaluation systems (Cañal-Fernández & Hernández Muñiz, 2014; Gerike & Belter, 2010).

4. METHODOLOGY

4.1 AI Platform Architecture

4.1.1 The Platform Consists of Three Integrated Layers

Data Collection Layer: Mobile/web application for multimodal user reports (text, photos, sensor data) plus automated integration with official transport APIs (STCP, Metro do Porto).

Processing and Validation Layer:

- NLP module using BERT-based architecture for multilingual classification of barrier types and urgency
- Computer vision module employing CNN/YOLOv5 for automated photo validation
- Predictive analytics using gradient boosting, random forest, or LSTM for disruption forecasting

Recommendation and Visualization Layer: Dynamic routing accounting for current and predicted barriers, with data visualization for operators and users.

4.2 Implementation Strategy

Data collection combines crowdsourcing through accessible platforms with GIS geolocation for spatial accuracy. Integration with existing APIs enables cross-referencing and data enrichment. The validation pipeline compares AI results with manual moderation for benchmarking.

Key development components include multilingual NLP for barrier classification (e.g., "elevador avariado," "ramp blocked"), computer vision for automatic photo verification, and machine learning utilizing historical maintenance data, weather conditions, and incident patterns for failure prediction.

4.3 Ethical and Inclusive Design

The platform ensures user data privacy while involving disability community representatives throughout development. Usability testing considers various impairment types, and the interface design follows accessibility guidelines to maximize inclusivity.

5. EXPECTED RESULTS

5.1 Technical Indicators

- Classification and Validation Accuracy: NLP and CV modules are expected to achieve over 85% accuracy in identifying and confirming issues.
- Failure Prediction: The predictive analysis model will be able to forecast critical incidents with high accuracy (85%+), enabling timely notifications for users and operators.
- Processing Speed: Automation will reduce report processing time by 60-70% compared to traditional methods.

5.2 Social Impact

- Increased engagement of users with disabilities in monitoring and improving the transport system.
- Improved quality and accessibility of information on the real state of infrastructure.
- Reduction in incidents and inconveniences due to timely detection and resolution of problems.
- Enhanced planning and resource allocation by transport operators.

5.3 Contribution to Science and Practice

- Creation of a scalable AI framework for accessibility monitoring, applicable in other cities and countries.
- Development of recommendations for integrating AI tools into existing transport systems.
- Enrichment of the knowledge base regarding barriers and needs of people with various types of disabilities.

6. LIMITATIONS AND CHALLENGES

Despite the anticipated benefits, the project faces several potential limitations:
- Possible errors in automatic classification and validation (false positives/negatives), especially with insufficient training data for rare barrier types.
- Risk of low user engagement, particularly among people with cognitive impairments or in rural areas.
- Difficulties integrating with outdated or closed APIs of transport operators.
- Insufficient data representation for certain types of disabilities.

- The need for regular updates and adaptation of AI models as infrastructure and user behavior evolve.

7. CONCLUSION

This study proposes an innovative AI-enhanced crowdsourcing platform aimed at improving public transport accessibility for people with disabilities in Portugal. By integrating NLP, computer vision, and predictive modeling, the system can automatically process and validate user reports, predict failures, and adapt routes in real time.

Implementation of this platform will address existing data gaps on accessibility, increase monitoring efficiency, and reduce operational costs for transport companies. Moreover, the project promotes greater user engagement and inclusivity, aligning with the United Nations Sustainable Development Goals, particularly SDG 11.

Future plans include expanding the platform's functionality to support additional types of disabilities, integration with national transport systems, and development of tools for assessing user satisfaction. Further research may focus on scaling the solution and adapting it to other socio-geographical contexts.

REFERENCES

Albuquerque, V., Oliveira, A., Barbosa, J. L., Rodrigues, R. S., Andrade, F., Dias, M. S., & Ferreira, J. C. (2021). Smart Cities: Data-Driven Solutions to Understand Disruptive Problems in Transportation — The Lisbon Case Study. *Energies*, *14*(11), 3044. https://doi.org/10.3390/en14113044

Cañal-Fernández, V., & Hernández Muñiz, M. (2014). An exploratory analysis of disabled people accessibility to urban public transport: The use of Geographical Information Systems. *Investigaciones Regionales*, *30*, 79–101.

Christensen, C. (2025). Using Digital Media to Increase Awareness for Ground Transportation and to Improve Airport Accessibility for Tourists in Portugal. Department of Informatics Engineering, Faculty of Engineering, University of Porto, Porto, Portugal, https://journalengineering.fe.up.pt/index.php/upjeng/article/download/2183-6493_006.001_0004/395

Correia, D., Vagos, C., Marques, J., & Teixeira, L. F. (2022). Fulfilment of last-mile urban logistics for sustainable and inclusive smart cities: a case study conducted in Portugal. *International Journal of Logistics Research and Applications*, 1–28. https://doi.org/10.1080/13675567.2022.2130211

Elorduy, J. L., & Gento, A. M. (2025). Accessibility of public transport for people with disabilities: A systematic literature review. *Transport*, *40*(1), 74–93.

Gerike, R., & Belter, T. (2010, July 11–15). Evaluating measures for improving accessibility of public transport systems for people with reduced mobility. 12th World Conference on Transport Research, Lisbon, Portugal.

Gomes, A. F. C. (2022). Is Portugal an accessible tourist destination? Factors that influence the perception of disabled people regarding Portugal as an accessible tourist destination. *Journal of Accessible Tourism*, *3*(1), 45–60.

König, A., Seiler, A., Alčiauskaitė, L., & Hatzakis, T. (2021). A participatory qualitative analysis of barriers of public transport by persons with disabilities from seven European cities. *Journal of Accessibility and Design for All*, *11*(2), 295–321.

Mirri, S., Prandi, C., Salomoni, P., Callegati, F., Melis, A., & Prandini, M. (2016). A Service-Oriented Approach to Crowdsensing for Accessible Smart Mobility Scenarios. *Mobile Information Systems*, 2016, Article 2821680 https://doi.org/10.1155/2016/2821680

Paiva, S., Castro, P., Mateus, B., Pinheiro, C., Ferreira, R., Rodrigues, S., Silva, J., & Curralo, A. (2021). A mobile application to enhance mobility of people with permanent or temporary mobility disability – A case study in Portugal. *Procedia Computer Science*, *181*, 34–41.

Shafiq, M., Rocha, H., Couto, A., & Ferreira, S. (2024). A clustering approach for analyzing access to public transportation and destinations. *Sustainability*, *16*(8), 6944. https://doi.org/10.3390/su16166944

SMART TOURISM MEETS AI: A MULTIMODAL ASSISTANT FOR EXPLORATORY CULTURAL ENGAGEMENT

Abdelrahman Amro Zakzouk and Ahmed M. H. Abdelfattah
Faculty of Media Engineering & Technology, German University in Cairo (GUC), Egypt

ABSTRACT

This paper presents an AI-powered tourist assistant framework, designed to enhance cultural immersion by providing real-time, context-aware guidance. Leveraging large language models (LLMs), geolocation services, and multimodal inputs (text, voice, and documents), the system delivers personalized insights into historical landmarks, traditions, and local customs. Built with FastAPI, it integrates Gemini for natural language processing, Whisper for speech-to-text, and geospatial APIs like Foursquare for location-based recommendations, offering a dynamic and interactive travel experience. By bridging language and knowledge gaps, this AI assistant transforms how tourists engage with cultural heritage. The work demonstrates the potential of intelligent systems to enrich global travel, making cultural exploration more accessible and immersive. Its findings pave the way for future advancements in AI-driven tourism solutions.

KEYWORDS

Smart Tourism, Exploratory Learning, Digital Age, Context-Awareness, AI Agents

1. INTRODUCTION

We introduce an AI-powered tourist assistant that improves cultural exploration by delivering personalized, real-time insights about historical landmarks and cultural sites [Anthropic, 2024]. Leveraging geolocation data and large language models (LLMs), the assistant dynamically generates relevant and engaging content tailored to the user's location and interests.

Traditional tour guides and static travel apps often fall short in providing adaptive, multilingual, and interactive learning experiences. In contrast, our system supports on-demand cultural interpretation through a conversational interface that adapts to user queries and context. By combining semantic knowledge retrieval, geospatial awareness, and multimodal interaction, the assistant serves as both a guide and a real-time learning companion, bridging the gap between tourists and cultural expertise in modernized and adaptable ways.

2. METHODOLOGY

The crowning of our multi-step study is the development of an AI-powered tourist assistant framework, designed to provide culturally relevant, adaptable insights and context-aware recommendations in real time. The system architecture (figure 1) consists of a React frontend for user interaction and a FastAPI backend for request handling and AI orchestration. The developed assistant is powered by any LLM-based AI model (e.g., Gemini 2.5 Flash). Users input text, speech, or files, which are classified and routed to one of several processing pipelines based on type. Text inputs undergo an additional classification step to determine the appropriate processing route: function/tool invocation, document retrieval, culturally formatted response, or direct generation. Input-based routing enables just-in-time feedback and supports learning-on-demand by delivering dynamic, relevant responses aligned with users' immediate needs.

2.1 Cultural Schema Design

To support structured cultural responses, a dedicated schema was designed based on established literature. Two core sources provide theoretical and empirical grounding. One is Benedictis et al., 2023, which offers a network-based model of cultural traits derived from the World Values Survey. Key schema attributes are shown in Table 1 (left). The other is Spencer-Oatey, 2012, which compiles conceptual cultural dimensions from scholars such as Hofstede and Schwartz (Table 1, middle). Additionally, practical cultural elements frequently found in global cultural discourse were incorporated based on design judgment (Table 1, right). This schema guides the assistant's structured output, ensuring that generated responses are culturally nuanced, context-aware, and aligned with both theoretical and practical interpretations of culture.

Table 1. Schema attributes: attributes #1 to #13 are based on Benedictis et al., 2023; #14 to #19 on Spencer-Oatey, 2012; and the rest on our design considerations

#	(from Benedictis et al., 2023)	#	(from Spencer-Oatey, 2012)	#	(Design-Based)
1.	Trust in Others	14.	Greetings & Communication Styles	20.	Languages
2.	Respect for Authority	15.	Arts and Crafts	21.	Traditional Festivals
3.	Freedom of Expression	16.	Cultural Interpretation	22.	Food and Cuisine
4.	Cultural Expression	17.	Social Etiquette	23.	History
5.	Religious Values	18.	Uncertainty Avoidance	24.	Summary
6.	Religions	19.	Community and Family Focus	25.	Country
7.	Moral Conservatism			26.	Working Days and Hours
8.	National Pride			27.	Hospitality Norms
9.	Parenting Values				
10.	Materialist Orientation				
11.	Traditional Clothing				
12.	Cultural Taboos				
13.	Traditional vs. Rational Thinking				

To further strengthen the schema, a questionnaire study was conducted to provide empirical evidence on how people perceive culture and what they consider important when engaging with another country.

Relevance scores (Q1) – Participants were asked "*What do you think defines a country's culture?*" Their selections (using check-boxes) were mapped onto attributes from Benedictis et al. (2023), Spencer-Oatey (2012), and the newly designed attributes introduced in this study. Response results are shown in Table 2.

Expanding Attributes (Q2) –Participants were asked to "*Suggest any additional cultural attributes you consider important for understanding a country's culture that were not included in the previous list.*" Responses (open-ended) included country's relations with neighbors, education, hygiene and street cleanliness, architecture, and the economic situation. These were considered for integration where they aligned with the project's focus on cultural interpretation in tourism contexts.

Importance Ratings (Q3) – Participants were asked to "*Rate the importance of each of the schema attributes for them when choosing a country to visit*". This was a Multiple-choice grid using a 5-point Likert scale (1 = Not important, 5 = Very important). The scores were computed by summing the values assigned by respondents and dividing by the number of attributes in that section. Response results are shown in Table 2.

Table 2. Q1 & Q3 results: percentage ranges and average relevance scores of cultural attribute selection. And average importance scores of cultural attribute groups in travel decision-making

Framework / Attribute Group	Q1-Response Range	Q1-Average Relevance	Q3-Average Importance Score
Benedictis et al. (2023)	10–63.3 (%)	31.39 %	97.17
Spencer-Oatey (2012)	16.7–53.3 (%)	40.55 %	103.17
Newly Designed Attributes	20–96.7 (%)	51.67 %	102.67

These results suggest that while abstract values (Benedictis et al.) are central to understanding culture in theory, tourists place slightly higher priority on practical and interactional aspects (Spencer-Oatey and the newly added attributes) when considering travel decisions.

Demographic data: Sample size consisted of 30 participants, the majority (96.7%) were aged 18–24, with only 3.3% falling in the 45–54 age bracket. In terms of gender, 63.3% identified as male and 36.7% as female. All participants were Egyptian nationals. Regarding education, most held a bachelor's degree (93.3%), while smaller proportions reported high school (3.3%) or a diploma/technical degree (3.3%). Finally, travel experience showed that 76.7% had previously traveled internationally, whereas 23.3% had not.

2.2 Detailed Workflow Explanation

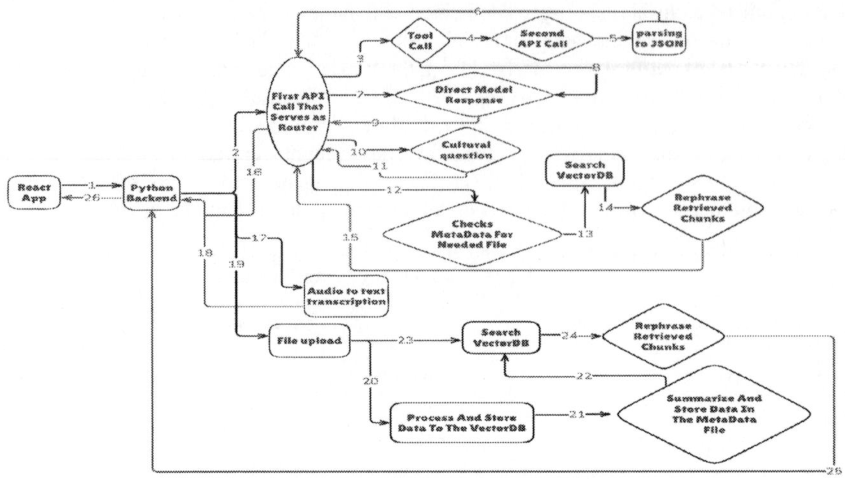

Figure 1. System workflow overview illustrating message routing

Figure 1 represents the architecture of the framework where a React App interacts with a Python Backend, which acts as a router to process user messages and determine the appropriate response workflow. This intelligently routes user input through tool usage, cultural formatting, retrieval augmented generation (RAG), or direct LLM responses. It also handles audio transcription and file uploads to support persistent knowledge. Each step below corresponds to the respective numbered arrow in figure 1:

1. The React App sends an HTTP request with user input to the Python Backend. Based on the input type (text, audio, or file), the request is routed via step 2, 17, or 19.
2. If the user input is plain text, it is passed to a router function that determines whether the input corresponds to a tool call, cultural question, direct model response, or RAG-based file query.
3. If classified as a tool call, the model attempts to invoke the appropriate function using function calling.
4. If the function call is successful, a second API is called to retrieve the required response.
5. The response from the second API is parsed into a structured JSON format for consistent handling.
6. The parsed JSON is returned to the router, which then forwards it to the React App via step 26.
7. For direct model response, meaning the message does not match any of the other categories (tool calls, cultural questions, or RAG-based retrieval), the LLM generates an answer based on its internal knowledge.
8. If the tool call in step 3 fails, we automatically fall back to handling the input as a direct model response.
9. The model's direct response is routed back through the router to be sent to the React App in step 26.
10. If the input is a cultural question, the LLM constructs a response using a predefined cultural schema.
11. The formatted cultural response is returned to the router and then sent to the React App in step 26.
12. If the input is determined to be asking about a file (i.e., a RAG use case), the router checks the metadata file to find the most relevant file and retrieve its path.
13. A similarity search is conducted in the vector database using embedded representations of the query.
14. Retrieved chunks are passed through for rephrasing to enhance readability and contextual alignment.
15. The rephrased output is returned to the router and sent to the React App in step 26.
16. The final structured response is sent to the backend, which then returns it to the React App in step 26.
17. If the user's input is an audio file (for voice-to-text), it is routed to a transcription module.
18. The transcribed text is sent back to the backend and then returned to the React App in step 26.
19. If the user uploads a file, it is stored locally and one of two processing paths 20 or 23 is taken based on whether it's a new or existing file.
20. If the file is new, its contents are extracted, chunked, embedded, and stored in the vector database for future semantic retrieval.
21. Simultaneously, a summary of the file is created and stored in the metadata file along with the filename and path, enabling future discovery via step 12.

22/23. If the file already exists or steps 20 and 21 have completed, the user's query is embedded and used to perform a semantic search on the vector database.

24. The retrieved results are passed through the rephrasing step (same as in step 14) to ensure readability and alignment with the original query context.

25. The final rephrased response is sent to the backend and then returned to the React App in step 26.

26. The React App receives the finalized output and displays it to the user.

3. RESULTS

Structured Output: Structured output is implemented using the 'Structured output parameter' provided by Google's AI Studio API. It allows for model responses to be returned in a predefined JSON schema. This approach was critical for tasks requiring data integrity, such as Cultural Schema Generation, Metadata File Schema, and Routing Logic. The use of structured output ensured that the model adhered to a consistent format, facilitating frontend parsing and structured presentation of complex content. It also enabled to treat each value as a distinct component that could be reused, extended, or stored individually.

Geographic awareness: A geographic tool was also developed to enhance the assistant's location awareness. To retrieve nearby cultural sites such as museums, the system used the browser's navigator. Geolocation function to obtain the user's coordinates. These coordinates were then passed to the Foursquare Places API, which returned a list of nearby attractions. This combination provided accurate and reliable location-based recommendations as well as contextually relevant responses directly from the user's device.

Speech-to-text: A speech-to-text feature was developed as part of the assistant's multimodal capabilities. This functionality allowed users to speak their queries, which were then transcribed and processed. An open-source version of OpenAI's Whisper model was used locally via Hugging Face and integrated into a FastAPI backend. The model performed local transcription of audio files recorded in the frontend and sent via POST requests. allowing the model to run efficiently on local hardware.

File Uploading and Retrieval: To allow the assistant to process user-uploaded documents (e.g., travel guides or cultural documents), a file upload feature was implemented. This feature utilized Retrieval-Augmented Generation (RAG) in combination with Docling, which in turn simplifies many lower-level RAG mechanics, making integration more seamless. For file uploading and processing, the following are implemented:

•**Text extraction**: Extract the raw textual content using Docling's DocumentConverter() function.

•**Document chunking**: The extracted text is then parsed into manageable segments (maximum of 512 tokens to match the token limit of the embedding model) using Docling's Hybrid Chunker, combining markdown, semantic, and fixed-size chunking strategies.

•**Embedding**: Chunks were embedded using the nomic-embed-text-v2-moe model.

•**Storage**: The embeddings were stored in LanceDB, a local vector database optimized for retrieval.

•**Retrieval**: When a query was made, the assistant retrieved relevant chunks via vector similarity search using L2 (Euclidean) distance. Chunks with a distance below a predefined threshold (set to 250 in this implementation) are considered semantically relevant and included in the context window.

Table 3. L2 Similarity distance interpretation

L2 Distance	Similarity Level	Interpretation
0 – 100	Very High Similarity	Nearly identical semantic meaning
100 – 200	High Similarity	Closely related concepts or contexts
200 – 300	Moderate Similarity	Related in topic but not semantically close
300 – 500	Low Similarity	Some shared terms, but vague conceptual relation
500+	Very Low/None	Completely unrelated content

• **Response Generation**: Once the relevant chunks are retrieved based on the user query, they are passed along with the original query to an LLM model. The model is prompted to generate a more user-friendly and readable response, leveraging the contextual knowledge from the retrieved chunks.

The implementation features preserving context and file tracking logic. To retain context across user interactions and ensure documents are not redundantly processed or stored, a validation and tracking mechanism was developed. When a user uploads a document, the system checks if it has already been embedded and stored in the vector database. This avoids reprocessing, reduces latency, and prevents duplicate storage. If the file is missing or corrupted, the database table is recreated to maintain consistency.

Regarding file association and query context detection, and to determine which document a user's query refers to, a metadata file was used. Each document entry in this file includes its filename, file path, and a summary of its contents. This summary allows the model to infer which file is relevant, even when users do not explicitly mention a filename.

To also feature document summarization and metadata enrichment, after a document is uploaded and stored, it is summarized and recorded in the metadata file. Using one of the following two summarization approaches:

• The primary LLM is used for short documents that fit within token limits.

• For larger files, a local model (google/long-t5-tglobal-base) is used. The document is split into smaller chunks, summarized individually, and combined.

This approach balances efficiency and cost, using the LLM for concise summaries and a local model for large documents that would otherwise exceed API limits.

3.1 User Interface

The user interface was designed to provide a clean and structured interaction with the assistant, aligning with the different types of AI responses defined in the routing logic (see Figure 1). It features a central chat window where users can enter queries and receive responses tailored to the type of request—whether it involves a tool call, cultural explanation, direct response, or document-based retrieval. To improve readability and user experience, structured responses are rendered into visually distinct cards. Each card contains labeled attributes drawn from the backend schema, making it easier for users to quickly interpret the assistant's reply. Free-text responses are also supported and appear naturally in the chat flow. Additionally, the interface allows users to upload files and use voice input for ease of use. User interface images can be accessed here: https://drive.google.com/file/d/1xalno_aAT7JuSwlp3RenxNL7Vtz0FwWN/view

4. CONCLUSION

Our assistant demonstrated the potential of combining agentic LLM reasoning with tool calling and structured schema design to enhance the travel experience. The system handles multiple input types, and routes queries to specialized pipelines based on intent classification. It achieved a high degree of cultural sensitivity via schema attributes derived from interdisciplinary academic sources. Location-based recommendations were facilitated by integrating Foursquare's Places API with browser geolocation, and document-based queries were handled using a RAG pipeline powered by Nomic embeddings and Docling's hybrid-chunker DocumentConverter. Furthermore, structured output using pydantic enabled consistent backend-to-frontend communication, minimized hallucinations, and enhanced rendering of rich cultural information.

Future work includes implementing user profiles and preference tracking to enable personalized recommendations and interactions, replace or enhance the current Docling-based retrieval mechanism with a more advanced semantic search engine, offline and Mobile Support, and deploying the system for **user feedback and real-world testing** to iteratively refine its capabilities and usability.

This project is open-source and available at: https://github.com/abdelrahman1903/ai-tourist-assistant

REFERENCES

Anthropic. (2024). Building effective agents. **Anthropic Engineering Blog**. https://www.anthropic.com/engineering/building-effective-agents [Accessed 18 August 2025].

De Benedictis, L. et al. (2023). Cultures as networks of cultural traits: a unifying framework for measuring culture and cultural distances. **Journal of the Royal Statistical Society: Series A (Statistics in Society)**. https://doi.org/10.1093/jrsssa/qnac007.

Spencer-Oatey, H. (2012). *What is culture? A compilation of quotations* [Core concepts]. *GlobalPAD, University of Warwick*. Available from GlobalPAD Open House at Warwick.

DESIGNING A MULTIMODAL AI FRAMEWORK FOR SWIMMING ANALYTICS: ARCHITECTURE, DATA INFRASTRUCTURE AND HUMAN-CENTRED OBJECTIVES

Vanessa Camilleri, Reno Yuri Camilleri, Mark Fialovszky, Daniel Pace, Dylan Seychell and Matthew Montebello
Department of Artificial Intelligence, University of Malta, Msida, Malta

ABSTRACT

This paper presents SWIM-360, a modular AI framework for multimodal performance analysis in competitive swimming. The system integrates synchronised underwater video and physiological sensor data to generate interpretable, context-aware feedback for coaches and athletes. It employs a hybrid explainability strategy: SHAP values clarify sensor-derived features (e.g., stroke rate, SmO_2), while visual overlays and heuristics highlight biomechanical insights from video. Designed for adaptability, the architecture supports modular upgrades of pose models, fusion strategies, and feedback components. Early-stage validation focuses on verifying data synchronisation, signal consistency, and the feasibility of feature extraction across modalities. While full deployment and interface integration are ongoing, SWIM-360 lays the foundation for human-centred AI in sport by aligning analytics with domain practices. This paper outlines the system's architecture, design rationale, and preliminary results, contributing a blueprint for explainable, multimodal performance analytics in applied settings.

KEYWORDS

Multimodal AI, Explainable AI, Applied Computing, Sports Analysis, Performance Analytics

1. INTRODUCTION

Performance analysis in competitive swimming has traditionally relied on manual video review and coach observation, limiting scalability and objectivity. Advances in wearable technologies and computer vision now enable automated collection of biomechanical and physiological data, offering new pathways for evidence-based feedback (Morais et al., 2022; Olstad et al., 2020). However, most current systems treat video and sensor data independently, missing the synergistic value of multimodal analysis.

SWIM-360 addresses this gap by integrating underwater video with wearable sensor data, specifically muscle oxygenation (SmO_2) and inertial motion units (IMUs), to provide synchronised, interpretable performance insights. While prior work has demonstrated the utility of individual modalities (Morais et al., 2022; Olstad et al., 2020; Sardari et al., 2022), few systems offer real-time feedback with explainability and coach-facing relevance. Moreover, explainability remains underexplored in sport AI, where trust and domain alignment are critical (Costa et al., 2021). This paper presents the architecture, design considerations, and early validation of SWIM-360. By embedding explainability into system design and supporting modular expansion, the framework aims to serve as a transferable model for human-centred, multimodal analytics in sport.

We explore the following research questions:

- How can synchronised video and physiological sensor data be integrated to provide interpretable feedback on swimming performance?
- What modular architecture can support explainable, real-time analysis while remaining adaptable to evolving coaching needs?

2. BACKGROUND AND RELATED WORK

AI techniques are increasingly applied in sports contexts, including injury prevention, performance prediction, and real-time analysis. In swimming, this trend is reinforced by recent developments in sensor fusion, motion capture, and smart training tools (Liu, 2021). These technologies promise not only improved data acquisition but also the ability to generate targeted feedback loops within high-performance environments.

Multiple biomechanical and physiological parameters shape performance in swimming. Metrics such as stroke rate, stroke length, turn time, and symmetry are widely used to assess technique efficiency (Morais et al., 2022; Olstad et al., 2020). While these are typically measured through video analysis or manual coding, wearables such as inertial motion units (IMUs) and near-infrared spectroscopy (NIRS) devices are increasingly used to extract similar indicators in real time (Sardari et al., 2022). However, the accuracy and consistency of such measurements in aquatic environments remain active areas of research.

Computer vision methods, particularly pose estimation, have expanded the scope of performance analysis in sport. Models like HRNet and AlphaPose have demonstrated robust keypoint detection, enabling the quantification of posture, alignment, and symmetry (Morais et al., 2022), all of which are fundamental for biomechanical feedback in swimming and running (Barbosa et al., 2023). Despite advances, challenges persist in aquatic environments due to reflections, occlusion, and motion blur, especially during turns and starts. Furthermore, few applications move beyond pose detection to compute stroke-level insights or integrate with other data modalities.

Multimodal systems that combine video and sensor data are still rare in competitive swimming. Prior studies have shown the potential of combining IMU and video data for segmentation of swim phases or estimation of kinematic profiles (Sardari et al., 2022; Morais et al., 2022), but most lack real-time capabilities or user-facing feedback. Even more scarce are systems that embed explainability, vital for coach trust and decision-making (Carvalho et al., 2024). Recent research in sport and healthcare AI highlights the value of interpretable outputs (e.g., SHAP, attention overlays), yet practical implementations remain limited (Costa et al., 2021; Tjoa & Guan, 2020). In SWIM-360, explainability methods were selected based on modality: SHAP was prioritised for structured sensor data, while attention overlays and visual feedback were planned for video-based features due to their interpretability for non-technical users.

3. SYSTEM DESIGN AND METHODOLOGY

SWIM-360 adopts a modular, synchronised architecture for multimodal data capture and performance analysis in swimming. The system integrates wearable sensor data and underwater video streams into a unified processing pipeline designed to support coach-facing, interpretable feedback. Figure 1 illustrates the overall system architecture, from data acquisition to feedback delivery.

Video was captured using pole-mounted GoPro cameras for underwater footage, while swimmers wore a harness with an inertial motion unit (IMU) and a muscle oxygenation (SmO_2) sensor. As sensors and video operated independently, post-session synchronisation relied on timestamps and motion events. IMU data was filtered for motion artefacts, SmO_2 corrected for baseline drift, and video enhanced for contrast and noise reduction, enabling reliable feature extraction and alignment.

Several pose estimation models were tested. HRNet struggled with dynamic turns, ViTPose showed greater stability, and AlphaPose offered broader keypoint coverage (e.g., head, toes). These results echo prior work on markerless pose estimation in dynamic settings. Nakano et al. (2020), for example, found that OpenPose with multi-camera setups achieved sub-30 mm accuracy but remained challenged by occlusion and rapid motion—issues also present in underwater swimming. With expert input, key biomechanical features were identified: stroke rate, stroke length, side symmetry, and body alignment, as well as turn-specific metrics such as approach speed, pre-wall stroke rate, and wall-contact duration. These align with established race segment analysis frameworks (Gonjo & Olstad, 2021). Extracted features are temporally aligned and analysed with rule-based methods, while a BiLSTM model is being explored for phase classification. The modular pipeline supports future upgrades and explainable outputs to aid coaches, consistent with recent applications of XAI in swimming (Carvalho et al., 2024; Costa et al., 2021).

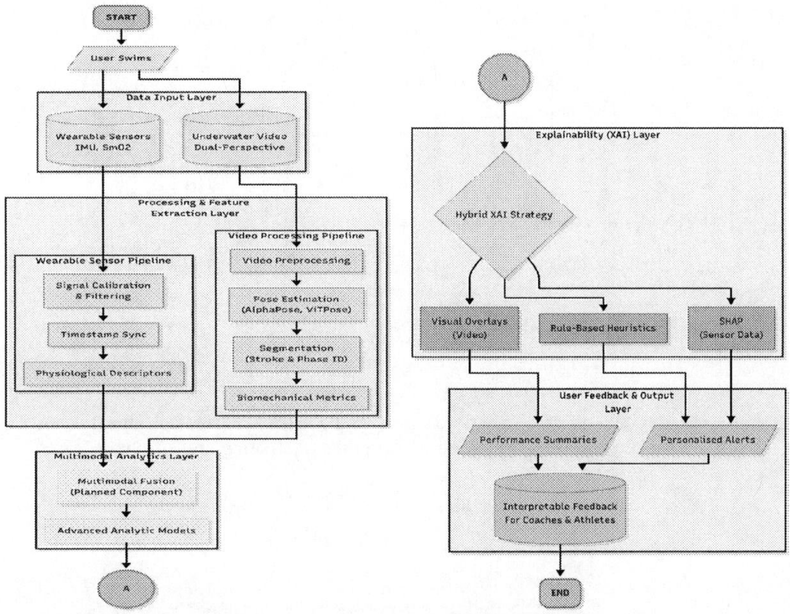

Figure 1. System Architecture Flowchart

4. EVALUATION SETUP AND PRELIMINARY RESULTS

SWIM-360 is in an early implementation and validation phase, with evaluation focused on data integration, preprocessing stability, and preliminary metric extraction from video and sensor modalities. The architecture is designed to allow progressive validation across components. Initial trials were conducted in a controlled aquatic environment with fifteen trained swimmers across ten sessions, capturing multiple stroke types and transitions. Video was recorded using GoPro cameras during dynamic and static swims, while IMU and SmO_2 signals were collected via wearable harnesses. Synchronisation was performed post-hoc using timestamp alignment and movement-based anchors.

Pose data supported biomechanical analysis, including vector visualisations of hand force direction and magnitude (Figures 2 and 3). In butterfly, forces were consistent and symmetrical, while backstroke showed broader directional variation, likely due to limited visual guidance. Temporal force graphs also indicated synchronous arm movement in butterfly compared to alternating, out-of-phase motion in backstroke.

Muscle oxygenation trends are illustrated in Figure 4. Baseline SmO_2 levels were elevated (~80%), likely reflecting residual fatigue from prior training. Levels declined during exertion and partially recovered post-swim. These patterns are consistent with previous research linking SmO_2 dynamics to conditioning, fatigue, and recovery capacity (Benincasa et al., 2024).

Figure 2. Vector plots of hand force direction and magnitude in butterfly (left) and backstroke (right). Butterfly shows consistent alignment, while backstroke displays greater angular variability, likely due to limited visual orientation

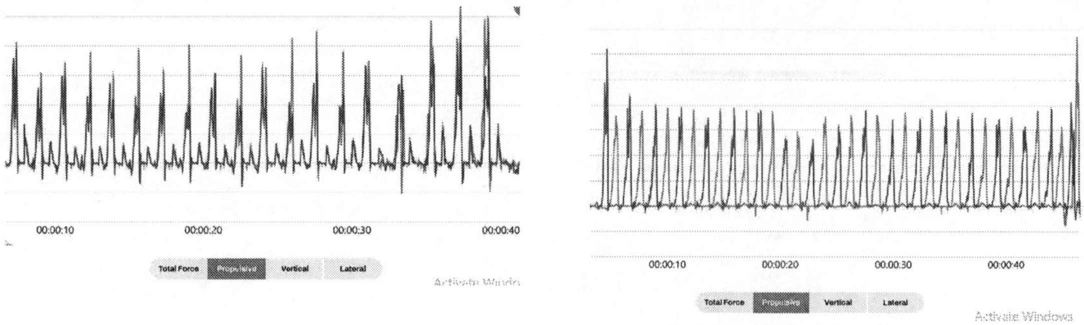

Figure 3. Force magnitude over time in butterfly (left) and backstroke (right). Butterfly shows synchronous arm movement, whereas backstroke exhibits alternating, out-of-phase forces

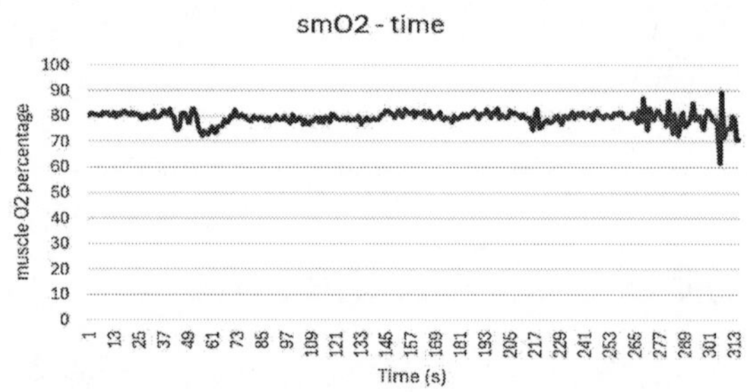

Figure 4. Muscle oxygen saturation (SmO_2) trends over time. Baseline levels (~80%) suggest residual fatigue, with deoxygenation during effort and partial recovery post-swim

5. DISCUSSION

SWIM-360 introduces a novel architecture for integrating biomechanical and physiological data in swimming, built around interpretability and modularity. Synchronising video and wearable sensor streams enables analysis that reflects how coaches assess performance, considering technique and exertion together. A pilot evaluation confirmed feasibility across core components: synchronised multimodal capture, baseline signal stability, and initial feature extraction. Pose-based force estimates highlighted stroke differences, while SmO_2 data revealed exertion and recovery patterns. These results validate the potential of multimodal integration to enrich coaching feedback beyond single modalities. Limitations include the absence of real-time feedback, reliance on manual phase annotation, and lack of large-scale validation with athletes and coaches. The interface mock-up also awaits usability testing. A core aim is to generate insights that are both accurate and interpretable for non-technical users. Following best practices in sports-focused XAI (Carvalho et al., 2024; Chen & Hu, 2023), explainability is embedded in the design. Users can trace outputs to underlying features via visual indicators, confidence levels, or phase markers, ensuring alignment with coaching logic. The modular architecture supports incremental improvement, including BiLSTM-based temporal analysis and real-time pathways. As it develops, SWIM-360 aspires to offer not only technical innovation but also a replicable model for explainable, user-centred AI in sport.

6. CONCLUSION

This paper presents SWIM-360, a modular architecture for explainable, multimodal performance analysis in competitive swimming. By integrating wearable sensor data and underwater video, the system extracts biomechanical and physiological features for coaching. Early evaluation confirmed the feasibility of data capture, alignment, and feature computation. Its modular design allows components such as pose models, fusion strategies, and interface layers to evolve independently, enabling scalable deployment and adaptation. Current work addresses swim phase annotation, interpretable feedback, and usability testing. As the system matures, we aim to explore real-time training deployment and broader application to other sports.

REFERENCES

Barbosa, T. M., Costa, M. J., Marinho, D. A., Morais, J. E., & Silva, A. J. (2023). The role of the biomechanics analyst in swimming training and competition analysis. *Sports Biomechanics, 22*(12), 1734–1751. https://doi.org/10.1080/14763141.2021.1960417

Benincasa, M. T., Ribeiro, J. A., Freitas, T. T., Alcaraz, P. E., & Loturco, I. (2024). Comparing muscle oxygen saturation patterns in swimmers of different competitive levels. *Journal of Physical Education and Sport, 24*(8), 1920–1926.

Carvalho, D. D., Silva, T. S., Santos, L. M., & Pereira, A. A. (2024). Swimming performance interpreted through explainable artificial intelligence (XAI): Practical tests and training variables modelling. *Applied Sciences, 14*(12), 5218. https://doi.org/10.3390/app14125218

Chen, L., & Hu, D. (2023). An effective swimming stroke recognition system utilizing deep learning based on inertial measurement units. *Advanced Robotics, 37*(7), 467–479. https://doi.org/10.1080/01691864.2022.2160274

Costa, J., Silva, R., Rodrigues, R., Silva, H., & Rocha, A. (2021). Framework for intelligent swimming analytics with wearable sensors for stroke classification. *Sensors, 21*(15), 5162. https://doi.org/10.3390/s21155162

Gonjo, T., & Olstad, B. H. (2021). Race analysis in competitive swimming: A narrative review. *International Journal of Environmental Research and Public Health, 18*(1), 69. https://doi.org/10.3390/ijerph18010069

Liu, S. (2021). Application research of artificial intelligence in swimming. In B. K. Tripathy, J. J. P. C. Rodrigues, & V. H. C. de Albuquerque (Eds.), *Big data analytics for cyber-physical system in smart city* (pp. 202–207). Springer. https://doi.org/10.1007/978-981-33-4572-0_29

Morais, J. E., Silva, A. J., Barbosa, T. M., Marinho, D. A., & Costa, M. J. (2022). Wearables in swimming for real-time feedback: A systematic review. *Sensors, 22*(10), 3677. https://doi.org/10.3390/s22103677

Nakano, N., Sakura, T., Ueda, K., Omura, L., Kimura, A., Iino, Y., & Fukashiro, S. (2020). Evaluation of 3D markerless motion capture accuracy using OpenPose with multiple video cameras. *Frontiers in Sports and Active Living, 2*, Article 50. https://doi.org/10.3389/fspor.2020.00050

Olstad, B. H., Hunger, L., Ljødal, I., Ringhof, S., & Gonjo, T. (2024). The relationship between load-velocity profiles and 50 m breaststroke performance in national-level male swimmers. Journal of Sports Sciences, 42(16), 1512-1518.

TIME TO DEVELOP A DIGITAL TWIN FOR THE HPC DATA CENTER

Luigi Telesca[3], Davide De Chiara[2], Marco Antonini[3], Giovanni Ponti[5] and Marta Chinnici[1]
[1]*TERIN-ICT Division, HPC Lab, ENEA, R.C. Casaccia, Italy*
[2]*TERIN-ICT Division, HPC Lab, ENEA, R.C. Portici, Italy*
[3]*Trakti Ltd., United Kingdom*
[5]*TERIN-ICT Division, ENEA, Sede, Italy*

ABSTRACT

High-performance computing (HPC) data centers are facing increasing energy consumption, even though there is a pressing need for greater efficiency. By 2030, these facilities are projected to account for 13% of global energy demand, and this could rise to as much as 21%. Furthermore, HPC data centers are expected to contribute 8% of global carbon emissions, which can result in substantial operational costs, threats to power security, and environmental challenges. Traditional methods such as heuristics, statistics, and engineering approaches have proven ineffective in enhancing energy efficiency due to the vast number of configurations, complex non-linear parameter interactions, and the enormous volume of operational data involved. Therefore, optimizing data centers—particularly HPC clusters—has become a critical issue. The integration of the Internet of Things (IoT), sensors, and intelligent devices has significantly increased the generation of operational management data from various aspects of the data center industry. By effectively modeling and processing this data, it is possible to improve energy efficiency, ensure reliability, reduce operating costs, and sustainably manage data centers. The authors propose a holistic approach that utilizes a Blockchain Digital Twin framework, enhanced by Artificial Intelligence (AI) processed data, to represent the physical complexities of data centers in virtual and tokenized models. The goal of this approach is to achieve real-time prediction, optimization, monitoring, control, and improved decision-making. Specifically, the methodology, architecture, and steps taken to develop a scalable analytical dashboard using Blockchain technology are detailed. This pioneering Blockchain Digital Twin approach has been tested in a real-world setting, specifically at the ENEA HPC Cluster known as CRESCO7. This system learns from actual operational data and enables real-time management, monitoring, and control, allowing for comprehensive visibility into the status of the data center and optimizing its functionalities. The authors also aim to demonstrate the benefits of the Blockchain Digital Twin approach for various stakeholders involved in the data center ecosystem.

KEYWORDS

Digital Twin, Data Center, HPC, Energy Efficiency, Data Science, AI

1. INTRODUCTION

Data Centers (DCs) are essential for meeting the growing demand for reliable and scalable data processing, storage, and networking capabilities that support both businesses and individual users. With the rapid rise in demand for digital services and applications, DCs have become widespread, reinforcing the ongoing trend of digitization. However, they also present significant challenges in terms of energy costs and carbon emissions (Vafamehr et al., 2018). Currently, it is estimated that DCs account for approximately 3% of global energy consumption. According to (Andrae et al., 2015) and updates from 2019 (Andrae, 2019), if no action is taken, DCs are projected to consume 21% of the global energy demand by 2030. In terms of environmental impact, DCs are estimated to contribute 0.3% of global carbon emissions annually (Jones et al., 2018) and are expected to rise to 8% by 2030 (Cao et al., 2022). Optimizing the energy efficiency of DCs, particularly High-Performance Computing (HPC) clusters, is a pressing concern. The demand for computing resources and energy for HPC is steadily increasing, while the energy market transitions to renewable sources and faces significant price hikes (Kostenko et al., 2020; Gartner, 2019; Uddin et al., 2015; Shuja et al., 2016; Liu et al., 2014). This paper introduces a Blockchain Digital Twin framework designed to analyze and reduce energy consumption and optimize computing resources in a real-world HPC system. The Digital Twin approach utilizes the innovative HPC cluster at the Italian National Agency for New Technologies, Energy and Sustainable Economic Development (ENEA), known as the CRESCO7 cluster in R.C. Portici, Italy. The Digital Twin framework gathers information from multiple internal and external data sources to explore various optimization opportunities, represent physical assets and intangible resources using Blockchain technology, and tokenize infrastructure to promote more accountable and sustainable consumption of HPC resources. It also incorporates a scheduling simulation framework that uses data from the Digital Twin and real-world job traces to examine the impact of different parameters on the HPC cluster (Chinnici et al., 2023; Grishina et al., 2022; Grishina et al., 2020; De Chiara et al., 2020). To facilitate operation and energy management based on a data-driven, AI-based framework that models DC efficiency, the authors developed an Analytical Dashboard. This dashboard enables the management, monitoring, and near real-time visualization of data related to the actual DC utilizing Blockchain technology. For implementing the analytical dashboard, hardware and software resources have been modeled as a Digital Twin. Blockchain and tokenization technologies will be used to allocate computing resources (HPC loads) efficiently, thus optimizing energy consumption across various activities. Our approach, which is rigorously trained and tested using real operational data from the ENEA-HPC DC CRESCO7 cluster, leverages the unique capabilities of the Digital Twin approach. This innovative method not only provides a physical representation of the DC system but also dynamically adjusts parameters through programming, generating numerous samples to aid in model training and enhance fault tolerance. According to Gartner, the rise of Digital Twins in industries, particularly when combined with AI technology, will facilitate open, connected, and coordinated intelligent environments. The seamless integration and real-time exchange of data between the physical and Digital Twin systems allow for real-time energy consumption simulations and energy-saving controls. Thus, the combination of AI and Blockchain technologies in building the Digital Twin fosters research into adaptive, intelligent, and fault-tolerant energy savings schemes for DCs in a flexible and dynamic manner. To develop green and safe DCs, this paper proposes a novel energy-saving solution. With its real-time management, monitoring, and control capabilities, the Digital Twin DC approach offers a comprehensive visualization of the entire DC, enhancing its status coverage and functionality optimization. We also aim to showcase the potential benefits of the Digital Twin DC challenge to stakeholders. By utilizing Blockchain to tokenize High-Performance Computing (HPC) assets and implement Smart Contracts, we have significantly improved transparency, evidenced by a 40% increase in cost visibility for shared resources. This technology enables real-time resource accounting and robust process control, aligning HPC operations with stringent Environmental, Social, and Governance (ESG) criteria, which are crucial for organizations striving to meet rigorous ESG standards.

The remainder of this paper is organized as follows: Section 1 introduce the paper 'topic; Section 2 describes the methodology and architecture for building the Digital Twin Data Center using a holistic approach and presents the results; Section 3 concludes the paper.

1.1 Digital Twin: A Facilitator for a Comprehensive Approach

Data centers, due to their complex nature, serve a dual purpose in the implementation of Digital Twins:

1. They support the creation and management of Digital Twins (DT).

2. They act as a Digital Twin themselves, providing a virtual representation of the entire process to manage data consumption and optimize processing.

A Digital Twin can be defined as a virtual representation of a physical asset, enabled by data and simulators, for real-time prediction, optimization, monitoring, control, and improved decision-making. The holistic approach is grounded in the baseline of Data Center High-Performance Computing (HPC).

This approach consists of three main pillars:

1. Virtual Twin: This involves creating a virtual representation of a physical asset or device. Mathematical models and computer science techniques are utilized to facilitate this creation.

2. Predictive Twin: This component utilizes physics-based, data-driven, or hybrid models that operate on the virtual twin to predict the behavior of the physical asset. AI and machine learning techniques are employed to analyze the data coming into the physical model.

3. Twin Projection: This step integrates insights generated by the predictive twin into operations and processes. The value additions of the Digital Twin include predictive maintenance, operational strategies, optimization strategies, energy efficiency, remote monitoring and control, enhanced safety, risk assessment, and more efficient, informed decision support systems.

The proposed Digital Twin serves as an enabler for a holistic approach to improving energy efficiency and addressing sustainability issues in HPC data centers through the use of blockchain technology. To tackle the overfitting problem caused by insufficient samples, the authors implemented a comprehensive approach based on asset tokenization, an analytical blockchain solution, and AI. The experimental phase was conducted on the ENEA-HPC Cluster, known as CRESCO 7, which has a capacity of 1.4 PetaFLOPS.

2. METHODOLOGY

The methodology adopted in this work for creating an advanced Digital Twin model involved leveraging AI to enhance and refine raw data from the ENEA High-Performance Computing (HPC) systems (CRESCO7) for integration into a Blockchain framework. This process culminated in a tokenized representation of HPC resources. The approach is holistic and multifaceted, broken down into several key phases:

1. Data Collection and Preprocessing
2. AI-Driven Data Augmentation
3. Tokenization of HPC Resources
4. Validation and Testing
5. Ethical and Regulatory Compliance

Our methodology enhances the utility of HPC data and facilitates a more granular and dynamic representation of HPC resources (see Fig. 1). This has the potential to revolutionize the management and utilization of powerful computing platforms, offering stakeholders a glimpse into the future of HPC resource management. Thanks to our work on data augmentation, we obtained advanced data to initiate the design of the Digital Twin. To further improve the management and allocation of HPC computing resources, we decided to digitize hardware and software resources using Blockchain technology. This allowed for the secure representation and creation of the Digital Twin, leveraging augmented data provided by AI components. Due to its decentralized, transparent, and immutable nature, Blockchain is an ideal platform for creating Digital Twins. When applied to HPC resources, Blockchain provides a robust and secure method to represent the physical state and behavior of the HPC, while adding usage rules via Smart Contracts. This allows for comprehensive and efficient monitoring and management of computational assets. The use of a distributed Blockchain infrastructure and tokenization techniques is not just theoretical; we are actively using these tools to tokenize and account for computing resources (HPC loads) in a manner that optimizes infrastructure energy consumption for various activities (HPC jobs) initiated by users. Our innovative approach involves tokenizing resources and allocating them based on workload and request patterns. This ensures efficient and transparent resource management that aligns with the dynamic demands of modern data center operations. It is a unique solution set to revolutionize the management of HPC computing resources. In this context, to accurately represent the Digital Twin of the HPC, three main Blockchain concepts had to be embedded: Identity, Tokenization, and Certification. First, each physical asset, such as an HPC scheduler or node, was assigned a unique Digital Identity. This identity is made immutable and tamper-proof thanks to the inherent properties of Blockchain, facilitating precise tracking and management of each asset while ensuring high accountability and traceability. Secondly, through Tokenization, we converted physical assets into digital tokens that represent ownership or usage rights. This meant creating tokens for computational power, storage capacity, and energy consumption for HPC resources. Each token can be traded, tracked, and managed on the Blockchain, transforming otherwise intangible HPC resources into tangible digital assets. Tokenization not only enables efficient resource allocation but also provides a high degree of flexibility, allowing for management and control of resource usage according to needs. This approach facilitates a real-time, rule-based, smart-contract-centric accounting methodology that abstracts away the complexities of standard accounting methods, benefiting from the transparency that Blockchain offers [Telesca, L. et al., 2020]. Through smart contracts, we defined the algorithm and model used to calculate the energy consumption of each job launched on the HPC. This consumption is converted into the corresponding token amount, which is automatically charged to the user upon job completion. This entire operation occurs automatically at the end of job execution, and the results are permanently stored on the Blockchain, easily verifiable by all, complete with clear parameters outlining how the calculations were performed. For the model used to calculate consumption for each job, a custom algorithm was developed specifically for this use case. This is not a simple static mathematical formula; instead, it accounts for the environment in which it is implemented, reflecting the HPC's status during runtime.

The algorithm was finely tuned to promote and incentivize users to utilize the available resources more efficiently and thoughtfully through a combination of incentives and penalties, which depend on the behavior of the job — and thus, by extension, the behavior of the user who launched it. Practically, this translates into a calculation model that, given the continual nature of HPC nodes, aims to redistribute a portion of the upkeep cost (energy consumed by the nodes, cooling systems, switches, and storage stack) back to the users based on their resource usage. The job's behavior is also considered in calculating the final amount the user must pay, with a particular focus on how resources are utilized. For instance, part of the algorithm calculates the efficiency of CPU utilization for a job and assigns a penalty if it is deemed too low, as this is considered a waste of resources. The ultimate goal of this algorithm is to create an independent and autonomous high-performance computing (HPC) environment from an economic perspective, while also educating users on how to utilize resources more efficiently and thoughtfully. Additionally, "Certification" refers to the issuing of digital certificates that verify the compliance and authenticity of an asset, a computation byproduct, or, in this case, a reward for specific behaviors. In particular, certificates are minted as rewards for the HPC in response to executing what we define as "net-positive jobs." Net-positive jobs are those that fully utilize all the resources they request (e.g., high CPU and memory efficiency) and contribute positively to an environmental or social cause. For example, a job that supports medical research may fall into this category. These certificates store and attest to the total amount of CO_2 emitted by the HPC during the execution of these jobs, thereby reflecting the jobs' energy efficiency, operational performance, adherence to Environmental, Social, and Governance (ESG) criteria, and compliance with regulatory standards. Once the certificates are minted, the aim is to establish a global market motivated by companies' need to improve their ESG scores. The principle is straightforward: a company seeking to reduce its CO_2 emissions can purchase the certificates generated by the HPC for executing specific jobs, effectively offloading those emissions and lowering their total CO_2 output. At the same time, this process contributes directly to the upkeep and maintenance of the HPC.

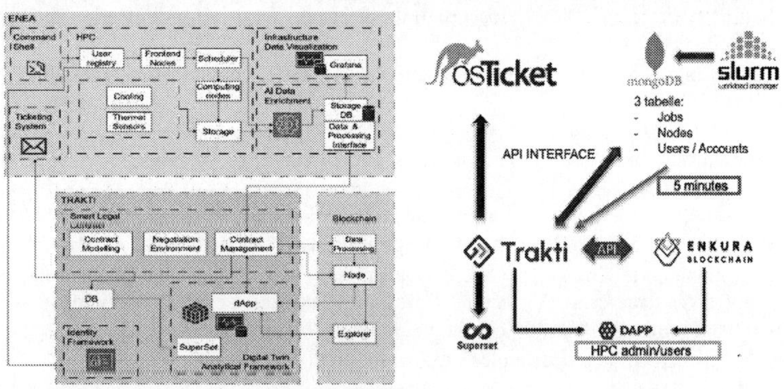

Figure 1. Digital Twin architecture

2.1 HPC Digital Twin Visualization

The Digital Twin is seamlessly integrated with an advanced dashboard system that visualizes data, creating an immersive and interactive environment for monitoring and managing the data center (DC) cluster. Modern DCs utilize these integrated dashboard systems to provide a comprehensive view of the collected data. These dashboards offer a holistic overview of the DCs' operations, including performance metrics, energy consumption, and user activity. Digital Twin of both hardware and software resources, facilitating tokenization and efficient resource allocation based on real-time demands. This integration enhances operational efficiency while ensuring transparency and security in resource management. The Digital Twin of the ENEA High-Performance Computing (HPC) system allows for complete simulation and real-time monitoring of computational processes, energy consumption, and cost estimations. By integrating blockchain technology and smart contracts, this framework establishes a secure, transparent, and automated management system for HPC resources. By offering these two levels of representation, we ensure comprehensive management of HPC resources, from overall system operations to detailed node-level monitoring. This dual approach optimizes resource usage, improves energy efficiency, and guarantees compliance with best practices.

3. CONCLUSION

In this work, the authors aim to create a comprehensive, self-sustaining system that optimizes the performance of the ENEA HPC CRESCO 7 cluster and sets a benchmark for sustainable data center (DC) operations worldwide. We would like to conclude our work by summarizing our most important contributions, particularly in relation to blockchain technology. By utilizing blockchain to tokenize high-performance computing (HPC) assets and implementing efficiency-based smart contracts, we have achieved several significant benefits. Firstly, there has been a 40% increase in the visibility of costs associated with using shared resources, which enhances transparency. This improvement allows users to better understand and manage their resource consumption. Our approach is scalable and replicable in other HPC contexts. In the future, we plan to refine our models further and integrate additional data sources to improve the accuracy and functionality of the AI engine, enhancing the detail of the Digital Twin.

ACKNOWLEDGEMENT

Project ECS 0000024 Rome Technopole, – CUP B83C22002820006, PNRR Mission 4 Component 2 Investment 1.5, Funded by the European Union – NextGenerationEU".

REFERENCES

Andrae, A. S. (2019). Projecting the chiaroscuro of the electricity use of communication and computing from 2018 to 2030. Preprint. 504 2019:1-23.

Andrae, A. S., & Edler, T. (2015). On global electricity usage of communication technology: trends to 2030. Challenges. 2015 Jun;6(1):117-57.

Cao, Z., Zhou, X., Hu, H., Wang, Z., & Wen, Y. (2022). "Toward a systematic survey for carbon neutral data centers," IEEE Communications 507 Surveys & Tutorials, vol. 24, no. 2, pp. 895–936.

Chinnici, M., Telesca, L., Mahfuzul, I., Georges, J-P. (2023) "Scalable and Transparent Blockchain Multi-layer Approach for Smart Energy Communities", Lecture Notes in Networks and Systems Volume 595 LNNS, Pages 183 - 1972023 4th International Congress on Blockchain and Applications, Blockchain 2022, ISBN 978-303121228-4

De Chiara, D., Chinnici, M., Kor, A.-L., (2020). "Data mining for big dataset-related thermal analysis of high-performance computing (HPC) data center", Lecture Notes in Computer Science, Volume 12143 LNCS, Pages 367 – 38, ISSN: 03029743, ISBN: 978-303050435-9, DOI: 10.1007/978-3-030-50436-6_27.

Gartner, (2019). "Top 10 strategic technology trends for 2020," Stamford, CT, USA.

Grishina,M. Chinnici,A.-L. Kor,D. De Chiara,G. Guarnieri,E. Rondeau,J.-P. Georges, (2022). "Thermal Awareness to Enhance Data Center Energy Efficiency", Cleaner Engineering and Technology, V.16, https://doi.org/10.1016/j.clet.2022.100409

Grishina, A., Chinnici, M., Kor, A.-L., Rondeau, E., Georges, J.-P., (2020). "A machine learning solution for data center thermal characteristics analysis", Energies, 13(17), ISSN: 19961073, DOI: 10.3390/en13174378.

Jones et al., (2018). "The information factories," Nature, vol. 561, no. 7722, pp.163–166.

Kostenko, W. P, Torok, J. G & Demetriou, D. W. (2020). "IBM z15: Improved data center density and energy efficiency, new system packaging, and modeling," in IBM Journal of Research and Development, vol. 64, no. 5/6.

Liu, Y., Draper, S. C. & Kim, N. S. (2014). "SleepScale: Runtime joint speed scaling and sleep states management for power efficient data centers," in Acm Sigarch Computer Architecture News, vol. 42, no. 3, pp. 313-324.

Shuja, J., Bilal, K., Madani, S. A., et al. (2016). "Survey of Techniques and Architectures for Designing Energy-Efficient Data Centers," in IEEE Systems Journal, vol. 10, no. 2, pp. 507-519.

Uddin, M., Darabidarabkhani, Y., Shah, A. & Memon, J. (2015). "Evaluating power efficient algorithms for efficiency and carbon emissions in cloud data centers: A review," in Renewable and Sustainable Energy Reviews, vol. 51.

Vafamehr A, & Khodayar, M. E., (2018). Energy-aware cloud computing. The Electricity Journal. 2018 Mar 1;31(2):40-9.

DIGITAL POLICIES: A STEP FORWARD FROM DIGITAL GOVERNMENT CONCEPT

Roberto Cortés-Morales
Computing Engineering School, Costa Rica Institute of Technology
Cartago, Costa Rica

ABSTRACT

This paper reviews the evolution of digital government as a concept shaped by both technological innovation and social transformation. Early definitions were largely focused on service delivery through online portals, described in models such as Layne and Lee's four stages and Fountain's G2C, G2B, and G2G interactions. A second stage, associated with open government, emphasized transparency, participation, and trust, while international organizations highlighted the need for governance and regulatory frameworks. The third stage reflects the impact of artificial intelligence, big data, and data-driven decision-making, while the smart city agenda emerged in parallel, linking urban innovation, sustainability, and quality of life. The review argues that traditional service-level typologies are no longer sufficient to explain current developments. We propose reframing digital government as digital policies, i.e., state-wide strategies aimed at creating public value and governing public goods. This perspective highlights digital transformation as a policy domain that addresses societal challenges across individuals, groups, communities, and the environment.

KEYWORDS

Digital Government, Public Policies, Public and Common Goods

1. INTRODUCTION

Digital government has become a central concept in public administration and policy. Early conceptions emphasized the digitalization of services through web portals to improve efficiency and accessibility (Fang, 2002). Foundational typologies framed interactions and maturity: Fountain's G2C/G2B/G2G schema and Layne & Lee's four-stage model became reference points for first-generation initiatives (Fountain, 2001; Layne & Lee, 2001). However, these service-oriented approaches only partially capture the broader governance transformations triggered by open data, citizen engagement, interoperability, and advanced analytics.

The purpose of this article is to review the conceptual evolution of digital government, to highlight how technological and social developments have reshaped its meaning, and to propose a reframing toward digital policies as a more comprehensive perspective. To this end, the article is structured into four main sections: Section 2 revisits the evolution of the concept in three stages and a parallel smart cities trajectory; Section 3 discusses the current capacities of digital technologies and their role in solving public problems; Section 4 advances a proposal for reframing digital government as digital policies; and the final section draws implications and conclusions.

2. METHODOLOGY: LITERATURE REVIEW PROTOCOL

This study follows a narrative literature review with systematic elements. Sources were identified through searches in Scopus, Web of Science, and Google Scholar, complemented by policy reports from international organizations such as the United Nations and the OECD. The time span covers 1995 to 2024, thereby capturing the trajectory from early web-based government initiatives to contemporary data-driven and AI-enabled governance. Core keywords included: digital government, e-government, open government, smart city/smart governance, big data, artificial intelligence, and digital public policy. Selection criteria prioritized conceptual and review articles with high citation impact, as well as comparative studies and reference reports. Case studies were considered selectively to illustrate trends.

The selection of sources followed a relevance and impact criterion. Foundational works that defined the field and are widely cited were included to trace the origins of the concept. Transitional contributions with high academic impact were prioritized to capture conceptual evolution. Finally, recent illustrative cases and policy reports were selected not only for their citation impact but also for their representativeness of diverse applications across regions and problem domains.

3. EVOLUTION OF THE CONCEPT OF DIGITAL GOVERNMENT

First stage of the concept can be identified as "service digitalization" ranging from 1995 to 2005 years. With the expansion of the Web, governments built portals to publish information and enable basic transactions. Layne and Lee (2001) described a growth path—cataloguing, transaction, vertical integration, horizontal integration—while Fountain (2001) mapped government interactions as G2C, G2B and G2G. Fang (2002) defined e-government as the use of ICT to improve efficiency, quality, and the citizen–state relationship. In parallel, Heeks (2003) warned that many projects failed in developing contexts due to 'design–reality gaps,' highlighting organizational and institutional constraints.

A second stage, going from 2005 to 2015 years emphasize on transparency and participation. The concept expanded toward openness, collaboration, and legitimacy. Digital Era Governance argued for reintegration, holistic delivery, and citizen-centric approaches, consolidating a new wave of digital governance (Dunleavy et al., 2006; Margetts & Dunleavy, 2013). Critical reviews cautioned that transparency's benefits can be overstated and require careful governance (Bannister & Connolly, 2012, 2014). In Latin America, open government advanced through co-creation among state, civil society, and academia (Criado & Ramírez-Alujas, 2012). Internationally, the OECD stressed regulatory frameworks, interoperability, and citizen trust (OECD, 2015).

From 2015 to current days "intelligent government", leveraging artificial intelligence, big data, blockchain, and predictive analytics shape the current stage. Janssen & Estevez (2015) introduced BOLD—Big and Open Linked Data—highlighting both transparency opportunities and privacy challenges. Janowski (2015) modeled an evolution from digitization and transformation toward engagement and contextualization, reflecting growing institutionalization and complexity. UN E-Government Surveys and OECD reviews document how digital government is increasingly seen as an ecosystem supporting decision-making, policy innovation, and resilience (UN, 2018, 2020, 2022, 2024; OECD, 2019, 2023).

Dealing with public solutions, it is needed also to consider the concept of smart cities that emerged as a framework that goes beyond service efficiency to encompass broader goals of urban sustainability and quality of life. Initiatives in domains such as smart-health, smart-environment, and smart-mobility illustrate that technology is not an end in itself, but rather a means to create more livable and inclusive cities (Nam & Pardo, 2011; Komninos, 2013; Anthopoulos, 2017). Smart city strategies emphasize that digital transformation requires ecosystems of actors—including local governments, private firms, universities, and civil society—working together to achieve sustainable and citizen-centred outcomes. Townsend (2013) stresses that smart cities combine data and civic innovation, while Chourabi et al. (2012) provide an integrative framework showing how governance, people, technology, and policy dimensions intersect. Meijer & Rodríguez Bolívar (2016) further argue that smart governance rests on three pillars: technological innovation, citizen collaboration, and legitimacy.

One can synthetize some conclusions by reviewing the evolution of the concept and the applications that may require a conceptual formalization: across stages and trajectories, the scope broadens from service efficiency to adaptive, data-driven governance. This sets the groundwork for shifting the unit of analysis from 'services' to public problems, and from 'executive modernization' to state-wide digital policies.

4. CURRENT ITC CAPACITIES AND PUBLIC PROBLEM-SOLVING

The capabilities of contemporary digital technologies enable government action across different problem domains. Rather than layering services, the emphasis is on policy's outcomes for individuals, groups, communities, and the environment. Illustrative experiences worldwide demonstrate how these capacities are reshaping public problem-solving. Typically, policies may be targeted to individuals, groups, communities or environment.

Policies for individuals may include digital security or identity systems such as India's Aadhaar have provided unique identification to more than a billion people, enabling targeted social protection and financial inclusion, while also raising debates on privacy and surveillance (Gelb & Clark, 2013; Khera, 2019). Similarly, mobile panic button applications in Mexico and Argentina connect victims of gender-based violence with emergency services in real time, showing how technology can enhance individual safety and rights protection (Frias, 2017; ONU Mujeres, 2020).

Considering policies for groups, data-driven equity and inclusion policies are emerging across sectors. The UK's National Health Service uses big data analytics to predict hospital demand and allocate resources efficiently (Raghupathi & Raghupathi, 2014; NHS England, 2018), while Estonia's e-education platforms extend access to learning opportunities, fostering mobility and inclusion for disadvantaged populations (Martens, 2010; OECD, 2016). These cases illustrate how collective needs can be addressed through analytics and platform-based solutions.

Regarding communities, digital tools support resilience and participatory democracy. Barcelona's Decidim platform allows residents to co-design urban policies and projects, institutionalizing digital participation (Calvo et al., 2019; Borge & Santamarina, 2020). Meanwhile, Singapore's IoT-enabled traffic monitoring improves public transport efficiency and safety in one of the world's most densely populated cities (Chourabi et al., 2012; Townsend, 2013). Both examples highlight how technology can strengthen community-level governance and infrastructure.

Finally environmental sustainability has become a critical domain for digital innovation. In the Netherlands, smart river sensor networks monitor water levels to prevent flooding (Van Alphen, 2016; Deltares, 2019). In Brazil, drones with IoT sensors monitor oil pipelines to detect leaks and mitigate ecological risks (Araujo et al., 2018). In Chile, satellite-based wildfire early-warning systems developed with CONAF and Google Earth Engine provide crucial data for environmental protection and disaster prevention (Gonzalez et al., 2018; CONAF, 2020). These cases show that the decisive question today is not how integrated an online portal is, but whether digital technologies contribute to solving concrete public problems under conditions of legitimacy, inclusiveness, and ethical safeguards (Bannister & Connolly, 2014; OECD, 2015).

5. FROM DIGITAL GOVERNMENT TO DIGITAL POLICIES

By examining previous sections, now is clear that the ITC impacts on public domains go beyond early stages of digital government concept and typologies. Moreover, strategies should consider a complex network of State powers, actors, resources, dimensions that are arranged to solve problems in the public space coming from the society, the economy, the politics or the administration or a combination of such dimensions (Cortés-Morales, 2017). Thus, the following aspects are proposed to be considered as one can propose to move from digital government to digital policies.

This paper proposes reframing the field from digital government—often associated with executive service delivery— to digital policies, i.e., coordinated public policies that involve the entire state: executive, legislative, and judicial branches, as well as autonomous institutions and local governments. This shift aligns the digital agenda with core policy cycle: agenda-setting, regulation, oversight, adjudication, and service delivery.

First, digital policies should be assessed against public value—legitimacy, trust, and collective utility—rather than efficiency alone (Moore, 1995). Drawing on Ostrom (1990, 2010), many digital outputs resemble public goods (non-rival, non-excludable) or help govern commons (e.g., open data, legal information, environmental monitoring). Thus, the digital turn is not merely administrative: it is a public goods and public value project. By setting a clear public value that creates or enhance a public good, it may prevents political risks on using ITC for non-desirable outcomes for society like undesirable surveillance among others.

Secondly it is necessary to overcome the service maturity ladders of digital government to a problem-oriented typology focused one where digital capabilities transform outcomes: Individuals (identity, protection, security); Groups (equity, inclusion, health); Communities (participation, infrastructure); Environment (sustainability, risk management). This typology complements the smart governance literature and better captures contemporary practice (Meijer & Rodríguez Bolívar, 2016; OECD, 2019, 2023; UN, 2018–2024).

Thus, research and practice should move beyond service-centric metrics to policy designs that integrate legitimacy, ethics, and distributional outcomes. For governments, 'digital by design' must be coupled with policy by design: capabilities for evidence-informed decision-making, safeguards for privacy and fairness, and institutional arrangements that sustain public goods at scale (Bannister & Connolly, 2014; OECD, 2015, 2023).

Finally, since policies should point to create or reinforce a public good as a mean to fix public issues (security, justice, non-polluted environment, employability, etc.), oriented to a specific target (individuals, groups, communities, environment) by allocating resources (political as laws, economic or administrative) and using the opportunities that information and communication technologies offers jointly with computer sciences methodologies. In summary, policies should point to solve problems characterized by any public goods. Once characterized, policy may identify resources into specific dimensions as well the target of the actions (individuals, communities, human groups, etc.). Finally, the policy lays on the capacities of the information technologies that could enable the solutions.

6. CONCLUSION

The concept of digital government has evolved from narrow service delivery models to a multidimensional paradigm that includes transparency, participation, intelligent governance, and smart urban development. This trajectory demonstrates the growing integration of technology, governance, and society. Future research and practice must move beyond the notion of digital government toward the design and implementation of digital policies.

Such policies, understood as state-wide strategies, are essential for generating public value and sustaining public goods. By reframing digital transformation in terms of public policies rather than services alone, governments can better address pressing societal challenges and ensure that technology serves as a catalyst for inclusive and sustainable governance.

REFERENCES

Anthopoulos, L., (2017). Understanding Smart Cities: A Tool for Smart Government or an Industrial Trick? Springer, Cham.

Araujo, A., Carvalho, P., Souza, R. & Santos, M., (2018). UAV-based inspection of pipelines in Brazil: Applications for environmental protection. Remote Sensing Applications: Society and Environment, 11, pp. 31–42.

Bannister, F. & Connolly, R., (2012). Defining e-government. eService Journal, 8(2), pp. 3–25.

Bannister, F. & Connolly, R., (2014). The Trouble with Transparency: A Critical Review of Openness in e-Government. Policy & Internet, 6(4), pp. 393–417.

Borge, R. & Santamarina, E., (2020). Deliberation and decision-making on digital platforms: The case of Decidim Barcelona. Policy & Internet, 12(3), pp. 325–345.

Calvo, E., Gomà, R. & Martí-Costa, M., (2019). Digital platforms for participatory democracy: The case of Barcelona's Decidim. Urban Studies, 56(7), pp. 1351–1368.

Chourabi, H., Nam, T., Walker, S., Gil-Garcia, J.R., Mellouli, S., Nahon, K., Pardo, T.A. & Scholl, H.J., (2012). Understanding smart cities: An integrative framework. Proceedings of the 45th Hawaii International Conference on System Sciences, pp. 2289–2297.

CONAF, (2020). Sistema de Alerta Temprana de Incendios Forestales en Chile. Corporación Nacional Forestal, Santiago.

Cortés-Morales, R. & Rodriguez-Arias, F., (2019). Open government proposal for transparency and information access in Costa Rica. In Proceedings of the 18th International Conference on WWW/Internet (ICWI 2019). IADIS Press, pp. 125–131.

Cortés-Morales, R., (2017). A Comprehensive Approach for E-Government Solutions. In: 2017 XLIII Latin American Computer Conference (CLEI). IEEE, pp. 1–8. https://doi.org/10.1109/CLEI.2017.8226452

Criado, J.I. & Ramírez-Alujas, Á., (2012). Gobierno abierto y reforma de la administración pública en Iberoamérica. Revista del CLAD Reforma y Democracia, 52, pp. 5–30.

Deltares, (2019). Smart monitoring for flood resilience. Delft: Deltares.

Dunleavy, P., Margetts, H., Bastow, S. & Tinkler, J., (2006). Digital Era Governance: IT Corporations, the State, and E-Government. Oxford University Press, Oxford.

Fang, Z., (2002). E-Government in Digital Era: Concept, Practice, and Development. International Journal of The Computer, the Internet and Management, 10(2), pp. 1–22.

Fountain, J.E., (2001). Building the Virtual State: Information Technology and Institutional Change. Brookings Institution Press, Washington, DC.

Frias, S.M., (2017). The "Panic Button": Mobile technology for tackling domestic violence in Mexico. Information Technologies & International Development, 13, pp. 1–10.

Gelb, A. & Clark, J., (2013). Identification for Development: The Biometrics Revolution. Center for Global Development, Washington, DC.

Gonzalez, M.E., Yebra, M., & Quintanilla, V., (2018). Satellite-based wildfire detection in Chile using MODIS and VIIRS data. Remote Sensing, 10(1), 123.

Heeks, R., (2003). Most eGovernment-for-Development Projects Fail: How Can Risks be Reduced? IDPM, University of Manchester, UK.

Janowski, T., (2015). Digital government evolution: From transformation to contextualization. Government Information Quarterly, 32(3), pp. 221–236.

Janssen, M. & Estevez, E., (2015). Big and Open Linked Data (BOLD) in government: A challenge to transparency and privacy. Government Information Quarterly, 32(4), pp. 363–368.

Khera, R., (2019). Aadhaar and food security in India. World Development, 127, 104–127.

Komninos, N., (2013). Intelligent Cities: Innovation, Knowledge Systems and Digital Spaces. Routledge, London.

Layne, K. & Lee, J., (2001). Developing fully functional e-government: A four-stage model. Government Information Quarterly, 18(2), pp. 122–136.

Margetts, H. & Dunleavy, P., (2013). The second wave of digital-era governance. Philosophical Transactions of the Royal Society A, 371(1987), 20120382.

Martens, H., (2010). Estonian e-education strategy: Building a digital learning culture. International Journal of Education and Development using ICT, 6(2), pp. 1–13.

Meijer, A. & Rodríguez Bolívar, M.P., (2016). Governing the smart city: A review of the literature on smart urban governance. International Review of Administrative Sciences, 82(2), pp. 392–408.

Moore, M., (1995). Creating Public Value: Strategic Management in Government. Harvard University Press, Cambridge, MA.

Nam, T. & Pardo, T.A., (2011). Conceptualizing smart city with dimensions of technology, people, and institutions. Proceedings of the 12th Annual International Conference on Digital Government Research, pp. 282–291.

NHS England, (2018). Next steps on the NHS Five Year Forward View. London: NHS England.

OECD, (2015). Government at a Glance 2015. OECD Publishing, Paris.

OECD, (2016). Innovating Education and Educating for Innovation: The Power of Digital Technologies and Skills. OECD Publishing, Paris.

OECD, (2019). Digital Government Review of Latin America and the Caribbean. OECD Publishing, Paris.

OECD, (2023). Government at a Glance 2023. OECD Publishing, Paris.

ONU Mujeres, (2020). Avances en la implementación de aplicaciones de seguridad para mujeres en América Latina. ONU Mujeres, Oficina Regional.

Ostrom, E., (1990). Governing the Commons: The Evolution of Institutions for Collective Action. Cambridge University Press, Cambridge.

Ostrom, E., (2010). Beyond Markets and States: Polycentric Governance of Complex Economic Systems. American Economic Review, 100(3), pp. 641–672.

Raghupathi, W. & Raghupathi, V., (2014). Big data analytics in healthcare: Promise and potential. Health Information Science and Systems, 2(3), pp. 1–10.

Townsend, A., (2013). Smart Cities: Big Data, Civic Hackers, and the Quest for a New Utopia. W.W. Norton, New York.

UN, (2018). United Nations E-Government Survey 2018: Gearing E-Government to Support Transformation towards Sustainable and Resilient Societies. United Nations, New York.

UN, (2020). United Nations E-Government Survey 2020: Digital Government in the Decade of Action for Sustainable Development. United Nations, New York.

UN, (2022). United Nations E-Government Survey 2022: The Future of Digital Government. United Nations, New York.

UN, (2024). United Nations E-Government Survey 2024. United Nations, New York.

Van Alphen, J., (2016). Flood risk management in the Netherlands: From flood defence to risk management and resilience. Journal of Flood Risk Management, 9(4), pp. 310–319.

Reflection Papers

ACCUMULATING COURSE OF EVENTS OF THE CONSIDERATION WORK IN LABORATORY SEMINARS WITH AN EMPHASIS ON ORAL DISCUSSION AND COMMENTS

Rui Igarashi[1], Sho Onami[1], Hiroki Nakayama[1], Ryo Onuma[1], Hiroaki Kaminaga[1], Youzou Miyadera[2] and Shoichi Nakamura[1]
[1]*Fukushima University, 1, Kanayagawa, Fukushima 960-1296, Japan*
[2]*Tokyo Gakugei University, 4-1-1, Nukuikita, Koganei, Tokyo 184-8501, Japan*

ABSTRACT

In the process of research activities, we deal with a variety of documents. For smooth execution of research, it is important to manage and share these documents satisfactorily and to understand the work circumstances. However, as the work progresses, the number of documents involved becomes enormous and difficult to manage. In particular, although oral discussions and comments provide important hints for understanding the work circumstances, they are difficult to accumulate and utilize. In this research, we have been aiming at developing a support system for accumulating course of events of the consideration work around laboratory seminars. In this paper, we first present a support framework for accumulating course of events of the consideration work with the emphasis on the accumulation of oral discussions and comments. We also describe the visual presentation of oral comments and their target slides by the system.

KEYWORDS

Understanding Course of Events of the Work, Oral Discussion and Comment, Laboratory Seminar Resources

1. INTRODUCTION

In the process of research activities, it is important to elaborate the work through repeated discussions with sharing results and progress of the work. Therefore, it is important to appropriately manage the documents used in the work, such as prepared presentation slides and papers, and to utilize them for understanding the work circumstances. However, as the work progresses, the increasing number of involved documents makes it challenging to manage them appropriately and to employ them effectively for understanding the work circumstances. In particular, oral discussions and the comments obtained during them are important for understanding the work circumstances, but are difficult to accumulate and utilize. To resolve these problems, there have been systems for version control of presentation materials (Morimoto et al., 2006; Wang, F et al., 2023; Hayama et al., 2007). However, these systems impose the burden of manually registering comments into the system each time a discussion occurs in order to accumulate oral comments. There have also been systems for automatically generating the minutes of discussion based on the analysis of oral comments (Sperrle et al., 2019; Tsuchida et al., 2010; Miura et al., 2019). However, these systems do not support the visualization of relationships between oral comments and research documents, nor between research documents. There is thus a strong need for effective support methods that enable the management of oral discussions and comments in conjunction with relevant documents.

In this research, we aim to develop a mechanism that automatically collects oral discussions and comments without imposing an additional burden on users, accumulates them by associating with related research documents, and enables to understand the work circumstances.

2. SUPPORT OVERVIEW

Figure 1 overviews the support for understanding the course of events of the consideration work in laboratory seminars. In this research, we have been developing a system environment that automatically collects and accumulates both the deliverables and the histories of research works performed by users on their PCs, such as writing papers, creating presentation materials, and searching or browsing published papers. Moreover, we have been developing methods to extract the deliverables and documents involved in the research works, as well as the relationships among them (called laboratory seminar resources), based on analysis of the work histories and the similarity of filenames and contents of research documents.

In addition, we accumulate oral discussions and comments in research seminars by associating them with research documents such as presentation slides used in seminar presentations. Furthermore, we present these laboratory seminar resources to users in a format so that they can understand the work circumstances (called elaboration context graph). These supports enable users to understand the work circumstances and histories by reviewing oral discussions and comments in conjunction with research documents.

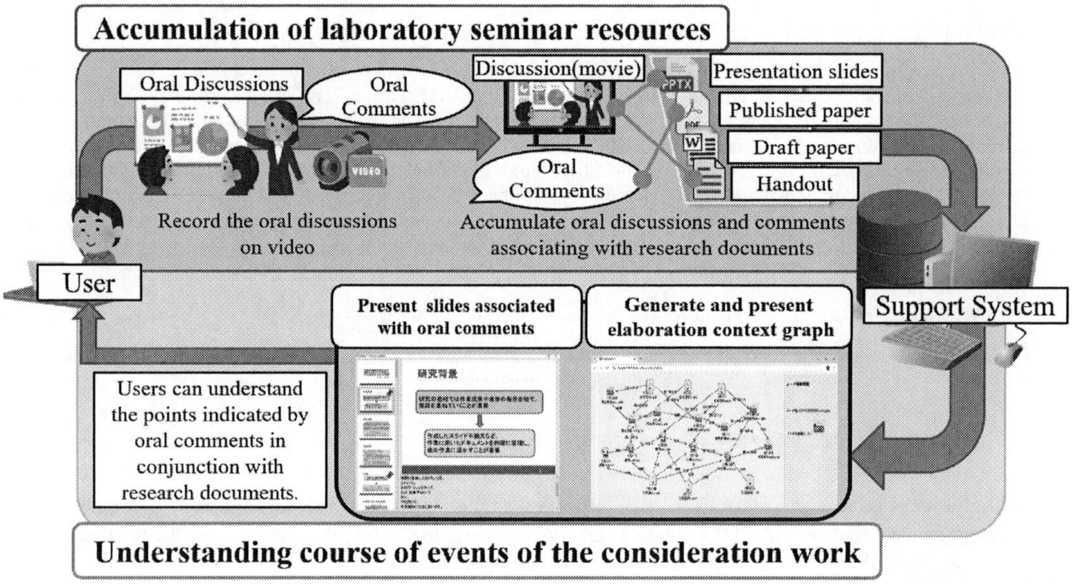

Figure 1. Support overview of accumulating course of events of consideration work in laboratory seminars

3. SYSTEM FOR ACCUMULATING COURSE OF EVENTS OF CONSIDERATION WORK

Users register videos capturing presentations in laboratory seminars and subsequent discussions into this system. Upon receiving a video, the system initially associates oral explanations with the corresponding slides by cross-referencing the date and time each explanation was given during the presentation with the slide presentation history. Users can easily review the oral explanations by selecting the thumbnails of slides displayed by this system. Furthermore, the system correlates oral remarks made in discussions after the presentation with the corresponding slides. This mapping is performed by comparing the timing of oral remarks with slide transitions and analyzing the occurrence status of key phrases extracted from the textualized oral remarks in the slides.

Based on this mapping, the system displays icons on the relevant slides corresponding to oral comments made during discussions (Figure 2). This allows users to easily identify slides to which oral comments have been given.

When a user selects the oral comment icon, the system highlights corresponding slide. Moreover, this system displays oral comments in text format. These displays enable users to easily confirm slides requiring further consideration by reviewing the discussions while checking the oral remarks.

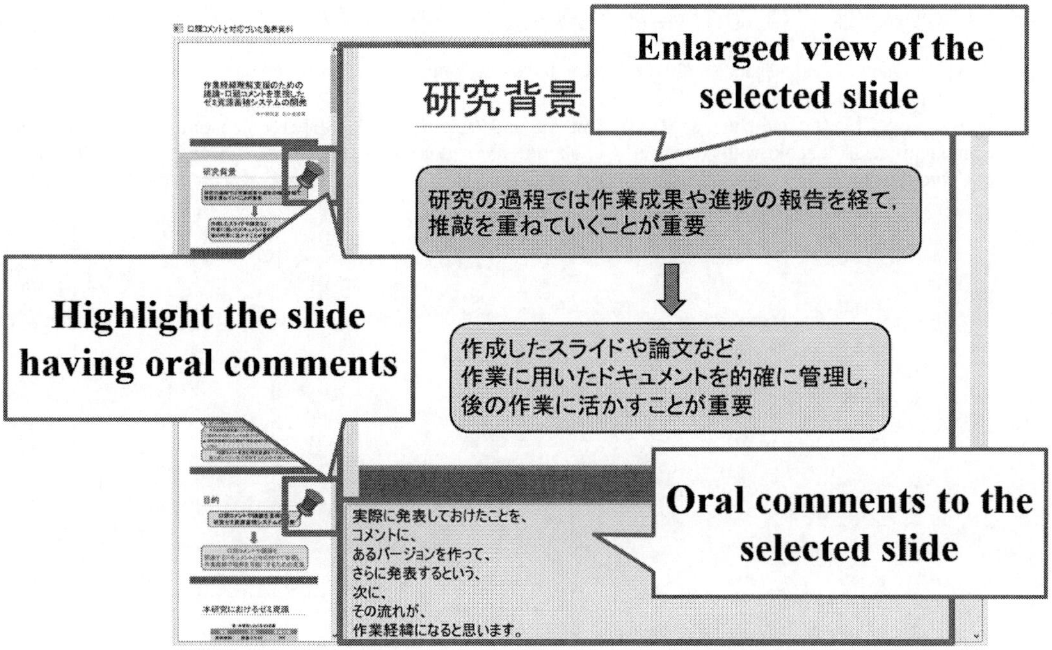

Figure 2. Display of oral comments in association with slides

4. CONCLUSION

In this paper, we described a framework for accumulating course of events of the consideration work in laboratory seminars with an emphasis on oral discussions and comments. We also overviewed a prototype system that displays oral comments by associating with slides.

Future work includes to further verify the effectiveness of our methods by applying the prototype to actual research work.

ACKNOWLEDGEMENT

This work was supported in part by the Ministry of Education, Culture, Sports, Science and Technology, Japan and by Japan Society for the Promotion of Science under Grant-in-Aid for Scientific Research (B) (No. 24K00446).

REFERENCES

Hayama, T., Yang, X., Susumu, Y. and Kunifuji, S. (2007). A Collaborative Notebook System that Provides Learning-knowledge Filtering. *IPSJ Journal*, Vol. 48, No. 8, pp. 2814-2822.

Miura, H., Takegawa, Y., Terai, A. and Hirata, K. (2019). Structuring of Discussion Based on Verbal and Non-verbal Information and Implementation of Interactive Minutes Generation System while Repeatedly Summarizing. *Journal of Japan Society for Fuzzy Theory and Intelligent Informatics*, Vol. 31, No. 1, pp. 1-10.

Morimoto, K., Shimada, H., Fujikawa, K. and Sunahara, H. (2006). The proposal of the version control system for presentation data, and the experiment of the progress management of the research. *IPSJ SIG Technical Reports*. Tokyo, Japan, pp. 245-250.

Sperrle, F., Sevastjanova, R., Kehlbeck, R., El-Assady, M. (2019). VIANA: Visual interactive annotation of argumentation. *Proceedings of the IEEE Conference on Visual Analytics Science and Technology (VAST)*. Vancouver, Canada, pp. 11-22.

Tsuchida, T., Ohira, S. and Nagao, M. (2010). Research Activity Support System Based on the Reuse of Seminar Contents. *IPSJ Journal*, Vol. 51, No. 6, pp. 1357-1370.

Wang, F., Liu, X., Liu, O., Neshati, A., Ma, T., Zhu, M., and Zhao, J. (2023). Slide4N: Creating Presentation Slides from Computational Notebooks with Human-AI Collaboration. *Proceedings of the 2023 CHI Conference on Human Factors in Computing Systems. Hamburg*, Germany, pp. 1-18.

A REVIEW OF TRAVEL RECOMMENDATION SYSTEM: APPROACHES, CHALLENGES AND FUTURE DIRECTIONS

Madhuri Debnath and Ashis Kumer Biswas
Computer Science and Engineering, University of Colorado Denver
Colorado, USA

ABSTRACT

The Travel Recommendation Systems (TRS) have emerged as essential tools in helping users plan personalized trips by filtering through vast amounts of information. These systems leverage various data sources and algorithms to suggest destinations, itineraries, accommodations, and activities tailored to user preferences and business satisfaction. This paper presents a comprehensive review of current approaches in Travel Recommendation System, classifies them based on methodologies. It also highlights the challenges associated with the system and the recent advancement in deep learning, social media integration, offering insights into promising future research directions.

KEYWORDS

Travel Recommendation System, Location-Based Social Network, Tourism, Deep Learning

1. INTRODUCTION

Tourism represents a major form of human activity and plays a vital role in global social and economic systems. A Travel Recommendation System (TRS) aims to assist users in discovering personalized travel plans by analyzing preferences, behaviors, and context. A TRS consists of two major steps: 1) finding the best points of interests (POIs) for visitors in a new city or various cities, and 2) schedule the POIs as an itinerary considering multiple constraints such as, time, budget, personal preferences etc. Finding interesting locations has the following challenges: 1) personal preferences, 2) temporal influences and 3) POI popularity (Debnath, M., 2018). The second step of travel route recommendation is to plan the set of locations with corresponding time information such that it maximizes user satisfaction. This paper aims to review the existing approaches and presents with the classification, data sources, challenges and promising future directions.

2. CLASSFICATION OF TRAVEL RECOMMENDATION SYSTEM

TRS can be categorized into two broad categories: 1) non-personalized systems compute a travel path from a set of POIs by maximizing the POI popularity or minimizing the required time to travel between one location to another location, and 2) personalized systems generate the travel path considering personal preferences and various constraints such as, individual's temporal influences, budget and diversity of preferences.

3. DATA SOURCES IN TRAVEL RECOMMEDATION SYSTEM

Data collection is one of the most important steps in recommendation generation system. The accuracy and evaluation of the system depend on the collection of real-life travel history of users. There are four types of popular data sources: 1) geo-tagged social media such as tweets and photos are a popular source for many

TRS, 2) location based Social Networks (LBSNs), such as data obtained through Foursquare, Gowalla, Facebook where users explicitly provide check-ins in specific locations, 3) transactional data, such as hotel bookings, activity reservations, users' locations, personal preferences and site popularity metrics.

4. CHALLENGES AND RECENT METHODOLOGIES

Travel recommendation systems may face several challenges, as they grow in complexity and scale. The followings are the few challenges: 1) cold-start problem due to the lack of sufficient data for new users or locations affects TRS quality, 2) data sparsity since most interactions belong in small portion of items, leading to higher sparsity in data, 3) privacy and ethical concerns rise with collection and analyses of personal and contextual data, 4) increasing computational cost for dynamic real time personalization.

Various tools and techniques have been utilized to generate the travel recommendations. (Debnath, M, 2018) presented a time-aware and preference-aware routes recommendation system. (Halder, S., 2022) proposed efficient itinerary recommendation via personalized POI selection and pruning using an adaptive MCTS algorithm. In recent advancement, deep neural models have demonstrated superior performance in this context. (Yang, 2017) introduced a deep learning model named *PACE* for POI recommendation, which combined semi-supervised learning and CF to learn user preferences for POIs. (Li, Y, 2017) proposed a convolutional neural network (CNN) model to capture spatial dependency. (Zhao, X., 2018) used reinforcement learning based technique to generate recommendations. (Ho, N., 2022) proposed a language model for learning POI embedding based on sequences of POI visits.

5. FUTURE DIRECTIONS AND CONCLUSIONS

Travel recommendation system is an important aspect of travel industry as it can help the industry grow by attracting billions of local and international visitors. Continued research is essential to overcome persistent challenges and create more intelligent, ethical, and user-centric travel recommendation. Therefore, there are still numerous directions that could be pursued in future: 1) generating explainable recommendations to provide justifications that will build trust in such TRSs, 2) generating sustainable and ethical tourism recommendations to promote responsible travel, 3) augmented and virtual reality integration can help to enable immersive exploration before travel, 4) cross-domain recommendations can be generated by integrating preferences across entertainment, dining, and lodging 5) federated Learning can be utilized by protecting privacy of the users by training models in a distributed manner.

REFERENCES

Debnath, M., Tripathi, P.K., Biswas, A.K. and Elmasri, R., (2018). November. Preference aware travel route recommendation with temporal influence. In *Proceedings of the 2nd ACM SIGSPATIAL Workshop on Recommendations for Location-based Services and Social Networks* (pp. 1-9).

Halder, S., Lim, K.H., Chan, J. and Zhang, X., (2022). Efficient itinerary recommendation via personalized POI selection and pruning. *Knowledge and Information Systems, 64*(4), pp.963-993.

Yang, C., Bai, L., Zhang, C., Yuan, Q. and Han, J., (2017). August. Bridging collaborative filtering and semi-supervised learning: a neural approach for poi recommendation. In *Proceedings of the 23rd ACM SIGKDD international conference on knowledge discovery and data mining* (pp. 1245-1254).

Li, Y., Yu, R., Shahabi, C. and Liu, Y., (2017). Diffusion convolutional recurrent neural network: Data-driven traffic forecasting. *arXiv preprint arXiv:1707.01926*.

Zhao, X., Zhang, L., Ding, Z., Xia, L., Tang, J. and Yin, D. (2018, July). Recommendations with negative feedback via pairwise deep reinforcement learning. In *Proceedings of the 24th ACM SIGKDD international conference on knowledge discovery & data mining* (pp. 1040-1048).

Ho, N.L. and Lim, K.H., (2022). December. Poibert: A transformer-based model for the tour recommendation problem. In *2022 IEEE International Conference on Big Data (Big Data)* (pp. 5925-5933). IEEE.

USABILITY OF GEOSPATIAL DATA VISUALIZATION IN VIRTUAL REALITY

Hossain Samar Qorbani, and Indratmo Indratmo
Department of Computer Science, MacEwan University, Edmonton, AB, Canada

ABSTRACT

This study presents a prototype virtual reality (VR) application designed to assess the usability of visualizing geospatial data using the Meta Quest 3 headset and Unity game engine. Motivated by the potential cognitive benefits of kinesthetic interaction and immersive exploration, the project incorporates multiple layers of urban data across global cities. Preliminary testing with eight users suggests positive reception toward VR-based spatial data visualization, particularly in terms of user engagement and perceived understanding. Usability was assessed with reference to Nielsen's 10 heuristics and the five quality components of usability: learnability, efficiency, memorability, error management, and satisfaction. Feedback highlighted the improvements needed in interface design and navigation controls. These findings suggest promising opportunities for VR as a tool for spatial data analysis, pending refinement and more rigorous empirical validation.

KEYWORDS

Virtual Reality, Geospatial Data, Usability, Spatial Visualization, Immersive Interaction

1. INTRODUCTION

With the proliferation of immersive technologies and the increasing accessibility of virtual reality (VR) headsets, there is growing interest in exploring VR beyond entertainment, particularly as a medium for data visualization. Traditional 2D visualizations on screens have dominated for decades; however, these methods are often insufficient for representing large, multidimensional, or spatially embedded datasets. As the complexity of the data increases, the need for more intuitive and interactive interfaces becomes critical.

This project examines the usability of VR as a tool for visualizing geospatial data, with a focus on user interaction and comprehension. The work is motivated by evidence suggesting immersive environments enhance memory recall and engagement through spatial perception and embodied interaction. We investigate whether VR-based interfaces enhance user interaction and comprehension of geographic data compared to screen-based approaches.

2. RELATED WORK

Data visualization is traditionally handled through two-dimensional dashboards displayed on computer screens. Although effective for many applications, this approach can limit user understanding, especially when working with complex, high-dimensional, or spatially rich datasets. With the increasing accessibility of virtual reality (VR) technology, researchers have begun to explore whether immersive environments can enhance user perception and interaction with data (Millais et al., 2018).

Recent studies suggest that VR can provide cognitive and usability benefits in data interpretation. Morales-Vega et al. (2024) developed a VR tool for visualizing dimensionality-reduced datasets using algorithms such as t-SNE and PCA and reported that users could more easily recognize patterns and clusters in 3D environments than in 2D. Similarly, Feng and Ge (2018) demonstrated that mapping high-dimensional data into a VR space using principal component analysis allowed users to gain a better understanding of its structure through movement and perspective shifting. These findings suggest that incorporating depth and kinesthetic interaction can help users interpret complex datasets more intuitively.

This idea is further supported by Hurter et al. (2024), who found that locomotion and proprioception in immersive environments facilitated users' recall of spatial data more accurately. Their study demonstrated that being able to move through and around data points created stronger memory associations, reinforcing the concept that spatial navigation plays a critical role in cognitive encoding. VR environments that utilize movement and embodied interaction may, therefore, have significant advantages over traditional interfaces when it comes to understanding complex or layered data.

In a survey on immersive analytics, Kraus et al. (2021) outlined the benefits of VR for abstract data visualization, emphasizing reduced cognitive workload and improved user satisfaction when working in immersive spaces. They categorize several immersive analytics systems and identify a growing trend toward incorporating natural movement, spatial context, and visual immersion into analytical workflows. Their findings underscore the need for interfaces that are both usable and accessible, leveraging these immersive features while remaining practical for end-users.

There are also examples of VR being used effectively in specific domains such as biology and infrastructure analytics. Zhang et al. (2019) developed BioVR, a platform for exploring genomic data, which demonstrated that users could more quickly understand structural relationships in VR than in 2D. Wang et al. (2023) explored a user-centered framework for data visualization in infrastructure inspection, concluding that immersive tools, when designed with user experience and control in mind, can support more informed decision-making. These findings align with our goal of evaluating usability in geospatial contexts, where both data complexity and user interpretation are essential.

Other researchers have focused on the role of interaction in immersive environments. Wei et al. (2022) demonstrated that user engagement improves when VR systems enable direct interaction with data elements. Sicat et al. (2019) also developed a system called DXR to support more intuitive creation of immersive visualizations, arguing that design tools must consider both technical constraints and how users mentally model the data.

Finally, earlier work by Drouhard et al. (2015) and Wegman and Symanzik (2001) demonstrated that immersive environments can support spatial reasoning in areas such as materials science and statistical analysis. These projects, though from earlier generations of VR, showed that immersive tools offer unique affordances for understanding spatial information, particularly when visualizations are tied to realistic physical cues or gestures.

These studies provide both a theoretical and practical basis for exploring VR-based geospatial visualization. While prior works have demonstrated the effective use of VR for specialized domains, few have systematically examined usability frameworks. Our work aims to contribute by applying Nielsen's usability heuristics and the five usability quality components, learnability, efficiency, memorability, error recovery, and satisfaction, to evaluate a geospatial VR tool.

3. METHODOLOGY

To explore the feasibility and usability of immersive geospatial visualization, we developed a prototype using Unity with the XR Interaction Toolkit, Figma for UI design, and the Meta Quest 3 headset. The development process involved integrating VR locomotion systems, designing user interfaces for toggling data layers, implementing adjustable opacity controls, and enabling seamless scene transitions between multiple cities (Edmonton, Paris, Tokyo). We used publicly available ArcGIS data layers due to SDK limitations that restrict layer access to publicly hosted tile or scene layers (Figure 1). Interface sketches and flow diagrams were produced early on to guide usability design, and these were refined as the technical constraints and opportunities of the ArcGIS SDK became clearer.

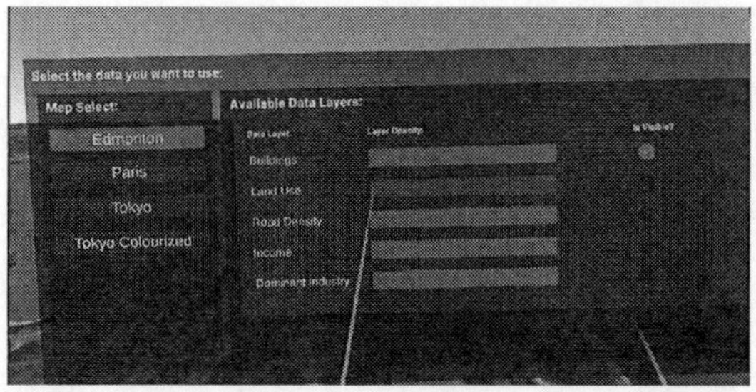

Figure 1. Figma design of the UI for navigating the different data layers and scenes available. Users can toggle the layers on or off and adjust the opacity of each layer

The application included a user interface that enabled users to toggle data layers, adjust opacity, view a legend, and switch between cities, as well as select a data layer to display (Figure 2). The interaction relied on locomotion and snap-turning, facilitated by a thumbstick for added comfort. Eight participants (N = 8) took part in a usability study. Each began in a tutorial scene to learn controls, then explored the scenes and interacted with the data. Following the exploration, they completed a Likert-scale survey and provided qualitative feedback.

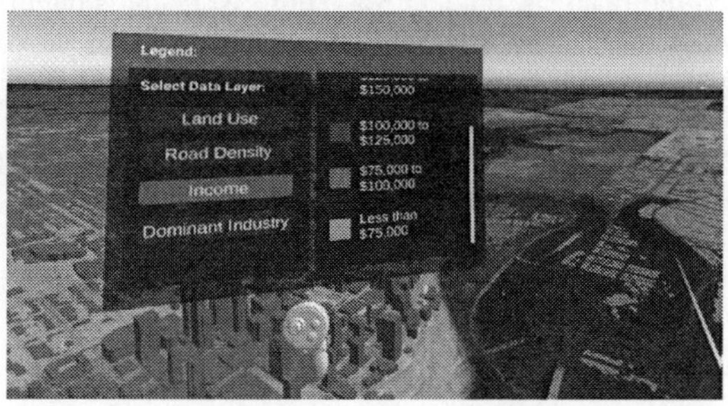

Figure 2. In-game view of the scene and corresponding legend, where the user can identify the meaning of color-coded data layers. In this instance, the user is referencing the legend to interpret the Income data layer

Challenges such as version control with Unity, limitations in Android builds, and SDK compatibility were encountered and resolved. In particular, the rendering quality of Android builds was insufficient for our goals, so we reverted to PC-tethered VR testing. The interface features, including a menu for data manipulation and a handheld legend to interpret map symbology, were iteratively developed to maximize usability and accessibility (Figures 3a and 3b).

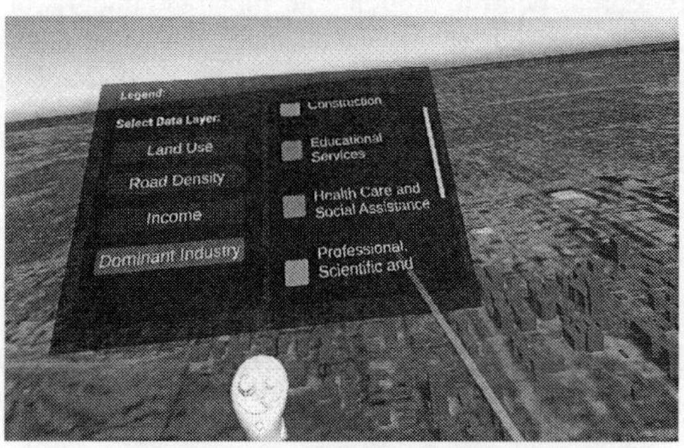

(a) color-coded data layers

(b) a city-wide view with certain data layers enabled

Figure 3. UI components: data layer, toggle menu, and in-game legend system

3.1 Design Goals and Participants

Design decisions were driven by Nielsen's 10 usability heuristics (e.g., visibility of system status, match between system and real world, user control, error prevention). For example, the toggles reflected the system status, the legends used real-world symbols, and the users could undo actions. We also targeted the five quality components of usability in interface design.

Demographics: All participants were university students or staff, with ages ranging from 22 to 41 years; four had prior experience with VR. While this is a small, exploratory sample, it provides preliminary insights into user needs and barriers.

3.2 User Testing Protocol and Usability Metrics

A usability evaluation was conducted with four participants using a structured pre-test, task-based test, and post-test questionnaire.

- The pretest demographics collected information on the participants' age, previous VR experience, and their familiarity with urban geography in Edmonton and other cities.
- Task-based testing involved users navigating through scenes, manipulating spatial layers, adjusting visual parameters, and interpreting legend data. Observations were made regarding their ability to navigate and change elevation within the 3D environment, use sliders to adjust building and layer opacity, interpret the legend's symbology, switch between cities and return to the original location, and interact with the user interface to assess its intuitiveness.

The post-test survey consisted of items on the Likert scale (1–7) to measure perceived clarity, intuitiveness, comfort, and usefulness of different interaction components. Open-ended comments were also collected for qualitative insight. Participants were encouraged to speak aloud during the session to capture real-time impressions. All tests were performed using a PC-connected Meta Quest 3, and each session lasted approximately 25 minutes.

4. RESULTS

Participants' responses were generally positive, though several areas for improvement were identified. All four users found movement within the 3D environment relatively intuitive, with three rating ease of movement as 5 or 6 (on a 7-point scale), and one slightly lower at 4. Similarly, scene navigation and map switching received strong ratings (5-7), suggesting that users appreciated the ability to explore different urban contexts. Layer visibility toggling and opacity adjustment were rated positively by three users (ratings of 6, 6, and 7), while one participant found the system less intuitive (rating of 3). The color scheme used in data representation received mixed feedback; three users rated it highly (5–7), but one gave a low rating (2), indicating a need for improved visual encoding. The legend was generally seen as helpful, though placement and integration with the UI raised usability concerns. Qualitative feedback focused on UI layout and navigation controls. Participants requested more precise layer toggling buttons, clearer controller mappings, and a floating UI panel that would follow the user's gaze rather than remaining static. Some users also expressed a desire for more explicit controls for vertical movement (ascend/descend) rather than relying on gaze direction.

5. DISCUSSION

Despite the limited sample size, user feedback aligns with known usability principles. High scores in satisfaction and efficiency support the potential of immersive data visualization, while issues in memorability and error handling point to areas for design improvement. The results of our usability study suggest a generally positive user experience, tempered by identifiable areas for improvement. Participants responded favorably to the immersive qualities of the VR environment and found the interface for controlling data layers largely intuitive. The average rating across categories such as ease of navigation, clarity of legends, and overall intuitiveness ranged between 5 and 6 out of 7. This indicates a strong baseline of usability despite the small participant pool. The iterative development process, including early user flow sketches, multiple UI prototypes, and a late-stage tutorial scene, significantly contributed to user comprehension. The pre-emptive inclusion of a tutorial scene was particularly beneficial for first-time VR users. Still, feedback highlighted issues with fixed UI placement and the lack of intuitive elevation control. Participants suggested allowing menus and legends to follow the user's position and including discrete controls for vertical movement, which would better accommodate different user preferences and familiarity levels.

From a methodological standpoint, the use of structured task-based evaluations combined with Likert-scale feedback proved effective. Observational notes during testing were invaluable in identifying the user pain points, particularly those not captured in the quantitative survey responses. For example, one participant struggled with opacity sliders, not due to confusion, but because of the precision required on the controller joystick, an issue that might be addressed through larger slider handles or haptic feedback. Given our use of spatial data embedded in realistic urban contexts, the application's potential for supporting urban planning or education became evident.

Familiarity with the city of Edmonton enhanced engagement for local participants, and expanding such local context features could further strengthen user connection in future work.

Although the sample size was small and exploratory in nature, the feedback we gathered offers strong validation of our design approach and highlights concrete steps for refinement.

6. CONCLUSION AND FUTURE WORK

We examined the usability of geospatial data visualization in virtual reality by developing and evaluating a Unity-based VR application. Initial feedback suggests that immersive environments offer advantages in engagement, spatial understanding, and interaction with layered geographic data. While participant responses were generally positive, key areas for improvement were identified in UI layout, movement mechanics, and SDK flexibility. Future work will focus on refining interaction design, particularly by enhancing menu accessibility and enabling vertical navigation through more intuitive input methods. Additionally, to support broader adoption, future iterations should allow users to import their own datasets and customize visual encodings. Transitioning away from SDK limitations and toward a more modular, extensible system may be necessary to achieve this. Through iterative improvements and broader testing, immersive geospatial data visualization may evolve into a practical tool for analysts, educators, and urban planners, providing a more immersive and intuitive way to explore complex spatial information. Future studies should expand participant diversity and incorporate A/B testing to compare VR against 2D dashboards using consistent task sets.

REFERENCES

Drouhard, M. et al. (2015). Immersive visualization for materials science data analysis using the Oculus Rift. In *2015 IEEE International Conference on Big Data (Big Data)*, pages 2825–2832. IEEE.

Feng, E. and Ge, X. (2018). Dataviz: Visualization of high-dimensional data in virtual reality.*F1000Research*, 7:1687.

Hurter, C. et al. (2024). Memory recall for data visualizations in mixed reality, virtual reality, 3d and 2d.*IEEE Transactions on Visualization and Computer Graphics*, 30(10):6691–6706.

Kraus, M., Fuchs, J., Sommer, B., Klein, K., Engelke, U., Keim, D., and Schreiber, F. (2021). Immersive analytics with abstract 3d visualizations: A survey. *Computer Graphics Forum*, 40(7):565–590.

Millais, P., Jones, S. L., and Kelly, R. (2018). Exploring data in virtual reality: Comparisons with 2d data visualizations. In *Extended abstracts of the 2018 CHI conference on human factors in computing systems*, pages 1–6. ACM.

Morales-Vega, J. C. et al. (2024). A virtual reality data visualization tool for dimensionality reduction methods. *Virtual Reality*, 28(1):41–56.

Wang, Z. et al. (2023). User-centric immersive virtual reality development framework for data visual- ization and decision-making in infrastructure remote inspections. *Advanced Engineering Informatics*, 57:102078.

Wei, T. et al. (2022). Virtual reality design in reading user experience: 3d data visualization with inter- action in digital publication figures. *Scientific Programming*, 2022:1–7.

Zhang, J. F. et al. (2019). Biovr: A platform for virtual reality-assisted biological data integration and visualization. *BMC Bioinformatics*, 20(1):78.

BEYOND OPTIMIZATION: RETHINKING SECURE RESOURCE ALLOCATION IN B5G NETWORKS UNDER ADVERSARIAL CONDITIONS

Sameer Ali and Helena Rifà-Pous
Internet Interdisciplinary Institute (IN3)
Center for Cybersecurity Research of Catalonia (CYBERCAT),
Universitat Oberta de Catalunya (UOC), Barcelona, Spain

ABSTRACT

The future mobile networks are transforming into multidimensional, adaptive networks, aka beyond 5G (B5G), where the digital services are delivered over network slices whose network definition is virtual. It is also important that such slices are available to users with a wide variety of needs on a safe and efficient basis. The current solutions are mainly aimed at ensuring that things are faster and reliable; however, in the majority of situations, they fail to give much consideration to the security threat from malicious users. This reflection paper examines the limitations of existing approaches and argues for embedding security mechanisms directly within resource allocation frameworks. It explores the integration of zero-knowledge proofs (ZKPs) for user verification and integer linear programming (ILP) for secure allocation, forming a unified adversary-aware model. This perspective encourages a shift from purely performance-driven strategies toward security-by-design methods capable of addressing dynamic threats in real time.

KEYWORDS

B5G Networks, Resource Allocation, Slice Spoofing, Zero-Knowledge Proofs, ILP Optimization, Network Security

1. INTRODUCTION

The most important problem occurs when mobile networks are evolving to B5G, and it is their efficient use of resources. One way of doing so is through a network slicing approach that breaks the physical infrastructure into virtualized slices, which other applications and customers can also share. B5G is making use of this technology. Instant real-time dynamic allocation of such slices is needed, and also, the number of tenants with different and varying needs is almost always too large. Many approaches to optimizing this have been suggested to cope with this complexity in the past (Abba Ari, et al.,2025), ILP models, reinforcement learning (Suh K, et al.,2022), and heuristic scheduling (Chen, et al.,2023). These have been good to enhance the performance quality, such as latency, throughput, and power efficiency.

Most current models, on the other hand, assume that everyone on the network is honest and willing to work together. This assumption is not valid in practical implementations. B5G networks are very vulnerable to security threats such as slice spoofing (Thanthrate A., et al.,2020), resource hijacking (Wang J., et al.,2022), and malicious overloads (Gokul N., et al.,2021). In these kinds of attacks, attackers pretend to be real users or services to get access to network resources they shouldn't have. Conventional optimization models seldom consider these cases, and only a limited number integrate methods to authenticate user validity or identify anomalous behavior during resource allocation (Chen L., et al.,2023).

The purpose of this research is the critical analysis of the foundations of deemed limitations of the existing methods and the justification of the paradigm shift. We would suggest that resource management at B5G should go beyond the capacity of strict optimization of the performance and that it must be intrinsically adversary-informed. The concept behind the creation of the main contribution is the intention to compile the cryptographic user verification, namely, the Zero-Knowledge Proofs (Khamesra A., et al.,2024), into the behavior-focused limitations in the optimization-based models. This sum becomes credible, limits the accessibility of adversarial influence, and allows threats to stop even before they happen during the resource distribution. The present research provides a prospective outlook on the development of robust and secure efficient frameworks of resources management on the next generation of wireless networks with respect to alignment of optimization, security and cryptography applied. According to Table 1, most of the currently available examples of model applied to the resource's allocation to B5G networks are focused on performance improvement of the services and do not focus on the risks of cyber-attacks. The intended method in place of this inserts security into the optimization correct itself through the cryptographic establishment and tracking of real-time behavior. This reinforces the framework against the human damaging conditions.

Table 1. Comparison of Existing vs. Proposed Resource Allocation Approaches in B5G

Criteria	Existing Models	Proposed Approach
Optimization Objective	Performance-centric (e.g., throughput, latency)	Security-aware and performance-balanced
Assumptions on User Behavior	Users are honest and cooperative	Users may be adversarial or malicious
Security Integration	External to optimization logic	Embedded within the optimization process
Authentication Mechanism	Token-based or absent	Zero-Knowledge Proof-based user verification
Anomaly Detection	Post-allocation monitoring (if any)	Real-time behavior tracking using decision variables
Simulation Conditions	Idealized, static environments	Realistic, attack-driven simulations

2. LITERATURE REVIEW: TRENDS AND GAPS

Existing approaches have tried to identify the best possible way of utilizing resources in a B5G network through mathematical optimization problems such as ILP (Martinovic J., et al.,2017), Mixed-Integer Nonlinear Programming (MINLP) (Liu L., et al.,2018), and heuristic algorithms. In the subsequent study, it is observed that the AI-based approaches, such as reinforcement learning, federated learning, and graph neural networks, have been incorporated to mitigate the changes in the network system in real-time (Zhao S., et al.,2023), (Liu T., et al.,2022), (Ji M., et al.,2024). Such models are an excellent way to handle big data and draw closer to an optimum when things are natural. However, these are more likely to overlook how the system responds to adversarial behavior (Ergu Y.A., et al.,2024).

Some research tries to improve security by separating known attacks, such as Denial of Service (DoS), and using encryption-based methods to keep data private (Javadpour A., et al.,2024), (Abd El-Latif, et al.,2020). Nevertheless, these strategies are constrained in their applicability and fail to provide proactive defense mechanisms during resource allocation. Most current models presume a safe environment and don't take into account real-time adversarial dynamics or hostile user strategies. Slice spoofing attacks (Nyangaresi V.O., et al.,2021), in which adversaries imitate legitimate slice behavior to acquire unauthorized resources, are predominantly unrepresented in optimization literature.

Also, authentication methods are generally separate from the logic that assigns resources, which makes it hard to combine user verification with resource assignments. Without integrated verification models, systems are open to hacking and unlawful use of resources. New study shows that cryptographic technologies like ZKP could help close this gap by allowing users to authenticate themselves without revealing any personal information throughout the optimization process (Farreras M., et al.,2024). Even though they could be useful, ZKPs are not used enough in existing B5G resource allocation frameworks.

3. CRITICAL ANALYSIS AND SOLUTION

A key constraint in modern models is their dependence on fixed assumptions on network behavior (Pandey C., et al.,2024). In a real-world B5G setting, resource needs change, users may act maliciously, and edge nodes can be hacked. In secure deployments, optimization models that don't expect or respond to these characteristics are inherently not good. Additionally, current simulations frequently occur in idealized environments, utilizing synthetic traffic and disregarding authentic attack patterns (Azizi A., et al.,2019). This discrepancy between theoretical models and practical realities engenders apprehensions regarding the applicability and resilience of proposed solutions.

There is also too much focus on boosting performance metrics at the cost of system integrity (Cui Z., et al.,2019). Quality of Service (QoS) is important, but it shouldn't come at the cost of letting attackers in. The absence of integrated security indicators or trust metrics in objective functions signifies a wasted opportunity for comprehensive design. If harmful activity isn't measured and limited (Bu G., et al., 2018), optimization solvers could accidentally give more weight to users who are in high demand and pose a high danger. Figure 1 displays the overall structure of the conceptual framework. It shows how slice spoofing attempts are found and stopped using a combination of ILP-based optimization and ZKP verification before resources are given out. This integration makes sure that only verified users can access network slices while also making sure that resources are used as efficiently as possible.

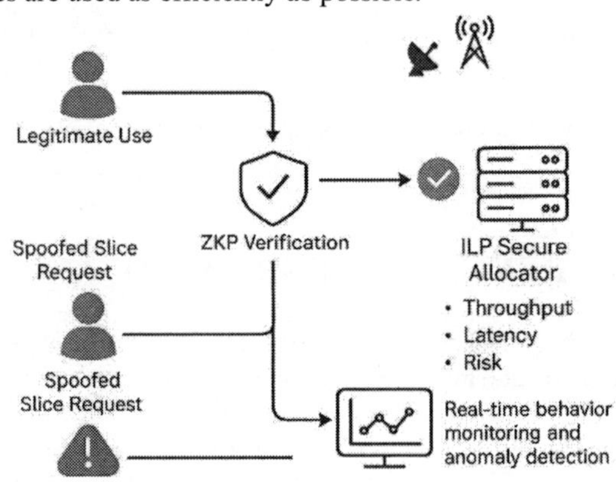

Figure 1. Adversary-aware B5G resource allocation using ILP optimization and ZKP-based spoofing defense

4. TOWARD ADVERSARY-AWARE ALLOCATION

This research supports a unified approach in which the embedding of security in process optimization will be employed. Another possible way to track suspicious behavior involves the implementation of decision variable-based tracking. It can be that in order to keep track of how many slices or resources are logged in by a user it can create new decision variables which would provide the information in real time as to whether or not something has gone wrong. Such actions may be incorporated into ILP models to determine the scope of diversity in use, and this will make it illegal to move laterally or benefit those people to gain additional privileges.

Also, with ZKPs (Bu G., et al.,2018), integrating into resource request, they enable the users to make statements which can be proved without compromising their identities and slice preferences. This will make privacy not lose and only those who have been verified will only be able to engage in the allocation process. Practically, such models may be tested under real threat circumstances in conjunction with adversary simulations like Mininet that are observed with the utilities in commercial products like Wireshark. Systems developed with adversary-aware design allow transfer to the stage of the proactive distribution of the resources, which provides maximum protection against such threats.

5. CONCLUSION

B5G networks require resource allocation mechanisms that are both performance-efficient and resilient to adversarial behavior. Integrating cryptographic verification with ILP optimization provides a promising direction. ZKPs ensure privacy-preserving user authentication, while ILP offers a structured way to balance multiple objectives under constraints. Embedding real-time behavioral tracking within allocation enables proactive defense against slice spoofing and similar attacks. This reflection encourages the research community to move beyond performance-only optimization. Future work should formalize adversary-aware ILP models, evaluate them under realistic threat scenarios, and explore their scalability in large-scale B5G deployments. Adopting security-by-design approaches will be essential for building trustworthy next-generation mobile networks.

ACKNOWLEDGEMENT

This work was supported by the Spanish Ministry of Science and Innovation through the PID2021-125962OB-C31 "SECURING" project. Additional funding was provided by the ARTEMISA International Chair of Cybersecurity (C057/23) and the DANGER Strategic Project of Cybersecurity (C062/23), both funded by the Spanish National Institute of Cybersecurity through the European Union NextGenerationEU and the Recovery, Transformation, and Resilience Plan.

REFERENCES

Abba Ari, A.A. *et al.*, "IoT-5G and B5G/6G resource allocation via learning algorithms," *IET Netw.*, vol. 14, no. 1, p. e70002, 2025.

Abd El-Latif, A.A. *et al.*, "Quantum-walk-based encryption for 5G IoT," *IEEE Trans. Netw. Serv. Manag.*, vol. 17, no. 1, pp. 118–131, 2020.

Azizi, A. *et al.*, "Profit maximization in 5G+ with aerial and ground BSs," *IEEE Trans. Mobile Comput.*, vol. 19, no. 10, pp. 2445–2460, 2019.

Bu, G. and Potop-Butucaru, M., "BAN-GZKP: Optimal zero-knowledge proof for WBANs," *Ad Hoc Netw.*, vol. 77, pp. 28–41, 2018.

Chen, L. *et al.*, "Abnormal behavior detection for power-5G terminals," in *Proc. SPIE ICCD*, vol. 12703, pp. 379–387, 2023.

Chen, Y.H., "Adaptive heuristic for network slicing resource management," *Int. J. Commun. Syst.*, vol. 36, no. 8, p. e5463, 2023.

Cui, Z. *et al.*, "Malicious code detection in 5G HetNets using RBM," *IEEE Netw.*, vol. 35, no. 2, pp. 82–87, 2021.

Ergu, Y.A. *et al.*, "Adversarial attacks on DRL-based O-RAN resource allocation," *IEEE Trans. Veh. Technol.*, 2024.

Farreras, M. *et al.*, "Network slicing dataset for AI-based B5G management," *Data in Brief*, vol. 55, p. 110738, 2024.

Gokul, N. and Sankaran, S., "Modeling and defense against resource depletion in 5G," in *Proc. IEEE INDICON*, pp. 1–7, 2021.

Javadpour, A. *et al.*, "5G slice mutation to overcome DDoS via RL," in *Proc. IEEE SIN Conf.*, pp. 1–9, 2024.

Ji, M. *et al.*, "GNN + DRL resource allocation for V2X," *IEEE IoT J.*, 2024.

Khamesra, A., Selvaraj, P., and Singh, I., "Data encryption in 6G via zero-knowledge proofs," in *Proc. IEEE I-SMAC*, pp. 577–585, 2024.

Liu, L. and Fan, Q., "MILP-based resource allocation in multi-cloudlets," *IEEE Access*, vol. 6, pp. 24533–24542, 2018.

Liu, T. *et al.*, "FL-assisted client selection for 5G/B5G vehicular networks," *IEEE Trans. Veh. Technol.*, vol. 72, no. 2, pp. 2280–2292, 2022.

Martinovic, J. *et al.*, "ILP formulations for cognitive radio resource allocation," *IEEE Wireless Commun. Lett.*, vol. 6, no. 4, pp. 494–497, 2017.

Nyangaresi, V.O. *et al.*, "Security and privacy preservation in 5G networks," in *Proc. IEEE TELFOR*, pp. 1–4, 2021.

Pandey, C. *et al.*, "5GT-GAN-NET: Internet traffic forecasting over 5G," *IEEE Trans. Mobile Comput.*, vol. 23, no. 11, pp. 10694–10705, 2024.

Suh, K. *et al.*, "Deep RL-based network slicing for B5G," *IEEE Access*, vol. 10, pp. 7384–7395, 2022.

Thantharate, A. *et al.*, "Secure5G: Deep learning for secure slicing," in *Proc. IEEE CCWC*, pp. 852–857, 2020.

Wang, J. and Liu, J., "Secure and reliable slicing in 5G/B5G vehicular networks," *IEEE Wireless Commun.*, vol. 29, no. 1, pp. 126–133, 2022.

Zhao, S., "Energy-efficient 5G resource allocation via reinforcement learning," *Sustain. Energy Technol. Assess.*, vol. 56, p. 103020, 2023.

ARTIFICIAL INTELLIGENCE FOR STUDENTS WITH ADHD IN HIGHER EDUCATION: A SYSTEMATIC REVIEW

João Guedes, Daiana M. de Oliveira, Sergio Santos Silva Filho
and Marcos Augusto Francisco Borges
Universidade Estadual de Campinas - UNICAMP
R. Paschoal Marmo, 1888, Brazil

ABSTRACT

Artificial intelligence (AI) has emerged as a transformative force across various sectors, including education and assistive technologies. Despite rapid advancement, there remains scope for research regarding its application in supporting neurodivergent students, particularly those with Attention Deficit Hyperactivity Disorder (ADHD) – within higher education settings. This systematic review aims to map the current body of literature by analyzing studies from 2024 onward, retrieved from Scopus, IEEE Xplore and PubMed databases. The findings show both the potential and the current limitations of AI-based interventions, indicating that this remains an emerging area of research. Future directions are fostered to encourage more inclusive and adaptive educational strategies using AI.

KEYWORDS

Artificial Intelligence, Attention Deficit Hyperactivity Disorder, Higher Education, Learning Disabilities, Assistive Technologies

1. INTRODUCTION

The rapid advancement of artificial intelligence (AI) technologies over the last decade has led to their integration into multiple domains of society, including healthcare, education and assistive technologies (Wang et. al, 2025; Zaheer and Akhtar, 2025). Among the many emerging applications, the use of AI to support neurodivergent students, including those with Attention Deficit Hyperactivity Disorder (ADHD), in higher education represents an area of research. Given the cognitive and behavioral profiles associated with ADHD, students often face challenges related to sustained attention, executive functioning and information processing, which may hinder academic performance in university settings (Sibley et. al, 2021). AI-based assistive technologies, ranging from adaptive learning systems to personalized organizational tools, have the potential to address these specific needs, promoting greater autonomy and academic success.

1.1 Study Motivation

In recent years, the popularization of generative AI tools such as ChatGPT, Midjourney, and DeepSeek has reshaped how individuals interact with digital content, offering new possibilities for personalization, support, and productivity (Lo, 2023). For students with ADHD, who may struggle with task management, sustained focus, and information organization, these tools could offer important academic support (Henning et al., 2021). Despite this potential, there remains a gap in systematic knowledge about how AI is being applied in higher education to support this population. This research was motivated by the need to map existing initiatives, identify effective practices, and highlight areas that still lack attention from academia and technology developers.

1.2 Study Objective

To understand the current state of research at this intersection, we conducted a systematic literature review following established methodological guidelines. Three major scientific databases were selected for the literature search: Scopus, IEEE Xplore, and PubMed. These databases were chosen based on their relevance and scope in their respective domains. Scopus was selected due to its broad multidisciplinary coverage and strong representation of educational and social sciences. IEEE Xplore was included as a key repository of engineering and computer science research, where the majority of technical AI innovations are published. PubMed, a leading database for biomedical and health-related research, was included to capture clinical and psychological insights regarding ADHD and the use of assistive technologies.

1.3 Search Strategy

The following base search strings were used, tailored to each database's syntax and scope:(AI OR artificial intelligence) AND (ADHD OR Attention Deficit Hyperactivity Disorder) AND (higher education OR university OR college).

In total, 208 articles were identified and examined: 12 from Scopus, 90 from IEEE Xplore, and 106 from PubMed. After applying all inclusion and exclusion criteria, only 4 articles were deemed eligible and included in the final comprehensive analysis. This selection underscores the scarcity of focused research at the intersection of AI, ADHD, and higher education, reinforcing the importance of this study.

1.4 Temporal Scope and Trends

To ensure that the review reflects the most current advancements in the field, only articles published from 2024 onward were included. This temporal filter is supported by a clear increase in publication volume in recent years (Wang et al., 2025). In PubMed database, for example, there is a marked surge in publications related to this topic beginning in 2023, with the number of relevant articles rising in 2024 (75 articles) and 2025 (25 articles at the time of this research), compared to an average of fewer than 10 articles per year before 2022. This trend suggests a growing academic and practical interest in AI applications in support of neurodivergent students, aligning with the broader popularization of generative AI tools such as ChatGPT, Midjourney, DeepSeek, and others (Lo, 2023).

2. METHODOLOGICAL RIGOR

Furthermore, to ensure methodological rigor, the Preferred Reporting Items for Systematic Reviews and Meta-Analyses (PRISMA) guidelines were followed throughout the review process (Moher et al., 2015). The PRISMA method is a standardized framework used for conducting systematic reviews, designed to enhance transparency and reproducibility. It consists of four key phases: identification, screening, eligibility, and inclusion. In this study, articles were first identified through the database queries, then screened based on titles and abstracts. Full texts were subsequently assessed for eligibility using predefined inclusion criteria, and finally, studies meeting all criteria were included in the analysis.

2.1 Research Questions and Goals

To guide the systematic review, the following research questions and goals were formulated:

• RQ1: What are the main applications of artificial intelligence to support students with ADHD in higher education?

– Goal: Identify and categorize AI-based tools, platforms, or systems specifically designed or adapted to assist university students with ADHD.

• RQ2: What results and impacts have been reported in studies regarding the use of AI-based assistive technologies for students with ADHD?

– Goal: Analyze reported outcomes regarding academic performance, attention span, engagement, and university adaptation among students using AI tools.

• RQ3: What are the limitations and challenges identified in the application of AI for supporting students with ADHD in universities?

– Goal: Understand barriers, technological limitations, ethical concerns, and gaps in implementation described in the current research.

2.2 Inclusion and Exclusion Criteria

The criteria for selecting articles in this systematic review are detailed below.

2.2.1 Exclusion Criteria

Studies were excluded based on the following criteria:

• Different population: Studies focusing on children or adolescents in primary or secondary education, or those investigating neurodivergent conditions other than ADHD.
• Generic technologies: Research not addressing AI.
• Lack of practical application: Theoretical articles without empirical evaluation.
• Older publications: Articles published before 2024.
• Nonscientific publications: Opinion pieces or non-peer-reviewed reports.
• Incompatible languages: Studies published in languages other than English, Portuguese, or Spanish without translation.
• Focus on diagnosis: Studies focusing solely on diagnosing ADHD rather than supporting learning.

2.2.2 Inclusion Criteria

Studies were included if they met the following criteria:

• Target population: Students with ADHD in higher education environments.
• Type of technology: Digital tools, AI-based platforms, assistive software.
• Measured outcomes: Academic performance, attention, retention, or university adaptation.
• Higher education focus: Context explicitly related to universities or adult education.
• Publication date: Between 2024 and 2025.
• Language: English, Portuguese, or Spanish

2.3 Quality Assessment

After the full-text reading and final selection phase, each included study was evaluated for quality based on how well it addressed the three predefined research questions. A three-point scale was used: 0 (does not address), 0.5 (partially addresses), and 1 (fully addresses), for a total possible score of 3 per study. This approach to quality assessment is consistent with established practices in systematic reviews of educational interventions (Gough et al., 2017). Only articles with a score equal to or greater than 2 were included in the final review.

Several studies were excluded at this stage for addressing ADHD or AI in a secondary way or for having no practical or assistive application relevant to higher education. This quality assessment process ensured that only the most relevant and comprehensive studies were included in our final analysis.

The quality scores assigned to each article are as follows:

• (Zhao et al., 2025): 3.0
• (Jafarian and Kramer, 2025): 3.0
• (Wilder and Stratchan, 2025): 3.0
• (Pomare et al., 2024): 2.0

3. ANALYSIS OF INCLUDED STUDIES

Zhao et al. (2025) This study aimed to investigate how students with disabilities, including ADHD, use generative AI tools (e.g., ChatGPT) for academic writing in higher education (Zhao et al., 2025). The research was informed by a prior interview study and AI-literacy model, surveying students regarding their use of generative AI and obtaining 124 valid responses from students with disabilities. This approach aligns with recent research on technology adoption among neurodivergent students (Henning et al., 2021).

Jafarian and Kramer (2025) evaluates the impact of AI-generated audio learning modules on students' academic performance, motivation, and reading engagement, particularly among those with ADHD symptoms (Jafarian and Kramer, 2025). The researchers employed a randomized controlled trial with 410 first-year Psychology students, with participants assigned to either the audio-learning condition (60%) or a control condition (40%). This methodological approach addresses a gap in the literature, as noted by several researchers who have called for more experimental studies in this field.

The objective of Wilder and Stratchan (2025) was to analyze how college students with ADHD perform in virtual job interviews using AI tools enhanced with eye-tracking and cognitive metrics (Wilder and Stratchan, 2025). The study involved 46 students with ADHD who completed a structured interview simulation using the Big Interview platform, coupled with eye-tracking data and cognitive assessments. This innovative approach combines multiple data sources to provide a comprehensive understanding of how students with ADHD interact with AI-enhanced environments.

Pomare et al. (2024) explores the integration of ChatGPT as an assistive technology for individuals with disabilities, with specific mention of its relevance for ADHD users (Pomare et al., 2024). The research delves into the potential of integrating ChatGPT with assistive technology to enhance accessibility, providing personalized communication and technological aid for users with varying requirements. This focus on personalization aligns with broader trends in adaptive learning technologies for neurodivergent students.

Considering RQs analysis, the reviewed literature:

- reveal several key applications of artificial intelligence designed to support students with ADHD in higher education environments. These applications can be categorized into three main areas: writing support, multimodal learning enhancement, and professional skills development;
- report several significant outcomes and impacts from the use of AI-based assistive technologies for students with ADHD in higher education. These impacts span academic performance, engagement, motivation, and skill development;
- highlight several significant limitations and challenges in the application of AI for supporting students with ADHD in higher education, despite the promising applications and positive impacts identified.

4. CONCLUSION

This systematic review has mapped the current landscape of research on AI applications for students with ADHD in higher education. Despite the limited number of studies meeting our inclusion criteria, the findings suggest that AI has significant potential to support this population across multiple domains of university life. The identified applications in writing support, multimodal learning, and professional skills development demonstrate promising approaches that align with the specific needs of students with ADHD.

However, substantial challenges remain, including technical limitations, accessibility barriers, ethical concerns, and implementation issues. Addressing these challenges will require collaborative efforts from researchers, educators, technology developers, and students themselves. Future research should focus on long-term outcomes, comparative effectiveness, implementation strategies, personalization mechanisms, ethical frameworks, and student perspectives.

As AI technology continues to evolve rapidly, there is an opportunity to develop more inclusive and adaptive educational environments that better support neurodivergent students. By building on the promising applications identified in this review and addressing the noted limitations and challenges, the field can move toward evidence-based practices that enhance educational equity and success for students with ADHD in higher education.

ACKNOWLEDGEMENT

This study was financed in part by the Coordenação de Aperfeiçoamento de Pessoal de Nível Superior – Brasil (CAPES) – Finance Code 001.

REFERENCES

Abdelnour, E., Carragher, N., Banaschewski, T., Brandeis, D., Asherson, P., and Stringaris, A. (2022). Cognitive and motivational pathways in adhd: A systematic review. *Neuroscience & Biobehavioral Reviews*, 139:104730.

Henning, A., Schrieber, L., Matte, B., Mota, N. B., Polanczyk, G. V., and Rohde, L. A. (2021). Adhd in college students: Developmental findings. *Attention Deficit and Hyperactivity Disorders*, 13:973–984.

Jafarian, N. R. and Kramer, A.-W. (2025). AI-assisted audio-learning improves academic achievement through motivation and reading engagement. *Computers and Education: Artificial Intelligence*, 8.

Lo, C. K. (2023). Generative ai in education: A framework for dialogue. *Educational Technology & Society*, 26(4):1–15.

Moher, D., Shamseer, L., Clarke, M., Ghersi, D., Liberati, A., Petticrew, M., Shekelle, P., and Stewart, L. A. (2015). Preferred reporting items for systematic review and meta-analysis protocols (prisma-p) 2015 statement. *Systematic Reviews,* 4(1):1. Published online 2015 Jan 1.

Pomare, Z. S., Hossain, G., Maguluri, D. S., and Prybutok, G. (2024). Chatgpt as assistive technology: Opportunities and challenges.

Ryan, R. M. and Deci, E. L. (2020). Intrinsic and extrinsic motivation from a self-determination theory perspective: Definitions, theory, practices, and future directions. *Contemporary Educational Psychology*, 61:101860.

Sibley, M. H., Arnold, L. E., Swanson, J. M., Hechtman, L. T., Kennedy, T. M., Owens, E., and Molina, B. S. (2021). Diagnosing adhd in adolescence. *Journal of the American. Academy of Child & Adolescent Psychiatry*, 60(7):859–872.

Sweller, J. (2020). Cognitive load theory and educational technology. *Educational Tech-nology Research and Development,* 68:1–16.

Wang, X., Jia, Q., Liang, L., Zhou, W., Yang, W., and Mu, J. (2025). Artificial intelligence in adhd: a global perspective on research hotspots, trends and clinical applications. *Frontiers in Human Neuroscience,* 19:1577585.

Wilder, T. L. and Stratchan, N. E. (2025). Artificial intelligence-enhanced interview suc-cess: Leveraging eye-tracking and cognitive measures to support self-regulation in college students with adhd. *Education Sciences*, 15(2):165.

Zaheer, A. and Akhtar, A. (2025). Artificial intelligence as a support to diagnose adhd: an insight of unorthodox approaches: a scoping review. *Child Neuropsychology*, pages 1–18.

Zhao, X., Cox, A., and Chen, X. (2025). The use of generative AI by students with disabilities in higher education. *The Internet and Higher Education*, 66.

PROMOTION OF VERIFYING THE AUTHENTICITY OF SOCIAL MEDIA POSTS BY EMPHASIZING THE USE OF OTHERS' REACTIONS

Leo Onodera[1], Ryo Onuma[1], Hiroki Nakayama[1], Hiroaki Kaminaga[1],
Youzou Miyadera[2] and Shoichi Nakamura[1]
[1]*Fukushima University*
1, Kanayagawa, Fukushima 960-1296, Japan
[2]*Tokyo Gakugei University*
4-1-1, Nukuikita, Koganei, Tokyo 184-8501, Japan

ABSTRACT

Social media have been widely used as a means of collecting information. However, countless posts exist on social media, and some contain false information, often causing confusion. Although it is important for users to verify the authenticity of posts on their own, such judgement is difficult for inexperienced. Although inexperienced individuals need clues to challenge themselves in discerning the authenticity of posts in order to accumulate meaningful experience, acquiring such clues is difficult. In this research, we have been aiming at developing methods to generate clues for verifying the authenticity of social media posts based on the analysis of others' reactions. This paper mainly describes methods for extracting noteworthy posts that require the verification of authenticity and for extracting useful others' reactions that contain descriptions expressing reasons or evidence. Finally, this paper describes an experiment using prototype and its results have suggested the basic effectiveness of our methods.

KEYWORDS

Experience in Determining Authenticity of Posts, Others' Reactions to Posts, Social Media, Information Literacy

1. INTRODUCTION

Social media has become a primary means for quickly obtaining the latest information due to its immediacy and easy accessibility. For instance, the penetration rate of social media in Japan reaches 81.5% (Ministry of Internal Affairs and Communications, 2023). However, posts on social media also contains information that differs from the truth as well as various speculations. To prevent users from suffering disadvantages due to false information, it is essential to have the ability to determine the authenticity of posts. Although this kind of ability is cultivated through experience in assessing the authenticity of posts, inexperienced individuals have difficulties in accumulating meaningful experience.

To resolve these problems, these have been systems for detecting disinformation on social media (Ahn and Jeong, 2019; Gupta et al., 2023; Jose et al., 2021; Matheven and Kumar, 2022; Mu et al., 2024; Singh and Patidar, 2022; Tanvir et al., 2019) and systems for collecting fake news using corrective posts (King and Escobari, 2025; Ma et al., 2023; Mannan and Nova, 2023; Nielsen and McConville, 2022; Shu et al., 2020). However, most of these existing systems primarily focus on automatically determining the authenticity of posts, and do not consider supporting inexperienced users in gaining experience to discern the authenticity of posts on social media themselves.

In this research, we have aimed to develop a mechanism that extracts and classifies others' reactions to posts on social media in order to present them to users as clues for discerning the authenticity of posts. Accordingly, we demonstrate a novel way to promote experience in discerning the authenticity of social media posts more realistically than existing methods.

2. SYSTEM OVERVIEW

Figure 1 overviews a system to generate the clues for identifying the authenticity of posts. When users attempt to identify the authenticity of posts, the support system extracts posts that should be examined on the basis of analyzing the particular expressions frequently used for pointing out fakes and presents them to the user. Receiving the user's selection of any post, the system collects others' reactions (replies and quote retweets) to the selected post. Next, this system extracts reactions from the collected others' that include reasons or evidences within the text body. Furthermore, the extracted reactions of others are classified by emotion. Finally, we visually present the extracted noteworthy posts along with corresponding others' reactions to users in an easy-to-understand format. These suggestions enable users to realistically challenge to judge themselves the authenticity of posts.

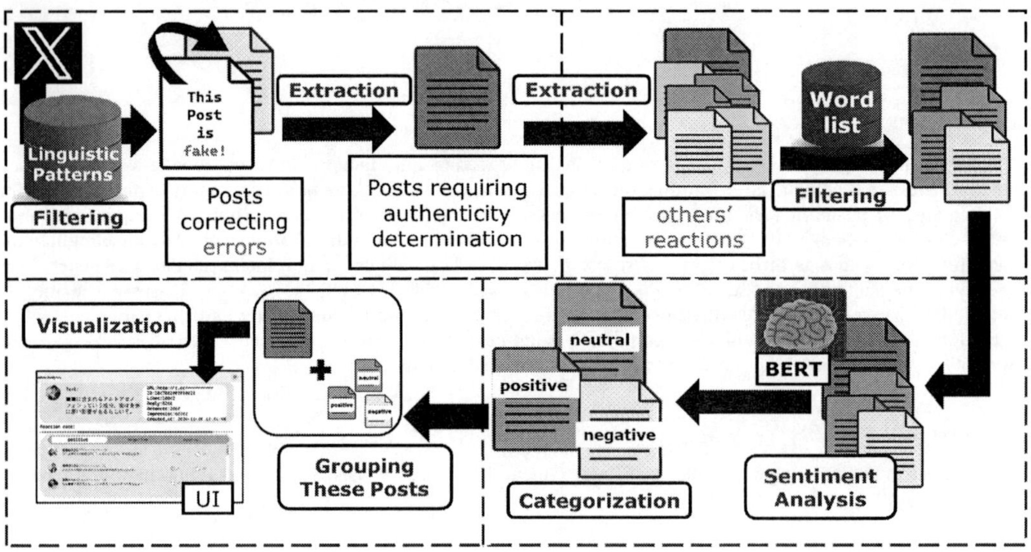

Figure 1. Overview of the system to generate the clues for identifying the authenticity of posts

3. METHOD FOR EXTRACTING POSTS REQUIRING AUTHENTICITY DETERMINATION

In this research, we extract posts that require authenticity determination by focusing on posts that point out errors in other posts. We define "quote retweets" and "replies" that indicate some errors in specific posts as correction posts, and the original posts targeted by these correction posts are regarded as noteworthy posts requiring authenticity determination. Figure 2 illustrates the relationship between correction posts and noteworthy posts requiring authenticity determination.

To extract correction posts, we employ the linguistic patterns that frequently appear in tweets pointing out errors (Murayama et al., 2020). Posts containing particular words or expressions that match these patterns are identified as correction posts. By searching for the target of the correction posts with their attributes such as reference IDs, we then extract the noteworthy posts that require authenticity determination.

4. EXTRACTION AND PRESENTATION OF OTHERS' REACTIONS

In this research, we extract replies and quote retweets to specific posts as others' reactions. However, these reactions from others are not necessarily all effective when determining the authenticity of a post. In order to extract others' reactions that are useful for authenticity judgment, we focus on those that include the descriptions expressing reasons or evidence. Specifically, we focus on particular expressions frequently used when presenting reasons or evidence, as well as conjunctions indicating sequential or contrasting relationships. We compile these into a list of conjunctions and a list of particular expressions. Furthermore, we extract others' reactions containing words included in these two lists respectively.

Next, we classify the extracted others' reactions into three sentiment categories—positive, negative, and neutral—in order to present them more effectively as clues for authenticity judgment. For this classification, we use BERT after performing fine-tuning using the collected actual others' reactions labeled with the above three sentiment categories as training data.

Finally, the noteworthy posts requiring authenticity determination are visually presented to users in association with the extracted and classified others' reactions as well as the overall impressions of the posts (Figure 3). Users attempt to judge the authenticity of noteworthy posts while referring to these suggestions.

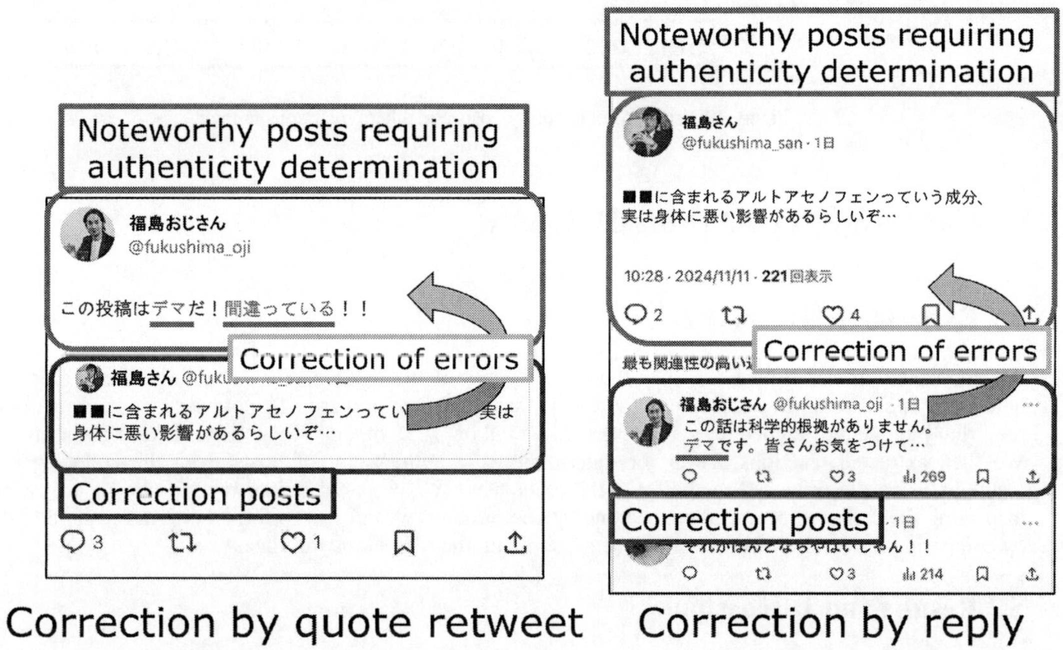

Figure 2. Relationship between correction posts and noteworthy posts requiring authenticity determination

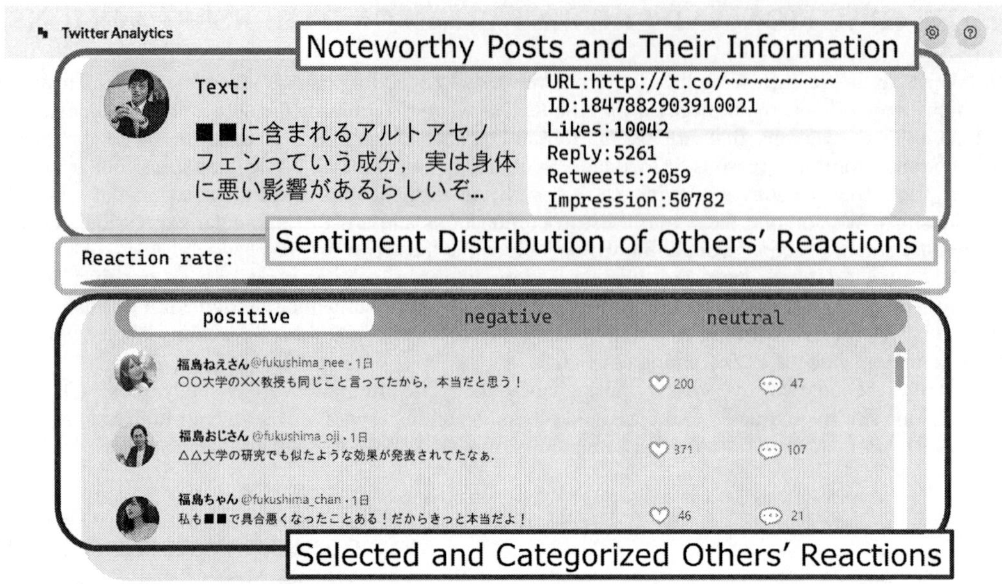

Figure 3. Display of noteworthy posts and others' reactions to them

5. EXPERIMENT AND DISCUSSION

5.1 Experiment Overview

We conducted an experiment to verify the effectiveness of the methods for extracting others' reactions to noteworthy posts requiring authenticity determination. First, we prepared 10 noteworthy social media posts requiring judgment of authenticity and collected a total of 7,058 others' reactions to them using a prototype. We then extracted reactions useful for determining the authenticity of posts from the collected others' reactions using the proposed method. On the other hand, we prepared the correct answer data by visually inspecting the collected others' reactions one by one. Finally, we calculated the precision, recall and F-value by comparing the result of extraction by the system with the correct answer data.

5.2 Results and Discussion

The results of extracting useful others' reactions are shown in Table 1. The findings indicate that the proposed method successfully extracted others' reactions containing reasons or evidence in a certain extent. On the other hand, the recall rate was relatively low. Since this experiment used the limited lists of particular expressions and conjunctions, improvement through their tuning is expected.

Table 1. Results of extracting others' reactions

Precision	Recall	F-Score
0.76	0.12	0.21

6. CONCLUSION

In this paper, we describe methods for promoting the experience of discerning the authenticity of posts on social media. Particularly, we described methods for extracting noteworthy posts requiring verification of authenticity from a large number of submissions, as well as methods for collecting others' reactions and then extracting and useful ones and classifying them.

Future work includes further verification and improvements of the methods for extracting and classifying others' reactions through careful experiments using actual social media posts.

REFERENCES

Ahn, Y.-C. and Jeong, C.-S., (2019), Natural language contents evaluation system for detecting fake news using deep learning. *Proceedings of 2019 16th International Joint Conference on Computer Science and Software Engineering (JCSSE)*, pp. 289-292.

Gupta, A., Batla, A., Kumar, C. and Jain, G., (2023), Comparative analysis of machine learning models for fake news classification. *Proceedings of 2023 3rd International Conference on Intelligent Technologies (CONIT)*, pp. 1-5.

Jose, X., Kumar, S. D. M. and Chandran, P., (2021), *Characterization, classification and detection of fake news in online social media networks. Proceedings of 2021 IEEE Mysore Sub Section International Conference (MysuruCon)*, Hassan, India, pp. 759-765.

King, K. K. and Escobari, D., (2025). Can Correction Messages Reduce the Spread of Fake News on Social Media? The Impact of Information Updates on the Effectiveness of Corrections. *Journal of Management Information Systems*, Vol. 42, No. 3, pp. 706-736.

Ma, Y., He, B., Subrahmanian, N. and Kumar, S., (2023), Characterizing and predicting social correction on Twitter. *Proceedings of the 15th ACM Web Science Conference*, pp. 86-95.

Mannan, I. and Nova, S. N., (2023), An empirical study on theories of sentiment analysis in relation to fake news detection. *Proceedings of 2023 International Conference on Information and Communication Technology for Sustainable Development (ICICT4SD)*, pp. 79-83.

Matheven, A. and Kumar, B. V. D., (2022), Fake news detection using deep learning and natural language processing. *Proceedings of 2022 9th International Conference on Soft Computing & Machine Intelligence (ISCMI)*, pp. 11-14.

Ministry of Internal Affairs and Communications, (2023) *Information and Communications in Japan 2023*. Ministry of Internal Affairs and Communications, Tokyo, Japan.

Mu, Y., Song, X., Bontcheva, K. and Aletras, N., (2024), Examining the limitations of computational rumor detection models trained on static datasets. *Proceedings of LREC-COLING 2024 (Language Resources and Evaluation Conference)*, Marseille, France, pp. 6739-6751.

Murayama, T., Wakamiya, S. and Aramaki, E., (2020). *Universal Fake News Collection System using Debunking Tweets.* arXiv, online.

Nielsen, D. S. and McConville, R., (2022), MuMiN: A large-scale multilingual multimodal fact-checked misinformation social network dataset. *Proceedings of the 45th International ACM SIGIR Conference on Research and Development in Information Retrieval (SIGIR)*, pp. 1-5.

Shu, K., Mahudeswaran, D., Wang, S., Lee, D. and Liu, H., (2020), FakeNewsNet: A data repository with news content, social context, and spatiotemporal information for studying fake news on social media. *Proceedings of the 2018 IEEE/ACM International Conference on Advances in Social Networks Analysis and Mining*, vol. 8(3), pp. 171-188.

Singh, A. and Patidar, S., (2022), A survey on fake news detection using machine learning. *Proceedings of 2022 4th International Conference on Advances in Computing, Communication Control and Networking (ICAC3N)*, Greater Noida, India, pp. 327-331.

Tanvir, A. A., Mahir, E. M., Akhter, S. and Huq, M. R., (2019), Detecting fake news using machine learning and deep learning algorithms. *Proceedings of 2019 7th International Conference on Smart Computing & Communications (ICSCC)*, Sarawak, Malaysia, pp. 1-5.

Posters

DIGITAL SEMANTIC NETWORK FOR FORENSIC INTELLIGENCE: GRAPH-BASED MACHINE LEARNING

Dmytro Uzlov[1], Oleksii Vlasov[1], Sergiy Yakovlev[1,2], Lyudmyla Kirichenko[1,2] and Denys Sadilo[1]
[1]*V.N. Karazin Kharkiv National University*
6 Svobody Sq., Kharkiv, 61022, Ukraine
[2]*Lodz University of Technology*
ul. Żeromskiego 116, 90-924 Lodz, Poland

ABSTRACT

This paper proposes an advanced approach to forensic intelligence by integrating graph-based machine learning techniques. We design a semantic network architecture that transforms fragmented and semi-structured crime records into structured knowledge graphs. These graphs serve as the foundation for embedding, classification, link prediction, and anomaly detection through advanced graph neural network (GNN) architectures. Our experimental evaluation on real-world criminal datasets demonstrates the efficacy of this approach in uncovering hidden relationships, forecasting crime patterns, and identifying entities of interest within forensic investigations.

KEYWORDS

Graph Machine Learning, Knowledge Graph, Forensic Intelligence, Graph Neural Networks, Spatiotemporal Prediction

1. INTRODUCTION

Modern crime analysis faces growing challenges due to the increasing volume, complexity, and fragmentation of available information. Traditional data systems often fail to capture the latent structure of criminal interactions, particularly when data originates from diverse, unstructured sources like investigation reports, witness statements, or surveillance summaries. Forensic intelligence systems require analytical frameworks that can go beyond surface-level correlations and identify deeper semantic and relational patterns within heterogeneous data. To address this gap, we propose a novel graph-based learning framework that transforms semi-structured textual crime data into semantic knowledge graphs. Unlike conventional tabular approaches, our system constructs a graph representation grounded in extracted subject–predicate–object (SPO) triples. These knowledge graphs allow for effective application of modern graph machine learning algorithms, including node embedding, link prediction, and graph neural networks (GNNs). What sets our approach apart is its end-to-end integration of natural language processing (NLP), semantic graph construction, and deep learning. The proposed system not only models complex relationships between criminal entities but also incorporates spatial and temporal metadata, enabling predictive analysis of crime dynamics. By doing so, we shift forensic intelligence from reactive investigation to proactive pattern discovery and risk assessment.

2. MATERIALS AND METHODS

The proposed system architecture includes several core stages: data preprocessing, semantic transformation, graph construction, embedding generation, and graph-based learning. The pipeline begins with entity and relation extraction from raw case files, producing SPO triples that are then assembled into a knowledge graph.

Figure 1 illustrates the architecture of our system.

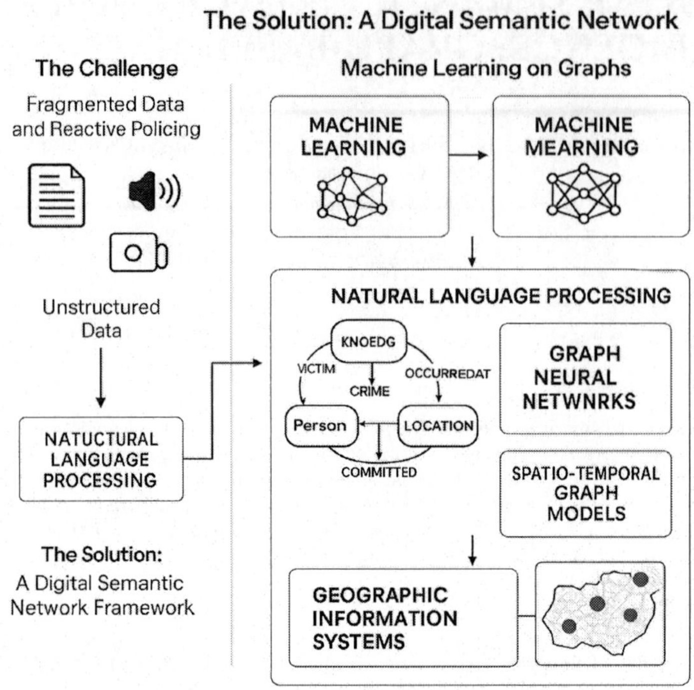

Figure 1. Architecture of the Proposed Graph-Based Forensic Intelligence System

The workflow starts with NLP modules for named entity recognition and relation extraction, followed by RDF triple formation. These triples are ingested into a graph database where each node represents a real-world entity (e.g., person, location, weapon) and edges correspond to observed or inferred relationships. This semantic layer serves as the foundation for all subsequent analysis.

To prepare the graph for machine learning, we generate low-dimensional node embeddings using Node2Vec and DeepWalk. These embeddings capture structural properties and neighborhood relationships, which are then utilized in supervised learning tasks. In particular, we train logistic regression and shallow neural classifiers to identify hidden links (e.g., unknown connections between suspects) and classify entities by role or behavior (e.g., victim, suspect, accomplice). We also employ unsupervised community detection (via the Louvain algorithm) to uncover clusters of entities that frequently co-occur or collaborate. Although the corresponding figure is omitted, our visual analysis revealed well-defined subgraphs aligning with known criminal networks and showing signs of hierarchical structure and inter-group links.

The framework incorporates Graph Neural Networks, including Graph Convolutional Networks (GCNs) and GraphSAGE, which aggregate information from a node's local neighborhood. Our implementation of GraphSAGE builds on inductive representation learning principles (Hamilton et al., 2017), enabling generalization to unseen nodes and adaptation to evolving forensic graphs. To capture temporal and geographic patterns, we enrich the graph with timestamps and location tags, employing spatio-temporal GNNs to predict crime hotspots and trace criminal activity propagation over time. These challenges align with multi-object control and probabilistic modeling in dynamic networks, where reliability and adaptability are critical (Rukkas et al., 2025).

3. RESULTS

We evaluated the framework using real-world structured crime data compiled from open law enforcement sources. Compared to traditional machine learning models operating on flat data, our graph-based system consistently demonstrated higher precision in identifying criminal relationships, especially in incomplete datasets. Community detection techniques successfully grouped entities into meaningful clusters, many of which aligned with known gangs or coordinated groups. These clusters often exhibited dense intra-group connections and sparse inter-group edges, reinforcing the interpretability of the model.

Our experiments also showed that incorporating Graph Attention Networks (GATs) improved model transparency by highlighting the most influential neighbors in classification tasks. For example, GATs helped identify key individuals whose connections significantly influenced the predicted role of others, a valuable feature for investigative prioritization.

Finally, spatio-temporal GNNs enabled dynamic forecasting of criminal activity, capturing regional trends and time-based escalation patterns. The system's outputs support both retrospective analysis and forward-looking threat assessments, making it highly applicable in operational settings.

4. CONCLUSION

This work introduces a comprehensive and scalable framework for forensic intelligence that leverages the strengths of semantic graph modeling and graph-based machine learning. Our method effectively transforms fragmented and semi-structured crime records into a unified knowledge graph, enabling advanced analytics that surpass conventional approaches in accuracy, interpretability, and predictive power.

The system's novelty lies in its holistic pipeline, which spans from semantic enrichment to spatio-temporal graph learning. This design provides law enforcement agencies with an actionable tool for real-time investigation and threat anticipation. The integration of GNNs and community detection methods enhances the system's ability to uncover hidden structures and infer missing links, while attention-based models contribute to greater transparency in the decision-making process. In future work, we plan to extend the framework by incorporating large language models to enhance entity extraction and by developing explainable AI modules to support human-in-the-loop investigation. Overall, our approach marks a significant step toward intelligent, adaptive, and ethically transparent forensic analysis.

REFERENCES

Hamilton, W., Ying, Z., & Leskovec, J. (2017). Inductive Representation Learning on Large Graphs. Advances in Neural Information Processing Systems (NeurIPS). https://10.48550/arXiv.1706.02216

Rukkas, K., Morozova , A., Uzlov, D., Kuznietcova, V., & Chumachenko, D. (2025). Efficiency and Reliability of Multi-Object Control Methods in Complex Networks. *Advanced Information Systems,* 9(1), 62–69. https://doi.org/10.20998/2522-9052.2025.1.07

SKY COMPUTING FOR SME: SIMPLIFYING MULTI-CLOUD COMPLEXITY

Henry-Norbert Cocos[†], Christian Baun[†] and Andreas U. Schmidt*
[†]*Frankfurt University of Applied Sciences, Department of Computer Science and Engineering, Nibelungenplatz 1, D-60318 Frankfurt am Main, Germany*
**Wilhelm Büchner Hochschule, Department of Computer Science, Hilpertstr. 31, D-64295 Darmstadt, Germany*

ABSTRACT

The evolution from traditional on-premise infrastructures to hybrid and multi-cloud architectures has transformed IT, enabling organizations to reduce vendor lock-in, optimize costs, and improve flexibility. However, managing resources across multiple clouds remains complex, especially for small and medium-sized enterprises (SMEs). This paper presents a vendor-agnostic multi-cloud framework focused on unified cost management through a standardized Cost API. The proposed architecture aims to simplify multi-cloud management, enabling more efficient and cost-effective operations. We conclude with the benefits of this approach and future research directions.

KEYWORDS

Sky Computing, Multi-Cloud, Vendor-Agnostic Framework, Cost Management, Cost API

1. INTRODUCTION

Cloud computing leverages virtualization and web technologies to deliver scalable services on demand. Since the late 2000s, organizations have increasingly adopted hybrid and multi-cloud strategies (Gundu et al., 2020) to access best-of-breed services, reduce dependency on single providers, and enhance business continuity and security through data distribution. Despite these advantages, multi-cloud environments introduce significant management challenges due to interoperability issues and lack of transparency (Jamshidi et al., 2016). Sky Computing seeks to address these challenges by abstracting resources across providers, enabling seamless service use.

2. STATE OF THE ART

Cloud service providers offer various pricing models, including static pricing (fixed rates), dynamic pricing (real-time adjustments), and pay-per-use or subscription models (Ibrahimi, 2017). Selecting the appropriate model is crucial for cost efficiency but can be complex in multi-cloud setups. Hybrid and multi-cloud architectures are now common, allowing organizations to distribute workloads for better availability and economic efficiency. However, they face persistent issues: lack of service transparency, API incompatibilities, and complex management requirements. With the rise of hybrid cloud, multi-cloud environments have become common, helping organizations avoid vendor lock-in and increase flexibility. These setups distribute services across providers, offering enhanced availability and economic efficiency. However, they also face challenges: lack of service transparency, API interoperability issues, and complex management (Ardagna, 2015; Barker et al., 2015).

While prior work focuses on pricing and resource efficiency, interoperability between cloud vendors remains underexplored. To address this, Stoica et al. (Stoica 2024; Stoica 2021) proposed Sky Computing as a framework for abstracting cloud provider services, enabling seamless cross-provider operations. The SkyPilot project at Berkeley exemplifies this vision, providing an intercloud broker for machine learning workloads.

Section 3 explores the current cloud landscape and Cloud Cost Management and Optimization Solutions for multi-cloud environments.

3. MANAGING COST IN MULTI-CLOUD

For SMEs, multi-cloud adoption offers flexibility and access to optimal services but complicates cost management and governance. Managing costs across providers is challenging due to differing billing models, hidden expenses (e.g., data transfer fees, idle resources), and the risk of overprovisioning. Effective cost management is essential to avoid waste and ensure efficient use of resources.

3.1 Cloud Cost Management and Optimization Solutions

Cloud Cost Management and Optimization (CCMO) tools are designed to address these challenges, offering features such as:

- **Data normalization:** Standardizing cost data from multiple providers for unified analysis.
- **Cost visualization:** Providing granular insights across services and infrastructure.
- **Cost optimization:** Delivering recommendations for savings, such as resizing or removing unused resources.
- **Budgeting:** Allowing tracking by team, project, or customer.
- **IT asset management:** Monitoring the lifecycle and utilization of IT assets.

While commercial CCMO tools offer comprehensive features (real-time monitoring, automated optimization, compliance checks), they often come with high licensing costs, which can be prohibitive for SMEs. Open-source alternatives (e.g., Komiser, OpenCost) support specific tasks but lack the full feature set required for complex, multi-cloud environments. Table 1 shows a list of CCMO tools on the market.

Table 1. CCMO tools on the market

Tool	Features	CSP support	Pricing
CloudZero [1]	- Real-time cost monitoring and allocation - Insights into costs per customer - Integration withpublic CSP, Kubernetes and SaaS platforms	AWS, Azure, GCP, Kubernetes, SaaS	- Free Plan: No. - Free Trial: No.
CloudHealth [2]	- Comprehensive cost management - Compliance and governance - Detailed reports and analyses	AWS, Azure, GCP, Oracle Cloud	- Cost: Up to $100,000 fixed price, then 3% of monthly expenses. Minimum fee of $1,000. - Free Trial: Yes, available.
Komiser [3]	- Cloud Asset Inventory - Cost management and analysis - Resource relationships visualizes the relationships between resources.	AWS, Azure, GCP, Civo, DigitalOcean, OCI, Linode, Tencent	Open Source
OpenCost [4]	- Real-time cost monitoring for Kubernetes - Cost optimization. - Integrations with open source tools.	AWS, Azure, GCP	Open Source

3.2 Cloud Cost API

An analysis of APIs from major cloud providers (AWS, GCP, Azure, IBM Cloud) reveals that all support detailed cost queries and usage tracking, with AWS, GCP, and Azure offering additional budget management APIs—IBM Cloud lacks this feature. These APIs enable granular cost breakdowns and facilitate automation

1 https://www.cloudzero.com/.
2 https://www.vmware.com/products/app-platform/tanzu-cloudhealth.
3 https://github.com/tailwarden/komiser.
4 https://opencost.io/.

and integration, though the depth and flexibility of cost monitoring tools differ between providers. This insight is crucial for developing a cost and risk management framework for SMEs, where cloud costs typically fall into base, usage-based, and support/management categories. Effective management depends on monitoring provisioned versus actual usage, leveraging pricing models, managing dynamic costs, and using predictive analytics. As multi-cloud environments grow more complex, SMEs face increasing challenges in optimization. Introducing an abstraction layer or intercloud broker can simplify vendor management and enable unified, flexible cloud operations without altering underlying services or APIs.

We propose developing an abstraction layer that acts as a marketplace, allowing end-users to interact with multiple vendors through a unified platform. This approach simplifies vendor engagement without requiring changes to the underlying services or APIs, enabling smarter negotiation and greater flexibility in cloud adoption. However, this first look into the APIs of cloud vendors is just a first step in the process. First inspections into the different APIs of the vendors show, that e.g. AWS Price List Bulk API returns more than 6 GB of raw data, which need to be filtered and analyzed. This raw data is not normalized nor up to date, since vendors can make frequent changes to the prices of their services. However further investigation needs to be done in this field, since the mentioned issues are only applicable to static pricing data and do not include the dynamic beahaviour of running services.

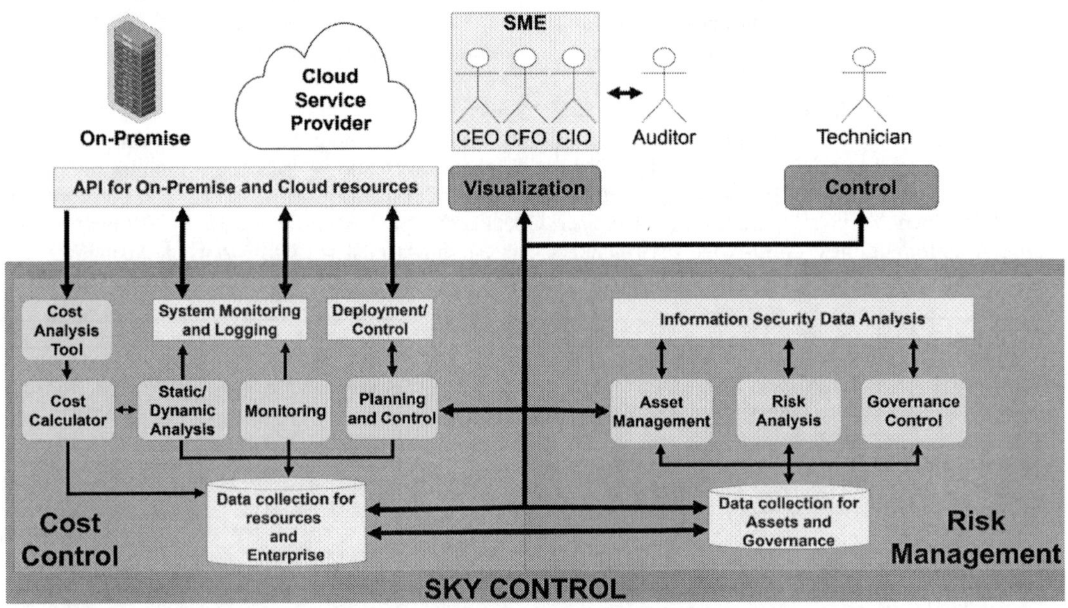

Figure 1. The SKY CONTROL architecture (Cocos et al., 2025)

4. SKY CONTROL: A VENDOR AGNOSTIC MULTI-CLOUD FRAMEWORK

The distributed nature of multi-cloud environments provides significant benefits for SMEs, such as flexibility and vendor independence, but also introduces challenges in workload management, cost transparency, and security governance across different cloud service providers (CSPs). SKY CONTROL (Cocos et al., 2025) addresses these challenges by offering a comprehensive framework for SMEs using multi-cloud infrastructures. The framework is designed to address the unique needs of SMEs operating in multi-cloud environments. Its core components are:

- **Unified Cost Control:** SKY CONTROL provides analytics and visualization for both on-premise and cloud resources, supporting static and dynamic cost analysis. It predicts price trends and enables planning across multiple providers through a standardized Cost API.

- **Risk Management:** The framework assesses risks based on asset criticality, data protection, and compliance requirements (e.g., C5 for German SMEs). It offers visual tools to support audits and governance.
- **Intercloud Broker:** Acting as a mediator between cloud and on-premise environments, the broker ensures seamless interoperability and optimal workload distribution. It supports both vertical (cloud-to-on-premise) and horizontal (cloud-to-cloud) migrations.

The benefits for SMEs are the following:

- Reduced complexity in managing multi-cloud environments
- Improved cost transparency and control
- Enhanced compliance and risk management
- Greater flexibility and resilience through vendor independence

As shown in Figure 1, the SKY CONTROL architecture emphasizes analyzing pricing, workload criticality, and governance to inform optimal workload placement. To support this, SKY CONTROL must first develop a conceptual model for evaluating decision factors, as optimality depends on multiple, often competing, dimensions.

5. CONCLUSION AND FUTURE WORK

Sky Computing and frameworks like SKY CONTROL represent a promising approach to overcoming the challenges of multi-cloud management. By providing abstraction, automation, and unified cost and risk management, SMEs can operate more efficiently and flexibly. Future work will focus on expanding provider support, refining workload placement strategies, and developing a market-ready solution that empowers SMEs to fully leverage modern cloud technologies.

REFERENCES

Ardagna, D. (2015). "Cloud and Multi-Cloud Computing: Current Challenges and Future Applications." In *2015 IEEE/ACM 7th International Workshop on Principles of Engineering Service-Oriented and Cloud Systems*, 1–2. https://doi.org/10.1109/PESOS.2015.8.

Barker, A., Varghese, B., and Thai, L. (2015). "Cloud Services Brokerage: A Survey and Research Roadmap." In *2015 IEEE 8th International Conference on Cloud Computing*, 1029–32. https://doi.org/10.1109/CLOUD.2015.144

Cocos, H.-N, Baun, C., and Kappes, M. (2025). "The Evolution of Cloud Computing Towards a Vendor Agnostic Market Place Using the SKY CONTROL Framework." In *Proceedings of the 15th International Conference on Cloud Computing and Services Science - CLOSER*, 211–18. SciTePress. https://doi.org/10.5220/0013361200003950.

Gundu, S. R., Panem C. A., and Thimmapuram, A. (2020). "Hybrid IT and Multi Cloud an Emerging Trend and Improved Performance in Cloud Computing." *SN Computer Science* 1 (5). https://doi.org/10.1007/s42979-020-00277-x.

Ibrahimi, A. (2017). "Cloud Computing: Pricing Model." *International Journal of Advanced Computer Science and Applications* 8 (6). https://doi.org/10.14569/IJACSA.2017.080658.

Jamshidi, P., Pahl, C., and Mendonça N. C. (2016). "Pattern-based Multi-cloud Architecture Migration." *Software: Practice and Experience* 47 (9): 1159–84. https://doi.org/10.1002/spe.2442

Stoica, I. (2024). "Sky Computing: Opportunities and Challenges." In *Studies in Systems, Decision and Control*, 15–27. Studies in Systems, Decision and Control. Cham: Springer Nature Switzerland.

Stoica, I., and Shenker, S. (2021). "From Cloud Computing to Sky Computing." In *Proceedings of the Workshop on Hot Topics in Operating Systems*, 26–32. HotOS '21. New York, NY, USA: ACM. https://doi.org/10.1145/3458336.3465301

MONITORING FRACTAL PROPERTIES OF TIME SERIES VIA HURST EXPONENT ESTIMATION AND LSTM-BASED DETECTION

Lyudmyla Kirichenko[1,2], Sergiy Yakovlev[1,2], Alexander Kirpich[3], Olha Matsyi[1] and Dmytro Chumachenko[4,5]
[1]Lodz University of Technology, ul. Żeromskiego 116, 90-924 Lodz, Poland
[2]V.N. Karazin Kharkiv National University, 6 Svobody sq., 61022 Kharkiv, Ukraine
[3]Georgia State University, 33 Gilmer St, SE Atlanta, GA 30303, United States
[4]Balsillie School of International Affairs, 67Erb St, W, N2L 6C2, Waterloo, ON, Canada
[5]National Aerospace University "Kharkiv Aviation Institute", 17 Vadyma Manka St, 61070 Kharkiv, Ukraine

ABSTRACT

Many technological, physical, and biological systems exhibit complex fractal behavior. Detecting changes in the fractal structure of time series is essential, as they may indicate transitions to anomalous or critical states. This study proposes a method for tracking such changes by monitoring the Hurst exponent using a sliding window and the Whittle estimator. To detect significant variations in the Hurst parameter, we apply LSTM autoencoders, which can capture temporal dependencies and identify deviations via reconstruction error. The model was trained on synthetic fractal time series with various types of Hurst dynamics, including abrupt shifts and gradual trends. Validation on both synthetic and real EEG data demonstrated the method's ability to detect meaningful structural changes.

KEYWORDS

Hurst Exponent, Fractal Analysis, LSTM Autoencoder, EEG, Anomalous Diffusion, Time Series

1. INTRODUCTION

It is now widely recognized that a significant number of technological, informational, physical, and biological processes possess a complex fractal structure. Fractal analysis has been extensively applied to model, analyze, and manage complex systems across various fields of science and engineering, as it enables the identification of hidden patterns and offers deeper insights into the internal organization of intricate dynamic processes (Gowrisankar & Banerjee, 2021).

The detection of changes in the fractal structure of time series is a relevant challenge, as such changes reflect transformations in the correlation, fractal, and frequency structures of the system, which may indicate the presence of critical states or anomalous operating modes. These changes may not be evident when using traditional spectral and correlation methods, as they manifest on different time scales and may exhibit nonlinear behavior. Within the framework of fractal analysis, a key indicator of structural changes is the Hurst parameter, which characterizes the long-term dependence and self-similarity of a time series. Monitoring the Hurst parameter by sliding window approach represents an effective approach to detecting changes in the fractal structure of time series. To address this challenge, the present study proposes the use of neural networks capable of efficiently processing sequential Hurst parameter estimates and detecting significant changes.

2. MATERIALS AND METHODS

The sliding window approach involves sequential analysis of the time series, where the Hurst parameter is estimated at each step using a fixed-size window with constant overlap. This method allows for the detection of local changes in fractal characteristics and provides a dynamic view of how the internal complexity of the process evolves over time. In each window, the Hurst exponent was estimated using the Whittle estimator (Zhang et al., 2024), which relies on a maximum likelihood method in the frequency domain. By minimizing the difference between the empirical and theoretical spectral densities, it yields stable estimates of the self-similarity parameter. This method is particularly effective for processes with long-range dependencies and has been successfully applied in various domains.

The estimation procedure results in a new time series representing the dynamics of the Hurst exponent. This transformation allows a shift in focus from the original data to its underlying fractal structure. Such a representation is more sensitive to long-term dependencies and can reveal changes in the system's organization that are not apparent through traditional signal analysis. To prepare the data for neural network processing, the Hurst exponent sequence was standardized, and overlapping segments of equal length were extracted. These segments were then used to train a Long Short-Term Memory (LSTM) autoencoder. LSTM networks are well suited for capturing temporal dependencies in sequential data and can effectively encode the internal patterns of fractal dynamics. The autoencoder was trained on sequences corresponding to typical (non-anomalous) behavior. During inference, deviations from learned patterns were identified through elevated reconstruction error. This makes it possible to detect various types of structural changes, including smooth drifts, abrupt jumps, and mixed patterns, within a unified framework.

3. RESULTS

A promising approach to detecting abrupt changes in the Hurst parameter and analyzing the fractal structure of time series is the use of LSTM autoencoders (Machine Learning Mastery, n.d.). Long Short-Term Memory (LSTM) networks have the ability to model complex temporal dependencies and effectively handle sequential data. The autoencoder architecture, consisting of an encoder and a decoder, enables the network to learn hidden patterns and structures in the data, providing a compact representation of the time series in a latent space.

Building on the LSTM autoencoder model trained on sequences of Hurst exponent values introduced in Kirichenko et al. (2024), this study proposes a generalized framework capable of detecting gradual, abrupt, and mixed-type anomalies across diverse types of time series.

In the context of Hurst parameter analysis, the autoencoder can be trained on normal (non-anomalous) behavior of the time series, which allows for the detection of deviations from typical behavior by analyzing the reconstruction error. After training the autoencoder on such data, a significant increase in the reconstruction error indicates changes in the fractal structure of the series, potentially signaling a transition of the system to a new state or the occurrence of anomalous phenomena.

For training the neural network, model fractal time series with various values of the Hurst parameter were used, in which the Hurst parameter exhibited different types of changes, including abrupt jumps, smooth trends, and random fluctuations. This allowed the creation of a training dataset encompassing various scenarios of fractal structure changes. After the training phase, the effectiveness of the developed approach was tested on model test data, which enabled an assessment of the network's ability to detect significant changes in the Hurst parameter and confirmed its suitability for analyzing complex time series.

Subsequently, the proposed method was applied to real electroencephalogram (EEG) time series recorded from patients experiencing abrupt emotional changes (Samnikolas, n.d.).

Analysis showed strong alignment between anomalies in the Hurst exponent and documented emotional responses, validating the method's applicability in biomedical domains.

4. CONCLUSION

This study demonstrates that analyzing the dynamics of the Hurst exponent using a sliding window approach, followed by anomaly detection via LSTM autoencoders, provides an effective framework for identifying structural changes in time series. The method successfully captures abrupt, gradual, and mixed-type anomalies, both in synthetic data and real EEG recordings, reflecting transitions in the internal complexity of the system.

Compared to traditional correlation and spectral methods, this approach offers improved sensitivity to multiscale and nonlinear changes by leveraging fractal properties. Its generality makes it applicable to various domains where long-range dependence is present.

Future work will explore adaptive thresholding and the extension of the framework to multivariate time series with complex fractal interactions.

ACKNOWLEDGEMENT

This study was partly funded by the IMPRESS-U joint program of the National Science Foundation (project no. 2412914), the National Science Center of Poland (project no. 2023/05/Y/ST6/00263), and the Office of Naval Research of the US National Academy of Sciences (project no. 7136).

REFERENCES

Gowrisankar, A., & Banerjee, S. (2021). *Frontiers of fractals for complex systems: Recent advances and future challenges. European Physical Journal Special Topics*, 230(23), 3743–3745. https://doi.org/10.1140/epjs/s11734-021-00376-7

Kirichenko, L., Shakhovska, N., & Kotenko, I. (2024). *Anomaly detection in fractal time series with LSTM autoencoders. Mathematics*, 12(19), Article 3079. https://doi.org/10.3390/math12193079

Machine Learning Mastery. (n.d.). *LSTM Autoencoders*. Retrieved April 12, 2025, from https://machinelearningmastery.com/lstm-autoencoders/

Samnikolas. (n.d.). *EEG dataset*. Kaggle. Retrieved April 12, 2025, from https://www.kaggle.com/datasets/samnikolas/eeg-dataset

Zhang, H. Y., Feng, Z. Q., Feng, S. Y., and Zhou, Y. (2024). *A survey of methods for estimating Hurst exponent of time sequence*. arXiv preprint arXiv:2310.19051. Retrieved April 12, 2025, from https://arxiv.org/pdf/2310.19051.pdf

DEEP LEARNING FORECASTS OF HEPATITIS A, B, AND C INCIDENCE IN WAR-TORN UKRAINE: A MULTIVARIATE LSTM APPROACH

Dmytro Chumachenko[1, 2], Mykola Butkevych[1], Tetyana Chumachenko[3], Alexander Kirpich[4], Lyudmyla Kirichenko[5, 6] and Olha Matsyi[5, 6]
[1]National Aerospace University "Kharkiv Aviation Institute"
17 Vadyma Manka St, 61070 Kharkiv, Ukraine
[2]Balsillie School of International Affairs
67Erb St, W, N2L 6C2, Waterloo, ON, Canada
[3]Kharkiv National Medical University
Nauky ave, 4, 61001 Kharkiv, Ukraine
[4]Georgia State University
33 Gilmer St, SE Atlanta, GA 30303
[5]Lodz University of Technology
ul. Żeromskiego 116, 90-924 Lodz, Poland
[6]V.N. Karazin Kharkiv National University
6 Svobody sq., 61022 Kharkiv, Ukraine

ABSTRACT

Viral hepatitis remains a major public health threat globally, yet Ukraine's surveillance capacity has been repeatedly destabilised by the Russian war, complicating resource planning for hepatitis A, B and C. We extracted 84 monthly case counts for each virus (January 2018 – December 2024) from the Public Health Centre of Ukraine registry and trained a two-layer Long Short-Term Memory network with a 12-month input window to generate 12-step forecasts. The model, optimised with Adam and early stopping, achieved mean-absolute-percentage errors of 5.40 % (acute HAV), 13.78 % (acute HBV), 17.13 % (chronic HBV), 26.34 % (acute HCV) and 23.89 % (chronic HCV) on the held-out 2024 horizon. Critically, cumulative MAPE remained below 1.5 % for all series. These findings demonstrate that a lightweight, CPU-deployable LSTM can deliver procurement-grade, year-ahead incidence forecasts for Ukraine's three principal hepatitides, offering a scalable decision-support tool aligned with the WHO 2030 elimination agenda.

KEYWORDS

Epidemic Model, Hepatitis A, Hepatitis B, Hepatitis C, LSTM, Deep Learning, Machine Learning

1. INTRODUCTION

Viral hepatitis remains one of the world's deadliest infectious diseases. The World Health Organization Global Hepatitis Report 2024 notes that hepatitis-related deaths now rival tuberculosis at 1.3 million per year, or ~3 500 every day, and warns that the 2030 elimination targets are slipping out of reach (World Health Organization, 2024). Achieving the required 90 % reduction in new infections demands reliable, forward-looking incidence estimates to steer vaccination, screening, and antiviral procurement in real time.

Ukraine presents a particularly urgent case. According to the Public Health Center (PHC) electronic registry, chronic hepatitis B prevalence approaches 1 % of the population, hepatitis C notifications have risen steadily since 2018, and large hepatitis A outbreaks continue to surface in conflict-affected oblasts. The 2022 escalation of the Russo-Ukrainian war has further destabilized surveillance by damaging laboratory infrastructure and delaying case reporting, amplifying non-stationarity in the national time series (Chumachenko et al., 2024). Recurrent neural networks, and particularly Long-Short-Term Memory (LSTM) architectures, excel at learning long-range, non-linear temporal dependencies and have repeatedly outperformed statistical baselines for tuberculosis (Yang et al., 2022), COVID-19 (Mello-Román and Martínez-Amarilla, 2025), and dengue (Chen and Moraga, 2025) forecasting.

Building directly on that validated architecture and using the data provided by PHC (January 2018 – December 2024), the paper aims to develop the LSTM model to generate 12-month forecasts for hepatitis A, B, and C. By holding the model specification and preprocessing pipeline constant across pathogens, we create the first unified deep learning baseline for Ukraine's three major hepatitis.

2. MATERIALS AND METHODS

Monthly counts of laboratory-confirmed hepatitis A (HAV), hepatitis B (HBV) and hepatitis C (HCV) cases were extracted from the open electronic registry of the Public Health Center (PHC) of the Ministry of Health of Ukraine. The data included 84 consecutive observations per virus (January 2018 – December 2024). Case definitions follow national guidelines: HAV is any symptomatic infection with laboratory confirmation; acute HBV/HCV require clinical onset within six months of exposure; chronic infection is defined by antigen (HBsAg) or RNA persistence ≥ 6 months. Completeness audits revealed no missing months, allowing the first 72 observations (2018-2023) to serve as the estimation set and the final 12 months (2024) as a strictly held-out test horizon. Two parallel series were created for each pathogen: raw monthly counts and cumulative totals, the latter reflecting procurement-relevant burden. All values in the training split were rescaled to the unit interval via min-max normalization to stabilize gradients. The inverse transform was applied to model outputs before evaluation. No imputation or outlier removal was required because surveillance streams contained neither gaps nor negative values.

Forecasts were generated with a compact two-layer LSTM network. Each input consisted of a 12-month sliding window mapped by two stacked LSTM blocks (64 hidden units per layer, dropout = 0.20) to a dense layer and a single linear output neuron that produced the next-month prediction. The configuration totals 171 251 trainable parameters. Separate networks were trained for HAV, HBV and HCV to accommodate pathogen-specific seasonality while preserving the same hyperparameter grid. Optimisation used the Adam algorithm (learning-rate 1×10^{-3}, batch-size 8) with early stopping after five epochs without validation-loss improvement. A maximum of 300 epochs was allowed.

3. RESULTS

Table 1 summarizes predictive accuracy on the 12-month hold-out slice (January-December 2024). Performance is reported as mean absolute percentage error (MAPE) and mean squared error (MSE) for the original monthly counts ("daily") and the cumulative series that drives procurement decisions.

Table 1. Results of simulation

Disease	MAPE (daily)	MSE (daily)	MAPE (cumulative)	MSE (cumulative)
Acute HAV	5.40 %	15.38	3.74 %	156137.14
Acute HBV	13.78 &	411.20	0.85 %	3362.44
Chronic HBV	17.13 %	76.26	0.82 %	3932.12
Acute HCV	26.34 %	168.98	0.28 %	68.24
Chronic HCV	23.89 %	36341.16	1.46 %	1256.34

The network achieved its lowest monthly error on acute HAV (MAPE = 5.40 %), indicating that the short-term seasonality of this predominantly outbreak-driven infection was well captured. HBV forecasts exhibited intermediate accuracy (MAPE ≈ 14–17 %), while the highest point-wise errors were observed for HCV (MAPE ≈ 24–26 %). This ranking mirrors the underlying signal-to-noise ratio: HAV incidence displays sharp but regular peaks, whereas HCV notifications are irregular and heavily influenced by screening campaign timing, complicating one-step prediction. MSE scale with absolute case counts: chronic HCV, the numerically largest series, recorded the highest MSE, even though its percentage error was comparable to that of acute HCV.

For programme planning, the cumulative trajectory is paramount. Across all five series, the cumulative MAPE remained below 4 %, with four under 1.5 %. Acute HCV, the most volatile monthly series, paradoxically delivered the tightest cumulative fit (MAPE = 0.28 %), demonstrating that over- and under-predictions at adjacent time steps tend to cancel when aggregated. Acute and chronic HBV stayed within a ±1 % envelope, comfortably meeting Ukraine's stock management tolerance threshold. HAV's comparatively larger cumulative MSE reflects its higher annual case total rather than poorer proportional accuracy.

The LSTM maintained sub-5 % monthly error for the outbreak-prone HAV series and sub-1 % cumulative error for both HBV streams, attesting to its ability to learn stable seasonal patterns while remaining resilient to war-related reporting shocks. Elevated monthly errors for HCV underscore the difficulty of forecasting diagnoses that depend on opportunistic screening. Nonetheless, the negligible cumulative deviation (< 1.5 %) confirms that the model remains serviceable for long-horizon procurement. The results validate the feasibility of a single architecture, trained without pathogen-specific tuning, to provide actionable forecasts.

4. CONCLUSION

This study demonstrates that a compact, two-layer LSTM architecture can be retrained without pathogen-specific tuning to generate reliable 12-month incidence forecasts for hepatitis A, B, and C in Ukraine. On a strictly held-out 2024 horizon, the network maintained ≤ 5 % mean-absolute-percentage error for the outbreak-prone HAV series and ≤ 1.5 % cumulative error for all five surveillance streams, thereby meeting operational thresholds for vaccine and antiviral procurement even under conflict-related reporting instability.

ACKNOWLEDGEMENT

This study was funded by National Science Foundation (project No. 2412914), National Science Centre of Poland (project No. 2023/05/Y/ST6/00263), Office of Naval Research (ONR), US National Academy of Science (US NAS) through Science & Technology Center in Ukraine (STCU) Project No. 7136, within the joint IMPRESS-U initiative entitled "Modeling and Forecasting of Infection Spread in War and Post War Settings Using Epidemiological, Behavioral and Genomic Surveillance Data".

REFERENCES

Chen, X. and Moraga, P. (2025). Forecasting dengue across Brazil with LSTM neural networks and SHAP-driven lagged climate and spatial effects. *BMC Public Health*, 25(1), p. 973. doi: 10.1186/s12889-025-22106-7.

Chumachenko, D., Bazilevych, K., Butkevych, M., Meniailov, I., Parfeniuk, Y., Sidenko, I. and Chumachenko, T. (2024). Methodology for assessing the impact of emergencies on the spread of infectious diseases. *Radioelectronic and Computer Systems*, 2024(3), pp. 6–26. doi: 10.32620/reks.2024.3.01.

Mello-Román, J.D. and Martínez-Amarilla, A. (2025). COVID-19 Data Analysis: The Impact of Missing Data Imputation on Supervised Learning Model Performance. *Computation*, 13(3), p. 70. doi: 10.3390/computation13030070.

World Health Organization (2024). *Global hepatitis report 2024: action for access in low- and middle-income countries.* [online] www.who.int. Available at: https://www.who.int/publications/i/item/9789240091672 [Accessed 11 Jul. 2025].

Yang, E., Zhang, H., Guo, X., Zang, Z., Liu, Z. and Liu, Y. (2022). A multivariate multi-step LSTM forecasting model for tuberculosis incidence with model explanation in Liaoning Province, China. *BMC infectious diseases*, 22(1), p. 490. doi: 10.1186/s12879-022-07462-8.

AUTHOR INDEX

International Association for Development of the Information Society (IADIS)
Rua Sao Sebastiao Da Pedreira
No. 100, 30, 1050-209
Lisbon, Portugal

ISBN 979-8-3313-2985-3

9 798331 329853

CURRAN ASSOCIATES INC.
proceedings.com